UN
Tel
Fax

For over a century the University Arms has been a leading Cambridge hotel. It combines the old-fashioned virtues of superior quality and service and the unhurried life of yesteryear with the most modern facilities available. Each of the 115 bedrooms has a private bathroom, colour television, radio, direct dial telephone, also Tea & Coffee making facilities. Its splendid oak panelled restaurant, adjacent to 'Parkers Piece' 25 acres of open parkland, offers an excellent wine list. Relax in the spacious Octagon Lounge by a log fire in winter or have a drink in one of three bars, including a specialist whisky bar.

AA ★★★★ RAC EGON RONAY

DE VERE HOTELS

More financial ideas

PERSONAL LOANS

Easy to arrange at competitive rates.

BANKING SERVICE

A full banking service with a £100 cheque guarantee card, automatic £500 overdraft and interest too.

Norwich and Peterborough

Norwich and Peterborough Building Society

See Yellow Pages for your local branch.

Chief Office: St. Andrew's House, St. Andrew's Street, Norwich NR2 4TR.
Telephone: Norwich (0603) 660081.
Administrative Centre: Peterborough Business Park, Lynch Wood, Peterborough PE2 0FZ.
Telephone: Peterborough (0733) 371371.

Member of The Building Societies Association. Member of LINK.
Personal loans are subject to status. Full written details of all services available on request
from any branch of the Society.

A member of the Norwich and Peterborough Group

BY APPOINTMENT TO
H.M. QUEEN ELIZABETH II
ROBE MAKERS

BY APPOINTMENT TO
H.R.H. DUKE OF EDINBURGH
ROBE MAKERS

BY APPOINTMENT TO
H.M. QUEEN ELIZABETH
THE QUEEN MOTHER
ROBE MAKERS

BY APPOINTMENT TO
H.R.H. PRINCE OF WALES
ROBE MAKERS

Ede & Ravenscroft Ltd., London.

Gown makers of distinction

Academic robes for Universities throughout the country

Academic robes also for hire

High class tailors

Shirt makers & Hosiers

Robe Makers and Tailors since the Reign of William and Mary in the year 1689

Ede and Ravenscroft

*71/72 TRUMPINGTON STREET,
CAMBRIDGE CB2 1RJ.
Telephone (0223) 350048*

The Student's Choice

Chambers English Dictionary is the bestselling single volume quality dictionary on the market today, with a huge range of words from the archaic to the ultra-modern, from science to literature, plus informal, colloquial and dialect words of everyday speech.
That's what makes it the only realistic choice for the student.

Standard	1 85296 000 0	£16.95
Concise	1 85296 010 8	£9.95
Pocket	1 85296 012 4	£5.50
Mini (Paperback)	1 85296 014 0	£1.95
Thesaurus	1 85296 016 7	£9.50

Chambers Dictionary of Synonyms and Antonyms
1 85296 350 6 Paperback £3.95

And for the scientist....

Chambers Science and Technology Dictionary
1 85296 150 3 Hardback £30.00
1 85296 151 1 Paperback £16.95

Chambers Biology Dictionary
1 85296 152 X Hardback £17.50
1 85296 153 8 Paperback £8.95
Pub: August

W & R Chambers Ltd
43-45 Annandale Street, Edinburgh EH7 4AZ

Cambridge University Press
The Edinburgh Building, Shaftesbury Road, Cambridge CB2 2RU

An opportunity to keep abreast of new ideas and the progress of legal reform

CAMBRIDGE LAW JOURNAL

- Acknowledged as influential in law reform, **CLJ** publishes articles on all aspects of law, with special emphasis on contemporary developments.

- In 'Case and Comment' distinguished contributors analyse recent judicial decisions, new legislation and current law reform proposals.

- Established over 60 years ago, this prestigious journal holds a leading place among the world's legal periodicals.

- Case notes and articles are designed to have the widest appeal to those interested in law, whether as practitioners, students, teachers, judges or administrators.

- **CLJ** contains an extensive section of book reviews.

"a highly respected academic title . . ."
Magazines for Libraries

Subscriptions Volume 48: March, July and November 1989 at £24.00; airmail £9.50 per year extra. To subscribe send remittance to: The Journals Subscription Manager, Cambridge University Press, The Edinburgh Building, Shaftesbury Road, Cambridge CB2 2RU.
ISSN 0008-1973

Cambridge Journals

Everyone's reading THE CAMBRIDGE REVIEW!

New Look
The first two years of the new-look CAMBRIDGE REVIEW have been a sell-out success. In its new form it contains some of the best and most accessible writing to be found anywhere on current intellectual developments and topical cultural themes.

What you've missed.....
Consider just some of the things that you missed by not reading some of the first issues of the new CAMBRIDGE REVIEW: Shirley Williams, Robert Rhodes James, Giles Radice and others debated the relation between 'Politics and Higher Education'; Max Perutz, Eric Ashby, Denis Noble and others pondered the future of Cambridge science, while the symposium of articles on 'Women in Cambridge' stirred up considerable controversy and is already figuring in references and on reading lists...In addition there have been new poems by internationally known poets like Donald Davie, Paul Muldoon, A.D. Hope, Kathleen Raine, Peter Scupham, Deborah Greger and Les Murray.

Subscriptions
THE CAMBRIDGE REVIEW (ISSN 0008-2007) is published quarterly by Cambridge University Press in March, June, October and December. 1989 subscription for an individual is £12 per year (£9 to a Cambridge address), £28 for companies and institutions (£18 to a Cambridge address). Send your order to: Journals Publicity Department, FREEPOST, Cambridge University Press, The Edinburgh Building, Shaftesbury Road, Cambridge CB2 1BR, England (No postage stamp needed if posted within UK) or write for a sample copy.

You can't afford not to read it !

Special reduced subscription rates for *students:*

Behavioral & Brain Sciences £26 *(normally £43)*
British Journal of Music Education £12 *(£16)*
Cambridge Law Journal £12 *(£24)*
English Today £12 *(£16)*
Geological Magazine £21 *(£82)*
Journal of Latin American Studies £15 *(£22)*
The Milbank Quarterly £15 *(£22)*
New Testament Studies £16 *(£25)*
Oceanus £17 *(£20)*
Visual Neuroscience £58 *(£84)*

Other reductions are available for members of certain societies.
We publish over 100 different journals. To find out more about them, write or telephone for the latest catalogue.

Journals Publicity Department
Cambridge University Press
The Edinburgh Building
Shaftesbury Road
Cambridge CB2 2RU
Tel: (0223) 325804

Cambridge

The British Isles: A History of Four Nations
HUGH KEARNEY
'... a refreshing book ... should be widely used to educate those who think they know about British history when in fact they know only English history'. Christopher Hill,
The New York Review of Books
'... a book into which much labour and thought, much knowledge and wisdom has been packed, which contains ... much that is unexpected and fascinating...' *The Spectator*
£17.50 net   0 521 33420 9   256 pp.

Now in paperback
Cambridge Commemorated
An Anthology of University Life
Compiled by **LAURENCE FOWLER** and **HELEN FOWLER**
Short Foreword by H.R.H. The Duke of Edinburgh, Chancellor of the University of Cambridge
'This is an excellent book, wonderful value for money, well-illustrated, perfect for dipping into, interesting on every page, stimulating to thought, and entertaining for idleness.'
The Cambridge Review
£9.95 net   Pb   0 521 38910 0

The Edinburgh Building, Cambridge CB2 2RU

QUESTION:
HOW DO I WRITE A GOOD ESSAY?
ANSWER:
READ THIS BOOK!

* helps with the problems of academic writing

* uses concrete examples from a variety of disciplines

* demonstrates an innovative approach to reading, taking notes, interpreting and analysing

* describes how to structure and develop essays

* shows how to make effective use of language

Paperback £5.95 net
0 521 36905 3

(Also available in hard covers £19.50 net 0 521 36005 6)

THE STUDENT'S WRITING GUIDE FOR THE ARTS AND SOCIAL SCIENCES
GORDON TAYLOR

CAMBRIDGE UNIVERSITY PRESS

IF £15 ISN'T ENOUGH TO GET YOU TO OPEN AN ACCOUNT OUR next OFFER IS A £30 VOUCHER.

If you think choosing the right bank is hard, think about choosing between the 1,374 different articles you could buy with our free £30 Next Directory voucher.

Or alternatively how you could impress some of your fellow freshers by taking them out for a curry, with £15 cash.

You see, with a Barclays student account you get interest on your money, the use of 5,000 cash dispensers nationwide, the advice of our Student Business Officers, preferential rates on overdrafts and on top of all that the choice of £15 cash or a Next Directory and a £30 voucher.

Whatever next? Some might say.

To find out about opening an account and the terms of the offer, call us free on **0800 400 100**.

+ + + YOU'RE BETTER OFF TALKING TO BARCLAYS

WRITTEN CREDIT DETAILS ARE AVAILABLE ON REQUEST FROM BARCLAYS BANK PLC (MEMBER OF IMRO), 94 ST. PAUL'S CHURCHYARD, LONDON EC4M 8EH. OFFER CLOSES 31ST DECEMBER 1989.

The balance of news, analysis and debate provided by **New Theatre Quarterly** is invaluable to all theatre enthusiasts.

Volume 5: February, May, August and November 1989

Subscription: £15 for individuals; £27 for institutions; £29 for institutions elsewhere. Airmail £10 extra per year.

Cambridge Opera Journal

A new journal for opera-lovers

For the first time, an interdisciplinary opera journal with articles on all aspects of this exciting area of study.

Volume 1: (Triannual) 1989

Subscription: £18 for individuals; £32 for institutions. Airmail £9.50 per year extra.

For further information, please write to Journals Publicity Department, **Cambridge University Press**, FREEPOST, Edinburgh Building, Shaftesbury Road, Cambridge CB2 1BR or 'phone (0223) 325804

THE CAMBRIDGE UNIVERSITY HANDBOOK

1989-90

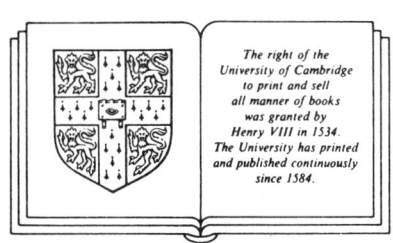

CAMBRIDGE UNIVERSITY PRESS

CAMBRIDGE
NEW YORK   PORT CHESTER
MELBOURNE   SYDNEY
1989

Published by the Press Syndicate of the University of Cambridge
The Pitt Building, Trumpington Street, Cambridge CB2 1RP
40 West 20th Street, New York, NY 10011, USA
10 Stamford Road, Oakleigh, Melbourne 3166, Australia

ISBN 0 521 38878 3

Printed in Great Britain by the University Press, Cambridge

78th Edition
Revised to 1 August 1989

CONTENTS

1	THE UNIVERSITY	*page* 1
	Officers	2
	Matriculation	10
	Affiliation	13
	Incorporation	19
	M.A. Degree by virtue of office	19
	M.A. status	20
	B.A. status	20
	The University Library	20
	The Fitzwilliam Museum	22
	Madingley Hall	23
2	THE COLLEGES	24
	Admission	25
	Overseas Candidates	26
3	UNIVERSITY EXAMINATIONS AND DEGREES	28
4	COURSES OF STUDY FOR DEGREES, DIPLOMAS, AND CERTIFICATES	47
	Anglo-Saxon, Norse, and Celtic	47
	Archaeology and Anthropology	53
	Architecture	75
	Chemical Engineering	85
	Classics	93
	Computer Science	110
	Development Studies	114
	Economics and Politics	115
	Education	140
	Engineering	166
	Electrical and Information Sciences Tripos	177
	Manufacturing Engineering Tripos	179
	Management Studies Tripos	181

CONTENTS

4 COURSES OF STUDY FOR DEGREES, DIPLOMAS, AND CERTIFICATES (*continued*)

English	page 187
Geography	202
History	208
History of Art	228
Land Economy	236
Latin-American Studies	247
Law	252
Mathematics	265
Medical Sciences	272
Medicine and Surgery	284
Modern and Medieval Languages	291
Music	337
Natural Sciences	347
Oriental Studies	390
Philosophy	415
Polar Studies	427
Social and Political Sciences	429
Theology and Religious Studies	441
Veterinary Medicine	478

5 RESEARCH AND COURSES OF ADVANCED OR FURTHER STUDY — 484

6 UNIVERSITY SCHOLARSHIPS AND OTHER AWARDS — 490

University scholarships	490
Awards offered by other bodies	516

7 THE UNIVERSITY CAREERS SERVICE — 522

8 TRAINING FOR THE MINISTRY — 524

INDEX — 526

PREFACE

The Cambridge University Handbook is designed to include most of the information, particularly about courses, which a prospective candidate for admission to Cambridge will need, and which an undergraduate will usually wish to have readily available.

The *Handbook* is not a substitute for the University Ordinances. Much of it is based on the Ordinances, and it contains an abridged account of some of them, but it must not be regarded as having the authority of the actual regulations. These are to be found in the latest edition of the *Statutes and Ordinances of the University of Cambridge* (published every three years*) and the *Amending Statutes and Supplementary Ordinances* (published in each year in which the Statutes and Ordinances are not published) as they are amended from time to time by Grace or by notice published in the *Cambridge University Reporter*.

A complete list of University administrative and teaching officers, members of University bodies, and representatives of the University on other bodies may be found in a special issue of the *Cambridge University Reporter* and also in the *Commonwealth Universities Yearbook*. A booklet entitled *University of Cambridge: Information and Regulations*, a copy of which is issued to every freshman, gives a full account of the regulations relating to residence and discipline and also information about medical and dental arrangements, libraries, and museums. The *Cambridge Admissions Prospectus* is published each year by the Cambridge Tutorial Representatives for the guidance of candidates applying between March and September for entry in October the following year. It contains details of individual Colleges, their Tutors, teaching Fellows, and Directors of Studies and may be obtained on application to any College or to the Cambridge Inter-Collegiate Applications Office, Kellet Lodge, Tennis Court Road, Cambridge CB2 1QA.

The Editor is grateful for help received from many quarters, and will be glad to have her attention drawn to any mistakes that may have been made.

* Latest edition, 1988.

UNIVERSITY REGISTRY
1 August 1989

1
THE UNIVERSITY

The University is a self-governing body; the legislative authority is the Regent House, which consists mainly of the teaching and administrative staff of the University and Colleges. The Senate, which consists of all holders of the M.A. or higher degrees, has now only certain formal duties, other than meeting for the discussion of Reports made by the Council of the Senate and other bodies. The chief administrative body of the University is the Council of the Senate, which is elected by the Regent House. The General Board of the Faculties co-ordinates the educational policy of the University and the Financial Board supervises its financial affairs.

The nominal and ceremonial head of the University is the Chancellor, who is elected for life. The Vice-Chancellor is a head of a College who is nominated for election by the Council of the Senate and normally holds office for two years. The Vice-Chancellor presides over Congregations of the Regent House, at which degrees are conferred, and is Chairman of the Council of the Senate and the more important of the many Boards and Syndicates which manage the affairs of the University.

Changes in the Ordinances, or regulations, of the University are proposed by the Board or Syndicate concerned in the form of reports which, after being approved for publication by the Council of the Senate, are published in the *Cambridge University Reporter*. Such reports can be commented on by members of the Senate at Discussions which are held once a fortnight in Full Term. A report may be amended after remarks made in a Discussion. Subsequently a Grace, which is a motion for the approval of recommendations made in a report, is submitted to a vote of the Regent House. Minor amendments of Ordinances are proposed in Graces which the Council of the Senate submit for the approval of the Regent House without the formality of Report and discussion. Ordinances may not infringe the University Statutes. The procedure for making amendments of the Statutes is the same as for the Ordinances, but such amendments require the approval of the Queen in Council, after the approval of the Regent House has been obtained.

The educational and research activities of the University are organized in Faculties, some of which are subdivided into Departments. All are answerable to the General Board of the Faculties. Through the Faculties, the University is responsible for lectures and laboratory work. The University also conducts all examinations and awards degrees; but it is the Colleges which select students for admission, arrange the tuition of undergraduates either individually or in small groups, and see to the welfare, both academic and personal, of undergraduates. All undergraduates admitted by the Colleges must, however, satisfy the University's matriculation requirements.

Cambridge University Reporter

The *Cambridge University Reporter* is the official newspaper of the University and is published every Wednesday in Full Term; extra numbers are published as occasion requires. The *Reporter* can be ordered from the Cambridge University Press Publishing Division, Edinburgh Building, Shaftesbury Road, Cambridge CB2 2RU. The annual subscription* is £30.60, post free, and the terminal subscription £10.20, post free. Single copies cost 60p each (£1.05 postage paid).

All University announcements and reports to the Regent House are published in the *Reporter* and there are the following special issues: the Lecture-list, which is published at the beginning of the Michaelmas Term (and costs £1.20, £2.30 postage paid), with lists of additions and corrections published at the beginning of the Lent and Easter Terms; the List of University Administrative and Teaching Officers, etc., which is published at the beginning of the Michaelmas Term; the Awards number which is published in November; the list of examination timetables which is published in April; the Class-list issue, which is published in July (students going out of residence before the results of their examinations are announced are able to arrange with some newsagents for the relevant issue to be posted to them); and the College Accounts (costing £1.70, £2.85 postage paid).

Administrative officers

Chancellor: His Royal Highness, The Prince Philip, Duke of Edinburgh, K.G., P.C., K.T., O.M., G.B.E.

Vice-Chancellor (1989/90): Professor D. G. T. Williams, M.A., LL.B., President of Wolfson College. (The Vice-Chancellor is elected, a year at a time, for two years, from among the Heads of Colleges.)

Proctors (1989/90): E. H. R. Ford, M.D., of Selwyn College, and C. F. Forsyth, LL.B., PH.D., of Robinson College. (The Proctors are disciplinary officers nominated by the Colleges in rotation.)

Registrary: S. G. Fleet, M.A., PH.D.

Secretary General of the Faculties: J. R. G. Wright, M.A.

Treasurer: M. P. Halstead, M.A., PH.D.

* This excludes the College Accounts.

Professors

(as from 1 October 1989)

Aeronautical Engineering (Francis Mond)	M. Gaster, M.A.
Agriculture (Drapers)	Vacant
American History (Paul Mellon)	Mrs C. Erickson, M.A.
American History and Institutions (Pitt)	N. Rosenberg (for the year 1989–90)
Anatomy	H. G. J. M. Kuypers, M.A.
Ancient History	M. K. Hopkins, M.A.
Ancient Philosophy (Laurence)	M. F. Burnyeat, M.A.
Ancient Philosophy and Science	G. E. R. Lloyd, MA., PH.D.
Anglo-Saxon (Elrington and Bosworth)	R. I. Page, LITT.D.
Animal Embryology (Charles Darwin)	R. A. Laskey, PH.D.
Animal Pathology	E. J. L. Soulsby, M.A.
Animal Welfare (Colleen Macleod)	D. M. Broom, M.A., PH.D.
Applied Economics	Hon. W. A. H. Godley, M.A.
Applied Economics	D. M. G. Newbery, M.A., PH.D.
Applied Mathematics	D. G. Crighton, M.A.
Applied Numerical Analysis (John Humphrey Plummer)	M. J. D. Powell, SC.D.
Applied Thermodynamics (Hopkinson and Imperial Chemical Industries)	K. N. C. Bray, B.A.
Arabic (Sir Thomas Adams's)	M. C. Lyons, M.A., PH.D.
Archaeology (Disney)	A. C. Renfrew, SC.D.
Architecture	P. B. Carolin, M.A.
Astronomy and Experimental Philosophy (Plumian)	M. J. Rees, M.A., PH.D.
Astronomy and Geometry (Lowndean)	Vacant
Astrophysics	D. Lynden-Bell, M.A., PH.D.
Biochemistry (Sir William Dunn)	Sir Hans Kornberg, SC.D.
Biology (Quick)	C. C. Wylie
Botany	R. G. West, SC.D.
Cell Biology (John Humphrey Plummer)	J. B. Gurdon
Cell Physiology	Lord Adrian, M.A., M.D.
Chemical Engineering (Shell)	J. F. Davidson, SC.D.
Chemistry	A. D. Buckingham, SC.D.
Chemistry	Lord Lewis, SC.D.
Chemistry (Alexander Todd Visiting)	Vacant
Chinese	D. L. McMullen, M.A., PH.D.

CAMBRIDGE HANDBOOK

Civil Law (Regius)	P. G. Stein, M.A., LL.B.
Classical Archaeology (Laurence)	A. M. Snodgrass, M.A., PH.D.
Clinical Biochemistry	C. N. Hales, M.D., PH.D.
Clinical Gerontology	Miss K-T. Khaw, M.A., M.B., B.CHIR.
Clinical Oncology (Cancer Research Campaign)	N. M. Bleehen, M.A.
Clinical Pharmacology	M.J. Brown, M.D.
Comparative Law	J. A. Jolowicz, M.A.
Comparative Philology	R. G. G. Coleman, M.A.
Computer Science	D. J. Wheeler, B.A., PH.D.
Computer Systems	R. M. Needham, M.A., PH.D.
Criminology (Wolfson)	A. E. Bottoms, M.A.
Divinity (Lady Margaret's)	Miss M. D. Hooker, M.A.
Divinity (Norris-Hulse)	N. L. A. Lash, D.D.
Divinity (Regius)	S. W. Sykes, M.A.
Earth Sciences	D. P. McKenzie, M.A., PH.D.
Ecclesiastical History (Dixie)	C. N. L. Brooke, LITT.D.
Economic History (1971)	B. E. Supple, PH.D.
Economics (1965)	P. Dasgupta, B.A., PH.D.
Economics (1970)	F. H. Hahn, M.A.
Economics (1988)	M. H. Pesaran, PH.D.
Education	D. H. Hargreaves, M.A., PH.D.
Electrical Engineering	A. N. Broers, B.A., PH.D.
Engineering (1875)	D. E. Newland, M.A.
Engineering (1966)	J.E.Carroll, SC.D.
Engineering (1966)	S. Williamson
Engineering (1966)	A. N. Schofield, M.A., PH.D.
Engineering (1971)	J. Heyman, M.A., PH.D.
Engineering (1974)	K. Glover, M.A.
Engineering (1977)	K. L. Johnson, M.A.
Engineering (Rank)	J. E. Ffowcs Williams, SC.D.
English (1966, Grace 1 of 1 Dec. 1965)	Mrs G.P.K.Beer, LITT.D.
English (1966, Grace 2 of 1 Dec. 1965)	Mrs A. Barton, PH.D.
English (1983)	D. S. Brewer, LITT.D.
English and American Literature	P.A.Tanner, M.A., PH.D.
English as an International Language	Mrs G. Brown, M.A.
English Law (Rouse Ball)	D. G. T. Williams, M.A., LL.B.

English Legal History	J. H. Baker, LL.D.
English Literature (King Edward VII)	Mrs M. S. Butler, PH.D.
English Literature	J. B. Beer, M.A., PH.D.
Ethology	**P. P. G. B. Bateson, SC.D.**
Experimental Psychology	N. J. Mackintosh, PH.D.
Financial Accounting (Price Waterhouse)	G. Whittington
Fine Art (Slade)	R. G. Cork, M.A., PH.D. (for the year 1989–90)
French (Drapers)	**P. J. Bayley, M.A. PH.D.**
Genetics (Arthur Balfour)	J. R. S. Fincham, SC.D.
Geography (1931)	M. D. I. Chisholm, M.A.
Geography (1974)	R. J. Chorley, SC.D.
Geology (Woodwardian)	I. N. McCave, SC.D.
Geophysics	R. S. White, M.A., PH.D.
German (Schröder)	R. C. Paulin, M.A.
Greek (Regius)	E. W. Handley, M.A.
Haematology	R. W. Carrell, M.A., PH.D.
Hebrew (Regius)	J. A. Emerton, D.D.
History and Philosophy of Science	M. L. G. Redhead, M.A.
History of Mathematics and Exact Sciences	D. T. Whiteside, PH.D.
History of the British Commonwealth (Smuts)	D. A. Low, PH.D.
History of Western Art	A. M. Jaffé, LITT.D.
Immunology (Sheila Joan Smith)	P. J. Lachmann, SC.D.
Imperial and Naval History (Vere Harmsworth)	D. K. Fieldhouse, LITT.D.
Industrial Relations (Montague Burton)	W. A. Brown
Information Engineering	F. Fallside, M.A.
International Law (Whewell)	D. W. Bowett, LL.D.
Italian (Serena)	**P. Boyde, M.A., PH.D.**
Land Economy	G. C. Cameron, M.A.
Latin (Kennedy)	**M. D. Reeve, M.A.**
Latin-American Studies (Simón Bolívar)	Vacant
Law	S. F. C. Milsom, M.A.
Laws of England (Downing)	G. H. Jones, LL.D.
Legal Science (Arthur Goodhart)	J. C. Smith, LL.D. (for the year 1989–90)
Linguistics	P. H. Matthews, LITT.D.

Magnetic Resonance (John Humphrey Plummer)	R. Freeman
Management Studies (Peat, Marwick and Mitchell)	S. R. Watson, M.A., PH.D.
Manufacturing Engineering	C. Andrew, M.A., PH.D.
Mathematical Astrophysics	N. O. Weiss, M.A., PH.D.
Mathematical Physics (1967)	J. C. Taylor, M.A., PH.D.
Mathematical Physics (1978)	H. K. Moffatt, B.A., PH.D.
Mathematical Statistics	D. Williams
Mathematics (Lucasian)	S. W. Hawking, PH.D.
Mathematics (Rouse Ball)	J. G. Thompson, M.A.
Mathematics for Operational Research (Churchill)	P. Whittle, M.A.
Medicinal Chemistry (Herchel Smith)	L. D. Hall
Medicine (1962)	T. M. Cox
Medicine (1987)	J. G. P. Sissons
Medieval and Renaissance English	Mrs G. L. Mann, M.A., PH.D.
Medieval Art	G. D. S. Henderson, M.A., PH.D.
Medieval History	R. B. Dobson, PH.D.
Medieval Latin Literature	E. P. M. Dronke, M.A.
Metallurgy (Goldsmiths')	D. Hull, M.A.
Mineralogy and Petrology	E. R. Oxburgh, M.A.
Modern History	D. E. D. Beales, LITT.D.
Modern History (Regius)	P. Collinson, M.A.
Modern Japanese Studies	R. J. Bowring, M.A., PH.D.
Modern Languages	H. B. Nisbet, M.A.
Morbid Anatomy and Histology	G. A. Gresham, M.D., SC.D.
Music	A. Goehr, M.A.
Natural Philosophy (Jacksonian)	Sir Alan Cook, SC.D.
Neurology	D. A. S. Compston
Neuroscience	**M. Burrows, M.A., PH.D.**
Neurosensory Physiology	F. W. Campbell, M.A.
Obstetrics and Gynaecology	S. K. Smith
Organic Chemistry (1702)	A. R. Battersby, SC.D.
Organic Chemistry (1987)	A. R. Fersht, M.A., PH.D.
Paediatrics	I. A. Hughes
Pathology	M. A. Ferguson-Smith, M.A.
Pharmacology (Sheild)	A. W. Cuthbert, M.A.
Philosophy	**D. H. Mellor, M.A., PH.D.**
Philosophy (Knightbridge)	T. J. Smiley, M.A. PH.D.
Physic (Regius)	D. K. Peters, M.A.
Physical Chemistry (1920)	D. A. King
Physical Chemistry (1978)	B. A. Thrush, SC.D.

THE UNIVERSITY

Physics (1966)	V. Heine, PH.D.
Physics (1966, Grace 19 of 1 Dec. 1965)	M. Pepper, SC.D.
Physics (1974)	B. D. Josephson, M.A., PH.D.
Physics (1986)	A. Howie, PH.D.
Physics (Cavendish)	Sir Samuel Edwards, M.A., PH.D.
Physiology	I. M. Glynn, M.D.
Physiology of Reproduction (Mary Marshall and Arthur Walton)	P. A. Jewell, M.A., PH.D.
Plant Biophysics	Miss E. A. C. MacRobbie, SC.D.
Political Economy	R. C. O. Matthews, M.A.
Political Science	Q. R. D. Skinner, M.A.
Political Theory	J. M. Dunn, M.A.
Psychiatry	E. S. Paykel, M.D.
Public Health	N. E. Day
Pure Mathematics	A. Baker, M.A., PH.D.
Pure Mathematics (Sadleirian)	J. H. Coates, PH.D.
Radio Astronomy (1971)	A. Hewish, M.A., PH.D
Radioastronomy	J. E. Baldwin, M.A., PH.D.
Radiology	T. Sherwood, M.A.
Slavonic Studies	A. G. Cross, M.A., PH.D.
Social Anthropology (William Wyse)	E. A. Gellner
Sociology	A. Giddens, M.A., PH.D.
Spanish	C. C. Smith, LITT.D.
Structural Biochemistry	R. N. Perham, SC.D.
Structural Mechanics	C. R. Calladine, SC.D.
Surgery	Sir Roy Calne, M.A.
Veterinary Clinical Studies	A. Steele-Bodger, M.A.
Zoology	G. Horn, SC.D.

Readers

(as from 1 October 1989)

Acoustics	A. P. Dowling, M.A., PH.D.
African History	J. Iliffe, M.A., PH.D.
Algebra	J. E. Roseblade, B.A., PH.D.
Ancient Philosophy	M. Schofield, M.A., PH.D.
Ancient Philosophy	D. N. Sedley, M.A.
Architecture and Urban Studies	M. Echenique, M.A.
Astrophysics	D. O. Gough, M.A., PH.D.
Atmospheric Dynamics	M. E. McIntyre, M.A.
Auditory Perception	B. C. J. Moore, M.A., PH.D.
Biochemistry (Sir William Dunn)	J. C. Metcalfe, M.A., PH.D.

Biochemistry of Macromolecules	Miss J. O. Thomas, SC.D.
Biological Fluid Dynamics	T. J. Pedley, SC.D.
Chemical Engineering	C. N. Kenney, SC.D.
Comparative Anaesthesia	L. W. Hall, M.A.
Computer Graphics	N. E. Wiseman, M.A., PH.D.
Cultural History	U. P. Burke, M.A.
Developmental Genetics	M. Ashburner, SC.D.
Early Christian and Jewish Studies	E. Bammel, M.A.
Economic and Social History	M. J. Hatcher, M.A.
Economics	R. E. Rowthorn, M.A.
Egyptology (Herbert Thompson)	J. D. Ray, M.A.
Elastodynamics	J. A. Hudson, M.A., PH.D.
Engineering	L. C. Squire, M.A.
Engineering Fluid Mechanics	D. J. Maull, M.A.
English Legal History	D. E. C. Yale, M.A., LL.B.
Experimental Embryology	M. H. Johnson, M.A., PH.D.
Fluid Mechanics	J. C. R. Hunt, M.A., PH.D.
Formal Methods in Computer Science	M. J. C. Gordon, B.A.
French Literature	Mrs D. Coleman, LITT.D.
Functional Analysis	G. R. Allan, M.A., PH.D.
Geochemistry	H. Elderfield, M.A.
Geophysical Dynamics	H. E. Huppert, SC.D.
Greek and Latin	J. Diggle, LITT.D.
Greek Language and Literature	C. F. L. Austin, M.A.
Hebrew and Aramaic	H. G. M. Williamson, D.D.
Historical Anthropology	A. D. J. Macfarlane, M.A., PH.D.
History and Philosophy of Science	N. Jardine, M.A., PH.D.
History of Social Thought	G. Stedman Jones, M.A.
Human Development	M. P. M. Richards, M.A., PH.D.
Indian Studies	F. R. Allchin, M.A.
Indian Studies	K. R. Norman, M.A.
Inorganic Chemistry	B. F. G. Johnson, M.A.
Inorganic Chemistry	M. Gerloch, SC.D.
Insular Latin Literature	M. Lapidge, LITT.D.
Invertebrate Physiology	J. E. Treherne, SC.D.
Law	J. A. Weir, M.A.
Law of Taxation	J. Tiley, M.A.
Literary History	H. H. Erskine-Hill, LITT.D.
Mathematical Analysis	D. J. H. Garling, M.A., SC.D.
Mathematical Biology	A. W. F. Edwards, SC.D.
Mathematical Physics	P. Goddard, M.A., PH.D.

Mathematical Physics	P. V. Landshoff, M.A., PH.D.
Mathematics of Systems	F. P. Kelly, M.A., PH.D.
Mechanical Metallurgy	J. F. Knott, PH.D.
Mesopotamian Studies	J. N. Postgate, M.A.
Microelectronics	H. Ahmed, PH.D.
Mineral Physics	E. K. H. Salje, M.A.
Modern and Contemporary History	C. M. Andrew, M.A., PH.D.
Modern European History	T. C. W. Blanning, M.A., PH.D.
Modern History	P. F. Clarke, LITT.D.
Modern Indian History	C. A. Bayly, PH.D.
Neuroendocrine Physiology	A. V. Edwards, SC.D.
Neuroendocrinology	J. Herbert, M.A., PH.D.
Neurophysiology	**J. G. Robson, M.A., PH.D.**
Organic Chemistry	D. H. Williams, SC.D.
Organic Chemistry	**A. J. Kirby, M.A., PH.D.**
Organic Chemistry	I. Fleming, SC.D.
Organic Chemistry	J. Staunton, M.A.
Pharmacology	E. K. Matthews, M.A.
Philosophy	T. R. Harrison, M.A., PH.D.
Physical Chemistry	R. M. Lambert, M.A.
Physical Chemistry	D. Husain, SC.D.
Physics of Geochemical Measurement	J. V. P. Long, M.A., PH.D.
Physiology	J. T. Fitzsimons, M.D., SC.D.
Plant Pathology	D. S. Ingram, SC.D.
Process Metallurgy	J. A. Charles, SC.D.
Psychological Criminology	D. P. Farrington, M.A., PH.D.
Pure Mathematics	B. Bollobás, SC.D.
Quantum Chemistry	N. C. Handy, M.A., PH.D.
Quaternary Palaeoclimatology	N. J. Shackleton, SC.D.
Sensory Physiology	A. C. Crawford, PH.D.
Smuts Reader	Vacant
Sociology and Politics	**G. P. Hawthorn, M.A.**
Structure and Properties of Materials	**L. M. Brown, M.A., PH.D.**
Therapeutic Immunology	**H. Waldmann, M.A., PH.D.**
Turbomachinery	N. A. Cumpsty, M.A., PH.D.
Turbomachinery Aerodynamics	J. D. Denton, B.A., PH.D.
Vision	**O. J. Braddick, M.A., PH.D.**
Zoology	**M. J. Wells, SC.D.**

Matriculation

Matriculation marks the formal admission of a student to membership of the University, and a College may not allow an unmatriculated student *in statu pupillari* to remain in residence after the division of his first term. Every candidate for matriculation must subscribe to the following declaration by signing the Matriculation Registration Form:

'I promise to observe the Statutes and Ordinances of the University as far as they concern me, and to pay due respect and obedience to the Chancellor and other officers of the University.'

A student is deemed to be matriculated from the beginning of the term in which a completed Matriculation Registration Form and satisfactory evidence of his qualification to matriculate are received by the Registrary.

To qualify for matriculation, a student must have been admitted to a College and, unless he is a Graduate Student or an Affiliated Student, or belongs to some other class of person approved by the Council of the Senate as qualified to matriculate, he must have satisfied the examination requirements for matriculation or be deemed by the Matriculation Board to have satisfied the examination requirements. In special circumstances (e.g. if a candidate's education has been seriously hampered by illness) the Matriculation Board have power to allow individual candidates to matriculate without fully satisfying the examination requirements.

A candidate will satisfy the examination requirements for matriculation if:

(*a*) he has obtained a pass in an examination in the Use of English or in an approved alternative,[1] or a Grade A, B, or C in English in G.C.S.E. or in a G.C.E. examination at Ordinary level in English Language,

---

[1] The following papers are approved: *Use of English* set by the Cambridge Local Examinations Syndicate, the Oxford and Cambridge Schools Examination Board, the Southern Universities' Joint Board for School Examinations, the Welsh Joint Education Committee, the Northern Ireland G.C.E. Committee, and the Associated Examining Board; *Test in English* set by the Joint Matriculation Board; *Certificate of Proficiency in Use of English* set by the Oxford Delegacy of Local Examinations; *English* (*Ordinary*, in which attainment of band A, B, or C constitutes a pass, or *Higher*) in the Scottish Certificate of Education; and *Certificate of Proficiency in English* set by the Cambridge Local Examinations Syndicate.

THE UNIVERSITY

(b) he has Grade A, B, or C in G.C.S.E. or in G.C.E. Ordinary level or a pass in G.C.E. Advanced Supplementary level in:
one language other than English,
one approved mathematical or scientific subject,
two other approved subjects,

and (c) he has passed at Advanced level in any two approved subjects; provided that a pass in the three Parts of the First M.B. Examination is deemed to be the equivalent of passes in two approved scientific subjects at Advanced level, and a pass in two Parts of the First M.B. Examination is deemed to be the equivalent of a pass in one approved scientific subject at Advanced level.

A list of approved subjects is published in the Cambridge Admissions Prospectus.

Examinations approved as alternatives to G.C.S.E. and G.C.E. examinations

A candidate will satisfy the examination requirements for matriculation, set out at (a) and (b) above, if he has in one or more of the following examinations passed at the prescribed standard in the subjects specified above:

(a) A School Certificate or Malaysia Certificate of Education in the medium of English, awarded by the Cambridge Local Examinations Syndicate; or a certificate of having passed in certain subjects in the examination for one of these certificates. Standard: a pass with credit or with the note 'very good' in a School Certificate.

(b) A Cambridge Higher School Certificate, or a certificate of having passed in certain subjects. Standard: a pass in a subject as a subsidiary subject or a principal subject (a pass in a principal subject is deemed to be a pass at Advanced level).

(c) A Scottish Certificate of Education or a certificate of having passed in certain subjects. Standard: attainment of band A, B, or C in the Ordinary Grade (a pass in the Higher Grade is deemed to be a pass at Advanced level).

Special provisions

Graduates of approved Universities. Graduates of an approved university may be deemed to have satisfied the examination requirements for matriculation.

Mature Students. A mature student who is recommended by a College as fit to undertake a course leading to an Honours Degree may be deemed by the Matriculation Board to have satisfied the examination requirements for matriculation.

Candidates from the Commonwealth or from the Republic of Ireland or from countries using a European language, other than English, as the medium of instruction.[1] A candidate who produces a certificate showing that he is qualified for admission without further examination to an approved university, in a country in the Commonwealth other than in India or Pakistan,[2] or in the Republic of Ireland or in a country using a European language, other than English, as the medium of instruction,[3] may be deemed by the Matriculation Board to have satisfied, or partly to have satisfied, the examination requirements for matriculation if his qualification for such admission includes either the passing of an examination, or the satisfactory completion of a course of study, in the subjects specified for General Certificates of Education.

Candidates from India or Pakistan. A candidate who has attained the first class in an examination leading to the degree of Bachelor of Arts or Bachelor of Science, or the first or second class in the Examination for the degree of Bachelor of Arts or Bachelor of Science, in any university of India or Pakistan approved for the purpose, may be deemed to have satisfied the examination requirements for matriculation provided that, in some examination leading up to the degree of Bachelor of Arts or Bachelor of Science in that university, he has passed in an Oriental language, in Mathematics or Science, and in English.

Candidates from the United States of America. A candidate edu-

---

[1] It is advisable that applications on behalf of such candidates should be submitted to the Matriculation Board before the student comes into residence. Unless the certificate shows on its face that it would admit the holder to a university, it should be accompanied by a sufficiently authenticated declaration by a government official or officer of a university, embassy, legation, or consulate of a specified country, testifying that the certificate would entitle the holder to enter, without further examination, on a regular course of study in a university. When certificates are in any other language than English, Latin, French, German, Italian, Portuguese, or Spanish, they should be accompanied by an English translation, attested by a public, diplomatic, or consular officer, or by a notary or public translator.

[2] Save for special cause, the Matriculation Board will exercise this power only when the candidate is ordinarily resident in the country in question.

[3] Save for special cause, the Matriculation Board will exercise this power only when the candidate is a national of the country in question or when his education has been conducted in the language of that country.

cated in the United States of America who has taken the tests of
the College Entrance Examination Board may be deemed to have
satisfied the examination requirements for matriculation if he has
taken the following tests and has attained therein a standard
approved by the Matriculation Board:

(*a*) The Scholastic Aptitude Test (Verbal and Mathematical
Sections).

(*b*) Achievement Tests in:
   (i) English Composition,
   (ii) one language,
   (iii) one of the following: Biology, Chemistry, Mathematics,
   Physics,
   (iv) American History and Social Studies, *or* European History
   and World Cultures, *or* Literature, *or* a second language,
   or a second subject from (iii).

*Candidates from Homerton College for the Qualifying Examination
in Education.* Members of Homerton College who at the end of their
second year of study in the College have passed an intermediate
examination conducted by the College for such candidates are
deemed to have satisfied the examination requirements for matriculation.

Affiliation

Any person who before matriculation in the University of Cambridge
has received or become qualified to receive a degree from another
institution for the education of adult students is entitled, on or after
matriculation, to be approved as an affiliated student, provided that
(*a*) when he or she became qualified for the degree he or she had been
a member of one or more such institutions for not less than three
academical years; (*b*) the degree has been approved for the purpose
by the Council of the Senate. In particular cases the Council of the
Senate may approve as an affiliated student a member or former
member of an institution for the education of adult students who does
not fulfil these requirements. Candidates for admission as affiliated
students should make initial enquiry to one of the Colleges.

A Tutor must apply for approval of a pupil as an affiliated student
not later than the division of the term next following that in which
the student first resides in the University, and approval has effect from
the beginning of his first term of residence. An affiliated student is
deemed to have satisfied the examination requirements for matriculation, and the first term of residence is reckoned as the fourth for

the purposes of the regulations for Triposes, degree examinations in Music, and degrees other than the Ordinary B.A. Degree or the M.Phil., M.Sc., M.Litt., and Ph.D. Degrees, and for studentships, scholarships, prizes, and other awards.

The effect of these provisions is that an affiliated student may proceed to the B.A. Degree with honours in two years, but that if he or she is a candidate for the Ordinary B.A. Degree three years will be necessary.

An affiliated student has the following additional privileges, but may not take Part II of any Tripos as the first Tripos examination later than the sixth term after his or her first term of residence, unless the regulations for a particular Tripos specifically allow it:

Anglo-Saxon, Norse, and Celtic

An affiliated student may take the Anglo-Saxon, Norse, and Celtic Tripos in his or her second year and, if he or she obtains honours, proceed to the B.A. Degree under the same conditions as if he or she had obtained honours in another Honours examination also.

Archaeology and Anthropology

An affiliated student may take Part II of the Archaeological and Anthropological Tripos in his or her second year under the same conditions as if he or she had obtained honours in Part I.

Architecture

An affiliated student may, if the Faculty Board permit, take Part IB of the Architecture Tripos in his or her first year.

Chemical Engineering

An affiliated student may, if the Chemical Engineering Syndicate permit, be a candidate either for Part I of the Chemical Engineering Tripos in his or her first year or for Part II in his or her first or second year under the same conditions as if he or she had obtained honours in Part I.

Classics

An affiliated student may take Part II of the Classical Tripos in his or her second year under the same conditions as if he or she had obtained honours in Part I or, if the Faculty Board of Classics permit, take Part II of the Tripos in his or her first year under the same conditions as if he or she had obtained honours in another Honours examination in the year next preceding.

Computer Science

An affiliated student may, if the Computer Syndicate permit, take Part IB of the Computer Science Tripos in his or her first year, and, if he or she obtains honours therein, Part II of the Computer Science Tripos in his or her second year.

Economics

An affiliated student may, if he or she passes or gains exemption from the Economics Qualifying Examination in Elementary Mathematics, take Part II of the Economics Tripos in his or her second year under the same conditions as if he or she had obtained honours in Part I.

Education

An affiliated student may take the Qualifying Examination for the Education Tripos in his or her first year and, if he or she passes that examination, the Tripos in his or her second year, and if he or she obtains honours in the Tripos, he or she may proceed to the B.A. Degree on the same conditions as if he or she had obtained honours in another Honours examination also.

Engineering, Electrical and Information Sciences

An affiliated student may, if the Faculty Board permit, take Part II of the Engineering Tripos, or the Electrical and Information Sciences Tripos, in his or her first or second year under the same conditions as if he or she had obtained honours in another Honours examination.

English

An affiliated student may take in his or her second year *either* Part I of the English Tripos, *or* Part II of the English Tripos subject to the regulation for that Part which applies to candidates who have not previously obtained honours in Part I of the English Tripos; and if he or she obtains honours, he may proceed to the B.A. Degree as if he or she had obtained honours in another Honours examination also.

Geography

An affiliated student may, if the Faculty Board permit, take Part II of the Geographical Tripos in his or her first or second year under the same conditions as if he or she had obtained honours in another Honours examination.

History

An affiliated student may, if the Faculty Board allow it in his or her case, (*a*) be a candidate for Part II in his or her first or second year or a candidate for Part I in his or her second year and (*b*) may proceed to the B.A. Degree after obtaining honours in either Part of the Tripos under the same conditions as if he or she had obtained honours in another Honours examination also, provided that a candidate offering either Part of the Tripos may be required by the Faculty Board to take an additional paper or papers.

History of Art

An affiliated student may take the History of Art Tripos in his or her second year and, if he or she obtains honours, proceed to the B.A. Degree under the same conditions as if he or she had obtained honours in another Honours examination also.

Land Economy

An affiliated student may take Part IB of the Land Economy Tripos in his or her first year and, if he or she obtains honours therein, Part II of the Land Economy Tripos in his or her second year.

Law

An affiliated student may, if the Faculty Board of Law permit, take Part II of the Law Tripos in his or her first or second year without having obtained honours in Part IB.

Management Studies

An affiliated student may, if the Faculty Board permit, take the Management Studies Tripos in his or her first or second year under the same conditions as if he or she had obtained honours in another Honours examination.

THE UNIVERSITY

Mathematics

An affiliated student may take Part II of the Mathematical Tripos in his or her first or second year under the same conditions as if he or she had obtained honours in Part IB of the Tripos.

Medical Sciences

An affiliated student may proceed to the B.A. Degree after obtaining honours in Part IA and Part IB of the Medical Sciences Tripos under the same conditions as if he or she had obtained honours in another Honours examination also.

Modern and Medieval Languages

An affiliated student may take Part II of the Modern and Medieval Languages Tripos in his or her second year under the same conditions as if he or she had obtained honours in Part I or, if the Faculty Board of Modern and Medieval Languages permit, in his or her first year under the same conditions as if he or she had obtained honours in another Honours examination in the year next preceding or in his or her third year after spending an authorized year abroad under the same conditions as if he or she had obtained honours in another Honours examination in the year next but two preceding.

Music

An affiliated student may take Part IB of the Music Tripos in his or her first year and, if he or she obtains honours therein, Part II of the Music Tripos in his or her second year.

Natural Sciences

An affiliated student may: (*a*) take Part IB of the Natural Sciences Tripos in his or her first year; (*b*) if the Faculty Board concerned permit, take Part II of the Natural Sciences Tripos or, if the History and Philosophy of Science Syndicate permit, take Section II of Part II (General) of the Natural Sciences Tripos, in his or her first or second year as if he or she had obtained honours in Part IB.

Oriental Studies

An affiliated student may take Part II of the Oriental Studies Tripos in his second year under the same conditions as if he or she had obtained honours in Part I of the Tripos or, if the Faculty Board of Oriental Studies permit, in his or her first year under the same conditions as if he or she had obtained honours in another Honours examination in the year next preceding; if the Faculty Board permit, he or she may take Part II (General) in his or her first year under the same conditions as if he or she had obtained honours in Part I of the Tripos.

Philosophy

An affiliated student may take Part IB of the Philosophy Tripos in the student's first or second year. If the student takes it in his or her second year and obtains honours, he or she may proceed to the B.A. Degree under the same conditions as if he or she had obtained honours in another Honours examination also. He or she may also take Part II in his or her first or second year without having obtained honours in any Honours examination; provided that, if he or she takes Part II under Regulation 6 for the Philosophy Tripos in his or her first year or in the year after being a candidate for another Honours examination, he or she must offer Papers B1 and B2 of Part II of the Classical Tripos, and that if he or she takes Part II under Regulation 6 in his or her second year and has not been a candidate for another Honours examination he or she must offer Papers B1, B2, and B3 of Part II of the Classical Tripos.

Social and Political Sciences

An affiliated student may proceed to the B.A. Degree after obtaining honours in Part II of the Social and Political Sciences Tripos in his or her second year under the same conditions as if he or she had obtained honours in another Honours examination also.

Theology and Religious Studies

An affiliated student may take in his or her second year Part II of the Theological and Religious Studies Tripos under the same conditions as if he or she had obtained honours in another Honours Examination in the year next but one preceding, and, if he obtains honours, proceed to the B.A. Degree.

No affiliated student may take Part II of a Tripos as his first Tripos Examination later than the sixth term after his first term of actual residence, unless the regulations for a particular Tripos specifically allow it.

Incorporation

A graduate of the University of Oxford or of Trinity College, Dublin may be admitted by incorporation to a degree which in the opinion of the Council of the Senate is equivalent to the highest degree which either of those Universities has conferred upon him or her provided that:

  (i) he or she has been matriculated as a member of the University;
  (ii) he or she has attained the age of twenty-four years or the Council of the Senate see fit to exempt him or her from this provision;
  (iii) he or she has satisfied the Council of the Senate that he or she qualified for his degree by residence as well as by passing the examinations and performing the exercises required;
  (iv) he or she has been admitted to a University office or a Headship or a Fellowship (other than an Honorary Fellowship) of a College or holds a post in the University Press specially designated under Statute J, and
  (v) if he or she holds a University office or a post in the University Press or a Fellowship of a College to which initially he or she was not appointed or elected to the retiring age, he or she has already held a University office or offices or such a post or posts in the University Press or a Fellowship or Fellowships (other than an Honorary Fellowship) of a College or of different Colleges, or any combination of these, for a total period, which need not be continuous, of at least three years.

Applications together with the necessary evidence must be sent direct to the Registrary.

M.A. Degree under Statute B, III, 6

The degree of Master of Arts may be conferred on a person qualified under Statute B, III, 6 provided that he satisfies conditions (i), (ii), (iv), and (v) specified above for incorporation. Applications together with the necessary evidence must be sent to the Registrary.

M.A. status

Certain persons may be granted the status of Master of Arts provided they have attained the age of twenty-four years and have been matriculated. These persons include Graduate Students or other persons to whom the Council have previously granted the status of Bachelor of Arts, for so long as they are not of standing to proceed to the degree of Master of Arts. Enquiries may be made at the University Registry.

A person holding M.A. status may not be a candidate for any examination leading to a B.A. or Mus.B. Degree nor may he or she compete for any emolument for which undergraduates only are eligible.

B.A. status

Graduate Students who are not graduates of the University and have not the status of Master of Arts have the status of Bachelor of Arts, as have certain Oxford graduates while in Cambridge. This status may also be conferred by the Council on other persons who have attained the age of twenty-one years and have been accepted for admission to a College and who are not reading for a B.A. or equivalent degree.

A person holding B.A. status may not be a candidate for any examination leading to a B.A. or Mus.B. Degree nor may he or she compete for any emolument for which undergraduates only are eligible.

The University Library

In the early fifteenth century, the first known catalogue of the University Library listed 122 books. There are now approaching five million books housed in the present Library, which comprises a building designed by Sir Giles Scott and opened in 1934 and an extension, to the designs of Gollins, Melvin, Ward and Partners, added to it in 1971. Under the provisions of the Copyright Act, the Library may claim a copy of every work published in the British Isles. Among the collections for which it is famous are Bishop Moore's library (30,000 volumes), the Bradshaw Collection of Irish books, the Wade collection of Chinese books, the Acton Historical Library (60,000 volumes), the Taylor-Schechter collection of Hebrew fragments from the Cairo Genizah, the Sir Geoffrey Keynes collection, the Bible Society Library, and important collections of incunabula – books printed before 1501 – and manuscripts.

Throughout its history the Library has provided open access to a large proportion of its books. Virtually all the stacks in the 1934 building are open-access, the closed-access stacks being concentrated in the 1971 extension, which also houses reading rooms for Manuscripts, for Rare Books, for Periodicals and Reserved Books, and for Official Publications. The 1934 building houses the main Reading Room (containing the principal collection of reference works: bibliographies, encyclopedias, dictionaries, etc.), the Map Room (with a collection of over one million maps and 10,000 atlases) and the Music Department. Details of these rooms and their times of opening are available at the Library.

The Library is open on Saturdays from 9 a.m. to 1 p.m. and on other weekdays from 9 a.m. to 7.15 p.m. (10 p.m. during the Easter Full Term). There is no entry to the Library during the last quarter of an hour before the time of closing.

The Library is closed on all Sundays, on Christmas Eve and the following days up to and including the New Year public holiday, on Good Friday and the three following days, on the August Bank Holiday, and from 16 to 23 September both days inclusive.

The day for the annual return of books is 15 September.

The Library is open to all members of the University on the production of a valid Reader's Ticket, for which application should be made in person at the Library during the opening hours of the Admissions Office. Currently registered Graduate Students and Bachelors of Medicine and Bachelors of Surgery may borrow not more than ten volumes from the Library's stock of loan materials. Not more than five volumes may be borrowed by undergraduates of at least six terms' standing, by Affiliated Students and by students who are graduates of any university and who are either following a course of study leading to a Tripos Examination or to a degree, diploma, or certificate of the University, or who are resident members of Ridley Hall, Westcott House, Westminster College, or Wesley House.

Those entitled to borrow ten volumes must return their books not later than eight weeks after borrowing or by the day for the annual return of books, whichever is earlier. Those entitled to borrow five volumes must return their books not later than the fourteenth day after the date of borrowing. Such books may not be borrowed again by the same person before the second day after their return.

The fine for not returning a book by the specified day is 30p for the first day and 10p for each subsequent weekday until the book is returned.

Copies of the Library's Regulations, Rules and Code of Practice of Established Usage are available on request and are posted in the Library. A leaflet, *Introduction for New Readers*, is given to all readers when they first register to use the Library. The *Readers' Handbook* is available on request in the Entrance Hall.

The Fitzwilliam Museum

In the Fitzwilliam Museum's collections the fine arts and the applied arts are both extensively represented. There are in addition departments of antiquities, of manuscripts and printed books and of coins and medals.

The principal feature of the Museum is the series of picture galleries occupying the whole of the upper floor. The collection covers a period from the late Middle Ages to the present day, and includes paintings from all the main European schools. Among those of outstanding quality is a group of Venetian pictures by Titian, Tintoretto, Bassano and Veronese. Drawings, water-colours, and prints, with Italian maiolica and some sculpture and furniture, are also shown in these galleries.

The main collections of applied arts, portrait miniatures, and illuminated manuscripts are displayed in the galleries on the lower floor, together with the antiquities, which comprise Egyptian and Western Asiatic Collections, and Greek and Roman Collections. Of high importance is the collection of ceramics, which is among the foremost in Great Britain; it is particularly strong in English pottery, but includes also many fine examples of English and Continental porcelain, and of Far Eastern Islamic wares. Another exceptional collection is that of English table glass. Other applied arts which are represented include silver (both English and Continental), metalwork, carvings, jewellery, textiles (including a very good collection of English samplers), fans, and arms and armour. A group of renaissance bronze statuettes, mostly Italian, and a series of medals from the work of Pisanello onwards, are displayed in association with the paintings.

The collection in the Coin Room is one of the most important in this country. It consists of a fully representative collection of coins, medals, and seals, including in particular very fine Greek coins and an unrivalled collection of medieval coins. Admission is for students only.

The Print Room contains another particularly good collection. Its chief riches are prints by Dürer and other early German masters, and by Lucas van Leyden, etchings by Rembrandt, and extensive series of English and French portrait prints, and of political caricatures.

The Library, open to members of the University and scholars, contains over 200,000 volumes. In addition there are 800 medieval manuscripts, many of them illuminated, and of the finest quality, and a collection of early printed books. The music collection of over 1,400 volumes is one of the best in Great Britain. Among other collections are autographs and literary manuscripts.

Special Exhibitions are held in the Adeane Gallery, the most considerable gallery for this purpose in East Anglia.

The Museum is open free to the public as follows:

Tuesdays to Fridays	Lower Galleries 10 a.m.–2 p.m.
	Upper Galleries 2 p.m.–5 p.m.
Saturdays	10 a.m.–5 p.m.
Sundays	2.15 p.m.–5 p.m.

(Subject to staff availability)

The Museum is closed from 24 to 31 December, on New Year's Day, and on Good Friday; and on Mondays, except on Easter Monday and on the Spring and August Bank Holidays. On these Mondays the Museum will be open as on Tuesdays to Fridays.

Madingley Hall

Madingley Hall, a country house four miles west of Cambridge, was acquired by the University in 1948 and is now administered by the Board of Extra-mural Studies. The Hall is used as a residential centre for adults who attend the 200 short courses (usually of one to five days' duration) which the Board organizes each year for the general public; and a similar number of conferences and courses is held there in conjunction with other public and educational institutions and with some commercial and industrial organizations. Up to sixty residents can be accommodated, mainly in single rooms.

All enquiries about the programme of public courses, arrangements for specially commissioned courses and conferences or residence at the Hall should be addressed in the first instance to the Director of Extra-mural Studies, Madingley Hall, Madingley, Cambridge, CB3 8AQ. Telephone: Madingley (0954) 210636.

2

THE COLLEGES

NOTE

Details of the individual Colleges, their Tutors, teaching Fellows, and Directors of Studies are included in the *Admissions Prospectus* which is published by the Cambridge Tutorial Representatives each year in March for the guidance of candidates applying between March and October for entry in the following year. The prospectus may be obtained on application to any College or to the Cambridge Intercollegiate Applications Office, Kellet Lodge, Tennis Court Road, Cambridge, CB2 1QJ. Because of the cost of postage, a leaflet printed on airmail paper and containing all essential information is usually sent to applicants from overseas.

General

Each College is a self-governing body; the control of its affairs rests with its Head and Fellows or, in some Colleges, with a smaller executive body elected by them from among themselves. There are **twenty-seven Colleges which admit both undergraduate and graduate** students in most subjects. Of these, Lucy Cavendish (for women only), St Edmund's and Wolfson Colleges admit only mature and affiliated undergraduates. The remaining twenty-four Colleges admit undergraduates of all types. Two Colleges (Newnham and New Hall) admit women only: the remainder admit both men and women (Christ's, Churchill, Clare, Corpus Christi, Downing, Emmanuel, Fitzwilliam, Girton, Gonville and Caius, Jesus, King's, Magdalene, Pembroke, Peterhouse, Queens', Robinson, St Catharine's, St John's, Selwyn, Sidney Sussex, Trinity, Trinity Hall). In addition to these Colleges, Hughes Hall admits a limited number of affiliated students, but no ordinary undergraduates. Homerton College admits men and women for the B.Ed. Degree course only, using a different application procedure from other Colleges. Clare Hall and Darwin College admit graduate students only.

Under the authority of the governing body of each College certain officers are responsible for College teaching and for the detailed work of its administration. They include Lecturers and Directors of Studies, one or more Bursars, one or more Deans, who are responsible for services in the College Chapel and sometimes for College discipline, the Praelector, traditionally known as the Father of the College, who presents its members for degrees, and, most important of all from the point of view of the undergraduate, one or more Tutors, who advise their pupils not only about their studies but also on every kind of problem arising out of College and University life on which they may need advice, and who represent them in all their dealings with the University. A Tutor controls the educational and business arrangements arising out of his pupils' relations with the College.

Admission

Full details of the procedure for admission to Cambridge are published annually in the *Cambridge Admissions Prospectus*, a copy of which is sent to all schools which prepare candidates for admission to universities. The prospectus may be obtained on application to any College or to the Cambridge Intercollegiate Applications Office (CIAO), Kellet Lodge, Tennis Court Road, Cambridge, CB2 1QJ. Application must be made both to Cambridge on a Preliminary Application Form obtainable from a College or from CIAO, and to the Universities Central Council on Admissions (UCCA, P.O. Box 28, Cheltenham, Glos., GL50 3SA) listing Cambridge as one of five choices of University on the UCCA application form.

The closing date for both forms to reach their destinations is 15 October of the year before that in which the applicant wishes to be admitted. Early application is helpful to the College of first preference and in the case of an Open Applicant to CIAO.

Homerton College uses a different application procedure from other Colleges. A full description of the B.Ed. course can be found in the Homerton prospectus, obtainable on request from Homerton College, Cambridge CB2 2PH.

Enquiries about admission for research or for any of the courses for graduates other than the course for the Certificate in Education should be made to the Secretary, Board of Graduate Studies, University of Cambridge, 4 Mill Lane, Cambridge, CB2 1RZ. Enquiries about the course for the Certificate in Education should be made to the Department of Education, 17 Trumpington Street, Cambridge, CB2 1QA.

Overseas Candidates

About 12 per cent. of the students in the University, or roughly 1,500, are from overseas. Most of them are graduates with a good degree when they come to Cambridge. The Colleges do not normally admit undergraduates who do not intend to work for one of the qualifications offered by the University and there are therefore limited facilities for overseas students who wish to spend 'a junior year' abroad or 'transfer year' at Cambridge. Twelve Colleges are, however, ready to accept a small number of such students. These Colleges are: Christ's, Clare, Corpus Christi, Girton, Lucy Cavendish (for mature and affiliated women students only), Newnham (women only), New Hall (women only), Peterhouse, Queens', Robinson, Selwyn and Sidney Sussex.

A student proposing to spend three years in Cambridge working for a B.A. Degree should apply to the Tutor for Admissions of one (and one only) of the Colleges stating his or her age, present qualifications, other qualifications which he or she may hope to obtain by the time of his or her admission, and his or her proposed subject of study. The applicant should do this preferably by 31 July but in any case not later than 15 October in the year before that in which he or she wishes to be admitted.

An applicant holding an approved degree of an overseas university may be granted the privileges of affiliation and can then be admitted to the B.A. Degree in two years instead of the usual three, after passing one Part only of a Tripos, generally Part II (see p. 13). High academic standards are required of intending candidates in all subjects. Applications to Colleges should be submitted as early as possible, preferably by 30 September (for admission in October of the following year), and otherwise by the closing date, which is 31 October – although some Colleges may consider applications received after the closing date.

A prospective graduate student should apply, in the first instance, to the Secretary of the Board of Graduate Studies, 4 Mill Lane, Cambridge, CB2 1RZ. In addition to being asked to complete an application form, he will be required to give particulars of his qualifications and the names of Professors or others under whom he has worked, and to whom reference can be made. He will also have to state his subject of research or give an outline of his proposed thesis. Information concerning fellowships, scholarships, grants, etc., for which prospective graduate students from Commonwealth countries are eligible, is contained in *Scholarships Guide for*

Commonwealth Postgraduate Students published by the Association of Commonwealth Universities (36 Gordon Square, London, WC1H 0PF) and which can be obtained from that address, or from booksellers.

If overseas students require further information about the University before applying to a College, they should write to the Registrary, The University Registry, The Old Schools, Cambridge, CB2 1TN, or, in the case of Graduate Students, to the Secretary of the Board of Graduate Studies.

Overseas students seeking admission as undergraduates (but not those seeking admission as affiliated students) must also submit an application form to the Universities Central Council on Admissions (U.C.C.A.). The U.C.C.A. handbook and application form can be obtained from the U.C.C.A. office, GPO Box 28, Cheltenham, Glos., GL50 3SA or, usually, from the students' High Commission or Government Agency in London. U.C.C.A. will inform an applicant what costs are involved and these must be prepaid. The application form must be returned by 15 October of the year previous to that in which admission is required. Even if a student has a preference for Cambridge, he will be well advised to mention on his U.C.C.A. form other universities by which he would wish to be considered if he fails to secure a place at the university of his first choice.

The Government introduced charges for overseas visitors for treatment under the National Health Service from 1 October 1982. These charges do not apply to students on a course at a university lasting over six months. Nevertheless, students are advised before arrival to consult their College Tutor regarding taking out a health insurance policy especially if dependants are involved. Overseas visitors from the E.C. countries and from those countries where there is a reciprocal agreement* are exempt from being charged under the N.H.S.

* Countries with reciprocal agreements are: Austria, Bulgaria, Czechoslovakia, German Democratic Republic, Gibraltar, Guernsey, Hong Kong, Hungary, Isle of Man, Jersey, Malta, New Zealand, Norway, Poland, Portugal, Romania, Sweden, Union of Soviet Socialist Republics, Yugoslavia.

3

UNIVERSITY EXAMINATIONS AND DEGREES

UNIVERSITY EXAMINATIONS

Most University examinations are held once in every academical year, towards the end of the Easter Term. The dates of most examinations are prescribed by Ordinance and may be found in the *Cambridge Pocket Diary*. The dates for 1989–90 may be found on pp. 35–8 of this volume.

Examination entry

The College is responsible for entering candidates *in statu pupillari* for examinations, but if a candidate fails to keep his Tutor fully informed of his intentions he may incur a fine for late entry.

A first list of candidates, then a corrected list, and lastly a final list with a programme giving the time and places of examinations, are published successively from December onwards and are posted in each College. Every candidate is expected to make certain that he has been correctly entered for his examination and to inform his Tutor at once if there is an error in his entry in any of the lists. Each candidate is supplied for this purpose with an entry verification card, which he is expected either to sign as correct or to amend to show his correct entry. Amendments lead to the issue of revised cards until the candidate signs one as correct.

Conduct in examinations

No candidate may enter an examination room later or leave earlier than thirty minutes after the beginning of a session except with the consent of the Supervisor or Senior Invigilator. A candidate may not take into an examination room or have in his possession during an examination any unauthorized book or paper, nor may he remove from the room any paper except the question paper and any books or papers which he may have been authorized to take in. During an examination a candidate may not communicate with any other candidate, nor may he leave his place except with the consent of the Supervisor or an Invigilator. Should a candidate act in such a way as to disturb or inconvenience other candidates, he shall be warned and may, at the discretion of the Supervisor, Invigilator, or Examiner, be dismissed from the session. Candidates attending a practical examination must comply with the safety requirements of the laboratory in which the examination is held.

Candidates may apply to the Examiners if they think that there is a misprint or other error in the paper, and also may inquire whether they may take some particular point for granted in answering a question. For these purposes an Examiner will be present for the first twenty minutes of each session.

Candidates affected by illness or other serious hindrance

If a candidate for any University examination, except one for which candidates are required to be Graduate Students or one leading to the M.B., B.Chir. Degrees or the Vet.M.B. Degree, is absent from the whole examination because of illness or other grave cause, the Council of the Senate may, after receiving proof of that cause and evidence of his attainments:

(i) give him leave to degrade, including leave, where required, to present himself as a candidate for the same examination;
(ii) allow him the examination;
(iii) allow him one, or, where that is consistent with the regulations for the Ordinary B.A. Degree, two Ordinary Examinations;
(iv) declare him to have attained the honours standard. This allowance is given only when the candidate would, if successful in the examination, have been declared by the Examiners to have attained the honours standard.

If a candidate is prevented by illness or other grave cause from attending part of the examination, the Examiners may be authorized by the Council of the Senate to declare him to have deserved honours or to have deserved to have passed the examination, whichever is appropriate. The Examiners may not make such a declaration unless they judge the candidate to have acquitted himself with credit in a substantial part of the examination and unless they either are unable to include him in the list of successful candidates or would otherwise have to award him a class that would in their opinion misrepresent his abilities. If the Examiners are unable to do so, the Council may take one of the four courses set out above.

If a candidate has been hindered by illness or other grave cause in preparing for an examination which he takes and fails, the Council may also take one of the four courses set out above.

It is very important that any examination candidate who

(1) *finds that his preparation for the examination is seriously hindered;*

(2) *withdraws from the examination;*

or (3) *completes it under a disability,*

should inform his Tutor of the fact and of the full circumstances, whatever the cause, at the earliest possible moment.

Examinations leading to the B.A. Degree

Examinations for honours leading to the B.A. Degree are known as Tripos Examinations. Most Tripos Examinations are divided into Parts but a few are undivided. It is possible to offer various combinations of subjects by taking Part I of a Tripos in one subject at the end of the first or second year and Part I or Part II of another Tripos, or one of the undivided Triposes, at the end of the third. An account of the regulations and subjects for each Tripos Examination and of the regulations governing the standing of candidates is given in the next chapter, and is summarized in the Table below.

A candidate obtains honours by the inclusion of his name in one of the classes or under the heading 'Declared to have deserved honours' in the class-list or by his being allowed the examination by the Council.

No one who is, or is qualified to be, a member of the Senate, or is, or has been, registered as a Graduate Student, shall be a candidate for honours in an honours examination.

Qualifying Examinations or Preliminary Examinations for Triposes are not honours examinations but 'examinations proper to an honours course'. In any year in which he does not take a Tripos Examination (or in certain subjects a Qualifying Examination) a candidate for honours is likely to be advised by his College to sit for a Preliminary Examination. Failure to take or pass a Preliminary Examination does not in itself debar a student from proceeding to a Tripos Examination.

EXAMINATIONS AND DEGREES

Tables of standing required for Honours Examinations

In the following tables standing is shown by reference to years and not to terms as in the Ordinances. The tables do not show any differing requirements in the numbers of papers to be offered by candidates according to their standing. No account is taken of the privileges of Affiliated Students. The tables are therefore only an approximate guide, and for complete accuracy the relevant Ordinances should be consulted.

I. Examinations taken as the first Honours Examination

Examination	Year of standing required
Anglo-Saxon, Norse, and Celtic	2
Archaeology and Anthropology, Part I	1
Architecture, Part I A	1
Classical, Part I	1 or 2
Computer Science, Part I A	1
Economics, Part I	1
Engineering, Part I A	1
Engineering, Part I B	2
English, Part I	1 or 2
Geographical, Part I A	1
Historical, Part I	2
Land Economy, Part I A	1
Law, Part I A	1
Law, Part I B	2
Mathematical, Part I A	1
Mathematical, Part I B	1 or 2
Medical Sciences, Part I A	1
Modern and Medieval Languages, Part I	1 or 2
Music, Part I A	1
Natural Sciences, Part I A	1
Oriental Studies, Part I	1 or 2
Philosophy, Part I A	1
Philosophy, Part I B	2, 3, or 4
Social and Political Sciences, Part I	1
Theological and Religious Studies, Part I	1

II. Examinations taken after one or more Honours Examinations

Examination	Year of standing required		Remarks
Anglo-Saxon, Norse, and Celtic	3 or 4	‡	
Archaeological and Anthropological, Part I	3	*	
Archaeological and Anthropological, Part II	3 or 4	‡	
Architecture Tripos, Part IA	2 or 3	*	Part IA of same Tripos must precede
[1]Architecture Tripos, Part IB	2, 3, or 4	*	Part IB of same Tripos must precede
[1]Architecture Tripos, Part II	3 or 4	‡	Specific requirements for preceding exam
Chemical Engineering, Part I	3 or 4	*	Part I of same Tripos must precede
Chemical Engineering, Part II	4 or 5	‡	Not after MML I with Latin or Greek
Classical, Part I	2, 3, or 4	‡	
Classical, Part II	3 or 4	‡	
Computer Science, Part IB	2 or 3	*	Not after Part IB
Computer Science, Part II (General)	3 or 4	*	Part IB of the same Tripos must precede
Computer Science, Part II	3 or 4	*	
[2]Economics, Part II			
(i)	3		After Part I of same Tripos
(ii)	3 or 4	‡	After any other Tripos
Education			
(i)	3, 4, or 5	*	Ed.Q.E. must immediately precede
(ii)	2		B.Ed. candidates (Homerton)
Electrical and Information Sciences	3 or 4	*	Part IA may not be the sole preceding exam
Engineering, Part IA	2 or 3		
Engineering, Part IB	2, 3, or 4	‡	
Engineering, Part II	3 or 4	‡	Part IA may not be the sole preceding exam
English, Part I	2, 3, or 4	‡	

[1] Candidates must have satisfied the Examiners in studio-work the preceding year.
[2] Candidates must be exempt, or obtain exemption, from E.Q.E.M.
* To be taken in the year after another Honours Examination.
† To be taken in the year next but one after another Honours Examination.
‡ To be taken in the year after or next but one after another Honours Examination.

EXAMINATIONS AND DEGREES

Examination	Year of standing required	Remarks
English, Part II	2, 3, or 4 ‡‡	
Geographical, Part I A	2 or 3 *	
Geographical, Part I B	2, 3, or 4 *	
Geographical, Part II		
(i)	3 or 4 ‡‡	Part I A may not be the sole preceding exam
(ii)	3 or 4 *	After Part I B
Historical, Part I	3 or 4 ‡‡	
Historical, Part II	3 or 4 ‡‡	
History of Art	3 or 4 ‡‡	
Land Economy, Part I B	3 or 4 *	
Land Economy, Part II	2	
Law, Part I B	3 or 4 *	Faculty Board may grant special permission
Law, Part II	2, 3, or 4 ‡‡	Part I B of same Tripos must precede. Faculty Board may grant special permission
	3 or 4 ‡‡	
Management Studies	3 or 4 †	Part I A may not be the sole preceding exam
Manufacturing Engineering, Part I	3 or 4 *	After Part I B or Part II Engineering
Manufacturing Engineering, Part II	4 or 5 *	Part I of same Tripos must precede
Mathematical, Part I A	2 or 3 *	
Mathematical, Part I B	2, 3, or 4 ‡‡	
Mathematical, Part II	2, 3, or 4 ‡‡	Part I A may not be the sole preceding exam
Mathematical, Part III	3 or 4 ‡‡	
Medical Sciences, Part I A	2 or 3 §	Not after NST I A including Physiology
Medical Sciences, Part I B	2, 3, or 4 *	Part I A must precede
Medical Sciences, Part II (General)	3 or 4 ‡‡	Section I or II only after Parts I A and I B. Section III only after NST I A and I B
Modern and Medieval Languages, Part I	2, 3, or 4 ‡‡	

* To be taken in the year after another Honours Examination.
† To be taken in the year next but one after another Honours Examination.
‡‡ To be taken in the year after or next but one after another Honours Examination.
§ The previous Honours Examination must have been taken not earlier than the candidate's second year.

Examination	Year of standing required		Remarks
Modern and Medieval Languages, Part II			
(i)	3 or 4	‡	If Honours obtained after first year
(ii)	3 or 4	†	If Honours obtained in first year. Or next but two if year spent abroad with approval of Faculty Board
Music, Part I B	2 or 3	*	
Music, Part II	3 or 4	*	Part I B of the same Tripos must precede
Natural Sciences, Part I A	3	*	
Natural Sciences, Part I B	2		
Natural Sciences, Part II (General)	3 or 4	§	
Natural Sciences, Part II	3 or 4	§	
Oriental Studies, Part I	2, 3 or 4	‡	
Oriental Studies, Part II			
(i) certain subjects	3 or 4	*	
(ii) certain subjects	3 or 4	†	Part I of the same Tripos must precede
Oriental Studies, Part II (General)	3 or 4		
Philosophy, Part I B	2, 3, or 4		Part I A may not be sole preceding exam
Philosophy, Part II	3, 4, or 5	‡	
Social and Political Sciences, Part II			
(i)	3		After Part I of the same Tripos
(ii)	3 or 4	‡	After any other Tripos
Theological, and Religious Studies, Part I	2, 3, or 4	*	
Theological and Religious Studies, Part II			
(i)	3, 4, or 5	†	After Part I or other Honours exam
(ii)	3, 4, or 5	*	After Honours exam other than Part I

* To be taken in the year after another Honours Examination.
† To be taken in the year next but one after another Honours Examination.
‡ To be taken in the year after or next but one after another Honours Examination.
§ The previous Honours Examination must have been taken not earlier than the candidate's second year.

EXAMINATIONS AND DEGREES

Dates of Examinations, 1989–90

Anglo-Saxon, Norse, and Celtic	
Preliminary	4 June 1990
Tripos	4 June 1990
Archaeology and Anthropology	
Tripos, Part I	6 June 1990
Preliminary for Part II	4 June 1990
Tripos, Part II	4 June 1990
Architecture	
Tripos, Part I A	6 June 1990
Tripos, Part I B	6 June 1990
Tripos, Part II	6 June 1990
Chemical Engineering	
Tripos, Part I	2 June 1990
Tripos, Part II	26 May 1990
Classics	
Preliminary for Part I	11 June 1990
Tripos, Part I	6 June 1990
Except Papers 10 and 11	24 and 25 Apr. 1990
Preliminary for Part II	4 June 1990
Tripos, Part II	4 June 1990
Diploma in Classical Archaeology	4 June 1990
Ordinary Examinations in Latin and Greek	11 June 1990
Computer Science	
Tripos, Part II	2 June 1990
Tripos, Part I A	2 June 1990
Tripos, Part I B	2 June 1990
Tripos, Part II (General)	2 June 1990
Diploma, Part A	2 June 1990
Development Studies	
Diploma	12 June 1990
Economics	
Tripos, Part I	8 June 1990
Preliminary for Part II	7 June 1990
Tripos, Part II	31 May 1990
Diploma	31 May 1990
E.Q.E.M.	6 Oct. 1989 and 25 Apr. 1990
Education	
Qualifying Examination	28 May 1990
Tripos	28 May 1990
Electrical and Information Sciences	
Tripos	29 May 1990
Engineering	
Tripos, Part I A	11 June 1990
Tripos, Part I B	6 June 1990
Tripos, Part II	29 May 1990
English	
Tripos, Part I	28 May 1990
Tripos, Part II	25 May 1990
Ordinary Examination	11 June 1990

Geography
Tripos, Part IA	6 June 1990
Tripos, Part IB	31 May 1990
Preliminary for Part II	31 May 1990
Tripos, Part II	31 May 1990

History
Preliminary for Part I	24 Apr. 1990
Tripos, Part I	6 June 1990
Preliminary for Part II	2 June 1990
Tripos, Part II	2 June 1990
Ordinary Examination	11 June 1990

History of Art
Preliminary	6 June 1990
Tripos	6 June 1990

Land Economy
Tripos, Parts IA, IB, and II	28 May 1990

Law
Tripos, Part IA	29 May 1990
Tripos, Part IB	29 May 1990
Tripos, Part II	29 May 1990
Examination in Criminal Law	2 Oct. 1989
LL.M. Examination	31 May 1990

M.Phil. Examinations
Archaeology	4 June 1990
Biological Anthropology	12 June 1990
Computer Speech and Language Processing	8 May 1990
Economics	12 June 1990
Economics and Politics of Development	12 June 1990
Finance	12 June 1990
Land Economy	12 June 1990
Latin-American Studies	12 June 1990
Medieval and Renaissance Literature	24 Apr. 1990
Musical Composition	12 June 1990
Oriental Studies	4 June 1990
Psychopathology	12 June 1990
Social Anthropology	4 June 1990
Theology	11 June 1990

Management Studies Tripos
29 May 1990

Manufacturing Engineering
Tripos, Part I	29 May 1990
Tripos, Part II	25 Apr. 1990

Mathematics
Tripos, Part IA	1 June 1990
Tripos, Part IB	6 June 1990
Tripos, Part II	4 June 1990
Tripos, Part III	4 June 1990
Diploma in Mathematical Statistics	11 June 1990

Medical Sciences
Tripos, Part IA	4 June 1990
Tripos, Part IB	26 May 1990
Tripos, Part II (General)	26 May 1990

EXAMINATIONS AND DEGREES

Medicine and Surgery
  First M.B. Examination   24 Sept. 1990
  Second M.B. Examination   2 July and 24 Sept. 1990
    (except Medical Sociology)
  Medical Sociology   16 Jan. and 2 July 1990
  Final M.B. Examination Part I   6 Dec. 1989, 17 Apr. and 20 June 1990
           Part II   4 Dec. 1989, 18 Apr. and 18 June 1990
           Part III   4 Dec. 1989 and 18 June 1990

Modern and Medieval Languages
  Preliminary for Part I   4 June 1990
  Tripos, Part I   4 June 1990
    Oral Examinations   21 Apr. 1990
  Preliminary for Part II   28 May 1990
  Tripos, Part II   28 May 1990
  C.C.K.   23 May 1990
    Oral Examinations   21 Apr. 1990
  Advanced Oral Examinations   8 Mar. 1990

Music
  Tripos, Part I A   4 June 1990
  Tripos, Part I B   28 May 1990
  Tripos, Part II   28 May 1990
  Mus.B. Examination   28 May 1990

Natural Sciences
  Tripos, Part I A   8 June 1990
  Tripos, Part I B   26 May 1990
  Tripos, Part II (General) Section I   26 May 1990
  Preliminary for Part II (General) Section II   30 May 1990
  Tripos, Part II (General) Section II   30 May 1990
  Preliminary for Part II   26 May 1990
  Tripos, Part II   30 May 1990

Oriental Studies
  Preliminary for Part I   4 June 1990
  Tripos, Part I   4 June 1990
  Tripos, Part II (General)   4 June 1990
  Tripos, Part II   4 June 1990

Philosophy
  Tripos, Part I A   28 May 1990
  Preliminary for Part I B   28 May 1990
  Tripos, Part I B   28 May 1990
  Preliminary for Part II   28 May 1990
  Tripos, Part II   28 May 1990

Social and Political Sciences
  Preliminary for Part II   1 June 1990
  Tripos, Part I   6 June 1990
  Tripos, Part II   1 June 1990

Theological and Religious Studies
  Tripos, Part I   1 June 1990
  Preliminary for Part II   1 June 1990
  Tripos, Part II   1 June 1990
  Diploma   11 June 1990

Veterinary Medicine
  Second Vet.M.B. Examination   2 July and 24 Sept. 1990
  Final Veterinary Examination, Part I   25 Sept. 1989 and 18 June 1990
  Final Veterinary Examination, Part II   25 Sept. 1989 and 11 June 1990
  Final Veterinary Examination, Part III   25 Sept. 1989 and 11 June 1990

Carus Greek Testament Prizes   11 Dec. 1989
Jeremie Prizes   4 Dec. 1989
Dr Lightfoot's Scholarships   24 Apr. 1990
Charles Oldham Shakespeare Scholarship   16 Mar. 1990
John Stewart of Rannoch Scholarships in Hebrew   24 Apr. 1990
Tyrwhitt's Hebrew Scholarships   8 May 1990
Whewell Scholarships in International Law   31 May 1990
Winchester Reading Prizes   2 May 1990

DEGREES

Degrees are conferred at Congregations in the Senate-House. These ceremonies are held three times in each term and once in the Long Vacation, usually on Saturdays at 2 p.m.* Although the degree of B.A. may be conferred at most Congregations, candidates for that degree are more likely, unless their circumstances are unusual, to be admitted to it on one of the two days in June set apart as days of General Admission to Degrees. Candidates may be admitted to degrees by proxy.

Entry of candidates

Any qualified person who wishes to take a degree should communicate with the Tutor or Praelector of his College. Anyone who wishes to proceed to the B.A. Degree on some date other than a day of General Admission, or to some other degree at any Congregation, should give early notice to his College. Except with the approval of the Vice-Chancellor, no degree other than those of B.A., LL.M., Mus.B., Vet.M.B., and B.Ed. may be conferred on a day of General Admission.

* The Congregation in March usually now starts at 1.30 p.m.

EXAMINATIONS AND DEGREES

Academical dress

In general, all men being admitted to degrees must wear at the ceremony in the Senate-House dark clothes, black shoes, white ties, and bands with their academical dress. Women wear a plain black or dark coat and skirt with a plain white blouse, or a plain black or dark dress, and black shoes; their stockings need not be black, but must not be of a bright colour.

A person being admitted to a degree by incorporation or to the degree of M.A. under Statute B, III, 6 wears the gown and hood of the degree that he is to receive. A graduate of the University being admitted to a degree wears the gown and hood of the highest degree that he has hitherto received from the University. A possessor of the status of B.A. or M.A. who is not a graduate of the University and is being admitted to a degree other than the degree of M.A. under Statute B, III, 6 or to a degree by incorporation shall wear the gown appropriate to his status and the hood of the degree, or of the higher of the two degrees, that he is to receive. An undergraduate being admitted to a degree wears his undergraduate gown, and the hood of the degree, or of the higher of the two degrees, that he is to receive.

The order of seniority of degrees is prescribed by Ordinance.

Presentation

At each Congregation, after supplicats (motions for the approval of the conferment of degrees) have been read by the Senior Proctor, degrees are conferred. When his turn comes, each candidate is led forward by the officer presenting him (generally, except for higher degrees, the Praelector of his College) who takes him, right hand by right hand, to the Vice-Chancellor and pronounces the formula of presentation, stating that the candidate is qualified for the degree by his character and his academic attainments. The candidate then kneels and places his hands together between those of the Vice-Chancellor, who pronounces the formula of admission to the degree. The graduate rises, bows to the Vice-Chancellor and withdraws. He may then leave the Senate-House at the next permissible opportunity.

Certificates of Degrees

Original certificates of degrees are issued without charge to all persons proceeding to degrees. A fee of £3 is charged for a *repetition* of a certificate of a degree; for a certificate issued from the Registry attesting matriculation or the passing of any examinations a fee of £5 is charged. The Registrary may issue on request a degree certificate of an alternative design bearing the arms of the University printed in colour, for which a fee of £15 is charged.

Bachelor of Arts by honours

A candidate for this degree must have kept or been allowed nine terms and have obtained honours

    (*a*) in Part II of any Tripos (except Section I of Part II (General) of the Natural Sciences Tripos), or in the Anglo-Saxon, Norse, and Celtic Tripos, the Education Tripos, the Electrical and Information Sciences Tripos, the History of Art Tripos, or the Management Studies Tripos;

or (*b*) in any two Honours Examinations, except that he may not count for this purpose (i) both Part IA and Part IB of the same Tripos, (ii) any two Parts IA, or (iii) both Part IB of the Natural Sciences Tripos and another Honours Examination (other than Part II of a Tripos);

    (*c*) in any three Honours Examinations.

If, however, he completed the examination requirement in any term earlier than his eighth he must *either* produce a 'Certificate of Diligent Study' (i.e. a certificate from his College that since completing this requirement he has been engaged upon academic studies suited to his attainments and has been regular and diligent therein), *or*, not earlier than in the last but one of the terms that he needs for a degree, pass an examination leading to the Ordinary B.A. Degree, the examination for the Diploma in Mathematical Statistics, or in Computer Science, or the LL.M. Examination (provided that if he elects to proceed to the LL.M. Degree he is not also entitled to proceed to the B.A. Degree). It is not possible for a candidate to qualify for the B.A. degree and a one-year M.Phil. degree simultaneously.

For details of other courses leading to the B.A. Degree with honours that are open to Affiliated Students, see p. 17.

The Ordinary degree of Bachelor of Arts

No candidates are admitted to the University as candidates at the outset for the Ordinary B.A. Degree and the degree is mainly intended for those who fail to pass a Tripos Examination or a Tripos Qualifying Examination and so become ineligible to proceed to the B.A. Degree by honours.

In order to qualify for the Ordinary degree a candidate must

    (*a*) keep nine terms;

    (*b*) accumulate three Ordinary Examinations.

A candidate cannot accumulate more than one Ordinary Examination by the end of his first year nor more than two by the end of his second year, nor, except with the permission of the Council of the Senate, may he take more than one examination leading to the Ordinary B.A. Degree in the same term, and then only after his second year.

Ordinary Examinations are accumulated as follows:

(i) A pass in a Preliminary Examination or a Tripos Qualifying Examination always counts as the equivalent of one Ordinary Examination, as does being classed in one language in Part I of the Modern and Medieval Languages Tripos or in a Part of a Tripos taken in a candidate's first year.

(ii) Being classed in a Part of a Tripos taken in a candidate's first year counts as the equivalent of one Ordinary Examination as does being classed in a Part of a Tripos taken in a candidate's second year if he already has one Ordinary Examination to his credit but otherwise that counts as the equivalent of two Ordinary Examinations.

(iii) An allowance of one Ordinary Examination may be made by the Council of the Senate to a candidate who has not passed a Preliminary Examination or a Tripos Qualifying Examination, and of one or two Ordinary Examinations to a candidate who has not passed a Tripos examination, but has performed sufficiently well to justify that allowance.

(iv) The Examiners may make an allowance towards the Ordinary B.A. Degree to a candidate for an Honours Examination who has not been classed but who has performed sufficiently well to justify it, which gives him one Ordinary Examination if he is in his first year or is in his second year and has one Ordinary Examination to his credit or is in his third year and has two Ordinary Examinations to his credit and otherwise two Ordinary Examinations.

(v) A pass in an actual Ordinary Examination counts as one Ordinary Examination. A performance of at least the standard for an allowance towards the Ordinary B.A. Degree in an Honours Examination which the Council of the Senate have allowed a candidate to take as though it were an Ordinary Examination counts either as one Ordinary Examination or as two, as the Council may decide.

The Ordinary Examinations in Greek, Latin, English, History, Law, certain Modern and Oriental Languages, Geography, Medical Sciences, Philosophy, Theology, and certain of the Natural Sciences are described where their subjects are dealt with in the following chapter.

Bachelor of Divinity

A candidate for the B.D. Degree must be a graduate of the University of at least five years' standing from admission to his first degree in the University (or in another University if he has also been admitted to the M.A. degree under Statute B, III, 6 or a degree by incorporation) and must submit a dissertation or published work; he must also establish his competent knowledge of Christian Theology.

Bachelor of Education

A candidate for the B.Ed. Degree must have kept five terms, passed the Ed.Q.E., obtained honours in the Education Tripos, and satisfied the Examiners for the Tripos in practical teaching ability.

Bachelor of Medicine

A candidate for the M.B. Degree must have kept three terms and have passed the prescribed examinations.

Bachelor of Music

A candidate for the Mus.B. Degree must have kept nine terms and have passed the two Sections of the prescribed examination.

Bachelor of Surgery

A candidate for the B.Chir. Degree must have kept three terms and have passed the prescribed examinations.

Bachelor of Veterinary Medicine

A candidate for the Vet.M.B. Degree must have kept nine terms and have passed the prescribed examinations, the last of which cannot be completed until the end of his sixth year.

Master of Arts

A candidate for the M.A. Degree must be a Bachelor of Arts of the University of at least two years' standing, and six or more years must have passed after his first term of residence. The College will usually notify its members when they are of standing to proceed to the M.A. Degree. Each candidate is required to give notice to the College of the day on which he proposes to take the degree.

Master of Law

A candidate for the LL.M. Degree must have kept three terms and passed the LL.M. Examination.

Master of Letters

A candidate for the M.Litt. Degree must be a registered Graduate Student who shall pursue a course of research under supervision, ordinarily for not less than six terms, and submit a dissertation embodying the results of his course (see Chapter 5).

Master of Music

A candidate for the Mus.M. Degree must be a Bachelor of Music of the University of at least two years' standing, and must pass the prescribed examination, which is in two Parts. Part I, which is held in March, is a written and oral examination. Part II is an exercise in the form of a musical composition, written for the occasion, and conforming to the detailed provisions of the regulations. A Bachelor of Music who has been approved for the degree of Mus.M. may be admitted to that degree three years after he has been admitted to the Mus.B.

Master of Philosophy

A candidate for the M.Phil. Degree must normally be a graduate of a university. To qualify for the degree he must pursue a course of study of either one year or two years under supervision and pass the prescribed examination. The examination after the two-year course consists of written papers, a thesis, and may include an oral examination. The examination after the one-year course consists of written papers or a thesis or both, and may include an oral examination on the thesis. No one may qualify simultaneously for the B.A. degree and the one-year M.Phil. degree.

Master of Science

A candidate for the M.Sc. Degree must be a registered Graduate Student who shall pursue a course of research under supervision, ordinarily for not less than six terms, and submit a dissertation embodying the results of his course (see Chapter 5).

Master of Surgery

A candidate for the M.Chir. Degree must be a holder, of at least five years' standing, of an approved medical degree and also a holder of a primary degree of the University or of the M.A. degree under Statute B, III, 6 or a degree by incorporation (in the latter two cases of at least two years' standing), must pass a clinical examination, and must submit a thesis or published work. Further details may be obtained from the Secretary of the M.Chir. Committee, at the Clinical School.

Doctor of Divinity

A candidate for the D.D. Degree must be a Bachelor of Divinity of the University of at least three years' standing or a holder, of at least twelve years' standing, of another degree of the University or a degree of another university (in the latter case holding also the M.A. degree under Statute B, III, 6 or a degree by incorporation), and must submit a dissertation or published work.

Doctor of Law

A candidate for the LL.D. Degree must be of at least eight years' standing from admission to his first degree of this University or of another University (in the latter case holding also the M.A. degree under Statute B, III, 6 or a degree by incorporation), and must submit proof of distinction by some original contribution to the advancement of the science or study of Law.

Doctor of Letters

A candidate for the Litt.D. Degree must be of at least eight years' standing from his first degree of this University or of another University (in the latter case holding also the M.A. degree under Statute B, III, 6 or a degree by incorporation), and must give proof of distinction by some original contribution to the advancement of science or of learning.

Doctor of Medicine

A candidate for the M.D. Degree must be a holder, of at least four years' standing, of an approved medical degree and also a holder of a primary degree of the University or of the M.A. degree under Statute B, III, 6 or a degree by incorporation (in the latter two cases of at least two years' standing). He must submit a dissertation specially composed for the purpose and may also submit published work in support of his dissertation. In certain circumstances he may be allowed to submit published work only. He will undergo a *viva voce* examination on work submitted, as well as on other medical subjects, and may be required to take a clinical examination.

Doctor of Music

A candidate for the Mus.D. Degree must be of at least eight years' standing from his first degree of this University or of another university (in the latter case holding also the M.A. degree under Statute B, III, 6 or a degree by incorporation), and must give proof of distinction in musical composition. He must submit not more than three works (printed or otherwise) including either an oratorio, an opera, a cantata, a symphony for orchestra, a concerto, or an extended piece of chamber music.

Doctor of Philosophy

A candidate for the Ph.D. Degree must be a registered Graduate Student who shall pursue a course of research under supervision ordinarily for not less than nine terms, and submit a dissertation embodying the results of his course (see Chapter 5). Under special regulations, a candidate may proceed to the Ph.D. Degree if he can give proof of a significant contribution to scholarship by the submission of published work and an oral examination. Candidature for the Ph.D. Degree under the special regulations is confined to graduates of the University who must be of at least six years' standing from admission to their first degree of this University or of another university (in the latter case holding also the M.A. degree under Statute B, III, 6 or a degree by incorporation).

Doctor of Science

A candidate for the Sc.D. Degree must be of at least eight years' standing from his first degree of this University or of another university (in the latter case holding also the M.A. degree under Statute B, III, 6 or a degree by incorporation), and must give proof of distinction by some original contribution to the advancement of science or of learning.

4

COURSES OF STUDY FOR DEGREES, DIPLOMAS, AND CERTIFICATES

ANGLO-SAXON, NORSE, AND CELTIC

The course of study leading to the Anglo-Saxon, Norse, and Celtic Tripos is primarily concerned with the culture and history of the British Isles between the departure of the Romans and the coming of the Normans. It provides a diverse education of general value or, if desired, a stage in the training of future scholars in this field. All the main forms of evidence can be studied, a student being free to place the emphasis where he chooses. For instance, he can pursue a principal interest in history or literature or in one region or period. If he is an historian, he can learn to correlate the various kinds of evidence and to read the documents in their original languages; if his interest is predominantly literary, he can study a literature of his choice against its cultural background and in comparison with other literatures. If he wishes, he can also extend his interest by studying, for example, Middle English as well as Old English, or the history of the Vikings in their homelands, or Celtic literatures until the end of the Middle Ages. He has an option of preparing a short dissertation to give some experience of research. No previous knowledge of the subjects studied is required, although some knowledge of Latin is useful.

This Tripos is not divided into Parts. A student can qualify for an Honours Degree by taking it, either first or second, in combination with a Part of some other Tripos, although an Affiliated Student can qualify for an Honours Degree on this Tripos alone. According to a student's interests it combines well with English, or History, or Modern and Medieval Languages, or Classics, or Archaeology and Anthropology, or History of Art, or Theological and Religious Studies. A student who is preparing for this Tripos after obtaining Honours in a Part of another Tripos may spend either one year or two, but the Department expresses a strong preference for two;* any other student spends two years. A student who is spending two years may take a Preliminary Examination at the end of his first year.

* If he wishes to spend two years, after spending two years obtaining honours in another Tripos, and is receiving an L.E.A. grant, he is strongly advised to apply through his Tutor for his grant for his fourth year not later than the beginning of his fourth term at the University.

The Anglo-Saxon, Norse, and Celtic Tripos[1]

The examination consists of the following papers:

1. England before the Norman Conquest

An introduction to the history and civilization of England from the age of the Anglo-Saxon settlements to the Norman Conquest. A candidate will be required to use primary sources in the original languages or in translation.

2. The Vikings

An introduction to the political, social, and religious history of the Vikings in their homelands and during their expansion to east and west. Their history in the British Isles is excluded in so far as it is included in Papers 1 and 3. Particular attention is paid to primary sources, notably those in Old Norse, with discussion of the historical value of the Sagas of Icelanders. A knowledge of Old Norse, although useful, is not essential. There will be recommended texts, including groups of Old Norse works to be read in translation.

3. The Celtic-speaking peoples from the fourth century to the twelfth

An introduction to the history and civilization of the Celtic-speaking peoples of the British Isles and Brittany from the collapse of the Roman Empire to the Norman invasions. A candidate will be required to use primary sources in the original languages or in translation.

4. Insular Latin language and literature (also serves as Paper 10 of Part I and Paper 16 of Part II of the English Tripos)

An introduction to the Latin prose and poetry of England, Wales, and Ireland during the early medieval period. An advanced knowledge of Latin is not expected when preparation is begun, although some knowledge of the language is desirable. There will be set texts in the original language and recommended texts in translation. A candidate will be required to show detailed knowledge of set texts and to write essays on recommended texts as well as on set texts.

5. Old English language and literature (also serves as Paper 9 of Part I and Paper 15 of Part II of the English Tripos)

An introduction to the language and literary characteristics of Old English prose and poetry. There will be set texts in the original language; a candidate will be required to translate passages from the set texts and an unseen passage of Old English, and to write essays on selected topics.

---

[1] A list of set texts and recommended reading may be obtained from the office of the Faculty of English.

ANGLO-SAXON, NORSE, AND CELTIC

6. Old Norse language and literature (also serves as Paper 11 of Part I and Paper 17 of Part II of the English Tripos)

An introduction to the language and literary characteristics of Old Norse prose and poetry. There will be set texts in the original language; a candidate will be required to translate passages from the set texts and an unseen passage of Old Norse, and to write essays on selected topics.

7A. Medieval Welsh language and literature I (also serves as Paper 12 of Part I and Paper 18A of Part II of the English Tripos)

An introduction to the language and literature of Wales from the beginnings to the end of the Middle Ages. There will be set texts in the original language, including selections from the 'Mabinogion', from the early poets, and from Dafydd ap Gwilym and other later poets, and there will also be recommended texts in the original language. A candidate will be required to translate an unseen passage of Middle Welsh and extracts from the set texts. He will be required also to write essays on selected topics and/or to comment on the linguistic or literary characteristics of passages from the recommended texts.

7B. Medieval Welsh language and literature II (also serves as Paper 18B of Part II of the English Tripos)

This paper is intended for those who have taken Paper 7A or have reached an equivalent standard when preparation is begun. There will be set and recommended texts in Old and Middle Welsh. A candidate will be required to translate extracts from these set texts, and to translate other passages, of which some will be drawn from the recommended texts and some will be unseen. There will be two further groups of set texts, one of them in Medieval Cornish and Breton and the other in Middle Welsh. A candidate will be required to translate extracts from either or both of these further groups of texts. He will be required also to write essays on selected topics in medieval Welsh, Cornish or Breton language and literature, or in comparative Celtic philology.

8A. Medieval Irish language and literature I (also serves as Paper 19A of Part II of the English Tripos)

An introduction to the language and literature of early medieval Ireland, in particular until the end of the tenth century. There will be set texts in the original language, including selections from the early lyric poetry and from the prose sagas and religious prose, and there will also be recommended texts in the original language. A candidate will be required to translate an unseen passage of Old Irish and extracts from the set texts. He will be required also to write essays on selected topics and/or to comment on the linguistic or literary characteristics of passages from the recommended texts.

8 B. Medieval Irish language and literature II (also serves as Paper 19 B of Part II of the English Tripos)

This paper is intended for those who have taken Paper 8 A or have reached an equivalent standard when preparation is begun. Irish language and literature from the beginnings to the end of the Middle Ages are studied. There will be set and recommended texts in the original language. A candidate will be required to translate extracts from the set texts, and to translate other passages, of which some will be drawn from the recommended texts and some will be unseen. He will be required also to write essays on selected topics in medieval Irish language and literature or in comparative Celtic philology.

9. Palaeography, diplomatic, and the editorial process

An introduction to the processes by which extant sources written in the languages studied for Papers 1-8 have been transmitted and of the scholarly methods by which these sources are converted into a usable form. The history of script, the manuscript as a physical object, the history of the forms of legal instruments, and the various editorial approaches and techniques are studied. A candidate will be required to answer a compulsory practical question and to write essays on selected topics.

10. Special subject I, specified by the Faculty Board of English from time to time

In a year for which a subject is specified, the paper will consist of a detailed consideration of a predominantly historical topic related to more than one field of study in the Tripos. A candidate will be required to use primary sources in the original languages or in translation. He will be expected to show a knowledge of relevant literary and linguistic evidence, and he will have to show familiarity with both Germanic and Celtic societies.

The subject specified for **1990** is The Norman Conquest of Britain.

11. Special subject II, specified by the Faculty Board of English from time to time.

In a year for which a subject is specified, the paper shall consist of a detailed consideration of a predominantly literary topic related to more than one field of study in the Tripos. A candidate will be expected to show knowledge of the relevant primary sources and familiarity with both Germanic and Celtic literatures.

The subject specified for **1990** is Literacy.

12. Anglo-Saxon England in the pagan period (also serves as one of the papers set for Paper 5 in Archaeology of Part II of the

Archaeological and Anthropological Tripos and Paper O9 of Part II of the Classical Tripos)

An introduction to the archaeology and history of the Anglo-Saxon peoples from the age of the settlements to c. 650. A candidate will be expected to show familiarity with archaeological, historical, and linguistic evidence.

13. Early medieval literature and its background (Paper 8 of Part I of the English Tripos)

14. Chaucer (Paper 3 of Part II of the English Tripos)

15. Medieval English literature, 1066–1500 (Paper 4 of Part II of the English Tripos)

16. History of the English language (Paper 13 of Part II of the English Tripos)

A candidate will be required to answer three questions from Section A only.

17. Medieval Latin literature, from 400 to 1300 (Paper 12 of Part II of the Modern and Medieval Languages Tripos)

18. The Teutonic languages, with special reference to Gothic, Anglo-Saxon, Early Norse, Old Saxon, and Old High German (Paper 121 of Part II of the Modern and Medieval Languages Tripos)

19. A subject in medieval European history
In **1990**: Rome's heirs: the German kingdom of Western Europe, 476–987 (Paper 15 of Part II of the Historical Tripos)

20. French literature, thought, and history, before 1300 (Paper 1 of Part II of the Modern and Medieval Languages Tripos)

A candidate who has spent two years preparing for the Tripos must offer six papers; a candidate who has spent one year in preparation is required to offer only five papers. No candidate can offer a paper he has already taken in another Tripos Examination. A candidate cannot offer both Papers 7A and 7B or both 8A and 8B; nor can he offer more than two of Papers 13–20.

A candidate may apply to the Faculty Board of English not later than the division of the Michaelmas Term for permission to submit a dissertation on any subject within the scope of the Tripos. The application must specify the proposed subject of the dissertation and the whole scheme of papers that the candidate intends to offer. A candidate whose application is granted shall offer one paper less than the number of papers that he would otherwise be required to choose. The Faculty Board may require that such a candidate shall not offer more than one paper from among Papers 13–20. The dissertation must show evidence of reading, of judgement and criticism, and of power of exposition, but not necessarily of original research, and shall be of not less than 5,000 and not more than 12,000 words in length (inclusive of notes and appendices). A candidate will be required to declare that the dissertation submitted is his own work and does not contain material which he has already used for a comparable purpose, and to give full references to sources used. The dissertation must be typewritten, and submitted to the Head of Department so as to reach him not later than the first day of Full Easter Term. The Examiners have power at their discretion to examine a candidate *viva voce* on the dissertation and on the general field of knowledge within which it falls.

The Preliminary Examination for the Anglo-Saxon, Norse, and Celtic Tripos

The examination consists of the following papers:

1. England before the Norman Conquest
2. The Vikings
3. The Celtic-speaking peoples from the fourth century to the twelfth
4. Insular Latin language and literature
5. Old English language and literature
6. Old Norse language and literature
7. Medieval Welsh language and literature
8. Medieval Irish language and literature
9. Palaeography

A candidate must offer three papers.

A student who is not a candidate for the examination may offer Paper 4 or 5 or 6 or 7 in accordance with the regulations for the Preliminary Examination for Part I of the English Tripos, and his marks will be communicated to his Tutor.

ARCHAEOLOGY AND ANTHROPOLOGY

There are in these subjects courses of study followed by candidates for:

The *Archaeological and Anthropological Tripos*, which is divided into two Parts.

The *Preliminary Examinations* for each subject of Part II of the Tripos.

The *M.Phil. Degree* (one-year course) *in Archaeology*, *Biological Anthropology*, and *Social Anthropology*.

Papers from this Tripos can be taken in the *Anglo-Saxon, Norse, and Celtic Tripos* (p. 47); in Part II of the *Classical Tripos* (p. 99) and in the Diploma in *Classical Archaeology* (p. 108); in Part II (General) of the *Medical Sciences Tripos* (special subject, Biological Anthropology) (p. 278); in the *Oriental Studies Tripos* (p. 390): in Part I of the *Social and Political Sciences Tripos* (p. 430); and in Part II of the *Theological and Religious Studies Tripos*.

The Archaeological and Anthropological Tripos

Part I

The first part of the Tripos provides an introduction to four interlocked but relatively discrete subjects: (*a*) Archaeology, (*b*) Biological Anthropology, (*c*) Social Anthropology, (*d*) Sociology.

The central field of study is the variation in cultural, social, and biological conditions of humankind and the different theoretical and practical ways in which such variation can be understood. This variation is viewed through the perspective of time since the appearance of the early precursors of human beings (which is dealt with by Biological Anthropology), over the millenia during which human beings developed their culture and societies (the subject matter of Archaeology), and in the variety of contemporary peoples ranging from Western society, developing new nations in Africa, Asia, and Latin America, rural peasantry, and tribal societies (the scope of Social Anthropology). Social anthropology is concerned with both contemporary and traditional societies, placing them in a comparative perspective, studying their interaction, and examining processes of evolution and social change. Sociology is the study of social institutions and processes, of the social context of ideas, and of the individual as a member of society, with its main emphasis on industrial societies.

The course of study for Part I of the Tripos lasts one year. It is anticipated that most candidates will confine their studies to three of the four subjects. There are two lecture courses in each subject. Candidates for Part I may be first-year undergraduates intending to go on to Part II of the Tripos or intending to transfer to another Tripos (e.g. Social and Political Sciences). The course is also open to third-year undergraduates from other Triposes (e.g. Medical Sciences).

Part II

Social Anthropology. The Part II in Social Anthropology is designed as a two-year course for those who have read some anthropology or sociology in the previous year. A modified version of the Part II to be taken in one year, is however available, for undergraduates who have previously taken a two-year Part I in a different Tripos. The first year of the two-year syllabus includes the study of subsidiary subjects, linguistics, social psychology, or statistics and computing. In the same year, students undertake work on a special region of the world, e.g. South Asia, Latin America, Europe, New Guinea, West Africa, or East Africa. Each year three of those areas are offered as options. All students take a paper on the Third World. The second year of the two-year course is directed to the four main areas of comparative institutional study, economics, religion, kinship and politics, and there are a number of other optional topics available, including anthropology and development, anthropological theory and urban and ethnic studies. The modified one-year Part II course requires students to take the anthropological theory paper, two of the main institutional papers and offers a choice for the fourth paper. Students taking the one-year course should consult their Directors of Studies as early as possible and are advised to undertake some preliminary reading.

The concerns of social anthropology are closely related to those of sociology, but include the full range, historical and geographical, of human societies and cultures. Attention is paid both to pre-industrial societies and to the non-industrial sectors of more complex ones, and to contemporary urban communities. With regard to methods, emphasis is placed upon techniques of intensive field research, use of comparative study, formal analysis, and sociological enquiry. The courses offered attempt to introduce students to the comparative study of politics, kinship, religion, and economy. Optional papers may be taken in theories of social dynamics, the study of social change, urban and ethnic studies, comparative medicine, population studies

ARCHAEOLOGY AND ANTHROPOLOGY

and development. Other topics include the study of myth and ritual, the role of women, systems of exchange, modes of production and reproduction, micro-politics, the ethnography of disputes, and the use of force.

Cambridge has a very distinguished tradition of social anthropological research and theory, going back to Sir James Frazer who was the leading and most influential anthropologist around the turn of the century. More recently, Professors Meyer Fortes, Sir Edmund Leach and Jack Goody have been recognised as international leaders in the subject. The tradition they have left behind involves the study of all aspects of human societies, from comparative investigations into economic systems to the study of cultural and religious symbolism. There is systematic research into the social organisation and ethos of advanced societies as well as simpler ones, and amongst advanced societies, both socialist and capitalist societies receive systematic attention. The Department is concerned with the classical theoretical questions about human society and with preparation for the practical application of anthropology in fields such as development in the Third World or ethnic and community relations in the developed world.

Biological Anthropology. Biological Anthropology can be taken as a two-year Part II course by students from Part I of the Tripos. The subjects examined at the end of the Preliminary year (which includes a long vacation course as an optional component) are shown below (p. 62). Human biology is studied at a much greater depth than in Part I, and students with no science background will find it challenging. First-year students intending to take Part II Biological Anthropology are advised to discuss their choice of Part I courses with a staff member.

Transfer to a two-year Part II in Biological Anthropology is also possible from other Triposes, especially Part IA of the Natural Sciences or Medical Sciences Triposes. A one-year course is available for students who have completed Part IB of the Medical Sciences Tripos or who have taken biological subjects in Part IB of the Natural Sciences Tripos. Students taking the one-year course are advised to attend during the preceding Long Vacation term.

The course for the Tripos Examination covers three main branches of biological anthropology:

(*a*) The comparative anatomy, ecology, behaviour, and evolution of the primates; the fossil evidence for hominid evolution in relation to the palaeoecological and archaeological records. (*b*) Biological variation in human populations and its genetic basis. The course stresses polymorphic systems, but also deals with continuous variation, including psychometric traits. (c) Human adaptability in different environments; ecological aspects of nutrition and disease; growth; biological aspects of demography. Students are also required to select one of several options for more detailed study, or to complete a project and submit a dissertation. Practical work includes biometric and laboratory studies, and the statistical analysis of data.

Archaeology. Archaeological research has made possible the study of human societies through long periods of time; the evidence is steadily improving in quality and variety.

The Part II Archaeology course, designed as a self-contained two-year study (which can be taken by undergraduates transferring from other disciplines without serious disadvantage), considers the theoretical premises upon which a study of the past can be based and the way in which that study has developed. Students also discuss and receive practical training in the field-methods used and in the retrieval and analysis of archaeological evidence in the laboratory. Teaching in comparative technology, both ancient and modern, is given from the University's museum collections.

Undergraduates also choose, from a range of area and period options, a series of problems to study in detail. These currently include early prehistory, later prehistoric and early historic Europe, Asian, African and Classical Archaeology. Other optional topics include ethnoarchaeology, experimental archaeology, quantitative archaeology, palaeoecology, prehistoric agriculture and the archaeology of the Americas and East Asia.

Practical experience is offered through participation in a number of departmental and other research projects.

Part I

Part I is taken at the end of the first year. It may also be taken at the end of his third year by a student who has obtained honours in another Tripos Examination in his second year. A candidate takes five papers; he shall be permitted but not required to select his papers from more than three groups.

Subjects of examination

The subjects of examination are as follows:

Group A. Archaeology

1. (a) The development of early societies

The paper will deal with the principles and history of Archaeology and with aspects of world prehistory, from the origins of human culture to the development of agriculture, social ranking, and state formation, with particular reference to the Near East (including Egypt), the Far East, and Mesoamerica.

2. The archaeology of Europe and neighbouring areas

The paper will examine the archaeological evidence for the origins of agriculture, metallurgy, urbanism, and civilization in Europe and neighbouring areas.

Group B. Biological Anthropology

3. Human biology, ecology, and population structure

Human biology and ecosystems. Climatic and nutritional adaptations in evolutionary and comparative perspective. The ecology of disease and growth. Genetic differences and their social implications. Biosocial influences on the structure of populations.

4. Prehistory and human evolution

Chronological and environmental frameworks for human evolution. Man as a primate: behaviour and adaptation. The evolution of hominids and their artefacts; technology and ecology.

Group C. Social Anthropology

5. Human societies: the comparative perspective (Also serves as Paper 3 of the SPS Part I Tripos)

The aims, scope and methods of social anthropology and its relation to other disciplines. A review of key themes in the comparative study of human societies, complex and simple, industrial and tribal, near and remote; patterns of subsistence, economic production and exchange; kinship, marriage and the family in their social context; government, law and social order and the play of power in decision making; religious values, their expression and realisation in ritual, church, and cult. The anthropology of Western society.

The course will include an in-depth study of one selected society, using both written and audio-visual materials, and it will provide the opportunity to take part in an optional practical study-project using anthropological techniques.

6. Culture, society, and communication

This paper examines the relations between culture and society and the way in which symbols sustain human art and society. Through a comparative perspective, it focuses on the nature and organisation of different symbolic systems such as language, writing, art, ritual, clothing, gesture, and spatial arrangements, and examines the way these systems are used for verbal and non-verbal communication, the way in which culture is transmitted through time and space, and the way in which people learn behaviour appropriate to their society and social statuses.

Group D. Sociology

7. Theoretical foundations of sociology

The scope of sociology. The development of sociological thought. Distinct concepts, modes of analysis, and methods of enquiry. An introduction to theoretical issues and debates in modern sociology.

8. Industrial societies (Also Paper 2 of SPS Part I Tripos)

The historical development of specialized political and economic institutions. Social and psychological effects of industrial conditions. Social stratification and occupational differentiation. Urbanism. Demographic factors and domestic organization in industrial society. Crime and delinquency.

Part II

Part II may be taken in the third or fourth year by a candidate who has obtained honours in a Tripos Examination one or two years before.

There is an examination for Part II in each of the following three subjects:

Social Anthropology, Biological Anthropology, Archaeology[1].

Every candidate for Part II must offer one of these subjects. The scheme of papers set in each subject is set out below. The rules for dissertations are as follows:

Dissertations

A candidate who chooses to offer a dissertation must submit his proposed title, together with a brief outline of the contents of the proposed dissertation, and a statement of the papers that he intends to offer in the examination, though his Tutor to the Secretary of the Faculty Board in accordance with any instructions issued by the Faculty Board and according to the timetable set out below. Each candidate must obtain the approval of the Faculty Board for his title according to the timetable set out below. After the Faculty Board have approved a candidate's proposed title no change may be made

[1] If a candidate offers Archaeology, he must provide evidence that he has undertaken archaeological excavation or fieldwork.

ARCHAEOLOGY AND ANTHROPOLOGY

in it without the further approval of the Faculty Board, provided that a candidate in Social Anthropology may submit a revised title by the division of the Lent Term for the approval of the Faculty Board. The length of a dissertation must be as set out below. Each dissertation must be typewritten unless a candidate has obtained previous permission from the Faculty Board to present his dissertation in manuscript, and shall be submitted through the candidate's Tutor so as to reach the Secretary of the Faculty Board not later than the division of the Easter Term in which the examination is held. Each dissertation must be accompanied by (*a*) a brief synopsis on a separate sheet of paper of the contents of the dissertation, and (*b*) a certificate signed by the candidate that it is his own original work, and that it does not contain material that has already been used to any substantial extent for a comparable purpose.

Subject	Date by which titles are to be submitted	Date by which approval is to be obtained	Length of dissertation: not more than
Social Anthropology	Second Monday of Full Michaelmas Term next preceding the examination	Last day of Full Michaelmas Term	6,000 words
Biological Anthropology	First Monday of Full Lent Term next preceding the examination	Division of Lent Term	10,000 words
Archaeology	Last day of Full Michaelmas Term next preceding the examination	Division of Lent Term	10,000 words

Note the length *excludes* footnotes, appendices, and bibliography.

Social Anthropology

A candidate taking the Tripos in two years must offer Papers 1–4, and

either (a) two papers from among Papers 5–7

or (b) one paper from among Papers 5–7, and a dissertation (on which he may be examined *viva voce*) on a topic approved by the Faculty Board which falls within the field of Social Anthropology, provided that a candidate may not submit a dissertation on a topic falling within the scope of any of the papers that he/she is offering in the examination.

A one year candidate must offer:

(i) two papers from among Papers 1–4.
(ii) Paper 6.
(iii) one other paper from among Papers 1–5 and 7.

The details of the papers are:

1. Non-industrial economics

The organization of production, consumption, and exchange. Wealth, capital, and labour. Land tenure and property. Technology and social organization. Social inequality. Systems of exchange.

2. Religion, ritual, and ideology (Also serves as Paper 37 of Part II of the Theological and Religious Studies Tripos).

Religion and magic, witchcraft, totemism, prophetic cults, mythology, and cosmology. Morality in relation to ritual practices and beliefs. Comparative religion. Symbolism and thought.

3. Kinship, marriage, and the family

The comparative study of the family, kinship, and kin groups; marriage, affinity, and divorce; bride-wealth and dowry; inheritance, succession, and descent; the organization of domestic groups; sex and procreation; changing family structures.

This paper attempts to cover the kinship and family of non-European, peasant, and industrial societies, but there is a sufficient choice of questions to enable students to concentrate upon two of these fields.

4. Political anthropology

Caste and class. Local, occupational, and other forms of groupings. Stateless societies and the evolution of the state. Kingship, chiefship, and

ARCHAEOLOGY AND ANTHROPOLOGY

achieved leadership. Stratification. Councils and courts. Micropolitics. Ritual aspects of government. Feud and warfare. Law and custom; sanctions. Judicial institutions.

5. Special topic in social anthropology

Candidates are required to offer one of a number of special subjects. The topics prescribed will be:

In **1990**: *Either* Visual Anthropology
        or   Anthropology and development.
In **1991**: *Either* Medical Anthropology
        or   Anthropology and development.

6. Anthropological theory

This paper will be divided into two sections:

Section A

Historical approaches; the definitions and origins of humanity; pre-agrarian communities; agrarian society; state formation, literacy, abstract religion; technological advances; social and gender division of labour; modes of production; the growth of cities; industrial society and its emergence; capitalism and socialism.

Section B

Theoretical approaches; evolutionism, functionalism, structuralism, Marxism, transactionalism, and other approaches: philosophy, sociology, anthropology; rationality and modes of thought; growing points in anthropology.

7. Urban and ethnic studies

Urban studies, based on intensive field research in Britain and elsewhere. Urbanized and urbanizing societies. The comparative study of city life, the urban workplace, the inner city; poverty and marginality. Country and town, and movement between them. Ethnicity, colour, and migration.

Biological Anthropology

A candidate must offer all the papers and a practical examination, except that he may, with the permission of the Faculty Board obtained before the division of the Lent Term next preceding the examination, submit in place of Paper 4

either (*a*) a dissertation[1],

or (*b*) one paper from Social Anthropology or Archaeology.

The practical examination may include or consist wholly of a *viva voce* examination. The Examiners will also take into account such practical work done by candidates during the courses leading to the examination as shall from time to time be determined by the Faculty Board of Archaeology and Anthropology.

The details of the papers are:

1. Human genetics and variation

This paper requires a knowledge of human genetics and variation, with particular emphasis on polymorphism in living populations.

2. Primate biology and evolution

This paper requires a knowledge of the biology of living Primates and of human and primate evolution.

3. Human ecology and adaptability

This paper covers various aspects of human ecology and adaptability, in particular climatic adaptation, epidemiology, growth, and population aspects of nutrition.

4. Special subject in biological anthropology

One of the following subjects:

For **1988** and **1989**: *Either* Primate behaviour *or* Topics in mammalian evolution *or* The human biology of a geographical region.

---

[1] See p. 58.

Archaeology

A candidate for Part II in Archaeology must offer
  (i) Papers 1 and 2,
  (ii) *either* Papers 3 and 4 set for any one of options A, B, C, E, F, and G,
      or any two of the papers set for option D,
  (iii) one paper chosen from among Papers 5(1) to 5(18) which he/she is not offering under (ii) above,
and (iv) a practical examination[1] which must include the submission of records of such practical work done during the courses leading to the examination as may be determined by the Faculty Board; such records must bear as an indication of good faith the signatures of the teachers under whose direction the work was performed;

provided that

  (1) a candidate who offers one of options A, B, C, F, and G may submit, in place of the paper prescribed under (iii) above, a dissertation[2] on a subject approved by the Faculty Board;
  (2) a candidate who offers option D may submit, in place of the paper prescribed under (iii) above, a thesis in accordance with the provisions for the Classical Tripos;
  (3) a candidate who offers option F, if he/she is not offering a dissertation under proviso (1) above, may submit, in place of Paper 3F, a dissertation[2] on a topic approved by the Faculty Board which falls within the field of Ancient India;
  (4) a candidate who offers option G, if he/she is not offering a dissertation[2] under proviso (1) above, may submit, in place of Paper 3G, a dissertation[2] on a topic approved by the Faculty Board which falls within the field of Ancient Mesopotamia;

(*b*) A candidate may be examined *viva voce* in the subjects of the papers that he/she has offered in the examination; such an examination may include questions relating to any dissertation that the candidate has offered and on the general field of knowledge within which it falls.

---

[1] A test of the candidate's power of recognizing and describing archaeological material with special reference to the areas and periods studied.
[2] See p. 58.

The details of the papers are:

1. History and scope of archaeology

The history of archaeological research. Its relations with the humanities and the natural sciences. Quaternary research. Prehistory and protohistory. Application of archaeological method to historical times.

2. Methods and techniques of archaeology

Field archaeology, including air photography. Excavation. Classification and dating. Identification and interpretation of finds. Limitations of archaeological data.

3, 4. The archaeology of a special area.

Option A. Palaeolithic and Mesolithic archaeology.

> Paper 3A. Palaeolithic and Mesolithic archaeology 1.
> Paper 4A. Palaeolithic and Mesolithic archaeology 2.

The prehistory of human societies from the earliest times up to the origins and spread of food-production; archaeology, geological sequence, and physical types.

Option B. Europe from the Neolithic Age to the end of the Early Iron Age.

> Paper 3B. Europe from the Neolithic Age to the end of the Early Iron Age 1.
> Paper 4B. Europe from the Neolithic Age to the end of the Early Iron Age 2.

The Archaeology of Crete, Greece, the Cyclades, Italy, and Sicily, from the Neolithic Age to the beginning of the historic period; and of Malta and the West Mediterranean Islands, Southern France, and Iberia, from the Neolithic Age to the Roman Conquest. The Archaeology of the Neolithic, Bronze, and Early Iron Ages in the British Isles, North-western, Northern, and Central Europe.

ARCHAEOLOGY AND ANTHROPOLOGY

Option C. Europe from the beginning of the Roman period to the end of the medieval period.

- Paper 3C. Europe from the beginning of the Roman period to the end of the medieval period 1.
- Paper 4C. Europe from the beginning of the Roman period to the end of the medieval period 2.

These papers will have particular reference to the north-western provinces of the Roman Empire, including Britain, to northern Europe during the migration and Viking periods, and to medieval Britain.

Option D. Classical archaeology.

- Paper D1. Prehellenic archaeology (Paper D1 of Part II of the Classical Tripos).
- Paper D2. A prescribed subject connected with early Hellenic archaeology or early Greek art (Paper D2 of Part II of the Classical Tripos).
- Paper D3. A prescribed subject connected with Classical (Greco-Roman) art of the archaeology of the Greek and Hellenistic world (Paper D3 of Part II of the Classical Tripos).
- Paper D4. Archaeology of the Western Provinces of the Roman Empire (Paper D4 of Part II of the Classical Tripos).

Option E. Ancient Egypt.

- Paper 3E. History of Ancient Egypt (Paper E. 22 of the Oriental Studies Tripos).
- Paper 4E. Art and archaeology of Ancient Egypt (Paper E. 19 of the Oriental Studies Tripos).

Option F. Ancient India.

- Paper 3F. Indian art and archaeology (500 B.C.–A.D. 400) (Paper In. 22 of the Oriental Studies Tripos).
- Paper 4F. Prehistory and protohistory of India (Paper In. 21 of the Oriental Studies Tripos).

Option G. Ancient Mesopotamia.

- Paper 3G. History of Mesopotamia (Paper As. 13 of the Oriental Studies Tripos).
- Paper 4G. Art and archaeology of Mesopotamia (Paper As. 16 of the Oriental Studies Tripos).

Paper 5. Special subject.

Not more than eighteen papers, numbered 5(1) to 5(18), on special subjects in archaeology, which may include papers set as Paper 3 or Paper 4 for any of options A, B, C, E, F, and G, and any papers set for option D.

There will be a practical examination to test the candidate's power of recognizing and describing archaeological material with special reference to the areas and the period studied.

The Special Subjects in Paper 5 for **1988** and **1989** are:

(1) African archaeology.
(2) Palaeoecology and primate evolution.
(3) Prehistoric agriculture.
(4) Ethnoarchaeology, experimental archaeology, and quantitative archaeology.
(5) Archaeology of the Americas.
(6) Anglo-Saxon England in the pagan period (Paper 12 of the Anglo-Saxon, Norse, and Celtic Tripos).
(7) Agriculture, industry, and trade of the North-Western Roman Provinces.
(8) Prehistory and protohistory of India (Paper In. 22 of the Oriental Studies Tripos).
(9) Aspects of East Asian archaeology.
(10) Akkadian specified texts (Paper As. 1 of the Oriental Studies Tripos).
(11) Art and archaeology of Mesopotamia (Paper As. 16 of the Oriental Studies Tripos).
(12) Special subject in Assyriology (Paper As. 15 of the Oriental Studies Tripos).
(13) Special subject in Egyptology (Paper E. 18 of the Oriental Studies Tripos).
(14) Prehellenic archaeology (Paper D1 of Part II of the Classical Tripos).
(15) Early Hellenic archaeology (Paper D2 of Part II of the Classical Tripos).
(16) Classical (Greco-Roman) art (Paper D3 of Part II of the Classical Tripos).
(17) Archaeology of the Western Provinces of the Roman Empire (Paper D4 of Part II of the Classical Tripos).
(18) Art and archaeology of ancient Egypt (Paper E. 19 of the Oriental Studies Tripos).

The Preliminary Examination for Part II, Social Anthropology

The examination consists of four papers as follows:

1. Theory, problems, and enquiry

2. Special areas

Candidates are required to offer one of the special areas specified by the Faculty Board for **1988**:
   (*a*) Europe.
   (*b*) Latin America.
   (*c*) West Africa.

3. A paper on one of the following subjects:

(*a*) General linguistics (Paper 111 of Part II of the Modern and Medieval Languages Tripos).
   (*b*) **Anthropology and social psychology.**
   (*c*) Anthropology, communication and the arts.

4. The Third World

Candidates must offer all four papers.

The Preliminary Examination for Part II, Biological Anthropology

The examination consists of three papers as follows:

1. Human biology

The paper is divided into Sections A and B, and candidates are required to answer at least one question from each section.

Section A covers topics in biochemistry including nucleic acids, protein synthesis, and gene expression. Section B covers topics in physiology and immunology.

2. Comparative anatomy, evolution and primate biology.

The paper covers methods of study and principles of functional anatomy and behaviour, growth and development, evolution and palaeoecology.

3. Practical

The practical examination covers the subjects examined in Papers 1 and 2 and may require statistical calculations. A candidate must also present for the inspection of the Examiners, not later than the division of the Easter Term, a record of practical work done by him. The records of practical work must be presented not later than the last Mondays of Full Michaelmas Term and Full Lent Term and by the division of the Easter Term.

Candidates must offer all three papers.

The Preliminary Examination for Part II, Archaeology

The examination consists of two papers as follows:

1. Aims and methods of archaeology.
2. Special areas.

Candidates are required to offer one of the special areas specified by the Faculty Board for **1989**: (*a*) Paleolithic and Mesolithic archaeology; (*b*) Europe from the Neolithic Age to the end of the Early Iron Age; (*c*) Europe from the beginning of the Roman Period to the end of the Medieval period; (*d*) Classical archaeology; (*e*) Ancient Egypt; (*f*) Ancient India; (*g*) Ancient Mesopotamia.

Examinations set in options (*a*), (*e*), (*f*) and (*g*) may each contain additional questions on one or more of the other options.

Candidates must offer both papers and a practical examination, which will consist of the submission of practical work done during the course.

Examinations for the M.Phil. Degree

(See p. 487)

The Faculty offers the following one-year postgraduate courses which lead to the M.Phil. Degree:

Archaeology.   Social Anthropology.
Biological Anthropology.

Archaeology

The scheme of examination, at the choice of the candidate, consists of Option A or Option B.

Option A. Archaeology

(*a*) a thesis, of not more than 15,000 words in length, including footnotes, appendices, but excluding bibliography, on a topic approved by the Degree Committee for the Faculty of Archaeology and Anthropology;

and

(*b*) three written papers, each of three hours' duration, as follows:
1. The principles of archaeology.
2. The practice of archaeology.
3. Aspects of world archaeology.

    This paper includes the following sections, from which every candidate, subject to the approval of the Degree Committee, must select one, on which he will be required to answer three questions:
    (i) Palaeolithic and mesolithic archaeology.
    (ii) Bio-archaeology.
    (iii) Mesopotamian archaeology.
    (iv) South Asian archaeology.
    (v) African archaeology.
    (vi) Later European prehistory.
    (vii) The archaeology of early historic Europe.
    (viii) The archaeology of ancient Egypt.
    (ix) Quantitative analysis.
    (x) Ethnoarchaeology.
    (xi) East Asian archaeology.
    (xii) Archaeology of the Americas.
    (xiii) Cultural resource management.

    The Degree Committee may announce, not later than the end of the Easter Term of the preceding academical year, that a particular section or sections are not available;

(*c*) a practical examination designed to test the candidate's powers of understanding evidence from survey and fieldwork, and of recognizing and describing archaeological material related to the section of Paper 3 selected by him.

The examination includes, at the discretion of the examiners, an oral examination upon the thesis and written papers.

Option B. Archaeological Heritage and Museums

(a) a thesis of not more than 15,000 words in length, including footnotes and appendices, but excluding bibliography, on a topic approved by the Degree Committee for the Faculty of Archaeology and Anthropology, which must fall within the field of study covered by Papers 4–6 in (ii) below;

and

(b) three written papers, each of three hours' duration, as follows:

Paper 4. The socio-politics of the past.

Paper 5. The management of the archaeological heritage.

Paper 6. Museum practice.

A candidate who chooses Option B shall undertake practical work during a period of experience spent either in a museum housing archaeological collections or in an institution concerned with some aspect of archaeological heritage management, the nature of the practical work and length of the period being determined by the Degree Committee for the Faculty of Archaeology and Anthropology. He/she shall present for the inspection of the Examiners a record of this practical work bearing, as an indication of the good faith of the record, the signature of the museum curator or heritage manager under whose supervision it was performed. A statement concerning the candidate's period of experience, certified by the Head of the Department of Archaeology, shall be submitted to the Examiners.

The examination may include, at the discretion of the Examiners, an oral examination upon the thesis and upon the general field of knowledge within which it falls.

Biological Anthropology

The course of study consists of lectures and seminars, plus appropriate practical work. The following areas of study form the syllabus for the course: primatology and palaeoanthropology; human variation; human ecology.

A knowledge of the topics covered in the courses for Part II Physical Anthropology is required.

The scheme of examination consists of:

1. (a) a thesis of not more than 20,000 words, including tables, footnotes, appendices, and bibliography, on a subject in biological anthropology approved by the Degree Committee for the Faculty of Archaeology and Anthropology;

and (b) two written papers, each of which may cover all the areas of study prescribed in the syllabus;

and (c) two pieces of submitted work, each of which may be either an essay of about 2,000 words or an equivalent exercise, on topics specified by the Degree Committee.

2. The examination may include, at the discretion of the Examiners, (a) an oral examination on the thesis and on the general field of knowledge within which it falls, and (b) additional oral examinations on each of the written papers and on the essays or exercises.

Social Anthropology

There are four options of which each student takes one: Option A. Social Anthropology; Option B. Social Anthropology with Special Reference to the Work of a Museum; Option C. Social Anthropology and the Community; Option D. Anthropology and Development. For Option A the syllabus provides for study of Social Anthropology with special reference to the following four areas: economics of non-industrial societies; politics; kinship and the family; ritual and religion. For Option B the syllabus provides for study of two of the above four areas from Option A together with Social Anthropology as it relates to the work of a museum. For Option C the syllabus provides for study of kinship and the family, and another Option A area; and *either* Anthropology and the Community *or* Anthropology in relation to *either* Medicine *or* Population Studies, as announced. For Option D the syllabus provides for the study of Anthropology and Development, together with two of the four areas listed under Option A.

The examination consists of *either* Option A *or* Option B *or* Option C *or* Option D, as follows:

Option A. Social Anthropology

(i) a thesis, of not less than 7,500 and not more than 10,000 words in length, including footnotes, tables, appendices, and bibliography, on a subject approved by the Degree Committee for the Faculty of Archaeology and Anthropology, which must not fall within the field of any paper or essay offered by the candidate under (ii) of this Option.

and

(ii) three written papers, to be chosen by the candidate, subject to the approval of the Degree Committee, from the following list of papers:

Paper 1. Social Anthropology with special reference to the economics of non-industrial societies.

Paper 2. Social Anthropology with special reference to politics.

Paper 3. Social Anthropology with special reference to kinship and the family.

Paper 4. Social Anthropology with special reference to ritual and religion.

Option B. Social Anthropology with special reference to the Work of a Museum

(i) a thesis, of not less than 7,500 and not more than 10,000 words in length, including footnotes, tables, appendices, and bibliography, on a subject approved by the Degree Committee for the Faculty of Archaeology and Anthropology, which has special reference to material culture, but which does not fall within the field of any paper or essay offered by the candidate under (ii) or (iii) of this Option.

and

(ii) two written papers, to be chosen by the candidate, subject to the approval of the Degree Committee, from Papers 1–4 under Option A above.

and

(iii) one written paper as follows:

Paper 5. Social Anthropology, with special reference to the Work of a Museum.

A candidate who chooses Option B must undertake practical work during a period of experience spent in a museum having anthropological collections, the nature of the practical work and the length of the period being determined by the Degree Committee for

ARCHAEOLOGY AND ANTHROPOLOGY

the Faculty of Archaeology and Anthropology. He must present for the inspection of the Examiners a record of this practical work bearing, as an indication of the good faith of the record, the signature of the museum curator under whose supervision it was performed. A statement concerning the candidate's period of experience, certified by the Head of the Department of Social Anthropology, must be submitted to the Examiners.

Option C. Social Anthropology and the Community

(i) a thesis, of not less than 7,500 and not more than 10,000 words in length, including footnotes, tables, appendices, and bibliography, on a subject approved by the Degree Committee for the Faculty of Archaeology and Anthropology, which has special reference to community organization, but which does not fall within the field of any paper or essay offered by the candidate under (ii)–(iii) of this Option.

and

(ii) two written papers from Option A above including paper 3;

and

(iii) *either* one written paper as follows:
   Paper 6, Anthropology and the Community;
   or an essay on *either* Anthropology in relation to Medicine, *or* Anthropology in relation to Population Studies, whichever of those subjects is announced by the Degree Committee for the examination in a particular year. Such an essay must not be more than 6,000 words in length, exclusive of footnotes, appendices, and bibliography.

Option D. Anthropology and Development

(i) a thesis, of not less than 7,500 and not more than 10,000 words in length, including footnotes, tables, appendices, and bibliography, on a subject approved by the Degree Committee for the Faculty of Archaeology and Anthropology, which has special reference to the application of anthropological theory to development policy and/or to a specific development project.

and

(ii) any two papers from Papers 1, 2, 3 and 4 under Option A above;

and

(iii) one written paper as follows:
   Paper 7. Anthropology and Development.

In place of any one or more of the written papers prescribed for any of the Options above, a candidate may, *with the special permission of the Degree Committee, granted after consideration of the candidate's experience and special qualifications*, offer the same number of essays, each not more than 6,000 words in length, exclusive of footnotes, appendices and bibliography, and each on a topic chosen by the candidate *with the Degree Committee's approval* from a list of alternative areas of study published from time to time by the Degree Committee. The candidate, after discussion with his supervisor, should propose to the Degree Committee by the first meeting of the Michaelmas Term what course of instruction he proposes to follow. The list of possible alternative areas include the following: Comparative Studies in Anthropology; the use of historical methods and sources; the use of computing in the Social Sciences; Psychology and Anthropology; Anthropology in relation to Medicine; Anthropology in relation to Population Studies; Linguistics and Anthropology; Myth, Folklore, and Oral Literature; Anthropology of Socialist Countries; the Anthropology of Inner Asia; Visual Anthropology. Additional topics, relating to the current teaching and research interests of members of the Department of Social Anthropology, may be specified on a yearly basis.

The examination normally includes an oral examination upon the thesis, and on the essays if they are offered, and on the general field of knowledge in which they fall. In exceptional circumstances, and at the Examiners' discretion, the requirement for an oral examination may be waived.

Further details of the courses of study may be obtained from the Department of Social Anthropology, Free School Lane, Cambridge, CB2 3RF.

ARCHITECTURE

A student reading architecture will attend courses in the School of Architecture and will take the appropriate examinations for the Tripos. These examinations are held in three stages: Part I A at the end of the first year, Part I B at the end of the second year, and Part II at the end of the third year. This three-year course leads to an Honours Degree and provides a basic education and training in architecture: it also qualifies for exemption from the Part I Examination of the Royal Institute of British Architects. The course concentrates on the study of known problems of building and of the built environment. Studies may be either individual or collective. They all involve the presentation of studio-work in which specialized studies are brought into relationship in the finished design and this studio-work forms the major educational process throughout the course. After taking the three-year course, a student may apply to take a further two-year course, leading to the Diploma in Architecture, which qualifies for exemption from the Part II Examination of the Royal Institute of British Architects. The course includes both the study of certain special subjects in the field of urban studies and studio-work.

The qualification for membership of the Royal Institute of British Architects can be obtained by the satisfactory completion of the School courses and the compulsory two years of practical training required by the Royal Institute of British Architects, one year of which should be taken before the Diploma course.

The Department of Architecture has also a centre of research work in the Martin Centre for Architectural and Urban Studies.

A one-year M.Phil Degree course is offered, with options in History and Philosophy of Architecture, or Environmental Design.

Students have the use of the Faculty Library, housed in the Department of Architecture, and in addition have available the library of the Fitzwilliam Museum and the University Library. Most College libraries also possess useful collections of reference works.

Recommended reading

The following books are recommended for reading by students coming to Cambridge to read Architecture:

S. Giedion, *Space, Time and Architecture*, Harvard University Press, 1973; E. H. Gombrich, *The Story of Art*, Phaidon, 1966; Le Corbusier, *Towards a New Architecture*, Architectural Press, 1946; N. Pevsner, *An Outline of European Architecture*, Penguin Books, 1943; S. E. Rasmussen, *Experiencing Architecture*, Chapman and Hall, 1959; Curtiss, *Modern Architecture since 1900*; J. Summerson, *The Classical Language of Architecture*, B.B.C. Publications, 1963, Methuen and Co., 1964.

Recommended for further reading

J. Summerson, *Heavenly Mansions and Other Essays on Architecture*, Cresset, London, 1949; J. Summerson, *Architecture in Britain 1630–1830*, Penguin Books, 1953; Reyner Banham, *Theory and Design in the First Machine Age*; Frampton, *Modern Architecture, a critical history*; Kevin Lynch, *Image of the City*; March and Steadman, *Geometry of the Environment*, RIBA Publications, 1971; Victor Olgyay, *Design with Climate*, Princeton University Press, 1963; R. Wittkower, *Architectural Principles in the Age of Humanism*, Academic Editions, London, 1973; Reyner Banham, *The Architecture of the Well-tempered Environment*, Mainstone; C. Norberg-Schulz, *Meaning in Western Architecture*, Studio Vista, 1975.

The Architecture Tripos

The Architecture Tripos consists of three Parts: Part I A, Part I B, and Part II. The normal programme for an undergraduate who intends to spend three years reading architecture will be as follows:

Part I A of the Tripos at the end of the first year;
Part I B of the Tripos at the end of the second year;
Part II of the Tripos at the end of the third year.

All candidates taking Part II should have taken Part I A and Part I B but provision is made for candidates who change to architecture after having spent one year in another subject.

ARCHITECTURE

Part I A

The examination for Part I A consists of three sections:

Section A. Six written papers as follows:

1. Introduction to the history of architecture

The paper deals with a selective introduction to the architectural history of Western Europe and North America from classical antiquity to the early twentieth century.

2. Approaches to architectural thought and practice

The paper deals with an introduction to theoretical writings on architecture from the mid-eighteenth century to the mid-twentieth century, related to the architectural practices of the time.

3. Introduction to design theory

The paper may include questions on the fundamental nature of architectural theory and some of the ways in which specific theories have been brought to bear in the design of particular buildings.

4. Fundamental principles of construction

The paper may include questions on the development of construction methods, the elementary principles of construction of small buildings, and the basic properties of construction materials.

5. Fundamental principles of structural design

The paper may include questions on the elementary principles of structural design of buildings, on simple statics, stress analysis, and strength of structural materials.

6. Fundamental principles of environmental design

The paper may include questions on the elementary principles of environmental control in buildings and servicing of buildings.

Section B. Studio-work.

Section C. Course-work.

A candidate for Part I A must offer all six papers in Section A; and for Section B, must present for the inspection of the Examiners, not later than the Monday before the first day of the written examination, a portfolio of studio-work carried out during the academical year in which he presents himself for the examination and attested by satisfactory evidence; and for Section C, must present for their inspection, by the same day, records in an appropriate form of course-work done by him, and bearing, as an indication of the good faith of the record, the signatures of the teachers under whose direction the work was performed.

Part I B

The examination for Part I B consists of three sections:

Section A. Five papers as follows:

1. Introduction to Architectural History

Periods from the architectural history of Europe and North America are specified from time to time. The periods in **1989** and **1990** will be:

(a) Housing in Britain, 1890–1979.
(b) Modern Movement in Europe between the wars.
(c) Iconography of Materials.
(d) Interpretations of Gothic.
(e) Renaissance Approaches to Antiquities.
(f) Aspects of American Architecture 1893–1973.
(g) To be announced.

2. Theories of architecture, urbanism, and design

This paper may include questions on
(a) the nature of architectural elements and systems, their mathematical description and analysis, and approaches to synthesis;
(b) concepts and ideals which, since the mid-eighteenth century, have contributed to the development of modern architectural theory;
(c) the development of modern urban theory, the mathematical description and analysis of urban systems, and approaches to urban design and policy.

3. Principles of construction

This paper may include questions on the principles governing the use of constructional elements in complex building types, properties of materials, dimensional co-ordination, analysis of simple methods of enveloping space.

4. Principles of structural design

This paper may include questions on the structural aspects of architectural design, the behaviour of structural elements under load, the use of load-bearing brickwork, steel, and reinforced concrete, systems of roof spanning and their calculation, the mathematical and graphical determination of simple structural systems.

5. Principles of environmental design

This paper may include questions on the principles of environmental control and functional design, the practical applications of the principles of thermal response, of acoustics, and of lighting in buildings, micro-climate, planning and designing for user needs.

Section B Studio-work.

Section C Course-work.

A candidate is required:

(*a*) to offer all five papers in Section A;

(*b*) for Section B, to present for the inspection of the Examiners, not later than the Monday before the first day of the written examination, a portfolio of studio-work attested by satisfactory evidence and carried out during the academical year in which he presents himself for examination;

(*c*) for Section C, to present for their inspection by the same day, records in an appropriate form of course-work done by him, and bearing, as an indication of the good faith of the record, the signatures of the teachers under whose direction the work was performed.

The Examiners are provided by the Head of the Department with assessments of all the course-work performed by the candidates of which records have been presented under (*c*).

Part II

The scheme of the examination for Part II consists of four sections. A candidate is required for Section A to offer Papers 1–4. These papers are as follows:

1. Advanced studies in the theoretical and historical aspects of architecture and urbanism

The paper is divided into a number of sections corresponding to the topics or periods in the theory and history of architecture and urbanism announced by the Faculty Board. The Faculty Board have power to debar a candidate from attempting a specified section or sections.

2. Advanced studies in construction methods, building technologies, and the properties of materials

3. Advanced studies in structural analysis and design related to special building types

4. Advanced studies in environmental analysis and design related to special functional requirements

Section B Studio-work.

Section C Course-work.

Section D A thesis on an approved subject in the history or theory of architecture and urbanism.

A candidate for Part II is required:

(*a*) for Section A, to offer Papers 1–4;
(*b*) for Section B, to present for the inspection of the Examiners, not later than the Monday before the first day of the written examination, a portfolio of studio-work carried out during the academical year in which he presents himself for examination and attested by satisfactory evidence;
(*c*) for Section C, to present for the inspection of the Examiners, by the same day, records in an appropriate form of the course-work done by him, and bearing, as an indication of the good faith of the record, the signatures of the teachers under whose direction the work was performed;
(*d*) for Section D, to submit a thesis on an approved subject in accordance with the details below.

The Examiners are provided by the Head of the Department with assessments of all the course-work performed by the candidates of which records have been presented under (*c*).

Each candidate must submit the proposed subject of his thesis through his Tutor to the Secretary of the Faculty Board not later than the end of the third quarter of the Michaelmas Term next preceding the examination and must obtain the approval of the Faculty Board for his subject not later than the end of that term.

The proposed subject must fall within a topic or period selected from a list of topics or periods in *either* the history of architecture and urban development *or* the theory of architecture, urbanism, and design; the list will be published by the Faculty Board not later than 1 June in the year next preceding the examination.

Each thesis must be between 7,000 and 9,000 words (inclusive of notes). Theses must be typewritten (unless previous permission has

ARCHITECTURE

been obtained to present it in manuscript) and must be submitted through the Tutor to the Secretary of the Faculty Board so as to reach him not later than the first day of Full Easter Term in which the examination is to be held.

In both Parts I and II the Examiners may impose such oral and practical tests as they think fit, and in drawing up the class-list they will take into account the candidate's performance in all such tests, and in the studio-work and course-work, as well as in the written papers and theses, together with the assessment of his course-work presented by the Head of the Department. A candidate may be required to attend a *viva voce* examination in the subject of any thesis he has submitted.

The Diploma in Architecture[1]

The Diploma is awarded to members of the University who have diligently attended a two-year course prescribed by the Faculty Board and have passed the First and Second Examinations for the Diploma.

The First and Second Examinations are held once a year during the last half of the Easter Term.

First Examination

The First Examination will consist of studio-work and course-work.

(a) The *studio-work* must be carried out during the academical year in which a candidate presents himself for examination, and must be submitted to the Examiners not later than the last Wednesday of Full Easter Term.

(b) The *course-work* must consist of three essays, each on a topic proposed by the candidate and submitted through his Tutor to the Secretary of the Diploma Committee so as to reach him not later than the end of the first quarter of the Lent Term; the candidate must obtain the approval of the Diploma Committee for his topics not later than the division of the Lent Term. A candidate must propose one topic in the history, theory, and practice of each of the following subject-areas: (i) architecture, (ii) urban and regional development, (iii) building technology.

---

[1] A candidate may not make use of material that he has already submitted in the examination for the M.Phil. Degree.

Each essay must be of not less than 2,500 words and not more than 3,000 words and must be submitted to the Examiners not later than the first day of Full Easter Term.

The essays must be in English and must be typewritten unless previous permission has been obtained from the Diploma Committee to present the written work in manuscript. A candidate will be called for a *viva voce* examination in connexion with the studio-work, and the essays.

Second Examination

A candidate for the Second Examination must work in Cambridge under the supervision of the Diploma Committee during three Full Terms of an academical year; provided that the requirement to work in Cambridge may for special reasons approved by the Diploma Committee be waived by the Committee for the whole or part of that period in respect of a particular candidate.

The Second Examination consists of studio-work and a dissertation. The studio-work must be carried out during the academical year in which the candidate presents himself for examination, and must be submitted to the Examiners not later than the last Wednesday of Full Easter Term. Each dissertation must relate to a topic approved by the Diploma Committee in the field of planning, architecture, or building technology. Each candidate must submit the proposed topics of his studio-work and of his dissertation through his Tutor to the Secretary of the Diploma Committee so as to reach him not later than the division of the Michaelmas Term, and must submit his dissertation to the Examiners not later than the first day of the Full Lent Term. Dissertations must be typewritten in English, and must be of not less than 10,000 words and not more than 20,000 words. A candidate may be called for a *viva voce* examination in connexion with the studio-work and the dissertation.

M.Phil Degree in Architecture

The Department of Architecture has established a one-year M.Phil. degree course in Architecture, with two options:

Option A: History and Philosophy of Architecture
Option B: Environmental Design

The courses consist of lectures, seminars and supervisions and the syllabuses are as follows:

Option A: *History and Philosophy of Architecture*

1. Problems of interpretation in Architecture

   The main intention of the course is to establish a basis for the interpretation and understanding of the current reality of architecture. The method developed in the course will follow the principles of contemporary phenomenology and hermeneutics. This approach will also be used in the interpretation of the broader historical background.

2. Selected themes from Architectural History

   The transition from the late Baroque to the Enlightenment separates Traditional from Modern culture. This period of transition will be used as a reference for the selection and interpretation of the following critical themes:

   (a) The problem of architectural order, its foundations and cultural context, with particular emphasis on the Classical and Christian tradition, and their culmination at the beginning of the eighteenth century.

   (b) The conditions of modernity, the role of scientific and historical knowledge in the formation of a new architectural thinking, the problems of cultural autonomy, historicism, style, representation and meaning.

Option B: *Environmental Design*

1. The history of environmental control in architecture

   The development of the theory and practice of environmental control in the eighteenth and nineteenth centuries, with particular reference to the technologies of heating, ventilation and artificial lighting, and to theories of acoustics.

2. Principles of architectural physics

   The physics of heat, light and sound as applied to buildings; the impact of climate on building design; the theory of comfort and its relationship to environmental design specifications.

3. Approaches to energy conservation in building design

   The design of the form and thermal properties of the building fabric; mechanical systems and their controls; ambient energy design.

The scheme of examination consists of:

(a) a thesis, of not more than 20,000 words in length, excluding appendices and bibliography, on a topic approved by the Degree Committee for the Faculty of Architecture and History of Art;

and, **for Option A,**

(b) an exercise consisting, subject to the approval of the Degree Committee, of **either**

   (i) three essays not exceeding 5,000 words each on topics to be chosen by candidates from the list of subjects published by the Degree Committee; provided that at the discretion of the Degree Committee a comparable exercise may be substituted for not more than one of the essays; **or**

   (ii) a drawn project on a topic approved by the Degree Committee;

or, **for Option B,**

(b) five essays or other exercises, each of not more than 3,000 words, on topics specified by the Degree Committee;

provided that, if a candidate for the M.Phil. Degree has previously been a candidate either for the First Examination or for the Second Examination for the Diploma in Architecture, he may not offer in the examination for the degree a thesis or an essay on a subject that overlaps significantly with the dissertation or with any of the essays that he offered for either of the Examinations for the Diploma.

The examination may, at the discretion of the Examiners, include an oral examination upon the thesis and upon the general field of knowledge within which it falls; such an oral examination may include questions relating to one or more of the other pieces of work submitted by the candidate under (b) above.

CHEMICAL ENGINEERING

In this subject there are courses of study followed by candidates for:

The *Chemical Engineering Tripos*, which is divided into two Parts.
Certificates of Advanced Study in Chemical Engineering.
Certificates of Post-graduate Study in Chemical Engineering.

Definition

A chemical engineer is concerned with industrial processes, products, and methods of operation, in which there are changes in the composition and properties of matter. These operations may involve chemical reactions, biological processes, changes of temperature or state, mixing or separation, size reduction or other chemical or physical operations.

Education and training

The Cambridge course is subject to continuous development and enhancement. The essential ground work of thermodynamics, chemical kinetics and fluid mechanics is thoroughly covered. Major subjects recently added are the application of computers to chemical engineering processes, biochemical engineering, and food processing. Safety, hazard and operability studies, process economics and optimisation, and industrial management are also included. In all aspects of the course, the application of scientific methods to a wide variety of industrial problems is taught.

Students who wish to study chemical engineering in Cambridge begin with either (i) the Natural Sciences Tripos, see p. 334, including certain compulsory subjects, or (ii) the Engineering Tripos, see p. 65. The choice between these alternatives is purely personal.

The course for Part I of the Chemical Engineering Tripos is fully accredited by the Institution of Chemical Engineers: students who obtain the BA degree after taking Part I of the Chemical Engineering Tripos satisfy all academic requirements of the Institution.

Most students find it worthwhile to take the fourth year course which leads to Part II of the Chemical Engineering Tripos and confers the Certificate of Advanced Study.

Details of the courses are set out on pp. 89–90.

Professional training is completed by a period of work in industry in a responsible post leading to Corporate Membership of the Institution of Chemical Engineers and Chartered Engineer status, see below.

Industries

Chemical engineering as an academic discipline grew out of the requirements of the oil and heavy chemical industries in which there is need to design process plant for large scale production. Examples are the refining of petroleum, the production of tonnage plastics, fertilisers and chemicals; chemical engineers have a significant involvement with the production of North Sea oil. A substantial proportion of chemical engineers work in process industries, their primary roles being those of plant design, management and construction.

However, research and development for new processes is an important activity for chemical engineers; it is essential for chemical engineers to be involved in the conception of a new process, working alongside research chemists and other scientists in industrial laboratories and on pilot plant.

Many chemical engineers work in the plant construction industry, in the design, construction and commissioning of large scale plant.

Modern developments in biotechnology have been pioneered by chemical engineers who have developed industrial applications of the new technology. Chemical engineers are increasingly employed in traditional biotechnology industries, e.g. food processing and brewing.

The development and production of new and highly sophisticated plastics and of composite materials, e.g. mixtures of carbon fibre or glass fibre with appropriate plastics has been pioneered by chemical engineers.

Improvement of the environment is an increasing preoccupation for chemical engineers. The cleaning up of gaseous, liquid and solid effluents from the power industries and from the chemical, nuclear and other industries are major challenges in which chemical engineers are central figures. For example, the removal of acid forming gases and of particulates from power station flue gases may generate major industries in the next decade.

CHEMICAL ENGINEERING

The Institution of Chemical Engineers

The relevant professional body is the Institution of Chemical Engineers, 165–171 Railway Terrace, Rugby CV21 3HQ. The Institution functions as a Qualifying Body, overseeing both academic qualifications and industrial training.

To obtain Corporate Membership, a period of industrial training and responsible experience, usually of 3 or 4 years' duration, is necessary. After suitable training and experience and the submission of a report to the Institution, election to Membership follows. Full details of the requirements may be obtained from the Institution. Corporate Membership of the Institution is a sufficient qualification for the title of 'Chartered Engineer', conferred by the Engineering Council.

Students who intend to be chemical engineers qualify for Student Membership of the Institution; they receive the Institution's publications and may attend meetings in a number of centres throughout the country.

After successfully taking Part I of the Chemical Engineering Tripos it is usual to become a Graduate Member of the Institution. There are special arrangements (a reduced fee) for Graduate Members of the Institution reading for Part II of the Chemical Engineering Tripos.

Career prospects

Over the years it has become apparent that the broad background, and the link with new technology, provided by chemical engineering courses is a good basis for a whole range of jobs both technical and non-technical. Compared with other branches of engineering and pure science, job prospects for chemical engineers have been good. Graduates from the Department have reached very senior positions in a wide range of profitable companies large and small; this success has clearly been based on their technical expertise. Other graduates in chemical engineering have been successful in diverse fields such as banking, accountancy and journalism.

The courses leading to both parts of the Chemical Engineering Tripos are as follows:

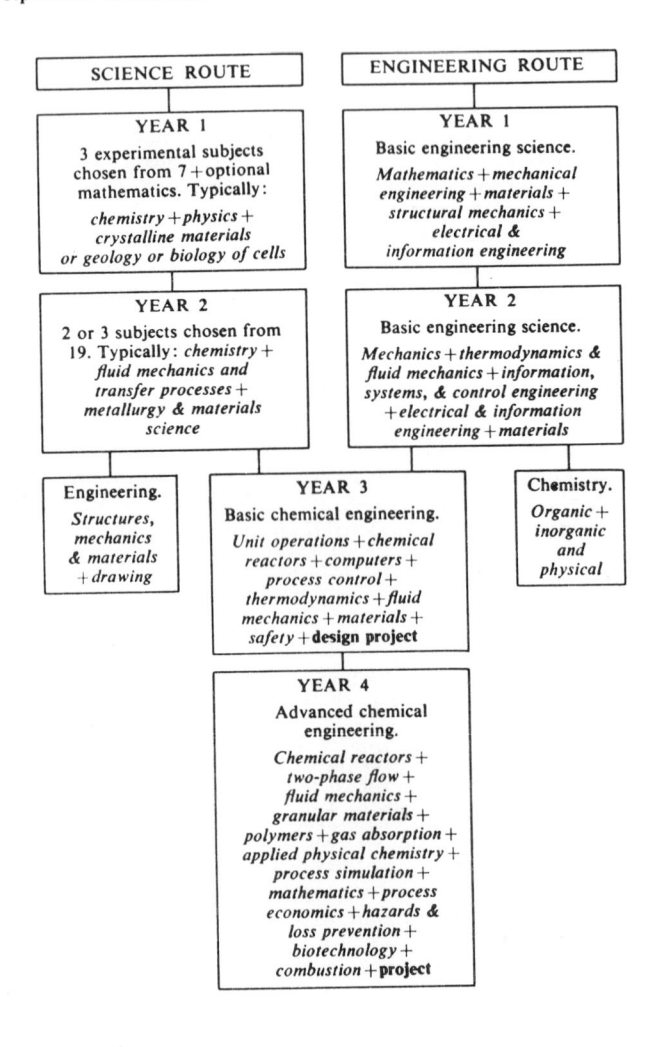

SCIENCE ROUTE

YEAR 1

3 experimental subjects chosen from 7 + optional mathematics. Typically:

chemistry + physics + crystalline materials or geology or biology of cells

YEAR 2

2 or 3 subjects chosen from 19. Typically: *chemistry + fluid mechanics and transfer processes + metallurgy & materials science*

ENGINEERING ROUTE

YEAR 1

Basic engineering science.

Mathematics + mechanical engineering + materials + structural mechanics + electrical & information engineering

YEAR 2

Basic engineering science.

Mechanics + thermodynamics & fluid mechanics + information, systems, & control engineering + electrical & information engineering + materials

---

Engineering.

Structures, mechanics & materials + drawing

YEAR 3

Basic chemical engineering.

Unit operations + chemical reactors + computers + process control + thermodynamics + fluid mechanics + materials + safety + **design project**

Chemistry.

Organic + inorganic and physical

YEAR 4

Advanced chemical engineering.

Chemical reactors + two-phase flow + fluid mechanics + granular materials + polymers + gas absorption + applied physical chemistry + process simulation + mathematics + process economics + hazards & loss prevention + biotechnology + combustion + **project**

The Chemical Engineering Tripos

The Chemical Engineering Tripos is divided into two Parts. Part I is normally taken at the end of the third year in the University and Part II at the end of the fourth year. Whilst Part I satisfies the academic requirements of the Institution of Chemical Engineers, Part II gives an opportunity to study the subject in greater depth, to consider recent advances, and to undertake some original work instead of the more usual laboratory classes. Candidates who satisfy the examiners for Part II, having already obtained the B.A. degree, are awarded a Certificate of Advanced Study.

The first two years at the University are spent reading for either the Natural Sciences Tripos, Part I B, or the Engineering Tripos, Part I B. Natural scientists who are going on to Chemical Engineering take Chemistry in their first year and Fluid Mechanics in their second year.

The choice between taking the Natural Sciences Tripos or Engineering Tripos first is largely personal. There is a natural tendency for students who are mainly interested in the construction and design of equipment to proceed via the Engineering Tripos and those who are mainly interested in the chemistry and physics of processes to proceed via the Natural Sciences Tripos. However, these subdivisions need not be permanent and a competent person with due practical training can move from one branch of the profession to the other without difficulty.

Part I

The course for Part I of the Chemical Engineering Tripos (which normally occupies the third undergraduate year) begins in the second week in July with a 'Long Vacation term' lasting about four weeks. The Tripos Examinations are held towards the end of May.

The examination consists of four written papers, each of which is of three hours' duration.

Papers 1, 2, and 3 will each be on Chemical Engineering Principles and will contain questions on applied chemistry, thermodynamics, fluid and particle mechanics, transfer processes, applied mathematics, control theory, and chemical engineering operations. They may also contain questions on technical and economic aspects of the chemical industry, industrial management, and other topics at the discretion of the Examiners.

Paper 4 will consist of two sections for which the examinations may be held on separate days:

Section 1. General Engineering, will be taken by candidates who have previously obtained honours in the Natural Sciences Tripos, Part I B, and will contain questions on selected aspects of engineering (for example, structures, mechanics, and materials of construction).

Section 2. Chemistry, will be taken by candidates who have previously obtained honours in the Engineering Tripos, Part I B.

The course for Part I includes experiments to illustrate chemical engineering principles.

An important feature of the Part I course is the *design project*. It is based on a problem such as might be encountered by a practising chemical engineer, that of manufacturing a given product from certain raw materials. There may be several alternative process routes which each student evaluates, using technical and economic criteria. One process route is then worked out in detail. Every candidate writes two independent reports: (1) a short report gives the initial assessment, and (2) a longer report which is submitted to the examiners later in the academic year.

An Affiliated Student or a student admitted to the examination for Part I by leave of the Chemical Engineering Syndicate will take the section prescribed for him or her by the Chemical Engineering Syndicate.

Part II

The Part II examination consists of four written papers each of which is of three hours' duration.

Papers 1, 2, 3, and 4 will contain questions on applied chemistry, thermodynamics, fluid and particle mechanics, applied mathematics, control theory, polymers, biotechnology, process simulation, hazard and operability states, and chemical engineering operations. The Examiners may also include questions on technical and economic aspects of the chemical industry, industrial management, and any chemical engineering topics of current interest, e.g. pollution problems.

Every student reading for Part II undertakes a project, usually in collaboration with another student, and supervised by a member of staff. Normally the work involves theoretical or experimental investigations or both. There is no other practical work during the year. Every candidate writes an independent report which is submitted to the Part II examiners. The work occasionally leads to a published paper; some of the best research in the department began with an exploratory Tripos project.

CHEMICAL ENGINEERING

Certificate of Advanced Study in Chemical Engineering

A Certificate of Advanced Study in Chemical Engineering is awarded to a member of the University who obtains honours in Part II of the Chemical Engineering Tripos having previously completed the examination requirements for the B.A. Degree.

Certificate of Post-graduate Study in Chemical Engineering

Certificates are awarded for advanced study and training in research in Chemical Engineering. A candidate must have been admitted as a Graduate Student, on the recommendation of the Degree Committee of the Faculty concerned, by the Board of Graduate Studies, who will fix the date of commencement of the candidature. A candidate must also *either* (*a*) have graduated, or have completed the examination and residence requirements for graduation, in the University, and have been classed in Part II of the Mathematical, Natural Sciences, or Engineering Tripos, or in the Chemical Engineering Tripos, *or* (*b*) if not a member of the University, satisfy the Degree Committee of fitness to study for the Certificate.

The course of instruction extends over three consecutive terms, but a candidate may be permitted in exceptional circumstances to spend up to two years in study for the Certificate.

The study and training include (*a*) courses of lectures, and (*b*) practical work carried out in one or more of the following ways: (i) experimental or theoretical exercises of an advanced type, (ii) training in research by means of assistance with a piece of research, (iii) training in research by means of an original research investigation, (iv) training in some technique.

Each candidate is required to submit a dissertation and to take an oral examination, which may include practical tests, on the subject of the dissertation and on the general field of knowledge within which it falls, and which may be supplemented by a written examination. In addition candidates may be required to take one or more written papers. By the end of the second term of candidature, a candidate must send to the Secretary of the Board of Graduate Studies the proposed title of the dissertation for approval by the Board. Two copies of the dissertation must be submitted to the Secretary of the Board of Graduate Studies during the third term of candidature, unless an extension has been granted; a statement of the sources from which his information is derived must be included.

A candidate for a Certificate may be allowed to count the whole or some part of the period for which he or she has been a candidate towards a course of research for the degree of Ph.D., M.Sc., or M.Litt., but if such an allowance is made he or she will not be entitled to receive a Certificate so long as he or she remains on the register of Research Students, nor subsequently if he or she should submit a dissertation for the degree of Ph.D., M.Sc., or M.Litt. A candidate is not entitled to receive a Certificate until he or she has kept at least three terms.

A candidate who is not awarded a Certificate may not be a candidate again nor be a candidate for any other Certificate of Postgraduate Study.

CLASSICS

In this subject there are courses of study followed by candidates for:

The *Classical Tripos*, which is divided into two Parts.

The *Preliminary Examinations* for Part I and Part II of the Classical Tripos.

Examinations for the Ordinary B.A. Degree in Greek *and in* Latin.

The *Diploma in Classical Archaeology*.

The Classical Tripos

The civilization of ancient Greece and Rome is of fundamental importance for the comparative study of societies and cultures and, more especially, for the understanding of the origins of modern Europe. The Classical Tripos approaches the study of classical antiquity through the original sources; and candidates for admission must possess a competent command at least of Latin. A good knowledge of Greek is, of course, an advantage but those with little or no Greek before acceptance are provided with intensive and systematic instruction in the language and the gap rapidly closes. The Tripos is usually completed in three years but may occupy four (see below under Part II). After reading Classics some students go on to further academic work and to teaching in schools and universities, but these do not represent a majority. Classical graduates follow a wide variety of careers and find that the Classical Tripos offers a valuable educational preparation for life in business, industry or administration.

The Tripos is divided into two Parts:

The course for Part I covers the main aspects of classical civilization: literature, history, philosophy, art and archaeology. All students take papers in Greek and Latin literature, together with two papers chosen from the other three fields of study. The course is intended to develop students' knowledge of the Greek and Latin languages; to give them the opportunity of learning about their chosen fields through the study of particular texts and other primary sources; and to introduce them to the techniques of classical scholarship. As well as serving as a preparation for more specialized classical studies, Part I is designed to provide a course of wide scope that is balanced and satisfying in itself. Thus it is suitable for candidates who intend to read another Tripos in their third year, particularly one of those to which a first-hand knowledge of the classical background is relevant, such as Archaeology and Anthropology, English, History, Law, Philosophy, or Theology.

It is usual to take Part I at the end of the second year of residence. The regulations in fact allow a student to take it at the end of the first year, but few will have read widely enough in the ancient authors before coming to Cambridge to do this with profit. Part I may also be taken after a Part I in another subject by candidates who attained a good standard in Greek and Latin at school, unless they have already offered classical Greek or Latin in Part I of the Modern and Medieval Languages Tripos.

Part II offers an opportunity for the student to explore in depth some particular aspect or aspects of the classical world and also, for those who wish, to investigate related aspects of other cultures and disciplines. The subject is divided into five groups of papers concerned with (A) Literature, (B) Philosophy, (C) History, (D) Art and Archaeology, (E) Language, representing five fields of study, and a sixth group, X, representing a combination of two or more of these fields of study. For their main field of study candidates (including those who spend two years reading for Part II) choose one of these groups A, B, C, D, E, X; they must offer at least two papers from the group and may offer three. These must be supplemented by additional papers, as detailed below. The options for additional papers include certain specially designated papers in other Triposes. These latter are at pesent chosen from the following Triposes: Anglo-Saxon, Norse, and Celtic, English, History, History of Art, Modern and Medieval Languages, Natural Sciences, Philosophy, and Theology.

Part II is usually taken at the end of the third year, but may be taken at the end of the fourth, i.e. after two years' study. The option of taking Part II after two years is commonly chosen by Affiliated Students who already hold a first degree from another University; it is also recommended for those candidates who attained a good knowledge of Greek and Latin at school but preferred to read Part I of another Tripos on coming into residence.

CLASSICS

Details of the examinations are as follows:

Part I[1]

Candidates are required to offer seven papers, each of three hours, as under:

Paper 1 or 2; Papers 3, 4, 5, and 6; and two papers chosen from among Papers 7–9. In **1991**, the two papers are to be chosen from among Papers 7–10.

In addition, a candidate may offer **Paper 10 or 11 or both** these papers. In **1991**, Papers 10 and 11 will be renumbered Papers 11 and 12.

The papers are:

1. Passages for translation from Greek authors

2. Less difficult passages for translation from Greek authors

The passages set will be selected from Homer and from Attic writers in prose and verse. The paper is intended for candidates who had little or no Greek at entrance.

3. Passages for translation from Latin authors

4. In **1990** and **1991**: Passages for translation from Greek and Latin authors

This paper will be divided into four sections. Section A will contain passages in Greek from works that appear in the schedule of texts prescribed for Paper 5. Section B will contain passages in Greek from other works. Section C will contain passages in Latin from works that appear in the schedule of texts prescribed for Paper 6. Section D will contain passages in Latin from other works.

Candidates for the Classical Tripos who offer Paper 1 will be required to translate six passages, three from Section A and three from Section C. Candidates for the Classical Tripos who offer Paper 2 will be required to translate six passages, of which not more than four and not less than three may be taken from Section C and the remainder from Section A.

Candidates offering Greek for the Modern and Medieval Languages Tripos, if they offer Paper 1, will be required to translate four passages, two from Section A and two from Section B. Candidates offering Greek for the Modern and Medieval Languages Tripos, if they offer Paper 2, will be required to translate four passages, two from Section A and two from Section B.

[1] The following papers, or the parts dealing with Greek, may be offered by candidates offering Classical Greek for Part I of the Modern and Medieval Languages Tripos: Papers 1, 2, 4, 5, 7, 8, 9, 10.

CAMBRIDGE HANDBOOK

Candidates offering Latin for the Modern and Medieval Languages Tripos will be required to translate four passages, two from Section C and two from Section D.

5. In **1990** and **1991**: Greek literature

This paper will consist of two sections. Section A will contain passages for analysis and appreciation chosen from a schedule of Greek texts which will be prescribed from time to time by the Faculty Board. Section B will contain essay questions on works chosen from the same schedule, and on other literary topics.

Candidates will be required to answer *either* four questions from Section A and one from Section B *or* two questions from Section A and two from Section B.

A candidate offering Paper 1 who chooses option (2) in Paper 5 will be required to choose questions pertaining to four different groups.

1. Homer, *Iliad* 3–6; *Iliad* 18–22; *Odyssey* 8–13*.

2. Hesiod, *Op.*; *Homeric hymns* 2 (Demeter), 3 (Apollo), 5 (Aphrodite), 7 (Dionysus); lyric & elegiac selection as in D. A. Campbell, *Greek lyric poetry* (Bristol 1982), but without choral lyric (see 3).

3. Choral lyric as in Campbell (Alcman, Stesichorus, Bacchylides); Pindar, *Pythians* as in G. Kirkwood, *Selections from Pindar* (Scholars Press 1982); Pindar, *Olympians, Nemeans, Isthmians,* as in Kirkwood.

4. Aeschylus, *Oresteia*.

5. Sophocles, *O.T.**; Sophocles, *Philoctetes*; Euripides, *Medea*.

6. Euripides, *Hippolytus*; Euripides, *Electra**; Sophocles, *Trachiniae*.

7. Aristophanes, *Frogs**; Aristophanes, *Clouds*; Menander, *Samia*.

8. Herodotus 1.1–94*; Herodotus 7.1–130; Thucydides 2.1–65.

9. Antiphon *Tetral.* 2, Andocides 1, Lysias 24, Demosthenes 5; Antiphon 5, Lysias 1, Demosthenes 54, Hyperides *Epitaphios*; Gorgias *Helen*, Lysias 16, Demosthenes 39, Lycurgus 1.

10. Plato, *Symposium*; Plato, *Phaedo**; Aristotle, *Poetics*.

11. Apollonius 3; Callimachus, *Hymns* 1, 2, 5, 6; selection of Hellenistic poetry as in N. Hopkinson, *A Hellenistic anthology* (C.U.P. 1988), but without Apollonius, Callimachus *Hymns*, Theocritus.

12. Theocritus 1–3, 6–7, 11; Theocritus 13–16, 18, 24, 28; Longus, *Daphnis & Chloe*.

* Two of the passages set in Section A of Paper 4, and two of those set in Section A of Paper 5, will be taken from the works marked with an asterisk.

6. In **1990** and **1991**: Latin literature

This paper will consist of two sections. Section A will contain passages for analysis and appreciation chosen from a schedule of Latin texts which will be prescribed from time to time by the Faculty Board. Section B will contain essay questions on works chosen from the same schedule, and on other literary topics.

Candidates will be required to answer *either* four questions from Section A and one from Section B *or* two questions from Section A and two from Section B. Candidates for the Classical Tripos who choose option (2) will be required to choose questions pertaining to four different groups.

1. Plautus, *Casina*; Terence, *Adelphoe*†; Seneca, *Thyestes*.

2. Catullus 61–68; Catullus 1–60, 69–116; Virgil, *Eclogues*.

3. Lucretius 1; Virgil, *Georgics* 3 & 4; Ovid, *Ars amatoria* 1.

4. Cicero, *Pro Caelio*; *Philippic* 2; *Tusc.* 1†.

5. Virgil, *Aeneid* 1, 12; 2, 4; 6, 8.

6. Horace, *Odes* 1†; *Odes* 4; *Epistles* 1.

7. Propertius 1; Tibullus 1; Ovid, *Amores* 1†.

8. Sallust, *Catiline*; Livy 5†; Tacitus, *Histories* 3.

9. Horace, *Satires* 1; Persius 1, 3, 5; Juvenal 1–5†.

10. Ovid, *Metamorphoses* 8; Lucan 6; Statius, *Thebaid* 10.

11. Seneca, *Apocolocyntosis*; Petronius, *Cena*; Apuleius, *Cupid & Psyche*.

12. Letters: Cicero as in D. R. Shackleton Bailey, *Cicero: Select letters* (C.U.P. 1980); Seneca *Ep.* 12, 18, 28, 47, 53, 90, 108, 114, 122; Pliny as in A. N. Sherwin-White, *Fifty letters of Pliny* (ed. 2, O.U.P. 1969).

7. Greek and Roman history

The paper contains questions on the following topics:

democratic Athens, Spartan government and society, reform and revolution in Republican Rome, the city of Rome, frontiers of the Roman Empire, Everyday life in the Roman Empire, and in **1991** later Roman Empire. and on the following topics relating to both Greece and Rome:

In **1990**: the ancient economy, education and literacy, images of power, political thought.

In **1991**: the ancient economy, education and literacy, images of power.

---

† Two of the passages set in Section C of Paper 4, and two of those set in Section A of Paper 6, will be taken from the works marked with a dagger.

8 Greek and Roman philosophy and theology with particular reference to Plato

This paper is divided into two sections. Section (*a*) contains questions on a prescribed dialogue or prescribed dialogues of Plato. Section (*b*) contains questions on ancient philosophers and philosophical systems and on religion. Candidates are required to answer four questions of which at least one and not more than two must be chosen from section (*a*).

Section (*a*):
In **1990** and **1991**: Plato, *Phaedo*.

9. Greek and Roman art and archaeology

The paper will include one question, Question 1, involving comments on photographs.

Candidates for the Classical Tripos will be required to attempt Question 1 and any three other questions.

Candidates offering classical Greek or classical Latin for Part I of the Modern and Medieval Languages Tripos, if offering Paper 9 as a whole paper, will be required to attempt Question 1 and any three other questions.

Candidates offering classical Greek for Part I of the Modern and Medieval Languages Tripos, if offering Paper 9 as a half-paper, will be required to attempt any two questions.

10. Translation from English into Greek prose and verse[1]

This paper is divided into two sections. Section (*a*) contains three passages of English prose for translation into Greek prose (two of which will be straightforward English translations from designated Greek prose authors), and one passage of English verse for translation into Greek iambics. Section (*b*) contains one passage of English verse for translation into Greek iambics, shorter than that set in section (*a*), and one passage of English verse for translation into Greek elegiacs. Candidates are required to attempt *either* one passage from section (*a*) *or* both passages from section (*b*).

The designated Greek prose authors are: Lysias and Plato.

11. Translation from English into Latin prose and verse

This paper is divided into two sections. Section (*a*) contains three passages of English prose for translation into Latin prose (two of which will be straightforward English translations from designated Latin authors), one passage of English verse for translation into Latin hexameters, and one passage of English verse for translation into Latin elegiacs. Section (*b*) contains one passage of English verse for translation into Latin hexameters

[1] Credit will be given for a knowledge of the general principles of Greek accentuation.

CLASSICS

and one passage of English verse for translation into Latin elegiacs, each shorter than the corresponding passage in section (*a*). Candidates are required to attempt *either* one passage from section (*a*) *or* both passages from section (*b*).

The designated Latin authors are: Cicero (Speeches) and the younger Seneca (Letters and Dialogues).

Papers 10 and 11 will be renumbered 11 and 12 with effect from 1 October 1990.

In **1991**: Paper 10. Greek and Latin philology and linguistics

The paper will be divided into four sections, (*a*) phonology, (*b*) lexicology, (*c*) morphology and syntax, and (*d*) pragmatics and discourse analysis. Most of the questions will require a knowledge of both Greek and Latin, but each section will contain some questions concerned exclusively with only one language. Candidates will be required to attempt four questions chosen from at least three sections.

Part II

Part II may be taken at the end either of the third or of the fourth year of residence, but no one, except an Affiliated Student, may be a candidate for honours in Part II unless he has already obtained honours in Part I or in another Honours Examination not more than two years before.

No student may present himself as a candidate for Part II on more than one occasion.

Subjects of examination[1]

The examination consists of papers assigned to five groups A, B, C, D, E, representing five fields of study, and to a sixth group, X, representing a combination of two or more of these fields of study, and certain papers from other Triposes (Group O).

A candidate who takes Part II in one year must offer

    (*a*) two papers belonging to a single group, chosen from among the six Groups A, B, C, D, E, X;

and *either* (*b*) two additional papers chosen from Groups A, B, C, D, E, X, and from the Schedule of Optional Papers;

---

[1] Advisers to students who wish to begin to read for Part II of the Classical Tripos are appointed annually; a list of the Advisers, together with the times at which they are available for interview, is published in the *Cambridge University Reporter* before or during the Easter Term.

or (c) one additional paper chosen from Groups A, B, C, D, E, X, and from the Schedule of Optional Papers, together with a thesis on a topic proposed by himself and approved by the Faculty Board;

provided that no candidate may offer more than three papers from Group D or more than two papers from Group X or more than one paper from the Schedule of Optional Papers.

A candidate who takes Part II in two years must offer

(a) two papers belonging to a single group, chosen from among the six Groups A, B, C, D, E, X;

and *either* (b) three additional papers chosen from Groups A, B, C, D, E, X, and from the Schedule of Optional Papers;

or (c) two additional papers chosen from Groups A, B, C, D, E, X, and from the Schedule of Optional Papers, together with a thesis, as prescribed in Regulation 24, on a topic proposed by himself and approved by the Faculty Board;

provided that no candidate may offer more than three papers from Group D or more than two papers from Group X or more than one paper from the Schedule of Optional Papers.

A candidate may be examined *viva voce* on the field of study of a group from which he offers two or more papers, provided that the scope of such an examination will be restricted to the subjects of the papers which the candidate has offered.

Details of the papers are:

GROUP A (LITERATURE)

Paper A1. A prescribed Greek author or authors, and a prescribed Latin author or authors

This paper contains questions on a Greek author or authors and on a Latin author or authors. The works prescribed are taken from among the major works of Greek and Latin literature.

In **1990** and **1991**: Homer, *Odyssey* and Virgil, *Aeneid*.

Paper A2. A prescribed Greek author

In **1990**: Sophocles, with special reference to *Electra* 1–250, 660–824, 1384–1510.

In **1991**: The later plays of Euripides, with special reference to *Bacchae*. The plays to be studied are *Heracles*, *Troades*, *Ion*, *Helen*, *Orestes*, *Bacchae*. The following passages of *Bacchae* are specified for textual comment: 1–63, 170–433, 604–659, 862–911.

CLASSICS

Paper A3. A prescribed Latin author

In **1990** and **1991**: Propertius, with special reference to Books I and IV. (Textual prescription: I, 16–22; IV, 8, 10, 11.)

Papers A2 and A3 are each divided into three sections:

Section A contains passages for textual comment, Section B contains passages for literary comment, and Section C contains essay questions. In each paper candidates will be required to answer three questions, at least one from Section A and at least one from Section B. Section A will include a question on palaeography, which is to be attempted only by candidates who choose to answer two questions from Section A; this question may require not only transcription but also textual criticism and a knowledge of the history of the text.

GROUP B (PHILOSOPHY)

Paper B1. Plato

This paper includes questions on a prescribed portion or portions of the works of Plato.

In **1990** and **1991**: *Euthydemus* and *Hippias Major*.

Paper B2. Aristotle

This paper includes questions on a prescribed portion or portions of the works of Aristotle.

In **1990**: Aristotle, *De anima* 1.1; 2.1–6, 12; 3.1–5.
In **1991**: Aristotle, *Physics* 2.

Paper B3. Ancient philosophers other than Plato and Aristotle from Thales to Marcus Aurelius

This paper will include (*a*) questions on a prescribed text or texts taken from, or relating to, one or more of the Presocratic philosophers, and (*b*) questions on a prescribed text or texts taken from, or relating to, one or more of the post-Aristotelian philosophers.

In **1990** and **1991**: Parmenides; Cicero, *De Fato*.

GROUP C (HISTORY)[1]

Paper C1. A prescribed period or subject of Greek history

In **1990** and **1991**: The Greeks and the Other.

---

[1] These papers may contain questions on the literary, epigraphical, and archaeological sources for the period or subject prescribed and questions that involve a knowledge of geography and topography and of the political, legal, and social antiquities of the period or subject prescribed; such questions will not require a technical knowledge of archaeology.

Paper C2. A prescribed period or subject of Roman history
In **1990** and **1991**: The city of Rome 200 B.C.–A.D. 200.

Paper C3. A prescribed subject taken from ancient history
In **1990** and **1991**: Egypt under Roman rule 50 B.C.–A.D. 300.

GROUP D (ARCHAEOLOGY)

Paper D1. Prehellenic archaeology

Paper D2. A prescribed subject connected with early Hellenic archaeology or early Greek art

In **1990** and **1991**: Early Hellenic archaeology.

Paper D3. A prescribed subject connected with Classical (Greco-Roman) art or the archaeology of the Greek and Hellenistic world

In **1990** and **1991**: Classical (Greco-Roman) art.

Paper D4. Archaeology of the Western Provinces of the Roman Empire

GROUP E (LANGUAGE)

Paper E1. Elements of comparative linguistics
This paper will cover the principles of the comparative method and of historical reconstruction and their applications to Indo-European phonology, morphology, syntax, and lexicon. A knowledge of the relevant phenomena in Vedic will be required.

[1]*Paper E2. The Greek language*
This paper will cover the history of the Greek language and its dialects to the late Hellenistic period.

In **1990** and **1991**:

The Language of Early Greek Poetry with special reference to Homer. The prescribed texts will be Homer, *Iliad* x, 194–468, Page, *Lyrica Graeca Selecta* (OCT). 109 (Alcaeus); 191, 203 (Sappho); 263 (Ibycus); West, *Dialectus ex Iambis et Elegis Graecis* (OCT). Archilochus 13, 122; Semonides 1; Solmsen & Fraenkel, *Inscriptiones Graecae ad inlustrandos dialectos selectae.* 8 (Lesbian); 12 (1–23) (Thessalian); 55, 56 (Eastern Ionic); 63, 64 (Central Ionic); Herodotus I, 86–7.

[1]*Paper E3. The Latin language*

This paper will cover the history of the Latin language to the end of the Roman Empire.

In **1990** and **1991**:

Vulgar Latin. The prescribed texts will be extracts from Plautus (*Cap.* 349–60, *Cu.* 610–21, *Ep.* 620–31, *Mi.* 393–405, *Ps.* 655–67, 1157–69, *ST.* 361–73, *Tru.* 241–55, all in Lindsay's OCT); imperial inscriptions from Pompeii, Rome and Gaul (*Select Latin Texts* 4.7, 10, 12, 14, 15, 16; 6.2, 3, 4, 6, 7; 13.1, 2, 3, 4, available in typescript copies from the Faculty Office); extracts from Petronius, *Vetus Latina, Appendix Probi, Itinerarium Egeriae, Lex Salica* and Gregory of Tours (as in G. Rohlfs *Sermo Vulgaris Latinus* (3rd ed., 1969) 2.6, 7, 13, 18.1 and 2, 25).

GROUP X

There will be not more than three papers in this group, X1, X2, X3, whose subjects will be prescribed from time to time by the Faculty Board of Classics. The subjects will be of an inter-disciplinary nature, requiring knowledge related to more than one of the fields of study represented by Groups A, B, C, D, and E.

In **1990** and **1991**: Paper X1: Rhetoric.
Paper X3: The human body in classical antiquity.

GROUP O

O1. General linguistics (Paper 111 of Part II of the Modern and Medieval Languages Tripos).

O2. Greek literature, thought, and history, since 1910 (Paper 104 of Part II of the Modern and Medieval Languages Tripos).

O3. Tragedy (Paper 2 of Part II of the English Tripos).

O4. History and Theory of literary criticism (Paper 9 of Part II of the English Tripos).

O5. Metaphysics (Paper 1 of Part I B of the Philosophy Tripos).

O6. History of political thought to *c.* 1750 (Paper 19 of Part I of the Historical Tripos).

O7. Medieval Latin literature from 400 to 1300 (Paper 12 of Part II of the Modern and Medieval Languages Tripos).

O8. Christian life and thought to A.D. 461 with reference to a special topic (Paper 21 A of the Theological and Religious Studies Tripos).

[1] Each of Papers E2 and E3 includes a compulsory question in which portions of the prescribed texts are set for translation and comment.

O9. Anglo-Saxon England in the pagan period (Paper 12 of the Anglo-Saxon, Norse, and Celtic Tripos).

O10. The transformation of the Roman world (Paper 12 of Part II of the Historical Tripos).

O11. Scientific ideas and practice from antiquity to the Renaissance (Paper 1 of Section II of Part II (General) of the Natural Sciences Tripos).

O12. The triumph of Classicism: architecture in England, and France, 1750–1830 (the pair of Papers 10–11 of the History of Art Tripos).[1]

Thesis

A candidate who chooses to offer a thesis must submit the proposed title of his thesis, together with a statement of the scheme of papers that he intends to offer through his Tutor to the Secretary of the Faculty Board so as to reach him not later than the fifth day of the Full Michaelmas Term next preceding the examination if he is taking the examination in one year, and not later than the last day of the Lent Term next but one preceding the examination if he is taking the examination in two years. In the case of a candidate taking the examination in one year, the topic of his thesis must be closely connected with the subject of a paper belonging to one of the six Groups A, B, C, D, E, X, provided that a candidate may not submit a thesis on a topic that falls within the general area of any of the papers that he is offering in the examination, and that a candidate who chooses to offer three papers from Group D may not submit a thesis on a topic that falls within the general area of that group. In the case of a candidate taking the examination in two years, the topic of his thesis must fall within the field of Classics and must not coincide substantially with the subject of any of the papers that he is offering in the examination. Each candidate must obtain the approval of the title of his thesis by the Faculty Board not later than the end of the third quarter of the Michaelmas Term next preceding the examination if he is taking the examination in one year, and not later than the end of the third quarter of the Easter Term next preceding the examination if he is taking the examination in two years. When the Faculty Board have approved a candidate's title, no change may be made to it, or to his scheme of papers, without the further approval of the Faculty Board. The length of the thesis must not exceed 10,000 words (inclusive of notes). A candidate will be

[1] This is suitable only for 2 year candidates.

required to give full references to sources used and to declare that the thesis is his own work and that it does not contain material which he has already used to any substantial extent for a comparable purpose. The Board will expect the thesis to show detailed knowledge of the relevant primary sources and to provide evidence of ability to select a topic of interest, to handle it in an enterprising manner and with sound and independent judgement, and to present it with clarity and precision. Except for Greek quotations, which may be written by hand, theses must be typewritten, unless a candidate has obtained previous permission from the Faculty Board to present his thesis in manuscript, and must be submitted to the Secretary so as to reach him not later than the first day of the Full Easter Term in which the examination is to held. The candidate will also be examined *viva voce*.

The Preliminary Examination for Part I

(each paper 3 hours)

The examination consists of six papers as follows:

1. Greek translation
2. Alternative Greek translation

The paper contains passages for translation from the following Greek books prescribed by the Faculty Board of Classics, together with two passages for unseen translation, one verse, one prose, from the authors of the prescribed Greek books:

In **1990**: Homer, *Odyssey* x. 133–574; Euripides, *Electra* (excluding lyrics); Lysias, I, 41–80; Plato, *Crito*; Thucydides, I, 1–23, 139–146.

In **1991**: Lysias, I; Euripides, *Electra* (excluding Lyrics) lines 1–111, 212–431, 487–698, 747–1146, and 1238–1359; Plato, *Crito*; Homer, *Odyssey* IX (105–end); Thucydides I (1–23, 139–146).

3. Latin translation
4. Classical questions

The paper contains questions on:

(*a*) Greek and Latin literature;
(*b*) Greek and Roman history from 800 B.C. to A.D. 337;
(*c*) Greek and Roman philosophy and theology;
(*d*) **Greek and Roman art and archaeology.**
(*e*) Greek and Latin philology and linguistics.

Candidates are required to answer four questions taken from any one or more of the above-named sections.

5. Greek prose and verse composition. Designated authors: Lysias and Plato

6. Latin prose and verse composition. Designated authors: Cicero (Speeches) and the younger Seneca (Letters and Dialogues)

Every candidate must offer *either* Paper 1 *or* Paper 2, and Papers 3 and 4. Papers 5 and 6 are optional, but the Examiners will give credit for proficiency in these papers; candidates are not required to attempt both prose and verse.

The Preliminary Examination for Part II

The papers for this examination are taken from among the papers for Part II of the Classical Tripos. It is usual for Affiliated Students to take the Preliminary Examination at the end of their first year. Every candidate must offer two papers, provided that no candidate may offer more than one paper taken from the schedule of Optional Papers.

The Examinations for the Ordinary B.A. Degree
Greek

The examination consists of *either* (*a*) the five following papers, all of which must be taken:

1, 2, and 3. Passages for translation into English from specified books: Homer, *Iliad* XVIII–XXI, *Odyssey* V–VII, Sophocles, *Philoctetes*, Euripides, *Hecuba*; Plato, *Phaedrus*.

4. Passages from unspecified books for translation into English, such passages being chosen from books comparable in style and difficulty to those specified for Papers 1, 2, and 3.

5. History and civilization, with special attention to the period 600–323 B.C.

or (*b*) the following papers from Part I of the Tripos:

either (i) Papers 1, 5, and 10,
or (ii) Papers 1, 4 (two Greek passages), and 5, and two questions from any one of Papers 7, 8, and 9,
or (iii) Papers 1 and 5 and two questions from each of two of Papers 7, 8, and 9.

CLASSICS 107

In the case of Paper 8 one question must be chosen from section (*a*) and one from section (*b*) of the paper. In the case of Paper 9 candidates may not answer Question 1.

For certain restrictions see the last paragraph under Latin, below.

Latin

The examination consists of *either* (*a*) the five following papers, all of which must be taken:

1, 2, and 3. Passages for translation into English from specified books: Lucretius III, Horace, *Odes*, III; Virgil, *Aeneid* X–XII; Livy V.

4. Passages from unspecified books for translation into English, such passages being chosen from books comparable in style and difficulty to those specified for Papers 1, 2, and 3.

5. History and civilization, with special attention to the period 78 B.C.–A.D. 117.

or (*b*) the following papers from Part I of the Classical Tripos:

either (i) Papers 3, 6, and 11,
or (ii) Papers 3, 4 (two Latin passages), and 6, and two questions from Paper 7 or Paper 9,
or (iii) Papers 3 and 6, and two questions from each of Papers 7 and 9.

In the case of Paper 9 candidates may not answer Question 1.

A student may not count towards the Ordinary B.A. Degree both the Special Examination in Latin or Greek and also anything that he may have to his credit as the result of the Preliminary Examination in Classics or Part I of the Classical Tripos; but in lieu of a Special Examination, a student who has passed the Preliminary Examination may take certain papers from Part I of the Tripos in one or the other language, and a student who has received an allowance on Part I of the Tripos or on the Preliminary Examination for his performance in one of the two languages may take certain papers from Part I of the Tripos in the other.

The Diploma in Classical Archaeology

A candidate for the Diploma in Classical Archaeology must be approved by the Faculty Board of Classics and must *either* be a graduate of the University who has obtained honours in Part I or Part II of the Classical Tripos *or* be a graduate of another university who has passed with honours in that university an examination of a standard and scope comparable to that of Part I or Part II of the Classical Tripos *or* have produced other evidence to satisfy the Faculty Board of his fitness to study for the Diploma.

Before being admitted to the examination for the Diploma a candidate must obtain a certificate, signed by the Secretary of the Faculty Board of Classics, of having received instruction in Classical Archaeology under the direction of the Faculty Board for at least two terms. The certificate must be sent to the Registrary by 1 May in the term in which the candidate wishes to take the examination.

The Diploma is awarded to members of the University who have obtained certificates of instruction in Classical Archaeology, passed the examination, and kept at least three terms. No one may be a candidate for the Diploma on more than one occasion.

Subjects of examination

The examination for the Diploma is partly written and partly oral; all candidates will be examined *viva voce* on the subjects of the papers and upon the subject of any extended essay that they have offered. The following papers are set:

1. Prehellenic archaeology.

2. A prescribed subject connected with early Hellenic archaeology or early Greek art.

3. A prescribed subject connected with Classical (Greco-Roman) art or the archaeology of the Greek and Hellenistic world.

4. Archaeology of the Western Provinces of the Roman Empire.

5. Greek and Roman epigraphy.

The paper is divided into two sections, (*a*) Greek epigraphy and (*b*) Roman epigraphy; candidates will be required to answer at least one question from each section. The paper will include facsimiles of inscriptions for transcription, translation, and comment.

6. Ancient coinage.

A candidate for the Diploma must offer:

either (*a*) if he has not previously offered any paper from Group **D** in Part II of the Classical Tripos, or if he has offered, or is deemed to have offered, one such paper, five papers chosen from among Papers 1–6;

or (*b*) if he has previously offered, or is deemed to have offered, two papers from Group **D** in Part II of the Classical Tripos, four papers chosen from among Papers 1–6, together with an extended essay of not less than 3,000 and not more than 5,000 words (inclusive of notes) on a topic which shall be proposed by himself and approved by the Faculty Board.

A candidate who offers an extended essay must submit the proposed title of his essay, together with a statement of the papers that he intends to offer in the examination, through his Tutor to the Secretary of the Faculty Board so as to reach him not later than the division of the Michaelmas Term next preceding the examination. The topic proposed for the essay must fall within the field of Classical Archaeology (including Classical art), and must not overlap substantially with the subject of any paper that the candidate intends to offer in the examination. Each candidate must obtain the approval of his title by the Faculty Board not later than the last day of the Full Michaelmas Term. When the Faculty Board have approved the title of a candidate's essay, no change shall be made to it, or to his scheme of papers, without the further approval of the Faculty Board. A candidate will be required to give full references to sources used and to declare that the essay is his own work and that it does not contain material which he has already used to any substantial extent for a comparable purpose. Except for Greek quotations, which may be written by hand, essays must be typewritten, unless a candidate has obtained previous permission from the Faculty Board to present his essay in manuscript, and must be submitted to the Secretary not later than the division of the term in which the examination is to be held.

COMPUTER SCIENCE

Computer science is the study of the design and use of digital computers. It extends from the principles upon which computers themselves work to the mathematical understanding of the semantics of programming languages, the principles of operating systems and computer networks, and the growing area of artificial intelligence.

Computer Scientists are people who understand the 'why' as well as the 'how' of these things, and they are needed wherever a broad view is necessary; they understand how large and complex systems are articulated and how problems may be solved in differing or complementary ways.

More and more of the practice of computing is being brought within the domain of proper theoretical understanding, and as this happens the intellectual scope and challenge of the subject increases too. The Cambridge courses are designed to give students advanced practical experience together with an understanding of principles which will outlast today's technology.

There are courses of study followed by candidates for:

The *Computer Science Tripos*.
The *Diploma in Computer Science*.

The Computer Science Tripos

There are two versions of the Computer Science Tripos. The normal course of study for a student in Computer Science is Part IA taken in the first year, followed by Part IB taken in the second year, and Part II in the third year leading to a B.A. Degree. The alternative is Part II (General) in the final year following Part I of some other Tripos.

Part IA

A candidate takes Part IA in his first year. Part IA serves as preparation for further Parts of the Tripos. Every candidate must submit a portfolio of assessed laboratory work and offer Papers 1 and 2. Every candidate must also offer the papers set for the subject Mathematics in Part IA of the Natural Sciences Tripos and the paper, and practical examination if any, set for one of the following subjects in Part I A of the Natural Sciences Tripos:

Biology of Cells	Geology
Chemistry	Physics
Crystalline Materials	

Papers 1 and 2 will be of such a nature as to test candidate's knowledge of the fundamentals of computer science. The subjects covered will include:

Programming in ML	Discrete Mathematics
Digital Electronics and Computer Design	Computer Systems

Part I B

A candidate may take Part I B in his second year if he has obtained honours in Part I A or in another Honours Examination in his first year. Every candidate must submit a portfolio of assessed laboratory work and offer Papers 3–6.

Papers 3–6 will be of such a nature as to enable candidates to show a specialised knowledge of four branches of computer science:

Computer Technology	Computer Systems
Theory of Computation	Programming

Part II

A candidate may take Part II in his third year if he has obtained honours in Part I B. Every candidate must submit a dissertation of up to 12000 words on an approved subject and offer Papers 7–9.

Papers 7–9 will cover applications including:

Specification and Verification	Special Architectures
Semantics of Computation	Artificial Intelligence
Real-time and Distributed Computing	

Part II (General)

A candidate may take Part II (General) in his third or fourth year if he has obtained honours in an Honours Examination in the previous year provided he has not previously obtained honours in Part I B of the Computer Science Tripos. Every candidate must submit a portfolio of assessed laboratory work and offer Papers 10–13.

Papers 10 and 11 will be of such a nature as to test candidates' knowledge of the fundamentals of computer science and computer technology. The subjects covered will include:

Digital Electronics and Computer Design	Data Structures and Algorithms

Papers 12 and 13 will be of such a nature as to enable candidates to show a specialised knowledge of computer science, including:

Computer Technology	Computer Systems
Theory of Computation	Artificial Intelligence
Programming Languages	

Diploma in Computer Science

Applicants for admission to the Diploma course should normally have at least a second-class Honours Degree in Mathematics, Science, or Engineering. The course covers the basic aspects of computer hardware and software, with additional material on topics such as data bases, data communication, computer graphics, numerical analysis and algebraic manipulation. Students have access to the computers in the Laboratory and have opportunities to follow up their own particular interests. The examination is in two Parts; Part A consists of four written papers taken near the end of the Easter Term, and Part B consists of a dissertation submitted during the following long vacation on an individually approved subject. Further information about the course may be obtained from the Head of the Computer Laboratory.

A candidate for the Diploma must be approved by the Computer Syndicate. He must satisfy the Syndicate that he has attained a standard in mathematics sufficiently high for him to profit by the course and must ordinarily be a graduate of a university. No one may be a candidate in the same year for the Diploma and for another Diploma or any Tripos.

An application for approval as a candidate should be sent, together with evidence of qualifications, to the Head of the Computer Laboratory so as to reach him well before the beginning of the Michaelmas Term in which the applicant wishes his candidature to begin. Applications are preferred between January and June prior to the start of the course. The course is approved by the Science and

Engineering Research Council for tenure of advanced course studentships. Application for a studentship is made on behalf of an eligible student who has been provisionally admitted to the course. The quota of grants for allocation is generally small in comparison with the number of applicants.

The course of instruction extends over one academical year and requires regular attendance at the Computer Laboratory. To be awarded the Diploma candidates must have passed both parts of the examination and must have kept at least three terms.

A candidate who has taken the examination for the Diploma may not count any part of the period during which he has been a candidate for it towards a course of research for the degree of Ph.D., M.Sc., or M.Litt. A candidate who fails in the examination may not be a candidate again.

M.Phil. Degree in Computer Speech and Language Processing

For details of this one-year course, see p. 185.

DEVELOPMENT STUDIES

Candidates wishing to undertake Development Studies at Cambridge should refer to the following entries:
  (i) P. 138. A course in the Economics and Politics of Development leading to the M.Phil. Degree is available in the Faculty of Economics and Politics.
  (ii) P. 245. A course leading to a Diploma in Development Studies is available under the Board of Graduate Studies and the Degree Committee of the Department of Land Economy.

Other courses which may be of interest are:

> The course leading to a Diploma in Economics (p. 137).
> The course leading to an M.Phil. in the Economics of Developing Countries.
> The course leading to an M.Phil. in Land Economy (p. 243).
> The course leading to an M.Phil. in Social Anthropology (p. 71).
> The course leading to an M.Phil. in Latin-American Studies (p. 247).
> The course leading to an M.Phil. in International Relations (p. 225).
> The course leading to an M.Phil. in the Sociology and Politics of Development.

ECONOMICS AND POLITICS

In this field the courses of study offered to candidates are:

The *Economics Tripos*.
The *Preliminary Examination* for Part II of the Economics Tripos.
The *Diploma in Economics*.
The *M.Phil. Degree*.

The Economics Tripos

The Economics Tripos, as it has developed, allows candidates a broad range of options. There is provision for the study of politics, training in the mathematical aspects of economics is on a firm basis and sociology is covered. It will appeal to those interested in the study of society, whatever their speciality in school may have been: students trained in mathematics will find as much scope for their abilities as those who have specialized in history, geography, or languages. The Faculty of Economics and Politics maintains its own computer system, together with a range of statistical programmes and databases, and students can use these to acquire practical experience in modern techniques of data analysis.

The Tripos is based on a solid core of economics, pure and applied. It examines employment and unemployment, economic growth, price fluctuations, international trade, resource allocation, the distribution of income, and so on. Those who read for the Tripos can also study cognate subjects such as economic history, politics, sociology, and statistics. The Tripos is divided into two Parts:

Part I is taken at the end of the first year;
Part II is normally taken at the end of the third year.

Many candidates read Economics for three years, but the system allows considerable flexibility. Candidates may often combine Part I of the Economics Tripos and Part II of another Tripos, or Part I of another Tripos and Part II of the Economics Tripos.

For studying economic principles at the Part II level it is a great help if candidates have a certain familiarity with elementary mathematical concepts. There is, therefore, an economics qualifying examination in elementary mathematics (E.Q.E.E.M.); this is normally taken in the candidates' Part I year, or just before starting the second year. The standard required is lower than for 'A' level in G.C.E. Candidates will be assisted to acquire the necessary understanding of elementary mathematics during their first year at Cambridge, and there are also provisions whereby certain people can be accepted for Part II without passing E.Q.E.E.M.

The examination for Part I, which is taken at the end of the undergraduate's first year, consists of four compulsory papers: three in selected aspects of political economy and one in British economic history. The scope of these papers is described in greater detail below. Even for those who do not intend to continue in economics this year of study will be valuable. It will give them more insight into many live issues on which sooner or later almost everyone has to form an opinion. Moreover, there are many careers in which a basic understanding of economic processes is a valuable professional qualification.

Part I of the Tripos provides an interesting consolidation and extension of studies for those who have taken economics at Advanced level, but it is in no way a requirement to have done so. The Tripos is also suitable for those with no previous study of the subject. It makes a particular appeal to students who have done some history at school, but whose main interests are in contemporary society; they will already know some of the background to the papers in economic history and politics, and will learn to analyse these subjects more rigorously. Part I will also be of interest to those who have done mathematics or natural sciences and are looking for a subject where they can apply their knowledge in a new field.

Part II provides the means to study several of the social sciences in some depth. At the end of the course everyone has to take three papers in economic principles and problems; in addition all candidates must take either three papers from a wide choice of optional subjects or one paper and a dissertation. It is possible to take special papers in industry, labour, economic theory, mathematical economics, banking and credit, public economics, the sociology and politics of welfare, the economic problems of underdeveloped countries, World Depression in the interwar years, Russian economic development since 1861, applied economic and social statistics, and the theory of statistics. In addition, the choice extends to papers from the Social and Political Sciences Tripos, on the social structure of modern Britain, comparative political systems, and the sociology and politics of developing areas with special reference to South Asia or Latin America. Subjects can be combined in many ways so as to suit those of varied tastes, abilities, and previous training.

Part II of the Tripos offers many opportunities to the undergraduates who in their last years at school specialized in mathematics, and find the mathematical method of thought congenial – they will be able to use mathematical methods in many parts of economic theory, and they will learn how the methods of mathematical statistics can be applied in quantitative studies and will get an idea of the computational problems involved. Such a training is essential to anyone who wants to become a mathematical economist or econometrician, and is also of great value to anyone contemplating a career in industry which calls for programming, operational research, or the use of computers. This field of work offers full scope to the mathematical qualities of clarity and rigour, and provides a challenging range of new problems in applied mathematics.

But a previous training in mathematics is by no means the only approach to economics. Much economic theory and useful quantitative work in applied economics and statistics can be handled without specialized mathematical training. Moreover, problems of economic policy also involve political and moral criteria which are essentially qualitative in nature. There is need for historical and institutional knowledge, and the ability to weigh the pros and cons of problems for which purely mathematical solutions are inadequate. People with a variety of gifts and tastes can gain from – and contribute to – the study of both economics and economic history.

Students may wish to consider the possibility of specializing in the study of sociology. By acquiring a knowledge of sociological theory and methods of social investigation students who are interested in such problems as social class, political authority, the family, work groups in industry, etc., will learn to study these subjects with some precision. By comparing the working of these social institutions in different societies, they will come to have a broader perspective on their own society.

Whatever discipline students may have followed when they take Economics Part II they will be enabled to study one social science in depth and see how it is related to allied social sciences. They will learn to combine rigorous and abstract reasoning with an understanding of the problems of public policy. Their judgement will be strengthened and they will acquire the habit of applying scientific methods to the analysis of social issues.

As in all other subjects, only a minority of those who read for the Economics Tripos go on to a career of academic teaching and research. There is, however, a growing number of specialized occupations available to graduates in the social sciences. Both in industry and the civil service economists are to an increasing extent employed in a professional capacity, while statisticians are employed in the civil service and in industry and commerce, where they are engaged in sales forecasting, marketing problems, the control of industrial processes, and so on. With the coming of high-speed computers, programming methods, and operational research techniques, a new field of specialized jobs has opened up. The development of market research and the increasing professionalization of social administration and personnel management provide new scope for the trained sociologist.

But the Economics Tripos is not designed just to produce academics or specialists. A large proportion of graduates in economics go into business, public administration, and professions such as accounting, where they can make use of the habits of thought they have acquired at the University. A particular trend in recent years is the growing proportion of Economics graduates who enter management consultancy and related fields. Experience slows that employees recognize the practical utility of a training in the social sciences, and young men and women with a good degree have no difficulty in obtaining interesting and well-paid jobs.

Copies of booklists may be obtained from Directors of Studies or from the Secretary, Faculty of Economics and Politics, Austin Robinson Building, Sidgwick Avenue, Cambridge, CB3 9DD.

Part I

Part I is taken at the end of the first year. The subjects are:

1, 2, and 3. Selected aspects of political economy

The topics on which questions are set are as follows:

(a) *Markets, rational agents, and concepts of equilibrium*: theory of the consumer: choice and demand; theory of the producer: costs and supply; supply, demand, and market equilibrium: relationship between partial and general equilibrium analysis; demand and supply in factor markets; market equilibrium under various forms of industrial structure; the analysis of market failure and the rôle of the state, with some empirical illustrations; elementary game theory and bargaining;

(b) *Employment, wages, and price-levels*: Keynes' general theory and developments stemming from it, such as the multiplier and accelerator; classical, Marxian, and neo-classical theories of employment and wage-level determination; introduction to business accounting; links between the theories and national income accounts, introduction to social accounts and the national income ('Blue Book'); fiscal management; elementary models of inflation, including their microeconomic aspects; a discussion of the empirical findings on the causes of inflation;

(c) *Money and credit*: introductory discussion of concepts such as money,

ECONOMICS AND POLITICS

interest, and credit, and their relationship to the determination of output, employment, and the price-level; the demand for money, the determination of interest rates, and wealth effects in Keynesian and Quantity theories of money and credit; the empirical evidence relating to these theories; the transmission mechanisms of monetary policy; the relationship between monetary policy and fiscal policy; essential features of the financial institutions of modern economics; data sources;

(*d*) *The balance of payments and international monetary problems*: components of the balance of payments and how balance of payments tables are set up; introduction to data sources; economic significance of various types of changes in the figures; recent trends in UK balance of payments; concepts of balance of payments equilibrium under various systems of international payments; exchange-rate variations and other adjustment mechanisms; interactions between internal and external factors;

(*e*) *Output, income distribution, and poverty*: concepts and conventions in measuring real GDP and productivity; measurement, theoretical explanations, and social and economic implications of various aspects of the distribution of income and wealth among persons and groups; redistribution of income by taxation and public expenditure; poverty and the efficacy of various measures for alleviating poverty.

All three papers will be based on a common core of economic analysis applied to the specified topics; however, the emphasis of each of the papers will differ, as follows:

Paper 1 will emphasize theoretical issues (and some questions may be set which require knowledge of the history of economic thought).

Paper 2 will emphasize the application of quantitative methods to these topics; candidates will be expected to have experience in using *National Income and Expenditure* (the 'Blue Book'), and will be expected to bring with them a copy of a specified issue of the *Monthly Digest of Statistics, Economic Trends Annual Supplement*, or any other publication specified by the Faculty Board from time to time. Candidates will also be expected to display knowledge of concepts and elementary quantitative methods for analysing problems relating to these topics, and to display ability to use elements of business accounting and specific statistical methods as follows: the use of tables, graphs, and frequency distributions in summarizing and organizing statistical data; summary measures of central tendency and dispersion, especially mean, median, mode, standard deviation, interquartile ratio, and coefficient of variation; Lorenz curves and their simple applications; the construction and economic interpretation of index numbers in common use, with particular reference to the Index of Retail Prices and the Index of Industrial Production; analysis of association between variables with the help of scatter diagrams using both economic and social data.

Paper 3 will stress the influence of political and some sociological considerations on these and related topics. It will be concerned with the interrelationship between the exercise of economic and political power, account being taken of conflicts of interest between, and the relative power of, different classes and groups in society, as well as the constraints imposed by the relationship between, and organization of, political and economic structures. It will consider the processes by which policies come to be formulated and the way in which employers' organizations, trade unions, the City, the military, the political parties, the media, and the bureaucracy of the State influence the decision-making process. It will analyse the rôle of the State in relation to employment and wage policy, international economic policy, the rate of economic growth, and poverty.

4. British economic history

This paper is concerned with three main themes in the industrial development of Britain between 1750 and 1939: the industrial revolution, problems of growth and trade in the mature economy up to 1914, and the slump and recovery of the inter-war years; it also covers some of the demographic and social changes associated with this industrial development. The specific topics which are covered in the course of the analysis of the main themes include the long-run growth of output, productivity, and the standard of living; the costs of growth; demographic changes; capital accumulation and technical progress; entrepreneurship; foreign trade, the export of capital, and the role of the Empire; changes in the industrial structure; the labour market; government economic policies. In addition, an attempt is made to demonstrate the relevance of simple theories of economic growth and development to the study of the historical development of the British economy.

Economics Qualifying Examination in Elementary Mathematics

The examination, which will consist of a single paper lasting three hours, will be held on the second day of Full Easter Term and the Friday before the first day of Full Michaelmas Term. The standard required is lower than that for 'A' level mathematics. The paper will be set in three sections, A, B, and C.

Candidates will be examined in the use of those concepts, notations, and methods in elementary mathematics which are commonly employed by lecturers and writers on elementary economic principles and quantitative economics. Section A will consist of questions on numerical techniques, Section B of questions involving graphical presentation and Section C of questions on the correct interpretation of the kind of mathematics students may meet in lectures or textbooks and on elementary economic theory done in a mathematical form. Questions in Section C will be given substantially more weight than those in Sections A and B, which will be weighted equally. Candidates will be expected to answer at least one question from each section. As a general guide, correct answers to four questions from Sections A and B together and one from Section C will be sufficient to enable candidates to pass the examination.

Candidates who are taking Part I of the Economics Tripos, but are certain that they will not wish to take Part II are not required to pass the E.Q.E.E.M., though they are advised to follow the lecture course.

The Faculty Board will grant exemption from taking the E.Q.E.E.M. to the following candidates for Part II of the Tripos:

(*a*) Those who have obtained honours in Part I of another Tripos and are regarded as suitable to be candidates for Honours in Part II of the Economics Tripos without having taken the E.Q.E.E.M. Candidates who have taken Part I in Mathematics, Engineering, or Natural Sciences would clearly be suitable for exemption in this category, and exemption would also be appropriate for candidates who have taken 'non-mathematical' Part Is if the Tutor considered that the Long Vacation before starting Economics should be devoted to preparation for the Economics course rather than the E.Q.E.E.M.

(*b*) Affiliated students regarded as suitable to be candidates for Honours in Part II of the Economics Tripos without having taken the E.Q.E.E.M.

In order to gain exemption under any of these headings a candidate's Tutor must submit a certificate to the Secretary of the Faculty Board, from whom blank certificates may be obtained.

The Faculty Board have provided that they shall waive the requirement to pass the E.Q.E.E.M. for candidates who have obtained honours in Part I of the Economics Tripos, and have failed to pass the E.Q.E.E.M., but are recommended by their Tutors for exemption.

In order to gain exemption under this heading a candidate's Tutor must submit a recommendation to the Secretary of the Faculty Board, from whom blank certificates may be obtained.

Part II

Part II is taken at the end of the third year, except that a candidate who has obtained honours in another Tripos may take it at the end of his fourth year.* Every candidate, except as provided below, must take

(*a*) Papers 1, 2, and 3, *and*
(*b*) *either* (i) three or four papers chosen from among Papers 4–18;†
    or (ii) one or two papers chosen from among Papers 4–18, together with a dissertation on an approved topic within the field of any one of Papers 4, 5, 7–10, and 13–18 or within a field from among other fields which the Faculty Board shall specify from time to time;

provided that

(1) each candidate must offer at least one paper from among Papers 4–12 and 16–18 or a dissertation on an approved topic within the field of any one of Papers 4, 5, 7–10, and 16–18 or within one of the other fields specified by the Faculty Board;

and (2) a candidate offering under (*b*)(ii) only one paper together with a dissertation will not be allowed to submit a dissertation on a topic within the field of that paper.

The Examiners in drawing up the class-list give a dissertation double the weight given to each of Papers 4–18, except that if under (*b*)(ii) above a candidate offers two papers and a dissertation they may give the dissertation equal weight if that would be to the candidate's advantage.

If under (*b*)(i) above a candidate offers four papers, the paper of these four on which the Examiners judge the candidate's performance to be least good will be taken into account only if that would be to the candidate's advantage, provided that at least one of Papers 4–12 and 16–18 will always be taken into account.

---

* A candidate who takes the examination in the year next after he has obtained honours in another Tripos shall be exempt from taking the E.Q.E.E.M. and offer Papers 1 and 2 and not less than two nor more than three papers chosen from among Papers 3–18. If he offers three such papers his performance in the one in which the Examiners judge his work to be least good shall only be taken into account if that would be to his advantage.

† Until further notice Paper 18 will not be set.

ECONOMICS AND POLITICS

If under (b)(ii) above a candidate offers two papers and a dissertation, the paper of these two on which the Examiners judge the candidate's performance to be less good will be taken into account only if that would be to the candidate's advantage; provided that account will always be taken of a paper if

either (a) the candidate's dissertation topic falls within the field of the other paper

or (b) the other paper is one of Papers 13–15 and the candidate's dissertation also falls within the field of one of Papers 13–15.[1]

The Faculty Board of Economics and Politics provide not later than 1 June each year a list of topics on which a dissertation may be submitted for the Tripos to be taken in the following year. Candidates may alternatively submit their own suggested topics for approval. A list of approved topics for the dissertation and details of the timetable and procedure for the submission of topics and of the dissertation are available from the Secretary, Faculty of Economics and Politics, Austin Robinson Building, Sidgwick Avenue, Cambridge, CB3 9DD.

The papers (each of 3 hours' duration except Paper 3) are: 1, 2, and

13. Economic principles and problems

These papers deal with the scope and method of economics, with fundamental ideas, and with the application of the methods of economic analysis to economic problems. The papers are designed to afford scope for the exercise of analytical power in abstract reasoning and in interpreting economic data. A few questions of a more advanced analytical character may be set, but the papers as a whole are so framed as to be within the competence of those who have not made a study of advanced methods of

---

[1] In considering their choice from among the alternative papers candidates should bear in mind that the number of alternatives is such that clashes between the times of lectures cannot be entirely avoided and that there will be clashes in connexion with the following combinations of papers:

(a) Paper 6 and Paper 4;
(b) Paper 6 and Paper 9;
(c) Paper 6 and Paper 16;
(d) Paper 6 and Paper 17;
(e) Paper 7 and Paper 14;
(f) Paper 12 and Paper 9;
(g) Paper 12 and Paper 14;
(h) Paper 12 and Paper 15;
(i) Paper 12 and Paper 16;
(j) Paper 12 and Paper 17.

Papers 13, 14 and 15 will clash with other optional papers.

[1] Paper 3 will be of 4 hours' duration.

analysis. A main object is to test the power of candidates to apply their theoretical reasoning to actual problems. Candidates are, therefore, expected to show a general knowledge and understanding of the role of the Government in economic affairs and of the workings and effects of the principal economic institutions in the fields of production and distribution, of money and banking, international economics, of employment, labour and wage determination. Knowledge of the British economy is a basic requirement. Candidates should be able to analyse British problems in their international setting. Some questions will be asked about international economic problems and institutions, and about the problems of different types of economy. The questions set will not require such detailed knowledge as may be appropriate in Papers 4–10, but an understanding of general principles. In Paper 3 candidates are required to answer one question only. Candidates are free to take to the examination their own copy of *Economic Trends Annual Supplement* for any year or any other publication specified by the Faculty Board from time to time, and will be told in advance what other statistical source material, if any, will be provided.

4. Labour

This paper has the following subject matter:

analysis of labour markets in relation to the determination of wages, conditions of work, and the distribution of employment; the market demand for labour by firms and other organizations, and the supply of labour by households; job selection and hiring procedures; discrimination, wage and salary differentials, and their relationship with the distribution of income and poverty; the concept of human capital; the influence of education on social mobility and occupational recruitment; labour turnover and lateral mobility;

power in trade unions, and its effects on union policy and labour markets; general features of British trade unionism, compared with other national movements; types of unions, and trends in union structure, growth, amalgamations and the TUC internal government; the relation between formal constitutions and the actual distribution of power; the shop steward system: its relation to formal constitutions, and to union leaders and members, and to the management of firms; union policies on collective bargaining, earnings distribution, employment and restrictive practices; strikes and other forms of industrial conflict; current issues in industrial relations, including legal controls on unions, strikes, and the collective bargaining system; other types of Government intervention in the labour market;

the causes of changes in the money wage-level, with special reference to

ECONOMICS AND POLITICS

the role of trade unions, wage and price interdependency; prices and incomes policies, with special reference to pay policies, possibilities and problems in the light of experience in the U.K. and other countries.

Candidates are expected to be familiar with the main empirical characteristics of the British labour market, including important recent studies, but they may also be asked questions relating to other countries.

Candidates are encouraged to consider the theoretical and factual issues involved in this paper in the light of both economic and sociological techniques of thought.

In this paper some questions may be set which permit candidates to show capacity to interpret and handle statistical evidence.

5. Economic theory and analysis

In this paper questions are set of a more advanced character than in Papers 1, 2, and 3, and the emphasis rests on the theoretical aspects of economics. The paper provides opportunity for the use of analytical methods of various types, but is so framed, taken as a whole, as to be within the competence of those who have no knowledge of advanced mathematics.

6. Mathematical economics

Candidates for this paper are examined in those parts of economic theory where mathematical methods of exposition offer particular advantages, e.g. of lucidity, conciseness, and rigour. They are expected to use such methods in the discussion of particular economic theories and economic models. In particular, it is a feature of this way of theorizing that assumptions are to be clearly stated and their relation to conclusions made precise.

Some questions in this paper will be marked with an asterisk. Extra credit will be given for answers to questions with asterisks, and a candidate will not obtain a first-class mark on the paper unless he completes at least one starred question. Relatively little credit will be given for answers to parts of questions.

7. Banking and credit

The paper has the following subject matter:

The nature of money and liquidity; demand for money by households and firms; the banking system; composition of the money stock and methods of control over money and credit; portfolio selection behaviour – especially that of banks and other financial intermediaries; the term structure of interest rates; capital markets and the finance of investment;

developments in world capital markets – the origins, growth, and effects of the Euro-dollar system; the implications of international financial flows for domestic monetary management and the exchange rate; intervention in domestic economic policies by the World Bank and the International Monetary Fund.

The objectives and instruments of monetary policies, including: implications for the financial efficiency of banks, both commercial and central, and other financial institutions; interconnexions between fiscal and monetary policies, and their mutual interaction with balance of payments and exchange rate policies.

The paper will require knowledge of the relevant theories, institutions, and recent events in the U.K. and the international financial system. Questions may be set relating to the practices of other countries.

In this paper some questions may be set which permit candidates to show capacity to interpret and handle statistical evidence.

8. Public economics

The paper has the following subject matter:

The structure and accounts of the public sector; the pattern of public expenditure and taxation; reasons for and against particular categories of public expenditure: 'public goods'; the role of taxes, charges, and subsidies in dealing with externalities; applications of cost benefit analysis in the public sector; public sector pricing and investment policy; methods of monitoring public expenditure and its efficiency; incidence of expenditure and taxes; a detailed study of the main categories of taxes levied on households and companies, and their comparative advantages; economics of the public debt and its management; interconnexions between fiscal and monetary policies.

The paper requires knowledge of the relevant theories, institutions, and recent events in the U.K. Questions may be set relating to the practices of other countries.

In this paper some questions may be set which permit candidates to show capacity to interpret and handle statistical evidence.

9. The economics of underdeveloped countries

This paper deals with the origins of underdevelopment and its changing character, with the factors which have led to differences in economic growth and structure and in income distribution and living standards in less developed market and socialist economies, and with the effects of different national and international policies designed to promote develop-

ECONOMICS AND POLITICS

ment. Candidates are expected to show familiarity with the theoretical issues involved, with the actual economic conditions, problems, and policies in a number of less developed countries, and with the impact of the sociopolitical environment in which such policies operate.

In this paper, some questions are set which give candidates an opportunity to make use, in writing their answer, of a brief amount of empirical data provided on the examination paper. Such questions are designed to test candidates' knowledge of development economics and do not require elaborate arithmetical or statistical computations. They carry no more weight than any other question. Candidates may be required to answer one of these questions, but in this event at least three such questions will be set.

10. Industry

This paper has the following subject matter:

the modern business enterprise: the firm seen as a social organization and as an economic decision-making unit; the sociology of large-scale organizations: theories of bureaucracy; the composition and behaviour of main social groups within the enterprise; technology and market in relation to the structure of management; the professional in the organization; conflicts within management systems;

the industrial worker: theories of alienation and involvement; workers' productive behaviour, responses to economic incentives, etc.; the distribution of power in the enterprise, methods of management control, and their effectiveness; the distribution of, and relationship between economic and political power in western capitalist societies; sociological aspects of ownership and control; the rise of the managerial 'class' and its ideologies;

implications of the internal organization and functioning of the enterprise for its economic performance; alternative behaviour hypotheses including profit-maximizing, utility-maximizing, and satisficing hypotheses; problems of testing these hypotheses; some of their theoretical implications for theories of the firm, including theories of the growth of firms, and of business concentration; the economic analysis of the transnational enterprise;

changes in the structure of British industry: goods and services, the location of industry, small and large firms; the role of vertical integration, diversification, and of research and development expenditure in the growth of firms; market structure, business behaviour, and market performance; barriers to entry, oligopolistic groupings etc.; the relationship between structure, behaviour, and performance: theory and empirical evidence; the Government and industry: alternative policy approaches to the problems of monopoly and competition; policy on restrictive practices and monopoly in Britain, and some international comparisons.

Candidates are encouraged to consider the theoretical and factual issues involved in this paper in the light of both economic and sociological techniques of thought. Opportunity is given to refer to the historical experience of different societies.

In this paper some questions may be set which permit candidates to show capacity to interpret and handle statistical evidence.

11. Applied economic and social statistics

This paper consists of a written examination of three hours' duration and the submission of an account of a project undertaken by the candidate. It does not require the use of any advanced mathematical methods nor are proofs or commitment to memory of formulae to be expected; it deals with the simpler ways in which statistical data and methods can assist in the study of economic and social problems. The written paper and the account of the project will carry equal weight. In the written paper the candidate will be required to answer a number of questions relating to statistical methods and sources and their applications and to show knowledge in each of these areas. Candidates will be expected to be familiar with, and to use where appropriate, shortened or approximate methods of calculation. Mathematical tables (including tables of logarithms) and a list of the more complicated statistical formulae will be provided.

The project to be undertaken by the candidate shall be chosen from a list of topics specified by the Examiners. This list will be published not less than two weeks before the last day of the Full Lent Term. Candidates will be required to submit an account of the project, in the form of an extended essay, by a date not later than one week after the first day of the Full Easter Term. This account, which must be in English, should not exceed 4000 words in length (inclusive of notes and appendices).[1] It should report the statistical sources and techniques used by the candidate as well as presenting the candidate's results and conclusions. Candidates are expected to show familiarity with the range of statistical techniques set out in paragraph (*a*) *Statistical methods* below, and to be able to select the appropriate techniques and data for the analysis of the topic which they have selected.

Candidates are expected to show a knowledge of each of the following:

(*a*) *Statistical Methods:*

(i) the use of tables, graphs, and frequency distributions in sum-

---

[1] One A4 page consisting largely of charts, statistics or symbols shall be regarded as the equivalent of 250 words; the contents of such pages must be presented so as to be readily legible.

marizing and organizing statistical data; summary measures of central tendency, dispersion and skewness; the construction and interpretation of index numbers;

(ii) the use of sample statistics; sampling distributions (large samples): sample mean, sample variance, difference between sample means, difference between sample proportions; sampling distributions (small samples from parent normal populations): difference between sample means where population variances are the same, ratio of sample variances;

(iii) an elementary treatment of point and confidence interval estimation and hypothesis testing: in each case, the sample statistics used are those enumerated in (ii);

(iv) chi-square hypothesis testing: goodness of fit of observed data to hypothetical distribution; independence of two-way classification;

(v) regression: statistical estimation of the classical linear regression model where errors are independently and normally distributed with common variance, sampling distributions of regression coefficients and correlation coefficients; estimation and hypothesis testing; extension of the classical linear regression model, including heteroscedasticity, autoregressive errors and errors in variables;

(vi) non-parametric testing; use of Kendall rank correlation coefficient (tau);

(vii) simpler methods of seasonal correction;

(viii) conduct and use of economic and social surveys.

(*b*) *Statistical Sources:*

The topics covered include national income and expenditure; the incomes and expenditures of firms and households; production; prices; overseas trade and payments; population and vital statistics; labour; households and families; education; housing; and crime. The major general source books of United Kingdom statistics and their use, especially the *Monthly Digest of Statistics, Economic Trends* (including the *Annual Supplement*), the *Annual Abstract of Statistics, National Income and Expenditure* ('Blue Book'), and such international source books as the *O.E.C.D. Main Economic Indicators*; how to seek more detailed statistical information not included in these general source books (e.g. in the *U.K. Balance of Payments*, in the *Family Expenditure Survey, The Census of Production, The Census of Population*).

(*c*) *Econometric applications:*

The candidates will be expected to show familiarity with major econometric studies in areas to be specified by the Faculty Board from time to time. The Board will also specify the particular studies to be covered. The candidates will be expected to show knowledge of the statistical and economic problems involved in analysis of economic issues in these areas.

Candidates will be required to cover the following areas and books and articles until further notice:

(i) Econometric studies of consumer behaviour with particular reference to the following:

S. J. Prais and H. S. Houthakker, *The Analysis of Family Budgets*, Chaps. 5–8; M. Friedman, *A Theory of the Consumption Function*, Chaps. 3 and 4; J. E. Davidson, D. F. Hendry, F. Srba, and S. Yeo, 'Econometric Modelling of the Aggregate Time-Series Relationship between Consumers' Expenditure and Income in the United Kingdom', *The Economic Journal*, Dec. 1978.

(ii) Econometric studies of the behaviour of firms with particular reference to the following:

A. Singh and G. Whittington, 'The Size and Growth of Firms', *The Review of Economic Studies*, Jan. 1975; R. L. Marris and A. J. B. Wood (Eds.), *The Corporate Economy*, Appendices A and B, pp. 389–427.

(iii) Econometric studies of U.K. imports with particular reference to:

H. S. Houthakker and S. P. Magee, 'Income and Price Elasticities in World Trade', *Review of Economics and Statistics*, May 1969; T. S. Barker, (Ed.), *Economic Structure and Policy*, Chap. 7; R. D. Rees and P. R. G. Layard, *The Determinants of U.K. Imports*, Government Economic Service, Occasional Paper No. 3, 1972.

(iv) Econometric studies of U.K. exports with particular reference to

M. Panič and T. Seward, 'The Problem of U.K. Exports', *Bulletin of the Oxford Institute of Economics and Statistics*, Feb. 1966; D. Stout, *International Price Competitiveness, Non-Price Factors and Export Performance*, N.E.D.O., 1977; T. S. Barker (Ed.), *Economic Structure and Policy*, Chap. 6.

(v) Econometric studies of pricing behaviour with particular reference to:

K. J. Coutts, W. A. H. Godley, and W. D. Nordhaus, *Industrial Pricing in the United Kingdom*, Chaps. 2–4.

(vi) Econometric studies of investment behaviour with particular reference to:

D. W. Jorgenson, 'Econometric Studies of Investment Behaviour: A Survey', *Journal of Economic Literature*, Dec. 1971; P. J. Lund, 'The Econometric Assessment of the Impact of

Investment Incentives', in A. Whiting (Ed.), *The Economics of Industrial Subsidies*, H.M.S.O.; M. Desai, *Applied Econometrics*, Chap. 6.

(vii) Econometric studies of output, productivity and employment with particular reference to:

Z. Hornstein, J. Grice, and A. Webb (Eds.), *The Economics of the Labour Market*, a Chapter by S. G. B. Henry; *Cambridge Economic Policy Review*, 1978, Chap. 3; W. A. H. Godley and J. R. Shepherd, 'Long-Term Growth and Short-Term Policy', *National Institute Economic Review*, Aug. 1964.

(viii) Macroeconometric models of the U.K. economy with particular reference to:

M. V. Posner, *Demand Management*, Chaps. 1–4 and 7; M. Desai, *Applied Econometrics*, Chap. 8.

(d) Interpretation and Use of Statistics:

Interpretation of the meaning and validity of statistical data; the use of statistics to assist in forming judgements about the course of events and in testing economic or sociological hypotheses. Considerable importance is attached to a candidate's performance in this aspect of the subject in both Parts of the examination.

12. The theory of statistics

Candidates for this paper are expected to show both an understanding of the theory of statistics and an ability to apply statistical methods to economic problems and to perceive the limitations and difficulties inherent both in data and methods. The use of slide-rules, calculators, and statistical tables is permitted in the examination.

The paper poses questions involving estimation, hypothesis testing, and forecasting primarily in the context of statistical models of particular use in economic and social studies: the models include multiple regression, multivariate regression and simultaneous equations models; particular emphasis is placed on such problems as serial correlation, errors in variables, and identification. In addition questions on such topics as Bayesian estimation and inference, the design and analysis of sample surveys, sequential sampling, and non-parametric procedures may be asked.

Candidates are expected to attempt not more than four questions. Relatively little credit is given for answers to parts of questions.

13. The social structure of modern Britain (Paper 4 of the Social and Political Sciences Tripos)

14. Comparative political systems (Paper 6 of the Social and Political Sciences Tripos)

15. A subject in the field of sociology and politics

Until further notice the subjects specified for this paper, from which candidates are required to select one, will be:

The sociology and politics of South Asia.

The sociology and politics of Latin America.

The sociology and politics of welfare.

The subjects are respectively the subject specified for Paper In. 28 of the Oriental Studies Tripos, and Paper 43 of Part IIB of the Social and Political Sciences Tripos.

16. A subject in economic history

This paper is entitled 'Economic development of Russia from 1860 to the present day'. Topics covered include the Emancipation of 1861, the Stolypin reforms, collectivization and other changes in land holding and the position of the peasantry; the condition of agriculture and its interaction with the industrial sector; the growth of industry and the industrial labour force; the contribution to economic growth of foreign capital and foreign trade; the role of the state in promoting economic development; the economic and political aspects of the policy debates of the 1920s; the system of planning and administration of the Soviet economy as it has developed since 1929.

The paper will be divided into two parts. Section A will include questions mainly on the pre-1917 period, Section B will include questions mainly on the post-1917 period. Questions requiring knowledge of both periods may be included in either section or in both sections. Candidates will be required to answer at least one question from each section.

Questions may be set on the current period, but candidates are not expected to have a detailed knowledge of the changes in the Soviet economy after 1965.

17. A subject in economic history

This paper is entitled 'World Depression in the interwar years'. Its main focus is on the causes and courses of the Great Depression of the 1930s, but the events of the 1920s including the inflation and deflation of 1919–21 also receive attention. Topics covered include the transfer problem and international monetary arrangements, the growth of protection and the development of trading blocs, monopolistic tendencies and changes in income distribution, technology and structural changes, the agrarian depression, and the comparative experience of different countries with regard to unemployment, especially following the trough of the cycle.

The main countries considered are Britain, France, Germany, U.S.A., and Japan, but the paper is not exclusively confined to these, and, in particular, the experience of some of the main primary producing countries is also studied.

18. A subject in economic history

This paper will not be set until further notice.

The Preliminary Examination for Part II

The examination is taken at the end of the second year and consists of the following papers:

Papers 1 and 2. Economic principles

These papers are concerned with the theoretical groundwork of the topics covered in Papers 1, 2, and 3 of Part II of the Economics Tripos, with emphasis on tools of analysis and their use. In Paper 2 some questions are included which deal with the history of economic thought.

Each of these papers contains one question which involves candidates in manipulating simple 'mathematical' models. The mathematical competence required is not higher than that required in passing E.Q.E.M. The required manipulative element accounts for approximately one third of the total weight to be accorded the question as a whole. The remaining two thirds is accounted for by a discursive element (which does not rule out but does not require further 'mathematical' manipulation). In both Paper 1 and Paper 2 the 'mathematical' question is set as one half of an either/or combination where the alternative question is in the same subject area as the 'mathematical' question but does not have a required 'mathematical' element.

Paper 3. Economic development

This paper provides an introduction to basic concepts and theories in development economics and to their application to the comparative industrialization and development experience of selected countries. It is designed to provide a useful foundation for candidates proposing to take Part II specialist options in development economics or in economic history, but it also constitutes a self-contained one-year course for those interested in studying this field but not necessarily planning to continue with it further.

The concepts and theories to be covered are: theories of imperialism; the concept and measurement of 'development'; the evolution of the structure of output and employment during the course of 'development'; interactions with the world economy (different foreign trade strategies; the rôle of foreign capital); the rôle of different sectors (agriculture, industry, and the services) in the development process; the rôle of the state; socio-economic issues (demography and income distribution).

The examination is in two sections. Section (1) includes purely analytical questions. Section (2) requires candidates to relate their analysis of theoretical issues to comparative historical evidence from countries including Germany, Japan, China, Brazil, and Kenya during the period covered in the lectures for this course. Candidates will be required to answer one question from Section (1) and two questions from Section (2).

Paper 4. Sociology

The scope of sociology. Basic sociological concepts and principles as seen in the analysis of: social stratification and mobility; population, community and family; political mobilization and political parties; social control and deviance; education and social structure; urbanization; religion; relations between economic activity and social organization in industrial and pre-industrial societies.

Paper 5. Economic and social statistics

This paper deals with the manner in which statistics contribute to the study of economic and social problems and to the discussion of issues of public policy. Its main purpose is to test the candidate's ability to analyse problems in applied economics and similar problems of a sociological type, by bringing to bear on them relevant economic or sociological theory, knowledge of statistical sources, and relatively simple statistical derivations. It does not require mathematical analysis.

The examination will consist of a four-hour paper which will be set in such a way that candidates will be required to answer two questions which directly test their ability to use statistical techniques, and one question of an applied economic or sociological character. The latter question will carry as much weight as the first two. Candidates are expected to be familiar with and to use, where appropriate, shortened or approximate methods of calculation. Numerical tables will be provided.

ECONOMICS AND POLITICS

Statistical techniques

The specific statistical techniques covered by the syllabus are given below:

(a) *The use of tables, graphs, and frequency distributions* in summarizing and organizing statistical data; summary measures of central tendency; dispersion and skewness; the construction and interpretation of index numbers.

(b) *The use of sample statistics:* sampling distributions (large samples): sample mean, sample variance, difference between sample means, difference between sample proportions; sampling distributions (small samples from parent normal populations): difference between sample means where population variances are the same, ratio of sample variances.

(c) *An elementary treatment of point and confidence interval estimation and hypothesis testing:* in each case, the sample statistics used are those enumerated in (b).

(d) *Regression:* statistical estimation of two-variable models where errors are independently and normally distributed with common variance; sampling distributions of regression coefficients and correlation coefficients; testing of hypotheses; estimation and interpretation of multiple regression coefficients (candidates will not be expected to estimate multiple regression equations with more than three variables).

(e) *Methods of Social Accounting*, including an introduction to the concept of an input–output table.

(f) *Economic time-series:* identification of the 'trend' and 'seasonal' components of economic time-series on the basis of simple assumptions.

Statistical sources

Candidates will be expected to have had experience in using the *Monthly Digest of Statistics*, the *Annual Abstract of Statistics, National Income and Expenditure* (the 'Blue Book'), *Economic Trends* including the Annual Supplement, and the *Handbook of International Economic Statistics for Use with the Cambridge Economics Tripos*; they should also have had more limited experience in seeking for more detailed information, not included in these general source books, in the *General Household Survey*, the *Family Expenditure Survey*, the *U.K. Balance of Payments* and the *Census of Population*.

Paper 6. Mathematics for economists and statisticians

This paper deals with those portions of linear algebra, differential and integral calculus, differential and difference equations, probability theory, and statistics which are the principal mathematical groundwork of the subjects covered in Papers 6 and 12 of Part II of the Economics Tripos.

The paper will be divided into three sections, in each of which there will be questions labelled (*a*), (*b*), and (*c*). In each section questions are in ascending order of difficulty from (*a*) to (*c*). Candidates can satisfy the Examiners in this paper by answering correctly one question labelled (*a*) from each section. Candidates can obtain progressively higher marks by answering correctly questions from harder categories.

Papers 1–4 and 6 are set for three hours each.

A candidate may offer all or any of the six papers specified above, provided that

(*a*) in order to be included in the list of candidates who have passed the examination
- (i) a candidate who has previously taken Part I of the Economics Tripos shall offer Papers 1, 2, and 5, and at least one other paper chosen from Papers 3, 4, and 6;
- (ii) a candidate who has previously taken a Tripos Examination in Mathematics, Natural Sciences, or Engineering shall offer Papers 1 and 2 and at least one other paper chosen from Papers 3, 4, and 5;
- (iii) any other candidate shall offer Papers 1 and 2 and at least one other paper chosen from Papers 3, 4, 5, and 6.

(*b*) if a candidate wishes to offer fewer papers than required under (*a*) above, his entry is made in accordance with Regulation 4 for entries and lists of candidates for examinations.

(*c*) if a candidate offers more papers than the minimum required under (*a*) above, his performance in the additional paper or papers will be taken into account by the Examiners only if that would be to his advantage.

(*d*) a candidate who offers Paper 6 may, in addition, submit such written work done by him during the course leading to the examination as shall from time to time be determined by the Faculty Board, bearing, as an indication of good faith, the signatures of the teachers under whose direction the work was performed. In drawing up the class-list the Examiners shall take account of this written work only if that would be to the candidate's advantage.

Candidates may use battery-powered electronic calculators.

The Diploma in Economics

Candidature for the Diploma in Economics is open to any member of the University who has not been classed in Part II of the Economics Tripos.

A candidate for the Diploma must be admitted as a Graduate Student. The Board of Graduate Studies will fix the date of commencement of his candidature.

At least three terms must have been kept by any candidate before he is qualified to receive the Diploma. He must pursue his studies for the Diploma in Cambridge under the direction of a Supervisor appointed by the Degree Committee and under any special conditions that the Committee may lay down in his case.

Not later than the fourth, nor earlier than the first, term after the term of the commencement of his candidature the candidate must satisfy the Examiners for Part II of the Economics Tripos in three papers, chosen from among the papers of Part II of the Economics Tripos and Paper 3 of the Preliminary Examination for Part II of the Economics Tripos, provided that one paper must be chosen from among Papers 1, 2, 3, 5, and 9 of Part II of the Economics Tripos, and that no candidate may offer both Paper 3 and Paper 11 of Part II. A candidate may elect to offer four papers subject to the approval of the Degree Committee, in which case his performance in the one paper in which the Examiners judge his work to be least good shall be taken into account only if that would be to his advantage. Subject to the approval of the Degree Committee, candidates for the Diploma who take Paper 11 of Part II may be permitted to make a different choice of questions from that available to candidates for the Tripos. The choice of papers must be approved by the Degree Committee, and in the three papers judged together the candidate must reach at least the standard of the first division of the second class. The Examiners will make a written report on each candidate's work to the Degree Committee.

Not earlier than the division of the second term, nor later than the end of the fourth term after the term of the commencement of his candidature, the candidate for the Diploma must send to the Secretary of the Board of Graduate Studies a thesis or essay not exceeding fifteen thousand words on a subject previously approved by the Degree Committee; the thesis or essay may, by special permission of the Board, be submitted later than the fourth term after the term of commencement of candidature. This thesis or essay will be referred to an Examiner appointed by the Degree Committee, who will report on it to the Degree Committee, who will consider the reports of the Examiners of the papers and of the thesis and will decide whether the candidate shall be entitled to receive the Diploma.

A Graduate Student who has been given leave by the Board of Graduate Studies to count the period or any part of it during which he has been a candidate for the Diploma towards a course of research for the degree of Ph.D., M.Sc., or M.Litt. will not be entitled to be awarded the Diploma so long as he remains on the register of Graduate Students, nor if he subsequently proceeds to the degree of Ph.D., M.Sc., or M.Litt.

M.Phil. Degree (one-year)

This is a qualification gained for advanced course work.

(a) M.Phil. in Economics

The examination takes the form of a three-hour written paper or an 8,000 word essay, or four essays each of not more than 2,000 words in length, or a combination of a three-hour written paper and a 4,000 word essay on each of four topics on which the Faculty offers M.Phil. courses; in place of one of these topics the candidate may submit an 8,000 word essay on a subject of his own choice which has been approved by the Degree Committee. In 1989–90, M.Phil. courses will be offered on Political Economy (five courses), Mathematical Economics (two courses), Applied Economics (one course), Econometrics and Applied Econometrics (two courses), Industrial Economics (four courses), Development Studies (three courses), and Industrial Relations (one course).

(b) M.Phil. in the Economics and Politics of Development

The examination takes the form of three three-hour written papers in (1) Theories of Development, (2) Sociology and Politics of Development, (3) Applied Economics for Development and either an 8,000 word essay on a subject of the candidate's own choice which has been approved by the Degree Committee or one course chosen subject to the approval of the Degree Committee from the courses offered in (a) above.

In place of the examination described above, a candidate may, by special permission of the Degree Committee, granted after considering the candidate's experience, special qualifications, and proposed topic, offer

> (i) a thesis of not more than 25,000 words in length, including footnotes, tables, appendices, and bib-

ECONOMICS AND POLITICS

liography, on a subject approved by the Degree Committee;

and (ii) three essays, each of not more than 4,000 words in length, including footnotes, tables, appendices, and bibliography, on subjects approved by the Degree Committee and falling respectively within the following fields:

1. Theories of development.
2. Sociology and politics of development.
3. Applied economics for development.

(*c*) *M.Phil. in Finance*

(i) The examination takes the form of an essay, of not more than 8,000 words (an A4 page consisting largely of statistics or symbols will be the equivalent of 250 words) in length, on a topic approved by the Degree Committe (but the Degree Committee may permit a particular candidate to offer, in place of the essay and in addition to those subjects that he is required to offer under (ii), one alternative subject);

and

(ii) three subjects chosen by the candidate with the approval of the Degree Committee from the list of subjects in Finance, published by the Degree Committee (a candidate may elect to offer four subjects chosen from that list with the approval of the Degree Committee, in which case the candidate's performance in the one subject on which the Examiners judge his work to be least good will be taken into account only if that would be to his advantage).

The alternative subject will be chosen *either* from the list published by the Degree Committee *or* from the list published for the M.Phil. course in Economics (see above).

The examination may include an oral examination upon the essays and the written papers.

Further details of the courses may be obtained from the Director of Graduate Studies, Faculty of Economics and Politics, Austin Robinson Building, Sidgwick Avenue, Cambridge, CB3 9DD.

EDUCATION

Introduction

The University of Cambridge is concerned with the following courses of study in the field of Education: (1) a one-year postgraduate course leading to the award of the Postgraduate Certificate in Education; (2) a two-year course for undergraduates and affiliated students leading to an Honours B.A. Degree with a Certificate in Education; (3) a two-year course, for students who have already completed two years of study at Homerton College, leading to the B.Ed. Degree; and (4) a one-year course leading to the M.Phil. Degree. There are also facilities for research and an opportunity for those who have already completed the Certificate in Education course at the University to submit work towards a Diploma in Education.

ONE-YEAR COURSE FOR THE POSTGRADUATE CERTIFICATE IN EDUCATION

Regulations for the granting of Qualified Teacher status to graduates make it necessary for all those graduating after 31 December 1973 to complete successfully a minimum of one year of professional teacher training. This means that new graduates cannot obtain appointments to teach in maintained schools in England and Wales without taking a Certificate course.

At the present time, many changes are taking place in schools, both in the social context and in new developments in curricula and teaching methods. Intending teachers need to be aware of the opportunities provided by these changes, and to be equipped to respond to them in a professional way. The Postgraduate Certificate course therefore seeks to combine the learning of practical teaching techniques with the analysis of contemporary professional practice in both its subject specific and general aspects.

The programmes offered are for students wishing to train to teach in either Primary or Secondary Schools.

General

Each year about 350 graduate students in the Faculty read for the Postgraduate Certificate in Education. All students must be members of a College (or an Approved Society). Cambridge graduates are usually allowed to continue membership of their own College for this extra year. Details of the application procedures are given on pp. 156.

Details of the Course

During the course students study methods of teaching particular subjects and examine wider educational issues in a very practical way, often involving school experience visits. There are also extended periods of supervised teaching practice.

The Secondary School Programme (S1 and S2)

There is a choice of two secondary programmes, S1 and S2, which vary according to the subject specialisms offered. The **S1 course** is organised by the University Department of Education and the **S2 course** by Homerton College. The range of subjects available in each of the two programmes is explained in the section dealing with the study of teaching methods.

General Principles of Educational Practice

The underlying issues in education are considered throughout the course in both S1 and S2 programmes. They are taught in various ways under the headings: Situations, Themes, Core Course and Special Topics.

Situations. These sessions occur during the first term. In interdisciplinary groups, students take part in discussions, simulations and role play exercises under the guidance of a member of staff. Each session presents a situation which might be encountered by a student or probationary teacher and considers possible courses of action. Related readings are also provided. The topics covered include:

classroom management and the motivation of pupils;
assessment of pupils' work and ability;
children with special educational needs;
curriculum issues;
language in the classroom;
equal opportunities;
relationships between teachers and parents;
the role of the teacher in the school and community.

Some of these sessions take place in local schools with experienced senior teachers.

Themes. Each theme is a lecture presentation of a major topic in education, such as discipline, and is linked with the Situations course.

Core Course. In the third term all students engage in further study of topics of particular concern in education, such as the relationship between schools, industry and the community; the role of public examinations; or the place of education in a multi-cultural society.

Special Topics. In the third term each student selects two Special Topics to study in some depth. A selection of options currently offered is as follows:

applications of Information Technology in education;
the use of simulation in the classroom;
a study of disaffected pupils;
an approach to health education in schools;
developments in the assessment of pupils;
links between education and industry;
the influence of social class on education.

The Study of Teaching Methods

Students follow either the S1 or the S2 programme. The range of subjects available in each programme are detailed below.

The S1 programme

Students select a main subject specialism from the following list.

Biology; Chemistry; Physics;
(all include a course in Combined Science)*

Classics; English; Modern Languages;
Geography; History; Religious Studies;
Mathematics†.

* A four-term course in *Combined Science with Intensive Physics and Chemistry* may also be available.

† A two-year *Mathematics conversion* PGCE course may also be available.

Applicants are normally expected to have a degree qualification in either their teaching subject or a closely related subject which will enable them to cover the full range of secondary work up to university entrance standard.

Work in Methods groups deals with all aspects of the teaching of particular school subjects including, for example, classroom organization and management, the subject as part of a school curriculum, techniques and problems of teaching and learning, preparation of appropriate teaching materials, assessment procedures etc. Each week, experienced serving teachers, acting as teacher-tutors, take part in Methods sessions.

The **English** Methods course is based on the principle of workshop activity. Students work mainly in groups and participate in drama work and personal writing. Skills are developed in educational technology, including the use of micro-computers in English teaching.

The **Classics** Methods course prepares students to teach Latin, Classical Studies, Ancient History and Greek, where students are appropriately qualified. Classical Studies graduates are welcome to apply but should normally have Latin to A-level standard. The first term's work is focused on school experience, the development of teaching materials and the use of audio-visual aids and computers. In the third term sixth-form work, examinations and the use of sites and museums are particularly considered.

Graduates with Joint Honours in Latin and a Modern Language can, by arrangement, follow a Methods course in Modern Languages/Latin.

Modern Languages specialists should offer two languages, one of which must be French or German, although all applicants must have some qualification in French. They must also have had a substantial period of residence abroad in a relevant country (e.g. as an English Assistant or as a student at a foreign university). Russian and Spanish may be offered also as subsidiary languages.

Much of the **Geography** Methods course consists of practical workshop sessions using a variety of resources, including micro-computers and inter-active video. The first term's work concentrates on preparation for teaching practice, but in the third term wider issues are studied and students work in groups on research topics related to school Geography. All students undertake some residential field-work with a school group.

In the **History** Methods course, through practical activity, students acquire a range of teaching approaches including the use of source materials, audio-visual aids, the Schools History project 13–16, computers, work sheets as well as drama and role-play. In the third term wider issues such as developments in assessment, sixth form teaching and teaching in a multi-cultural society are examined.

The **Religious Studies** course offered by the University Department of Education introduces students to the wide range of teaching methods and skills which can be used to make the subject interesting and relevant to modern adolescents. Workshops are held on the use of videos, computers, source materials, artefacts, drama and role play. Visits are arranged to various faith communities. From the beginning of the course students are encouraged to work with pupils in the classroom and help is provided by experienced teachers with lesson planning and preparation, often drawing on resources within the Department. New ways of teaching for GCSE are explored and there are opportunities for sixth form work. Emphasis is also laid on the ethical and social dimensions of modern RS teaching. Students are encouraged to develop their own interests and skills through individual project and group work. A particular opportunity exists for involvement in Personal and Social Education through a course run by an experienced teacher.

The one-year *Mathematics* course is intended for graduates whose first degree has entailed a substantial study of Mathematics, including those with degrees in Computer Science, Engineering and Physics.

The **Mathematics** Methods course provides the opportunity for the development of appropriate resources for school use, design of course units and planning of single lessons. Some of the material can be tried out immediately in school: students visit schools once a week in the first term in order to observe teachers and work with small groups, or even whole classes in some cases. In addition, new, controversial, important and difficult aspects of mathematics learning and teaching are examined in the first and third terms. There is a wide choice of type of school available for teaching practice in terms of age-group (11–16, 13–18 or 11–18) and location. Student preferences are taken into account and it is usually possible to arrange the practice to be near the student's home if that lies within 50 miles of Cambridge. Mature students, particularly those who have careers in industry or who have been bringing up children are encouraged to apply. With a strong interest in multi-cultural education, the Mathematics team encourage applicants from ethnic minority communities.

Science in schools is undergoing a period of major development and change. The National Curriculum will require that all pupils undertake a science course which is broad and balanced. This means that in future school science courses may range from those where Biology, Chemistry and Physics are co-ordinated, though still taught separately, to those where the science is fully integrated. In any case, pupils up to the age of 16 will no longer be able to choose only one or two subjects from the traditional separate sciences. The PGCE S1 course reflects these developments in two ways:

(1) Graduates who wish to train as teachers of Science are first asked to choose a specialist separate Science subject and will join a

Biology, Chemistry or Physics group. The intention is to help students gain teaching expertise in their chosen subject specialism up to A Level. School science departments still need teachers who take particular responsibility for biological, chemical or physical aspects of their courses at all stages. The separate sciences will be taught in the 16–19 age range for the foreseeable future and good specialist teachers are always in demand.

(2) We arrange a substantial amount of *Combined Science* activities for all intending teachers of Science, irrespective of their individual specialisms. Throughout our Combined Science course, students:

* study aspects of science education common to all sciences
* work in many laboratory-based practical sessions
* examine widely-used school science courses
* have opportunities for individual study
* where possible, observe and teach Science lessons during school experience.

This experience of training in both specialist and combined science education should prepare new science teachers for the variety of courses they may meet in schools. The DES Bursary scheme at present applies to the Chemistry and Physics options.

The **Biology** Methods course is available to applicants with graduate qualifications in any of the Biological Sciences and offers specialist preparation for all secondary levels, including sixth-form teaching. The work has a strong practical focus and includes special consideration of environmental and health-related biological issues.

The **Chemistry** course is available to graduates whose degree course included Chemistry (e.g. chemistry, biochemistry, materials science, metallurgy, earth sciences). The course concentrates on the development of a wide range of skills required for teaching chemistry/science up to A level. There is an emphasis on participation, planning and practical work. The course includes experience in schools, the management of laboratory-based lessons, techniques of assessment, work with computers and audio-visual aids, field work, and how to use resources outside school.

The **Physics** course is based on discussion and practical laboratory experience. The physics-based Programmes of Study from the National Curriculum and GCSE are the main focus in the first term, which equips students to undertake teaching practice in a variety of schools. Many topics, such as electronics, sixth-form teaching and field work are chosen by the student group each year to fit in with their special interests. Applications are welcome from physicists, physical scientists and engineers.

Supplementary Courses Additional optional courses are also available in Combined Science, Drama, Educational and Information Technology, Electronics, Games, Latin, Religious Studies.

Additional Courses and Activities open to all Students

Throughout the year all students are given the opportunity to acquire skills in educational technology (including, for example, TV and audio recording, graphics and display and the use of film, slide and overhead projectors) and some 'hands-on' experience with microcomputers. It is intended that all students will gain an appreciation of the use of microcomputers in education during the course.

The S2 Programme

Students choose two subject methods courses. The first teaching subject receives slightly greater emphasis than the second. First subjects are chosen from those listed below:

Biology	French
Chemistry	German
Physics	Music
Mathematics	Religious Studies
English	

Students who choose English as a first teaching subject must follow a second subject in Drama.

Science students must choose a second Science, but Chemistry and Physics students, if qualified, may choose Mathematics.

Students with first subject French or German should normally offer the other language as a second subject, but other choices are possible.

Modern Language students should have had a substantial period of residence abroad in the appropriate country.

Religious Studies students must follow a second-subject course in Personal and Social Education.

All other applicants must choose a second teaching subject, in which they are suitably qualified, from one of the groups given below which does **not** contain their first subject.

A	B	C	D
Biology	German	Chemistry	English
French	Music	Religious Studies	P.E. (Games)
Mathematics*	Physics		

* A Special Initiative Two-Year PGCE course in **Mathematics**

(and if desired, a second subject) may be offered to candidates with degrees in subjects other than Mathematics or Engineering, but having some Mathematics in their degree.

Applicants are normally expected to have a degree qualification which will enable them to cover the full range of secondary work. Acceptance for a second subject is normally dependent upon students having some element of that subject or a related subject in their degree or having studied the subject to at least A level. It is not possible to change from one methods group to another at any time after acceptance without reapplication.

Work in methods groups deals with all aspects of the teaching of particular school subjects and each first subject methods tutor works in close liaison with a member of staff specialising in professional and educational studies. Between them they devise a programme geared to the specific needs of the subject, including classroom organisation and effective classroom control, the subject as part of the curriculum, preparation of appropriate teaching materials, assessment procedures etc. Experienced serving teachers regularly take part in methods sessions and appropriate school experience usually occupies one day each week of the time allocated to methods work.

Biology. In the Michaelmas Term course, in association with the programmes of Science Education and their second (science) subject, students are expected to look closely at biological topics that are typical of current GCSE syllabuses. These also form the basis of lesson preparation for the school visits. The topics chosen are ones which usually present some learning difficulty to children. The Easter Term course examines issues which have arisen from the Lent Term Teaching Practice and looks forward to the probationary year.

Chemistry. In the Michaelmas Term the emphasis is on reinforcing the notion that learning and teaching Chemistry can be fun. This is linked to modes of co-operative learning using laboratory investigations, teacher demonstrations and group seminar papers. The Easter Term offers the opportunity for reflection on performance and the development of teaching materials for the probationary year, including the use of computers in Chemistry. A-level topics are also examined in this term.

Science Education. This course contains weekly sessions that are common to all S2 Science graduates. In the Michaelmas Term these include the planning of science lessons; and production of resources; laboratory management; the aims, objectives and the sequencing of lessons; safety in laboratories; microteaching exercises; control and discipline and the opportunity to teach in local schools on two days per week. The Easter Term programme is held jointly with the S1 students and looks at a variety of issues which are currently under review in Science Education.

Physics. The S2 Physics course (Michaelmas Term) is designed to prepare students to teach physics or the physics component of a combined science or integrated science scheme to GCSE level. A wide variety of experimental situations are examined as well as some elements derived directly from GCSE, such as in-course assessment and the applications of physics to the world of work. In the Easter Term there is an opportunity to examine further issues for the 11–16 teacher, but also to consider some topics in A-level physics. Topics such as electronics and interfacing with the computer are tackled in this term.

English. The S2 English Methods Course involves reading, discussion, written work and practical preparation for teaching. It aims to enable students to evolve some kind of framework with which to appraise the variety of classroom language uses and to understand developmental aspects of children's responses to literature. First choice students establish a continuing contact with the English department of a local secondary school, working alongside teachers and pupils to develop the full range of language and reading activities.

Drama. Drama is a separate but related course taken by all students intending to do English as their first choice subject. The first part of the course aims to give students a knowledge of the principles and practice involved in using drama and theatre as learning processes. The second part of the course explores methods appropriate to the teaching of dramatic texts and provides opportunities for students to develop skills in the practical aspects of play production.

French and German. The Modern Languages course aims to provide opportunities for students to plan, try out and evaluate a wide range of teaching strategies, materials and ideas. An emphasis is put on encouraging pupil participation and on realistic, practical, communicative activities for use in the classroom. Each language is catered for separately in order to provide appropriate methodological examples, to illustrate the materials and facilities which are available for teaching it and to deal with the areas of interest, strengths and learning difficulties which are peculiar to it.

Mathematics. The course aims to encourage students to examine a variety of approaches to the teaching of mathematics to pupils at all levels of attainment up to and including A-level. Time is spent in the Mathematics department of a local secondary school where students are encouraged to develop their own teaching strategies supported by teachers and tutors. The role of calculators and computers, comparison of different teaching styles, pupil involvement and learning, the use of practical materials, the relevance of mathematics, and assessment will all be considered in discussion on effective teaching of a variety of topics.

Music. The course lays emphasis on Music as a practical, creative art, involving a wide range of styles from a variety of cultures. Composing, performing and listening are regarded as the core activities in musical education and their function in the classroom is explored through lectures, workshops, video and school observation and practice. This practical emphasis is supported by a detailed study of such issues as 'Curriculum planning', 'How children learn music', 'Music and New Technology' and 'Music in a multi-Cultural Society'.

Religious Studies. The Religious Studies course aims to make students aware of how and why the aims of the subject have changed since 1944. The course includes planning lessons for teaching religions, handling ethical issues, and exploring the relationship between experience and interpretation in the classroom. Careful study is made of teaching strategies suited to different ages and abilities and materials used by teacher and pupil, ranging from agreed syllabuses, books and artifacts to other written and audio-visual resources. Students gain first hand experience of different faith communities and teaching in class before undertaking their full term teaching practice.

Personal and Social Education. This option is available only to those students who select Religious Studies as their first teaching subject. The course seeks to prepare students to share in a school's programme of Personal and Social Education in both tutorials and class teaching situations. Attention is given to both principles and materials involved in constructing schemes for pastoral and tutorial work and a syllabus and material for classroom use.

Physical Education (Games). This is offered as a Second Subject Course only. Its purpose is to provide students with opportunities for developing competence, confidence and enthusiasm for teaching a selection of winter and summer, indoor and outdoor, team and individual games, as a foundation for subsequent teaching within a secondary school Physical Education department.

School Experience and Teaching Practice

There are three elements of school experience and teaching practice in the course.

Initial experience in a primary or secondary school

Students are required to undertake a two-week period of school experience which now forms part of the course as far as term dates are concerned, before the university based part of the course begins. Students on the S1 programme spend this time in a maintained primary school, students on the S2 programme in a maintained comprehensive school. Students arrange their initial school experience through their own Local Education Authority, although pre-printed letters are provided for the purpose by the Faculty. Each student is provided with an observation guide which gives a clear indication of what to look for and find out about the school.

Work in schools in the Michaelmas Term

During the Michaelmas Term there are frequent opportunities to visit schools and to work with children. Wherever possible, students are encouraged to participate in lessons and discuss them with experienced teachers.

At least one visit is made to the school in which the student will undertake the main teaching practice.

Main teaching practice

The main practice, lasting a full school term, begins after Christmas, at the beginning of the school term. Each student is supervised by a member of the school staff who will help, advise and arrange a programme to include time for preparation and regular discussion of work. Lecturers from the Faculty visit all students during the term.

Extended Professional Experience

Towards the end of the Easter Term students will have the opportunity to spend three weeks working on an individually designed project of their choice.

The Primary School (P) Programme

Applicants should normally be graduates holding a degree in a primary school curriculum subject or a closely related subject. The course consists of three main components:

1. General principles of educational practice

EDUCATION

2. Methods of teaching specific elements of the primary school curriculum.

3. School experience and teaching practice.

1. General Principles of Educational Practice

During the Michaelmas Term and the first part of the Lent and Easter Terms, major themes concerned with schools and teaching with particular reference to the junior school age range are presented. These will include the growth of cognition, the development of language, personal and social development, multi-cultural education and the education of children with special needs. Whenever possible these sessions are followed by visits to local junior schools to enable students to engage in follow up exercises, or as a preliminary to discussions back in college. These sessions provide the theoretical background to practical curriculum course activities and clarify the link between theory and practice. The course is intended to focus the attention of students on the role of teacher, the developing child and the society beyond the classroom.

Special topics. All students on the primary course follow two special topics which provide the opportunity to study in more depth two further aspects of educational theory related to junior school teaching. One topic aims to develop an understanding and appreciation of the importance of issues concerning the nature and justification of the primary school curriculum through philosophical reflection. The other provides some understanding of the social context in which the primary school operates.

2. Methods of Teaching

Michaelmas Term

During the Michaelmas Term all students take the following methods courses, which consider different aspects of the junior school curriculum, and introduce different ways in which children explore their world. All courses have a strongly practical bias and involve regular contact with children and teachers from local primary schools. The common aim is to enable students to become confident, enthusiastic and informed teachers in the primary classroom.

Art. The aim of the work in this course is twofold. Firstly to give students some understanding of the experience gained from working with various materials. Secondly to investigate ways in which children may be stimulated and encouraged to obtain this kind of experience. The main approach to the work lies in observation of the environment in conjunction with the use of different media leading to the development of an ability to handle a number of materials and an inventive approach to work in schools.

Drama. This course introduces drama specifically as a process through which learning and understanding can be developed with children. It looks at the ways in which a fictional context can be explored with children and at a variety of teaching strategies which can be employed within such a context. Consideration is given to the degree to which other areas of the curriculum can supply appropriate content for this process and to the reasons for choosing drama as a way of working.

Language. This course combines the two important curriculum areas of English and the Teaching of Reading. Beginning with self-appraisal of the students' own range of reading and use of different skills and strategies, the nature of the reading process is examined and ways and means of encouraging children to read and to help them develop their reading for a variety of purposes is explored. The course also covers the extensive range of topics subsumed within the English curriculum of the primary school, variously adapted to meet the needs of different age-groups, different types of organisation and the range of abilities to be found in the primary classroom. It is concerned with how children learn to put ideas and feelings into words and to communicate them to others orally, with helping children to write both vividly and accurately and with finding the kind of topics on which children enjoy writing. It involves discussion of ways of teaching spelling, punctuation and basic grammatical points and the correction and assessment of children's work. The enjoyment of poetry, how to choose and introduce it, projects in English, group-work on a theme and English topic work are also discussed.

Geography. The course is intended to help students to plan topic work which will include awareness, understanding and concern for the environment, both in the locality and in the wider world. Emphasis is placed on identification of objectives, key ideas, first-hand sources and the preparation of themes and projects which can be used in primary schools.

History. The course considers the nature of historical evidence and strategies for engaging children in problem-solving historical detective work. It also identifies ways in which History topics can extend children's skills and develop imaginative involvement in the past through practical classroom activities. A large variety of historical sources, teaching aids and materials are evaluated and students investigate the local environment as a basis for historical work in school.

EDUCATION

Mathematics. The course places great emphasis on fostering the confidence and enthusiasm of students for mathematics. They are helped to use and develop their own mathematical knowledge by studying the methods by which junior children learn the subject. Students will be prepared to teach up to and including level 6 of the National Curriculum attainment targets. Consideration is given to topics likely to be met in primary mathematics and to methods of teaching these including practical activities, the use of apparatus and games. Particular emphasis is given to the place of the calculator and to mathematical investigations.

Music. The common course aims to show how students whose musical skill may be limited can undertake a variety of activities with juniors. Approaches to composition, classroom music making and listening are studied within a practical framework. There is also a consideration of musical development in children and the place of music within the total curriculum.

Physical Education. The course builds from an appreciation of the broad concept of human movement, through a consideration of the importance of movement to the primary age child, to a knowledge and understanding of the areas in which movement work can be developed in the junior school. It includes both the theory of the main branches of the subject and practical work in a variety of activities. It also considers the relevance of health education within the curriculum of the primary school.

Religious Studies. This course introduces students to the way in which the aim of the subject has changed in recent years from a concern to teach for belief or to initiate pupils into the Christian faith, to helping them to understand the nature of religion. It deals with the contribution which can be made at the junior school level to achieving this overall aim. This is achieved by the exploration of ideas about religion through discussion based on the experience of resources related to the teaching of religious education.

Science. This course is designed with graduates in non-scientific subjects in mind. It introduces them to methods, source materials and resources for a broad based range of scientific enquiry appropriate for pupils in junior schools. It involves practical activities which might be undertaken in the classroom, and consideration of the different ways of organising group or individual investigations.

Lent Term

During the Lent Term in addition to continuation of the Language, Mathematics and Physical Education courses, the emphasis in methods courses will be on integrated work. There will be three bands in which all students will be involved:

Humanities. This course uses the content and methods of the subject areas of History, Drama and Religious Studies to indicate ways of integrating them to form a coherent set of learning experiences within the primary school.

CDT. Students are introduced to a range of design skills and craft techniques to enable an approach to this important emerging area of primary school practice with confidence and enthusiasm. A practical problem solving approach is developed along with ways of working which will enhance children's skills, challenge their thinking and decision making abilities, and increase their confidence and self worth through achievement.

Expressive Arts. The course is intended to help students to make links between the various expressive arts and to enable them to initiate and develop integrated arts projects in the primary school.

Easter Term

During the Easter Term there will be a continuation of methods work in Language, Mathematics, Physical Education and Computing. In addition each method area will offer short intensive courses designed to enable suitably qualified students to examine the role of the specialist subject teacher in the primary school and the contribution they might make as team leaders in curriculum development.

3. School Experience and Teaching Practice

There are three elements of school experience and teaching practice in the course.

Initial experience in a primary school. Students are required to undertake a home-based two-week period of school experience at the start of the course. This should be spent in a maintained primary school and students arrange this experience through their own Local Education Authority, although pre-printed letters are provided for the purpose by the Faculty. Each student is provided with a structured observation guide which gives a clear indication of what to look for and find out about the school.

Work in schools. During the Michaelmas, Lent and Easter Terms as part of the college-based course there are frequent opportunities to visit schools and to work with teachers and children. Whenever possible students are encouraged to participate in lessons and to discuss them with experienced teachers.

At least one visit is made to teaching practice schools before the start of each practice.

Main teaching practices. There are two block teaching practices, one in the second half of the Lent Term and one in the second half of the Easter Term. These provide students with practice opportunities in contrasting schools and with two different age ranges, with a period in college for reflection in between. Each student is supervised by a member of the school staff in close cooperation with a member of the college staff, who visits fortnightly to observe lessons and discuss progress.

Postgraduate Certificate Examination

The assessment of the course is based on a combination of submitted work and assessment of performance in the teaching practice. The examination has the following three Sections:

Section I. Educational Theory

(a) a number of professional exercises and assignments and one essay dealing with the principles of educational practice, based on the Situations and Themes course and other general courses given during the year;

(b) two long essays (or equivalent pieces of work) on subjects from the two Special Topics in educational theory which have been chosen for study.

Section II. Course work on teaching methods

(a) one or two pieces of submitted work;

(b) an assessment of the student's contribution to the courses in teaching methods.

Section III. Practical teaching

Assessment by the Examiners on the basis of teaching practice reports from the schools concerned and from lecturers supervising the practice.

For those who fail in any Section of the examination, re-examination is possible on not more than two occasions subject to the permission of the Faculty Board and under conditions set in each case by the Faculty Board and the Examiners. Re-examination must normally take place within two years of the initial failure. A candidate failing in practical teaching is normally required to take a full school term of teaching practice in a subsequent academical year.

Award of the Certificate

The award of the Postgraduate Certificate in Education of the University of Cambridge is made to candidates who diligently attend and satisfactorily complete the course, and who satisfy the Examiners in Section III and in the examination as a whole. Such candidates will be recommended to the Department of Education and Science for the grant of Qualified Teacher Status.

Admission to the Course

Applications are welcomed from candidates from a wide variety of academic, social and ethnic backgrounds. Applicants should be graduates or have qualifications that are recognised as degree equivalent. For students choosing to teach at Secondary level this will normally be in the chosen subject specialism, or a closely related subject. Students must also hold G.C.E. O-Level or GCSE passes in Mathematics and English Language, or equivalent qualifications. (For G.C.E. and GCSE examinations taken in June 1975 or thereafter, a pass is regarded as Grade A, B or C.)

Full details of the application procedure are available in the Faculty of Education's P.G.C.E. prospectus, available on request from the Assistant Secretary of the Department of Education, 17 Trumpington Street or from the Registrar, Homerton College, from whom Faculty application forms are also available.

All applicants are required to register their application with the Graduate Teacher Training Registry (G.T.T.R.). Full details are given in the P.G.C.E. prospectus, but applicants should note that applications will not be considered until the Faculty application forms, G.T.T.R. forms and references have all been received. As well as being accepted by the Faculty of Education, students must also be accepted by a College before being offered a place on the course. It is not, however, necessary to make a separate application for a College place. Students will not normally be accepted without interview.

Grants

Similar procedures apply in obtaining grants for the course as for undergraduate grants. Students will be told how to go about obtaining the grant once they are offered a place on the course. Arrangements can be made for students who are unable to obtain grants to enter as private students. Details of fees involved are supplied on request. The University fee is the normal undergraduate University Composition Fee. Colleges also charge fees, normally at their undergraduate rate.

Term dates and residence

The PGCE course has different term dates from those of the University Full Terms. Details of exact dates will be supplied to students by the Faculty in good time before the start of the course.

TWO-YEAR EDUCATION TRIPOS COURSE (B.A. AND B.ED. DEGREES)

The course, which is at Part II stage, is open to two groups of students: firstly, undergraduates who have completed two years of study and have passed their Part I examinations, and affiliated students who already hold degrees from other universities. These students proceed to the B.A. Degree with a Certificate in Education. Secondly, students matriculated by Homerton College who have already undertaken two years' work in the College and who proceed to the B.Ed. Degree.

Both groups of students follow similar courses and are taught together, with the exception of certain courses specially arranged for B.A. students in the Michaelmas Term. Both groups take the same examinations – Qualifying Examination in Education at the end of the first year, and Education Tripos at the end of the second year. Students entering the course are required to have passed O-level English Language and Mathematics.

The aim of the course is to provide for those who intend to follow careers in Education, many as teachers but others in educational administration, counselling and guidance or educational research. The arrangements for the Tripos seek to make it possible for all students to follow a coherent, sustained course in which professional training and the study of educational theory are integrated and in which there is an opportunity for some students to carry further the study of a subject other than education.

The course covers the main Sections of the examination and assessment in practical teaching. The examinations and their Sections as they will be for the academical year 1989–90 are set out below.

Qualifying Examination in Education (taken at the end of the first year)

This examination comprises three Sections:

Section I. Teaching Studies. Assessment is made of course work carried out on teaching in an area of the curriculum or a special age-range of children. There are two assignments, which relate to courses taken during the year.

Section II. Candidates for the BEd degree take **two** two-hour papers chosen from the following four papers. Candidates for the BA Degree with a Certificate in Education will take **three** two hour papers, chosen from the following papers, together with an essay of not more than 5000 words on a topic that falls within the field of one of these papers.

The papers are:

Paper 1. Psychology of education

This paper deals with the growth of understanding, motivation, and topics in the field of Language Development and Social Communication.

Paper 2. Philosophy of education

This paper deals with two main subject areas, (*a*) the philosophy of learning and teaching, and (*b*) the aims and content of the curriculum.

Paper 3. Sociology of Education

This paper deals with 'the social context of schooling' and will be concerned with educational policy – the national context; studies of locality and their impact on education; the institutional context of schooling and its relationship to educational policy and provision.

Paper 4. History of Education (specified periods)

The period specified for examination in **1989** is:

Hierarchy and egalitarianism in English schooling, 1830–1965

Elementary schooling for the masses contrasted with more advanced schooling for a small élite; the growth of interconnections between the two systems and their partial assimilation in recent times; the development of meritocratic schooling, in idea and practice; the methods and purposes of secondary selection; social class and educational opportunity, 1830–1965.

Section III. This Section is taken by candidates for the BEd Degree only. Each candidate normally offers two papers in one or two of the subjects in the schedule listed below. Details of the papers which may be offered are published a year before the examination. This notice will indicate where a dissertation may be substituted for a paper.

EDUCATION

Schedule of subjects:

Archaeology and Anthropology (Archaeology)*
Classics
Economics
Engineering*
English
Geography
History
History of Art
Mathematics
Modern and Medieval Languages (French, German,† Italian,† Russian,† Spanish†)
Music
Natural Sciences (Biology,[1] Chemistry, Physics, History and Philosophy of Science)
Oriental Studies
Social and Political Sciences
Theology and Religious Studies

Education Tripos

Candidates for the B.Ed. Degree take

    (i) either subject A or subject B from Section I
    (ii) one paper from among Papers 1–4 in Section II in the same subject as one of those offered for the Qualifying Examination the previous year
and   (iii) either a second paper from Section II or a written paper or exercise from Section III or a paper from Section IV.

Candidates for the B.A. Degree with a Certificate of Education take

    (i) either subject A or subject B from Section I
    (ii) two papers from among Papers 1–4 in Section II in the same subjects as ones offered for the Qualifying Examination the previous year
and   (iii) either a third paper from Section II or a paper from Section IV.

Candidates for either degree may offer a dissertation in place of not more than one paper from among those prescribed for Sections I, II and IV.

The examination comprises four Sections:

Section I. Curriculum Studies

Subject A. The primary school curriculum.
Subject B. The secondary school curriculum.

* Candidates may not offer two papers in this subject.
† By special application.
[1] Biology includes animal biology, biology of cells, environmental biology, **biology of organisms, biological resources, and plant biology.**

Each subject will be examined by means of a written paper and an essay of not more than 3,000 words on a topic chosen by the candidate from a list of topics specified by the Faculty Board from time to time.

Section II. Educational Theory

Paper 1. Psychology of education

This paper deals with social psychology and the development of personality, together with the topics specified for Paper 1 of Section II of the Qualifying Examination.

Paper 2. Philosophy of Education

This paper deals with social, political and moral values in relation to:

(*a*) the educational system.

(*b*) the role of the school.

(*c*) classroom teaching and learning.

Paper 3. Education, Society and the State

Until further notice this paper will be entitled 'Schools, policy and practice: special topics'. The paper will be concerned with four specified topics, of which previous notice will be given, complementing themes studied for the Qualifying Examination. Candidates will be expected to answer questions in two of the four topics.

Paper 4. Special topics in the modern history of education

This paper will comprise of topics of which previous notice will be given, complementing the themes studied for the Qualifying Examination.

Paper 5. A special subject in education studies specified by the Faculty Board from time to time

Until further notice the subjects specified for this paper will be:

A. *Comparative education: education in contemporary France*

This subject will be primarily concerned with the changes within the educational system which have taken place under the Fifth Republic. An awareness of the political, social, historical, and economic background, and of parallel problems in education in Britain, will be expected.

EDUCATION

B. *Comparative education: theory and practice of Communist education*

This subject will be mainly concerned with Marxist educational ideas and their practical application as seen in the educational institutions of socialist countries, and will deal with the period from the Communist Manifesto to the present with references to influences from, and developments within, other pre-Marxist and Marxist 'schools' and periods. An awareness of the political, social, historical, and economic background, and of parallel problems in education in Britain, will be expected.

C. *Research methods in education*

Basic statistical techniques; test construction; research design and criticism; use of computer-assisted analysis.

Section III. A subject other than Education

Written papers and other exercises in a subject offered by the candidate in Section III of the Qualifying Examination. The Faculty Board of Education, shall specify for each subject the combinations of the papers and other exercises that may be offered for this section, and shall also specify which of the papers may be replaced by a dissertation; may specify papers and other exercises for this section as follows;

either (a) a written paper taken from another University Examination (including the Music Tripos), provided that a candidate may be allowed to submit a dissertation instead in a case where this is permitted in the regulations for the examination concerned;

or (b) a combination consisting of one such written paper and either a practical examination or the submission of course-work or notebooks, as specified in the regulations for the examination concerned;

or (c) a thesis, dissertation, or other exercise equivalent to a three-hour paper, as prescribed in the regulations for another University Examination;

or (d) a specially set written paper;

or (e) in Music, a specially set practical examination.

Section IV. Additional Professional Studies
Paper 6. A special subject in professional studies
Until further notice the subjects specified for this paper will be:

Literature and children

This paper is concerned with the following topics:

Poetry, novels, and short stories written specifically for children: realism, fantasy, fairy tales, and folk tales, novels about schools, the concept of character development in fiction, traditional and contemporary poetry from a variety of cultures.

Adult works, and ways in which some may be made accessible to children in school.

Concepts of children's literature: notions of excellence and taste, 'quality' books and popular books, narrative as a primary act of mind, children as critics, changing attitudes to, and historical perspectives on, children's literature.

School experience and teaching practice

Before the course starts, B.A. students undertake a two-week period of observation in a school. During their first year, they have opportunities for observation in schools. Before the beginning of the final teaching practice all students undertake a one-week period of school experience (a mixture of observation and teaching). This is carried out in the school in which the main teaching practice takes place. The main practice occupies most of the schools' autumn term (irrespective of University Term dates).

Award at the end of the course

A student who has obtained honours in the Tripos, and is qualified to proceed to the B.A. Degree, receives a Certificate in Education, if he has satisfied the Examiners in practical teaching ability. This is the recognised qualification for teaching. Students who have qualified for the B.A. Degree and the Certificate in Education are recommended to the Department of Education and Science for the award of Qualified Teacher Status, provided they satisfy the conditions in force at the time.

Candidates from Homerton who are classed in the Education Tripos and satisfy the Examiners in practical teaching proceed to the Honours B.Ed. Degree, a recognised qualification for teaching.

EDUCATION

Enquiries and Admissions

For Cambridge undergraduates, enquiries and applications should be directed through College Tutors, but any interested students can obtain further preliminary information from the Secretary of the Department of Education at 17 Trumpington Street. Early application during an undergraduate's second year is advised.

The course leading to the B.A. Degree and Certificate in Education is open to affiliated students (see p. 148).

Applicants for the B.Ed. Degree should approach Homerton College.

Grants

Candidates for the B.Ed. Degree – the two-year Education Tripos course is the second half of a known four-year course and is, therefore, covered by initial grant.

Candidates for the B.A. Degree – in order to qualify for an award from a Local Education Authority for the course, undergraduates at Cambridge must obtain the written permission of their College Tutor to the transfer onto the Education Tripos course by 31 December of their second year of undergraduate study. They must also, by the same date, inform their Local Education Authority of their intention to transfer.

Affiliated Students – grants are awarded at the discretion of their Local Education Authority, but most Local Education Authorities are reluctant to support students who wish to work at undergraduate level for a second 'first' degree.

ONE-YEAR COURSE FOR THE M.PHIL. DEGREE

The Faculty of Education offers a one-year advanced course leading to the award of the M.Phil. Degree. The examination is by a combination of a thesis (not exceeding 15,000 words in length) on an approved topic and submitted essays.

In 1989–90, M.Phil. courses will be offered in Curriculum Design and Organisation, Mathematical Education, and The Psychological Investigation of Intellectual Development.

Further details of the courses and of entrance requirements may be obtained from the Secretary of the Department of Education, 17 Trumpington Street, Cambridge CB2 1QA.

RESEARCH IN EDUCATION

Applications are welcomed from those who wish to carry out research in Education for the M.Litt., M.Sc., or Ph.D. Degrees, which are degrees by dissertation.

The research interests of members of the teaching staff of the Faculty available to supervise research include developmental psycholinguistics; classroom interaction; curriculum development, planning and evaluation; education in certain overseas countries; analysis and evaluation of teaching; moral and social education; mathematical education; philosophy of education; social psychology in relation to education; sociology of education; history of education; urban education. Enquiries about other subjects should, however, be made as it may be possible to arrange the necessary supervision. Acceptance of a candidate for research will be dependent on the availability of suitable facilities and of specialist supervision in Cambridge.

Applicants are advised to write first of all to the Secretary of the Department of Education, 17 Trumpington Street, Cambridge, CB2 1QA, who will provide further details of the application procedure and refer the enquiry to an appropriate member of staff. Details of the applicant's qualifications and experience should be included in the letter together with a statement of about 1000 words outlining the nature of the research it is proposed to undertake, the main reason for choosing this subject and how it relates to previous knowledge and experience. The statement should also indicate, as far as is practicable, the methods the applicant proposes to use and the main types of sources to be consulted.

Formal applications for admission should be made as instructed to the Board of Graduate Studies. The statement on the research proposed will also have to be attached to the application. A detailed bibliography is not required. Further details are given in the Graduate Studies Prospectus which may be obtained from the Secretary of the Board of Graduate Studies, 4 Mill Lane, Cambridge, CB2 1RZ.

UNIVERSITY DIPLOMA IN EDUCATION

Graduates who have completed a course of study in the Department of Education since 1952, and have received the Certificate in Education or the Postgraduate Certificate in Education, are eligible without further residence as candidates for the University Diploma in Education. They must write a thesis of 15,000–20,000 words on an approved topic in the field of Education. Those graduates who obtained a Certificate in Education from the University of Cambridge Education Syndicate in or before 1951 should consult the Secretary of the Degree Committee of the Faculty of Education as to their eligibility.

At least one year from the award of the Certificate in Education must have elapsed before a topic is proposed, and at least two years before a thesis is submitted.

The full regulations may be obtained on application to the Secretary of the Degree Committee, 17 Trumpington Street, Cambridge, CB2 1QA.

ENGINEERING

In this subject there are courses of study which may be followed by candidates for:

The *Engineering Tripos*, which is divided into three Parts, Part I A, Part I B, and Part II.

The *Electrical and Information Sciences Tripos*, which is not divided into Parts.

The *Manufacturing Engineering Tripos*, which is divided into two Parts, Part I and Part II, with a Certificate in Manufacturing Technology.

The *Management Studies Tripos*, which is not divided into Parts.

The *degree of M.Phil. in Computer Speech and Language Processing.*

Certificates of Postgraduate Study in Engineering.

Postgraduate Certificate in Design, Manufacture and Management

Professional engineers may be employed in one of several fields (for example: aeronautical, chemical, civil, control, electrical, information, mechanical, nuclear, or production engineering) and their work may be in design, development, research, production, management, or sales. Before they can acquire the necessary specialist knowledge they must follow a course in the basic elements of engineering science. This begins at school, with mathematics and physics as the essentials, and may be continued in the Engineering Tripos at Cambridge.

In Parts I A and I B of the Engineering Tripos, covering the first two years of study, the student continues his study of applied mathematics. His knowledge of applied physics is developed, but emphasis is placed upon applications of direct importance to the engineer: electricity, magnetism and electronics with their application to the design of electrical machines, circuits, and control mechanisms; the strength and properties of materials and the analysis and design of structures in which they may be used; thermodynamics and its utilization in the design of engines for power production, as well as refrigeration; the application of mechanics to the design and manufacture of machinery; and fluid mechanics and its use in civil engineering as well as the design of aircraft, engines, and machines.

This general course is taken by all Cambridge engineering undergraduates, but some specialization is provided within Part I B. It is important to note that the student entering the Department is not immediately required to make the choice of his specialist field of engineering (e.g. civil, mechanical, or electrical).

Following this wide-ranging course in engineering science given in

ENGINEERING

Parts I A and I B, the student may take Part II of the Engineering Tripos or the Electrical and Information Sciences Tripos, or the Management Studies Tripos, each of which is for one year. The student may also take the Manufacturing Engineering Tripos or the Chemical Engineering Tripos (details on p. 83) both of which last for a further two years. Advanced courses are offered in Part II of the Engineering Tripos, and in the Electrical and Information Sciences Tripos. The student is required to concentrate on a few subjects and to study these in depth. He may specialize entirely in a major engineering field such as aeronautical, civil, electrical or mechanical engineering, but alternatively he may opt to take papers in a variety of subject areas depending on his interests and abilities.

The Management Studies Tripos replaces and expands the former option within the Engineering Part II. The course is open to all third year students but most of those taking it will have previously studied Engineering, Economics, Mathematics or Natural Sciences. It is designed for those who wish to pursue a career in management and should appeal to students interested in accountancy, management consultancy, general management or operational research.

The Manufacturing Engineering Tripos provides the student with opportunity for extended study of manufacturing technology, design and production management. It is normally taken after reading Parts I A and I B of the Engineering Tripos and is itself in two parts covering two years of study. Much of the final year of this Tripos, that is the fourth year as an undergraduate, is spent carrying out projects in manufacturing industry.

Experimental laboratory work and computing are important parts of the undergraduate courses in engineering, as is training in engineering drawing, which is a vital means of communication for the professional engineer.

At the Postgraduate level the Department offers advanced courses as well as opportunities for Research. A one-year Postgraduate Certificate in Design, Manufacture, and Management provides an introduction to the procedures and problems of design, manufacture and management in industry. About three-quarters of this course takes place in industrial firms throughout the United Kingdom, and much of the time is spent in project work. A one-year course leading to the M.Phil. Degree is available in Computer Speech and Language Processing; lecture courses are examined in the Lent Term and a major research project is then undertaken.

Most areas of Engineering research are pursued in the Department. The majority of research students are registered for the Ph.D. Degree which provides an extensive training in research and is

expected to take three years. A few students register for the M.Sc. which is expected to take two years or for the Certificate of Postgraduate Study which is for one year. Many students also register for the Ph.D. Degree after completing the M.Phil. or Certificate of Postgraduate Study, the time spent on these courses counting towards the three years required for the Ph.D.

Entrants to Postgraduate courses and research degrees come from many British and Overseas Universities. Those who received their Undergraduate training in the Department often spend a period in industry before returning to academic work.

It should be emphasized that academic training is only part of the education of a professional engineer. Even with a research degree, a graduate cannot become a chartered engineer or a corporate member of a professional engineering institution without a period of practical experience in a responsible position.

The Engineering Tripos

The Engineering Tripos consists of three Parts, Part I A, Part I B, and Part II. During the first year all students follow similar courses, which lead to Part I A at the end of the year. At the end of the second year candidates for the Part I B Examination will take five papers and two more chosen from a group of four. A student who has obtained honours in Part I B or in another Tripos may take Part II in his second, third, or fourth year.

Part I A of the Engineering Tripos

The papers for Part I A consist of the following:

1. Mathematics.
2. Mechanical engineering.
3. Materials and structural mechanics.
4. Electrical and information engineering.

Each paper will be set for three hours and every candidate must offer all four papers.

The Examiners take into account course work done during the year.

Details of these papers are as follows:

1. Mathematics

The paper consists mainly of questions on: vector methods, including vector calculus; ordinary differential equations; functions of several variables, including simple partial differential equations; series approximations, including Fourier series; linear algebra; numerical and computational methods for the above topics.

2. Mechanical engineering

The paper consists mainly of questions on: statics; kinematics and dynamics of a particle; the work equation applied to mechanisms; modelling and analysis of dynamical systems with one or two degrees of freedom; basic concepts of thermodynamics; the first and second laws; the application of these laws and of the conservation of mass and momentum to flow processes; the thermodynamic properties of pure substances.

3. Materials and structural mechanics

The paper consists mainly of questions on: the properties of engineering materials (including the moduli, strength, toughness, fatigue strength, creep strength, corrosion resistance, and wear resistance); the physical origins of the properties; the selection and use of materials in given engineering applications; equilibrium and displacements of bodies and assemblies; pin-jointed frameworks; states of stress and strain; constitutive equations; tubes and shafts; elastic and plastic theories of bending and torsion; buckling of struts; vibration of beams.

4. Electrical and information engineering

The paper consists mainly of questions on: simple electrical networks containing active and passive devices with elementary analogue and digital applications; the principles and uses of computers and microprocessors in information engineering; fundamental concepts of electromagnetic phenomena with elementary applications.

Part IB of the Engineering Tripos

The papers for Part IB are as follows:

1. Mechanics.
2. Thermodynamics and fluid mechanics I.
3. Information, systems, and control engineering.
4. Electrical engineering.
5. Materials.
6. Thermodynamics and fluid mechanics II.
7. Electrical and information engineering I.
8. Electrical and information engineering II.
9. Structural mechanics.

Each paper will be set for three hours.

Every candidate must offer Papers 1–5 and two papers chosen *either* from Papers 6, 7 and 8 *or* from Papers 6, 7 and 9.

The Examiners take into account course work done during the year.

No candidate can obtain honours unless he has satisfied the Examiners

(*a*) that he has qualified in a practical course approved by the Faculty Board in one of the following subjects:
   (i) surveying,
   (ii) mechanical engineering,
   (iii) electrical engineering;
(*b*) that he has such workshop or equivalent experience as may be determined from time to time by the Faculty Board of Engineering.

Details of the papers are as follows:

1. Mechanics

The paper consists mainly of questions on: rigid body statics applied to engineering problems; particle dynamics; rigid body dynamics in two dimensions; vibrations; kinematics and dynamics of simple machines; elementary treatment of gyroscopic action.

2. Thermodynamics and fluid mechanics I

The paper consists mainly of questions on: fossil fuels and the application of thermodynamic principles to combustion; other sources of energy including nuclear energy; heat transfer by conduction, radiation, and convection; heat exchangers; fluid statics; kinematics of fluid motion; dynamics of fluid motion including the effects of viscosity; model testing.

3. Information, systems, and control engineering

The paper consists mainly of questions on: basic principles of information and signal analysis, analogue and digital signals, power and energy spectra; basic principles of communication, encoding and decoding information, effects of noise, examples of communication systems; basic principles of systems and control, elementary control systems analysis, and design techniques.

4. Electrical engineering

The paper consists mainly of questions on: methods of electrical instrumentation; electrical power, underlying principles of electrical machines; electronic circuit techniques.

5. Materials

The paper consists mainly of questions on: the properties of engineering materials (mechanical properties, chemical properties, electrical, magnetic, and optical properties); the origins of these properties and their control by processing; the selection and use of materials in given engineering applications.

6. Thermodynamics and fluid mechanics II

The paper consists mainly of questions on thermodynamics of power plant (including steam and gas turbine cycles and reciprocating internal combustion engines), refrigeration, properties of pure substances, consideration of maximum/minimum work, gas liquefaction, turbomachinery; fluid motion including free-surface flow and effects of compressibility and two-dimensional potential flow.

7. Electrical and information engineering I

The paper consists mainly of questions on: principles of digital systems and control; related digital electronics; basic principles of acquisition, storage, and manipulation of digital information in computing systems, networking, use of computers in communication and control; fundamentals of optics applied to engineering; a further treatment of topics falling within the scope of Papers 3 and 4.

8. Electrical and information engineering II

The paper consists mainly of questions on: basic semiconductor physics; principles of operation and fabrication of semiconductor devices and integrated circuits; the fundamental laws of electromagnetism; transmission and reception of electromagnetic waves; a further treatment of topics falling within the scope of Papers 3, 4, and 5.

9. Structural mechanics

The paper consists mainly of questions on: the application of the bound theorems of plasticity to engineering problems; strength and deformation of soil bodies; elastic analysis of statically-indeterminate structures.

Part II of the Engineering Tripos

The papers in Part II are as follows:

- G 1. Structures I
- G 2. Structures II
- G 3. Soil mechanics
- G 4. Geotechnical engineering
- G 5. Civil engineering fluid mechanics
- G 6. Position fixing
- G 7. Dynamics
- G 8. Vibrations
- G 9. Mechanical power transmission
- G 10. Stress analysis and vibration
- G 11. Mechanics of solids
- G 12. Materials I
- G 13. Materials II[2]
- G 14. Mechanical design
- G 15. Thermodynamics and heat transfer
- G 16. Nuclear power engineering
- G 17. Internal combustion engines
- G 18. Turbomachinery
- G 19. Fluid mechanics I
- G 20. Fluid mechanics II
- G 21. Noise generation and control
- G 22. Aircraft aerodynamics
- G 23. Economics
- G 24. Technology, work, and society
- G 25. Dynamic systems and optimization
- E 1. Electrical circuits[1]
- E 2. Devices and VLSI[1]
- E 3. Information engineering I[1]
- E 9. Control systems[1]
- E 10. Electrical power and drives[1]
- P 2. Organization and control of manufacturing systems[2]
- M 2. Models for management[3]

Every candidate for Part II must offer five of the papers above, at least three of which must be chosen from one of the following groups:

(1) Group A: Papers G 1, G 2, G 3, G 4, G 5, and G 11;
(2) **Group B: Papers G 7, G 8, G 9, G 10, G 11, G 12, G 14, and E 9;**
(3) **Group C: Papers G 11, G 12, G 13, and G 14;**
(4) **Group D: Papers G 15, G 17, G 18, G 19, G 20, and G 22;**
(5) **Group E: Papers E 1, E 2, E 3, E 9, and E 10;**
(6) Group F: Papers E 3, E 9, and G 25;

[1] Papers E 1, E 2, E 3, E 9, and E 10 are papers in the Electrical and Information Sciences Tripos.

[2] Papers G 13 and P 2 are papers in Part I of the Manufacturing Engineering Tripos.

[3] Paper M 2 is a paper in the Management Studies Tripos.

ENGINEERING

provided that

(i) Paper G 2 may not be offered without Paper G 1;
(ii) Paper G 4 may not be offered without Paper G 3;
(iii) Paper G 10 may not be offered with Paper G 8 or Paper G 11;
(iv) for Group C both Papers G 12 and G 13 shall be offered;
(v) Paper G 17 may not be offered without Paper G 15;
(vi) Paper G 18 may not be offered without Paper G 19;
(vii) Paper G 20 may not be offered without Paper G 19;
(viii) Paper G 22 may not be offered without Papers G 19 and G 20;
(ix) Paper G 25 may not be offered by a candidate who chooses Group A, B, C or D;
(x) no candidate may offer the five papers E 1, E 2, E 3, E 9, and E 10;
(xi) Paper G 23 may not be offered by a candidate who has previously obtained honours in Part I of the Economics Tripos.

The Examiners take into account course-work done during the year. A candidate must satisfy the Examiners that he has industrial or equivalent experience.

The details of the papers are as follows:

G 1. Structures I

The paper consists mainly of questions on the general principles of structural mechanics and their application to the elastic and plastic behaviour of structures, including buckling.

G 2. Structures II

The paper consists mainly of questions on the analysis and design of structures, including plates and shells, under static and dynamic loading conditions.

G 3. Soil mechanics

The paper consists mainly of questions on the general principles of soil mechanics and on the analysis of earthworks, foundations, and soil structures.

G 4. Geotechnical engineering

The paper consists mainly of questions on the properties and behaviour of soils and rocks, and on the analysis and design of earthworks, foundations, and soil structures.

G 5. Civil engineering fluid mechanics

The paper consists mainly of questions on fluid loads on structures, pollution, flood control; loose-boundary hydraulics, coastal engineering.

G 6. Position fixing

The paper consists mainly of questions on orbital motion, satellite geodesy, geodetic astronomy, time, physical geodesy, geodetic surveying, and position fixing and navigation systems.

G 7. Dynamics

The paper consists mainly of questions on the principles of mechanical dynamics, including their application to wheeled vehicles, rotors and gyroscopic instruments, inertial navigation, and the motion and uses of artificial satellites.

G 8. Vibrations

The paper consists mainly of questions on the theory of vibrations, including random and non-linear vibrations, and the causes, measurement, isolation, and suppression of vibrations in machinery and structures.

G 9. Mechanical power transmission

The paper consists mainly of questions on mechanical power transmission and tribology.

G 10. Stress analysis and vibration

The paper consists mainly of questions on the application of elasticity and plasticity, and vibrations in machines and structures.

G 11. Mechanics of solids

The paper consists mainly of questions on elasticity, plasticity, and their applications.

G 12. Materials I

The paper consists mainly of questions on the physical and chemical properties of engineering materials and the influence of those properties on the selection and use of materials.

G 13. Materials II (also serves as a paper in Part I of the Manufacturing Engineering Tripos)

The paper consists mainly of questions on the properties of metals and non-metallic materials which are of significance in manufacturing processes, and the effect of production processes upon the properties and functioning of materials.

G 14. Mechanical design

The paper consists mainly of questions on formal design methods, engineering optimization, and mechanical design and analysis.

G 15. Thermodynamics and heat transfer

The paper consists mainly of questions on thermodynamic principles, chemical thermodynamics, and heat and mass transfer.

G 16. Nuclear power engineering

The paper consists mainly of questions on nuclear engineering (fission and fusion), superconductivity and its applications, and electrothermal industrial processes.

G 17. Internal combustion engines

The paper consists mainly of questions on combustion and emissions, spark ignition and diesel engines, unsteady gas dynamics, and turbocharging.

G 18. Turbomachinery

The paper consists mainly of questions on the fluid mechanics of turbomachinery and jet engines.

G 19. Fluid mechanics I

The paper consists mainly of questions on the equations of fluid motion, boundary layers, and incompressible and compressible flow.

G 20. Fluid mechanics II

The paper consists mainly of questions on unsteady flows, numerical fluid mechanics, turbulence, and real fluid flows.

G 21. Noise generation and control

The paper consists mainly of questions on the generation and propagation of sound, sound sources including flow-induced vibrations, simple properties of sound waves, and techniques for the measurement and analysis of noise.

G 22. Aircraft aerodynamics

The paper consists mainly of questions on performance and stability of aircraft, wing theory, stalling, and drag estimation.

G 23. Economics.

The paper consists mainly of questions on the economic analysis of markets and decision making, factors affecting wages, profits and prices, company accounts and finance, factors affecting the level of activity and employment in the economy as a whole.

G 24. Technology, work, and society

The paper consists mainly of questions on relations between technology, work organization, employment, and social change. (This paper will include questions on the topics covered by Course D.[1])

G 25. Dynamic systems and optimization

The paper consists mainly of questions on stochastic processes, time series analysis, and optimization methods. (This paper will deal with the topics covered by Courses G and H.[1])

E 1. Electrical circuits[2]

The paper consists mainly of questions on the fundamental theory of electrical circuits with passive and active devices using digital and analogue techniques, applications to the design and operation of practical circuits using integrated circuits, optical elements, and microprocessors.

E 2. Devices and VLSI[2]

The paper consists mainly of questions on the construction, design, and operation of electronic and optical devices in their discrete and integrated form, integration techniques and design procedures for such devices, and applications to systems.

E 3. Information engineering I[2]

The paper consists mainly of questions on fundamental techniques and concepts used in communications, computing, software, and the analysis or control of systems.

E 9. Control systems[2]

The paper consists mainly of questions on multivariable linear control systems, control system design techniques, optimal and adaptive control, system identification, robotics, process control systems, and electrical drives and positioning systems.

E 10. Electrical power and drives[2]

The paper consists mainly of questions on the fundamental principles of the control, conditioning, flow, and use of electrical power.

---

[1] Defined by Management Studies Tripos; see pp. 181–183.

[2] **Papers E 1, E 2, E 3, E 9, and E 10 are papers in the Electrical and Information Sciences Tripos.**

ENGINEERING

P 2. Organization and control of manufacturing systems[1]

The paper consists mainly of questions on quality control, inventory control, the control of manufacturing operations, and information systems for manufacturing.

M 2. Models for management[2]

The paper consists mainly of questions on the use of formal models of management systems.

The Electrical and Information Sciences Tripos

The Electrical and Information Sciences Tripos is not divided into Parts. A student who has obtained honours in another Tripos (other than Part I A of the Engineering Tripos) may be a candidate in his third or fourth year. An Affiliated Student may, if he obtains permission from the Faculty Board of Engineering, be a candidate in his first or second year.

The papers are as follows:

E 1. Electrical circuits.[3]
E 2. Devices and VLSI.[3]
E 3. Information engineering I.[3]
E 4. Mathematics for Electrical and Information Sciences.
E 5. Communication systems
E 6. Optical and microwave communications
E 7. Information engineering II.
E 8. Device physics
E 9. Control systems.[3]
E 10. Electrical power and drives.[3]

Every candidate must offer five of the papers above, at least three of which must be chosen from Papers E 1, E 2, E 3, and E 4.

The Examiners take into account course-work done during the year.

[1] Paper P 2 is a paper in Part I of the Manufacturing Engineering Tripos.
[2] Paper M 2 is a paper in the Management Studies Tripos.
[3] Papers E 1, E 2, E 3, E 9, and E 10 also serve as papers in Part II of the Engineering Tripos.

Details of the papers are as follows:

E 1. Electrical circuits[1]

The paper consists mainly of questions on the fundamental theory of electrical circuits with passive and active devices using digital and analogue techniques, applications to the design and operation of practical circuits using integrated circuits, optical elements, and microprocessors.

E 2. Devices and VLSI[1]

The paper consists mainly of questions on the construction, design, and operation of electronic and optical devices in their discrete and integrated form, integration techniques and design procedures for such devices, and applications to systems.

E 3. Information engineering I[1]

The paper consists mainly of questions on fundamental techniques and concepts used in communications, computing, software, and the analysis or control of systems.

E 4. Mathematics for Electrical and Information Sciences

The paper consists mainly of questions on mathematical and computational theory and techniques associated with aspects of physical electronics, circuit analysis, electrical communications, and information and control theory.

E 5. Communication systems

The paper consists mainly of questions on a more advanced treatment of topics covered in Paper E 3, on the fundamentals of transmission, coding, decoding, and recovery of information both in digital and analogue form, and advanced techniques of communications using electronic methods.

E 6. Optical and microwave communications

The paper consists mainly of questions on the fundamentals of generation, radiation, and propagation of electromagnetic waves in radio, microwave, and optical form, and engineering techniques and methods used to make radio, microwave, and optical devices and systems.

---

[1] Papers E 1, E 2, E 3, E 9, and E 10 also serve as papers in Part II of the Engineering Tripos.

ENGINEERING

E 7. Information engineering II

The paper consists mainly of questions on a more advanced treatment of topics covered in Paper E3, on the principles and techniques used in artificial intelligence, recognition and processing of visual and audio information, applications of these principles and techniques in robotics, and hardware required to effect these principles.

E 8. Device physics

The paper consists mainly of questions on a more advanced treatment of topics covered in Paper E 2, on the fundamentals of physical principles and construction of electrical devices and integrated circuits, quantum theory of semiconductor materials and lasers, and advanced measurement techniques of physical electronics.

E 9. Control systems[1]

The paper consists mainly of questions on multivariable linear control systems, control system design techniques, optimal and adaptive control, system identification, robotics, process control systems, electrical drives and positioning systems.

E 10. Electrical power and drives[1]

The paper consists mainly of questions on the fundamental principles of the control, conditioning, flow and use of electrical power.

The Manufacturing Engineering Tripos

The Manufacturing Engineering Tripos consists of two Parts, Part I and Part II. The course for the Tripos is one of those specially designated by the University Grants Committee as a high-quality first-degree course with a pronounced orientation towards manufacturing industry. A student who has obtained honours in Part IB of the Engineering Tripos may take Part I of the Manufacturing Engineering Tripos normally in his third year. If he obtains honours in Part I of that Tripos, he may then proceed to Part II in a fourth year.

Part I of the Manufacturing Engineering Tripos

The examination consists of five written papers, each of three hours' duration. The Examiners take into account course work undertaken during the year. In order to obtain honours a candidate must satisfy

---

[1] See footnote on p. 178.

the Examiners that he has appropriate industrial or equivalent experience.

The written papers are as follows:

P 1. Design and manufacture
P 2. Organization and control of manufacturing systems.[1]
P 3. Management economics and accounting.
M 1. Human resources.[2]
G 13. Materials II.[1]

Details of the papers are as follows:

P 1. Design and manufacture

The paper consists of eight questions, divided into two sections of four questions each. Section I focuses on design of products and Section II on manufacturing systems, including their design. Candidates will be required to attempt not more than two questions from each of Sections I and II.

P 2. Organization and control of manufacturing systems[1]

The paper consists mainly of questions on quality control, inventory control, the control of manufacturing operations, and information systems for manufacturing. (This paper will include questions on the topics covered by Course I.[3])

P 3. Management economics and accounting

The paper consists mainly of questions on the economic and financial aspects of industrial management. (This paper will include questions on the topics covered by Course A.[3])

M 1. Human resources (Paper M 1 of the Management Studies Tripos)

The paper consists mainly of questions on organizational theory and behaviour, industrial relations, the operation of labour markets, personnel management, and labour law.

G 13. Materials II[1]

The paper consists mainly of questions on the properties of metals and non-metallic materials which are of significance in manufacturing processes, and the effect of production processes upon the properties and functioning of materials.

[1] Papers P 2 and G 13 also serve as papers in Part II of the Engineering Tripos.
[2] Paper M 1 also serves as Paper M 1 of the Management Studies Tripos.
[3] Defined by the Management Studies Tripos; see pp. 181–183.

Part II of the Manufacturing Engineering Tripos

The examination consists of two written papers, each of three hours' duration. The Examiners also take into account and attach considerable weight to course work undertaken during the year. In order to obtain honours a candidate must satisfy the Examiners that he has appropriate industrial or equivalent experience.

The scope of the written papers is as follows:

1. Technological aspects of production engineering.
2. Managerial aspects of production engineering.

A **Certificate of Advanced Study in Manufacturing Technology** is awarded to a member of the University who obtains honours in Part II of the Production Engineering Tripos having previously completed the examination requirements for the B.A. Degree.

The Management Studies Tripos

The Management Studies Tripos consists of one Part only. A student who has either (i) obtained honours in an Honours Examination in the first, second or third term after his first term of residence and has subsequently been successful in a Preliminary Examination or (ii) obtained honours in an Honours examination in the fourth, fifth or sixth term after his first term of residence may be a candidate in his third year. An affiliated student may, if he obtains permission from the Faculty Board of Engineering, be a candidate in his second year.

The papers are as follows:

M 1. Human resources.
M 2. Models for management.
M 3. Economics and finance.
M 4. Special topics I.
M 5. Special topics II.

Every candidate must offer all five papers.

The Examiners take into account course work undertaken during the year. In order to obtain honours a candidate must satisfy the Examiners that he has appropriate industrial, commercial, or equivalent experience.

Details of the papers are as follows:

M 1. Human resources

The paper consists mainly of questions on organizational theory and behaviour, industrial relations, the operation of labour markets, personnel management, and labour law.

M 2. Models for management

The paper consists mainly of questions on the use of formal models of management systems.

M 3. Economics and finance

The paper consists mainly of questions on the economic analysis of markets and decision making, the measurement and analysis of company performance, company accounts, investment appraisal, and company finance.

M 4. Special topics I and M 5. Special topics II

For these papers candidates are required to answer questions on the topics covered by four of the courses listed below which are not already covered by their other papers.

Course A. Economic policy issues

This course covers topical issues in local, national, and international public economies, and factors affecting financial markets and the level of economic activity.

Course B. Industrial economics

This course covers the theoretical and empirical analysis of industrial structure, the links between industrial structure and performance, mergers, industrial policy, and competition policy.

Course C. Industrial organization

This course covers industrial sociology, including comparative perspectives, job design, division of labour, and occupational trends.

Course D. Sociology of technological change

This course covers the social and economic consequences of technological innovation, and industrial relations in Britain and other industrialized countries.

Course E. Data analysis

This course covers survey methods, data presentation, and statistical procedures.

Course F. Decision making

This course covers decision theory and its applications to individual and group decision making.

Course G. Optimization and the theory of algorithms

This course covers optimization theory and the theory of algorithms.

Course H. Dynamic systems modelling

This course covers stochastic processes and time series analysis.

Course I. Production control

This course covers the control of manufacturing operations and the control of materials.

Course J. Multivariate statistics

This course covers multiple regression, principal components, discriminant analysis, and cluster analysis.

Course K. Financial Management

This course covers the management of corporate assets and liabilities.

Course L. Marketing

This course covers the principles and practice of marketing.

Course M. Information management

This course covers the technical and social aspects of information systems in management.

Workshop and Industrial experience Qualifications

The regulations for the Engineering Tripos, the Electrical and Information Sciences Tripos, the Manufacturing Engineering Tripos, and the Management Studies Tripos require candidates to furnish evidence of practical experience in industry or, for immigrants to the Management Studies Tripos, in commerce.

Candidates for Part IB of the Engineering Tripos are required to spend a minimum of four weeks obtaining 'hands on' experience of manufacturing in mechanical, electrical, or civil engineering. If possible this experience is obtained with a company but the Department also sponsors suitable courses at Government Training Centres; applications should be made to the Workshops Superintendent in the Department.

Candidates for Part II of the Engineering Tripos, or for the Electrical and Information Sciences Tripos, who have already obtained the Part IB Engineering Tripos workshop qualification, are required to spend four weeks in industry in close contact with the workforce. Some flexibility is permitted in satisfying this requirement. The Department will allow candidates to reverse the order in which they obtain their practical experience required for Parts IB and II.

Candidates for Part II of the Engineering Tripos or for the Electrical and Information Sciences Tripos who have not taken Part IA or Part IB of the Tripos will be required to obtain four weeks of experience of either type in order to qualify for honours. Candidates for Part I or for Part II of the Manufacturing Engineering Tripos or the Management Studies Tripos must obtain appropriate industrial or commercial experience under guidance from the Department.

A document is available from the Superintendent of Workshops, University Department of Engineering, Cambridge, CB2 1PZ, clearly setting out the details of the requirements for Workshop and Industrial Qualifications.

Students and prospective students would be well advised, before entering an industrial establishment for the purposes of satisfying the Tripos regulations, to obtain this document and if necessary to consult the Workshops Superintendent of the Department, who will inform them whether their intended period of training will in fact give them the required qualifications. It should be noted that these qualifications must be obtained *before* the relevant Tripos Examination is taken. Students are encouraged to complete their full requirements by the end of their second year; many have completed them before beginning as undergraduates and eight weeks or more of training on an industrial course with a company will normally fulfil all the industrial experience requirements of all courses.

Exemptions from the Examinations of Professional Institutions

The Engineering Institutions

New graduates with an engineering degree are not yet fully qualified. It is necessary to have further professional training and experience in industry before becoming a Chartered Engineer. The exact requirements for registration depend on the particular field of engineering. However, the Cambridge Engineering courses are accepted as meeting the technical educational requirements of the following institutions, subject to appropriate options being taken:

Institution of Civil Engineers
Institution of Electrical Engineers

Institution of Mechanical Engineers
Institution of Production Engineers
Institution of Structural Engineers

Council of Engineering Institutions (C.E.I.)

Part I of the Engineering Tripos exempts from Parts I and II of the C.E.I. Examination provided that it is followed by the award of a degree.

Examinations for the M.Phil. Degree

Candidates for the M.Phil. Degree must have been admitted to the status of Graduate Student by the Board of Graduate Studies on the recommendation of the Degree Committee of the Faculty of Engineering.

The Department offers the following one-year postgraduate course which leads to the M.Phil. Degree:

Computer Speech and Language Processing

This course is intended for students who have a good first degree in engineering, computer science, physics, mathematics, linguistics or experimental psychology.

Students will follow an introductory course of lectures aimed at bringing students of differing backgrounds nearer to a common basis. There will be integrated main lecture courses on speech and language processing together with shorter lecture courses on the adjacent subjects of phonetics, linguistics, psycholinguistics and experimental psychology. There will be experimental and computer-based coursework and a project forms an important part of the overall course and is the subject of a thesis submitted as part of the Examination.

The scheme of examinations consists of:
- (*a*) two written papers, each of which may include questions on computer speech and language processing;
- (*b*) not less than five and not more than eight essays or exercises of a length and on topics approved by the Degree Committee for the Faculty of Engineering;
- *and* (*c*) a thesis, of not more than 15,000 words in length, including footnotes, appendices and bibliography, on a subject approved by the Degree Committee.

The Examination shall include an oral examination upon the thesis and the general field of knowledge in which it falls.

The scope of the written papers is defined as follows.

Papers 1 and 2

Knowledge of speech and language from the viewpoints of phonetics, linguistics, cognitive science and computer processing and the application of this knowledge in speech analysis, recognition and synthesis and in syntactic parsing, semantic interpretation and text and discourse planning.

Postgraduate Certificate in Design, Manufacture, and Management

A one-year Postgraduate Course in Design, Manufacture, and Management is run by the Department in co-operation with Lancaster University. It is designed to be an alternative to the first year of postgraduate training in industry and is approved for this purpose by the Institution of Mechanical Engineers and by the Institution of Production Engineers. The Course leads to the award of a Postgraduate Certificate.

A candidate for the Certificate shall ordinarily be a graduate of a university or polytechnic and must be approved by the Faculty Board of Engineering.

Application for admission to the Course should be sent to the Head of the Department of Engineering, Engineering Laboratory, Trumpington Street, Cambridge, CB2 1PZ, by 1 May of the year in which the student wishes to begin the Course.

ENGLISH

In this subject there are courses of study followed by candidates for:

The *English Tripos*, which is divided into two Parts.
The *Ordinary Examination* in English for the Ordinary B.A. Degree.

The English Tripos

The course of study for the English Tripos covers English language and literature from 1066 to the present day, with primary reference to the literature of the British Isles; with reference to classical literature and to post-classical European literatures in their relations with English literature, life and thought; and with reference also to American literature and to other literatures in English. Anglo-Saxon (Old English) is not compulsory; it is an optional subject in both Parts of the Tripos, and those intending to read it should make arrangements to do so as early as possible, preferably in their first year.

The Tripos is divided into two Parts. Part I is devoted principally to English literature; Part II includes various options involving classical and other literatures, and the history of ideas. This will be seen in the detailed syllabus that follows. A dissertation may be substituted in Part I for one specified paper in the Tripos. A dissertation is compulsory in Part II; a further dissertation may be offered as one of the optional elements in Part II.

Part I takes two years; Part II normally takes one year, though it is possible to spend two years on this Part. The ordinary assumption, however, is that the whole Tripos is a three-year course.

The school subjects most relevant to the Tripos, besides English itself, are Classics, Modern Languages and History. It is generally desirable that intending candidates should have taken an A level in one classical or modern European Language.

Either Part of the Tripos may be combined with a Part of another Tripos. The most suitable combinations are with Classics, Modern and Medieval Languages, or History. Students who have read Part I of any of these Triposes might well change to English for their second Part. Students who intend to change to English, either Part I or Part II, in their third year, after taking some other Tripos in their second year, should try to give some time to reading English literature during the first two years. They should also try to attend during that period some of the relevant courses of lectures provided by the

Faculty of English. It is also possible to change to other Triposes after reading Part I English. Impulsive last-minute changes are not recommended; students are advised to form some comprehensive idea of the course they intend to pursue, whether both Parts of the English Tripos, or English combined with some other subject, as early as possible. On all these matters they should consult their Tutors and Directors of Studies.

Part I*

The papers in Part I* are as follows:

1. English literature and its background, 1300–1550.
2. English literature and its background, 1550–1700.
3. English literature and its background, 1700–1830.
4. English literature and its background, since 1830.
5. Shakespeare.
6. Literary criticism.
7. Foreign language and literature; passages for translation and comment.
8. Early medieval literature and its background (also serves as Paper 14 of Part II, and as Paper 13 of the Anglo-Saxon, Norse, and Celtic Tripos).
9. Old English language and literature (Paper 5 of the Anglo-Saxon, Norse, and Celtic Tripos).
10. Insular Latin Language and Literature (Paper 4 of the **Anglo-Saxon, Norse, and Celtic Tripos**).
11. Old Norse language and literature (Paper 6 of the Anglo-Saxon, Norse, and Celtic Tripos).
12. **Medieval Welsh language and literature** (Paper 7 A of the Anglo-Saxon, Norse, and Celtic Tripos).
13. History of the English Language (Paper 13 of Part II).

Each paper is set for three hours except Paper 6 which is set for three and a half hours.

Every candidate for Part I must offer Papers 1 and 5 and

either   (*a*) Papers 2–4; and two papers from among Papers 6, 7, 8, 9, and 13;

or   (*b*) two papers from among Papers 2–4; and three papers from among Papers 6, 7, 8, 9, and 13;

* See p. 189 on the submission of an original composition in English for Part I.

ENGLISH 189

or (*c*) two papers from among Papers 2–4; two papers from among Papers 6, 7, 8, 9, and 13; and one paper from among Papers 10–12;

provided that

(i) a candidate who offers two papers from among Papers 8–12 must offer at least one of Papers 8 and 9;

(ii) a candidate may, in substitution for one of Papers 2–5, submit a dissertation on a topic of literary interest falling within the scope of that paper, except that (1) no candidate may submit a dissertation of which the main emphasis is on literature written in a foreign language and (2) if a candidate submits a dissertation in substitution for Paper 2 it must not be wholly or largely on Shakespeare.

If a candidate chooses to submit a dissertation, the topic must be approved by his Director of Studies and the approved topic notified through his Tutor to the Secretary of the Faculty Board not later than the end of the Full Michaelmas Term next preceding the examination. A dissertation must not be more than 5,000 words in length (inclusive of notes and appendices, although appendices additional to this word limit may be allowed in special circumstances subject to the approval of the Faculty Board not later than the division of the Lent Term next preceding the examination) and must be accompanied by a list of the books and articles used in its preparation. A candidate is required to declare that the dissertation is his own work and does not contain material which he has already used to any substantial extent for a comparable purpose. A candidate may be called for *viva voce* examination in connexion with his dissertation. The dissertation must be typed, in English, with proper attention to style and presentation, marked with the candidate's name and College and the Part of the Tripos for which he is a candidate, and sent through his Tutor to the Secretary of the Faculty Board so as to reach him not later than the third day of the Full Easter Term in which the examination is to be held.

The scope of the papers in Part I is as follows:

1. English literature and its background, 1300–1550

Medieval texts are prescribed for special study; and passages are set from them for translation or explanation or both. Questions are set both on the literature and on the life and thought of the period. All candidates are expected to show such knowledge of the life and thought of the period as is necessary for understanding its literature.

For **1990**: Chaucer, *Troilus and Criseyde*, Book III; *Sir Gawain and the Green Knight*, lines 1998–2530; *Piers Plowman*, B Text, Passus 18, 'Harrowing of Hell' (ed. A. V. C. Schmidt, Everyman, 1978).

For **1991**: Chaucer, *Troilus and Criseyde*, Book III (Riverside Chaucer, ed. Larry D. Benson); *Sir Gawain and the Green Knight*, lines 1–490 (ed. J. R. R. Tolkein and E. V. Gordon, rev. N. Davis; *Piers Plowman*, B Text, Passus 18, 'Harrowing of Hell' (ed. A. V. C. Schmidt, Everyman).

2. English literature and its background, 1550–1700

Questions are set both on the liteature and on the life and thought of the period. All candidates are expected to show such knowledge of the life and thought of the period as is necessary for understanding its literature.

A special topic will be prescribed for **1990**: Literature and kingship.

Prescribed texts will be announced for **1991**, in place of the special topic.

3. English literature and its background, 1700–1830

Questions are set both on the literature and on the life and thought of the period. All candidates are expected to show such knowledge of the life and thought of the period as is necessary for understanding its literature.

A special topic will be prescribed for **1990**: Literature and nature.

Prescribed texts will be announced for **1991**, in place of the special topic.

4. English literature and its background, since 1830

Questions are set both on the literature and on the life and thought of the period. All candidates are expected to show such knowledge of the life and thought of the period as is necessary for understanding its literature.

A special topic will be prescribed for **1990**: Literature and money.

Prescribed texts will be announced for **1991**, in place of the special topic.

5. Shakespeare

Questions are set requiring explanation and discussion of passages of a specific work or works. Questions are also set on other works of Shakespeare and matters of historical and critical interest relevant to his works.

For **1990** and **1991**: *Henry IV, Parts 1 and 2*.

6. Literary criticism

Questions on literary criticism (critics or critical works may be specified or recommended for study); passages of English prose or verse for explanation, comment and appreciation.

ENGLISH

Specified critics for **1990**: Johnson and Coleridge.
Specified critics for **1991**: Johnson, Coleridge and Eliot.

The following works have been specified for special study:

(for **1990** and **1991**):

Johnson: (i) from *Lives of the Poets*, the lives of Cowley, Milton, and Gray.
(ii) The Preface to his edition of Shakespeare and the notes on the following plays: *Love's Labour's Lost, Henry IV, Parts 1 and 2, King Lear, Macbeth, Hamlet,* and *Othello*.

Coleridge: (i) *Biographia Literaria* (Chapters i–iv, xiii–xxii, and xxiv).
(ii) The following extracts from Coleridge's *Shakespearean Criticism* in two volumes, ed. T.M. Raysor (Everyman): vol. 1, section I the Notes on *Romeo and Juliet, Hamlet, Othello, King Lear, Macbeth, Love's Labour's Lost,* and *The Tempest*.

(for **1991**):
Eliot: *Selected essays* (Faber 1932).

7. Foreign language and literature; passages for translation and comment

The paper includes one passage for unseen translation and one passage for comment from a prescribed text or texts in the following languages for which there is a candidate: classical Greek, French, German, Italian, classical Latin, medieval Latin, Russian, and Spanish. Candidates are not required to show knowledge of more than one of these languages.

The prescribed texts for each language in **1990** are:

French	J.-P. Sartre, *Les mots*.
German	G. Büchner, *Dantons Tod, Woyzeck*, in *Werke und Briefe*, ed. Werner Lehmann (D.T.V., no. 2065).
Greek	Sophocles, *Philoctetes* (Cambridge Greek and Latin Classics edition).
Italian	Dante, *Vita Nuova*.
Latin (classical)	Virgil, *Eclogues*, ed. R.G.G. Coleman, C.U.P., 1977.
Latin (medieval)	Alan of Lille, *De planctu naturae*, ed. N. M. Haring, extracted from *Studi Medievali*, no. 19 (1978), 795–879.
Russian	Dostoyevsky, *Notes from Under Ground*.
Spanish	J.-L. Borges, *Ficciones*, ed. G. Brotherston and P. Hulme (London: Harrap, 1976).

The prescribed texts in **1991** will be as in **1990**, except:
French   Racine, *Athalie*

8. Early medieval literature and its background

The period covered by this paper is 1066–*c*. 1350. English and French texts are prescribed for special study: and passages are set from them for translation or explanation or both. Questions are set on the English texts of the period; there are also questions on French texts, whether written in England or on the Continent, which stand in a significant relation to them. A list of topics may be prescribed on which optional questions will be set. Candidates are expected to show such knowledge of the life and thought of the period as is necessary for the understanding of its literature.

Prescribed texts in **1990** and **1991**. *La Chanson de Roland*, ed. Whitehead, lines 1671–1760, 2375–2475; *Le Mystère d'Adam*, ed. P. Aebischer or P. Noomen, lines 205–357; Chrétien de Troyes, *Yvain*, ed. Reid, lines 269–482; Marie de France, *Lais*, ed. Ewert: 'Laustic', 'Chevrefoil'; *The Owl and the Nightingale*, ed. Stanley, lines 1043–1290; *Ancrene Wisse*, ed. Shepherd, p. 15, line 12, to p. 23, line 8; *King Horn* (Cambridge M.S.), ed. McKnight, EETS, o.s. (1901, repr. 1962), lines 801–1298.

Prescribed topics in **1990** and **1991**. The Bayeux Tapestry, The Life of Christina of Markyate, The *Tristan* story, The Other World, The 'Katharine Group' texts, Courtliness.

9. Old English language and literature

10. Insular Latin Language and Literature (Paper 4 of the Anglo-Saxon, Norse, and Celtic Tripos)

11. Old Norse language and literature (Paper 6 of the Anglo-Saxon, Norse, and Celtic Tripos)

12. Medieval Welsh language and literature I (Paper 7A of the Anglo-Saxon, Norse, and Celtic Tripos)

Part II

The papers for Part II are as follows:

GROUP A (Compulsory Papers)

1. Practical criticism.
2. Tragedy (also serves as Paper O3 of Part II of the Classical Tripos).

Group B(i)

3. Chaucer (also serves as Paper 14 of the Anglo-Saxon, Norse, and Celtic Tripos).
4. Medieval English literature, 1066–1500 (also serves as Paper 15 of the Anglo-Saxon, Norse, and Celtic Tripos).
5. Special period of English literature (taken from the period after 1500 and before 1700).
6. Special period of English literature (taken from the period after 1700).
7. Special subject I.

Group B(ii)

8. English moralists.
9. History and theory of literary criticism.
10. The novel.
11. American literature.
12. Special subject II.

Group C(i)

13. History of the English language (Paper 16 of the Anglo-Saxon, Norse, and Celtic Tripos).
14. Early Medieval literature and its background (Paper 8 of Part I of the English Tripos).
15. Old English language and literature (Paper 5 of the Anglo-Saxon, Norse, and Celtic Tripos).

Group C(ii)

16. Insular Latin Language and Literature (Paper 4 of the **Anglo-Saxon, Norse, and Celtic Tripos**).
17. Old Norse language and literature (Paper 6 of the Anglo-Saxon, Norse, and Celtic Tripos).
18A. **Medieval Welsh language and literature I (Paper 7A of the Anglo-Saxon, Norse, and Celtic Tripos).**
18B. **Medieval Welsh language and literature II (Paper 7B of the Anglo-Saxon, Norse, and Celtic Tripos).**
19A. **Medieval Irish language and literature I (Paper 8A of the Anglo-Saxon, Norse, and Celtic Tripos).**
19B. **Medieval Irish language and literature II (Paper 8B of the Anglo-Saxon, Norse, and Celtic Tripos).**
20. French literature, thought, and history, from 1594 to 1700 (Paper 5 of Part II of the Modern and Medieval Languages Tripos).

21. **French literature, thought, and history, from 1690 to 1789** (Paper 6 of Part II of the Modern and Medieval Languages Tripos).
22. **French literature, thought, and history, from 1789 to 1898** (Paper 7 of Part II of the Modern and Medieval Languages Tripos).
23. **French literature, thought, and history, since 1890** (Paper 8 of Part II of the Modern and Medieval Languages Tripos).
24. A special period or subject in French literature, thought, or history (Paper 11 of Part II of the Modern and Medieval Languages Tripos, in any year in which the subject announced by the Faculty Board of Modern and Medieval Languages has been approved for this purpose by the Faculty Board of English).
25. **Dante** (Paper 14 of Part II of the Modern and Medieval Languages Tripos).
26. **Medieval Latin literature from 400 to 1300** (Paper 12 of Part II of the Modern and Medieval Languages Tripos).
27. **A special subject in Comparative Literature** (i) and (ii) (Papers 123 and 124 of Part II of the Modern and Medieval Languages Tripos).
28. **General linguistics** (Paper 111 of Part II of the Modern and Medieval Languages Tripos).

Each paper is set for three hours except Paper 1 which is set for three and a half hours. The Faculty Board announce in every year one or more special subjects for Paper 7; they may in addition announce one or more special subjects for Paper 12. A question paper shall be set for each subject so announced and for which there is a candidate, and if a candidate offers one or both of these papers he shall in each case declare in his entry for the examination which subject he intends to offer.

Every candidate for Part II must offer:

(*a*) a dissertation on a subject in English literature;
(*b*) both papers from Group A;
(*c*) *either* two papers chosen from Groups B and C *or* one paper chosen from Groups B and C and a second dissertation;

provided that:

(i) a candidate may not offer any paper that he has previously offered for another Honours Examination;
(ii) a candidate may not offer both Paper 9 and one of the Special Subjects for Paper 12 if the Faculty Board have specified that

ENGLISH

it may not be so combined when announcing that Special Subject; nor more than one of the papers from Group C(ii); nor both Papers 18 A and 18 B or both 19 A and 19 B;

(iii) a candidate who has obtained honours in Part I of the English Tripos or any allowance on that examination towards a degree may not offer both Papers 5 and 6;

(iv) every candidate who has not previously obtained honours in Part I of the English Tripos must offer *either* at least one paper from Group B(i), *or*, in substitution and if he has obtained leave from the Faculty Board, one paper chosen from among Papers 1-5 of Part I of the English Tripos. An application for leave to offer one of these Part I papers must be sent through the candidate's Tutor to the Secretary of the Faculty Board so as to reach him not later than the division of the Michaelmas Term next preceding the examination and shall state the whole scheme of papers which the candidate proposes to offer, including the topic of his required dissertation and topic of his second dissertation (if offered). In determining whether to approve such an application the Faculty Board will take into consideration both the overall balance of the proposed scheme and the potential overlap between the papers to be offered under it. After the Faculty Board have approved a candidate's proposed scheme of papers, no change may be made in the scheme without the approval of the Faculty Board.

The dissertation under (*a*) above must be of not less than 5,000 and not more than 7,500 words in length (inclusive of notes and appendices, although appendices additional to this word limit may be allowed in special circumstances subject to the approval of the Faculty Board not later than the division of the Lent Term next preceding the examination), and must be on a topic in English literature approved by the candidate's Director of Studies. The approved topic must be notified to the Secretary of the Faculty Board not later than the end of the Full Michaelmas Term next preceding the examination. A candidate may, if he wishes, choose a topic in the same field as that of any of the papers that he is offering. A candidate will be required to give full references to the sources used and to declare that the dissertation is his own work and does not contain material which he has already used to any substantial extent for a comparable purpose. A dissertation must show evidence of reading, of judgement and criticism, and of power of exposition. It must be typed, in English, with proper attention to style and presentation, marked with the candidate's name and College and the Part of the Tripos for which he is a candidate, and sent through the candidate's Tutor to the Secretary of the Faculty Board so as to reach him not later than the third day of the Full Easter Term in which the examination is to be held. A candidate may be called for *viva voce* examination in connexion with his dissertation.

Second Dissertation

A candidate for Part II who chooses under (*c*) above to offer only *one* paper from Groups B and C must submit a second dissertation in English of not less than 5,000 and not more than 7,500 words in length (inclusive of notes and appendices, although appendices additional to this word limit may be allowed in special circumstances subject to the approval of the Faculty Board not later than the division of the Lent Term next preceding the examination). This dissertation may be on any topic in the field of English and related studies, as indicated by the range of the English Tripos as a whole, excluding those papers not set by the Examiners for the English Tripos and the Anglo-Saxon, Norse, and Celtic Tripos which has been approved by the Faculty Board, provided that:

(i) if he is offering one of the papers from Group B(ii) the dissertation must be on a topic in English literature unless the Faculty Board (after considering the proposed topics of his dissertation and the whole scheme of the papers he intends to offer) allow him to submit a second dissertation on any topic in the field of English and related studies as indicated by the range of the English Tripos as a whole;

(ii) if he is offering one of the papers from Group C(ii), the dissertation must be on a topic in English literature.

Subject to the foregoing provisions, a candidate may choose a topic in the same field as that of any of the papers that he is offering, except that, if the topic of the dissertation which he is offering under (*a*) is in the field of one of his papers, the Faculty Board may at their discretion decline to allow for the second dissertation a topic in the field of the same paper. A candidate must give full references to the sources used and declare that the dissertation is his own work and does not contain material which he has already used to any substantial extent for a comparable purpose; a dissertation must show evidence of reading, of judgement and criticism, and of power of exposition. Each candidate must submit the proposed topic of his dissertation together with that of his dissertation required under (*a*), and the whole scheme of the papers he intends to offer, through his Tutor, to the Secretary of the Faculty Board so as to reach him not later than the division of the Michaelmas Term next preceding the examination. In determining whether to approve such an application the Faculty Board will take into consideration both the overall balance of the proposed scheme and the potential overlap between the subjects to be offered under it. After the Faculty Board have approved a candidate's proposed scheme of subjects, no change may be made in the scheme without the approval of the Faculty Board. The Secretary will communicate its approval or rejection to the candidate's Tutor. Whether the proposed topic is approved or not, a candidate may submit a revised topic so as to reach the Secretary of the Faculty Board by the division of the following Lent Term; topics received after that date will be considered by the Faculty Board only in the most exceptional circumstances. Dissertations must be typewritten, with proper attention to style and presentation, marked with the candidate's name and College and the Part of the Tripos for which he is a candidate, and must be sent through his Tutor to the Secretary of the Faculty Board so as to reach him not later than the third day of the Full Easter Term in which the examination is to be held. A candidate may be called for *viva voce* examination in connexion with his dissertation.

Original Compositions in Part I and Part II of the Tripos

A candidate may submit an original composition in English of not more than 5,000 words (exclusive of notes). This, if of sufficient merit, will be taken into account by the Examiners, who may examine him *viva voce* upon it. The submission of non-literary material is not allowed. Compositions must be typewritten, marked with the candidate's name and College and the Part of the Tripos for which he is a candidate, and must be sent through his Tutor to the Secretary of the Faculty Board so as to reach him not later than the third day of the Easter Full Term in which the examination is to be held.

The scope of the papers in **Part II** is as follows:

1. Practical criticism

    Passages of English prose and verse for critical comment.

2. Tragedy

    Tragedy ancient and modern in connexion and comparison with English Tragedy.

3. Chaucer

Candidates are expected to show a full and detailed knowledge of the works of Chaucer. Questions are set on those works and on Chaucer's relationship to his contemporaries and to the life and thought of his age.

4. Medieval English literature, 1066–1500

A specific literary subject is prescribed for special study. It is of a kind to require reading in early as well as in the late medieval English literature and may involve the study of related texts from other languages.

For **1990**: Medieval Romance.

For **1991**: Arthurian Literature.

5. Special period of English literature (taken from the period after 1500 and before 1700)

Candidates are required to show a substantial knowledge of the literature of the period prescribed together with its life and thought.

For **1990** and **1991**: 1579–1603.

6. Special period of English literature (taken from the period after 1700)

Candidates are required to show a substantial knowledge of the literature of the period prescribed together with its life and thought.

For **1990** and **1991**: 1785–1830.

7. Special Subject I

The work of an author or of a group of authors, or a literary topic or genre, or a period not already prescribed for Papers 5 or 6, within the field of English literature, is prescribed for special study. Relevant texts may be recommended for study from time to time. The Faculty Board may from time to time prescribe a number of such special subjects of which one may be offered by candidates for this paper.

In **1990** and **1991**:

(*a*) Shakespeare and the development of English literature: Shakespeare and Jonson.
(*b*) Dryden and Restoration Literature.
(*c*) Henry James.
(*d*) Twentieth-century English poetry.

8. English moralists

Moral and philosophical aspects of English literature in relation to the history of philosophical thought. Candidates are expected to make full use of their existing interests in poetry, drama, and the novel. They are also given opportunities to show knowledge of English intellectual history including topics in moral, social, and political philosophy. Relevant foreign as well as English moral and philosophical authors may be specified or recommended for special study.

9. History and theory of literary criticism

The paper comprises historical, critical, and comparative questions on works and problems in the history of literary criticism and also of literary theory from the fourth century B.C. to the present day. A sufficient number of questions are set to enable candidates to choose questions on a limited chronological period (including the modern period).

10. The Novel

A critical and historical study of the novel, with special reference to the period from 1830 to 1930. Candidates are expected to have studied English novels in relation to selected foreign novels, American and European, and relevant foreign as well as English works may be recommended for study. Questions are also set on the history of the novel, including works and authors before 1830 and after 1930.

11. American literature

The subject covered by the paper is American literature from 1820 to the present day. Questions will be set on the literature and on the life and thought of the period. A list of books may be recommended for special study. All candidates will be expected to show such knowledge of the life and thought of the period as is necessary for understanding its literature.

The books recommended for **1990** and **1991** are: James Fenimore Cooper. *The Deerslayer*; Ralph Waldo Emerson, 'The American Scholar', 'Self Reliance', 'Nature', 'The Over-Soul' (from *Essays, First Series*); 'The Poet', 'The Transcendentalist' (from Lectures on *The Times*); Henry David Thoreau, *Walden*; Nathaniel Hawthorne, *The Scarlet Letter*; Herman Melville, *Moby Dick*; Walt Whitman, *Song of Myself*; Mark Twain, *The Adventures of Huckleberry Finn*; Emily Dickinson, *Selected Poems* (ed. Ted Hughes); Henry James, *The Bostonians*; F. Scott Fitzgerald, *The Great Gatsby*; Wallace Stevens, *Selected Poems* (Faber); William Faulkner, *Absalom, Absalom!*; William Carlos Williams, *Selected Poems* (ed. Charles Tomlinson); Eugene O'Neill, *Long Day's Journey into Night*.

12. Special Subject II

For a year for which a subject is announced for this paper, the work of an author or of a group of authors, or a literary topic or genre, or a period not already prescribed for Paper 5, or 6, or 7, is prescribed for special study.

Relevant foreign texts as well as English texts may be recommended for study from time to time. The Faculty Board may from time to time prescribe a number of such special subjects of which one may be offered by candidates for this paper.

(*a*) In **1990** and **1991**: Comedy and drama.

(*b*) In **1990** and **1991**: Gender and writing: 1879–1941.

13. History of the English language (also serves as Paper 13 of Part I and Paper 16 of the Anglo-Saxon, Norse, and Celtic Tripos)

The paper will be set in three sections. Sections A and B will contain passages for comment and analysis. Section C will contain questions on the historical development and structure of English (including phonology, syntax, semantics, and literary style). A list of set texts will be published for each of Sections A and B, the list for Section A relating to the period up to *c.* 1600 and the list for Section B relating to the period since *c.* 1500.

Candidates offering this paper for the English Tripos will be required to answer one question from Section A or Section B and two questions from Section C. Candidates offering this paper for the Anglo-Saxon, Norse, and Celtic Tripos, or for Part II of the Modern and Medieval Languages Tripos, will be required to answer one question from Section A and two questions from Section C.

For *Section A* in **1990**: *Early English Verse and Prose*, ed. Bennett and Smithers, VI (Dame Sirith), X (Layamon), XV (Interludium), XVI (Peterborough Chronicle), XVIII Section C (Ancrene Wisse).

For *Section B* in **1990**: Jonson, *Bartholomew Fair*, Wycherly, *The Country Wife*.

The list of texts prescribed for Sections A and B in **1991** is available from the English Faculty Office on request.

Paper 24. A special period or subject in French literature, thought or history (Paper 11 of Part II of the Modern and Medieval Languages Tripos, in any year in which the subject announced by the Faculty Board of Modern and Medieval Languages has been approved for this purpose by the Faculty Board of English)

Subject for special study: Modern critical theory.

The Faculty Board of English have given notice that a candidate who offers this paper in the English Tripos may not also offer Paper 9 of Part II of the English Tripos (History and theory of literary criticism).

The Preliminary Examination for Part I

There will be no Preliminary Examination for Part I in **1990**, and **until further notice.**

ENGLISH

The Examination in English for the Ordinary B.A. Degree

The examination consists of three papers chosen by the candidate from among Papers 1–6 of the papers set for Part I of the English Tripos, including at least one paper from among Papers 1, 2, and 5.

The papers and schedules in any year will be the same as those for Part I of the English Tripos.

A student may not count towards the Ordinary B.A. Degree both the Ordinary Examination in English and also anything he may have to his credit as the result of the Preliminary Examination for Part I of the English Tripos or Part I of the English Tripos.

GEOGRAPHY

In this subject there are courses of study followed by candidates for:

The *Geographical Tripos*, which is divided into three Parts.
The *Preliminary Examination* for Part II of the Tripos.
The *Ordinary Examination* in Geography for the Ordinary B.A. Degree.

The Geographical Tripos

Normally more than a hundred undergraduates are admitted each year to the Department of Geography. Almost all of these spend three years reading geography and take all Parts of the Geographical Tripos; no subsidiary subject is required. A few people, however, take a Part of the Geographical Tripos either before or after a Part of some other Tripos.

University geography differs from school geography in that it places greater stress upon analysis and provides opportunity for more intensive specialization in specific branches or areas. This is particularly true of Part II of the Tripos.

The normal programme for an undergraduate who intends to spend three years reading geography is as follows:

1. Part I A of the Tripos at the end of the first year.
2. Part I B of the Tripos at the end of the second year.
3. Part II of the Tripos at the end of the third year.

The course for Part I A aims at providing a general all-round training in the subject. It comprises teaching in Physical Geography, Environment and Resources, Contemporary Human Geography, Historical Geography, Geographical ideas and in the application of field and quantitative techniques and the making and use of maps. In Part I B, a candidate must offer at least one paper in each of the three main branches of the subject and a compulsory paper in ideas and methods but otherwise may specialize. The course for Part II permits a candidate *either* to specialize *or* to draw his or her options widely within the discipline. A candidate has also to write a short dissertation on some area or topic, which will be taken into account by the Examiners.

The school subjects most relevant to the Tripos, besides geography itself, include mathematics, physical and biological sciences, geology, economics, and history. A modern language is also desirable, and a good general education is an important asset. A candidate who has not taken geography at school would not necessarily be at a disadvantage if his or her other subjects were cognate.

Undergraduates who transfer to the Geographical Tripos after taking a Part of some other Tripos may spend one year on Part IA or Part IB, or either one year or two years on Part II. Such undergraduates should consult their Directors of Studies well in advance on the question of preliminary reading, and this applies particularly to those who intend to read for Part II, owing to its more specialized nature. Some undergraduates who transfer, and some Affiliated Students, are not required to submit a dissertation for Part II. Triposes that combine most readily with parts of the Geographical Tripos include Archaeology and Anthropology, History, Economics, Social and Political Sciences, Law, Natural Sciences (which includes Geology) and Land Economy.

General

The Geographical Tripos consists of three Parts, Part IA, Part IB and Part II. Students may not present themselves for more than one Part in the same term, and no student can be entered for the same Part more than once. Examiners may take account in each Part of the Tripos of laboratory and field work done by the candidates during their courses.

Part IA

Part IA is normally taken in the first year, or in the second year by a candidate who has obtained Honours in some other Tripos examination. The examination consists of five papers, all of which must be offered. In addition, candidates must submit to the Examiners, in accordance with arrangements to be specified by the Head of the Department of Geography, records of practical exercises undertaken by the candidate. The maximum marks allocated to Paper 5 and to the submitted work, which shall be equal, shall together be equal to the maximum marks allocated to one of the other papers. The five papers are as follows:

1. Physical geography

Aspects of geomorphology, climatology and related subjects in physical geography.

2. Environment and resources

Introduction to biogeography, population geography and natural resources.

3. Contemporary human geography

Aspects of economic, social and political geography, and related subjects in contemporary human geography.

4. Historical geography

Introduction to historical geography, with particular reference to the British Isles.

5. Geographical ideas and methods

Introduction to the history, philosophy, and methodology of geography.

Part I B

Part I B is normally taken in the second year, either after a candidate has obtained honours in Part I A of the Geographical Tripos, or in another honours examination. The papers for Part I B are as under; a candidate must offer Paper 1 and in addition one paper from each of Groups A, B, and C, and any other two papers.

1. Geographical ideas and methods
Development of geographical ideas; techniques of analysis.

Group A

2. Human geography I
Geography of economic activities.

3. Human geography II
Economic and social aspects of urban geography.

4. Human geography III
The human geography of developing countries.

5. Political geography
The geography of political problems and issues.

Group B

6. Historical geography I
The historical geography of North America.

7. Historical geography II
The historical geography of cities.

8. The cultural geography of a prescribed area

Either one or two areas will be prescribed; candidates will be expected to show knowledge of *one* area.
   In **1990**: Middle America.

9. The geography of a prescribed area
   In **1990**: Melanesia.

Group C

10. **Physical geography I**
    Process geomorphology.

11. **Physical geography II**
    Physical geography of the tropics.

12. **Physical geography III**
    Landforms and environmental change.

Part II

Part II may be taken in the third or fourth year, either in the year next after a candidate has obtained honours in Part I B, or in the year or next year but one after he has obtained honours in another honours examination (other than Part I A). The papers in Part II are as follows; a candidate must offer any five papers:

1. **Human geography I**
   The human geography of the United Kingdom.

2. **Human geography II**
   The human geography of advanced countries.

3. **Human geography III**
   Urban problems, planning, and policy.

4. **Historical geography I**
   The geography of medieval Britain.

5. **Historical geography II**
   The geography of the Industrial Revolution in Britain.

6. **Historical geography III**
   The historical geography of France.

7. Historical geography IV
   The methodology of historical geography.

8. Physical geography I
   Fluvial geomorphology.

9. Physical geography II
   Quaternary environments.

10. Physical geography III
    A topic in physical geography.
    In **1990**: The physical geography of the ocean world.

11. Physical geography IV
    Glacial studies.

12. Biogeography
    Geographical aspects of ecosystems.

13. Environment and conservation
    Environmental problems, planning and policies in developed countries.

14. Spatial analysis, remote sensing and cartography
    Spatial information systems, remote sensing and image analysis, automated cartography and mapping models.

15. The geography of South Asia

16. The geography of the U.S.S.R.

17. The geography of Latin America

Dissertations for Part II

A candidate for Part II, except for

(*a*) an affiliated student; and

(*b*) a student who has not obtained honours in either Part I A or Part I B and takes Part II in the year after he has obtained honours in another Tripos

must submit a dissertation on some geographical subject. The subject of the dissertation must be approved by the Head of Department not later than the division of the Michaelmas Term preceding the examination. The text must not exceed 9,000 words and must be submitted in typescript (unless permission has been obtained to submit it in manuscript) not later than the division of the Lent Term preceding the examination. The examiners may examine a candidate *viva voce* upon it.

The Preliminary Examination for Part II

The papers in this examination are taken from amongst the papers for Part IB of the Tripos. Each candidate must offer four of those papers.

The Ordinary Examination in Geography for the Ordinary B.A. Degree

The examination consists of the five papers for Part IA of the Geographical Tripos.

A student may not count towards the Ordinary B.A. Degree both the Ordinary Examination in Geography and also anything he may have to his credit as the result of Part IA or Part IB of the Geographical Tripos.

HISTORY

In this subject there are courses of study followed by candidates for:
The *Historical Tripos*, which is divided into two Parts.
The *Preliminary Examination* for each Part of the Tripos.
The *Ordinary Examination* in History for the Ordinary B.A. Degree.
The *Diploma in Historical Studies*.
M.Phil. Degree in *International Relations*.

The Historical Tripos

The Historical Tripos is designed to allow the study of a wider range of historical subjects than is normally available at school, and to provide an opportunity for the investigation of these subjects at a deeper level, and from a greater variety of standpoints, than is possible in a school curriculum. Cambridge has for many years been strong in social and economic, as well as in political, religious and intellectual, history; candidates can choose from papers ranging chronologically from ancient Greece and Rome to the present day, and geographically from Britain and Europe to extra-European countries. There is increasing opportunity, as the course unfolds, to study the subject through primary source materials. The teaching system, based on a combination of lectures, seminars, and individual tuition, is intended to stimulate a spirit of historical enquiry, and to encourage undergraduates, by weighing and assessing the evidence, to reach their own conclusions.

The Tripos is divided into two Parts, the examination for Part I normally being taken at the end of the second year, and the examination for Part II normally at the end of the third year. The Preliminary Examination, held at the end of the third term of the first year, does not affect the degree classification.

The two principles governing the organization of the Tripos are:

(*a*) the provision of opportunities for increasing specialization over the course of the three-year period of study,

(*b*) the provision of an increasingly wide choice of subjects as the course proceeds.

All candidates for Part I take a General historical problems paper. A candidate is required to choose at least one of the five periods of English political and constitutional history and English economic and social history. He also makes three further choices from among papers covering other periods of English history, seven periods of European history, two periods in the History of political thought, Expansion of Europe, North American history since 1607, and The West and the 'Third World' from the First World War to the present day. In total a candidate takes six papers in Part I.

In Part II there is a wide range of subjects, and their time span is narrower. There are opportunities to study aspects of British or European history in greater depth than in Part I; there are 'specified' subjects devoted to a particular theme or topic or to comparative studies; there are papers on extra-European history, on the History of political thought, and on Political Philosophy; and there are 'special' subjects which vary from time to time, and which allow close examination of short periods with particular attention to primary documents.

A candidate for Part II may choose to offer a dissertation of between 7,000 and 15,000 words on a topic in substitution for one of his Part II papers, but not in place of a 'special' subject.

Compulsions governing the choice of subjects in Part II are as follows:

(a) All candidates must take a 'special' subject.

(b) Candidates who in Part I of the Historical Tripos took no paper which fell mainly in a period before 1750 must take at least one such paper in Part II.

(c) Candidates who in Part I of the Historical Tripos took no European paper must take at least one such paper in Part II.

Subject to his abiding by these provisos, a candidate in Part II can therefore, if he wishes, confine himself entirely to one general field, selecting his three subjects from either English, or European, or extra-European history; alternatively, he can range as widely as he likes, choosing something from each.

While the great majority of undergraduates reading history have specialized in history at school, this is not essential. Freshness of approach is often preferable to historical erudition, and a good working knowledge of French and German, for example, is likely to prove of considerably more value than close acquaintance while still at school with the more specialized products of modern historical scholarship. The best preparation for the Historical Tripos, before coming to Cambridge, consists of wide general reading and the cultivation of an interest in the present as well as in the past.

Although the full course in History at Cambridge is a three-year course, the division of the Tripos into two Parts makes it possible for an undergraduate to study History for only one or two of his three years and to take one Part of a Tripos in another subject for the remainder of his time at the University. It would be possible, therefore, to combine one Part of the Historical Tripos with one Part of another Tripos, such as Law, or Archaeology and Anthropology, or Fine Arts. While Part I of the Historical Tripos is a two-year course, and Part II is normally a one-year course, there is also an extended version of Part II, covering two years, for candidates who have taken Part I of another Tripos at the end of their first year, and wish to switch to Part II of the Historical Tripos.

Part I

Part I may be taken at the end of the second year of residence, or one or two years after obtaining honours in another Honours Examination, but not later than a candidate's fourth year. The scheme of examination is as follows:

Section A – *General Historical Problems*

1. General historical problems.

Section B – *English Political and Constitutional History*

2. English political and constitutional history, 500–1450.

3. English political and constitutional history, 1200–1600.

4. English political and constitutional history, 1450–1750.

5. English political and constitutional history, 1600–1870.

6. English political and constitutional history, since 1750.

Section C – *English Economic and Social History*

7. English economic and social history, 500–1450.

8. English economic and social history, 1200–1600.

9. English economic and social history, 1450–1750.

10. English economic and social history, 1600–1870.

11. English economic and social history, since 1750.

Section D – *European History*

12. European history, 776 B.C.–A.D. 284.

13. European history, 31 B.C.–A.D. 962.

HISTORY

14. European history, 284–1250.

15. European history, 962–1500.

16. European history, 1250–1715.

17. European history, 1500–1871.

18. European history, since 1715.

Section E – *Political Thought*

19. History of political thought to *c.* 1750 (also serves as Paper O 6 of Part II of the Classical Tripos).

20. History of political thought since *c.* 1750.

Section F – *Extra-European History*

21. Expansion of Europe since the fifteenth century to the First World War.

22. North American history since 1607.

Section G – *Additional Historical Subjects to be set from time to time*

23. The West and the 'Third World' from the First World War to the present day.

24. A subject in any aspect of History specified by the Faculty Board from time to time.

A candidate for Part I must offer papers as follows:

(*a*) if he takes the examination in the fourth, fifth, or sixth term after his first term of residence, or in the year next but one after he has obtained honours in another Honours Examination, or if he is an Affiliated Student who has been given leave by the Faculty Board to take Part I in the fourth, fifth, or sixth term after his first term kept, Paper 1 and five other papers;

(*b*) if he takes the examination in the year next after he has obtained honours in another Honours Examination, Paper 1 and four other papers;

provided that

(i) he offers at least one paper from Section B, at least one paper from Section C, and at least one paper from Sections D–G;

(ii) if he offers more than one paper either from Section B or from Section C or from Section D, he must not choose papers within that Section which overlap chronologically:

(iii) no candidate who has obtained honours in either Part of the Classical Tripos can offer Paper 12 or 13;

(iv) the Faculty Board may specify from among Papers 2–24 a paper or papers which an Affiliated Student who is a candidate under this regulation may or may not offer.

The details of these papers are as follows:

1. General historical problems

The purpose of this paper is to test candidates' ability to handle questions of historical method and broad historical themes. In particular, candidates are expected to show greater skill at sustained and wide-ranging historical analysis than is possible in the other Tripos papers, and to demonstrate their capacity to strike a balance between generalized argument and detailed examples.

Candidates are required to answer one question.

Some of the questions are designed to enable candidates to display a knowledge of historical theory and method, including the nature of historical explanation, the boundaries and connexions between different fields of historical study, relations with other disciplines, and critical analysis of the methods, concepts, and types of evidence used by historians.

Other questions are designed to test candidates' ability to deploy a connected argument supported by historical illustration about major themes of human development.

2–6. English political and constitutional history, from A.D. 500 to the present day

In these papers candidates are required to show knowledge of political and constitutional aspects of English history within the specified period. Candidates may also be required to show knowledge of Irish, Scottish, and Welsh history and diplomatic history, where relevant to the period studied. Candidates are expected to show evidence of their ability to use and interpret contemporary documents. In each paper three questions must be answered, but no question will be specified as compulsory.

7–11. English economic and social history, from A.D. 500 to the present day

In these papers candidates are required to show knowledge of economic, social, and cultural aspects of English history within the specified period.

Candidates may also be required to show knowledge of Irish, Scottish, and Welsh history, where relevant to the period studied. Candidates are expected to show evidence of their ability to use and interpret contemporary documents. In each paper three questions must be answered, but no question will be specified as compulsory.

12–18. European history, from 776 B.C. to the present day

These papers survey European history in the periods concerned, in its political, constitutional, cultural, economic, and social aspects. Each paper is set in two sections. In one section the major emphasis is on political and constitutional history; in the other section the major emphasis is on economic, social, intellectual, and cultural history. Candidates are also required to show knowledge of general aspects of European history. Candidates are required to answer three questions, at least one question from each section.

19. History of political thought to *c.* 1750

20. History of political thought since *c.* 1750

These papers deal with political ideas and arguments in relation to the general historical contexts in which they arose. Each paper is divided into two sections. Section A consists of questions on the prescribed texts. Section B contains questions of two types. Some will be designed to test knowledge of general trends and issues in the history of political thought. These questions will be based on the list of texts prescribed for Section A, and on a further list of subsidiary texts announced by the Faculty Board. Other questions in Section B will allow particular themes and concepts from the prescribed texts to be analysed in greater detail, as well as allowing comparative studies to be made of those themes and concepts which recur in several of the prescribed texts. In each paper three questions must be answered. One but not more than one question must be taken from Section B.

21. Expansion of Europe from the fifteenth century to the First World War

This paper deals comparatively with the growth of political, economic, and cultural relations between Europe and the rest of the world since 1400; and with their effects in world history. The subject consists of an historical introduction to the institutions and culture of the major societies of Africa and Asia; comparative analysis of the motives and forms of the expanding wealth and power of Europe; the effects of European expansion upon indigenous societies and the emergence of modern nationalisms: the politics and economics of European colonization and the development of colonial nationalism in the Americas (excluding the United States after 1776), Australasia, and North and South Africa; the general theory of imperialism and nationalism in the modern world.

22. North American history since 1607

This paper concentrates on the history of those parts of North America which now form the United States. Candidates are required to answer three questions.

23. Subject specified in **1989** and **1990**: The West and the 'Third World' from the First World War to the present day

This paper surveys the historical interaction between the West and the 'Third World' since 1918 in its political, economic, and strategic aspects. It deals with the effects of world economic fluctuations and of the two World Wars on Western societies and the development of modern nationalist movements; Western attempts at political and strategic adjustment including the process of decolonization; the emergence of the 'new states' and their evolution since independence; the nature and relevance of modern theories of imperialism, neo-colonialism, and under-development. Attention is given to those aspects of the social and economic structure of overseas societies that are pertinent to the explanation of major political trends.

Part II*

Part II may be taken one or two years after obtaining honours in Part I, or in any other Honours Examination, but not later than a candidate's fourth year. The scheme of examination is as follows:

Section A – *Special Subject*

1. Sources paper
2. Essay paper

Each candidate must choose one Special Subject from a list of Special Subjects published by the Faculty Board. With each of the subjects original

---

* Candidates for Part II in 1990, who have previously taken Part I of the Historical Tripos and who did not offer in that Part a paper in European History, may meet the requirement to take a European History paper in Part II by offering one of the following papers: Papers 7, 8, 11, 12, 14, 15, 18, 20, 21, 22, and 24.

HISTORY 215

authorities are specified some of which may be in a foreign language. A candidate is required to take two three-hour Special Subject examination papers. One of the papers deals exclusively with the original authorities; in the other paper three questions have to be answered.

In **1990** the special subjects will be:

- *A. The city of Rome (Paper C2, Part II of the Classical Tripos)
- *B. The English gentry, 1440–1480
- *C. Conquerors and conquered in the lands of the Crown of Aragon
- D. No subject specified
- E. No subject specified
- *F. Thomas Hobbes
- G. The Whigs and the crisis of the Old Order in Britain, 1828–35
- H. The drafting and ratification of the United States Constitution, 1787–88
- I. The transfer of power and partition of India, 1942–1947
- J. The churches and social problems in Britain, 1883–1914
- K. Rethinking the role of the State: Economic and social policy, 1922–35
- L. Revolution and colonial confrontation in Buganda, 1884–1931
- M. The Russian Revolution (1917–1921)

In **1991** the special subjects will be:

- A. The city of Rome (Paper C2 of Part II of the Classical Tripos).
- B. Conquerors and conquered in the lands of the Crown of Aragon
- C. The English gentry, 1440–80
- D. The English town in the later Middle Ages: London, York, and Cambridge
- E. Perceptions and uses of the past in sixteenth-century England
- F. Politics and the arts in the age of Louis XIV
- G. Thomas Hobbes
- H. The drafting and ratification of the United States Constitution, 1787–88
- I. The Whigs and the crisis of the Old Order in Britain, 1828–35

* **Candidates who have previously taken Part I and who did not offer in that Part a paper falling mainly in the period before 1750 will be able to meet the requirement to take a pre-1750 paper in Part II by offering one of the subjects** marked with an asterisk.

J. The 'national question' in France, 1830–70
K. The churches and social problems in Britain, 1883–1914
L. Revolution and colonial confrontation in Buganda, 1884–1931.
M. The Russian Revolution, 1917–21
N. Rethinking the rôle of the State: economic and social policy, 1924–37
O. The transfer of power and partition of India, 1942–47

Section B – *Political Thought*

3. The history of political thought up to *c.* 1750 (also serves as Paper 47 of Part II of the Social and Political Sciences Tripos).

4. The history of political thought since *c.* 1750.

Papers 3 and 4 deal with political ideas and arguments in relation to the general historical contexts in which they arose. Each paper is divided into two sections. Section A consists of questions on prescribed texts. Section B contains questions of two types. Some will be designed to test knowledge of general trends and issues in the history of political thought; these questions will be based on the list of texts prescribed for Section A and on a further list of subsidiary texts announced by the Faculty Board. Other questions in Section B will allow particular themes and concepts from the prescribed texts to be analysed in greater detail, and will also allow comparative studies to be made of those themes and concepts which recur in several of the prescribed texts. In each paper three questions must be answered; one question, but not more than one, must be taken from Section B.

5. Political philosophy (also serves as Paper 20 of Part II of the Social and Political Sciences Tripos).

This paper centres on the study of the nature and ends of the state, the grounds of political obligation, and the study of the main theories which have influenced the structure and functions of governments in the modern world. Candidates are expected to show some knowledge of modern intellectual movements and some ability to discuss political concepts and broad political issues in a critical and independent way. The main concepts and issues to be considered are as follows: the understanding of politics and of society generally; the question of the relations between political thought and action, and of the limitations on the possibility of political action; the concepts of authority, power and security; contract, rights, and representation; liberty, social justice, equality, welfare, and the public interest; the relations between law, moral attitudes, and political behaviour.

HISTORY

Section C – *Comparative and Thematic Studies*

6. A subject in economic history
For **1990** and **1991**: Business, literature and society, 1750–1950.

7. A subject in the history of international relations
For **1990** and **1991**: Europe and the rise of the Superpowers: international relations since 1815.

8. A subject in the history of ideas since *c.* 1500
For **1990** and **1991**: Socialism in its nineteenth century context.

9. A subject in comparative and thematic studies
For **1990** and **1991**: Revolution (Paper 7 in Part II of the Social and Political Sciences Tripos).

10. A subject in comparative and thematic studies
For **1990**: Marriage in England, 1500–1800.
For **1991**: No subject specified.

11. A subject in comparative economic and social history
In **1990** and **1991**: European society and the First World War; Britain, France, Germany, 1914–20.

Section D – *Topics in English or European or English and European history*

12. A subject in ancient history
For **1990** and **1991**: The transformation of the Roman world, A.D. 284–476 (also serves as Paper O 10 of Part II of the Classical Tripos).

13. A subject in medieval English history
For **1990** and **1991**: The Black Death and its aftermath.

14. A subject in medieval European history
In **1990** and **1991**: Byzantium and its neighbours (*c.* 900–1204).

15. A subject in English or European or English and European history in the medieval period
In **1990** and **1991**: Rome's heirs: the German kingdom of Western Europe, 476–987.

16. A subject in English or European or English and European history in the medieval period
In **1990** and **1991**: Religious thought in Oxford and Cambridge, 1370–1714.

17. A subject in English or European or English and European history in the early modern period

In **1990** and **1991**: The British problem, *c.* 1534–*c.* 1707.

18. A subject in English or European or English and European history in the early modern period

In **1990**: The political culture of Spain and its Italian possessions in the early modern period.

In **1991**: No subject specified.

19. A subject in modern English history

For **1990** and **1991**: Deviance, law, and social order in England, 1750–1914.

20. A subject in modern European history

For **1990** and **1991**: Continuity and change in France since the French Revolution.

21. A subject in English or European or English and European history in the modern period.

In **1990** and **1991**: Economic development and economic backwardness in modern Europe: Britain, Germany, Russia, Italy.

22[1]. A subject in English or European or English and European history in the modern period.

In **1990** and **1991**: European history since 1871.

23. A subject in English or European or English and European history

For **1990** and **1991**: Seventeenth century British America.

24. A subject in English or European or English and European history.

For **1990** and **1991**: The struggle for mastery in Germany, 1740–1880.

Section E – *Extra-European history*

25. A subject in African history

For **1990** and **1991**: The history of Africa from *c.* 1800 to the present day.

The paper deals with the history of the entire African continent. Candidates are expected to show a general grasp of the processes of African

---

[1] Paper 22 may not be offered by a candidate who has offered Paper 18 in Part I.

HISTORY

history including the principles of African social, economic, and political organization, the growth of African states and empires, the changes brought about by European influences, the emergence of modern nationalism, the terms of decolonization, and the problems of post-colonial government and economy. While candidates will be allowed to give special attention to one or more geographical regions, they will also be given the opportunity to draw comparisons between them. The paper is not divided into sections, but for purposes of both specialization and comparison, the continent will be considered to have the four following regions: North and North East Africa, including central and eastern Sudan, Ethiopia, and Somalia; South and South Central Africa, including Angola and Mozambique; East Africa, including Rwanda and Burundi; Western Africa, including the western Sudanic zone and Zaire (Congo).

26. A subject in Asian history

For **1990** and **1991**: The history of the Indian Sub-Continent from the late eighteenth century to the present day.

This paper will, until further notice, be entitled 'The History of the Indian Sub-Continent from the late eighteenth century to the present day'. The paper will be broadly concerned with the development of the Indian sub-continent during the specified period. Candidates will be expected to show knowledge of the working of indigenous political and socio-religious systems; the rise and operation of British rule; the development of nationalism and Muslim separatism; social and religious movements; economic, educational and social developments (including land questions); India's place within the British Imperial system and its relations with the outer world; the transfer of power and the partition of India; and the nature of economic, social and political change in the sub-continent as a whole since independence.

27. A subject in North American history

In **1990**: Economic and social history of the U.S.A., 1815–85.
In **1991**: No subject specified.

28. A subject in extra-European history specified by the Faculty Board

For **1990** and **1991**: Independence and revolution: Mexico, 1790 to the present day.

29. A subject in extra-European history

For **1990** and **1991**: The history of the Commonwealth from 1839 to the present day.

In this paper Commonwealth history is understood to mean a survey of Imperial and Commonwealth history from 1839 to the present day in its political, constitutional, economic, and strategic aspects. Candidates are expected to show knowledge of the more important contemporary documents bearing on the subject.

Knowledge of the internal history of individual Commonwealth countries is required only in so far as is necessary for an understanding of the emergence, development, and working of the Commonwealth as a whole.

A candidate for Part II must offer

(*a*) if he takes the examination in the year next after he has obtained honours in Part I of the Historical Tripos or in another Honours Examination, or if he is an Affiliated Student who has been given leave by the Faculty Board to take Part II in the first, second, or third term after his first term kept, Section A (Papers 1 and 2) and

either two papers from Sections B–E

or one paper from Sections B–E and a dissertation on a topic approved by the Faculty Board within the range of the Historical Tripos as a whole, provided that a candidate must not submit a dissertation on a topic falling within the scope of any of the papers that he is offering in Part II;

(*b*) if he takes the examination in the year next but one after he has obtained honours in Part I of the Historical Tripos or in another Honours Examination, or if he is an Affiliated Student who has been given leave by the Faculty Board to take Part II in the fourth, fifth, or sixth term after his first term kept, Section A (Papers 1 and 2) and

either four papers from Sections B–E

or three papers from Sections B–E and a dissertation on a topic approved by the Faculty Board within the range of the Historical Tripos as a whole, provided that a candidate must not submit a dissertation on a topic falling within the scope of any of the papers that he is offering in Part II:

provided that

(i) no candidate may offer any paper that he has previously offered as a candidate for another Honours Examination;

HISTORY

(ii) the Faculty Board may give notice before the end of the Easter Term in the academical year next but one preceding the examination that a candidate who offered a particular paper or combination of papers in Part I of the Historical Tripos may not offer a particular paper or papers from Section D of Part II;

(iii) no candidate who has obtained honours in Part II of the Classical Tripos may offer Paper 12;

(iv) no candidate may offer in Papers 1 and 2 a subject which he has already offered in Group C of Part II of the Classical Tripos;

(v) no candidate who has previously offered Paper 19 in Part I of the Historical Tripos may offer Paper 3;

(vi) no candidate who has previously offered Paper 20 in Part I of the Historical Tripos may offer Paper 4;

(vii) no candidate may offer both Paper 3 and Paper 4;

(viii) the Faculty Board may specify from among Papers 3–29 a paper or papers which an Affiliated Student who is a candidate under this regulation may or may not offer;

(ix) a candidate who has previously obtained honours in Part I of the Historical Tripos but who did not offer in that Part a paper from among

either Papers 2–5, 7–10, 12–17 and 19

or Papers 23 and 24 (if available, and if the subject specified for the paper fell mainly in a period before 1750)

must offer in Part II

either Papers 1 and 2, provided that the special subject selected by the candidate is one which has been announced by the Faculty Board as a subject falling mainly in the period before 1750

or one of the following papers, provided that the period specified for the paper is a subject falling mainly in the period before 1750:

Papers 3, 8, and 12–18;

Papers 23, 24, and 27–29 (if available);

(x) a candidate who has previously obtained honours in Part I of the Historical Tripos but who did not offer in that Part a paper from among Papers 12–18 must offer in Part II a paper from among 14, 20, and any other papers on a subject in

European history specified by the Faculty Board from time to time[1];

A candidate for Part II who chooses to offer a dissertation must submit the proposed title of his dissertation through his Tutor to the Secretary of the Faculty Board so as to reach him not later than the first Monday of the Full Michaelmas Term next preceding the examination; with his proposed title the candidate shall submit the number and title of each paper that he intends to offer. Each candidate must obtain the approval of the title of his dissertation by the Faculty Board not later than the end of the Full Michaelmas Term next preceding the examination. After the Faculty Board have approved a candidate's proposed dissertation title no change may be made to it without the approval of the Faculty Board, but a candidate may submit a revised title to the Secretary of the Faculty Board by the division of the following Lent Term for the approval of the Faculty Board. Titles received by the Faculty Board after that date shall be considered only in the most exceptional circumstances. Each dissertation must be typewritten, unless permission has been given to present it in manuscript (and if this is considered insufficiently legible, it may have to be resubmitted in typescript), of not less than 7,000 and not more than 15,000 words in length (inclusive of footnotes and appendices, but exclusive of bibliography), must show knowledge of primary sources, and must be submitted through the candidate's Tutor so as to reach the Secretary of the Faculty Board not later than the end of the first week of Full Term in which the examination is held. A dissertation shall not bear the candidate's name, but shall be accompanied by a coversheet signed by the candidate certifying that it is his own original work, that it does not contain material that he has already used to any substantial extent for a comparable purpose, and that the dissertation does not exceed the word limit. A candidate shall also supply with his dissertation a brief synopsis on a separate sheet of paper of the contents of the dissertation. A candidate will be required to give full references to sources used. The Examiners will have power at their discretion to examine a candidate *viva voce* on his dissertation and on the general field of knowledge within which it falls.

---

[1] In **1991** the papers will be: 7, 8, 11, 12, 14, 15, 18, 20, 21, 22 and 24.

HISTORY

The Preliminary Examination for Part I

The examination consists of five papers as follows:

1. General historical problems (Paper 1 of Part I).
2. English history: political and constitutional.
3. English history: social and economic.
4. European history from 776 B.C. to the present day.
5. Translation of foreign language passages.

Every candidate must offer Paper 5, unless he has obtained honours in another Tripos or is an Affiliated Student or is certified by his Tutor to have qualified for matriculation with the help of a non-European language, and two of Papers 1–4.

Paper 1 will be framed to enable candidates to display a knowledge of general aspects of history. Candidates will be required to answer one question.

The papers on English history run from the Anglo-Saxon period to the present day, and therefore encompass all five of the separate periods of English history set in Part I of the Historical Tripos. In Paper 2 candidates are required to show knowledge of political and constitutional aspects and also of general aspects of English history. Candidates may also be required to show knowledge of Irish, Scottish, and Welsh history and diplomatic history, where relevant to the period studied. Candidates are expected to show evidence of their ability to use and interpret contemporary documents. Three questions must be answered but no question will be specified as compulsory. In Paper 3 candidates are required to show knowledge of economic, social, and cultural aspects and also of general aspects of English history. Candidates may also be required to show knowledge of Irish, Scottish, and Welsh history, where relevant to the period studied. Candidates are expected to show evidence of their ability to use and interpret contemporary documents. Three questions must be answered, but no question will be specified as compulsory.

Paper 4 on European history covers the chronological span from 776 B.C. to the present day. The paper is set in two sections. In one section the major emphasis is on political and constitutional history; in the other section the major emphasis is on economic, social, intellectual, and cultural history. Candidates are also required to show knowledge of general aspects of European history. Candidates are required to answer three questions at least one of which must be chosen from each section.

In Paper 5 candidates are required to translate into English passages written in a foreign language. Two passages will be set in Latin, two in French, and two in German. One passage will be set in Greek, one in Spanish, one in Italian, and one in Russian. Candidates are expected to satisfy the Examiners in one passage in Latin or French or German, and in one additional passage which may be in Latin, in French, in German, or in one of the other languages set. Dictionaries may be used in the examination.

The Preliminary Examination for Part II

The papers for this examination are taken from among the papers for Part II of the Historical Tripos. A candidate who wishes to be classed must offer any three papers, except Paper 1 or Paper 2, or a paper which he would not be permitted to offer if he were a candidate for the Tripos examination.

The Examination in History for the Ordinary B.A. Degree

The examination consists of the following four papers, all of which must be taken:

1. General historical problems.
2. English history: political and constitutional.
3. English history: social and economic.
4. European History from 776 B.C. to the present day.

The papers in any year are the same as those for the papers in the Preliminary Examination for Part I.

The Diploma in Historical Studies

The Diploma is primarily but not exclusively intended to provide for those who intend to proceed to a research degree in Cambridge after taking three terms postgraduate course in advanced historical studies. Candidature is open to students who, on the recommendation of the Degree Committee for the Faculty of History, have been admitted to the status of Graduate Student by the Board of Graduate Studies. Applications must be submitted to the Secretary of the Board of Graduate Studies, together with a statement of the candidate's previous studies, attainments, and qualifications.

HISTORY

Candidates must submit a dissertation of not less than 15,000 or more than 30,000 words (including notes and appendices) on a subject approved by the Degree Committee. Each candidate must submit to the Secretary of the Degree Committee, not later than the division of the term in which his candidature begins, the proposed title of the dissertation. Each candidate must submit two copies of his dissertation to the Secretary of the Board of Graduate Studies not later than the last day of Full Term in the third term of his candidature, provided that the Board may, on the recommendation of the Degree Committee, allow him to submit it at a later date.

Candidates are examined orally on the subject of their dissertation and on the general field in which it falls.

The M.Phil. course (one-year) in International Relations

The course of study includes lectures, seminars, and individual supervision. It is designed to give a general understanding of the nature and development of the modern international system, an appreciation of the nature and problems of the contemporary world, and an opportunity for the candidate to study at greater depth a subject suited to his needs and interests in those areas.

The syllabus of the course of study is as follows:

The rise of the nation-state and the modern system of relations between states; statecraft and diplomacy and their historical development; the concepts of national interest, balance of power, and international community; the roles of power and war; the relationship between the super-powers; the relationship between states at different stages of development; the theories of deterrence; modern international law and its development; the relationship of international law, policy, and economics; the legal and economic aspects of regional integration; international institutions and their development; the role of the U.N. and its agencies; the law of armed conflict and peaceful settlement of disputes; the economics of international trade and finance; the economics of growth and development; comparisons and contrasts between the economic development of different social systems.

The scheme of examination consists of (*a*) **a thesis of not more than 25,000 words in length, including tables, footnotes, and appendices, but excluding bibliography, on a subject approved by the Degree** Committee for the Faculty of History; and (*b*) essays, each not exceeding 2,000 words in length and on a set topic falling within one of the following fields, provided that not more than one topic is chosen from any particular field:

International history and politics.
Theory of international relations.
Strategic studies.
International economics.
International law.

The examination includes an oral examination upon the thesis and on the general field of knowledge within which it falls.

The M.Phil. course (one-year) in Medieval History

The course offers candidates the opportunity to study an aspect of medieval history in considerable depth and to write a thesis of up to 25,000 words on the topic chosen. The course also provides a specific training in the auxiliary disciplines of medieval history (palaeography and diplomatic, medieval Latin, research methods and resources), and to enhance the candidate's understanding of the Middle Ages by focusing on the historical writing of the period or on medieval archaeology.

By the beginning of the academic year candidates should have a basic understanding of Latin grammar and the ability to translate straightforward Latin texts. For those who need it, an intensive introductory course in medieval Latin will be available in the period immediately before the beginning of the academic year. Candidates without a formal qualification in Latin are advised to attend this introductory course.

COURSE OF STUDY

THE FIRST HALF OF THE COURSE of study covers:

1. Medieval Latin palaeography and auxiliary studies
2. Sources, methods, and bibliography
3. *Either* (a) Historical writing in the Middle Ages
   Or (b) Medieval archaeology

In both these courses candidates will have the opportunity to specialize in particular areas of interest in addition to their more general work.

This half of the course will be examined in April by a practical test in palaeography and a technical description (of not more than 5,000 words in length), of a medieval manuscript of class of records; by a critical bibliography of an approved area of study (containing not more than 100 items); and by two essays (each not exceeding 5,000 words in length), on topics within which of the two fields the student has chosen from 3(a) or 3(b) above.

THE SECOND HALF OF THE COURSE is devoted to the preparation and writing of the research thesis after consultation with the supervisor. This thesis must be submitted by the end of August and will be followed by an oral examination on the thesis and on the general field of knowledge within which it falls.

HISTORY OF ART

The History of Art Tripos is intended for those who wish to study the history, criticism, and theory of the figurative arts as well as of architecture. The course does not provide studio-work in practical art.

To be entered as a candidate for the History of Art Tripos, it is necessary to have obtained honours in Part I of any other Tripos or to be accepted by the University as an Affiliated Student.

The courses and Tripos requirements are so arranged as to enable candidates to prepare to take Group (i) in one year, or Group (ii) in two* years. Candidates for Group (ii) are required to take a Preliminary Examination at the end of their first year of study.

The Head of the Department of the History of Art is responsible for arranging the teaching and for the issue of lists of recommended books. Teaching consists of lectures and classes in the Department (Scroope Terrace), and in the Fitzwilliam Museum. The Slade Professor of Fine Art is a member of the Faculty. His classes in the Department and his public lectures to the University are arranged in conjunction with the teaching of the Department.

Lectures and classes given by the staff of the Department are extensively augmented with teaching given by visitors appointed for their outstanding abilities in those fields of Art History related to the subjects of special study.

Prospective candidates, after consulting their College Tutors and present Directors of Studies, should arrange to call on the Director of Studies in the History of Art for their College as early in their Cambridge careers as possible, and *in any case not later than one week before the end of the Easter Full Term preceding the year in which they would begin to read specifically for the History of Art Tripos*, in order to discuss their likely suitability and plans for preliminary study and travel. Preparation for reading History of Art at Cambridge should include: as much looking at buildings and works of art in the original as may be feasible in this country and abroad; attendance at the Slade lectures, and at other 'open lectures' on the arts; an ability to read French at least, and, desirably, German or Italian or both. Really inadequate reading knowledge of these principal languages of Europe may debar candidates not only from satisfactory access to the documentary sources, but also from using secondary material

---

* If a candidate wishes to spend two years, after spending two years obtaining honours in another Tripos, and is receiving an L.E.A. grant, he is strongly advised to apply through his Tutor for his grant for his fourth year not later than the beginning of his fourth term at the University.

HISTORY OF ART

of critical importance. Total incapacity to cope with Latin sentences, even with a dictionary, is no less a handicap to those who wish to concentrate particularly on Medieval or Renaissance subjects.

Prospective candidates should make every effort to read the few books in the list below. These books have been selected as offering classic examples of the principal approaches to those fundamental problems of interpretation and method in art history with which undergraduates should become familiar before beginning their work for the History of Art Tripos. The number of books on this basic list has been kept to a minimum. Most are very easily obtainable; and all can be read in English. The styles of approach represented, and many of the problems and ideas involved, are applicable generally beyond the ostensible limits of each book's chosen field. Copies of other lists of books currently recommended for particular courses may be obtained by applying to the Secretary, University of Cambridge Department of the History of Art, 1 Scroope Terrace, Cambridge. Reference may be made to the Head of the Department of the History of Art at the same address for such other information about the courses and requirements as is not contained in the *Handbook*.

Some foreign travel during vacations is virtually essential. Grants towards the cost of this are generally obtainable either through special funds administered by Colleges, or, with the recommendation of the Department, from Local Education Authorities. But undergraduates must expect to have to provide a part of what is needed from their own resources. The Department as such can dispose of no finance for travel.

For books undergraduates have use of the Faculty Library housed at Scroope Terrace, from which they may borrow, and of the Fitzwilliam Museum Library nearby, where they may work but not borrow, besides the University Library, which is particularly rich in source books from the mid-sixteenth to the early nineteenth century. An increasing number of books of importance in modern criticism is becoming obtainable at more reasonable prices as paperbacks; and College Libraries are co-operating most helpfully in making available to their undergraduates additional copies of the most used books of general interest.

Recommended reading

The following books are recommended to all proposing to read for the History of Art Tripos:

C. Baudelaire, *The Painter of Modern Life and other essays*, ed. J. Mayne,

London, 1964; M. Baxandall, *Painting and Experience in Fifteenth Century Italy*, Oxford, 1972; M. Baxandall, *The Limewood Sculptors of Renaissance Germany*, New Haven and London, 1980; O. Benesch, *The Art of the Renaissance in Northern Europe*, London, 1965; A. Braham, *The Architecture of the French Enlightenment*, London, 1980; B. Berenson, *The Italian Painters of the Renaissance*, London, 1952; J. Burckhardt, *The Civilisation of the Renaissance in Italy*, tr. S. G. C. Middlemore, London, 1945; J. Connors, *Borromini and the Roman Oratory*, Cambridge, Mass., 1980; R. Fry, *Cézanne: a study of his development*, London, 1927; J. Gage, *Colour in Turner*, London, 1969; M. Girouard, *The Victorian Country House*, New Haven and London, 1979. E. H. Gombrich, *Art and Illusion*, London, 1960; F. Haskell, *Patrons and Painters*, New Haven, 1980. F. Haskell and N. Penny, *Taste and the Antique*, New Haven, 1981. G. Henderson, *Early Medieval*, (style and civilization), Harmondsworth, 1972, repr. 1977; L. Heydenreich and W. Lotz, *Architecture in Italy 1400–1600*, Harmondsworth, 1974. M. Jaffé, *Rubens and Italy*, Oxford, 1977; H. W. Janson, ed., *Sources and Documents in the History of Art*, Prentice-Hall Inc., Englewood Cliffs, New Jersey; P. Joannides, *The Drawings of Raphael*, Oxford, 1983; A. Katzenellenbogen, *The Sculptural Programs of Chartres Cathedral*, Baltimore, 1959; E. Mâle, *The Gothic Image*, London, 1913, repr. 1961; R. Middleton and D. Watkin, *Neoclassical and 19th Century Architecture*, New York, 1980; J. M. Montias, *Artists and Artisans in Delft in the Seventeenth Century*, Princeton, 1982; G. Morelli, *Italian painters: Critical studies of their works*, tr. C. J. Ffoulkes, London, 1892; O. Pächt, *The Rise of Pictorial Narrative in Twelfth-Century England*, Oxford, 1962; E. Panofsky, *Renaissance and Renascences in Western Art*, Stockholm, 1960; E. Panofsky, *Studies in Iconology*, New York, 1962; N. Pevsner, *An Outline of European Architecture*, London, 1960; M. Podro, *The Critical Historians of Art*, New Haven, 1983; J. Reynolds, *Discourses on Art*, ed. R. Wark, San Marino, 1959; J. Rykwert, *The First Moderns: The Architects of the Eighteenth Century*, Cambridge, Mass., and London, 1980; F. Saxl, *Lectures*, London, 1957; M. Schapiro, *Word and Image*, Leyden, 1972; M. Schapiro, *Late Antique, Early Christian and Mediaeval Art*: Selected papers, London, 1980; G. Scott, *The Architecture of Humanism*, London, 1914; J. Summerson, *Architecture in Britain 1530–1830*, London, 1983; J. White, *The Birth and Rebirth of Pictorial Space*, London, 1957; H. Wölfflin, *Principles of Art History*, tr. M. D. Hottinger, London, 1932; H. Wölfflin, *Classic Art*, London, 1952.

The scheme of examination is as follows:

The Tripos consists of one Part. A student who has obtained honours in another Honours Examination may take the Tripos in

HISTORY OF ART

his third or fourth year. A student may not be a candidate for the Tripos on more than one occasion, or be a candidate for another University examination in the same term. The scheme of the examination is as follows:

Paper 1. Approaches to the History of Art, with reference to works of criticism

This paper deals with the influence of writers of classical antiquity upon the Renaissance approach to art and architecture; with changing attitudes towards both antiquity and the Middle Ages in the eighteenth century; with nineteenth-century and twentieth-century theoretical and critical approaches to art and architecture; and with recent developments in art historical methods, the growth of connoisseurship, formal and stylistic criticism, and sociological and iconographical interpretations of works of art and architecture.

and such number of **pairs of papers** on special subjects as the Faculty Board may announce from time to time. There will be no less than six pairs of such papers on special subjects. Each pair of papers will deal with a particular person, subject, or period in the History of Art. In each pair of papers, the second paper will consist of photographs of works of art requiring comment and interpretation.

A candidate for the Tripos must offer

(i) if he takes the examination in the year next after he has obtained honours in another Tripos, Paper 1; two pairs of papers on special subjects; and a thesis of between 7,000 and 9,000 words on a subject approved by the Faculty Board dealing with a particular person, work of art, subject, or period in the History of Art.

(ii) if he takes the examination in the year next but one after he has obtained honours in another Tripos, three pairs of papers on special subjects; and a thesis of between 7,000 and 9,000 words on a subject approved by the Faculty Board dealing with a particular person, work of art, subject, or period in the History of Art. Theses must be typewritten, unless previous permission has been obtained to present the thesis in manuscript.

The pairs of papers on special subjects in **1990** will be as follows:

2 and 3. Religious art of the High Middle Ages in Northern Europe

The option investigates techniques of pictorial narrative in painting and sculpture, mainly of the twelfth and thirteenth centuries; the variety of interplay of pictorial imagery and the written word, in 'literal' illustrations, captions, inscribed verbal dialogue, etc.; the emergence in this period of new narrative and devotional subjects; the imagery of the saints; and the 'visionary' element in some representations of sacred scenes or persons. Special attention will be paid throughout to the evidence contained in illuminated books such as Psalters and Apocalypses in Cambridge collections.

4 and 5. The Interaction of Painting and Sculpture in Central Italy 1400–1500

This option covers the period from the competition for the second set of bronze doors for the Florentine Baptistry, won by Lorenzo Ghiberti in 1401, to the early stages of work by Michelangelo on the tomb of Pope Julius II in the first decade of the next century. It will concentrate mainly on developments in Tuscany, the most active centre for advanced and experimental work, but the activities of Tuscan sculptors in other parts of Italy, notably Bologna, Ferrara, Padua, Rome, and Venice, will also be considered, with occasional attention paid to indigenous developments where they seem of particular interest. Given the variety and richness of work produced in this period and the number of artists of universally recognized genius, the basic approach will be monographic. The vast and varied *oeuvre* of Donatello, whose career spans two-thirds of the fifteenth century, will receive close attention as will the early work of Michelangelo and that of Jacopo della Quercia, Ghiberti, Antonio Federighi, the Rossellino Brothers, Agostino di Duccio, Desiderio da Settignano, Pollaiuolo, Verrocchio, and Andrea Sansovino. There will also be some examination of more general questions such as the rôle of different types of patronage, the relation between painting and sculpture, the development of portraiture, and that of relief sculpture.

6 and 7. Dürer and his time

A study of Dürer as a painter, an engraver, a draughtsman, and a theorist demonstrates his paramount place in the Northern Renaissance. His travels will be studied and the impact of new ideas and forms on the development of his art. This will involve a comparative analysis of Italian and Northern trends. However, the principal aim will be to show the place of Dürer's production within his social and cultural environment (humanist, popular, religious, etc). This approach should allow an understanding, not only of the artistic, but also of the cultural aspects of Dürer's art.

HISTORY OF ART 233

8 and 9. The patronage of Louis XIV

This option deals with the architectural and artistic policies of Louis XIV. It begins with the projected re-planning of Paris, with its focus on the east front of the Louvre, the re-making of the Tuileries gardens, and the extension of the city to St-Germain-en-Laye. With Louis' decision to transfer his residence and court to Versailles, Paris was superseded as a centre of activity and Versailles became the centre of the realm. This course naturally concentrates on the massive enlargement of the chateau, its embellishment with paintings and sculpture, the laying-out of the vast gardens and their decoration, and the re-planning of the town. Close attention is paid to Le Vau and Mansart among the architects, Le Nôtre among the landscape architects, and Le Brun as the designer, entrepreneur, and organizer of the painted schemes and the sculpture.

10 and 11. The Triumph of Classicism: Architecture in England and France, 1750–1830

The paper concentrates on the attempts to revitalise the classical tradition, firstly by a return to first principles involving new investigations of ancient Greek and Roman architecture, and secondly by the theory and practice of the Picturesque which sought to turn architecture into a language of emotional communication. The implications of this shift from classic to neo-classic are studied through an investigation of the work of Stuart, Adam, Chambers, Dance, Soane, Nash and Cockerell in England, Soufflot, Peyre, De Wailly, Boullée and Ledoux in France.

12 and 13. Fontainebleau and the French Renaissance 1494–1598

This paper deals with artistic and cultural developments in France, from the invasion of Italy by Charles VIII to the end of the Wars of Religion. The topic has many interesting aspects, such as the impact of Italian artists (from Leonardo da Vinci, who died in France, to Rosso, Primaticcio and Niccolo dell'Abate), the role of royal patronage, and the production of artists working independently of the 'Fontainebleau School.' Links between art and literature will be investigated, as will the use of allegorical and emblematic imagery, often with political overtones. Special attention will also be given to the decorative arts. The aim of the course will be to assess all these developments within the culture of the time.

14 and 15. Art in England and France during the Revolutionary and Napoleonic Period

This course will survey painting in England and France from 1785 to c.1820. It will concentrate on the impact on painting in France of the Revolution and the Empire and reactions, both positive and negative, to French developments in English Art. Interchange and cross-traffic between the two countries will be given considerable attention. Among the artists to be discussed in some detail will be Barry, Blake, Constable, David, Gericault, Girodet, Gros, Ingres, Turner, West and Wilkie.

16 and 17. Early Medieval Art in North-West Europe

The option traces the rise of early medieval art in the British Isles and on the Continent in the eighth and ninth centuries. Monuments of Insular and Carolingian art will be studied with a view to establishing the character and range of Early Christian works accessible as models. This will involve the critical assessment of the cultural achievements of the period, from the production of accurate facsimiles of earlier works, through interpretative free adaptations, to totally new departures in imagery and design. The problem of the dating of works in Ireland, Pictish Scotland, and Anglo-Saxon England relative to their Carolingian counterparts will be investigated. Other topics to be studied include the status of the illuminated book in the hierarchy of church treasures, the expression in art of royal and ecclesiastical authority, and the development of pictorial narrative in various media. Finally the option will evaluate the contribution which the period made to the art of the later Middle Ages, notably to Suger's St-Denis and Eadwine's Christchurch, Canterbury.

There will be eight pairs of special subjects in **1991**:

Papers 2 and 3 will be the same as Papers 2 and 3 in 1990.
Papers 4 and 5 will be the same as Papers 4 and 5 in 1990.
Papers 6 and 7 will be the same as Papers 6 and 7 in 1990.
Papers 8 and 9 will be the same as Papers 8 and 9 in 1990.
Papers 10 and 11 will be the same as Papers 10 and 11 in 1990.
Papers 12/13 will be The Mask and the Face: European Portraiture from Hogarth to Hockney.

Portraits are one of the most frequently-encountered art-forms, especially in Cambridge, and yet they have been very little studied in their own right. This Special Subject looks at the problems surrounding the interpretation of faces and figures, beginning with Hogarth's discrimination between 'character' and 'caricature', and the new 'scientific' physiognomics of the Enlightenment. It traces the ways in which portrait artists in Europe have drawn on other genres, such as history-painting, landscape and still-life to articulate their subjects, and considers the effect of photography on portrait-conventions. Among the artists discussed are Hogarth, Reynolds, Gainsborough, Batoni, Raeburn, David, Goya, Ingres, Gillray, The Pre-Raphaelites, Manet, Van Gogh, Picasso, Kokoschka, Dix, Beaton and Hockney.

Papers 14 and 15 will be the same as Papers 14 and 15 in 1990.
Papers 16 and 17 will be the same as Papers 16 and 17 in 1990.

The Preliminary Examination for the History of Art Tripos

The Examination in **1990** consists of a paper entitled 'Approaches to the history of art, with reference to buildings and works of art in and around Cambridge', together with certain papers from among the History of Art Tripos, namely Paper 1 (Approaches to the History of Art, with reference to works of criticism) and one pair of papers on a special subject, chosen from a list of subjects specified by the Faculty Board of Architecture and History of Art, which will be available in the Tripos the following year.

The paper entitled 'Approaches to the History of Art, with reference to buildings and works of art in and around Cambridge' covers a wide range of art historical materials and methods through study of accessible works of art and architecture. Candidates are expected to have examined the nature of the artistic problems confronted in individual works, to have gained a knowledge of the practices, attitudes, and theories of the respective periods of those works, and to have noted the changes in attitude towards the works that are characteristic of subsequent periods.

LAND ECONOMY

In this subject there are courses of study followed by candidates for:

The *Land Economy Tripos*, Parts I A, I B, and II.
The *M.Phil.* (*one-year*) in Land Economy.
The *Diploma* in Development Studies.

Land economy is the study of the use, development and management of land, other natural resources and the built environment. Drawing upon theories and concepts from economics, law and quantitative methods, the student analyses how the private sector allocates resources, what implications this has for society and why and how governments seek to alter private processes. Though the analysis concentrates upon economically advanced countries, the experience of selected low income countries is also covered.

The Land Economy course encourages students to develop an understanding of complex economic, political and administrative questions. For example, how can the efficiency and profitability of industries dealing with the land, natural resources and buildings be improved? How should private development objectives be balanced against the need to conserve social assets? Can the divisive effects of uneven economic development (whether within the nation, region or city) be ameliorated? In poor countries, what should governments do in the face of the explosive growth of urban areas and rural depopulation?

The development of an analytical capacity to tackle complex questions such as these provides a stimulating education for students who take Land Economy courses for all nine terms, or mix some Land Economy courses with those of another Tripos. Moreover, the explicit emphasis in coursework upon the interactions of the private and public sectors fits students of Land Economy, after graduation, to enter either of these sectors.

There are no special requirements for entry to the Department other than those required by the College and the University. Candidates who have specialised in sciences, social sciences or arts subjects at school have found Land Economy a subject in which they can further develop their skills and interests. Further advice on admissions procedure for prospective land economists may be obtained by telephoning or writing to the Secretary for Undergraduate Information at the Department.

Students can read Land Economy for one, two or three years. The coursework progresses from basic principles (particularly those drawn from economics and law) in the first year, to more advanced analysis and vocational applications in the second and third years. In their first year (Part IA) all students take introductory courses in economics, business and administrative law, accounting and data evaluation and a topics course on land, environment and structural change in the United Kingdom. In the second year those who have completed the Land Economy I A must take an advanced economic theory paper, a law paper and three others from a range of six on offer. Others beginning Land Economy in the second year must take the accounting and data evaluation course (unless specifically exempted), a law paper, an advanced economic theory paper and two others.

In the second year students may select courses which lead to a specific professional career, as for example, Chartered Surveying, or choose courses with a view to a range of jobs in business or administration within either the public or private sectors.

In the third year students have the maximum freedom to select those courses which most suit their interests, skills and professional objectives. Five papers, or four papers and a long essay based on a seminar course, have to be offered.

The coursework and supervisions in small groups are supplemented by field trips within the United Kingdom. Recent visits have included an examination of the role of a major shopping centre in a new town, the redevelopment of the London Docklands, the economics and management of public and private forests and the effectiveness of the public inquiry system as exemplified by Sizewell.

The Department has a large number of research projects funded by foundations, research councils, government departments and international agencies. Findings from the research are publicised and serve to stimulate the teaching programme.

Students who pass certain specified Tripos exams are exempted from the professional exams of the Royal Institution of Chartered Surveyors (RICS) in any one of three divisions – general practice, rural practice, and planning and development. When subsequently they pass a test of professional competence examination they can become a full professional associate and use the letters ARICS. Similar opportunities exist for those who wish to become a professional member of the Incorporated Society of Valuers and Auctioneers.

The employment prospects of graduates in Land Economy are

excellent. There is a wide range of opportunities in occupations dealing with land management, planning and development, in both urban and rural contexts, and in many other academic, professional, industrial and government spheres. Some graduates enter the surveying profession, in both public and private sectors. Others find interesting careers in banking and other financial institutions, in consultancy, in management, agriculture, and in urban and regional analysis.

The papers in the Tripos are divided into four groups and are as follows:

Group I

1. Introduction to economics

An introduction to economic concepts and theory and to the economic environment in which the private sector, governments, and public organizations operate.

2. Business and administrative law

An introduction to legal method, to the English legal system, and to government (central and local) in England and Wales, and an outline of important areas of law for business and commerce.

3. Accounting and data evaluation

An introduction to principles of accounting and data evaluation for use in private business and public organizations.

4. Land, environment, and structural change

Major economic, demographic, institutional, and technological changes and their impact upon the natural and built environments of the United Kingdom.

Group II

5. Economic theory and spatial analysis

Economic theory, including choice theory, production theory, the theory of markets, welfare theory, and growth theory, macro-economic modelling and policy, and selected topics of specific relevance to land economy.

6. Finance and investment analysis

Methods of financial and investment analysis used in business and management and in the public sector for administration and policy decisions, together with key aspects of the economic environment for investment.

7. Urban and regional economic analysis

The economic analysis of urban and regional development and of policies designed to influence them, including taxation and public finance and central–local relations.

GROUP III

8. Land, environment, and planning law

An introduction to the basic principles of land, environmental, and planning law in England and Wales, and in Scotland, and to the restrictions, both common law and statutory, on land use.

9. Business law

Aspects of law relevant to business and commerce, including the law of contract, company law, the law of agency, the law relating to fair trading and competition, the law of intellectual property and employment, and the law of insolvency.

GROUP IV

10. The built environment

Elements of building design and construction and the impact of social, economic, legal, and technological factors on the built environment.

11. Land markets and public policy

The nature and operation of urban and rural land markets, and policies for public intervention in land markets and in the process of property development.

12. Law and economics

The relationship between the disciplines of law and economics, including economic theories and analysis of law, the part played by economic theory in legal reasoning, the rôle of law in allocating resources and in correcting market failures, and economic and legal theories of value and of compensation.

Group V

13. Landlord and tenant law

The land law of England and Wales of particular relevance to the relationship of landlord and tenant: the common law of leases and of the rights and obligations of the parties to leases, and statutory regulation of residential, business, and agricultural tenancies.

14. Land use planning

The law, administration, practice, and theory of land use planning in Great Britain.

15. Valuation theory and practice

Economic, proprietary, and statutory influences on land value and the valuation of interests in land.

16. Agriculture, forestry, and rural development

The development and current patterns of agriculture, forestry, and the rural sector generally in the United Kingdom and an analysis of policies directly related to rural development.

17. Land policy and development economics

The rôle of land, agriculture, and natural resources in the growth and development of low income countries and their relationships to richer countries.

Part I A

A candidate must offer all four papers in Group I.

Part I B

A candidate must offer papers as follows:
- (a) if he has previously obtained honours in Part I A, he must offer five papers chosen from Groups II–IV, which will include Paper 5 and at least one of Paper 8 and Paper 9;
- (b) if he has not previously obtained honours in Part I A, he must offer:
    - (i) *either* Paper 2 *or* Paper 8;
    - (ii) Paper 3 and Paper 5;
    - (iii) two other papers chosen from Groups II–IV;

provided that a candidate who has obtained honours in Part I of the Economics Tripos, Part IA of the Engineering Tripos, Part IA of the Geographical Tripos, Part IA of the Mathematical Tripos, or Part IA of the Natural Sciences Tripos, or who has been granted exemption from the requirement to offer Paper 3, may offer instead a further paper chosen from Groups II–IV. Exemption to offer Paper 3 may be given to any candidate for honours who satisfies the Board that he has passed an examination of an acceptable standard in statistics or quantitative methods. Application for such exemption must be made in writing through the candidate's Tutor to the Secretary of the Board not later than the end of the second week of the Full Michaelmas Term preceding the examination; the candidate will be notified of the Board's decision not later than the division of the Michaelmas Term.

Part II

A candidate for honours must offer papers as follows:
  (*a*) if he has previously obtained honours in Part IB he must:
   either offer five papers chosen from Groups II–V, including at least two from Group V,
   or offer four papers chosen from Groups II–V, including at least one from Group V, and in addition participate in a seminar course and submit an essay not exceeding 10,000 words in length on a subject prescribed by the Board or chosen by him from a number of subjects so prescribed,
  provided that he may not offer any paper which he has previously offered in another Honours Examination;
  (*b*) if he has not previously obtained honours in Part IB he must offer five papers chosen from Groups II–V, including at least one from each group.

A candidate wishing to take part in a seminar course must make application through his Tutor to the Secretary of the Board before the end of the Full Easter Term next preceding the year in which he wishes to take part. The Board has power to accept or reject applications, having regard to the number of candidates who apply to take part in each course, and the Secretary of the Board will notify each candidate, before 31 July, of the acceptance or rejection of his application. Late applications, provided that they are submitted not later than the end of the first week of Full Michaelmas Term in the academical year in which the seminar course is to be conducted, may be accepted at the discretion of the Board. Further information on approved topics for the essay and details of the time-table and procedure for the submission of topics and of the essay are available from the Secretary, Board of Land Economy, 19 Silver Street, Cambridge, CB3 9EP.

Higher Degrees

The interdisciplinary nature of land economy is reflected in the wide range of economic, legal and social problems being studied by graduate students in the Department, both in an urban and a rural setting and in developed and developing countries. Recent research ranges from private home ownership and inner-city development to the impact of development programmes in rural regions; from the sale of council houses to leisure facilities and land-use planning; from the integration of immigrants in British cities to economic development in the Scottish Highlands; from the spatial impact of industrial development in Nigeria to land reform programmes in Sri Lanka and agricultural planning in Ghana.

It is possible to read for research degrees over one, two, or three years, for the M.Phil., M.Litt., or M.Sc. and Ph.D. respectively. All are examined by dissertation only. For the M.Phil. there is a prescribed course of instruction in some aspects of research methodology. In all cases candidates are encouraged to attend University lectures and seminars relevant to their chosen topic. In addition the Department offers an M.Phil. by coursework which allows for specialisation in urban and regional economics, agricultural and rural development and economic and land use planning in low income countries.

Regular Departmental seminars are arranged to encourage research students to expound their latest discoveries and benefit from the exchange of ideas and constructive criticism of their colleagues and staff. The Department has excellent computing facilities.

Awards for postgraduate study

The Board of Land Economy offer annually one Harold Samuel Studentship to finance studies leading to higher degrees. A successful applicant will be required to pursue research in economic, legal, or social matters relating to the use, tenure, or development of land. Candidature is open, but tenure of a studentship is conditional upon the student becoming a registered graduate student of the University. The electors will normally require a candidate to have obtained an honours degree in land economy, law, economics, geography, politics, sociology, history, agricultural economics, or town and country planning.

The Department also offers an M.E.P.C. studentship for students undertaking an M.Phil. by thesis. The terms of the award are similar to those of the Harold Samuel Studentship.

Graduates in these and other relevant subjects wishing to undertake research in the department are eligible for certain studentships and other awards offered by Colleges. Details of these can be obtained from Tutors' offices.

British students and others qualified by residence may be eligible for a studentship offered by the Economic and Social Research Council, the Natural Environment Research Council, the Ministry of Agriculture or other public body. These awards are highly competitive.

Further information on graduate facilities, awards, and application procedures, and on the Harold Samuel and M.E.P.C. Studentships in particular, may be obtained from the Secretary for Research Studies at the Department.

M.Phil. Degree

The scheme of examination for the one-year course of study in Land Economy will consist, at the choice of the candidate, of *either* Option A *or* Option B, as follows:

Option A

The examination consists of a thesis, of not more than 30,000 words in length, inclusive of diagrams, footnotes, bibliography, and appendices, on a subject approved by the Degree Committee for the Department of Land Economy. The examination includes an oral examination on the thesis, and on the general field of knowledge within which it falls.

Option B

For this Option the Degree Committee will publish a list of subjects for the examination to be held in the academical year next following; this list, which is divided into two groups, will include not less than five of the subjects specified in the two groups and may include not more than five additional subjects prescribed by the Degree Committee. In publishing the list the Degree Committee will announce whether each subject in the list shall be examined by a three-hour written paper, or by an essay of not more than 8,000 words in length which if the Degree Committee approve may deal with two distinct topics within the field of the subject, or by four essays each dealing with a distinct topic within the field of the subject and each of not more than 2,000 words in length, or by a three-hour written paper in addition to an essay, of not more than 4,000 words in length, dealing with a single topic in the field.

The examination consists of:

(a) an essay, of not more than 8,000 words* in length, on a topic approved by the Degree Committee, provided that the Degree Committee may permit a particular candidate to offer, in place of the essay and in addition to those subjects that he is required to offer under (b) below, one subject chosen with the approval of the Degree Committee from the list of subjects published by the Degree Committee;

and

(b) three subjects chosen by the candidate with the approval of the Degree Committee from that list of subjects, provided that each candidate shall offer at least one subject from each of the two groups; and provided also that a candidate may elect to offer a fourth subject chosen from that list with the approval of the Degree Committee, in which case the candidate's performance in the one subject in which the Examiners judge his work to be least good shall be discounted.

At the discretion of the Examiners the examination may include an oral examination on the essays and the written papers and on the general field of knowledge within which they fall.

The list of subjects in the two groups are:

Group 1. General subjects

1. Research methodology.
2. Investment analysis: public and private sectors.

Group 2. Special subjects

3. Urban and regional analysis.
4. Urban land markets and housing, policies and planning.

* One A4 page consisting largely of statistics or symbols shall be regarded as the equivalent of 250 words.

5. National planning and economic policy.

6. Agriculture, food and land policies in low-income countries.

7. Agriculture, environment, and rural development in developed countries.

Each subject will be examined by a three-hour written paper.

Diploma in Development Studies

The Diploma in Development Studies is a one-year course-work postgraduate qualification of an inter-disciplinary nature. The course is designed to provide a programme of study for those concerned with problems of underdevelopment and the formulation, planning and execution of development policies. The course is the responsibility of the Board of Graduate Studies and the Degree Committee for the Department of Land Economy, advised by a Committee of Management with representation from the relevant Faculties and Departments concerned with the subject matter of the teaching, namely, Economics and Politics, Geography, Land Economy, Social Anthropology, and Social and Political Sciences. Candidates are able to follow such other courses of lectures in other departments of the University which may be relevant to their particular needs and interests in the development context.

The examination consists of three written papers, each of three hours, as follows:

1. Theories of development

This paper offers the basic grounding required to understand development processes by introducing and explaining fundamental concepts and by showing how they have been applied to the analysis of development problems at the local, national, and international levels.

The aim is to survey ideas and ideologies of development in economic and social thought since the late eighteenth century; the contributions of the various social sciences to the subject, especially since the Second World War; theories of modernization and dependency; developing countries in the international system; global and national environmental issues.

2. Rural and urban development planning

This paper deals with development planning at the sectoral and local levels in the national context, and especially with the ways in which urban and rural communities can affect and are affected by it. Special attention will be paid to case studies, plans, and projects.

Rural development: land tenure, conversion and reform; individual, co-operative, and collective models and comparative post-reform performances; social and economic change at the village level; the penetration of capitalism in peasant economies; rural labour markets, household decision-making; cultural inhibitions with regard to development; popular religious and social dissent.

Urban development: urbanization theories in national and regional planning; migration determinants and dynamics; transformation of class structures and the emergence of an urban working class; urban management, finance, and housing policies; rural/urban inter-relationships.

3. The political economy of development

This paper deals with contemporary economic and political processes in developing countries. One aim is to develop students' competence in the numerical analysis of national income accounts and the application of social cost-benefit analysis, within the framework of an understanding of the political economy of development. The topics covered include macro- and micro-economics and their application to planning in poor and middle-income countries at the national, sectoral, and project levels. Another aim is to examine political processes both at the national level and at the local level: the role of the state, the bureaucracy, political parties, and the military, and relationships between the state and small-scale communities will be analysed. Emphasis will be placed on the effective contribution that economic theory and quantitative techniques can make to the practice of development planning, given the economic, political, and administrative constraints arising in these economies.

(See also M.Phil. Degree in the Economics and Politics of Development, p. 138.)

LATIN-AMERICAN STUDIES

M.Phil. (one-year course) in Latin-American Studies

The M.Phil. Degree in Latin-American Studies is intended to meet the needs and interests of graduates wishing either to gain knowledge of Latin America in preparation for a career associated with that part of the world, or to broaden their existing knowledge on an interdisciplinary basis before proceeding to further study and research for a higher degree. Candidates need not have any previous training in specifically Latin-American areas of study, although such experience would of course be an advantage. They will be expected, however, to have obtained a reading knowledge of the Spanish or Portuguese languages before coming into residence, or to be prepared to do so within the first weeks of residence.

To qualify for the M.Phil. Degree, a candidate must pursue the prescribed course and pass the examination. He must also reside for three terms. To be admitted as a candidate, an applicant must normally be a graduate and must be admitted to the status of Graduate Student by the Board of Graduate Studies.

A candidate may not take the examination on more than one occasion nor may he be a candidate for any other University examination in the same term.

Applications should be sent to the Secretary of the Board of Graduate Studies by 15 July of the academical year next preceding that in which he wishes to take the examination, including evidence of proficiency in Spanish or Portuguese.

A candidate pursues his studies for the M.Phil. Degree in Cambridge under a Supervisor appointed by the Degree Committee of the Faculty of Earth Sciences and Geography.

The scheme of examination, which includes an oral examination on any thesis submitted and upon the general field of knowledge in which it falls, consists of:

> (*a*) a thesis, not exceeding 15,000 words in length, including footnotes, tables, appendices, and bibliography, on a subject approved by the Degree Committee for the Faculty of Earth Sciences and Geography, which shall fall within the field of the group of papers in which the candidate offers two written papers;

and (*b*) three written papers, each of three hours, to be chosen by the candidate, subject to the approval of the Degree Committee, from the list of papers below. Each candidate must offer two papers from any one group together with any one paper from another group.

Group A

1. The agrarian sociology of the Andean zone

Institutions of land tenure from pre-Incaic period to the present day; ecological adaptations of the peasant economy; theories of peasant economy and capitalist agriculture; social movements and the impact of agrarian reform.

2. A topic in Andean agrarian sociology

Candidates must answer questions on one of the following topics: the historical development of peasant society and its economy; the impact of international trade on the establishment of capitalistic forms of agriculture; agrarian reform and peasant movements in Chile, Bolivia, and Peru; *la violencia* in Colombia; *indigenismo* and the *indigenista* novel.

3. Social anthropology of the Andean Zone and Upper Amazon

The ethnography of the Amerindian population of the Andes and the forest areas east of the Andes; ethnohistory, with particular reference to the interaction between highlands and lowlands; social organization, including demography, patterns of residence, kinship, local-level politics in relation to both Hispanic rule and national institutions; social and economic aspects of feasts; mythology and ritual with emphasis on comparison between highlands and lowlands and on syncretism with Catholicism; ethnic relations and their implications at the economic and social level and the syncretism of belief systems.

Group B

4. The history of Mexico

The effects of Spanish conquest; demographic movements during the colonial period; the rise of the great estate; fluctuations in the mining economy; Creole patriotism; independence and the conflicts between Liberals and Conservatives; positivism and the export economy; the revolution and the P.R.I.; agrarian reform and modern industrialization.

5. A topic in the history of Mexico

Candidates must answer questions on one of the following topics: Conquest society in New Spain, 1519-70; Bourbon Mexico, 1763-1810; the Mexican Revolution, 1910-40.

Group C

6. Spanish American literature

The poetry, essay, short story and novel in Spanish America since Independence. Candidates will study major authors individually (e.g. Rulfo, Paz) and/or works grouped thematically (e.g. the indigenist novel, the novel of dictatorship).

7. Two Spanish-American authors

The following options are available:

(i) César Vallejo and Pablo Neruda.
(ii) Jorge Luis Borges and Julio Cortázar.
(iii) José María Arguedas and Mario Vargas Llosa.
(iv) Carlos Fuentes and Alejo Carpentier.

Group D

8. Archaeology and ethnohistory of Mesoamerica and the Andean Zone

Prehispanic archaeology: earliest food production and sedentism, origins of ranking and stratification, early chiefdom and state formation, origins of urbanism, development of writing systems, and state religion. Late prehispanic and contact period ethnohistory: varieties of sociopolitical organization (empires, kingdoms, peasant communities), intellectual life, Mesoamerican trade and markets, Andean verticality and redistribution.

9. A topic in the archaeology and ethnohistory of either Mesoamerica or the Andean Zone

Candidates must answer questions on one of the following topics: urbanism and settlement patterns in Mesoamerica or the Andes; ecology and economics of prehispanic Mesoamerican or Andean societies; Aztec or Inca imperial organization and its precursors; Amerindian and sixteenth-century Spanish historical writings.

Group E

10. Urban sociology of Latin America

Dependent urbanization; classic and contemporary marginality theory; labour migration to cities; employment in cities; social mobilization among low-income groups, urban social movements and social change; survival strategies and social networks; comparative social welfare policies.

11. Issues in urban planning of Latin America

The history of economic planning and urban physical planning in Latin America; the politics and functions of planning; modes of housing production; the effectiveness of urban development policies since 1970; urban fiscal crisis and state intervention; community participation and planning.

12. Politics and sociology of economic development in Latin America

Theories of development and dependency; structural change and social movements in the countryside and agrarian reform; populism, corporatism, and the state in the industrialization process; bureaucratic authoritarian regimes; party political systems and grassroots political participation; trade unions; the Church.

Group F

13. Economics of modern Latin America

Post-war trends in the economic development of Latin America; industrialization and trade policies within a comparative framework; inflation and monetary developments; income distribution changes and their consequences; the role of the state; issues related to 'dependency' theory.

14. A topic in the economics of modern Latin America

Candidates must answer questions on one of the following topics: the effect of economic growth on absolute and relative income; changes among the urban and rural poor; aspects of planning; fiscal structures and public investment; problems of international finance and foreign investment.

A candidate may, by special permission of the Degree Committee, granted after considering the candidate's experience, special qualifications, and proposed topic, offer in place of (*a*) and (*b*) above a thesis of not less than 20,000 and not more than 30,000 words in length, including footnotes, tables, appendices, and bibliography, on a topic approved by the Degree Committee.

LATIN-AMERICAN STUDIES

Every candidate must submit a proposed thesis topic to the Secretary of the Degree Committee for the Faculty of Earth Sciences and Geography not later than the division of the Michaelmas Term next preceding the examination. The Secretary will communicate to the candidate the Degree Committee's acceptance or rejection of his choice of topic not later than the end of Full Michaelmas Term.

Candidates must submit two copies of their thesis to the Secretary of the Board of Graduate Studies not later than the division of the Easter Term in which the examination is held, unless the Board grant an extension.

Further details of the course can be obtained from the Director of the Centre of Latin-American Studies, History Faculty Building, West Road, Cambridge.

LAW

In this subject there are courses of study followed by candidates for:

The *Law Tripos*.
The *Examination in Criminal Law*.
The *Ordinary Examinations* for the Ordinary B.A. Degree.
The examination for the degree of *Master of Law*.
The *Diplomas in Legal Studies* and *International Law*.
The *M.Phil. Degree in Criminology* (one-year course).

The University law course is intended to give a deeper appreciation of the working of legal rules and institutions than is obtainable from a merely vocational training. It seeks to do this by providing an opportunity to see law in its historical and social context and to examine its general principles and techniques. The problems studied involve questions of interpretation, of logical reasoning, of ethical judgement, of political liberty and social control.

Lawyers play many parts in society. They are employed not only in private practice but in the civil service, local government, the legal departments of industrial and commercial firms and banks, and international organizations. While a Law degree is not at the moment necessarily a sufficient qualification for practice in these fields, the intending lawyer will derive a benefit from reading Law at the University that he will not otherwise obtain from his later training; and it is therefore very desirable that the future practitioner should include at least some Law in his University course.

Many undergraduates read Law who have no intention of becoming professional lawyers, particularly those who intend to go into industrial management, commercial life or accountancy. The study of Law provides an intellectual discipline in a subject of wide human interest.

A student who intends to read Law at the University need not have taken any particular subject at school. Some knowledge of History is desirable, particularly in relation to the later study of Constitutional and International Law; but there is no reason why a student who has shown ability in any school subject should not read Law. Many highly successful Law students come from purely scientific backgrounds.

LAW

Preliminary reading list

Students thinking of reading Law may be helped to make up their minds by reading the relevant section on Law in *University Choice*, ed. Klaus Boehm (Pelican Books), and should then study Glanville Williams: *Learning the Law* (Stevens paperback) and R. M. Jackson: *The Machinery of Justice in England*. Lord Denning's books: *The Discipline of the Law*, *The Due Process of Law*, *What Next in the Law* and *The Closing Chapter*, may also be of interest.

The following list is intended to provide, before a student comes into residence, a background to the subjects included in the first year's work, not to those in later years.

Roman law. R. H. Barrow: *The Romans* (Penguin Books); C. F. Kolbert: *The Digest of Justinian* (Penguin Books); J. A. Crook: *Law and Life of Rome*.

Criminal law. R. M. Jackson, *Enforcing the Law* (Penguin Books, but out of print) *or* Barnard, *The Criminal Court in Action* (3rd ed.); Glanville Williams, *The Proof of Guilt* (1963); Barbara Wootton, *Crime and Penal Policy* (1981); H. L. A. Hart, *Punishment and Responsibility* (Oxford Paperbacks); Rupert Cross, *The English Sentencing System* (1981).

Constitutional Law. H. Street, *Freedom, the Individual and the Law* (Penguin, 1982); S. A. de Smith, *Constitutional and Administrative Law* (Penguin, 1981).

Law of Tort. R. W. M. Dias and B. S. Markesinis, *Tort Law* (1984). J. A. Weir, *Casebook on Tort* (1988), Introduction; G. L. Williams and B. A. Hepple, *Foundations of the Law of Tort* (1984).

Visiting law courts

Any available opportunity should be taken of visiting law courts, and of working for a short time in a solicitor's office. Little will be learned about the substance of the law by listening, without preparation, to a case in court, but it will give greater insight into some of the problems that will be studied in the University.

The Law Tripos

The papers for the Law Tripos are divided into four groups and are as follows:

Group I
1. Roman law I.
2. Constitutional law.
3. Criminal law.
4. Law of tort.

Group II
10. Law of contract.
11. Land law.
12. International law.
13. Roman law II.

Group III
20. Administrative law.
21. Family law.
22. Legal history.
23. Criminology.
24. Criminal procedure and criminal evidence.
25. Equity.

Group IV
40. Commercial law.
41. Labour law.
42. Principles of conveyancing law.
43. Company law.
44. Contract and tort II.
45. Conflict of laws.
46. European Community law.
47. French law.
48. Jurisprudence.
49. Prescribed subjects (half-papers).

Each paper is of three hours' duration, except Paper 49 for each subject of which the examination consists of a half-paper of two hours' duration.

Part IA of the Tripos

This will be taken in the first year. A candidate must offer all the papers for Group I.

Part IB of the Tripos

This will be taken in the second year by a student who has obtained honours in Part IA of the Law Tripos or in another Honours Examination, or who has not yet obtained honours in an Honours Examination. A candidate must offer five papers chosen from among Papers 2 and 4 and Groups II and III, provided that he may not offer any paper which he has previously offered; and a candidate who has not previously obtained honours in Part IA may apply to the Faculty Board for leave to offer Paper 1, Roman law I, in substitution for any of the papers specified above.

Part II of the Law Tripos

This will normally be taken in the third year. A candidate must:

either offer five papers chosen from among Paper 3 (Criminal Law) and Groups III and IV,

or offer four papers chosen from among Paper 3 (Criminal Law) and Groups III and IV, and in addition participate in a seminar course and submit an essay in a subject prescribed by the Faculty Board or chosen by him from a number of subjects so prescribed,

provided that he may not offer any paper which he has previously offered.

Prescribed subjects (half-papers) (Paper 49)

The prescribed subjects (half-papers) are as follows:

In **1989/90**: Procedural law, crime and criminals, intellectual property, law and philosophy, law and ethics of medicine, taxation.

Seminar subjects

A candidate may choose to substitute for one paper of Part II participation in a seminar course, together with the submission of an essay.

The procedure for prescribing the subjects and for notifying a candidate's intention of participating in a seminar course, are as follows:

(*a*) Subjects prescribed will be provisionally notified to Directors of Studies by the Faculty Board and will be published in the *Reporter* before the end of the Lent Term preceding the year in which seminars on the subjects are to be conducted. The subjects provisionally notified for seminar courses in **1989–90** are:

The family in society. Explanations of criminal behaviour. The sociology of law. Human rights. Securities regulation.

(*b*) A candidate wishing to take part in a seminar course must send his application to the Secretary of the Faculty Board before the end of the Full Easter Term preceding the year in which he wishes to take part. The Board has power to accept or reject applications, having regard to the number of candidates who offer to take part in each course, and the Secretary of the Faculty Board of Law will notify each candidate, before 31 July, of the acceptance or rejection of his application. Later applications, provided that they are submitted not later than the end of the first week of the Full Michaelmas Term in the academical year in which the seminar course is to be conducted, may be accepted at the discretion of the Board and, if an application is accepted, the candidate will be notified before the division of the Michaelmas Term.

(c) Subjects prescribed by the Faculty Board will be published in the *Reporter* before the end of the Long Vacation period of residence preceding the year in which seminar courses are to be conducted. Any subject prescribed by the Faculty Board may be withdrawn by the Faculty Board upon notice given in the *Reporter* within the first three weeks of the Full Michaelmas Term in the academical year in which the seminar course was to have been conducted. Each candidate who has applied to take part in that seminar course will be informed of its withdrawal by the Secretary of the Faculty Board.

(d) A lecturer conducting a seminar course will set each candidate an essay upon a given subject. Essays must not, without the consent of the lecturer, exceed 12,000 words including footnotes and appendices. Each essay must state the sources from which it is derived and must be prefaced with a declaration signed by the candidate that it represents his own work unaided except as may be specified by him in the declaration. Each candidate must also declare that he has retained a photocopy of the essay submitted by him. The essay must be sent to the Secretary of the Faculty Board to reach him not later than the seventh day of the Full Easter Term in the year in which the examination is to be held. A candidate who submits his essay at a later time may be penalized. If the Examiners consider that an essay is not sufficiently legible, they may require that it be resubmitted in typescript.

Examination in Criminal Law

This examination will be held at the beginning of each academical year for candidates wishing to read Law for one year only. It consists of one paper, of three hours' duration, covering the same syllabus as the paper set for Paper 3 in the preceding Easter Term. The examination will enable an undergraduate reading Law for one year only to gain exemption from all six core subjects of the first part of the professional examinations by offering one subject (Criminal Law) and the remaining five in Part I B.

Exemption from professional examinations in England and Wales

As a result of the recommendations of the Ormrod Committee on Legal Education the professional bodies agreed to restrict entry into the legal profession (with some exceptions) to graduates. This change was to have occurred in 1978: it was then postponed to 1980 and is now being reconsidered altogether. Under the agreed scheme there was to have been a Common Professional Examination, common to both branches of the profession, but this never materialized. Both branches of the profession still have their independent qualifying examinations.

To gain exemption from those examinations a graduate will normally be required to have taken six 'core' subjects, as part of his degree course, before proceeding to his vocational training and the final (or Part II) examination. These six subjects, with the corresponding Cambridge papers, are:

1. Constitutional and administrative law (Paper 2).
2. Law of contract (Paper 10).
3. Criminal law (Paper 3).
4. Land law (Paper 11).
5. Law of tort (Paper 4).
6. Law of trusts (Equity) (Paper 25).

A student who reads Law for one year at Cambridge will normally take Paper 3 (Criminal law) as a single paper, preferably in October, and offer the remaining five papers in the Law Tripos. Students reading Law for two or more years will have no difficulty including all six core subjects in their courses. It is understood that graduates who have not taken all the core subjects in their degree courses will be allowed to take the missing subjects in examinations held by the professional bodies.

At present there are no exemptions from the Part II professional examinations. Subjects taken at Cambridge may not, however, be repeated in Part II of the Bar Examinations.

Intending barristers

Applications for exemption must be made on forms which are obtainable from The Secretary, Council of Legal Education, Gray's Inn Place, London, WC1 5DX. The applicant should also request the Registrary of the University as soon as possible after publication of the University class-lists to inform the Council of Legal Education of the applicant's class or marks in the relevant examination or papers. A fee of £5 must accompany this request but no further fee is payable in respect of any subsequent request. The Council of Legal Education will inform the applicant whether exemption has been granted.

Intending solicitors

Applications for exemption must be made to the Secretary of The Law Society, 113 Chancery Lane, London, WC2A 1PL, on a form obtainable from him or from a Director of Studies.

Each year the University sends to the Law Society a list of those intending solicitors who have passed the six 'core' subjects, and an applicant whose Director of Studies, has given notification that he has passed in these subjects need not request a certificate from the Registrary, nor make individual application to the Law Society.

The Examinations in Law for the Ordinary B.A. Degree

Law Ordinary Examination I consists of three papers chosen from among groups I–III of the groups of papers for the Law Tripos.

Law Ordinary Examination II consists of three papers chosen from among Groups III–IV of the groups of papers for the Law Tripos.

A candidate for either of the Ordinary Examinations may not offer any paper which he has taken in a previous year in an examination which he has passed or on which he has received an allowance.

A student who has passed either of the examinations may not be a candidate again for the same examination.

The degree of Master of Law

The LL.M. Degree can be obtained by Cambridge graduates and also by graduates of other universities and, in exceptional cases, by other students who have passed an examination in law. The regulations for admission to the LL.M. have recently been changed and there are certain transitional provisions.

(*a*) A Cambridge graduate who takes the LL.M. Examination will normally do so in his fourth year. A Cambridge graduate is entitled to present himself as a candidate for the LL.M. provided that he has proceeded to the B.A. Degree and

either (i) has obtained honours, or has attained the honours standard in Part I of the Law Tripos before 1980, or in Part IB or Part II before 1989,

or (ii) has before 1 October 1987 been called to the Bar or admitted as a solicitor in England and Wales or in Ireland, or admitted as an advocate or a law agent in Scotland.

A person who fulfils these conditions may be allowed by his College to return into residence for that year, but does not need to keep further terms and may therefore, if he wishes, take the examination while out of residence. Cambridge graduates who do not fulfil these conditions will not be entitled to present themselves as candidates for the LL.M. as of right, nor take the examination while out of residence, but will have to seek admission to the course in accordance with paragraph (*c*) below.

(*b*) A graduate of another university who has been admitted as an Affiliated Student may, on application through his tutor, apply for leave to be a candidate for the LL.M. Examination in his second or later year if he has obtained honours in Part IB or Part II of the Law Tripos in a preceding year but has not proceeded to the B.A. Degree. The Faculty of Law does not usually grant leave unless the applicant has obtained class I or II:1 honours in that examination.

(*c*) A student who is not qualified under either of the two preceding paragraphs may be allowed by the Degree Committee of the Faculty to take the LL.M. Examination after keeping at least two terms, if he satisfies the Committee that by reason of his previous study of law he is qualified to engage in postgraduate study of law at an advanced level. In giving approval the Committee may require a student to obtain such class or grade as they may think fit in any examination taken or to be taken by the student. On passing the LL.M. Examination the student may then proceed to the LL.M. Degree when he has kept three terms.

Any student who wishes to be a candidate for the LL.M., whether falling within paragraph (*a*), (*b*), or (*c*), must apply *not later than 31 January preceding the year in which the examination takes place* Applications by persons who are members of the University must be made to the Secretary of the Degree Committee through the Director of Studies in Law for the College of which the applicant is a member. Applications by persons who are not members of the University should be made to the Board of Graduate Studies.

The following papers, each of three hours' duration, are prescribed for the LL.M. Examination to be held in **1990**:

1. Taxation.
2. *Conflict of laws.
3. Restitution and remedies.
4. International sales.
5. Securities regulation.
6. History of English civil and criminal law, 1154–1485.
7. History of English civil and criminal law, 1485–1710.
8. Sources and literature of English law, 1200–1800.
9. History of European private law since 1500.
10. Law and practice of civil liberties.
11. Judicial review of administration action.
12. Jurisprudence.
13. Comparative aspects of private and procedural law.
16. Current problems in criminal law.
17. Private law and political theory.
21. Law of peace.
22. Law of the Sea.
23. Law of armed conflict, use of force, and peacekeeping.
24. Pacific settlement of disputes.
25. *European Community law.
26. Corporate law and finance.

A candidate must offer either four of the prescribed papers or three such papers and a thesis, which must be not less than 5,000 and no more than 15,000 words in length. The proposed title of a thesis must

* **No candidate may offer both Paper 2 and Paper 25 without leave of the Faculty Board of Law.**

be submitted to the Faculty Board not later than the division of the Michaelmas Term in the academical year in which the candidate presents himself for the examination and the title must be approved by the last day of the Full Michaelmas Term. The approval of the Faculty Board will not normally be given to a topic which falls within the scope of any of the papers which the candidate is offering in the examination, nor will they normally approve a topic which falls within the scope of one of the other prescribed papers. In approving the topic the Faculty Board may direct that it shall qualify a candidate for the inclusion of his name in the class-list as having satisfied the Examiners in a particular section. Candidates intending to submit a thesis are requested to consult the Faculty's *Notes for Guidance* contained in the *LL.M. Handbook*.

Each thesis must be prefaced by a declaration signed by the candidate that it represents his own work unaided except as may be specified by him in the declaration, and that the work has been done principally in the academical year in which he presents himself for the examination; and must contain a statement of, or notes on, the sources from which the thesis is derived, including any written work which the candidate has previously submitted or is concurrently submitting for any other degree, diploma, or similar qualification at any university or similar institution.

The thesis must be submitted to the Secretary of the Faculty Board of Law not later than 1 May preceding the examination.

The syllabuses and recommended reading lists for the prescribed papers may be obtained from the Secretary, Faculty Board of Law, Old Syndics Building, Mill Lane, Cambridge, CB2 1RX.

The Diplomas in Legal Studies and International Law

A candidate for the Diploma in Legal Studies or the Diploma in International Law must be admitted as a Graduate Student, on the recommendation of the Degree Committee of the Faculty of Law, by the Board of Graduate Studies, who will fix the date of commencement of his candidature. At least three terms must have been kept by a candidate before he is qualified to receive a Diploma. He must study for it in the University for at least three terms under the direction of a Supervisor appointed by the Degree Committee and under any special conditions that the Committee may prescribe in his case, but a candidate who is a graduate of the University may, on the recommendation of the Degree Committee and with the approval of the Board of Graduate Studies, study at a university or institution outside England as a satisfaction in whole or in part of the requirement of study for a Diploma.

Not earlier than the end of the second, nor, except by special permission of the Degree Committee, later than the end of the fifth term after the term in which his candidature commenced, a candidate must send to the Secretary of the Board of Graduate Studies, with the prescribed fee, a thesis on a subject, previously approved by the Degree Committee, which falls within the field of Comparative Law or of International Law. The thesis must not exceed 20,000 words except with the special permission of the Degree Committee. It must afford evidence of serious study by the candidate, and of his ability to discuss a difficult problem critically. The Secretary of the Board of Graduate Studies will send the thesis to the Degree Committee, who after referring it to an Examiner, and considering his report, and the reports of the Supervisor will resolve that the Diploma be awarded or refused. The Degree Committee may allow a candidate to re-submit his thesis within a time limit fixed by them which will normally not extend beyond the end of the term following the notification of this decision.

A Graduate Student who has been given leave by the Board of Graduate Studies to count the period or any part of it during which he has been a candidate for the Diploma towards a course of research for the degree of Ph.D., M.Sc., or M.Litt., will not be entitled to be awarded the Diploma so long as he remains on the register of Research Students nor if he subsequently proceeds to the degree of Ph.D., M.Sc., or M.Litt.

The Examination in Criminology for the M.Phil. Degree (one-year course)*

This is a postgraduate degree obtainable in one academic year. It is open to graduates with a good degree in any subject, although in practice the majority of students have degrees in law, psychology or social or political sciences. The scheme of examination consists of:

(*a*) an exercise in designing a proposal for, or in critically evaluating, a project of empirical research on a subject chosen from a list announced by the Examiners; a candidate's report on his research exercise must not exceed 3,000 words, including notes and appendices;

and

(*b*) a thesis of not more than 15,000 words, including notes and appendices, on a topic approved by the Degree Committee for the Faculty of Law, falling within one of the following areas of study:

>The sociology of crime and deviance
>Psychiatric and psychological aspects of crime and its treatment
>The aims, effects, and problems of penal measures
>The development of criminal law and the administration of criminal justice

and

(*c*) five essays, each of not more than 3,000 words in length, chosen by the candidate from lists of topics announced by the Examiners.

The examination may include, at the discretion of the Examiners, an oral examination upon the thesis and on the general field of knowledge within which it falls, and such an oral examination may include questions relating to one or more of the other pieces of work submitted by the candidate under (*a*) and (*b*) above.

In place of sections (*a*), (*b*), and (*c*) of the above scheme a candidate may, by special permission of the Degree Committee for the Faculty of Law granted after considering his experience, special qualifications, and proposed topic, offer a thesis of not more than

---

* Applications for admission to the course should be submitted to the Board of Graduate Studies for consideration by the Institute of Criminology, which is part of the Faculty of Law and provides the relevant teaching.

30,000 words in length, including notes and appendices, on a criminological topic approved by them. The Examiners may, at their discretion, examine the student orally upon the thesis and on the general field of knowledge within which it falls.

MATHEMATICS

In this subject, which is regarded as including mathematical physics, there are courses of study followed by candidates for:

The *Mathematical Tripos*, which is divided into four Parts.
The *Certificate of Advanced Study in Mathematics*.
The *Diploma in Mathematical Statistics*.

There are also courses of study in Computer Science (cf. p. 110) suitable to be taken after Part IA of the Mathematical Tripos.

The Mathematical Tripos

The Tripos is divided into four Parts, IA, IB, II, and III. The normal course of study for a student in Mathematics is Part IA taken in the first year, followed by Part IB taken in the second year, and Part II in the third year leading to a B.A. Degree. Some students then stay on for a fourth year to take Part III.

Part IA

A candidate may take Part IA in his first year, or, if he has obtained honours in another Tripos, in the year after doing so but not later than his third year. In addition to serving as a preparation for further Parts of the Tripos, Part IA provides a suitable course for students who wish to have only an introduction to mathematics and its applications before taking up their main subject (which might be physics, theoretical physics, chemistry, engineering, economics, computer science, etc.).

Candidates may offer *either* Option (*a*): Pure and Applied Mathematics *or* Option (*b*): Mathematics with Computer Science. Candidates for Option (*a*) must offer Papers 2, 3 on Pure Mathematics and Papers 1, 4 on Applied Mathematics. Candidates for Option (*b*) must offer Papers 2, 4 together with Paper 5 on Pure and Applied Mathematics and Paper 6 on Computer Science; they must also undertake laboratory work on computer hardware.

Courses of lectures for Option (a) are given on the following topics:

Analysis I (24).
*Analysis II (24).
Algebra I (Vector Spaces) (24).
*Algebra II (Groups) (24).
*Probability and its
  Applications (24).
Vector Calculus (24).
*Linear Systems (24).
Newtonian Dynamics and
  Special Relativity (24).
*Electrodynamics (20).
*Potential Theory (16).

Those courses indicated by * are given in two versions, Standard and Fast. Attendance at a Fast version will lead to a slightly larger choice of questions in the examination. Numbers of lectures are given in parentheses after course titles. Candidates for Option (b) omit the courses on Newtonian Dynamics and Special Relativity and Analysis II and replace them with the following:

Programming and Data Structures (16).

Discrete Mathematics (16).

Introduction to Computer Hardware (16).

Part I B

A candidate may take Part I B in his first or second year, or, if he has obtained honours in another Honours Examination, one or two years after doing so but not later than his fourth year. Four papers, each of three hours, will be set for examination and every candidate must offer all four papers. Courses given for Part I B are of three types: core courses, which each candidate should attend most of; additional courses, which each candidate is advised to attend between one-half and two-thirds of; and a computing course. Core courses are given in two versions, Standard and Fast. The examination papers will be of cross-section type with the number of questions on each course in proportion to the number of lectures for that course; in the case of a core course this is taken to be the number of lectures for the Standard version. The course Computational Projects, which comprises lectures and practical work, is assessed on the basis of notebooks handed in by the candidates, and no questions are set on it in the examination; the maximum credit available is about equivalent to that for a normal sixteen-hour lecture course, and the credit gained is added directly to the credit gained in the examination

Courses of lectures are given for the Part I B year on the following topics (where two numbers are given after the title of a core course the first refers to the number of lectures in the Standard version and the second to the number in the Fast version):

Core courses

Complex variable (24, 16). Mathematical Methods (24, 24).
Algebra III (16, 16).   Quantum Mechanics (16, 16).
Statistics (16, 16).

Additional courses

Logic (12).   Numerical Analysis (16).
Rings (12).   Markov Chains (16).
Further Topics in Algebra (12).   Principles of Dynamics (24).
Analysis III (24).   Fluid Dynamics I (24).
Geometry (12).   Relativistic Electrodynamics (16).
Optimisation (16).

Computing course

Computational Projects

Part I B of the Mathematical Tripos provides a firm foundation for a later more specialized study of pure mathematics or mathematical physics or other applications of mathematics. It is also possible to transfer at this stage to another Tripos, for example Natural Sciences or Engineering, or to Computer Science or Management Studies; a student should first seek advice on whether he is adequately prepared for the proposed new course of study.

Part II

A candidate who has obtained honours in Part I B or in any other Honours Examination except Part I A may take Part II one or two years after doing so, but not later than his fourth year. Four papers are set for examination and every candidate must offer all four papers. The first three of these contain concisely stated problems of medium length, commonly based on a piece of bookwork which may also be asked for. These papers are of cross-section type. The fourth paper contains one question on each course; the questions are designed to test the candidate's proficiency at sustained exposition of a topic, and not more than three may be attempted. Candidates are expected to be familiar with the content of about 136 lectures. No questions are set in the examination on the course Computational Projects in Applied

Mathematics; credit is gained by the submission of notebooks by the candidate, and the maximum credit obtainable is approximately equivalent to that available for a twenty-four-lecture course. Students may be examined on any combination of the following courses of lectures, but the Secretary of the Faculty Board cannot always guarantee to arrange times of lectures so as to avoid clashes, especially over widely disparate subject-areas.

Groups (16).
Graph Theory (24).
Measure Theory (24).
Differential Analysis and
 Geometry (24).
Algebraic Geometry (24).
Algebraic Topology (24).
Linear Analysis (24).
Theory of Numbers (16).
Set Theory and Logic (16).
Stochastic Processes (16).
Principle of Statistics (24).
Convex Optimization (24).
Dynamic Stochastic
 Systems (16).
Probability Theory (24).
Communication Theory (24).
Nonlinear Differential
 Equations (24).
Dynamical Systems (16).
Solitons and Nonlinear
 Waves (12).
Methods of Mathematical
 Physics (24).

Representation Theory (16).
Galois Theory (24).
Riemann Surfaces (24).
Elementary Quantum
 Electronics (12).
Electrodynamics of
 Media (24).
Waves (24).
Cosmology (12).
Statistical Physics (24).
Foundations of Quantum
 Mechanics (24).
Partial Differential and
 Integral Equations (24).
Mechanics of Solids (24).
Fluid Dynamics II (24).
Applications of Quantum
 Mechanics (24).
Numerical Analysis (16).
General Relativity (16).
Approximation Methods (12).
Mathematical Economics (12).

Computing course

Computational Projects in Applied Mathematics.

Part III and the Certificate of Advanced Study in Mathematics

A candidate may take Part III in his third or fourth year if he has obtained honours in a Part of any Tripos Examination. In practice candidates from Cambridge have almost invariably taken either Part II of the Mathematical Tripos or Part II of the Natural Sciences Tripos in Physics or Theoretical Physics in the preceding year.

A graduate from another university or other applicant may take Part III in his first year provided he obtains the permission of the Degree Committee of the Faculty of Mathematics and is admitted by a College. The normal requirement is a first class degree in mathematics, physics, or engineering. Those interested in this possibility are invited to write to either the Head of the Department of Applied Mathematics and Theoretical Physics (Silver Street) or the Head of the Department of Pure Mathematics and Mathematical Statistics (16 Mill Lane) for further information. Technically, candidates who take Part III on this basis are not candidates for honours since they do not obtain a degree, but their results are published and classified in the same manner as for the other candidates, although on a separate list.

Graduates of Cambridge or of another university who attain the honours standard in the examination for Part III are awarded the Certificate of Advanced Study in Mathematics.

The subjects of the examination are those which have been treated in lecture courses during the academical year. There are normally about sixty such courses, which range over the whole extent of pure mathematics, statistics and the mathematics of operational research, applied mathematics and theoretical physics. They are designed to cover those advanced parts of the subjects which are not normally given in first degree courses but which are an indispensable preliminary to independent study and research. Although many candidates are prospective Research Students, Part III also provides a valuable course in mathematics and in its applications for those who want further training before taking posts in industry, teaching, or research establishments.

Papers of two or three hours' duration are set on courses of sixteen or twenty-four lectures respectively. Candidates must either offer papers whose total duration is not more than nineteen hours, or they must offer papers whose total duration is not more than sixteen hours together with an essay on one of the assigned set of topics. Each essay must state the sources consulted and must be prefaced with a declaration signed by the candidate that it represents his own work unaided except as may be specified by him in his declaration. The Examiners may examine a candidate *viva voce* on the subject of his essay. Candidates have a free choice of the combination of courses which they offer, though naturally they tend to select groups of cognate courses. The final decision about which courses to offer and whether to submit an essay does not have to be made until the end of the first quarter of Easter Term.

Weekly supervision classes are provided for Part III students taking courses in the Department of Applied Mathematics and Theoretical Physics and there is a teaching officer of the Department who advises them on courses of study, future careers, and other similar matters. There is a work room and small library available for their exclusive use in the Department.

Students taking courses given by members of the staff of the Department of Pure Mathematics and Mathematical Statistics receive informal teaching in addition to the lecture courses; this varies from course to course according to need. There is a work room in the Department for the exclusive use of Part III students, who are also encouraged to use the Departmental Library.

The Diploma in Mathematical Statistics

The aim of the Diploma course is to equip graduates of predominantly mathematical preparation for the vocation of statistician. To this end it includes, not merely classes in mathematical and applied statistics as such, but also classes in probability, operational research, and other relevant options. The course normally extends for nine months from 1 October. Candidates have to be approved for admission to the course by the Degree Committee of the Faculty of Mathematics, which requires evidence of previous familiarity with probabilistic and statistical ideas as well as evidence of substantial mathematical competence.

Instruction for the course is given at the Statistical Laboratory in the Department of Pure Mathematics and Mathematical Statistics, 16 Mill Lane, Cambridge, under the general supervision of the Director of Studies for the Diploma in Mathematical Statistics, to whom completed application forms should be sent by 8 March if possible.

Classes, practicals, etc., are given at the Statistical Laboratory. Candidates are also required to undertake a practical project, which may come from some other university department, or local industry or research units. Considerable importance is attached to this project; the project report is assessed and taken into account by the Examiners.

Each candidate is assigned two Supervisors; one is normally a University teaching officer in the Statistical Laboratory and the other is normally a member of the Department in which the candidate is to do his practical work.

A wide variety of fields of application is usually open to candidates within, for example, the sciences, medicine, agriculture, economics, engineering, operational research, criminology and linguistics.

Only a small number of candidates can work in any one applied field in a given year, and so intending candidates should suggest as wide as possible a range of practical topics in which they are or are prepared to become interested.

The examination consists of three theory papers (statistical theory and detailed methodology, probability and applications, stochastic processes and methods of operational research) and one practical paper. BBC micro-computers with Torch disc drives are used in the practical examination, and all candidates receive instruction in the use of the University mainframe computer, and have access to this and the micro-computers throughout the course.

Candidates are encouraged to attend seminars and to be aware of research activity in the Laboratory. It is not uncommon for Diploma students to continue with a Ph.D., either in the U.K. or abroad. They also find careers in industry, computing, actuarial work, the Civil Service, consulting in statistics and operational research, and teaching.

MEDICAL SCIENCES

The Medical Sciences Tripos*

The Medical Sciences Tripos can be read by candidates for Medical or Veterinary Degrees during their preclinical studies.

Parts I A and I B of the Tripos contain subjects which enable candidates to satisfy certain requirements for Medical and Veterinary Degrees and Section I of Part II (General) is taken by those who wish to spread the study of these subjects over three rather than two years. The subjects are treated as scientific disciplines without undue vocational bias.

All candidates read Anatomy, Biochemistry, Medical Genetics, and Physiology in their first year for Part I A. A course in Medical Sociology is also given but is not examined in the Tripos; medical students have to pass a Second M.B. Examination in this; Medical Sociology may be deferred to the second or third year of the Medical Sciences Tripos. There is also a course in Medical Statistics with subsequent in-course assessment in Part I B and Part II (General) Section I practical classes. Undergraduates may then choose between the two-year and the three-year preclinical courses.

If they choose the former, they will read for Part I B Anatomy and Physiology, Neurobiology, Pathology, Pharmacology and Psychology if they are medical students or Veterinary Anatomy, Pathology, Pharmacology and General and Special Veterinary Physiology if they are veterinary students. In their third year they have a number of options. They may offer Section II of Part II (General) which comprises **either** two of the Special Subjects History of Medicine, Pathology, Biological Anthropology, and Social Psychology **or** Special Subject Pathology together with two Elective Subjects from about ten listed below. Alternatively, they may offer Part II or Part II (General) of the Natural Sciences Tripos. Those undergraduates who wish to proceed to a Clinical Medicine course which is less than three years (which is provided at Cambridge but not at London) must spend their third year reading a subject which is approved by the General Medical Council as constituting a 'year of medical study'. The Council's ruling is, however, liberal and such subjects as History and Philosophy of Science, Biological Anthropology, Computer Science, Management Studies, Social and Political

---

* The structure of this Tripos is currently under reveiew. The Part I B examination structure may be changed in the Michaelmas Term 1990 if proposals before the University are approved.

MEDICAL SCIENCES

Sciences, and Zoology are among those approved by the Faculty Board of Clinical Medicine. If a three-year clinical course is to be taken (as provided at London) then the third undergraduate year may be spent reading for any Tripos (e.g. History of Art; Law; Philosophy).

Undergraduates who choose to do the *three-year* preclinical course postpone Pathology and Pharmacology until their third year. For Part I B they take the same Anatomy and Physiology as in the two-year course; if medical students, they take also the same Neurobiology and Psychology, and an Elective Subject chosen from a list of six; if veterinary students, they take the Veterinary Anatomy and General and Special Veterinary Physiology of the two-year course but instead of Psychology and an Elective Subject, they have a course in Animal Behaviour.

Such undergraduates spend their third year reading for Section I of Part II (General), taking the same Pathology and Pharmacology courses as in the two-year course and also reading an Elective Subject from the list of ten. Veterinary students take a further course in Animal Behaviour.

Transfers to the Medical Sciences Tripos are usually from the Natural Sciences Tripos. This may happen after Part I A provided that the undergraduate's College is willing to make one of its limited quota places available. Such candidates take the two-year preclinical course, reading for Parts I A and I B of the Medical Sciences Tripos in their second and third years. Undergraduates who have read Physiology in Part I A of the Natural Science Tripos read Pathology instead of Physiology in Part I A of the Medical Sciences Tripos and omit Pathology in Part I B. Transfers from other Triposes require detailed advice. The provisions for Affiliated Students are similar to those in the Natural Sciences Tripos.

Part I A

Candidates are required to take the following papers for Part I A:

Anatomy
Biochemistry
Medical Genetics
Physiology

but those who have already offered Physiology in Part I A of the Natural Sciences Tripos take Pathology instead of Physiology.

A suitable previous training for this Tripos is Chemistry, Physics, and *either* Biology (or Zoology) *or* Mathematics to Advanced Level in the General Certificate of Education. Candidates lacking Biology or Mathematics are advised to read these subjects if they are spending a third year in the sixth form.

The course is given by members of the Departments of Anatomy, Biochemistry, Community Medicine, Genetics, and Physiology.

Teaching in anatomy includes lectures on the anatomy of tissues, on cytology and cytogenetics, and on early embryology. Practical classes relate to these subjects. Medical students dissect the limbs and trunk and lectures are given on certain aspects of the anatomy of these parts. Veterinary students dissect the dog and receive some alternative lectures.

There is a course of general biochemistry which includes lectures on the structure, functions, and biosynthesis of the components of living tissues: proteins, nucleic acids, carbohydrates, fats, hormones, vitamins, etc. The course includes studies of enzymes, the liberation and utilisation of energy, metabolic processes and their control in animals, plants, and micro-organisms. The practical classes are designed to introduce students to biochemical methods and their application to the study of living systems. Lectures on medical genetics are integrated with relevant biochemistry.

The physiological systems covered in the first year include nerve, neuromuscular transmission, muscle, circulation, respiration, excretion, water balance, digestion, absorption, and thermo-regulation. There are related practical classes in experimental physiology and in histology.

Lectures on Medical Sociology and on Medical Statistics are also given but are not examined in the Tripos. However, Medical Sociology is a subject in the Second M.B. Examination.

The Part I A examinations taken at the end of the first year are as follows:

Anatomy. **The written paper consists of three sections, Sections A, B, and C, containing questions on, respectively, general anatomy, human anatomy, and veterinary anatomy. Section A will include cell and tissue anatomy, aspects of human biology, and developmental anatomy. Section B will include questions on topographical and functional anatomy. Section C will include questions on the topographical and functional anatomy of the dog. The questions in Sections B and C will deal mainly with the general architecture of the body and will not require a detailed knowledge**

MEDICAL SCIENCES

except of the most important regions dissected during the first year. The practical examination may include a *viva voce* examination.

Biochemistry. The written paper will require a knowledge of the chemical processes associated with the life and growth of animals, plants, and micro-organisms. There will be a practical examination which will not involve laboratory work but may include data handling questions and questions on practical aspects of the subject.

Medical Genetics. The paper will require a knowledge of the principles of heredity as their application to human or veterinary medicine.

Physiology. The written paper will be the paper in Physiology in Part IA of the Natural Sciences Tripos; it will be of such a nature as to test the candidate's understanding of the broad principles of Physiology. There will be most emphasis on the physiology of nerve and neuromuscular transmission, muscle, autonomic nervous system, cardiovascular system, respiration, kidney, salt and water balance, digestion, absorption and temperature regulation.

In the practical examination candidates will be examined in histology and experimental physiology.

Pathology. The paper and practical will be those in Part IB of the Medical Sciences Tripos.

Part IB

Every candidate must offer the written papers and practical examinations for the subjects of Part IB in accordance with one of the following options (*a*)–(*f*):

- (*a*) Anatomy and Physiology, Neurobiology, Psychology, one Elective Subject.
- (*b*) Anatomy and Physiology, Neurobiology, Pathology, Pharmacology, Psychology.
- (*c*) Anatomy and Physiology, Neurobiology, Pharmacology, Psychology.
- (*d*) General Veterinary Physiology, Special Veterinary Physiology, Veterinary Anatomy.
- (*e*) General Veterinary Physiology, Pathology, Pharmacology, Special Veterinary Physiology, Veterinary Anatomy.
- (*f*) General Veterinary Physiology, Pharmacology, Special Veterinary Physiology, Veterinary Anatomy.

Undergraduates offering options (*a*) or (*d*) take Pathology and Pharmacology in their third year. Those taking options (*c*) or (*f*) must have offered Pathology in Part IA.

The course is given by members of the Departments of Anatomy, Experimental Psychology, Pathology, Pharmacology, and Physiology, together with contributions from many others in the Elective Subjects.

Teaching in Anatomy includes lectures and practical classes on embryology, morphology, and radiological anatomy. Medical students dissect the head and neck and receive lectures relating to this part. They later dissect the brain and study the structure of the central nervous system at a microscopic level. Veterinary students study the anatomy of birds and domestic ungulates and receive some alternative lectures. There are also courses in neuroanatomy and the anatomy of reproduction. The latter is integrated with the teaching of the physiology of reproduction in a course of Reproductive Biology.

The Physiology lectures also deal with endocrinology and, for medical students the teaching of neurophysiology is integrated with neuroanatomy in a course of Neurobiology. Veterinary students receive separate lectures in Neurophysiology.

There is a course in general pathology which includes the variations which may occur in the structure and functions of living tissues and organs and discusses the causes of such changes. The course includes cellular pathology, immunology, microbiology, and virology. Practical classes are an important feature of the course and are integrated as far as possible with the lectures.

Lectures in pharmacology deal with the general principles of drug action and on the specific effects of some drugs. They continue with a consideration of selective toxicity and the effects of drugs on the endocrine, nervous, cardiovascular, and respiratory systems.

Short courses of lectures in psychology and in animal behaviour are also given.

The examinations taken at the end of the second year are as follows:

Anatomy and Physiology

The written paper will consist of two sections. Section A will contain questions on the anatomy and embryology of the head and neck. Section B will contain questions on endocrinology and reproductive biology. The practical examination, which may include a *viva voce* examination, will similarly be divided into two sections.

MEDICAL SCIENCES

General Veterinary Physiology

The written paper will contain questions on endocrinology, reproductive biology, and neurophysiology. The practical examination, which may include a *viva voce* examination may contain questions that involve data handling.

Neurobiology

The written paper will require knowledge of the structure and functions of the central nervous system and of the special sense organs. In the practical examination candidates will be examined in neuroanatomy and in experimental neurophysiology; questions may be included which require an elementary knowledge of statistical procedures.

Pathology. The examination will require an understanding of the damage caused to the structure and function of cells, tissues, and organs of higher animals and man by both living and inanimate agents. Knowledge will be required of the biology of viruses, bacteria, fungi, protozoa and metazoa as parasites, of immunological and other responses induced by these agents, and of the genetic, social, epidemiological, and preventive aspects of disease. The practical examination will include laboratory work.

Pharmacology. The written paper will require knowledge of the actions of drugs on whole organisms and mammalian systems, including the central nervous system, and also of the mode of drug action at the cellular, sub-cellular, and molecular levels. There will be a practical examination which will not involve laboratory work. In the written paper and in the practical examination questions may be included which require an elementary knowledge of statistical procedures.

Psychology. The paper will require knowledge of experimental psychology and some of its applications to medicine. Particular topics include learning and memory; perception and information processing; intelligence and development; emotion and its physiological basis; and social psychology.

Veterinary Anatomy

The paper will contain questions on cell and tissue anatomy, neuroanatomy and relevant embryology, and the comparative anatomy of domestic animals, including avian anatomy. The practical examination may include a *viva voce* examination.

Special Veterinary Physiology

The paper will contain questions on veterinary physiology, particularly of herbivorous animals

Elective Subjects. The list for any year will be announced by the division of the Easter Term preceding the year in which the Examination is to be held. The following are the subjects for 1990:

Human nutrition
History of medicine
†Human genetics and variation
Medical ethics
†Medical statistics and computing
Social aspects of medicine

The examination in each will consist of one written paper.

Part II (General)

Candidates take the examination for Section I or II, provided that they do not offer

(*a*) any subject or Special Subject that they have previously offered in the Natural Sciences Tripos;

(*b*) an Elective Subject which they have previously offered in Part I B of the Medical Sciences Tripos.

(*c*) not more than one Elective from any one group (see below).

SECTION I

This is designed for undergraduates taking the three-year preclinical course. Candidates offer the papers and practical examinations in Pathology and Pharmacology; a paper in an Elective Subject; and, if Veterinary students, the paper in Animal Behaviour.

Pathology. The examination will be the same as that in Pathology in Part I B.

Pharmacology. The examination will be the same as that in Pharmacology in Part I B.

Animal Behaviour. The paper will require knowledge of material on animal behaviour presented in the courses both for Part I B and for Part II (General).

† Candidates will be required to present to the Examiners on the first day of the written examination note-books containing a record of the practical work done by them.

MEDICAL SCIENCES

Elective Subjects. The list for any year will be announced by the division of the Easter Term preceding the year in which the Examination is to be held. They are divided into four groups (A to D). The subjects in **1990** are as follows:

- (A) †Human genetics and variation.
- (A) Human nutrition.
- (A) Topics in clinical physiology.
- (B) History of medicine.
- (B) †Medical statistics and computing.
  Medical ethics
- (C) Social aspects of medicine.
- (C) *Biology of parasitism.
- (C) Human reproduction.
- (D) Medical aspects of neurobiology.

The examination in each will consist of one written paper.

SECTION II

This is designed for undergraduates taking the two-year preclinical course who want to do a third year of preclinical study but not to take a single-subject Part II from the Natural Sciences Tripos.

Candidates offer **either** the papers, essay if any, and practical examination if any, prescribed for *two* of these special subjects:

> Biological Anthropology   **Pathology**
> History of Medicine   Social Psychology

or the Special Subject Pathology together with two Elective Subjects provided not more than one is chosen from each of the groups.

Biological Anthropology. A candidate shall offer written papers as follows:

either 1. ***Human genetics and variation*** **(The paper of an Elective subject for the Tripos, or in any year in which no such subject has been announced, Paper 1 in Physical Anthropology of Part II of the Archaeological and Anthropological Tripos),**

† Candidates will be required to present to the Examiners on the first day of the written examination note-books containing a record of the practical work done by them.

* **Candidates will be required to submit to the Examiners, not later than the first day of Full Easter Term, an essay of not more than 4,000 words on a subject approved by the Faculty Board.**

and	2. *Human ecology and adaptability* (Paper 3 in Physical Anthropology of Part II of the Archaeological and Anthropological Tripos);
or	3. *Primate biology and evolution* (Paper 2 in Physical Anthropology of Part II of the Archaeological and Anthropological Tripos),
and	4. *Primate behaviour* (A special subject in physical anthropology prescribed for Paper 4 in Physical Anthropology of Part II of the Archaeological and Anthropological Tripos).

Any practical examination shall include those parts of the practical examination in Biological Anthropology from Part II of the Archaeological and Anthropological Tripos that relate to the subjects of the written papers offered, and may include or consist wholly of a *viva voce* examination.

History of Medicine. The examination consists of two written papers as follows:

1. *Medicine and Natural Philosophy from antiquity to the end of the Seventeenth Century*
    (Paper 7 of Part II of the Natural Sciences Tripos.)

2. *Medicine, Science and Society from the Eighteenth Century*
    (Paper 8 of Part II of the Natural Sciences Tripos.)

Pathology. The examination is the same as that in the Special Subject in Part II (General) of the Natural Sciences Tripos.

Social Psychology. The written papers will be as follows:

1. *The individual in society* (Paper 10 of Part II of the Social and Political Sciences Tripos).

2. *The psychology of development* (Paper 11 of Part II of the Social and Political Sciences Tripos).

Transfers to Medicine read Part IA of the Medical Sciences Tripos in their second year and Part IB in their third year. If they have offered Physiology in Part IA of the Natural Sciences Tripos in the first year they offer Pathology from Part IB of the Medical Sciences Tripos in Part IA instead of in Part IIB.

MEDICAL SCIENCES

Exemption from Subjects of the Second M.B. and the Second Veterinary M.B. Examinations

A student shall be entitled to exemption from a subject of the Second M.B. and the Second Veterinary M.B. Examination if he is deemed by the Joint Exemptions Committee to have attained a satisfactory standard, as prescribed by the Faculty Board of Clinical Medicine, or the Clinical Veterinary Medicine Syndicate, in one of the corresponding subjects[1] of the Medical Sciences Tripos or the Natural Sciences Tripos, as shown in the following tables:

Subjects in Second M.B. Examination		Subjects in Tripos Examinations
Anatomy A		Medical Sciences Tripos, Part IA, Anatomy (Sections A and B);
Anatomy B		Medical Sciences Tripos, Part IB, Anatomy and Physiology (Section A)
Biochemistry		Medical Sciences Tripos, Part IA, Biochemistry;
	or	Natural Sciences Tripos, Part IB, Biochemistry and Molecular Biology;
	or	Natural Sciences Tripos, Part II (General), Biochemistry and Molecular Biology.
Medical Genetics		Natural Sciences Tripos, Part IA, Biology of Cells.
	or	Medical Sciences Tripos, Part IA, Medical Genetics.
Medical Statistics		In-course assessment.
Medical Sociology		None.
Neurobiology		Medical Sciences Tripos, Part IB, Neurobiology.
Pathology		Medical Sciences Tripos, Part IA, Pathology;
	or	Medical Sciences Tripos, Part IB, Pathology;
	or	Medical Sciences Tripos, Part II (General), Section I, Pathology;
	or	Natural Sciences Tripos, Part IB, Pathology;
	or	Natural Sciences Tripos, Part II (General), Pathology.
Pharmacology		Medical Sciences Tripos, Part IB, Pharmacology;
	or	Medical Sciences Tripos, Part II (General), Section I, Pharmacology;
	or	Natural Sciences Tripos, Part IB, Pharmacology;
	or	Natural Sciences Tripos, Part II (General), Pharmacology.
Physiology A		Medical Sciences Tripos, IA, Physiology;
	or	Natural Sciences Tripos, Part IA, Physiology.

Subjects in Second M.B. Examination	Subjects in Tripos Examinations
Psychology	Medical Sciences Tripos, Part IB, Psychology;
	or Natural Sciences Tripos, Part IB, Experimental Psychology.
	or Natural Sciences Tripos, Part II (General), Section I, Experimental Psychology.
Reproductive Biology and Endocrinology	Medical Sciences Tripos, Part IB, Anatomy and Physiology (Section B);
	or Medical Sciences Tripos, Part IB, General Veterinary Physiology
Endocrinology	*or* Natural Sciences Tripos, Part IB, Physiology;
	or Natural Sciences Tripos, Part II (General), Physiology.

Subjects in Second Vet.M.B. Examination	
Biochemistry	Medical Sciences Tripos, Part IA, Biochemistry;
	or Natural Sciences Tripos, Part IB, Biochemistry and Molecular Biology;
	or Natural Sciences Tripos, Part II (General), Biochemistry and Molecular Biology.
Medical Genetics	Natural Sciences Tripos, Part IA, Biology of cells;
	Natural Sciences Tripos, Part IA, Medical Genetics.
Medical Statistics	In course assessment
Pathology	Medical Sciences Tripos, Part IA, Pathology;
	or Medical Sciences Tripos, Part IB, Pathology;
	or Medical Sciences Tripos, Part II (General), Section I, Pathology;
	or Natural Sciences Tripos, Part IB, Pathology;
	or Natural Sciences Tripos, Part II (General), Pathology.
Pharmacology	Medical Sciences Tripos, Part IB, Pharmacology;
	or Medical Sciences Tripos, Part II (General), Section I, Pharmacology;
	or Medical Sciences Tripos, Part II (General), Section III, Pharmacology;
	or Natural Sciences Tripos, Part IB, Pharmacology;
	or Natural Sciences Tripos, Part II (General), Pharmacology.
Physiology A	Medical Sciences Tripos, Part IA, Physiology;
	or Natural Sciences Tripos, Part IA, Physiology.
Veterinary Anatomy A	Medical Sciences Tripos, Part IA, Anatomy (Sections A and C);
Veterinary Anatomy B	Medical Sciences Tripos, Part IB, Veterinary Anatomy;

Subjects in Second Vet.M.B. Examination	Subjects in Tripos Examinations
Veterinary Physiology	Medical Sciences Tripos, Part IB, Special Veterinary Physiology.
Physiology B	Medical Sciences Tripos, Part IB, General Veterinary Physiology (Section C); *or* Medical Sciences Tripos, Part IB, Anatomy and Physiology (Section B), *together with* Medical Tripos, Part IB, Neurobiology; *or* Natural Sciences Tripos, Part IB, Physiology; *or* Natural Sciences Tripos, Part II (General), Physiology

M.Phil. course in History of Medicine

This is a one-year course aimed to give an insight into the historical background of the subject of medicine, to provide a suitable training for doctors and those already working in fields related to the history of medicine who intend to undertake scholarly historical work as an adjunct to their professional practice, and to act as a conversion course for further formal training in the field of History of Medicine.

The scheme of examination consists of a thesis, of not more than 15,000 words in length, including footnotes and appendices, but excluding bibliography, on a topic approved by the Degree Committee for the Faculty of Clinical Medicine, and four essays, each of about 3,000 words in length, on topics approved by the Degree Committee and related to the following areas:

(i) Life sciences and medicine up to and including the seventeenth century.

(ii) Life sciences and medicine in the eighteenth and nineteenth centuries.

(iii) A topic to be chosen by the candidate from a list announced by the Degree Committee. These topics afford the candidate the opportunity to study with various University Departments which have interests related to the History of Medicine, and they cover a wide area of study.

At least one essay must be offered from each area, but only one essay may be offered from area (iii).

The examination may include an oral examination upon the thesis and essays, and on the general field of knowledge in which they fall.

MEDICINE AND SURGERY

The two degrees, Bachelor of Medicine and Bachelor of Surgery, commonly abbreviated to M.B., B.Chir., are qualifications for provisional registration under the Medical Act, 1983. Full registration is obtained after completing one year's pre-registration service. (Overseas nationals (non-E.E.C.) are advised to familiarise themselves with the changes in the Immigration Rules effective from 1 April 1985 regarding work permit arrangements following pre-registration service.) The course of study falls into three periods: study for the First M.B. Examination (the premedical period); study for the Second M.B. Examination (the preclinical period); and study for the Final M.B. Examination (the clinical period). The University does not offer a course to prepare students for the First M.B. Examination, and Cambridge Colleges do not normally admit medical students until they have passed or gained exemption from that examination, the commonest method of qualifying for exemption being by means of G.C.E. 'A' level passes in appropriate subjects.

Until 1976 when the Clinical School opened at Addenbrooke's Hospital, all pre-clinical students, when they had graduated with a B.A. Degree and passed or been exempted from the Second M.B. Examinations, proceeded to one of the London teaching hospitals or another university medical school for their clinical course. Now there are a hundred places each year on the Cambridge Clinical Course which lasts for two years and three months. The remainder of the pre-clinical students continue to go to the medical school of another university for their clinical training and return to take the Cambridge Final M.B. unless they have the option of taking the examination of the university at which they have undertaken their clinical training. All students taking the Cambridge Final M.B. must have been awarded a degree approved for this purpose before entering upon clinical training.

The course of study for the M.B., B.Chir., excluding the pre-medical period and pre-registration year, is five years and one term for those students who pursue their clinical studies in Cambridge and six years for the remainder of the students.

Until recently there were separate regulations and examinations for students doing their clinical training in Cambridge and for those who had done clinical courses in other universities. These have now been amalgamated into a single set of regulations for the M.B., B.Chir. Degrees.

Candidates preparing for the Second M.B. Examination in

MEDICINE AND SURGERY

Cambridge normally read the Medical Sciences Tripos, which gives the opportunity to obtain exemption from all Second M.B. subjects (except Medical Sociology) provided students obtain honours in the Tripos and reach the prescribed standard in the appropriate subjects. (In a similar way, it is also possible to obtain many Second M.B. exemptions by satisfactory performance in appropriate examinations in the Natural Sciences Tripos.) Students, however, must sit the actual Second M.B. Examination in Medical Sociology.

For full details of the structure of the Medical Sciences Tripos see page 270. Many students complete the necessary exemptions in the first two years of their undergraduate preclinical course. Those who wish to proceed to clinical studies at Cambridge (where the course is shorter than at other universities) **must** spend the third preclinical year reading a subject approved as a 'year of medical study'; this is in order to satisfy the requirements of the General Medical Council. This condition is not unduly restrictive, as the list of approved subjects includes not only courses in the Medical Sciences Tripos but also many courses in the Natural Sciences Tripos and some others including Biological Anthropology in Part II of the Archaeological and Anthropological Tripos; certain courses in the Social and Political Sciences Tripos; or courses leading to the Computer Sciences Tripos or Management Studies Tripos. At the end of the third year students will be eligible for the award of the B.A. Degree.

Arrangements can be made, subject to the availability of places, for undergraduates who have begun by reading a Tripos other than the Medical Sciences Tripos to transfer to Medicine. In addition students who have taken a preclinical course in another university and have obtained a degree normally with honours in an appropriate subject may also be considered for entry to the clinical course in Cambridge. Each case raises individual problems and it is the practice of the Faculty Board of Clinical Medicine to consider individual cases on their merits and make the necessary recommendations.

The Final M.B. Examination consists of three Parts. Part I (Pathology) may be taken after fourteen months of clinical study, Part II (Obstetrics and Gynaecology) after eighteen months (or, from 1991, sixteen months), and Part III (Medicine including Clinical Pharmacology and Therapeutics, and Surgery) after two years and two months clinical study in the University or after two years and eight months of clinical study elsewhere. Each candidate must before completing the Final Examination provide evidence of five years of medical study by producing certificates of diligent attendance on certain courses of lectures and practical instructions in each year in an approved institution (either three years of pre-clinical medical study in the University or elsewhere and two years and two months clinical study in the University *or* two years of pre-clinical medical study in the University and two years and eight months of clinical study elsewhere).

The following is a brief description of each of the examinations leading to the M.B. and B.Chir. Degrees.

First M.B. Examination

The three Parts of the examination are: I (Chemistry), II (Physics), and III (Elementary Biology). The examinations are held once a year, in September. The examination may be taken by any matriculated student or an unmatriculated student who is certified to be or to have been a *bona fide* candidate for admission to a College.

The Faculty Board of Clinical Medicine may exempt from one or more Parts of the First M.B. Examination a student who has passed other appropriate examinations in relevant subjects (including appropriate examinations at other universities). Although individual cases will be considered as necessary, many students' qualifications are covered by the general rules summarised below.

Currently exemptions may be secured by passes in suitable examinations in the General Certificate of Education (GCE) Advanced Level, Advanced Supplementary Level and Ordinary Level, in the General Certificate of Secondary Education (GCSE) or in other recognised examinations as specified below:

(*a*) From Part I of the First M.B. Examination by passing at Advanced Level in Chemistry, or Physical Science.

(*b*) From Part II of the First M.B. Examination by passing

either (i) at Advanced level in Physics, or Physical Science, or Physics-and-Mathematics, or Engineering Science;

or (ii) at Advanced level in Mathematics or Statistics, and also at Ordinary level or in the GCSE in Physics, or Physical Science, or Physics-with-Chemistry, or in one of the double-award Science examinations at Ordinary level or in the GCSE, provided that students counting a double-award Science examination in the GCSE towards exemption shall be required to attain Grade A in both subjects of the double award;

or (iii) at the Higher Grade in Physics in the Scottish Certificate of Education at Grade B or above

MEDICINE AND SURGERY

and also at Ordinary level or in the GCSE in Mathematics;

or (iv) at Advanced Supplementary level in Physics and also at Ordinary level or in the GCSE in Mathematics.

(*c*) From Part III by passing

either (i) at Advanced level in Biology, or Human Biology, or Botany, or Zoology;

or (ii) at Advanced level in Mathematics or Statistics, and also at Grade B or above at Ordinary level or in the GCSE in Biology, or Human Biology, or Botany, or Zoology, or at Grade B or above in both subjects of a double-award Science examination at Ordinary level, or at Grade A in both subjects of a double-award Science examination in the GCSE;

or (iii) at Higher Grade in Biology at Grade B or above in the Scottish Certificate of Education;

or (iv) at Advanced Supplementary level in Biology and also at Ordinary level or in the GCSE in Mathematics.

(*d*) A student may not count an Advanced Level pass in Mathematics or Statistics as contributing towards exemption from both Part II and Part III of the First M.B. Examination.

(*e*) A student may not count Advanced Supplementary Level passes in Physics and in Biology towards exemption from Parts II and III respectively of the First M.B. Examination unless he has in addition passed at Advanced Level in Mathematics or Statistics.

(*f*) The following are regarded for this purpose as the equivalent of a pass at GCE Advanced Level:

(i) a pass in the Scottish Certificate of Sixth Year Studies;

(ii) a pass at Grade 5 or above in the International Baccalaureate in a subject taken at the Higher level.

(*g*) The following is regarded for this purpose as the equivalent of a pass at GCE Ordinary Level (Grade A, B or C):

(i) a pass in the Scottish Certificate of Education Ordinary Grade examination at Grade 1, 2, or 3 (for examinations taken before 1986, Grade A, B or C is required).

(*h*) The following are regarded for this purpose as the equivalent of a pass in the GCSE (Grade A, B, or C):

        (i) a pass in the International GCSE at Grade A, B, or C;

        (ii) a pass in the Scottish Certificate of Education Standard Grade examination at Grade 1, 2, or 3.

(*i*) A student who has obtained honours or has reached the honours standard in an appropriate subject of the Natural Sciences Tripos is entitled to exemption from the corresponding Part of the First M.B. Examination, as shown in the following table:

Subject in Natural Sciences Tripos	*First M.B. Examination*
Chemistry.	
Biochemistry.	Part I
Biochemistry and Molecular Biology.	
Materials Science and Metallurgy.	
Physics.	Part II
Fluid Mechanics.	
Anatomy.	
Biochemistry.	
Biochemistry and Molecular Biology.	
Biological Resources.	
Animal Biology.	
Applied Biology.	
Biology of Cells.	
Ecology.	
Biology of Organisms.	
Plant Biology.	
Botany.	Part III
Genetics.	
Molecular Cell Biology.	
Pathology.	
Pharmacology.	
Physiology.	
Psychology.	
Physiology and Psychology.	
Experimental Psychology.	
Zoology.	

Note. Students seeking admission to the University to read for the Medical Sciences Tripos must also satisfy the Examination requirements for matriculation.

Second M.B. Examination

The Second M.B. Examination consists at present of the subjects Anatomy A, Anatomy B, Biochemistry, Neurobiology, Pathology, Pharmacology, Physiology A, Reproductive Biology and Endocrinology, Medical Genetics, Medical Statistics, Medical Sociology, and Psychology. Candidates for the M.B., B.Chir. Degrees must pass or gain exemption from all subjects of the Second M.B. Examination before they may take any Part of the Final M.B. Examination. A student will not normally be admitted to the clinical course at Cambridge until he has completed all the requirements of the Second M.B. Examination, although postponement of the examinations in Medical Genetics, Medical Sociology and Psychology may be permitted.

A candidate for the Second M.B. Examination, or for exemption from it, must (*a*) have completed the First M.B. Examination by having passed or been granted exemption from it; (*b*) diligently attended approved courses of instruction appropriate to the subject or subjects in which he proposes to present himself; (*c*) if he is a candidate for an examination in Anatomy, produce evidence of having satisfactorily dissected the appropriate parts of the human body; (d) have obtained honours in an Honours examination or, being over the standing to obtain honours in the Medical Sciences Tripos, to have attained the honours standard therein, or to have obtained a degree with honours of a university other than Cambridge or other degree deemed appropriate by the Faculty Board for this purpose. The Faculty Board may waive requirement (*a*) on condition that it is satisfied before the candidate takes any Part of the Final M.B. Examination.

Except for the subject Medical Statistics, the Second M.B. Examination in each subject consists of a written examination paper and, where appropriate, a practical examination. The examinations are held in June and September, except for Medical Sociology which is in January and June. The Second M.B. requirement in Medical Statistics is met by in-course assessment of practical exercises during the Medical Sciences Tripos course.

Candidates may present themselves for re-examination in the subjects of the Second M.B. Examination within limits prescribed by the regulations.

The Final M.B. Examination

The Final M.B. Examination is divided into three Parts, as follows:

Part I. Pathology.
Part II. Obstetrics and Gynaecology.
Part III. (*a*) Medicine including Clinical Pharmacology and Therapeutics.
(*b*) Surgery.

Under present regulations, Parts I and II are held in April, June and December and Part III in June and December each year. From 1991, Parts I and II will be held in late February or early March, June and December; Part III will continue to be in June and December. With the exception of resit candidates, the first sitting of Part II in each calendar year (i.e. the April sitting under current regulations) is open only to candidates who have pursued their clinical studies at Cambridge. Before taking any part of the Final M.B. Examination a candidate must have completed the First and Second M.B. Examinations and produced evidence of satisfactory attendance on the approved courses of clinical instruction appropriate to that Part.

Not less than six weeks before taking Part III for the first time, a candidate for that Part is required to submit to the Clinical Dean an essay of not more than 3,000 words on a subject related to medicine.

The Parts of the Final M.B. Examination may be taken either together or separately except that a candidate will be required to have passed Part I before presenting himself as a candidate for Part III unless he has been given special permission by the Faculty Board.

Re-examination in the Parts of the Final M.B. Examination, or in a Section of Part III, is allowed within limits prescribed by the regulations.

MODERN AND MEDIEVAL LANGUAGES

In this subject there are courses of study followed by candidates for:

The *Modern and Medieval Languages Tripos*, which is divided into two Parts (pp. 291 and 292).
A *Preliminary Examination* for Part II of the Tripos (p. 332).
Advanced Oral Examinations in modern languages (p. 333).
Certificates of Competent Knowledge in modern languages (p. 334).
Ordinary Examinations in certain modern languages for the Ordinary B.A. Degree (p. 335).
The *M.Phil. in Linguistics* (*one-year course*) (p. 335).

The Modern and Medieval Languages Tripos

The Modern Languages Tripos is normally a four-year course in two Parts, which must be taken separately. In Part I the emphasis is on language rather than on the intellectual aspects of the course. In Part II the converse is true. A very wide range of modern languages is available: Czech with Slovak, Dutch, French, German, Italian, Modern Greek, Polish, Portuguese, Russian and Spanish. Under certain conditions papers in the History of Catalan and Medieval Latin Literature may be offered in Part I. Other languages may also be approved. With the exception of French and German, candidates may choose languages they have not studied at school. Details are given on pp. 295–297 of the conditions under which Classical and Oriental languages can be offered.

Part I[1]

Part I consists of a written and an oral examination. A candidate must offer two languages at the same standard and may sit the written examination at the end of the first or the second year. It is possible to offer both languages in the same year, whether first or second; it is also possible to 'split' Part I, offering one language at the end of the first year, and the other language at the end of the second. To be classed in Part I a candidate must be classed in both languages taken.

Those candidates who offer two languages which they have already studied at school normally sit both their languages at the end of their first year. Where a candidate begins the study of a new language at Cambridge, it is usual either to 'split' Part I or to sit both languages

---
[1] Further details on pp. 293 ff.

at the end of the second year. A candidate's College can often give advice concerning the possibility of taking up a new language and can indicate what preliminary steps, for example a summer course or a period abroad, are desirable.[1]

Part II

A wide range of options is available in Part II as can be seen from the scope of Schedule II, published below. Candidates must offer from that Schedule four or five papers depending on whether they spend one or two years in preparation for Part II; the details are set out on p. 305. In addition to their schedule II papers or papers equivalent to them, candidates must offer two language papers, an Essay paper and a Translation and Composition paper; generally these papers are offered in the same language, but a candidate who wishes to do so can sit the Essay paper in a language different from that of the Translation and Composition paper.

It is possible to specialize in the language and literature of one country or to choose papers from a variety of literatures or languages; the course can thus be virtually 'tailor-made' for the individual concerned. While the great majority of papers in Part II are concerned with the literature, history and thought of a particular period and country, there are also papers on the history of individual languages, on comparative literature and comparative philology, on phonetics, on general and historical linguistics, on specified periods of history and on the history of the visual arts, on the history of linguistic thought and on the relationships between literature and the visual arts. As well as the papers listed in Schedule II, candidates have available to them papers from Part II of the Classical Tripos and also certain papers from the English Tripos, the Historical Tripos and from the Anglo-Saxon, Norse, and Celtic Tripos. Details of those papers are given on pp. 307–8. Before offering any papers from the Oriental Studies Tripos, a candidate must have the permission of the Faculty Boards concerned.

In Part II candidates may offer a dissertation in addition to their papers from Schedule II or as an alternative to one of them. A candidate may offer both an 'alternative' and an 'additional' dissertation if the specified conditions are fulfilled (p. 311).

Study Abroad

Candidates spend a compulsory year abroad as part of the preparation for Part II; they will thus spend four years reading for their degree. Such candidates must satisfy the Faculty Board that they will spend the year abroad either studying at a university *or* in some approved teaching post, *or* in a form of employment which has been approved by the Faculty Board. Application forms, to be obtained from the Faculty Office, are to be submitted by the Division of the Lent Term before the year to be spent abroad.

Part I

Candidates may take Part I in the first or second year or, if they have obtained honours in another Tripos, one or two years after doing so but not later than their fourth year. Candidates for Part I must choose one of three options: under option A, they may offer two languages in their first year, or in their first year after obtaining honours in another Tripos: under option B, they may offer two languages in their second year, or in their second year after obtaining honours in another Tripos; under option C, they may offer one language in their first year of study for Part I and their second language in the following year. If they choose either option B or C they will have to offer one additional paper as set out below.

Candidates for Part I are required to take papers in Composition, Translation, and Essay, and in a selected period of literary study, and to take an oral examination, in each of two languages. Candidates may combine one modern European language with either classical Latin or classical Greek, or an Oriental language, though in this last instance it is necessary for candidates to seek, through their College, the permission of the Faculty Board of Modern and Medieval Languages and the Faculty Board of Oriental Studies. The following modern European languages are available to candidates for Part I of the Modern and Medieval Languages Tripos; Czech (with Slovak), Dutch, French, German, Italian, Modern Greek, Polish, Portuguese, Russian and Spanish. Hungarian is also currently available. Other European languages may be offered subject to the permission of the Faculty Board. Certain combinations of cognate languages may not be permitted. However Spanish may be combined with Portuguese, Latin with Italian, and Classical Greek with Modern Greek. The attention of students is particularly drawn to the value, in both academic and career terms, of taking less commonly studied languages, and of learning at university languages not offered at schools. The Faculty buildings are equipped to receive programmes from foreign countries, and this, together with the language laboratory, offers considerable advantages both for those beginning a new language and for those increasing their familiarity with one language which they have already studied.

The examination in each modern language consists of two Sections:

Section A. Three language papers and an oral examination:

A1. Passages from works in the foreign language for translation into English or for linguistic commentary.

In French, German, Italian, Portuguese, and Spanish the passages are chosen from works not earlier than 1500, in Danish and Swedish from works not earlier than 1600, in Russian from works not earlier than 1700, and in Czech (with Slovak), modern Greek, Norwegian and Polish from works not earlier than 1800.

A2. Passages from English to be translated into the foreign language.

A3. An essay in a foreign language chosen from a paper of subjects half of which shall bear on the literature, history, thought, and language of the country concerned, and all of which shall demand reasoned exposition.

Oral Examination for Part I

An oral examination is an integral component of Part I in all the scheduled languages except Classical Greek and Latin and is assessed as the equivalent of half a written paper. The examination consists of three parts: (*a*) dictation, (*b*) reading aloud, including the reading of isolated words and phrases as a phonetic test, and (*c*) conversation on one of a number of prescribed topics involving reasoned argument. The list of topics from which the candidates may choose is published in the year before that in which the examination takes place and usually incorporates the topics set in the essay paper for Part I in the year in which the list is published. The oral examinations are held at the beginning of the Easter Term, some weeks before the written papers are taken.

A list of the topics prescribed for the oral examinations in 1990 may be obtained from the Faculty Office.

The language laboratories at Sidgwick Avenue are available to undergraduates, both to improve their fluency in languages which they already know and to assist them in learning new languages.

Section B. Papers listed in Schedule I, relating to the literature, history, thought, and language of the country the language of which may be offered, together with specified supplementary papers.

Certain papers are marked with an asterisk: a paper so marked may be offered only by a candidate who (*a*) is offering the language in the second year of study for the Tripos, and (*b*) is offering at the same examination one of the papers in Schedule I relating to the same language that is not marked with an asterisk.

Candidates who offer two modern languages in their first year of study for Part I under option A must take in each language Papers A1, A2, A3, and the oral examination, and one Section B paper chosen from among the papers listed in Schedule I that are not marked with an asterisk. Candidates who offer two modern languages in their second year of study for Part I under Option B must offer

(*a*) four papers in one language, and the oral examination, as specified in option A,

(*b*) five papers consisting of
  (i) four papers in the second language, as specified for a language in option A,
  (ii) an additional paper chosen from among the papers listed in Schedule I, which may be *either* a paper (whether marked with an asterisk or not) in the second language, *or* one of the supplementary papers,

and the oral examination in each language.

A candidate who offers two modern languages in successive years under option C must take four papers and the oral examination in the first year in one language as under option A, and five papers and the oral examination in the second language in the second year as in (*b*) of option B. For candidates in Arabic the regulations are slightly different (see below).

Candidates who begin the course intending to choose option A may at the end of their first year change to option C should they fail in one of the languages offered under option A. Similarly candidates who begin having chosen option C may change to option B if they fail in the language in which they have been examined at the end of their first year. In both cases however the candidates will be prohibited from offering again the language in which they have failed. They must offer a different language in its place and, if they are changing from option A to option C, they must offer in it five papers (as in (*b*) of option B).

To obtain honours in Part I a candidate must reach the honours standard in each of the two languages studied either on the same occasion (under option A or option B) or in successive years (under option C).

Arabic

Candidates wishing to offer Arabic with a modern European language will need to have permission of both the Faculty Board of Modern and Medieval Languages and the Faculty Board of Oriental Studies.

Classical Greek and Classical Latin

(*a*) The following papers shall be set in classical Greek and classical Latin, if candidates desire to present themselves therein:

51. Passages for translation from Greek authors (Paper 1 of Part I of the Classical Tripos).*
52. Less difficult passages for translation from Greek authors (Paper 2 of Part I of the Classical Tripos).*
53. Passages for translation from Latin authors.
54. Passages for translation from Greek and Latin authors (Paper 4 of Part I of the Classical Tripos).*
55. Greek literature (Paper 5 of Part I of the Classical Tripos).*
56. Latin literature (Paper 6 of Part I of the Classical Tripos).*
57. Greek and Roman history (Paper 7 of Part I of the Classical Tripos).*
58. Greek and Roman philosophy and religion with particular reference to Plato (Paper 8 of Part I of the Classical Tripos).*
59. Greek and Roman art and architecture (Paper 9 of Part I of the Classical Tripos).*
60. Translation from English into Greek prose and verse (Paper 10 of Part I of the Classical Tripos.)*
61. Translation from English into Latin prose and verse (Paper 11 of Part I of the Classical Tripos).*
62. Virgil.

* For the supplementary regulations for these papers which apply to candidates offering classical Greek or classical Latin in the Modern and Medieval Languages Tripos, see the supplementary regulations for the Classical Tripos.

MODERN AND MEDIEVAL LANGUAGES

(*b*) A candidate who offers under Regulation 18(*b*) one modern language and classical Greek shall take written papers and an oral examination in the modern language as prescribed in Regulation 19, and in classical Greek the following written papers:

(A) A candidate who chooses option A of Regulation 19 shall offer:
  (i) Paper 51 or Paper 52;
  (ii) Paper 54;
  (iii) Paper 55;
  (iv) *either* any one of Papers 57–60,
       or two half-papers, each consisting of two questions from one of Papers 57–59.

(B/C) A candidate who chooses option B of Regulation 19 and does not offer an additional paper in his modern language, or who chooses option C of that regulation and offers classical Greek on the second occasion, shall offer the papers specified for option A and an additional paper which may be
  either one of the supplementary papers,
  or a further paper chosen from Papers 57–60,
  or two half-papers, each consisting of two questions from one of Papers 57–59;

provided that
(1) any candidate may offer Paper 60 in addition to the papers, or papers and half-papers, which he is required to offer under this paragraph;
(2) no candidate may offer more than two half-papers;
(3) any candidate offering a half-paper shall be allowed one and a half hours only.

(*c*) A candidate who offers under Regulation 18(*b*) one modern language and classical Latin shall take written papers and an oral examination in the modern language as prescribed in Regulation 19, and in classical Latin the following written papers:

(A) A candidate who chooses option A of Regulation 19 shall offer Papers 53, 54, 56, and 62.

(B/C) A candidate who chooses option B of Regulation 19 and does not offer an additional paper in his modern language, or who chooses option C of that regulation and offers classical Latin on the second occasion, shall offer the papers specified for option A and an additional paper which may be
  either one of the supplementary papers,
  or Paper 57,
  or Paper 59;

provided that any candidate may offer Paper 61 in addition to the papers which he is required to offer under this paragraph.

(*d*) In determining the place in the class-list of any candidate who has offered either Paper 60 or Paper 61 as an additional paper, the Examiners shall give credit for proficiency in that paper. A mark of distinction, *G* or *L* respectively, shall be attached to the names of those candidates who, in offering either Paper 60 or Paper 61, acquit themselves with credit in that paper. A mark, *g* or *l* respectively, shall be attached to the names of those candidates who, in offering either Paper 60 or Paper 61, satisfy the Examiners in that paper.

The papers for Section B of Part I are as follows:

SCHEDULE I[1] (PAPERS FOR SECTION B OF PART I)

FRENCH

3. French literature, thought, and history in the seventeenth century (with special reference to particular periods or topics to be prescribed from time to time).
4. French literature, thought, and history in the eighteenth century (with special reference to particular periods or topics to be prescribed from time to time).
5. French literature, thought, and history in the nineteenth century (with special reference to particular periods or topics to be prescribed from time to time).

GERMAN

6. Aspects of the history of the German language.
7. Introduction to German medieval literature.
*8. German literature, thought and history, from 1620 to 1700.
9. German literature, thought, and history, from 1770 to 1832.
10. German literature, thought, and history, from 1815 to 1890.
*11. German literature, thought, and history, from 1880 to 1914.

ITALIAN

*12. Introduction to the structure and varieties of the Italian language.
†13. Introduction to Dante and his age.
†14. (*a*) Introduction to Dante and his age, and (*b*) the literature of the Risorgimento.
15. Introduction to the Italian Renaissance.
16. Italian literature, thought, and history, since 1880.

[1] Those papers marked with an asterisk may only be taken at the end of two years.

MODERN AND MEDIEVAL LANGUAGES

SLAVONIC

*18. Introduction to the study of Kievan and Muscovite Russia.
 19. Russian literature and thought, from 1799 to 1900.
*20. Russian literature, thought, and history, from 1891 to 1934.
 21. Czech and Slovak literature, thought, and history, from 1774 to 1939.
*22. Czech drama from 1813 to 1939.
 23. Polish literature, thought, and history, from 1795 to 1914.
 24. Polish literature and thought, from 1918 to 1956.
[1]*25. Serbian literature, history, and institutions, from 1168 to 1389.
[1]26. Serbian and Croatian literature, thought, and history, since 1800.

SCANDINAVIAN

(only for those already in residence)

*27. Danish literature, thought, and history, from 1870 to 1918.
 28. Danish literature, thought, and history, from 1918 to the present day.
*29. Norwegian literature, thought, and history, from 1870 to 1918.
 30. Norwegian literature, thought, and history, from 1918 to the present day.
*31. Swedish literature, thought, and history, from 1870 to 1918.
 32. Swedish literature, thought, and history, from 1918 to the present day.

SPANISH

*33. An introduction to the history of the Peninsular languages.
*34. Medieval Spain.
 35. Spanish literature, thought, and history in the sixteenth century.
*36. Cervantes and the Golden Age novel, from 1500 to 1616.
*37. Benito Pérez Galdós and the nineteenth-century novel.
 38. Spanish literature, thought, and history in the twentieth century.
*39. Argentina and Mexico since 1830.

DUTCH

*40. The early history and literature of the Netherlands.
*41. Vondel.
*42. The literature, thought, and history of the Netherlands, from 1830 to 1918.
 43. The literature, thought, and history of the Netherlands, from 1880 to 1939.

† No candidate may offer both Papers 13 and 14.
[1] Those interested in Papers 25 and 26 should consult the Department of Slavonic Studies.

CAMBRIDGE HANDBOOK

PORTUGUESE
*44. Portuguese literature, thought, and history, from 1495 to 1580.
45. Portuguese literature, thought, and history, since 1825.

MODERN GREEK
*46. Greek literature, thought, and history, from 1453 to 1700.
47. Greek literature, thought, and history, since 1800.

SUPPLEMENTARY PAPER
*48. Medieval Latin literature.

The following texts and periods have been prescribed, and authors and topics specified, for these papers in **1990** and **1991**:

SCHEDULE I
PAPERS FOR SECTION B OF PART I IN 1990
FRENCH

Paper 3. French literature, thought, and history, in the seventeenth century, with special reference to the period 1630–1700, and to the following:
  Corneille; Descartes, *Discours de la méthode*; Mme de Lafayette, *La Princesse de Clèves*; La Fontaine, *Fables*; La Rochefoucauld, *Maximes*; Molière; Pascal, *Pensées* (ed. L. Lafuma, Editions du Seuil, Collection 'Points'); Racine; Church and society in France, 1630–1700.

Paper 4. French literature, thought, and history, in the eighteenth century, with special reference to the period 1715–1789, and to the following:
  Lesage, *Gil Blas*; Montesquieu, *Lettres persanes*; Voltaire, *Zadig*, *Candide*, either *Le Philosophe ignorant* or *Lettres philosophiques*; Rousseau, *Les Rêveries du promeneur solitaire*; Diderot, *Le Neveu de Rameau*; Marivaux, *Le Jeu de l'amour et du hasard*, *La Double Inconstance*, *Les Fausses Confidences*; Prévost, *Manon Lescaut*; Beaumarchais, *Le Barbier de Séville*, *Le Mariage de Figaro*; Laclos, *Les Liaisons dangereuses*; The rôle of the *parlements* in eighteenth-century France; Watteau.

†*Paper 5. French literature, thought, and history, in the nineteenth century*, with special reference to the period 1830–70, and to the following:
  Stendhal, *Le Rouge et le noir*; Balzac, *La Cousine Bette*; Flaubert, *Madame Bovary*; Hugo, *Les Contemplations*; Nerval, *Les Chimères*, *Sylvie*; Gautier, *Emaux et camées*; Baudelaire, *Les Fleurs du Mal*; Romantic drama; the Revolutions of 1848; Utopian thought, 1830–51.

GERMAN

Paper 6. Aspects of the history of the German language
  A thorough knowledge of the following passages is required: Joseph Wright, *Grammar of the Gothic Language*, Oxford, 1954, pp. 210–40; Wilhelm Braune, *Althochdeutsches Lesebuch*, Tübingen, 1969 (or subsequent editions), Passage XX sections 3–6; M. O'C. Walsh, *A Middle High German Reader*, Oxford, 1974, Section VII; Alfred Götze, *Frühneuhochdeutsches Lesebuch*, Göttingen, 1958, Sections 5, 8, 11 (234–399), 13, 14 (93–149), 22 (1–18 and 59–110), 25h, 27b, 30, 36 (1–90).

Paper 7. Introduction to German medieval literature
  A thorough knowledge of the following works is required: *Minnesang vom Kürenberger bis Wolfram* (ed. Max Wehrli, Altdeutsche Übungstexte, Nr. 4), the poems of Der von Kürenberg, Friderich von Husen, Heinrich von Morungen, Hartman von Ouwe; Gottfried von Strassburg, *Tristan und Isold* (ed. F. Ranke, Altdeutsche Übungstexte, Nr. 3), lines 10803–12568.
  A general knowledge of the following works is required: Wolfram von Eschenbach, *Parzival*,

† For those students who did the Prelims Part I in 1989, the list of prescribed texts is as originally published (*Reporter*, 1987–88, p. 267).

MODERN AND MEDIEVAL LANGUAGES

Book v (ed. E. Hartl, Altdeutsche Übungstexte, Nr. 12); Walther von der Vogelweide, *Gedichte* (ed. Max Wehrli, Altdeutsche Übungstexte, Nr. 5), sections I, II, III, IV, VIII; Wernher der Gartenære, *Meier Helmbrecht* (any available edition).

*Paper 8. *German literature, thought, and history, from 1620 to 1700*

    (*a*) Texts for close study: *Deutsche Barocklyrik* (ed. M. Wehrli); Gryphius, *Papinianus* (rowohlts Klassiker); Grimmelshausen, *Die Landstörtzerin Courasche* (Reclam or dtv).

    (*b*) A general knowledge of the period, with principal reference to Opitz, Spee, the Nuremberg School. Fleming, Gryphius, Lohenstein, Hofmannswaldau, Grimmelshausen, Beer, Reuter, Günther.

Paper 9. *German literature, thought, and history, from 1770 to 1832*, with special reference to the following:

Goethe, *Faust I* (dty 980 or Reclam 1); *The Penguin Book of German Verse*, pp. 169–319, plus a duplicated selection of lyric poems which can be obtained from the German Department Office; Kleist, *Michael Kohlhaas; Die Marquise von O...; Das Erdbeben in Chili* (available in Kleist, *Erzählungen*, dtv edition, or Reclam nos. 218, 7670, and 1957).

A general knowledge of the period, with principal reference to Goethe, Schiller, Lessing, Herder, Novalis, Hölderlin, and Kleist.

Paper 10. *German literature, thought, and history, from 1815 to 1890*

    (*a*) Texts for close study: Büchner, *Dantons Tod* (Manchester University Press, ed. Jacobs, third edition, 1971); Stifter, *Bunte Steine* (Goldmann Klassiker, 7547); H. Heine, *Gedichte* (Reclam 8988/89), plus a duplicated selection of further poems by Heine which can be obtained from the German Department Office.

    (*b*) A knowledge of the literature, history, and thought of the period, with principal reference to Grillparzer, Hebbel, Heine, Büchner, Mörike, Droste, Keller, Stifter, Nietzsche, Storm, and Meyer.

*Paper 11. *German literature, thought, and history, from 1880 to 1914*

    (*a*) Texts for close study: Fontane, *Effi Briest* (ed. Keitel and Nürnberger, Ullstein); Wedekind, *Erdgeist* and *Die Büchse der Pandora* (ed. Unger and Vinçon, Goldmann); Rilke, *Neue Gedichte I* (Insel Taschenbuch 49).

    (*b*) A knowledge of the literature, history, and thought of the period, with principal reference to Fontane, Hauptmann, Thomas Mann, Heinrich Mann, Hofmannsthal, Schnitzler, Wedekind, Sternheim, Rilke, Stefan George, Trakl, Nietzsche.

ITALIAN

*Paper 12. *Introduction to the structure and varieties of the Italian language*

A general study of the present-day structure and varieties of Italian, together with a study of the general linguistic background.

†Paper 13. *Introduction to Dante and his age*, with special reference to the following:

Dante, *Vita nuova, Inferno, Purgatorio, Convivio* (Book I).
Prescribed topic: Dante's concept of Language.

†Paper 14. (*a*) *Introduction to Dante and his age*, and (*b*) *the literature of the Risorgimento*

    (*a*) Dante, *Vita nuova, Inferno*.
    Prescribed topic: The History of Florence, 1250–1313.
    (*b*) Manzoni, *I promessi sposi*; Leopardi, *I canti*.
    Prescribed topic: The Risorgimento in Italy up to and including the year 1861.

Paper 15. *Introduction to the Italian Renaissance*, with special reference to the following subjects:

    (*a*) Boccaccio, *Decameron*, I, 1–3, III, IV, VI, VII, 1–5, X, 10;
    (*b*) Petrarch, *Selected poems*, eds. Griffith and Hainsworth (M.U.P.);
    (*c*) Ariosto, *Orlando furioso*, selection, ed. Calvino (Einaudi);
    (*d*) Giotto, The Arena Chapel; Masaccio, The Brancacci Chapel; Ghiberti, The Florentine Baptistery Doors; Piero della Francesca, The Legend of the True Cross.
Students will be expected to show knowledge of at least three of the four subjects.

Paper 16. *Italian literature, thought, and history, since 1880*

    (*a*) Texts for close study: Verga, *I Malavoglia*; D'Annunzio, *Alcyone*; Pirandello, *Enrico IV*; Svevo, *La coscienza di Zeno*; Moravia, *Gli Indifferenti*; Gozzano, *I colloqui*; Ungaretti,

---

* See Regulations 17 and 19 (*Ordinances*, pp. 409–410).
† No candidate may offer both Papers 13 and 14.

L'Allegria; Montale, *Ossi di seppia*; Bassani, *Il giardino dei Finzi Contini*; Pavese, *La luna e i falò*; Sciascia, *Il contesto*.

(b) A general knowledge of the period with special reference to Italian political history from 1918 to the present day.

SLAVONIC

*Paper 18. *Introduction to the study of Kievan and Muscovite Russia*, with special reference to the following:

Texts: Сказание...Бориса и Глеба; Повесть о разорении Рязани Батыем;

Topics: Christian culture in the Kievan period; The emergence of Muscovy (Ivan III–Ivan IV); The reign of Aleksei Mikhailovich.

Paper 19. *Russian literature and thought, from 1799 to 1900*, with special reference to the following:

Texts: Pushkin, Медный всадник; Gogol', Повесть о том, как поссорился Иван Иванович с Иваном Никифоровичем; Lermontov, Герой нашего времени; Leskov, Леди Макбет Мценского уезда; Turgenev, Вешние воды.

Topics: Poetry 1800–1820; Chaadaev; the work of Dostoevskii to 1849; the work of Tolstoi after 1878, with special reference to Исповедь, Смерть Ивана Ильича, Хозяин и работник.

*Paper 20. *Russian literature, thought, and history, from 1891 to 1934*, with special reference to the following:

Texts: Chekhov, Невеста, Дом с мезонином, Палата No. 6, В овраге, Дама с собачкой; Blok, *Poems* (ed. A. Pyman); Anna Akhmatova, Четки; Bunin, Жизнь Арсеньева; Fadeev, Разгром; Olesha, Зависть.

Topics: Pobedonostsev; Early Russian Marxism (1894–1905); The revolution of 1905 and the First and Second Dumas; The revolutions of 1917; The rise of Stalin (1917–1928); The collectivization of agriculture (1928–1933).

Paper 21. *Czech and Slovak literature, thought, and history, from 1774 to 1939*, with special reference to the following:

Texts: Mácha, *Máj*; Havlíček, *Křest sv. Vladimíra*; Neruda, *Povídky malostranské*; Vrchlický, *Hudba v duši*; Karásek, *Posvátné ohně*; Machar, *Golgatha*; Olbracht, *Nikola Šuhaj*; Čapek, *Povětroň*; Krasko, *Básnické dielo*; F. Král, *Cesta zarúbaná*.

Topics: Czech *or* Slovak Romanticism; The Czech Decadent movement; Czech and Slovak Proletarian poetry; The Slovak social novel (1918–1939).

*Paper 22. *Czech drama from 1813 to 1939*, with special reference to the following:

Tyl, *Paličova dcera*; Bozděch, *Baron Görtz*; Mrštíkové, *Maryša*; Hilbert, *O Boha*; Dyk, *Posel*; Langer, *Periferie*; Bratří Čapkové, *Ze života hmyzu*; Konrád, *Kvočna*.

Paper 23. *Polish literature, thought, and history, from 1795 to 1914*, with special reference to the following:

Mickiewicz, *Sonety krymskie*; Słowacki, *Kordian*; Norwid, *Vade-mecum*; Prus, *Powracająca fala*; Sienkiewicz, *Nowele*; Wyspiański, *Noc listopadowa*.

Paper 24. *Polish literature and thought, from 1918 to 1956*, with special reference to the following:

Żeromski, *Przedwiośnie*; Pollak-Matuszewski, *Poezja polska 1914–1939*; Witkiewicz, *Szewcy*; Gombrowicz, *Ferdydurke*; Miłosz, *Wiersze* (London, 1967); Borowski, *Pożegnanie z Marią*.

*Paper 25. *Serbian literature, history, and institutions, from 1168 to 1389*, with special reference to the following:

Texts: Stojan Novaković, Примери књижевности и језика старога српско-словенскога (Beograd, 1909): pp. 209–17, 219–24, 229–38, 240–5, 247–68; N. Radojčić, Законик цара Душана (S.A.N. Beograd, 1960).

Topics: The work of St Sava; The history of Serbia from 1168 to 1355; The development of the Serbian biography; The causes leading to the Serbian defeat at Kosovo in 1389.

Paper 26. *Serbian and Croatian literature, thought, and history, since 1800*, with special reference to the following:

(a) Ivan Mažuranić, *Smrt Smail-age Čengijića*; Branko Radičević, *Pesme*; L. K. Lazarević *Pripovetke*; Miroslav Krleža, *Povratak Filipa Latinovicza*; Ivo Andrić, *Na Drini Ćuprija*; Dobrica Ćosić, *Daleko je sunce*.

(b) Topics; The work of Vuk Karadžić; The history of the first and second Serbian risings 1804–1830; The Illyrian Movement; *Seoska pripovetka*; The *Moderna* and Croatian literature 1897–1914.

* See Regulations 17 and 19 (*Ordinances*, pp. 409–410).

MODERN AND MEDIEVAL LANGUAGES 303

SCANDINAVIAN

*Paper 27. *Danish literature, thought, and history, from 1870 to 1918*, with special reference to the following:

J. P. Jacobsen, *Fru Marie Grubbe, Digte og Udkast*; Herman Bang, *Haabløse Slægter*; Henrik Pontoppidan, *Skyer*; Sophus Claussen, *Lyrik* (ed. F. J. Billeskov J.); Johannes V. Jensen, *Kongens Fald, Digte*; Martin Andersen Nexø, *Pelle Erobreren, Barndom*.

Paper 28. *Danish literature, thought, and history, from 1918 to the present day*, with special reference to the following:

Hans Kirk, *Fiskerne*; Karen Blixen, *Syv fantastiske Fortællinger*; Tom Kristensen, *Hærværk*; William Heinesen, *De fortabte Spillemænd*; Klaus Rifbjerg, *Anna (jeg) Anna*; Tove Ditlevsen, *Digte*; Kirsten Thorup, *Baby*.

*Paper 29. *Norwegian literature, thought, and history, from 1870 to 1918*, with special reference to the following:

Henrik Ibsen, *Et Dukkehjem*; Alexander Kielland, *Garman og Worse*; Jonas Lie, *Familjen på Gilje*; Arne Garborg, *Bondestudentar*; Bjørnstjerne Bjørnson, *Over Ævne I*; Henrik Ibsen, *John Gabriel Borkman*; Knut Hamsun, *Pan*; Sigrid Undset, *Jenny*.

Paper 30. *Norwegian literature, thought, and history, from 1918 to the present day*, with special reference to the following:

Johan Falkbergert, *Den fjerde nattevakt*; Knut Hamsun, *Landstrykere*; Nordahl Grieg, *Nederlaget*; Sigurd Hoel, *Møte ved milepelen*; Johan Borgen, *Lillelord*; Terjei Vesaas, *Fuglane*; G. Reiss-Andersen, *Digt i utvalg 1921–1962*; Dag Solstad, *25. Septemberplass*.

*Paper 31. *Swedish literature, thought, and history, from 1870 to 1918*, with special reference to the following:

August Strindberg, *Röda rummet, Tjänstekvinnans son I, Dödsdansen*; Selma Lagerlöf, *Gösta Berlings saga*; Gustaf Fröding, *Samlade dikter*; v. Heidenstam, *Dikter* and *Nya Dikter*; Hjalmar Söderberg, *Den allvarsamma leken*; Hjalmar Bergman, *Blå blommor*.

Paper 32. *Swedish literature, thought, and history, from 1918 to the present day*, with special reference to the following:

Hjalmar Bergman, *Markurells i Wadköping*; Birger Sjöberg, *Kriser och kransar*; Pär Lagerkvist, *Gäst hos verkligheten*; Harry Martinson, *Aniara*; Lars Ahlin, *Sjätte munnen*; Lars Gyllensten, *Barnabok*; Stig Dagerman, *Ormen*; Lars Andersson, *Snöljus*.

SPANISH

*Paper 33. *An introduction to the history of the Peninsular languages*

A general study of the present-day structures and basic external histories of Castilian and *either* Portuguese *or* Catalan. The following texts are set for special linguistic study:

Castilian: María de Maeztu, *Antología Siglo XX: Prosistas españoles*, Part two (col. Austral); Federico García Lorca, *La zapatera prodigiosa*; *Oxford Book of Spanish Verse*, 2nd ed. nos. 179–85, 189–93, 200–6, 219–27.

Portuguese: G. de Castilho (ed.), *Os melhores contos portugueses* (2. serie), pp. 1–97; *Contos do Brasil* (Harrap), pp. 1–57; *Oxford Book of Portuguese Verse*, 2nd ed. nos. 180–7, 200–5, 227–31, 250–4.

Catalan: J. Gili, *Introductory Catalan Grammar*, 2nd ed., pp. 122–52.

*Paper 34. *Medieval Spain*

A general study of the literature in connexion with the historical and cultural background during the Middle Ages, with special reference to narrative poetry.

Paper 35. *Spanish literature, thought, and history in the sixteenth century*, with special reference to the following:

(a) Texts for close study: Fernando de Rojas, *La Celestina*; the complete poems of Garcilaso de la Vega; San Juan de la Cruz, with special reference to his poetry; Gil Vicente, *Don Duardos, Auto de la Sibila Casandra*; Alfonso de Valdés, *Diálogo de las cosas ocurridas en Roma*; Lope de Vega, *Los comendadores de Córdoba, El remedio en la desdicha, El castigo del discreto*; Anon., *La vida de Lazarillo de Tormes*.

(b) General topics: the Spanish Inquisition; the Spanish monarchy; El Greco; the life of St Teresa.

---

* See Regulations 17 and 19 (*Ordinances*, pp. 409–410).

CAMBRIDGE HANDBOOK

*Paper 36. *Cervantes and the Golden Age novel from 1500 to 1616*, with special reference to the following:
  Amadís de Gaula (selections); *Lazarillo de Tormes*; Jorge de Montemayor, *La Diana*; Mateo Alemán, *Guzmán de Alfarache* (selections); Miguel de Cervantes, *Don Quijote*, *El celoso extremeño*, *La fuerza de la sangre*, *El coloquio de los perros*.

*Paper 37. *Benito Pérez Galdós and the nineteenth-century novel*, with special reference to the following:
  Benito Pérez Galdós, *Bailén*, *Prim*, *Ángel Guerra*, *La de Bringas*, *Misericordia*; Fernán Caballero, *La Gaviota*; P. A. de Alarcón, *El escándalo*; José María de Pereda, *Sotileza*; Juan Valera, *El comendador Mendoza*; Leopoldo Alas, *La Regenta*; E. Pardo Bazán, *La cuestión palpitante*.

Paper 38. Spanish literature, thought, and history in the twentieth century
  (a) A general knowledge of the period, with principal reference to the following: the 1898 generation; *modernismo*; *poesía popular*; the Second Republic and the Civil War; Franco's Spain; the Spanish novel 1939–1960 and its setting in post Civil War Spain.
  (b) Texts for close study: Unamuno, *Tres novelas ejemplares y un prólogo*; Antonio Machado, *Soledades, Galerías y otros poemas*, *Campos de Castilla*; Baroja, **either** *Aurora roja* **or** *El Mayorazgo de Labraz*; Ortega y Gasset, *Ideas sobre la novela*; Juan Ramón Jiménez, *Segunda antolojía poética*; García Lorca, *El amor de don Perlimplín con Belisa en su jardín*; Valle-Inclán, *Los cuernos de don Friolera*.

*Paper 39. Argentina and Mexico since 1830
  A general study of their history and culture, with special reference to the following: Argentina: Federalism and the Capital Question, economic development, literature; Mexico: the *Reforma*, the Empire of Maximilian, Porfirio Díaz, the novel and poetry.
  Prescribed texts for detailed study: José Hernández, *Martín Fierro*; D. F. Sarmiento, *Facundo, o civilización y barbarie*; Leopoldo Lugones; Julio Cortázar, *Los premios*, *Rayuela*; Mariano Azuela, *Los de abajo*; Juan Rulfo, *Pedro Páramo*; Mexican poetry in the twentieth century; Carlos Fuentes, *Cambio de piel*.

DUTCH

*Paper 40. *The early history and literature of the Netherlands*, with special reference to the following:
  (a) Texts for close study: Maerlant, *Van den Lande van Oversee* and *Der Kerken Glaghe* (Spectrum van de Nederlandse Letterkunde 3); *Lanceloet en het hert met de witte voet* and Segher Diengotgaf, *Tprieel van Troyen* (Spectrum...1); Keuze uit het *Geuzenliedboek* (Spectrum...7); *Een suverlijc boecxken* (Spectrum...4).
  (b) General topics: Middle Dutch Arthurian romances; The early history of the Low Countries.

*Paper 41. *Vondel*, with special reference to the following:
  Vondel, *Gijsbreght van Aemstel* and *Joseph in Dothan* (Spectrum van de Nederlandse Letterkunde 13); *Lucifer*; *Adam in Ballingschap*; *Kleine gedichten* (Spectrum...9); *Verovering van Grol* and *De getemde Mars* (Spectrum...7).

Paper 42. *The literature, thought, and history of the Netherlands, from 1830 to 1918*
  To be available only after consultation.

Paper 43. *The literature, thought, and history of the Netherlands, from 1880 to 1939*, with special reference to the following:
  (a) Texts for close study: *Een nieuw geluid. De Tachtigers in proza en poëzie* (Spectrum van de Nederlandse Letterkunde 23); *Zit stil en reis* (Spectrum...25); Couperus, *Eline Vere*; L. van Deyssel, *Een liefde*; M. Emants, *Een Nagelaten Bekentenis*; Nescio, *Titaantjes, De Uitvreter*; A. van Schendel, *De Waterman*; Heyermans, *Uitkomst*; F. Bordewijk, *Karakter*; G. Walschap, *Houtekiet*.
  (b) General topic: Naturalism in the Netherlands.

PORTUGUESE

*Paper 44. *Portuguese literature, thought, and history, from 1495 to 1580*, with special reference to the following:
  Gil Vicente, *Sátiras sociais* (ed. Saraiva); Sá de Miranda, *Cartas*, *Basto*; Bernardim Ribeiro, *Menina e moça*; António Ferreira, *Castro*; Camões, *Os Lusíadas*.

Paper 45. *Portuguese literature, thought, and history, since 1825*, with special reference to the following:
  Almeida Garrett, *Viagens na minha terra*, *Frei Luís de Sousa*; Camilo Castelo Branco, *A Brasileira de Prazins*; Antero de Quental, *Sonetos*; Cesário Verde, *Poesias*; Eça de Queiroz, *O Primo Basílio*.

* See Regulations 17 and 19 (*Ordinances*, pp. 409–410).

MODERN AND MEDIEVAL LANGUAGES   305

MODERN GREEK

*Paper 46. *Greek literature, thought, and history, from 1453 to 1700*

    (a) Texts for close study: *Ανακάλημα της Κωνσταντινόπολης* (ed. Kriaras); *Η φυλλάδα του γαϊδάρου* (ed. L. Alexiou); Bergadis, *Απόκοπος*; *Η Βοσκοπούλα* (ed. S. Alexiou 1971); S. Alexiou, *Κρητική Ανθολογία* (2nd ed. 1969); G. Chortatsis, *Ερωφίλη* (ed. Xanthoudidis); V. Kornaros, *Ερωτόκριτος*, Book I (ed. S. Alexiou).

    (b) Topics: the Orthodox Church; the Greek community in Venice; Turkish rule in mainland Greece; the Turco-Venetian war of 1645–1669; Cretan drama; developments in verse form.

Paper 47. *Greek literature, thought, and history, since 1800*

    (a) Texts for close study: D. Solomos, *Ο Κρητικός, Ο Πόρφυρας, Οι Ελεύθεροι Πολιορκημένοι*; K. Palamas, *Ίαμβοι και Ανάπαιστοι, Οι Καημοί της Λιμνοθάλασσας*; A. Karkavitsas, *Ο Ζητιάνος* (ed. Mastrodimitris 1980); C. P. Cavafy, *Ποιήματα*, Vol. I (ed. Savvidis); G. Seferis, *Μυθιστόρημα*; G. Theotokas, *Λεωνής*; S. Myrivilis, *Ο Βασίλης ο Αρβανίτης*; O. Elytis, *Άσμα ηρωικό και πένθιμο για το χαμένο ανθυπολοχαγό της Αλβανίας*; D. Chatzis, *Το τέλος της μικρής μας πόλης*; K. Tachtsis, *Το τρίτο στεφάνι*.

    (b) Topics: the War of Independence; the School of the Ionian Isles; the 'Great Idea'; the language question 1888–1920; the First World War and the Asia Minor Disaster; the political history of Greece since the Second World War.

SUPPLEMENTARY SUBJECT

*Paper 48. *Medieval Latin Literature*

    This subject will include Medieval Latin literature up to A.D. 1000, with special reference to the following:

    Augustine, *Confessiones* (publ. Loeb or Budé), Book VIII; Einhard, *Vita Karoli Magni*; *The Oxford Book of Medieval Latin Verse* (ed. F. J. E. Raby), nos. 9–118; *Carmina Cantabrigiensia* (ed. K. Strecker or W. Bulst).

SCHEDULE I
PAPERS FOR SECTION B OF PART I IN 1991
FRENCH

Paper 3. *French literature, thought, and history, in the seventeenth century*, with special reference to the period 1630–1700, and to the following:

    Corneille; Descartes, *Discours de la méthode*; Mme de Lafayette, *La Princesse de Clèves*; La Fontaine, *Fables*; La Rochefoucauld, *Maximes*; Molière; Pascal, *Pensées* (ed. L. Lafuma, Editions du Seuil, Collection 'Points'); Racine; Church and society in France, 1630–1700.

Paper 4. *French literature, thought, and history, in the eighteenth century*, with special reference to the period 1715–1789, and to the following:

    Lesage, *Gil Blas*; Montesquieu, *Lettres persanes*; Voltaire, *Zadig, Candide*, either *Le Philosophe ignorant* or *Lettres philosophiques*; Rousseau, *Les Rêveries du promeneur solitaire*; Diderot, *Le Neveu de Rameau*; Marivaux, *Le Jeu de l'amour et du hasard, La Double Inconstance, Les Fausses Confidences*; Prévost, *Manon Lescaut*; Beaumarchais, *Le Barbier de Séville, Le Mariage de Figaro*; Laclos, *Les Liaisons dangereuses*; The rôle of the *parlements* in eighteenth-century France; Watteau.

Paper 5. *French literature, thought, and history, in the nineteenth century*, with special reference to the period 1830–1870, and to the following:

    Stendhal, *Le Rouge et le noir*; Balzac, *La Cousine Bette*; Flaubert, *Madame Bovary*; Hugo, *Les Contemplations*; Nerval, *Les Chimères, Sylvie*; Gautier, *Emaux et camées*; Baudelaire, *Les Fleurs du Mal*; Romantic drama; the Revolutions of 1848; Utopian thought, 1830–51.

GERMAN

Paper 6. *Aspects of the history of the German language*

    A thorough knowledge of the following passages is required: Joseph Wright, *Grammar of the Gothic Language*, Oxford, 1954, pp. 210–40; Wilhelm Braune, *Althochdeutsches Lesebuch*,

* See Regulations 17 and 19 (*Statutes and Ordinances*, pp. 388–9).

Tübingen, 1969, passage XX, sections 3–6; M. O'C. Walshe, *A Middle High German Reader*, Oxford, 1974, section VII; Alfred Götze, *Frühneuhochdeutsches Lesebuch*, Göttingen, 1958, sections 1(a), 3(b), 8, 11(b) (lines 197–233), 12(b), 13, 16 (lines 1–81), 19(a), 20(d), 26(c), 27(b), 31(a) (lines 1–34).

Paper 7. *Introduction to German medieval literature*

A thorough knowledge of the following works is required: *Minnesang vom Kürenberger bis Wolfram* (ed. Max Wehrli, Altdeutsche Übungstexte, Nr. 4), the poems of Der von Kürenberg, Friderich von Husen, Heinrich von Morungen, Hartman von Ouwe; Gottfried von Strassburg, *Tristan und Isold* (ed. F. Ranke, Altdeutsche Übungstexte, Nr. 3), lines 10803–12568.

A general knowledge of the following works is required: Wolfram von Eschenbach, *Parzival*, Book v (ed. E. Hartl, Altdeutsche Übungstexte, Nr. 12); Walther von der Vogelweide, *Gedichte* (ed. Max Wehrli, Altdeutsche Übungstexte, Nr. 5), sections I, II, III, IV, VIII; Wernher der Gartenære, *Meier Helmbrecht* (any available edition).

*Paper 8. *German literature, thought, and history, from 1620 to 1700*

(a) Texts for close study: *Deutsche Barocklyrik* (ed. M. Wehrli); Gryphius, *Papinianus* (rowohlts Klassiker), Grimmelshausen, *Die Landstörtzerin Courasche* (Reclam or dtv).

(b) A general knowledge of the period, with principal reference to Opitz, Spee, the Nuremberg School. Fleming, Gryphius, Lohenstein, Hofmannswaldau, Grimmelshausen, Beer, Reuter, Günther.

Paper 9. *German literature, thought, and history, from 1770 to 1832*, with special reference to the following:

Goethe, *Faust I* (dtv 980 or Reclam 1); *The Penguin Book of German Verse*, pp. 169–319, plus a duplicated selection of lyric poems which can be obtained from the German Department Office; Kleist, *Michael Kohlhaas*; *Die Marquise von O...*; *Das Erdbeben in Chili* (available in Kleist, *Erzählungen*, dtv edition, or Reclam nos. 218, 7670, and 1957).

A general knowledge of the period, with principal reference to Goethe, Schiller, Lessing, Herder, Novalis, Hölderlin, and Kleist.

Paper 10. *German literature, thought, and history, from 1815 to 1890*

(a) Texts for close study: Büchner, *Dantons Tod* (Manchester University Press, ed. Jacobs, third edition, 1971); Stifter, *Bunte Steine* (Goldmann Klassiker, 7547); H. Heine, *Gedichte* (Reclam 8988/89), plus a duplicated selection of further poems by Heine which can be obtained from the German Department Office.

(b) A knowledge of the literature, history, and thought of the period, with principal reference to Grillparzer, Hebbel, Heine, Büchner, Mörike, Droste, Keller, Stifter, Nietzsche, Storm, and Meyer.

*Paper 11. *German literature, thought, and history, from 1880 to 1914*

(a) Texts for close study: Fontane, *Effi Briest* (ed. Keitel and Nürnberger, Ullstein); Wedekind, *Erdgeist* and *Die Büchse der Pandora* (ed. Unger and Vinçon, Goldmann); Rilke, *Neue Gedichte I* (Insel Taschenbuch 49).

(b) A knowledge of the literature, history, and thought of the period, with principal reference to Fontane, Hauptmann, Thomas Mann, Heinrich Mann, Hofmannsthal, Schnitzler, Wedekind, Sternheim, Rilke, Stefan George, Trakl, Nietzsche.

ITALIAN

*Paper 12. *Introduction to the structure and varieties of the Italian language*

A general study of the present-day structure and varieties of Italian, together with a study of the general linguistic background.

†Paper 13. *Introduction to Dante and his age*, with special reference to the following:

Dante, *Vita nuova, Inferno, Purgatorio, Convivio* (Book I).
Prescribed topic: Dante's concept of Language.

†Paper 14. (a) *Introduction to Dante and his age*, and (b) *the literature of the Risorgimento*

(a) Dante, *Vita nuova, Inferno*.
Prescribed topic: The History of Florence, 1250–1313.

(b) Manzoni, *I promessi sposi*; Leopardi, *I canti*.
Prescribed topic: The Risorgimento in Italy up to and including the year 1861.

---

* See Regulations 17 and 19 (*Statutes and Ordinances*, pp. 388–9).
† No candidate may offer both Papers 13 and 14.

Paper 15. Introduction to the Italian Renaissance, with special reference to the following subjects:
   (a) Boccaccio, *Decameron*, I, 1-3, III, IV, VI, VII, 1-5, X, 10;
   (b) Petrarch, *Selected poems*, eds. Griffith and Hainsworth (M.U.P.);
   (c) Ariosto, *Orlando furioso*, selection, ed. Calvino (Einaudi);
   (d) Giotto, The Arena Chapel; Masaccio, The Brancacci Chapel; Ghiberti, The Florentine Baptistery Doors; Piero della Francesca, The Legend of the True Cross.
   Students will be expected to show knowledge of at least three of the four subjects.

Paper 16. Italian literature, thought, and history, since 1880
   (a) Texts for close study: Verga, *I Malavoglia*; D'Annunzio, *Alcyone*; Pirandello, *Enrico IV*; Svevo, *La coscienza di Zeno*; Moravia, *Gli Indifferenti*; Gozzano, *I colloqui*; Ungaretti, *L'Allegria*; Montale, *Ossi di seppia*; Bassani, *Il giardino dei Finzi Contini*; Pavese, *La luna e i falò*; Sciascia, *Il contesto*.
   (b) A general knowledge of the period with special reference to Italian political history from 1918 to the present day.

SLAVONIC

*Paper 18. Introduction to the study of Kievan and Muscovite Russia, with special reference to the following:
   Texts: Сказание...Бориса и Глеба; Ilarion, Слово о законе и благодати; Повесть о разорении Рязани Батыем; Сказание о Дракуле; Повесть о Ерше Ершовиче.
   Topics: Christian culture in the Kievan period; The emergence of Muscovy (Ivan III–Ivan IV); The reign of Aleksei Mikhailovich.

Paper 19. Russian literature and thought, from 1799 to 1900, with special reference to the following:
   Texts: Pushkin, Медный всадник; Gogol', Повесть о том, как поссорился Иван Иванович с Иваном Никифоровичем; Lermontov, Герой нашего времени; Leskov, Леди Макбет Мценского уезда; Turgenev, Вешние воды.
   Topics: Poetry 1800–1820; Chaadaev; the work of Dostoevskii to 1849; the work of Tolstoi after 1878, with special reference to Исповедь, Смерть Ивана Ильича, Хозяин и работник.

*Paper 20. Russian literature, thought, and history, from 1891 to 1934, with special reference to the following:
   Texts: Chekhov, Невеста, Дом с мезонином, Палата No. 6, В овраге, Дама с собачкой; Blok, *Poems* (ed. A.Pyman); Anna Akhmatova, Четки; Bunin, Жизнь Арсеньева; Fadeev, Разгром; Olesha, Зависть.
   Topics: Pobedonostsev; Early Russian Marxism (1894–1905); The revolution of 1905 and the First and Second Dumas; The revolutions of 1917; The rise of Stalin (1917–1928); The collectivization of agriculture (1928–1933).

Paper 21. Czech and Slovak literature, thought, and history, from 1774 to 1939, with special reference to the following;
   Texts: Mácha, *Máj*; Havlíček, *Křest sv. Vladimíra*; Neruda, *Povídky malostranské*; Vrchlický, *Hudba v duši*; Karásek, *Posvátné ohně*; Machar, *Golgatha*; Olbracht, *Nikola Šuhaj*; Čapek, *Povětroň*; Krasko, *Básnické dielo*; F.Král, *Cesta zarúbaná*.
   Topics: Czech *or* Slovak Romanticism; The Czech Decadent movement; Czech and Slovak Proletarian poetry; The Slovak social novel (1918–1939).

*Paper 22. Czech drama from 1813 to 1939, with special reference to the following:
   Tyl, *Paličova dcera*; Bozděch, *Baron Görtz*; Mrštíkové, *Maryša*; Hilbert, *O Boha*; Dyk, *Posel*; Langer, *Periferie*; Bratři Čapkové, *Ze života hmyzu*; Konrád, *Kvočna*.

Paper 23. Polish literature, thought, and history, from 1795 to 1914, with special reference to the following:
   Mickiewicz, *Sonety krymskie*; Słowacki, *Kordian*; Norwid, *Vade-mecum*; Prus, *Powracająca fala*; Sienkiewicz, *Nowele*; Wyspiański, *Noc listopadowa*.

Paper 24. Polish literature and thought, from 1918 to 1956, with special reference to the following:
   Żeromski, *Przedwiośnie*; Pollak-Matuszewski, *Poezja polska 1914–1939*; Witkiewicz, *Szewcy*; Gombrowicz, *Ferdydurke*; Miłosz, *Wiersze* (London, 1967); Borowski, *Pożegnanie z Marią*.

* See Regulations 17 and 19 (*Statutes and Ordinances*, pp. 388–9).

*†*Paper 25. *Serbian literature, history, and institutions, from 1168 to 1389*, with special reference to the following:

Texts: Stojan Novaković, Примери књижевности и језика старога српско-словенскога (Beograd, 1909): pp. 209–17, 219–24, 229–38, 240–5, 247–68; N. Radojčić, Законик цара Душана (S.A.N. Beograd, 1960).

Topics: The work of St Sava; The history of Serbia from 1168 to 1355; The development of the Serbian biography; The causes leading to the Serbian defeat at Kosovo in 1389.

†Paper 26. *Serbian and Croatian literature, thought, and history, since 1800*, with special reference to the following:

(a) Ivan Mažuranić, *Smrt Smail-age Čengijića*; Branko Radičević, *Pesme*; L.K. Lazarević *Pripovetke*; Miroslav Krleža, *Povratak Filipa Latinovicza*; Ivo Andrić, *Na Drini Ćuprija*; Dobrica Ćosić, *Daleko je sunce*.

(b) Topics: The work of Vuk Karadžić; The history of the first and second Serbian risings 1804–1830; The Illyrian Movement; *Seoska pripovetka*; The *Moderna* and Croatian literature 1897–1914.

SPANISH

*Paper 33. *An introduction to the history of the Peninsular languages*

A general study of the present-day structures and basic external histories of Castilian and *either* Portuguese *or* Catalan.

*Paper 34. *Medieval Spain*

A general study of the literature in connexion with the historical and cultural background during the Middle Ages, with special reference to narrative poetry.

Paper 35. *Spanish literature, thought, and history in the sixteenth century*, with special reference to the following:

(a) Texts for close study: Fernando de Rojas, *La Celestina*; the complete poems of Garcilaso de la Vega; San Juan de la Cruz, with special reference to his poetry; Gil Vicente, *Don Duardos*, *Auto de la Sibila Casandra*; Alfonso de Valdés, *Diálogo de las cosas ocurridas en Roma*; Lope de Vega, *Los comendadores de Córdoba*, *El remedio en la desdicha*, *El castigo del discreto*; Anon., *La vida de Lazarillo de Tormes*.

(b) General topics: the Spanish Inquisition; the Spanish monarchy; El Greco; the life of St Teresa.

*Paper 36. *Cervantes and the Golden Age novel from 1500 to 1616*, with special reference to the following: *Amadís de Gaula* (selections); *Lazarillo de Tormes*; Jorge de Montemayor, *La Diana*; Mateo Alemán, *Guzmán de Alfarache* (selections); Miguel de Cervantes, *Don Quijote, El celoso extremeño, La fuerza de la sangre, El coloquio de los perros*.

*Paper 37. *Benito Pérez Galdós and the nineteenth-century novel*, with special reference to the following: Benito Pérez Galdós, *Bailén, Prim, Angel Guerra, La de Bringas, Misericordia*; Fernán Caballero, *La Gaviota*; P.A. de Alarcón, *El escándalo*; José María de Pereda, *Sotileza*; Juan Valera, *El comendador Mendoza*; Leopoldo Alas, *La Regenta*; E. Pardo Bazán, *La cuestión palpitante*.

Paper 38. *Spanish literature, thought, and history in the twentieth century*

(a) A general knowledge of the period, with principal reference to the following: *la generación del '98; modernismo*; the Spanish novel 1940–1960; the decline and fall of the monarchy in Spain in the twentieth century; the Civil War and Franco's Spain; post-Franco Spain.

(b) Texts for close study: Unamuno, *Tres novelas ejemplares y un prólogo*; Antonio Machado, *Soledades, galerías y otros poemas, Campos de Castilla*; Salinas, *La voz a ti debida*; Baroja, *El árbol de la ciencia*; Valle-Inclán, *Los cuernos de don Friolera* with Garcia Lorca, *El amor de don Perlimplin*; Ortega y Gasset, *La deshumanización del arte*.

*Paper 39. *Argentina and Mexico since 1830*

A general study of their history and culture, with special reference to the following: Argentina; Federalism and the Capital Question, economic development, literature; Mexico: the *Reforma*; the Empire of Maximilian, Porfirio Díaz, the novel and poetry.

Prescribed texts for detailed study: José Hernández, *Martín Fierro*; D.F. Sarmiento, *Facundo*; the short stories of Julio Cortázar, specifically *Relatos* (Alianza), vol. 3; J.L. Borges, *El informe de Brodie*; Manuel Puig, *Boquitas pintadas*; Mariano Azuela, *Los de abajo*; Juan Rulfo, *El llano en llamas*; Octavio Paz, *La estación violenta*; Carlos Fuentes, *Aura, Gringo viejo*; Rosario Castellanos, *Balún Canán*.

---

* See Regulations 17 and 19 (*Statutes and Ordinances*, pp. 388–9).
† Candidates who are interested in this paper should consult the Head of the Department of Slavonic Studies.

MODERN AND MEDIEVAL LANGUAGES

DUTCH

*Paper 40. *The early history and literature of the Netherlands*, with special reference to the following:

(a) Texts for close study: Maerlant, *Van den Lande van Oversee* and *Der Kerken Glaghe* (Spectrum van de Nederlandse Letterkunde 3); *Lanceloet en het hert met de witte voet* and Segher Diengotgaf, *Tprieel van Troyen* (Spectrum...1); Keuze uit het *Geuzenliedboek* (Spectrum...7); *Een suverlijc boecxken* (Spectrum...4).

(b) General topics: Middle Dutch Arthurian romances; The early history of the Low Countries.

*Paper 41. *Vondel*, with special reference to the following:

Vondel, *Gijsbreght van Aemstel* and *Joseph in Dothan* (Spectrum van de Nederlandse Letterkunde 13); *Lucifer*; *Adam in Ballingschap*; *Kleine gedichten* (Spectrum...9); *Verovering van Grol* and *De getemde Mars* (Spectrum...7).

Paper 42. *The literature, thought, and history of the Netherlands, from 1830 to 1918*
To be available only after consultation.

Paper 43. *The literature, thought, and history of the Netherlands, from 1880 to 1939*, with special reference to the following:

(a) Texts for close study: *Een nieuw geluid. De Tachtigers in proza en poëzie* (Spectrum van de Nederlandse Letterkunde 23); *Zit stil en reis* (Spectrum...25); Couperus, *Eline Vere*; L. van Deyssel, *Een liefde*; M. Emants, *Een Nagelaten Bekentenis*; Nescio, *Titaantjes, De Uitvreter*; A. van Schendel, *De Waterman*; Heyermans, *Uitkomst*; F. Bordewijk, *Karakter*; G. Walschap, *Houtekiet*.

(b) General topic: Naturalism in the Netherlands.

PORTUGUESE

*Paper 44. *Portuguese literature, thought, and history, from 1495 to 1580*, with special reference to the following:

Gil Vicente, *Sátiras sociais* (ed. Saraiva); Sá de Miranda, *Cartas, Basto*; Bernardim Ribeiro, *Menina e moça*; António Ferreira, *Castro*; Camões, *Os Lusíadas*.

Paper 45. *Portuguese literature, thought, and history, since 1825*, with special reference to the following:

Almeida Garrett, *Viagens na minha terra, Frei Luís de Sousa*; Camilo Castelo Branco, *A Brasileira de Prazins*; Antero de Quental, *Sonetos*; Cesário Verde, *Poesias*; Eça de Queiroz, *O Primo Basílio*.

MODERN GREEK

*Paper 46. *Greek literature, thought, and history, from 1453 to 1700*

(a) Texts for close study: *Ανακάλημα της Κωνσταντινόπολης* (ed. Kriaras); *Η φυλλάδα του γαϊδάρου* (ed. L. Alexiou); Bergadìs, *Απόκοπος*; *Η Βοσκοπούλα* (ed. S. Alexiou 1971); S. Alexiou, *Κρητική Ανθολογία* (2nd ed. 1969); G. Chortatsis, *Ερωφίλη* (ed. Xanthoudidis); V. Kornaros, *Ερωτόκριτος*, Book I (ed. S. Alexiou).

(b) Topics: the Orthodox Church; the Greek community in Venice; Turkish rule in mainland Greece; the Turco-Venetian war of 1645–1669; Cretan drama; developments in verse form.

Paper 47. *Greek literature, thought, and history, since 1800*

(a) Texts for close study: D. Solomos, *Ο Κρητικός, Ο Πόρφυρας, Οι Ελεύθεροι Πολιορκημένοι*; K. Palamas, *Ίαμβοι και Ανάπαιστοι, Οι Καημοί της Λιμνοθάλασσας*; A. Karkavitsas, *Ο Ζητιάνος* (ed. Mastrodimitris 1980); C. P. Cavafy, *Ποιήματα*, Vol. I (ed. Savvidis); G. Seferis, *Μυθιστόρημα*; G. Theotokas, *Λεωνής*; S. Myrivilis, *Ο Βασίλης ο Αρβανίτης*; O. Elytis, *Άσμα ηρωικό και πένθιμο για το χαμένο ανθυπολοχαγό της Αλβανίας*; D. Chatzis, *Το τέλος της μικρής μας πόλης*; K. Tachtsis, *Το τρίτο στεφάνι*.

(b) Topics: the War of Independence; the School of the Ionian Isles; the 'Great Idea'; the language question 1888–1920; the First World War and the Asia Minor Disaster; the political history of Greece since the Second World War.

SUPPLEMENTARY SUBJECT

*Paper 48. *Medieval Latin Literature*

This subject will include Medieval Latin literature up to A.D. 1000, with special reference to the following:

Augustine, *Confessiones* (publ. Loeb or Budé), Book VIII; Einhard, *Vita Karoli Magni*; *The Oxford Book of Medieval Latin Verse* (ed. F. J. E. Raby), nos. 9–118; *Carmina Cantabrigiensia* (ed. K. Strecker or W. Bulst).

* See Regulations 17 and 19 (*Statutes and Ordinances*, pp. 388–9).

The Faculty Board may allow candidates to be examined in subjects or papers other than those specified if, in the Board's opinion, the languages of the subjects offered possess literature adequate for examination purposes and if the Board are satisfied that the requisite teaching is available. Applications must be made not later than the division of the Michaelmas Term before the examination. Permission may be refused to a candidate who wishes to offer two closely allied languages. The following language and papers have been approved for the Part I examinations in **1990** and **1991**:

Hungarian

1. **Hungarian literature, thought, and history, from 1906 to 1956.**
2. **Hungarian literature, thought, and history, from 1849 to 1906.**

The following texts have been prescribed for these papers in **1990** and **1991**:

Hungarian literature, thought, and history, from 1906 to 1956, with special reference to the following:

    Kaffka, *Szinek és évek*; Füst Milán, *Összes versei*; Kosztolányi, *Néró, a véres költő*; Illyés, *Puszták népe*; Radnóti, *Tajtékos ég*; Déry, *Niki*.

**Hungarian literature, thought, and history, from 1849 to 1906*, with special reference to the following:

    Jókai Mór, *Az aranyember*; Arany László, *A délibábok hőse*; Madách Imre, *Az ember tragédiája*; Mikszáth Kálmán, *Az uj Zrinyiász*; Reviczky Gyula, *Összes versei*.
    For general reading the relevant parts of the following works are recommended: Szerb Antal, *Magyar irodalomtörténet*; Denis Sinor, *History of Hungary*.

Part II

Candidates for Part II must offer:

- (*a*) *either* (i) four papers, if they take the examination in the year next after that in which they have obtained honours in another Honours Examination;
-     *or* (ii) five papers, if they take the examination in the year next but one after that in which they obtained **honours in another Honours Examination;**

- (*b*) **an essay in a medieval or modern foreign language linked with** at least one of their options;

---

* See Regulations 17 and 19 (*Statutes and Ordinances*, pp. 388–9).

and
  (*c*) a paper containing one passage of English for translation into a foreign language to which the papers of their choice appertain and one passage of that language for translation into English.

Certain papers are common to Schedules I and II; candidates may not offer from Schedule II any paper which they have previously offered in Part I.

A year spent studying abroad, with the permission of the Faculty Board (see *Study abroad*, p. 292), will be disregarded for the purpose of calculating a candidate's standing for option (i) or (ii) under (*a*) above.

Dissertations

With certain exceptions, which may vary from time to time, a candidate may choose to offer a dissertation on a subject approved by the Faculty Board which lies within the field of one or more of the papers listed in Schedule II (see p. 317). Candidates may offer a dissertation

(*a*) as an *alternative* to one of their four or five papers mentioned in (*a*) (i) and (ii) above, so that they offer either three papers and a dissertation or four papers and a dissertation, together with the requisite language papers. (This is known as a dissertation under Regulation 27(*a*)(i).) The following restrictions apply however:

  (i) the candidate must already have attained at least the second class standard in a paper within the field of which the subject of his dissertation lies, in the Preliminary Examination for Part II. In the case of certain papers it will be sufficient for a candidate to have been placed at least in the second class in Part I and to have offered there a paper within the field of which the subject of the dissertation lies.*

  (ii) no candidate may offer a written paper within the field of which the subject of the dissertation lies. If the subject lies within the field of more than one paper the Board will

---

* The Faculty Board have specified that these papers from Schedule I should be the following:

French: 3, 4, 5   Italian: 13, 16   Slavonic: 20,
taken either one or two years after matriculation;
and Modern Greek: 46, taken two years after matriculation.

decide which paper or papers the candidate shall be permitted to offer.

(b) in *addition* to the papers which they are required to take for Part II (known as a dissertation under Regulation 27(b)). Such additional dissertations are not subject to the restrictions listed under (a) above.

Candidates may offer a dissertation under either (a) or (b) above, or they may offer two dissertations, one under (a) and one under (b). If a candidate proposes to offer two dissertations the Faculty Board will not approve subjects which substantially overlap. The Examiners will treat the mark for an 'alternative' dissertation as the exact equivalent of a mark for a written paper, but the mark for an 'additional' dissertation will be taken into account only if that would be to the candidate's advantage.

The procedure for dissertations for Part II is as follows: candidates must submit their proposed subject through their Tutor on the form provided by the Faculty Office so as to reach the Secretary of the Faculty Board not later than the third Friday of the Full Michaelmas Term preceding the examination, stating whether the dissertation is additional to their papers, or an alternative to one of them, which they must specify. If they wish subsequently to vary their proposal, further dates apply; details of these may be obtained from the Faculty Office. A dissertation offered under (a) above must be in English, but quotations from primary sources must be in the language of the original. A dissertation offered under (b) may be written in a modern foreign language instead of English if the Faculty Board in or after approving the subject so agree. The dissertation must be typewritten, except where a non-Roman or symbolic typeface is necessary and cannot be provided. In these cases, hand-written or photocopied extracts may be inserted. The dissertation must normally be not less than 8,000 words and in any case not more than 10,000 words in length (inclusive of notes and appendices but exclusive of bibliography). A dissertation within the field of comparative literature, whether offered under (a) or (b), must concern the literature of at least two languages. Two copies of the dissertation must be submitted through the candidate's Tutor so as to reach the Secretary of the Faculty Board not later than the first weekday in March preceding the examination. The Examiners may examine a candidate *viva voce* on the dissertation; the *viva voce* examination will be in English, or, if a candidate has offered a dissertation written in a modern foreign language, in the language in which it has been

MODERN AND MEDIEVAL LANGUAGES 313

written. The dissertation must be identified by a motto only and must be accompanied by an envelope containing the name of the candidate and the college, with a declaration signed by the candidate that the dissertation is his or her own work.

Papers from other Triposes[1]

A candidate may offer not more than two of the following papers from other Triposes in place of an equivalent number of Part II subjects:

Classical Tripos: any paper from Part II other than from the Schedule of Optional Papers, except that no candidate may offer both Paper E 1 and Paper 111 of Part II of the Modern and Medieval Languages Tripos; both Paper E 4 and Paper 120 of the Modern and Medieval Languages Tripos in any year if the Faculty Boards of Classics and of Modern and Medieval Languages in announcing the texts or subjects prescribed for those papers respectively have indicated that those papers may not in that year be offered in combination by a candidate for the Modern and Medieval Languages Tripos; a subsidiary paper in Group E and another paper from the same group; in any year from a group other than Group E a subsidiary paper and another paper from the same group if the Faculty Board of Classics in announcing the subjects prescribed for those papers have indicated that the particular combination of papers concerned may not in that year be offered by a candidate for the Modern and Medieval Languages Tripos.

English Tripos, Part II: Paper 2, Tragedy; Paper 3, Chaucer; Paper 4, Medieval English literature, 1066–1500; Paper 9, History and theory of literary criticism; Paper 13, History of the English language. English Tripos Paper 12; Gender & Writing: 1879–1941

Anglo-Saxon, Norse, and Celtic Tripos, Paper 2, the Vikings; Paper 4, Latin literature of the British Isles, 400–1100; Paper 5, Old English language and literature; Paper 6, Old Norse language and literature; Paper 7A, Medieval Welsh language and literature I; Paper 7B, Medieval Welsh language and literature II; Paper 8A, Medieval Irish language and literature I; Paper 8B,

---

[1] The Faculty Board have specified all the papers from other Triposes as papers on which candidates may not offer dissertations. Candidates spending a year abroad should not offer themselves for examination in these papers in the Preliminary Examination for Part II of the Modern and Medieval Languages Tripos without consulting with the Secretaries of the Faculty Boards concerned since these subjects may change between the Preliminary Examination and Part II of the Modern and Medieval Languages Tripos for which they will be candidates two years later. If there is any uncertainty, Directors of Studies should inform undergraduates that it would be advisable to study the relevant paper after rather than before their year abroad in order to allow time, if necessary, for a change of plan.

Medieval Irish language and literature II; Paper 11, Special subject II; provided that no candidate can offer both Papers 7A and 7B; or both Papers 8A and 8B; or Paper 2 if he offers Paper 50 from Schedule II.

Historical Tripos, Part II, Paper 20, A subject in modern European history (in any year in which the subject 'Continuity and change in France since the French Revolution' has been prescribed by the Faculty Board of History).

The list of papers for the Part II examination is as follows:

Schedule II* (Papers (other than essay and translation papers) for Part II)

Romance
French and Provençal

1. French literature, thought, and history, before 1300.
2. Occitan literature, thought, and history, before 1356.
3. French literature, thought, and history, from 1300 to 1510.
4. French literature, thought, and history, from 1510 to 1622.
5. French literature, thought, and history, from 1594 to 1700.
6. French literature, thought, and history, from 1690 to 1789.
7. French literature, thought, and history, from 1789 to 1898.
8. French literature, thought, and history, since 1890.
9. The history of the French language.
10. Literature and the Visual Arts in France, 1527–1914.

Medieval Latin

12. Medieval Latin literature, from 400 to 1300.

Italian

13. Italian literature, life, and history, before 1400.
14. Dante.
15. Italian literature, thought, and history, from 1400 to 1600.
x16. A special subject in Italian culture: The visual arts in Central Italy, 1405–1505.
17. Italian literature, thought, and history, since 1815.
x18. The history of the Italian language.

Spanish

20. Spanish literature, life, and history, before 1492.
21. Spanish literature, thought, and history, from 1492 to 1700.

* An x against a paper means that it is a paper on which candidates may not offer a dissertation.

MODERN AND MEDIEVAL LANGUAGES

22. Cervantes.
23. **Spanish literature, thought, and history, after 1820.**
24. A special period or subject in Spanish literature, life, or history: Literature in Catalan.
x[1]25. **The history of the Peninsular languages.**
26. Topics in Spanish-American history, 1492–1960.
27. A special subject in Latin-American history or literature. (This paper has been suspended until further notice.)
28. Latin-American literature.

PORTUGUESE

31. Portuguese literature, life, and history, before 1497.
32. Portuguese literature, thought, and history, from 1497 to 1700.
33. Portuguese literature, thought, and history, since 1700.

GERMANIC
GERMAN

40. German literature, thought, and history, before 1500.
41. German literature, thought, and history, from 1500 to 1700.
42. German literature, thought, and history, from 1700 to 1805.
43. Goethe.
44. German literature, thought, and history, from 1797 to 1890.
45. German literature, thought, and history, since 1890.
46. A special period or subject in German literature, thought, or history: The German historical imagination, 1750–1945.
47. **The history of the German language.**

SCANDINAVIAN

(Candidates should consult the Secretary of the Faculty Board before deciding to offer these papers.)

50. Humanism, Reformation, and Renaissance in Scandinavia, from 1500 to 1700.
51. Pietism, Enlightenment, and the Age of Liberty in Scandinavia, from 1700 to 1800.
52. Romanticism, Realism, and Reaction in Scandinavia, from 1800 to 1865.
53. Henrik Ibsen.
54. August Strindberg.
56. Modernism in Scandinavia from 1918 to 1965.

[1] Every candidate will be expected to show a knowledge of the history of *either* Spanish *or* Portuguese or both, but he may be allowed to offer the history of Catalan in place of, or in addition, to these.

Dutch

70. The literature, life, and history of the Netherlands, before 1570.
71. The literature, life, and history of the Netherlands, from 1570 to 1730.
72. The literature, life, and history of the Netherlands, from 1730 to 1880.
x73. The literature, life, and history of the Netherlands, since 1880.
x74. The history of the Dutch language.

Slavonic

80. Russian literature, life, and culture, before 1300.
81. Russian literature, life, and culture, from 1300 to 1676.
82. Russian literature, life, and culture, from 1676 to 1801.
83. Russian literature and thought, from 1801 to 1883.
84. Russian literature and thought, since 1883.
x85. Russian history, from 1801 to 1964.
x86. The history of the Russian language.
87. Czech literature, thought, and history, before 1620.
88. Czech and Slovak literature, thought, and history, since 1620.
x89. The history of the Czech and Slovak languages.
90. Polish literature, thought, and history, before 1795.
91. Polish literature, thought, and history, since 1795.
x92. The history of the Polish language.
93. Serbian and Croatian literature, thought, and history, before 1700.†
94. Serbian and Croatian literature, thought, and history, since 1700.†
x95. The history of the Serbo-Croat language.†
97. A special period or subject in the literature, thought, or history of the Slavs: Dostoevskii.

Modern Greek

x100. Greek literature, thought, and history, from 867 to 1204.
x101. Greek literature, thought, and history, from 1204 to 1453.
102. Greek literature, thought, and history, from 1453 to 1700.
103. Greek literature, thought, and history, from 1700 to 1910.
104. Greek literature, thought, and history, since 1910.
105. The history of the modern Greek language.

Linguistics

111. General linguistics.
112. Phonetics.
113. The history of linguistic thought.
114. Historical linguistics.

† Papers 93, 94 and 95 are not available after 1990 and those interested should consult the Head of the Department of Slavonic Studies.

MODERN AND MEDIEVAL LANGUAGES

COMPARATIVE STUDIES

¹×120. Vulgar Latin and Romance philology, with special reference to Old French, Occitan, Spanish, and Portuguese.
121. The Teutonic languages, with special reference to Gothic, Anglo-Saxon, Early Norse, Old Saxon, and Old High German.
²×122. The Slavonic languages, with special reference to Old Church Slavonic.
³123. A special subject in Comparative literature (i): European Satire, 1500–1850.
³124. A special subject in Comparative literature (ii): Avant-garde movements in Europe, 1910–1939.

The following texts and periods have been prescribed, and authors and topics specified, for these papers in 1990 and 1991:

SCHEDULE II

PAPERS (OTHER THAN ESSAY AND TRANSLATION PAPERS) FOR PART II IN 1990

Note: Candidates for papers marked with an asterisk (*) who intend to spend a year abroad should not offer themselves for examination in these papers in the Preliminary Examination for Part II of the Modern and Medieval Languages Tripos without consulting with the Secretary of the Faculty Board of Modern and Medieval Languages, since these variable subjects may change between the Preliminary Examination and Part II of the Modern and Medieval Languages Tripos for which they will be candidates two years later.

ROMANCE

French and Provençal

Paper 1. French literature, thought, and history, before 1300.

Paper 2. Occitan literature, thought, and history, before 1356, with special reference to the following:
  Les chansons de Guillaume IX, duc d'Aquitaine, 1071–1127, ed. A. Jeanroy (C.F.M.A. 9); Les Poésies du troubadour Marcabru, ed. J.-M.-L. Dejeanne (Toulouse, 1909; repr. Johnson Reprint Corporation, New York etc., 1971, and Slatkine, Geneva, 1971); Bernard de Ventadour: chansons d'amour, ed. M. Lazar (Paris: Klincksieck, 1966); Les Poésies de Peire Vidal, ed. J. Anglade, 2. éd. revue (C.F.M.A. 11); Les Troubadours I, Jaufre, Flamenca, Barlaam et Josaphat, 2. éd. revue (Paris: Desclée Brouwer, 1979).

Paper 3. French literature, thought, and history, from 1300 to 1510.

Paper 4. French literature, thought, and history, from 1510 to 1622.

Paper 5. French literature, thought, and history, from 1594 to 1700.

Paper 6. French literature, thought, and history, from 1690 to 1789.

Paper 7. French literature, thought, and history, from 1789 to 1898.

Paper 8. French literature, thought, and history, since 1890.

Paper 9. The history of the French language, with special reference to the following:
  C. W. Aspland, A Medieval French Reader (O.U.P., 1979), extracts nos. 1, 2, 3, 6, 9, 12, 15, 21, 23, 26, 30; P. Rickard, La Langue française au XVIe siècle. Étude suivie de textes (C.U.P., 1968), extracts nos. 3, 4, 9b, 15, 18, 24, 28, 39, 46; C. F. de Vaugelas, Remarques sur la langue française (ed. Streicher; Slatkine, 1934, reprinted 1970) and A. Arnauld et C. Lancelot, Grammaire générale et raisonnée (ed. H. E. Brekle; Friedrich Frommann Verlag, 1966).

**Paper 10.* A special subject in French culture: Literature and the visual arts in France, 1527–1914, with special reference to one of the following: The First School of Fontainebleau; Poussin and classicism; Diderot and 'le Retour à l'antique'; Representation in the nineteenth century (Romanticism to Impressionism); Fins et débuts de siècle.

Paper 11. A special period or subject in French literature, thought, or history: Modern critical theory
  Particulars of this special subject were published in Reporter 1987–88, p. 541.

CAMBRIDGE HANDBOOK

Medieval Latin

Paper 12. Medieval Latin literature, from 400 to 1300, with special reference to the following:

Boethius, *Consolatio Philosophiae* (ed. S.J.Tester or K.Büchner), Book II; Bernardus Silvestris, *Cosmographia* (ed. P.Dronke), Book I; *Camina Burana* (dtv edition): the satires 12–34, the love-songs 62–90, the plays 227 and 16*; The Archpoet, *Poems* (*Die Gedichte des Archipoeta*, publ. Reclam); *Ruodlieb* (publ. Reclam), Sections I–VII.

Italian

Paper 13. Italian literature, life, and history, before 1400, with special reference to thirteenth-century poetry, Petrarca, and Boccaccio, in connexion with the following:

Poeti del Duecento (ed. G.Contini), selections from Giacomo da Lentini, Guido delle Colonne, Stefano da Messina, Guittone d'Arezzo, Jacopone da Todi, Guido Guinizelli (I–x and xx), Guido Cavalcanti and Cino da Pistoia (I–xxIII); *Novellino*; Dino Compagni, *La Cronica* [(publ. Le Monnier); Petrarca, *Rime* (ed. G.Gontini, publ. Einaudi), *Secretum* (pp. 21–215 of *Prose*, publ. R. Ricciardi); Boccaccio, *Decameron*.

Paper 14. Dante, with special reference to the following:

Divina Commedia, Vita nuova, Rime, Monarchia.

Paper 15. Italian literature, thought, and history, from 1400 to 1600, with special reference to the following areas:

(a) Alberti, Poliziano, and fifteenth-century Florentine culture;
(b) Machiavelli, Guicciardini, and the historical background;
(c) Ariosto, Tasso, and the epic;
(d) Michelangelo, Castiglione, and High Renaissance culture.

Students will be expected to show knowledge of at least three of the four areas.

**Paper 16. A special subject in Italian culture*

The visual arts in central Italy, 1405–1505, with special reference to the following:

(a) writings on the theory and practice of painting: Alberti, *Della pittura*, ed. Grayson; Leonardo, *Scritti scelti*, ed. A.M.Brizio, U.T.E.T., pp. 174–246; Vasari, *Vite scelte*, ed. A.M.Brizio, U.T.E.T., pp. 67–117, 127–34, 191–224, 239–71, 361–89;
(b) the sculpture of Ghiberti, Donatello, and Verrocchio;
(c) the paintings of Masaccio, Fra Angelico, Filippo Lippi, Uccello, Domenico Veneziano, Piero della Francesca, Botticelli, and Leonardo (with particular attention to works in the galleries of Cambridge, London, and Florence).

Paper 17. Italian literature, thought, and history, since 1815, with special reference to the following:

Foscolo, *Le ultime lettere di Jacopo Ortis, Dei sepolcri*; Manzoni, *I promessi sposi*; Leopardi, *I canti*; Nievo, *Le confessioni di un Italiano*, Chs. I–x; Verga, *Mastro don Gesualdo*; D'Annunzio, *Il piacere*; Pirandello, *Sei personaggi in cerca d'autore, Il fu Mattia Pascal*; Gozzano, *I colloqui*; Fogazzaro, *Piccolo mondo antico*; Svevo, *La coscienza di Zeno*; Montale, *Ossi di seppia, Le occasioni*; Croce, *Breviario d'estetica*; Calvino, *Se una notte d'inverno un viaggiatore*.

Paper 18. The history of the Italian language, with special reference to the following:

Dionisotti and Grayson, *Early Italian Texts* (2nd ed.), passages 1–6, 9, 11–13, 15–16, 18, 19(c), (e), (f), 20(b), (c), (d), 21(a), 23, 25; Dante, *De vulgari eloquentia*; Fòffano, *Prose filologiche: La Questione della Lingua*; Bembo, *Le prose della volgar lingua*.

Spanish

Paper 20. Spanish literature, life, and history, before 1492, with special reference to the following:

(a) Spanish Ballads (ed. C.C.Smith, Oxford), and J.G.Cummins, *The Spanish Traditional Lyric* (Oxford); *Poema de mio Cid* (ed. C.C.Smith, Oxford or Cátedra); Berceo, *Milagros de Nuestra Señora* (any edition); Juan Ruiz, *Libro de buen amor* (ed. J.Joset, Clásicos Castellanos, 2 vols.); Juan Manuel, *El conde Lucanor* (ed. J.M.Blecua, Castalia); Diego de San Pedro, *Cárcel de amor* (any edition), and a selection from *Cancionero general* (ed. J.M.Aguirre, Anaya).
(b) The Reconquest, with particular reference to the eleventh century; the culture of Moslem Spain; the reign and works of Alfonso X (extracts from *Siete Partidas* and *Estoria de España* in *Antologia de Alfonso X*, ed. A.Solalinde, Austral or Granada); Fifteenth-century Castile, with particular reference to race and class (extracts from F.Pérez de Guzmán, *Generaciones y semblanzas*).

MODERN AND MEDIEVAL LANGUAGES 319

Paper 21. Spanish literature, thought, and history, from 1492 to 1700, with special reference to the following:

Fray Luis de León and the Counter-Reformation in Spain; the plays of Lope de Vega; the picaresque novel; Luis de Góngora; Francisco de Quevedo; Baltasar Gracián, *El Criticón*.

Paper 22. Cervantes

Paper 23. Spanish literature, thought, and history, after 1820, with special reference to the following:

Bernito Pérez Galdós; Miguel de Unamuno; the Spanish novel after 1960; *poesía pura*; surrealism.

*Paper 24. A special period or subject in Spanish literature, life, or history

Literature in Catalan, with special reference to the following:

Ramon Llull; the chronicles; humanism; Ausiàs March; 'la decadència'; 'la renaixença'; J.Verdaguer; N.Oller; A.Guimerà; 'modernisme'; 'noucentisme'.

Paper 25. The history of the Peninsular languages, with special reference to the following:

(*a*) D.J.Gifford and F.W.Hodcroft, *Textos lingüísticos del medioevo español* (Oxford, 1966), passages 3, 6, 8–37, 38, 43, 45, 49–52, 53–4, 57, 59, 60–1, 72, 74, 81, 92, 95–6, 102, 105–6, 112, 114, 120; *Poema de Mio Cid* (ed. C.C.Smith, Madrid, 1976), *Cantar I*; Juan de Valdés, *Diálogo de la lengua* (Clásicos castellanos).

(*b*) *Oxford Book of Portuguese Verse* (pp. 1–137); Rodrigues Lapa (ed.), *Crestomatia arcaica*; *Historiadores quinhentistas* (*Textos literários*); Camões, *Os Lusiadas*, canto I.

Paper 26. Topics in Spanish-American history, 1492–1960

Paper 27. A special subject in Latin-American history or literature. This paper is suspended until further notice.

Paper 28. Latin-American literature, with special reference to the following:

(*a*) Hernández, *Martín Fierro*; Rubén Dario and *modernista* poets; López Velarde; Villaurrutia; Vallejo; Neruda; Octavio Paz.

(*b*) Sarmiento, *Facundo*; Rodó, *Ariel*; Azuela, *Los de abajo*; Güiraldes, *Don Segundo Sombra*; Gallegos, *Doña Bárbara*; Octavio Paz, *El laberinto en la soledad*; Borges; Carpentier; Rulfo; Cortázar; Fuentes; García Márquez; Vargas Llosa; Onetti.

Portuguese

Paper 31. Portuguese literature, life, and history, before 1497, with special reference to the following:

Crestomatia arcaica (ed. J.J.Nunes); The Galician-Portuguese Lyric; *Cantigas de escarnho e maldizer* (ed. Rodrigues Lapa); Fernão Lopes, *Crónica de Dom João I* (Part 1); Dom Duarte, *Leal Conselheiro*; Zurara and the early phase of Portuguese expansion; *Cancioneiro Geral*.

Paper 32. Portuguese literature, thought, and history, from 1497 to 1700, with special reference to the following:

Gil Vicente, Sá de Miranda, Bernardim Ribeiro, António Ferreira, Damião de Góis, Camões, Mendes Pinto.

Paper 33. Portuguese literature, thought, and history, since 1700, with special reference to the period 1820 to 1935, and to the following authors:

Almeida Garrett, Herculano, Castelo Branco, Quental, Eça de Queiroz, Oliveira Martins, Fernando Pessoa, Aquilino Ribeiro.

GERMANIC

German

Paper 40. German literature, thought, and history, before 1500, with special reference to the following, from which passages may be set for translation and comment:

Braune, *Althochdeutsches Lesebuch* (1969 edition†), sections xx, 5–7; xxiii, 1; xxviii–xxxi; xxxii, 1, 4, 7, 14; xxxiv; xxxvi; xlii; xliii; Gottfried von Strassburg, *Tristan und Isold* (ed. Ranke, Verlag Francke, Bern); Wolfram von Eschenbach, *Parzival* (ed. Hartl, Verlag Francke, Bern); Wehrli (ed. Verlag Francke, Bern), *Minnesang vom Kürenberger bis Wolfram* (the poems of Der von Kürenberg, Friderich von Husen, Heinrich von Morungen, and Wolfram von Eschenbach); Wehrli (ed.): Walther von der Vogelweide, *Gedichte* (Verlag Francke, Bern), sections ii, iii, iv, vii, viii, x.

Paper 41. German literature, thought, and history, from 1500 to 1700

† Candidates using other editions are advised to check with the more detailed list obtainable from the Department of German.

Paper 42. German literature, thought, and history, from 1700 to 1805‡
    Subjects in history for special study: Frederick the Great *and* Political, Social, and Literary Aspects of the Aufklärung.
    Subject in thought for special study: German Idealism with special reference to *Deutscher Idealismus*, ed. R. Bubner (Reclam 9916), pp. 29–280.

Paper 43. Goethe†

Paper 44. German literature, thought, and history, from 1797 to 1890†
    Subjects in history for special study: The Revolution of 1848 *and* The Foundation of the Second German Empire.
    Subject in thought for special study: Theories of Tragedy with special reference to the following: Schelling, *Philosophie der Kunst* II.2.*y*. 'Die dramatische Poesie' (ed. Wissenschaftliche Buchgesellschaft, 1980, pp. 331–80); Hegel, *Ästhetik*, Dritter Teil. Dritter Abschnitt. Drittes Kapitel. C. III. 3. 'Die Arten der dramatischen Poesie und deren historische Hauptmomente'; Schopenhauer, *Die Welt als Wille und Vorstellung* I, §§ 33, 34, 49, 51, 52; Nietzsche, *Die Geburt der Tragödie*.

Paper 45. German literature, thought, and history, since 1890
    Subjects in history for special study: The Weimar Republic *and* National Socialism.
    Subject in thought for special study: Theories of the Unconscious with special reference to S. Freud, *Abriß der Psychoanalyse*, *Das Unbehagen in der Kultur*; C. G. Jung, *Die Beziehungen zwischen dem Ich und dem Unbewußten*; A. and M. Mitscherlich, 'Die Unfähigkeit zu trauern-womit zusammenhängt: eine deutsche Art zu lieben', in *Die Unfähigkeit zu trauern. Grundlagen kollektiven Verhaltens* (Munich, 1967), pp. 13–85.

*Paper 46. A special period or subject in German literature, thought, or history
    The German historical imagination, 1750–1945
    No prescribed texts are published but lists of recommended reading are available in the Department of German, Room 25, RFB.

Paper 47. The history of the German language, with special reference to the following, from which passages will be set for translation and comment:
    Braune, *Althochdeutsches Lesebuch* (1969 ed.‡), sections VI; X; XII; XIII (*a*); XIX; XX, 5–7, XXIII, 1; XXXII, 6, 14; XXXVI; XLIV, *Heliand*, lines 1–53; Walshe, *A Middle High German Reader* (Oxford, 1974), pp. 53–5, 91–101, 119–32, 137–45; S. Singer, *Mittelhochdeutsches Lesebuch*, sections I, IV, X (lines 1–117), XII, XV; A. Götze, *Frühneuhochdeutsches Lesebuch*, sections 2*a*, *c*; 4*b*; 9*a*; 12*b*; 15*c*, 16 (lines 61–121); 20*d*; 22 (lines 1–65); 25; 27*a* (lines 1–179); 33*b*; 37 (lines 1–76).

Scandinavian

Paper 50. Humanism, Reformation, and Renaissance in Scandinavia, from 1500 to 1700

Paper 51. Pietism, Enlightenment, and the Age of Liberty in Scandinavia, from 1700 to 1800

Paper 52. Romanticism, Realism, and Reaction in Scandinavia, from 1800 to 1865

Paper 53. Henrik Ibsen

Paper 54. August Strindberg

Paper 56. Modernism in Scandinavia, from 1918 to 1965

Dutch

Paper 70. The literature, life, and history of the Netherlands, before 1570, with special reference to the following:
    (*a*) Texts for close study: *Wie wil horen een goed nieuw lied? Liederen en gedichten uit de Middeleeuwen* (Spectrum van de Nederlandse Letterkunde 4, omitting *Een suverlijc boecxken*); *Het Roelantslied* (Spectrum…1); *De reis van Sinte Brandane* and *Beatrijs* (Spectrum…2); *Lanseloet van Denemerken* (Spectrum…5).
    (*b*) General topics: Medieval and sixteenth-century drama; The Burgundian Netherlands.

Paper 71. The literature, life, and history of the Netherlands, from 1570 to 1730, with special reference to the following:
    Hooft, *Sonnetten* (Spectrum van de Nederlandse Letterkunde 9), Uit het seste boek van *Neederlandsche Histooriën* (Spectrum…7); Huygens, *Zede-printen* (Spectrum…10); Bredero, *Lied-boeck* (Spectrum…9), *Spaanschen Brabander* (Spectrum…12); Vondel, *Jeptha*.

---

† Questions on Goethe's *Faust*, Part I, may be set in connexion with Papers 42, 43, and 44.
‡ Candidates using other editions are advised to check with the more detailed list obtainable from the Department of German.

MODERN AND MEDIEVAL LANGUAGES

Paper 72. *The literature, life, and history of the Netherlands, from 1730 to 1880*
  To be available only after consultation.

Paper 73. *The literature, life, and history of the Netherlands, since 1880*, with special reference to the following:
  (*a*) Texts for close study: Vestdijk, *Terug tot Ina Damman*; Elsschot, *Het Dwaallicht*; M. Nijhoff, *Lees maar, et staat niet wat er staat*; Hermans, *Het behouden huis*; G.K. van het Reve, *De Avonden*; H. Claus, *Suiker*; J. Wolkers, *Terug naar Oegstgeest*; H. Mulisch, *De Aanslag*.
  (*b*) General topics: The post-war novel; Modernist poetry.

Paper 74. *The history of the Dutch language*, with special reference to the following:
  De Oudnederlandse (*Oudnederfränkische*) *Psalmfragmenten* (ed. H. Cowan, 1957); Van Loey, *Middelnederlands Leerboek*, nos. 21–5, 28, II–VIII, XXVI, 29, 37, 38, 61*a*, 71, 74, 77, 79; A. Weijnen, *Zeventiende-eeuwse Taal*, texts 6, 7, 14, 22, 40, 42.

SLAVONIC

Paper 80. *Russian literature, history, and culture, before 1300*, with special reference to the following:
  Повесть временных лет, 912–1054; Житие Феодосия Печерского; Повесть об ослеплении Василька; Моление Даниила Заточника; Житие Авраамия Смоленского; Житие Александра Невского.

Paper 81. *Russian literature, history, and culture, from 1300 to 1676*, with special reference to the following:
  Задонщина; Житие митрополита Петра; Житие Сергия Радонежского; Хожение Афанасия Никитина; Домострой; Житие протопопа Аввакума.

Paper 82. *Russian literature, history, and culture, from 1676 to 1801*, with special reference to the following:
  (*a*) Kantemir, Сатиры I–II; Lomonosov, Ода на взятие Хотина; Sumarokov, Димитрий самозванец; Fonvizin, Недоросль; Chulkov, Пригожая повариха; Kniazhnin, Несчастье от кареты; Derzhavin, На смерть князя Мещерского, Фелица, Видение Мурзы, Водопад; Karamzin, Бедная Лиза, Наталья боярская дочь.
  (*b*) Prokopovich, Слово на погребение Петра Великого; Catherine II, Наказ and other legislative acts, in *Russia under Catherine the Great*, ed. P. Dukes; Shcherbatov, О повреждении нравов; Radischev, Путешествие из Петербурга в Москву.
  (*c*) The development of St Petersburg; Russia and the West: Anglo-Russian relations: Publishing; Classicism and Sentimentalism.

Paper 83. *Russian literature and thought, from 1801 to 1883*, with special reference to the following:
  (*a*) Texts for close study, passages from which may be set for comment: Pushkin, Евгений Онегин; Tolstoi, Анна Каренина.
  (*b*) Topics: The lyric poetry of Pushkin, Lermontov, and Tiutchev; the novels of Herzen, Goncharov, and Turgenev; drama from Griboedov to Ostrovskii; satirical prose from Gogol' to Saltykov-Shchedrin; the utopian and anti-utopian novel; aesthetics and literary criticism from Belinskii to Tolstoi; the Slavophile controversy; Populism from Herzen to Lavrov; conservative thought from Karamzin to Pobedonostsev.

Paper 84. *Russian literature and thought, since 1883*, with special reference to the following:
  The drama, 1890–1916, in relation to the plays of Chekhov, Andreev, Maiakovskii and theories of drama with reference to Stanislavskii and Meierkhol'd; the poetry of Blok, Maiakovskii, Mandel'shtam, Voznesenskii; Belyi as a novelist; literature and the State, 1917–34; early Soviet prose with special reference to Zamiatin, Babel', and Olesha; the Soviet novel, with special reference to Leonov, Sholokhov, and Platonov; Bulgakov; Pasternak; Solzhenitsyn; the *povest'* since 1956 with special reference to Trifonov, Shukshin, Rasputin; Russian women poets with special reference to Akhmatova, Tsvetaeva, and Ratushinskaia.

Paper 85. *Russian history, from 1801 to 1964*, with special reference to the following:
  (*a*) Documents for close study in relation to their historical setting: N. M. Karamzin, Записка о Древней и Новой России; Десятилетие министерства народного просвещения 1833–43 гг. ("Эпоха Николая I" под ред. М. О. Гершензона, 1910, стр. 115–18); P. L. Lavrov, Исторические Письма; S. Iu. Witte, Воспоминания (ed. Moscow, 1960), Vol. I, chs. 10, 14, 16, 18; Vol. II, chs. 19, 27, 38, 45, 51; Vol. III, chs. 52, 56, 61, 62; V. I. Lenin, Апрельские Тезисы (Полн. Собр. Соч., 5th ed. 1962), Vol. XXXI (March–April 1917), pp. 99–118, 123–4, 530–2; О задачах хозяйственников...I. V. Stalin, "Вопросы Ленинизма", II–е изд, 1945, стр. 322–30).
  (*b*) The period 1801–1894.
  (*c*) The period 1894–1964.

Paper 86. The history of the Russian language, with special reference to the following, from which passages will be set for translation and comment:

Obnorsky and Barkhudarov, Хрестоматия по истории русского языка (Moscow, 1952 and 1949), Parts I and II.
Part I: no. 1, pp. 14–16; no. 4, pp. 20–21; no. 8; no. 10; no. 12, pp. 39–40, lines 1–56; no. 13, pp. 44–46, lines 1–22; no. 17, p. 60, lines 29–63; no. 25; no. 30, pp. 114–19, lines 1–164; no. 44, pp. 174–5; no. 49, pp. 203–4; no. 53, pp. 230–1; no. 55, p. 239; no. 59, III, pp. 257–9; no. 64; no. 66, III, pp. 305–6; no. 67, pp 309–10; no. 68, pp. 317–18.
Part II: p. 83, no. 1; p. 99, no. 16; p. 144; pp. 254–5.

Paper 87. Czech literature, thought, and history, before 1620, with special reference to the following, from which passages may be set for translation and comment:

Výbor z české literatury od počátků po dobu Husovu (ed. B. Havránek et al., Prague, 1957), pp. 108–19, 134–5, 139–43, 153–67, 171, 177–80, 200–8, 212–17, 248–60, 317–21, 335–47, 360–81, 394–405, 414–16, 426–9, 498–515, 575–8; Výbor z české literatury doby husitské (ed. B. Havránek et al., Prague, 1963–64), vol. I, pp. 192–7, 281–3, 357–9, 391–5; vol. II, pp. 45–51; *Rada zhovadilých zvieřat*.

Paper 88. Czech and Slovak literature, thought, and history, since 1620, with special reference to the following:

Komenský, *Labyrint světa a Ráj srdce*; Mácha, *Máj*, *Krkonošská pouť* and lyrical poems; Světlá, *Vesnický román*; Hlaváček, *Básnické dílo*; Zeyer, *Tři legendy o krucifixu*; Čapek-Chod, *Turbina*; Durych, *Rekviem*; Nezval, *Básně noci*; Vančura, *Pole orná a válečná*; Hlinka, *Už není návratu*; Hviezdoslav, *Ežo Vlkolinský*; Šikula, *Majstri*.

Paper 89. The history of the Czech and Slovak languages, with special reference to the following, from which passages will be set for translation and comment:

Chrestomatie k vývoji českého jazyka (ed. J. Porák, Prague, 1979), pp. 35–40, 41–8, 112–14, 152–4, 269–71, 321–3, 352–4 (lines 100–70), 375–7; Antológia staršej slovenskej literatúry (ed. J. Mišianik, Bratislava, 1981), pp. 45–7, 181–5, 211–15, 549–50, 827–9.

Paper 90. Polish literature, thought, and history, before 1795, with special reference to the following:

Kochanowski, *Pieśni*; Sęp Szarzyński, *Rytmy abo wiersze polskie*; Skarga, *Kazania sejmowe*; K. Opaliński, *Satyry*; Trembecki, *Wiersze wybrane*; Staszic, *Przestrogi dla Polski*.

Paper 91. Polish literature, thought, and history, since 1795, with special reference to the following:

Malczewski, *Maria*; Mickiewicz, *Dziady III*; Słowacki, *Balladyna*; Norwid, *Pierścień Wielkiej Damy*; Prus, *Lalka*; M. Dąbrowska, *Noce i dnie*, vols. I–II.

Paper 92. The history of the Polish language, with special reference to the following, from which passages will be set for translation and comment:

St. Vrtel-Wierczyński, Wybór tekstów staropolskich (1963 edition), pp. 3–8, 12–15 (*Kazania* IV–VI), 34–5 and 42–3 (*Kazania* 1 and 9), 44–7, 65–9, 70–4 (*Genesis*, I–III), 114–16, 120–3, 158–61, 162–7, 188–90, 210–15, 297–300, 317–20.

Paper 93. Serbian and Croatian literature, thought, and history, before 1700, with special reference to the following:

Sava, *Žitije svi Simeona* (ed. Ćorović); Konstantin Filozof, *Žitije Stefana Lazarevića* (ed. Bašić, Srp. knj. zad.), Marko Marulić, *Judita*, Djore Držić, *Radmioi Ljubmir*; Petar Hektorović, *Ribanje i ribarsko prigovaranje*; Marin Držić, *Dundo Maroje*; Ivan Gundlić, *Dubravka*; *Osman*; Ivan Bunić, *Plandovanja*.

Paper 94. Serbian and Croatian literature, thought, and history, after 1700, with special reference to the following:

Dositej Obradović, *Život i priključenija*; P. P. Njegoš, *Gorski Vijenac*; Laza Kostić, *Maksim Crnojević*; Ante Kovačic, *U registraturi*; the Poetry of Vojislav Ilić; A. B. Simić, *Preobraženja*; Borisav Stanković, *Koštana*; Miroslav Krleža, *Gospoda Glembajevi*; Ivo Andrić, *Travnička Hronika*; Miloš Crnjanski, *Seobe 1*; Momčilo Nastasijević, *Pet lirkskih krugova*; Vladan Desnica, *Zimsko letovanje*; Miodrag Bulatović, *Crveni petao leti prema nebu*; Dragutin Mihailović, *Kad cvetaju tikve*; Miodrag Pavlović, *Izabrane pesme*.

Paper 95. The history of the Serbo-Croat language, with special reference to the following, from which passages will be set for translation and comment:

Vondrák, Cirkevněslovanská chrestomatie (Brno, 1925), pp. 148–9; M. Pavlović, Примери историског развитка српскохрватског језика, pp. 29–30, 33–8, 42–5, 50–1, 63–7, 70–3, 83–8, 91–7, 101–4, 106–9, 166–73, 176–84.

*Paper 97. A special period or subject in the literature, thought, or history of the Slavs:

Dostoevskii.

MODERN AND MEDIEVAL LANGUAGES 323

MODERN GREEK

Paper 100. Greek literature, thought, and history, from 867 to 1204, with special reference to the following:
Constantine Porphyrogenitus, *De Administrando Imperio* (ed. Moravcsik-Jenkins), chs. 1–22; John Mavrogordato, *Digenes Akrites* (Oxford, 1956); Hesseling-Pernot, *Poèmes Prodromiques*; Cecaumenos, *Strategicon* (ed. Wassiliewsky-Jernstedt); Nicetas Choniates (ed. van Dieten), pp. 275–354; Anna Comnena, *Alexias* (Teubner edition), Books X–XIII.

Paper 101. Greek literature, thought, and history, from 1204 to 1453, with special reference to the following:
Χρονικόν του Μωρέως (ed. Schmitt), pp. 184–506; Καλλίμαχος και Χρυσορρόη (ed. Pichard); Διήγησις του Αχιλλέως (ed. Hesseling); Βέλθανδρος και Χρυσάντζα (ed. Kriaras); M. Falieros, Ερωτικά 'Όνειρα (ed. van Gemert); Michael Ducas (ed. Grecu), chs. 35–42; Makhairas, Χρονικόν της Κύπρου (ed. Dawkins), sections 449–525.

Paper 102. Greek literature, thought, and history, from 1453 to 1700, with special reference to the following:
E. Georgillas (texts to be specified); *Poèmes d'amour en dialecte chypriote* (ed. Siapkaras-Pitsillidès); G. Chortatsis, Κατζούρμπος (ed. L. Politis), Πανώρια (ed. Kriaras 1975); V. Kornaros, Ερωτόκριτος (ed. S. Alexiou); Η θυσία του Αβραάμ (ed. Megas, 2nd ed., 1954); M. A. Foskolos, Φορτουνάτος (ed. Vincent); I. A. Troilos, Βασιλεύς ο Ροδολίνος.

Paper 103. Greek literature, thought, and history, from 1700 to 1910, with special reference to the following:
'Άνθη Ευλαβείας (ed. Karathanasis); το δημοτικό τραγούδι: (a) Κλέφτικα (ed. A. Politis), (b) της ξενιτιάς (ed. Saunier); A. Christopoulos, Λυρικά (ed. Tsantsanoglou); A. Matesis, Ο Βασιλικός; D. Solomos, Ποιήματα (ed. L. Politis 1948); A. Kalvos, Ωδαί; Makriyannis, Απομνημονεύματα Book I (ed. Vlachoyannis), E. Roidis, Η Πάπισσα Ιωάννα; G. Vizyinos, Νεοελληνικά Διηγήματα (ed. Moullas); A. Papadiamantis, Αυτοβιογραφούμενος (ed. Moullas), Η Φόνισσα; K. Palamas, Ο Δωδεκάλογος του Γύφτου.

Paper 104. Greek literature, thought, and history, since 1910, with special reference to the following:
C. Cavafy, Ποιήματα, Ανέκδοτα ποιήματα (ed. Savvidis); K. Theotokis, Η Τιμή και το Χρήμα; S. Myrivilis, Η Ζωή εν Τάφω; G. Seferis, Ποιήματα; K. Politis, *Eroica* (ed. Mackridge); O. Elytis, Προσανατολισμοί; N. Kazantzakis, Βίος και Πολιτεία του Αλέξη Ζορμπά, Ο Χριστός Ξανασταυρώνεται; S. Plaskovitis, Το φράγμα; M. Douka, Η Αρχαία Σκουριά; T. Sinopoulos, Συλλογή II.

Paper 105. The history of the modern Greek language, with special reference to the following:
Malalas, Book XVIII (Bonn edition); Hesseling-Pernot, *Poèmes Prodromiques*, pp. 48–83; *Le Roman de Phlorios et de Platzia Phlore* (ed. Hesseling), lines 1–426; M. Phalieros, Ιστορία και 'Όνειρο (ed. van Gemert); M. A. Foskolos, Φορτουνάτος (ed. Vincent), pp. 108–134; Makriyannis, Απομνημονεύματα Book II (ed. Vlachoyannis); D. Solomos, *Dialogue on the Language*; J. Psycharis, Το Ταξίδι μου, chs. 1–8; N. Kazantzakis, Ασκητική.

LINGUISTICS

Paper 111. General linguistics
Paper 112. Phonetics
Paper 113. The history of linguistic thought
Paper 114. Historical linguistics

Details may be obtained from the Department of Linguistics.

COMPARATIVE STUDIES

Paper 120. Vulgar Latin and Romance philology, with special reference to Old French, Occitan, Italian, Spanish, and Portuguese
Every candidate will be expected to show a knowledge of two at least of the Romance languages. Prescribed texts:
Vulgar Latin: G. Rohlfs, *Sermo Vulgaris Latinus* (3rd ed., 1969), passages 5, 7, 8, 13, 17, 18, 25, 29, 34 (i).
Romance Languages: R. Sampson (ed.), *Early Romance Texts*, passages 50–65 (French), 31–49 (Provençal), 73–90 (Italian), 11–22 (Spanish), 1–10 (Portuguese).

Paper 121. The Teutonic languages, with special reference to Gothic, Anglo-Saxon, Early Norse, Old Saxon, and Old High German
Every candidate will be expected to show a knowledge of Gothic and of two at least of the other languages. Prescribed texts from which passages for translation and comment will be selected:
Gothic: St Mark's Gospel, as contained in Wright's *Grammar of the Gothic Language*.
Old High German: Braune, *Althochdeutsches Lesebuch* (1969 edition†), sections V, 2; VIII Cap. III; X; XX; XXIII, 14; XXXII, 7, 12; XLI.

† Candidates using other editions are advised to check with the more detailed list obtainable from the Department of German.

Old Saxon: Holthausen, *Altsächsisches Elementarbuch* (1921), pp. 201–22.
Anglo-Saxon: *Sweet's Anglo-Saxon Reader*, rev. D. Whitelock (Oxford, 1967), nos. II, VIII, XVI, XXI, XXV, lines 1–76.
Old Norse: E. V. Gordon, *An Introduction to Old Norse*, rev. A. R. Taylor, nos. II, III, VIII, X.

Paper 122. The Slavonic languages, with special reference to Old Church Slavonic

Every candidate is expected to show a knowledge of Old Church Slavonic and of at least two other Slavonic languages. Passages will be set for translation and comment from the following specified texts in Old Church Slavonic:

R. Auty, *Handbook of Old Church Slavonic*, part II, *Texts and Glossary*, passages nos. 1 a (pp. 24–7 (Matth. vii)), 2 b, xv, 4 (pp. 52–4), 5 c, 6 b, 9 b, 11 b, 13 i, 14.

*†*Paper 123. A special subject in comparative literature* (i)

European satire, 1500–1850

The paper will be in three sections: A. Formal and theoretical
B. Thematic
C. Historical

A short list of basic texts to be read by all candidates, and reading lists, are available from the Department of Other Languages, Room 25, RFB.

*†*Paper 124. A special subject in comparative literature* (ii)

Avant-garde movements in Europe, 1910–1939

The paper will be in three sections:

A. Experiments in Form
B. Explorations of the Unconscious
C. Art and Society

Candidates will be required to answer *three* questions, not more than two from any one section.

There are no prescribed texts, but a list of reading suggestions is available from the Faculty of Modern and Medieval Languages.

SCHEDULE II

PAPERS (OTHER THAN ESSAY AND TRANSLATION PAPERS) FOR PART II IN 1991

Note: Candidates for papers marked with an asterisk (*) who intend to spend a year abroad should not offer themselves for examination in these papers in the Preliminary Examination for Part II of the Modern and Medieval Languages Tripos without consulting with the Secretary of the Faculty Board of Modern and Medieval Languages, since these variable subjects may change between the Preliminary Examination and Part II of the Modern and Medieval Languages Tripos for which they will be candidates two years later.

ROMANCE

French and Occitan

Paper 1. French literature, thought, and history, before 1300.

Paper 2. Occitan literature, thought, and history, before 1356, with special reference to the following:

Les chansons de Guillaume IX, duc d'Aquitaine, 1071–1127, ed. A. Jeanroy (C.F.M.A. 9); Les Poésies du troubadour Marcabru, ed. J.-M.-L. Dejeanne (Toulouse, 1909; repr. Johnson Reprint Corporation, New York etc., 1971, and Slatkine, Geneva, 1971); Bernard de Ventadour: chansons d'amour, ed. M. Lazar (Paris: Klincksieck, 1966); The Women Troubadours, ed. M. Bogin (Paddington Press, 1976; also available in French translation as Les Femmes Troubadours); La Chanson de Sainte Foi d' Agen, ed. A. Thomas (C.F.M.A. 45) or E. Hoepffner (Publ. de la Fac. des Lettres de l'Université de Strasbourg fasc. 32); Flamenca, ed. R. Lavaud and R. Nelli, in Les Troubadours II (Paris: Desclée Brouwer, 1979).

Paper 3. French literature, thought, and history, from 1300 to 1510.

Paper 4. French literature, thought, and history, from 1510 to 1622.

Paper 5. French literature, thought, and history, from 1594 to 1700.

Paper 6. French literature, thought, and history, from 1690 to 1789.

Paper 7. French literature, thought, and history, from 1789 to 1898.

Paper 8. French literature, thought, and history, since 1890.

MUSIC

Paper 9. The history of the French language, with special reference to the following:

C.W. Aspland, *A Medieval French Reader* (O.U.P., 1979), extracts nos. 1, 2, 3, 6, 9, 12, 15, 21, 23, 26, 30; P. Rickard, *La Langue française au XVIe siècle. Étude suivie de textes* (C.U.P., 1968), extracts nos. 3, 4, 9*b*, 15, 18, 24, 28, 39, 46; C. F. de Vaugelas, *Remarques sur la langue française* (ed. Streicher; Slatkine, 1934, reprinted 1970) and A. Arnauld et C. Lancelot, *Grammaire générale et raisonnée* (ed. H. E. Brekle; Friedrich Frommann Verlag, 1966).

*Paper 10. *A special subject in French culture*: *Literature and the visual arts in France, 1527–1914*, with special reference to one of the following: The First School of Fontainebleau; Poussin and classicism; Diderot and 'le Retour à l'antique'; Representation in the nineteenth century (Romanticism to Impressionism); *Fins et débuts de siècle*.

Paper 11. A special period or subject in French literature, thought, or history: *Modern critical theory*
Particulars of this special subject were published in *Reporter*, 1987–88, p. 541.

Medieval Latin

Paper 12. Medieval Latin literature, from 400 to 1300, with special reference to the following:

Boethius, *Consolatio Philosophiae* (ed. S.J. Tester or K. Büchner), Book I; Hrotsvitha, *Calimachus* and *Abraham* (ed. H. Homeyer or F. Bertini); Abelard, *Historia calamitatum* (ed. J. Monfrin); Héloïse, *Epistolae* I–II (ibid.); Hugh Primas, *The Oxford Poems* (ed. C.J. McDonough or W. Meyer); Bernardus Silvestris, *Cosmographia* (ed. P. Dronke), Book II.

Italian

Paper 13. Italian literature, life, and history, before 1400, with special reference to thirteenth-century poetry, Petrarca, and Boccaccio, in connexion with the following:

Poeti del Duecento (ed. G. Contini), selections from Giacomo da Lentini, Guido delle Colonne, Stefano da Messina, Guittone d'Arezzo, Jacopone da Todi, Guido Guinizelli (I–x and xx), Guido Cavalcanti and Cino da Pistoia (I–xxIII); *Novellino*; Dino Compagni, *La Cronica* [(publ. Le Monnier); Petrarca, *Rime* (ed. G. Gontini, publ. Einaudi), *Secretum* (pp. 21–215 of *Prose*, publ. R. Ricciardi); Boccaccio, *Decameron*.

Paper 14. Dante, with special reference to the following:

Divina Commedia, *Vita nuova*, *Convivio* I, IV.

Paper 15. Italian literature, thought, and history, from 1400 to 1600, with special reference to the following areas:

(*a*) Alberti, Poliziano, and fifteenth-century Florentine culture;
(*b*) Machiavelli, Guicciardini, and the historical background;
(*c*) Ariosto, Tasso, and the epic;
(*d*) Michelangelo, Castiglione, and High Renaissance culture.

Students will be expected to show knowledge of at least three of the four areas.

Paper 16. A special subject in Italian culture
The visual arts in central Italy, 1405–1505, with special reference to the following:

(*a*) writings on the theory and practice of painting: Alberti, *Della pittura*, ed. Grayson; Leonardo, *Scritti scelti*, ed. A. M. Brizio, U.T.E.T., pp. 174–246; Vasari, *Vite scelte*, ed. A. M. Brizio, U.T.E.T., pp. 67–117, 127–34, 191–224, 239–71, 361–89;
(*b*) the sculpture of Ghiberti, Donatello, and Verrocchio;
(*c*) the paintings of Masaccio, Fra Angelico, Filippo Lippi, Uccello, Domenico Veneziano, Piero della Francesca, Botticelli, and Leonardo (with particular attention to works in the galleries of Cambridge, London, and Florence).

Paper 17. Italian literature, thought, and history, since 1815, with special reference to the following:

Foscolo, *Le ultime lettere di Jacopo Ortis*, *Dei sepolcri*; Manzoni, *I promessi sposi*; Leopardi, *I canti*; Nievo, *Le confessioni di un Italiano*, Chs. I–X; Verga, *Mastro don Gesualdo*; D'Annunzio, *Il piacere*; Pirandello, *Sei personaggi in cerca d'autore*, *Il fu Mattia Pascal*; Gozzano, *I colloqui*; Fogazzaro, *Piccolo mondo antico*; Svevo, *La coscienza di Zeno*; Montale, *Ossi di seppia*, *Le occasioni*; Croce, *Breviario d'estetica*; Calvino, *Se una notte d'inverno un viaggiatore*.

Paper 18. The history of the Italian language, with special reference to the following:

Dionisotti and Grayson, *Early Italian Texts* (2nd ed.), passages 1–6, 9, 11–13, 15–16, 19(c), (e), (f), 20(b), (c), (d), 21(a), 23, 25; Dante, *De vulgari eloquentia*; Fòffano, *Prose filologiche: La Questione della Lingua*; Bembo, *Le prose della volgar lingua*.

CAMBRIDGE HANDBOOK

Spanish

Paper 20. Spanish literature, life, and history, before 1492, with special reference to the following:
   (*a*) Spanish Ballads (ed. C.C.Smith, Oxford), and J.G.Cummins, *The Spanish Traditional Lyric* (Oxford); *Poema de mio Cid* (ed. C.C.Smith, Oxford or Cátedra); Berceo, *Milagros de Nuestra Señora* (any edition); Juan Ruiz, *Libro de buen amor* (ed. G.B.Gybbon-Monypenny, Castalia); Juan Manuel, *El conde Lucanor* (ed. J.M.Blecua, Castalia); Diego de San Pedro, *Cárcel de amor* (any edition), and a selection from *Cancionero general* (ed. J.M.Aguirre, Anaya).
   (*b*) The Reconquest, with particular reference to the eleventh century; the culture of Moslem Spain; the reign and works of Alfonso X (extracts from *Siete Partidas* and *Estoria de España* in *Antologia de Alfonso X*, ed. A.Solalinde, Austral or Granada); Fifteenth-century Castile, with particular reference to race and class (F.Pérez de Guzmán, *Generaciones y semblanzas*). *y semblanzas*).

Paper 21. Spanish literature, thought, and history, from 1492 to 1700, with special reference to the following:
   Fray Luis de León and the Counter-Reformation in Spain; the plays of Lope de Vega; the picaresque novel; Luis de Góngora; Francisco de Quevedo; Baltasar Gracián, *El Criticón*.

Paper 22. Cervantes

Paper 23. Spanish literature, thought, and history, after 1820, with special reference to the following:
   Benito Pérez Galdós; Miguel de Unamuno; the Spanish novel after 1960; *poesía pura*; surrealism.

*Paper 24. A special period or subject in Spanish literature, life, or history
   Literature in Catalan, with special reference to the following:
   Ramon Llull; the chronicles; humanism; Ausiàs March; 'la decadència'; 'la renaixença'; J.Verdaguer; N.Oller; A.Guimerà; 'modernisme'; 'noucentisme'.

Paper 25. The history of the Peninsular languages, with special reference to the following:
   (*a*) D.J.Gifford and F.W.Hodcroft, *Textos lingüísticos del medioevo español* (Oxford, 1966), passages 3, 6, 8–37, 38, 43, 45, 49–52, 53–4, 57, 59, 60–1, 72, 74, 81, 92, 95–6, 102, 105–6, 112, 114, 120; *Poema de Mio Cid* (ed. C.C.Smith, Madrid, 1976), *Cantar I*; Juan de Valdés, *Diálogo de la lengua* (Clásicos castalia).
   (*b*) *Oxford Book of Portuguese Verse* (pp. 1–137); Rodrigues Lapa (ed.), *Crestomatia arcaica*; *Historiadores quinhentistas* (*Textos literários*); Camões, *Os Lusiadas*, canto I.

Paper 26. Topics in Spanish-American history, 1492–1960

Paper 27. A special subject in Latin-American history or literature. This paper is suspended until further notice.

Paper 28. Latin-American literature, with special reference to the following:
   (*a*) Hernández, *Martín Fierro*; Rubén Darío and *modernista* poets; López Velarde; Villaurrutia; Vallejo; Neruda; Octavio Paz.
   (*b*) Sarmiento, *Facundo*; Rodó, *Ariel*; Azuela, *Los de abajo*; Güiraldes, *Don Segundo Sombra*; Gallegos, *Doña Bárbara*; Octavio Paz, *El laberinto en la soledad*; Borges; Carpentier; Rulfo; Cortázar; Fuentes; García Márquez; Vargas Llosa; Onetti.

Portuguese

Paper 31. Portuguese literature, life, and history, before 1497, with special reference to the following:
   Crestomatia arcaica (ed. J.J.Nunes); The Galician-Portuguese Lyric; *Cantigas de escarnho e maldizer* (ed. Rodrigues Lapa); Fernão Lopes, *Crónica de Dom João I* (Part I); Dom Duarte, *Leal Conselheiro*; Zurara and the early phase of Portuguese expansion; *Cancioneiro Geral*.

Paper 32. Portuguese literature, thought, and history, from 1497 to 1700, with special reference to the following:
   Gil Vicente, Sá de Miranda, Bernardim Ribeiro, António Ferreira, Damião de Góis, Camões, Mendes Pinto.

Paper 33. Portuguese literature, thought, and history, since 1700, with special reference to the period 1820 to 1935, and to the following authors:
   Almeida Garrett, Herculano, Castelo Branco, Quental, Eça de Queiroz, Oliveira Martins, Fernando Pessoa, Aquilino Ribeiro.

GERMANIC

German

Paper 40. German literature, thought, and history, before 1500, with special reference to the following, from which passages may be set for translation and comment:

Braune, *Althochdeutsches Lesebuch* (1969 edition†), sections xx, 5–7; xxiii, 1; xxviii–xxxi; xxxii, 1, 4, 7, 14; xxxiv; xxxvi; xlii; xliii; Gottfried von Strassburg, *Tristan und Isold* (ed. Ranke, Verlag Francke, Bern); Wolfram von Eschenbach, *Parzival* (ed. Hartl, Verlag Francke, Bern); Wehrli (ed. Verlag Francke, Bern), *Minnesang vom Kürenberger bis Wolfram* (the poems of Der von Kürenberg, Friderich von Husen, Heinrich von Morungen, and Wolfram von Eschenbach); Wehrli (ed.): Walther von der Vogelweide, *Gedichte* (Verlag Francke, Bern), sections ii, iii, iv, vii, viii, x.

Paper 41. German literature, thought, and history, from 1500 to 1700

Paper 42. German literature, thought, and history, from 1700 to 1805‡

Subjects in history for special study: Frederick the Great *and* Political, Social, and Literary Aspects of the Aufklärung.

Subject in thought for special study: German Idealism with special reference to *Deutscher Idealismus*, ed. R. Bubner (Reclam 9916), pp. 29–280.

Paper 43. Goethe‡

Paper 44. German literature, thought, and history, from 1797 to 1890‡

Subjects in history for special study: The Revolution of 1848 *and* The Foundation of the Second German Empire.

Subject in thought for special study: Theories of Tragedy with special reference to the following: Schelling, *Philosophie der Kunst* ii.2.γ. 'Die dramatische Poesie' (ed. Wissenschaftliche Buchgesellschaft, 1980, pp. 331–80); Hegel, *Ästhetik*, Dritter Teil. Dritter Abschnitt. Drittes Kapitel. C. iii. 3. 'Die Arten der dramatischen Poesie und deren historische Hauptmomente'; Schopenhauer, *Die Welt als Wille und Vorstellung* i, §§ 33, 34, 49, 51, 52; Nietzsche, *Die Geburt der Tragödie*.

Paper 45. German literature, thought, and history, since 1890

Subjects in history for special study: The Weimar Republic *and* National Socialism.

Subject in thought for special study: Theories of the Unconscious with special reference to S. Freud, *Abriß der Psychoanalyse, Das Unbehagen in der Kultur*; C. G. Jung, *Die Beziehungen zwischen dem Ich und dem Unbewußten*; A. and M. Mitscherlich, 'Die Unfähigkeit zu trauern-womit zusammenhängt: eine deutsche Art zu lieben', in *Die Unfähigkeit zu trauern. Grundlagen kollektiven Verhaltens* (Munich, 1967), pp. 13–85.

**Paper 46.* A special period or subject in German literature, thought, or history

The German historical imagination, 1750–1945

No prescribed texts are published but lists of recommended reading are available in the Department of German, Room 25, RFB.

Paper 47. The history of the German language, with special reference to the following, from which passages will be set for translation and comment:

Braune, *Althochdeutsches Lesebuch* (1969 ed.†), sections vi; x; xii; xiii (*a*); xix; xx, 5–7, xxiii, 1; xxxii, 6, 14; xxxvi; xliv, *Heliand*, lines 1–53; Walshe, *A Middle High German Reader* (Oxford, 1974), pp. 53–5, 91–101, 119–32, 137–45; S. Singer, *Mittelhochdeutsches Lesebuch*, sections i, iv, x (lines 1–117), xii, xv; A. Götze, *Frühneuhochdeutsches Lesebuch*, sections 2*a*, *c*; 4*b*; 9*a*; 12*b*; 15*c*, 16 (lines 61–121); 20*d*; 22 (lines 1–65); 25; 27*a* (lines 1–179); 33*b*; 37 (lines 1–76).

Scandinavian

Paper 50. Humanism, Reformation, and Renaissance in Scandinavia, from 1500 to 1700

Paper 51. Pietism, Enlightenment, and the Age of Liberty in Scandinavia, from 1700 to 1800

Paper 52. Romanticism, Realism, and Reaction in Scandinavia, from 1800 to 1865

Paper 53. Henrik Ibsen

Paper 54. August Strindberg

Paper 56. Modernism in Scandinavia, from 1918 to 1965§

---

† Candidates using other editions are advised to check with the more detailed list obtainable from the Department of German.
‡ Questions on Goethe's *Faust*, Part i, may be set in connexion with Papers 42, 43, and 44.
§ Candidates who are interested in this paper should consult the Secretary of the Faculty Board.

Dutch

Paper 70. The literature, life, and history of the Netherlands, before 1570, with special reference to the following:

(a) Texts for close study: *Wie wil horen een goed nieuw lied? Liederen en gedichten uit de Middeleeuwen* (Spectrum van de Nederlandse Letterkunde 4, omitting *Een suverlijc boecxken*); *Het Roelantslied* (Spectrum...1); *De reis van Sinte Brandane* and *Beatrijs* (Spectrum...2); *Lanseloet van Denemerken* (Spectrum...5).

(b) General topics: Medieval and sixteenth-century drama; The Burgundian Netherlands.

Paper 71. The literature, life, and history of the Netherlands, from 1570 to 1730, with special reference to the following:

Hooft, *Sonnetten* (Spectrum van de Nederlandse Letterkunde 9), Uit het seste boek van *Neederlandsche Historiën* (Spectrum...7); Huygens, *Zede-printen* (Spectrum...10); Bredero, *Liedboeck* (Spectrum...9), *Spaanschen Brabander* (Spectrum...12); Vondel, *Jeptha*.

Paper 72. The literature, life, and history of the Netherlands, from 1730 to 1880

To be available only after consultation.

Paper 73. The literature, life, and history of the Netherlands, since 1880, with special reference to the following:

(a) Texts for close study: Vestdijk, *Terug tot Ina Damman*; Elsschot, *Het Dwaallicht*; M. Nijhoff, *Lees maar, et staat niet wat er staat*; Hermans, *Het behouden huis*; G.K. van het Reve, *De Avonden*; H. Claus, *Suiker*; J. Wolkers, *Terug naar Oegstgeest*; H. Mulisch, *De Aanslag*.

(b) General topics: The post-war novel; Modernist poetry.

Paper 74. The history of the Dutch language, with special reference to the following:

De Oudnederlandse (Oudnederfrankische) Psalmfragmenten (ed. H. Cowan, 1957); Van Loey, *Middelnederlands Leerboek*, nos. 21–5, 28, II–VIII, XXVI, 29, 37, 38, 61a, 71, 74, 77, 79; A. Weijnen, *Zeventiende-eeuwse Taal*, texts 6, 7, 14, 22, 40, 42.

SLAVONIC

Paper 80. Russian literature, history, and culture, before 1300, with special reference to the following:

Повесть временных лет, 912–1054; Житие Феодосия Печерского; Повесть об ослеплении Василька; Моление Даниила Заточника; Житие Авраамия Смоленского; Житие Александра Невского.

Paper 81. Russian literature, history, and culture, from 1300 to 1676, with special reference to the following:

Задонщина; Житие митрополита Петра; Житие Сергия Радонежского; Хожение Афанасия Никитина; Домострой; Житие протопопа Аввакума.

Paper 82. Russian literature, history, and culture, from 1676 to 1801, with special reference to the following:

(a) Kantemir, Сатиры I–II; Lomonosov, Ода на взятие Хотина; Sumarokov, Димитрий самозванец; Fonvizin, Недоросль; Chulkov, Пригожая повариха; Kniazhnin, Несчастье от кареты; Derzhavin, На смерть князя Мещерского, Фелица, Видение Мурзы, Водопад; Karamzin, Бедная Лиза, Наталья боярская дочь.

(b) Prokopovich, Слово на погребение Петра Великого; Catherine II, Наказ and other legislative acts, in *Russia under Catherine the Great*, ed. P. Dukes; Shcherbatov, О повреждении нравов; Radishchev, Путешествие из Петербурга в Москву.

(c) The development of St Petersburg; Russia and the West; Anglo-Russian relations; Publishing; Classicism and Sentimentalism.

Paper 83. Russian literature and thought, from 1801 to 1883, with special reference to the following:

(a) Texts for close study, passages from which may be set for comment: Pushkin, Евгений Онегин; Tolstoi, Анна Каренина.

(b) Topics: The lyric poetry of Pushkin, Lermontov, and Tiutchev; the novels of Herzen, Goncharov, and Turgenev; drama from Griboedov to Ostrovskii; satirical prose from Gogol' to Saltykov-Shchedrin; the utopian and anti-utopian novel; aesthetics and literary criticism from Belinskii to Tolstoi; the Slavophile controversy; Populism from Herzen to Lavrov; conservative thought from Karamzin to Pobedonostsev.

Paper 84. Russian literature and thought, since 1883, with special reference to the following:

The drama, 1890–1916, in relation to the plays of Chekhov, Andreev, Maiakovskii and theories of drama with reference to Stanislavskii and Meierkhol'd; the poetry of Blok, Maiakovskii, Mandel'shtam, Voznesenskii; Belyi as a novelist; literature and the State, 1917–34; early Soviet prose with special reference to Zamiatin, Babel', and Olesha; the Soviet novel, with special reference

MODERN AND MEDIEVAL LANGUAGES 329

to Leonov, Sholokhov, and Platonov; Bulgakov; Pasternak; Solzhenitsyn; the *povest'* since 1956 with special reference to Trifonov, Shukshin, Rasputin; Russian women poets with special reference to Akhmatova, Tsvetaeva, and Ratushinskaia.

Paper 85. *Russian history, from 1801 to 1904*, with special reference to the following:

(a) Documents for close study in relation to their historical setting: Н. М. Карамзин, *Записка о Древней и новой России*, ed. R. Pipes, Cambridge, Mass., 1959, стр. 52–63, 102–119; 'Дело Н. И. Пестеля', in *Восстание декабристов*, под ред. М. Н. Покровского, Москва-Ленинград, 1927, том 4, стр. 93–121; С. С. Уваров, 'Десятилетие Министерства народного просвещения 1833–43гг', in Эпоха Николая I, под ред. М. О. Гершензона, Москва, 1910, стр. 115–25: 'Манифест 19 февраля 1861г', in *Крестьянская реформа в России 1861 года* под ред. К. А. Софроненка, Москва, 1954, стр. 29–36: 'Программа и письмо исполнительного комитета партии Народная воля' in Хрестоматия по истории СССР, под ред. С. С. Дмитриева, Москва, 1948, том, 3, стр. 359–61, 368–70: С. Ю. Витте, 'О положении русской промышленности', in *Хрестоматия по истории СССР*, под ред. С. С. Дмитриева, Москва, 1948, том 3, стр., 187–94.

(b) The period 1801–1860.

(c) The period 1860–1904.

Paper 86. *The history of the Russian language*, with special reference to the following, from which passages will be set for translation and comment:

Obnorskii and Barkhudarov, Хрестоматия по истории русского языка (Moscow, 1952 and 1949), Parts I and II.

Part I: no. 1, pp. 14–16; no. 4, pp. 20–21; no. 8; no. 10; no. 12, pp. 39–40, lines 1–56; no. 13, pp. 44–46, lines 1–22; no. 17, p. 60, lines 29–63; no. 25; no. 30, pp. 114–19, lines 1–164; no. 44, pp. 174–5; no. 49, pp. 203–4; no. 53, pp. 230–1; no. 55, p. 239; no. 59, III, pp. 257–9; no. 64; no. 66, III, pp. 305–6; no. 67, pp 309–10; no. 68, pp. 317–18.

Part II: p. 83, no. 1; p. 99, no. 16; p. 144; pp. 254–5.

Paper 87. *Czech literature, thought, and history, before 1620*, with special reference to the following, from which passages may be set for translation and comment:

Výbor z české literatury od počátků po dobu Husovu (ed. B. Havránek et al., Prague, 1957), pp. 108–19, 134–5, 139–43, 153–67, 171, 177–80, 200–8, 212–17, 248–60, 317–21, 335–47, 360–81, 394–405, 414–16, 426–9, 498–515, 575–8; *Výbor z české literatury doby husitské* (ed. B. Havránek et al., Prague, 1963–64), vol. I, pp. 192–7, 281–3, 357–9, 391–5; vol. II, pp. 45–51; *Rada zhovadilých zvieřat*.

Paper 88. *Czech and Slovak literature, thought, and history, since 1620*, with special reference to the following:

Komenský, *Labyrint světa a Ráj srdce*; Mácha, *Máj, Krkonošská pouť* and lyrical poems; Světlá, *Vesnický román*; Hlaváček, *Básnické dílo*; Zeyer, *Tři legendy o krucifixu*; Čapek-Chod, *Turbina*; Durych, *Rekviem*; Nezval, *Básně noci*; Vančura, *Pole orná a válečná*; Hlinka, *Už není návratu*; Hviezdoslav, *Ežo Vlkolinský*; Šikula, *Majstri*.

Paper 89. *The history of the Czech and Slovak languages*, with special reference to the following, from which passages will be set for translation and comment:

Chrestomatie k vývoji českého jazyka (ed. J. Porák, Prague, 1979), pp. 35–40, 41–8, 112–14, 152–4, 269–71, 321–3, 352–4 (lines 100–70), 375–7; *Antológia staršej slovenskej literatúry* (ed. J. Mišianik, Bratislava, 1981), pp. 45–7, 181–5, 211–15, 549–50, 827–9.

Paper 90. *Polish literature, thought, and history, before 1795*, with special reference to the following:

Kochanowski, *Pieśni*; Sęp Szarzyński, *Rytmy abo wiersze polskie*; Skarga, *Kazania sejmowe*; K. Opaliński, *Satyry*; Trembecki, *Wiersze wybrane*; Staszic, *Przestrogi dla Polski*.

Paper 91. *Polish literature, thought, and history, since 1795*, with special reference to the following:

Malczewski, *Maria*; Mickiewicz, *Dziady III*; Słowacki, *Balladyna*; Norwid, *Pierścień Wielkiej Damy*; Prus, *Lalka*; Irzykowski, *Pałuba*.

Paper 92. *The history of the Polish language*, with special reference to the following, from which passages will be set for translation and comment:

St. Vrtel-Wierczyński, *Wybór tekstów staropolskich* (1963 edition), pp. 3–8, 12–15 (*Kazania* IV–VI), 34–5 and 42–3 (*Kazania* I and II), 44–7, 65–9, 70–4 (*Genesis*, I–III), 114–16, 120–3, 158–61, 162–7, 188–90, 210–15, 297–300, 317–20.

†Paper 93. *Serbian and Croatian literature, thought, and history, before 1700*, with special reference to the following:

Sava, *Žitije svi Simeona* (ed. Ćorović); Konstantin Filozof, *Žitije Stefana Lazarevića* (ed. Bašić, Srp. knj. zad.), Marko Marulić, *Judita*, Djore Drzić, *Radmioi Ljubmir*; Petar Hektorović, *Ribanje i ribarsko prigovaranje*; Marin Držić, *Dundo Maroje*; Ivan Gundlić, *Dubravka*; *Osman*; Ivan Bunić, *Plandovanja*.

† Candidates who are interested in this paper should consult the Head of the Department of Slavonic Studies.

†*Paper 94.* Serbian and Croatian literature, thought, and history, since 1700, with special reference to the following:

Dositej Obradović, *Život i priključenija*; P.P. Njegoš, *Gorski Vijenac*; Laza Kostić, *Maksim Crnojević*; Ante Kovačic, *U registraturi*; the Poetry of Vojislav Ilić; A.B. Simić, *Preobraženja*; Borisav Stanković, *Koštana*; Miroslav Krleža, *Gospoda Glembajevi*; Ivo Andrić, *Travnička Hronika*; Miloš Crnjanski, *Seobe 1*; Momčilo Nastasijević, *Pet lirkskih krugova*; Vladan Desnica, *Zimsko letovanje*; Miodrag Bulatović, *Crveni petao leti prema nebu*; Dragutin Mihailović, *Kad cvetaju tikve*; Miodrag Pavlović, *Izabrane pesme*.

†*Paper 95.* The history of the Serbo-Croat language, with special reference to the following, from which passages will be set for translation and comment:

Vondrák, *Cirkevněslovanská chrestomatie* (Brno, 1925), pp. 148–9; M. Pavlović, Примери историког развитка српскохрватског језика, pp. 29–30, 33–8, 42–5, 50–1, 63–7, 70–3, 83–8, 91–7, 101–4, 106–9, 166–73, 176–84.

Paper 96. Russian history from 1905 to the present, with special reference to the following:

(a) Documents for close study in relation to their historical setting: 'Манифест 17 октября 1905г', in *Хрестоматия по истории СССР 1861–1917гг* под ред. С.С. Дмитриева, Москва, 1970, стр. 373–75; С.Ю. Витте, 'Письмо о Манифесте 17 октября 1905г', in С.Ю. Витте, *Воспоминания царствования Николая II*, The Hague, 1958, том 2, стр. 2–5; 'Доклады начальника Петербугского охранного отделения...', in *Рабочее движение в Петрограде в 1912–1917гг*, под ред. Ю.И. Кораблева, Ленинград, 1958, стр. 225–30, 232–39; В.И. Ленин, 'Апрельские тезисы', in *Сочинения*, Москва, 1962, том 31, стр. 99–100, 103–18, 123–24; 'Заседания ЦК РСДРП/б/, январь-февраль.1918г', in *Протоколы центрального комитета РСДРП/б/. Август 1917–февраль 1918*, Москва, 1958, стр. 167–80, 197–208, 211–18; И.В. Сталин, 'О задачах хозяйственников', in И.В. Сталин, *Вопросы Ленинизма*, Москва, 1945, стр. 322–30; Н.С. Хрущев, 'Доклад на закрытом заседании XX съезда КПСС', in Бранко Лазич, *Исторический очерк...*, Лондон, 1986, стр. 59–70, 95–103.

(b) The period 1905–1921.

(c) The period 1921 to the present.

**Paper 97.* A special period or subject in the literature, thought, or history of the Slavs:
Dostoevskii.

MODERN GREEK

Paper 100. Greek literature, thought, and history, from 867 to 1204, with special reference to the following:

Constantine Porphyrogenitus, *De Administrando Imperio* (ed. Moravcsik-Jenkins), chs. 1–22; John Mavrogordato, *Digenes Akrites* (Oxford, 1956); Hesseling-Pernot, *Poèmes Prodromiques*; Cecaumenos, *Strategicon* (ed. Wassiliewsky-Jernstedt); Nicetas Choniates (ed. van Dieten), pp. 275–354; Anna Comnena, *Alexias* (Teubner edition), Books x–xiii.

Paper 101. Greek literature, thought, and history, from 1204 to 1453, with special reference to the following:

Χρονικόν του Μωρέως (ed. Schmitt), pp. 184–506; Καλλίμαχος και Χρυσορρόη (ed. Pichard); Διήγησις του Αχιλλέως (ed. Hesseling); Βέλθανδρος και Χρυσάντζα (ed. Kriaras); M. Falieros, Ερωτικά Όνειρα (ed. van Gemert); Michael Ducas (ed. Grecu), chs. 35–42; Makhairas, Χρονικόν της Κύπρου (ed. Dawkins), sections 449–525.

Paper 102. Greek literature, thought, and history, from 1453 to 1700, with special reference to the following:

E. Georgillas (texts to be specified); *Poèmes d'amour en dialecte chypriote* (ed. Siapkaras-Pitsillidès); G. Chortatsis, Κατζούρμπος (ed. L. Politis), Πανώρια (ed. Kriaras 1975); V. Kornaros, Ερωτόκριτος (ed. S. Alexiou); Η θυσία του Αβραάμ (ed. Megas, 2nd ed., 1954); M.A. Foskolos, Φορτουνάτος (ed. Vincent); I.A. Troilos, Βασιλεύς ο Ροδολίνος.

Paper 103. Greek literature, thought, and history, from 1700 to 1910, with special reference to the following:

'Άνθη Ευλαβείας (ed. Karathanasis); το δημοτικό τραγούδι: (a) Κλέφτικα (ed. A. Politis), (b) της ξενιτιάς (ed. Saunier); A. Christopoulos, Λυρικά (ed. Tsantsanoglou); A. Matesis, Ο Βασιλικός; D. Solomos, Ποιήματα (ed. L. Politis 1948); A. Kalvos, Ωδαί; Makriyannis, Απομνημονεύματα Book I (ed. Vlachoyannis), E. Roidis, Η Πάπισσα Ιωάννα; G. Vizyinos, Νεοελληνικά Διηγήματα (ed. Moullas); A. Papadiamantis, Αυτοβιογραφούμενος (ed. Moullas), Η Φόνισσα; K. Palamas, Ο Δωδεκάλογος του Γύφτου.

Paper 104. Greek literature, thought, and history, since 1910, with special reference to the following:

C. Cavafy, Ποιήματα, Ανέκδοτα ποιήματα (ed. Savvidis); K. Theotokis, Η Τιμή και το Χρήμα; S. Myrivilis, Η Ζωή εν Τάφω; G. Seferis, Ποιήματα; K. Politis, *Eroica* (ed. Mackridge); O. Elytis, Προσανατολισμοί; N. Kazantzakis, Βίος και Πολιτεία του Αλέξη Ζορμπά, Ο Χριστός Ξανασταυρώνεται; S. Plaskovitis, Το φράγμα; M. Douka, Η Αρχαία Σκουριά; T. Sinopoulos, Συλλογή II.

† Candidates who are interested in this paper should consult the Head of the Department of Slavonic Studies.

MODERN AND MEDIEVAL LANGUAGES 331

Paper 105. The history of the modern Greek language, with special reference to the following:

Malalas, Book XVIII (Bonn edition); Hesseling-Pernot, *Poèmes Prodromiques*, pp. 48–83; *Le Roman de Phlorios et de Platzia Phlore* (ed. Hesseling), lines 1–426; M.Phalieros, Ἱστορία καὶ Ὄνειρο (ed. van Gemert); M.A.Foskolos, Φορτουνάτος (ed. Vincent), pp. 108–134; Makriyannis, Ἀπομνημονεύματα Book II (ed. Vlachoyannis); D.Solomos, *Dialogue on the Language*; J.Psycharis, Τὸ Ταξίδι μου, chs. 1–8; N.Kazantzakis, Ἀσκητική.

LINGUISTICS

Paper 111. General linguistics
Paper 112. Phonetics
Paper 113. The history of linguistic thought
Paper 114. Historical linguistics

Details may be obtained from the Department of Linguistics.

COMPARATIVE STUDIES

Paper 120. Vulgar Latin and Romance philology, with special reference to Old French, Occitan, Italian, Spanish, and Portuguese

Every candidate will be expected to show a knowledge of two at least of the Romance languages. Prescribed texts:

Vulgar Latin: G.Rohlfs, *Sermo Vulgaris Latinus* (3rd ed., 1969), passages 5, 7, 8, 13, 17, 18, 25, 29, 34 (i).

Romance Languages: R.Sampson (ed.), *Early Romance Texts*, passages 50–65 (French), 31–49 (Provençal), 73–90 (Italian), 11–22 (Spanish), 1–10 (Portuguese).

Paper 121. The Teutonic languages, with special reference to Gothic, Anglo-Saxon, Early Norse, Old Saxon, and Old High German

Every candidate will be expected to show a knowledge of Gothic and of two at least of the other languages. Prescribed texts from which passages for translation and comment will be selected:

Gothic: St Mark's Gospel, as contained in Wright's *Grammar of the Gothic Language*.

Old High German: Braune, *Althochdeutsches Lesebuch* (1969 edition†), sections V, 2; VIII Cap. III; X; XX; XXIII, 14; XXXII, 7, 12; XLI.

Old Saxon: Holthausen, *Altsächsisches Elementarbuch* (1921), pp. 201–22.

Anglo-Saxon: Sweet's *Anglo-Saxon Reader*, rev. D.Whitelock (Oxford, 1967), nos. II, VIII, XVI, XXI, XXV, lines 1–76.

Old Norse: E.V.Gordon, *An Introduction to Old Norse*, rev. A.R.Taylor, nos. II, III, VIII, X.

Paper 122. The Slavonic languages, with special reference to Old Church Slavonic

Every candidate is expected to show a knowledge of Old Church Slavonic and of at least two other Slavonic languages. Passages will be set for translation and comment from the following specified texts in Old Church Slavonic:

R.Auty, *Handbook of Old Church Slavonic*, part II, *Texts and Glossary*, passages nos. 1*a* (pp. 24–7 (Matth. vii)), 2*b*, xv, 4 (pp. 52–4), 5*c*, 6*b*, 9*b*, 11*b*, 13*i*, 14.

‡Paper 123. A special subject in comparative literature (i)

European satire, 1500–1850

The paper will be in three sections: A. Formal and theoretical
B. Thematic
C. Historical

A short list of basic texts to be read by all candidates, and reading lists, are available from the Department of Other Languages, Room 25, RFB.

‡Paper 124. A special subject in comparative literature (ii)

Avant-garde movements in Europe, 1910–1939
The paper will be in three sections:

A. Experiments in Form
B. Explorations of the Unconscious
C. Art and Society

Candidates will be required to answer *three* questions, not more than two from any one section.

There are no prescribed texts, but a list of reading suggestions is available from the Faculty of Modern and Medieval Languages.

† Candidates using other editions are advised to check with the more detailed list obtainable from the Department of German.
‡ No candidate may offer both Papers 123 and 124.

As in the case of Part I (see above, p. 304), the Faculty Board may allow candidates to be examined in subjects or papers other than those specified. The following additional language and papers have been approved for the Part II examination in **1990** and **1991**.

1. Hungarian literature, thought, and history, before 1825.
2. Hungarian literature, thought, and history, since 1825.
3. The history of the Hungarian language.

Paper 1. Hungarian literature, thought, and history, before 1825, with special reference to the following: Balassi Bálint, *Összes versei*; Zrinyi Miklós, *Szigeti veszedelem*; Mikes Kelemen, *Törökországi levelek*; Csokonai Vitéz Mihály, *A méla Tempefői*; Katona, *Bánk bán*.

Paper 2. Hungarian literature, thought, and history, since 1825, with special reference to the following: Petőfi Sándor, *Összes versei*; Kemény Zsigmond, *Zord idő*; Mikszáth, *Különös házasság*; Kosztolányi, *Osszes versei*; Weöres, *A hallgatás tornya*; Konrád, *A látogató*.

Paper 3. The history of the Hungarian language, with special reference to the following, from which passages may be set for translation and comment: Bisztray-Kerecsényi, *Régi magyar próza*; Horváth János, *Magyar versek könyve*; *Hét évszázad magyar versei*, Vol. 1.

The Preliminary Examination for Part II

In the Preliminary Examination for Part II there are set, if there are candidates, any of the papers in Schedule II of the Tripos, and any additional paper that may have been approved by the Faculty Board. A candidate must offer three papers selected from Schedule II, together with *either* an essay in a medieval or modern foreign language *or* a paper containing a passage of English for translation into a foreign language and a passage of that language for translation into English. The essay or the translation paper must be in a language relating to at least one of the papers chosen by the candidate. A candidate may offer, in place of one or two of the Part II papers, one or two papers chosen from among

either Papers 2, 4, 5, 6, 7, and 8 of the Preliminary Examination for the Anglo-Saxon, Norse, and Celtic Tripos;

or any paper from Part II of the Classical Tripos, other than from the optional papers, except that no candidate may offer:

(i) both E1 (Classical Tripos) and Paper 113;
(ii) both E3 (Classical Tripos) and Paper 120 (subject to such announcement having been made beforehand);

MODERN AND MEDIEVAL LANGUAGES

or Papers 2, 3, 4, 9, 12 and 13 of Part II of the English Tripos.

Paper 12, Special Subject II, Option (*b*) (in any year in which the subject 'Gender and writing: 1879–1941' has been prescribed for this option by the Faculty Board of English);

Historical Tripos, Part II, Paper 20, A subject in modern European history (in any year in which the subject 'Continuity and change in France since the French Revolution' has been prescribed by the Faculty Board of History).

The prescribed works, authors, and topics for **1990** are the same as those for Part II of the Tripos in **1991** with the following exceptions:

(The papers are numbered as in Schedule II for Part II of the Tripos.)

Paper 14. Dante, with special reference to the following:
   Divina Commedia.

Paper 40. German literature, thought, and history, before 1500, with special reference to the following, from which passages may be set for translation and comment:

   Braune, *Althochdeutsches Lesebuch* (1969 edition‡), sections XXVIII; XXX; XXXII, 6, 7, 10, 21; XXXVI; XLIV, A. Aus dem Heliand: II, Aus III, Aus XXXV; Wolfram von Eschenbach, *Parzival* (any edition), lines 1, 1–4, 8; 114, 5–179, 12; 224, 1–319, 19; 433, 1–502, 30; 792, 10–806, 3; 827, 1–30; Wehrli (ed. Verlag Francke, Bern), *Minnesang vom Kürenberger bis Wolfram* (the songs of Der von Kürenberg, Friderich von Husen, Heinrich von Morungen, and Wolfram von Eschenbach).
   A general knowledge of the following is required: Gottfried von Straßburg, *Tristan und Isold* (ed. Ranke, Verlag Francke, Bern); Walther von der Vogelweide, *Gedichte* (ed. Wehrli, Francke Verlag, Bern), sections I, II, III, IV, V, VII, VIII, X.

Paper 47. The history of the German language, with special reference to the following, from which passages will be set for translation and comment:

   Wilhelm Braune, *Althochdeutsches Lesebuch*, Tübingen, 1969, passages I (1), II (3), V (2), VI, X, XII, XIII (a) and (b), XIX, XX (5) to (7), XXI (1), XXIII (1), XXXII (16) to (18), XXXVI, XLIV (lines 2902–2973); M. O'C. Walshe, *A Middle High German Reader*, Oxford, 1974, pp. 91–101, 119–32, 137–45; S. Singer, *Mittelhochdeutsches Lesebuch*, Berne, 1945, Sections I, X (lines 1–117); XV; A. Götze, *Frühneuhochdeutsches Lesebuch*, Göttingen, 1958, section 1 (a), 3 (b), 4 (b), 5 (a), 9 (a), 12 (b), 15 (c), 20 (d), 21 (lines 1–75), 22 (lines 1–65), 25 (a) (b) (f) (h), 26 (c), 27 (a) (lines 1–88), 30, 33 (b).

Paper 121. The Teutonic languages, with special reference to Gothic, Anglo-Saxon, Early Norse, Old Saxon, and Old High German

   Every candidate will be expected to show a knowledge of Gothic and of two at least of the other languages. Prescribed texts from which passages for translation and comment will be selected:
   Gothic: St Mark's Gospel, as contained in Wright's *Grammar of the Gothic Language*.
   Old High German: Wilhelm Braune, *Althochdeutsches Lesebuch*, Tübingen, 1969, sections XIII, XX (5) to (7). XXIII (1), XXV, XXXII (12). XXXVI. XXXVIII, XLI.
   Old Saxon: Holthausen, *Altsächisches Elementarbuch* (1921), pp. 201–22.
   Anglo-Saxon: *Sweet's Anglo-Saxon Reader*, rev. D. Whitelock (Oxford, 1967), nos. II, VIII, XVI, XXI, XXV, lines 1–76.
   Old Norse: E. V. Gordon. *An Introduction to Old Norse*, rev. A. R. Taylor, nos. II, III, VIII, X.

Advanced Oral Examinations

Any candidate for Part II may be a candidate for an Advanced Oral Examination in any of the modern languages available in the

Tripos. The Examination is also open to candidates who have obtained honours in Part I or who have been awarded a Certificate of Competent Knowledge in a Modern Language. The examination consists of four parts: (*a*) reading aloud; (*b*) oral précis; (*c*) prepared discourse; (*d*) conversation.

Certificates of Competent Knowledge in modern languages

A student who has satisfied the examination requirements for matriculation or the Matriculation Board and kept at least two terms may in any one year be a candidate for a Certificate of Competent Knowledge in one of the languages (other than classical Latin or classical Greek) specified for Part I of the Modern and Medieval Languages Tripos, provided that no student may be a candidate for a Certificate in a language which he or she is in the same term offering as a candidate for honours in the Tripos. A candidate may enter for Certificates in more than one language, and can be a candidate for a Certificate on more than one occasion. In each language there will be an oral examination and a written examination which will consist of three papers of three hours each as follows:

1. Passages from works in the foreign language for translation into English.
2. Passages from works in English to be translated into the foreign language.
3. An essay in the foreign language.

The form, scope, and standard of Papers 1 and 2 will be the same as that of the corresponding papers in Part I of the Modern and Medieval Languages Tripos. The essay must be chosen from a paper of subjects some of which will bear on the literature, history, thought, and language of the country concerned, and all of which will demand reasoned exposition. The oral examination will be similar in format and standard to the oral examination in Part I (see above, pp. 293–4) and must be taken in the same term in which the written papers for the Certificate are taken.

A candidate who wishes to offer any language other than Czech (with Slovak), Dutch, French, German, Italian, Modern Greek, Polish, Portuguese, Russian or Spanish must first obtain permission from the Faculty Board in accordance with the regulations for the Tripos. Applications must be made before the division of the Michaelmas Term before the examination.

To obtain a Certificate of Competent Knowledge the candidate must attain a standard not lower than the second class.[1]

A list of the topics prescribed for the oral examinations for the Certificate of Competent Knowledge in 1990 will be available from the Faculty Office.

Examinations in modern languages for the Ordinary B.A. Degree

There are Ordinary Examinations in Czech (with Slovak), Dutch, French, German, Italian, Modern Greek, Polish, Portuguese, Russian and Spanish. In each language the examination consists of an oral examination and three written papers:

(1) Passages from works in the foreign language for translation.

(2) Passages of English for translation into the foreign language.

(3) An essay in the foreign language on a subject of a general character.

The written papers and the prescribed topics for the oral examinations in any year are the same as *either* (*a*) those for the Preliminary Examination for Part I of the Tripos, *or* (*b*) those for Part I of the Tripos.

A student who has been classed in, or received an allowance on, the Preliminary Examination for Part I of the Modern and Medieval Languages Tripos, or who has received an allowance on Part I of the Tripos, shall not offer option (*a*).

Students may not count towards the Ordinary B.A. Degree both the Ordinary Examination in a modern language and also anything that they have to their credit in the same language as the result of another examination.

M.Phil. in Linguistics

A one-year course leading to the degree of Master of Philosophy is offered by the Department of Linguistics. Candidates will normally be expected to possess at least a good Upper Second Class degree or its equivalent. The course will comprise: (*a*) lectures and classes in theoretical and practical linguistics, phonetics (general and English, including tones and intonation), phonology, grammar and semantics; (*b*) intensive study, through lectures, seminars or directed studies, of at least one other subject, such as psycholinguistics, socio-

---

[1] For the purposes of the Ordinary B.A. Degree, a candidate who attains this standard is deemed to have passed a Special Examination, and a candidate who does not do so may be allowed a Special Examination.

linguistics, historical linguistics, the history of linguistics, instrumental phonetics, language learning and bilingualism, literary stylistics. The course on phonetics will include a practical test. One week after the end of the Lent Term candidates must submit two essays of not more than 4,000 words each, falling respectively within the fields of (i) phonetics and phonology, (ii) grammar and meaning. A list of topics for each field will be prescribed by the Degree Committee. At the end of the Easter vacation candidates will submit a third essay of not more than 7,000 words in another field; they will also submit a dissertation of not more than 15,000 words at the end of the Easter Term. The subjects of the third essay and of the dissertation are to be approved by the Degree Committee.

MUSIC

The Music Tripos

The Music Tripos consists of three Parts: Part I A, Part I B, and Part II.

The normal programme for an undergraduate who intends to spend three years reading music will be as follows:

> Part I A of the Tripos at the end of the first year
> Part I B of the Tripos at the end of the second year
> Part II of the Tripos at the end of the third year

The attainment of honours in Part I B is an essential qualification for taking Part II.

Part I A

Subjects of examination

1. Harmony

Candidates will be required to compose a complete theme and set it as it might appear in a classical sonata, write an accompaniment for a given melody in an eighteenth- or early nineteenth-century idiom, and write simple variations on a ground or chord sequence.

2. Counterpoint

Candidates will be required to work counterpoint *either* in sixteenth-century style in not more than four parts, *or* as academic species in not more than four parts; *and* write a fugal exposition in not more than four parts.

3. Subjects in the history of Music I

The paper will be divided into two sections, each containing questions on one subject or period in the development of European music. Candidates will be required to answer three questions, at least one from each section.

The subjects in **1990** will be:
  Melody, mode and word
  Origins of Twentieth Century music

4. Subjects in the history of music II and notation

The paper will be divided into two sections. The first section will contain questions on a subject in the development of European music; candidates will be required to answer one question. In the second section, a facsimile from a period related to that subject will be provided for transcription and editing, with extracts from modern editions for comment.

The subject in **1990** will be:

Music in Purcell's London

5. Analysis and set work

The paper will be divided into two sections. In the first, compositions, or extracts from compositions of the period 1700–1750 will be provided for analysis and comment. For the second section, an extended movement in the Viennese classical style will be prescribed not less than two weeks before the date of the written paper; candidates will be permitted to bring unmarked copies of the score into the examination, and will be required to answer questions on it. Candidates will be required to answer three questions, at least one from each section.

Practical examination

Aural tests will include a memorization test (melodies), dictation exercises (four-part chorale harmonization and three-part counterpoint), a mistake-spotting test, and aural analysis (a movement from the period 1700–1830).

Keyboard tests will include the reading of a score of a string quartet, of a vocal score with C clefs, the harmonizing of a given melody, and the realizing of a figured bass at the keyboard.

A candidate must offer all five papers and take the practical examination.

Part I B

Subjects of examination

1. Stylistic composition (also serves as Paper 6 of Part II)

Candidates will be required to demonstrate their knowledge of a composer's distinctive style by completing settings of which only one part throughout or the *incipit* alone will be provided in the examination paper. Candidates will be given a choice of settings and will be required to answer questions on one or more of the composers prescribed. The composers prescribed are:

For **1990**: Byrd, Palestrina.

2. Subjects in the history of music I and ethnomusicology

The paper will be divided into three sections. Sections A and B will each contain questions on a subject or period in the history of European music before 1750. Section C will contain questions on ethnomusicology. Candidates

MUSIC

will be required to answer three questions.

The subjects in **1990** will be:

Music in England 1547–1625
Monteverdi
Maqam from Tunis to Tashkent

3. Subjects in the history of Music II

The paper will be divided into two sections. Section A will contain questions on subjects or periods in the history of European music after 1750. Section B will contain general questions on the history of music and ethnomusicology. Candidates will be required to answer three questions, as follows: *either* three questions from Section A, covering at least two subjects or periods *or* two questions from Section A and one from Section B.

The subjects in **1990** will be:

Opera buffa in the eighteenth century
The Symphony from Berlioz to Mahler
1945–1958 Post-war music

4. Analysis

Short pieces or extracts of extended forms, including compositions of twentieth-century composers, will be provided in the examination for analysis and comment.

5. Musical acoustics

Nature of sound; noise and musical sound; transmission of sound, especially in relation to buildings. Sound production and the acoustics of musical instruments. Temperament. Hearing. Principles of recording and reproduction. Candidates will be expected to show an understanding of the physical principles involved, but questions demanding a specialized knowledge of mathematics or physics will not be asked.

Portfolio of Tonal Compositions

Candidates will be required to submit a portfolio of two tonal compositions and a recording of one of them on cassette tape. The compositions shall be in different forms chosen from the following: ritornello, variations, scherzo and trio, rondo, binary (aria-form) or ternary slow movement, sonata.

In place of one of the two compositions, candidates may submit a through-composed song or group of songs, each of which must possess a clear and appropriate formal structure, for solo voice and pianoforte accompaniment. Each composition or group of songs shall be of not more than five minutes' duration and shall be for an ensemble of not more than five players. One composition may be for solo keyboard, but melody instruments may be used only in ensemble. Candidates will be responsible for providing the cassette, but quality of recorded sound will not contribute to the final mark.

Practical examination

Aural tests will include a memorization test (two-part counterpoint), a mistake-spotting test, aural analysis, and a test related to the perception of orchestral timbres.

Keyboard tests will include reading an orchestral score, realizing a figured bass at the keyboard, harmonizing a melody, and transposition.

A candidate for Part IB shall offer Papers 2–5, take the practical examination and offer *either* Paper 1 *or* the portfolio of tonal compositions. The portfolio, if offered, must be submitted through the candidate's Tutor to the Chairman of Examiners so as to reach him not later than the fifteenth day of Full Easter Term and the compositions must have been written during the previous twelve months. Each work must be initialled by the lecturer or supervisor under whose direction the work was done, as an indication that he approves the submission.

Part II

Subjects of examination

1. Fugal forms

Candidates will be required to compose *either* a fugue in not more than four parts from a choice of subjects, *or* a chorale prelude or chaconne with fugal elements on a given chorale or bass.

2. Set works

Candidates will be required to choose one from the list of prescribed compositions and to answer questions on it. They will be permitted to bring copies into the examination.

The set works in **1990** will be:
  Haydn: Quartets, Op. 50
  Tchaikovsky: *Sleeping Beauty* ballet music
  R. Strauss: *Salomé*
  Bartok: Quartets 1–6
  Stravinsky: *Petrushka, Rite of Spring*

3 and 4. Notation of early music I and II

Candidates will be required to transcribe and edit from original sources, and to evaluate editorial practices and techniques. Paper 4 will include **questions on the history of notation, the relationship between notation and composition, and questions on appropriate periods of the history of music falling within the period 1350–1650.**

5. History of Performance Practice and Test of Performance

The study of notations, performance conventions, instrumental techniques and, where relevant, organology. The test of performance shall be undertaken as follows:

Test of performance

Either (a) on an historical instrument or in accompaniment on an historical instrument

For option (*a*) candidates will be required to demonstrate the technical and musical aspects of performance on their chosen instrument, by presenting a recital of not longer than twenty-three minutes' playing time which shall include one piece set by the Examiners after consultation with the candidate during the Michaelmas Term preceding the examination. Candidates must inform the Secretary of the Faculty Board not later than the division of that term of the instrument chosen, and details of the complete programme must be sent through the candidate's Tutor to the Secretary of the Faculty Board for approval, so as to reach him not later than the fourth day of the full Lent Term preceding the examination. The candidates will be questioned by the Examiners on matters relevant to their recitals.

or (b) on a modern instrument or in accompaniment on a modern instrument
or (c) in singing

For options (*b*) and (*c*) the test will consist of a recital of not more than twenty-three minutes' playing time, including a piece or a song (or songs) prescribed not later than the end of the Michaelmas Term preceding the examination. Candidates must inform the Secretary of the Faculty Board not later than the division of that term of the instrument chosen or type of voice, and details of the complete programme must be sent through the candidate's Tutor to the Secretary of the Faculty Board for approval, so as to reach him not later than the fourth day of the full Lent Term preceding the examination.

Candidates for the Test of Performance should note that they must make their own arrangements to provide an accompanist or page turner or both, if required, and that they should bring to the examination two copies of the pieces to be performed.

6. Stylistic composition (see Paper 1 of Part IB)

7–12. Additional papers

Additional papers may include subjects such as those shown in the following list: Ars Nova, Asian musics, Stravinsky, Elgar, Organ music of J. S. Bach.

The papers in **1990** will be:

Paper 7. Performance Practice in non-Western music
Paper 8. Dufay's isorhythmic motets
Paper 9. Franck and his School
Paper 10. Wagner's *Ring*
Paper 11. Advanced analysis

Portfolio of tonal compositions (see Part I B)

Portfolio of free compositions

Candidates will be required to submit a portfolio of four compositions which shall include a fugal composition and a setting of words in not less than three vocal parts. The compositions must be presented in normal staff notation.

Dissertation

A dissertation, of not less than 6,000 and not more than 7,000 words (exclusive of appendices), on a musical subject of the candidate's choice approved by the Faculty Board falling wholly or substantially outside the subjects chosen by the candidate for any of Papers 7–12 that he may choose to offer. The subject of the dissertation proposed by the candidate must be submitted through his Tutor to the Secretary of the Faculty Board so as to reach him not later than the fourth day of the Full Lent Term preceding the examination and approval must be obtained from the Faculty Board not later than the division of the Lent Term.

Interview

The Examiners are empowered for the purpose of drawing up the class-list for Part II to request a candidate to present himself for interview on matters arising from the examination, but they shall take account of that interview only if it would be to the candidate's advantage.

A candidate for Part II shall offer

(*a*) Papers 1 and 2, together with one paper chosen from Papers 7–12,
and
(*b*) three other papers chosen from Papers 3–12, provided that a candidate may substitute for any one or more of the papers that

he would otherwise offer under this sub-paragraph the same number of alternative exercises chosen from the following options:
  (i) the portfolio of tonal compositions
  (ii) the portfolio of free compositions
  (iii) the dissertation
      provided always that
(1) no candidate who offered Paper 1 in Part I B shall offer Paper 6;
(2) no candidate who offered the portfolio of tonal compositions in Part I B shall offer option (i).
(3) if a candidate offers Paper 4 he shall also offer Paper 3.

The portfolio of tonal compositions or free compositions, if offered, must be submitted in the same manner as the portfolio of tonal compositions in Part I B (see above).

The dissertation, if offered, must be submitted through the candidate's Tutor to the Chairman of Examiners so as to reach him not later than the eighth day of Full Easter Term. The Examiners shall have power to require the candidate to resubmit his dissertation in typescript if, in their opinion, the original work submitted is not sufficiently legible.

The degree of Bachelor of Music

A student who has obtained honours in any Part of the Music Tripos may, in his third year or later, be a candidate for the Mus.B. Examination (he cannot in the same year be a candidate both for the Mus.B. and for any other University examination except that for the Certificate of Competent Knowledge in a Modern Language).

The examination consists of two Sections, as follows:

Section I

An instrumental or vocal recital. Candidates must submit a programme lasting approximately ninety minutes of instrumental or vocal music. From this the Examiners will hear a recital of at least forty minutes' music. Each candidate must be responsible for providing his own accompanist and page turner, where required, and must provide an additional copy of the works for the Examiners.

Section II

(*a*) A dissertation of between 10,000 and 15,000 words (excluding appendices) on a subject chosen from a list of subjects announced by the Faculty Board not later than the division of the Easter Term of the year preceding the examination concerned.

The subjects announced for **1989** are:

The earliest motets.
Eighteenth-century organ music.
Nineteenth-century solo piano music.
Historical treatises and performance tutors.
Choral institutions and performance during the fifteenth and sixteenth centuries.
Methods of musical notation, 1925–1975.
Twentieth-century composers as their own interpreters.
Opera in the twentieth century.
Acoustical properties of instruments and their influence on performance.

(b) A paper of three hours' duration on the background of the subject of the candidate's dissertation. A candidate may be examined orally on questions arising from his recital or dissertation.

The two Sections of the examination must be taken together, whether at a candidate's first attempt or at any subsequent attempt, except that if a candidate has failed in not more than one Section he may be allowed to present himself for re-examination in that Section alone.

A candidate must send to the Secretary of the Faculty Board of Music, not later than the division of the Michaelmas Term preceding the examination, a list of the works that he proposes to perform, for approval by the Faculty Board, and, not later than 1 December preceding the examination, the subject of his dissertation. He must submit his dissertation to the Secretary not later than the eighth day of Full Easter Term.

M.Phil. Degree in Musical Composition

This is a one-year course of study in Musical Composition. The examination consists of:

(a) Two written papers, each of three hours' duration:

1. Analytical studies in the music of a composer, including appropriate consideration of the background and literature about his work.

MUSIC

2. *either* (i) The problems and methods of teaching composition in a period of the history of music,

   or (ii) the theories and philosophies of twentieth-century music.

The candidate's choice of composer for Paper 1 and, if he chooses Paper 2(i), of a period of the history of music, will be subject to the approval of the Degree Committee for the Faculty of Music.

(*b*) Two compositions which must be notated in a conventional manner:
   (i) a composition incorporating fugal elements, requiring not less than five and not more than ten minutes to perform, for five-part chorus or for at least three melody instruments and piano;
   (ii) a composition, requiring not less than twelve and not more than fifteen minutes to perform, for a large chamber ensemble or orchestra with or without soloists and/or chorus; this composition may be in any idiom of the candidate's choice.

The composition must be submitted to the Secretary of the Board of Graduate Studies not later than 31 August.

The examination will at the Examiners' discretion include an oral examination.

M.Phil. Degree in Musicology

This is a one-year course of study in Musicology. The scheme of examination consists of *either* Option A *or* Option B, as may be determined by the Degree Committee in the case of each candidate, as follow:

Option A. Musicology

(*a*) a thesis of not more than 25,000 words in length (including tables, footnotes, and appendices, but excluding bibliography, musical examples, and transcriptions) on a subject in the history of music approved by the Degree Committee for the Faculty of Music;

and

(*b*) an exercise consisting of:
   either (i) a transcription of a piece or pieces of music, with editorial commentary and full introduction,

or (ii) a full analysis of a piece or pieces of music.
The candidate's choice of music will be subject to the approval of the Degree Committee.

Option B. Ethnomusicology

(*a*) a thesis of not more than 12,000 words in length (including tables, footnotes, and appendices, but excluding bibliography, musical examples, and transcriptions) on a subject in ethnomusicology approved by the Degree Committee for the Faculty of Music;

and

(*b*) a written account of the candidate's fieldwork accompanied by a collection of annotated sound recordings made by the candidate;

and

(*c*) a transcription and analysis of a piece or pieces of recorded music. The candidate's choice of music shall be subject to the approval of the Degree Committee.

A candidate who chooses Option B must undertake a period of fieldwork whose nature and length will be subject to the approval of the Degree Committee.

The thesis and exercise (Option A) or the thesis, written account of fieldwork and the transcription and analysis (Option B) must be submitted to the Secretary of the Board of Graduate Studies not later than 31 August.

The examination may, at the Examiners' discretion, include an oral examination on the thesis and other written work and on the general field of knowledge within which they fall.

NATURAL SCIENCES

In the Natural Sciences there are courses of study followed by candidates for:

The *Natural Sciences Tripos*, which is divided into four Parts.

The *Preliminary Examinations for Part II and for Section II of Part II (General) of the Natural Sciences Tripos*.

Ordinary Examinations in the Natural Sciences for the Ordinary B.A. Degree.

Certificates of Post-graduate Study in Natural Science.

The *M.Phil. Degree* (one-year courses) in *Biological Science, History and Philosophy of Science, Physics, Plant Breeding,* and *Quaternary Research*.

The Natural Sciences Tripos

The Natural Sciences Tripos is divided into four Parts – I A, I B, II, and II (General). It is possible for a candidate to take all four Parts, which will take him four years, but normally he spends three years on taking three Parts. Part I A has to be taken in a candidate's first year (except that a candidate transferring from another Tripos may take Part I A in his third year). Part I B has to be taken in a candidate's second year, and Part II or Part II (General) in his third or fourth year.

It is possible to transfer, after passing Part I A or Part I B, to another Tripos. The new subjects taken up will depend on the candidate's interests, but common transfers are to Law or Economics after either Part I A or Part I B, and to Part II Engineering, Electrical and Information Sciences, Computer Science, Management Studies, or Part I Chemical Engineering after Part I B. Transfer to the Mathematical Tripos after Part I A, Part I B, or Part II is also possible and may be appropriate for those interested in theoretical physics. Transfer to Medicine is a special case, on which detailed advice is required, but in general it may be said that it is possible for a candidate who has passed Part I A to complete in another two years all courses necessary to prepare him for clinical work, either (if he has not read Physiology in Part I A) by transfer to the Medical Sciences Tripos, or by reading appropriate subjects in Part I B of the Natural Sciences Tripos and then transferring to the Medical Sciences Tripos.

Transfers from other Triposes to the Natural Sciences Tripos are also possible. Some intending physicists may find it worthwhile to take Part IA of the Engineering or of the Mathematical Tripos and then transfer to Part IB Natural Sciences in Advanced Physics and Mathematics, and Part II Natural Sciences in Physics and Theoretical Physics. Transfer to Part II Genetics from other Triposes, especially the Medical Sciences Tripos, may be made. Transfer to Part II Psychology is also possible in certain circumstances, particularly from the Philosophy Tripos, and various Triposes provide a satisfactory basis for transfer to History and Philosophy of Science in Part II (General).

An affiliated student may: (*a*) take Part IB of the Tripos in his first year; (*b*) if the Faculty Board concerned permit, take Part II of the Tripos or, if the History and Philosophy of Science Syndicate permit, take Section II of Part II (General) of the Tripos, in his first or second year as if he had obtained honours in Part IB.

Part IA

Candidates are required to offer three of the following subjects for Part IA:

Biology of Cells
Biology of Organisms
Chemistry
Crystalline Materials
Geology
Physics
Physiology

They may also offer Mathematics, Biological Mathematics, or Elementary Mathematics for Biologists as a fourth subject if they wish to do so.

The structure of Part IA is such as to encourage the study of at least one subject not previously studied by a candidate at school. The knowledge that candidates are assumed already to possess is indicated in the descriptions of each subject. Candidates offering Physics or Chemistry need to have studied that subject to Advanced level in the G.C.E. Examination, but the teaching of the other experimental subjects in Part IA is so designed as to provide for candidates with no previous knowledge of those subjects.

Biology of Cells. The course aims to provide a basic introduction to biology at the molecular and cellular level, and considers what cells are, what they look like, and how they work. The Biology of Cells course is complete in its own right, but it also provides a useful introduction to further studies in biology, biochemistry and genetics, for both biologists and non-biologists. The course is organized jointly by the Departments of Biochemistry, Botany, Genetics, and Zoology. All Lecturers for the course issue printed lecture notes.

In the first term, the lectures deal with the basic structure of cells and macromolecules, with the structure and function of cell membranes, and with the essential biochemistry of cell metabolism. The second term's lectures are concerned with viruses; with genetics (including the organization and inheritance of genetic information) and nucleic acid and protein synthesis; and with cell growth and multiplication. Lectures in the Easter Term consider aspects of development; recognition processes; and a specialized cell function (motility).

The practical side of the course is organized so that, as far as possible, the experiments are related to the subject matter of the concurrent lecture course.

Past experience shows that the course appeals to students who have no 'A' level Biology as well as to those who have. This former group is attracted by the ability increasingly to understand biological events in molecular terms; however, students will find it useful to have done some preliminary reading before coming up. Although students who have 'A' level Biology will find that some of the material presented is apparently familiar to them, the depth of treatment and the differences in viewpoint distinguish this course significantly from 'A' level Biology. Knowledge of 'A' level Chemistry is assumed, and students would be unwise to take the course without this qualification.

Biology of Organisms. As its title implies, this course is intended to complement the Biology of Cells course: most, but not all, students studying 'Organisms' also study 'Cells'. The course is given jointly by the Departments of Botany, Genetics, and Zoology and aims at introducing students to the variety of multicellular organisms, their adaptations, and the genetical mechanisms underlying adaptation in general.

The first term will deal with animals. The first eighteen lectures will include brief descriptions of who's who in the animal world, and cover such comparative topics as the effects of scale on animal structure and physiology, metabolic rates and the cost of transport, flight, life in moving fluids, and the colonisation of land and freshwater. Each of the major phyla will be used as a basis for the discussion of general 'across the board' topics. Thus, for example, Crustacea, moulting and hormonal control, excretory systems; Mollusca, structural materials, hermaphroditism, filter feeding, and buoyancy; Annelida, hydrostatic skeletons, circulation and blood pigments. The last six lectures will add a historical dimension, considering the origins of animal diversity in relation to the changing ecology of the Earth's surface over the last 10^9 years. Linked to the lectures are practical classes that will include dissections, and observation of living animals.

The second term deals with two major groups of organisms: the seed plants (16 lectures) and the fungi (8 lectures). The general aim is to show what has led to the wide distribution and diversity of these groups during evolution. The lectures on seed plants deal with the integration of plant structure, biochemistry, physiology and development throughout the life cycle. In the first part of the course examples of relatively unspecialized types from different seed plant groups are considered. Subsequently a wide range of plant types is analysed in the same way so as to illustrate adaptations which enable seed plants to colonize a variety of environments. Finally, the lectures summarize the interactions between plants in plant communities. The lectures on fungi, in addition to considering their diversity, mode of growth, nutrition and genetics emphasize their ecology and role in the carbon cycle and their inter-relations with seed plants as parasites. The practical classes are closely related to the lectures and involve both observation and experiment.

In the third term there is a consideration of the processes of evolution. This course is designed to consider the mechanisms which may have influenced the development and diversification of life on earth. After a brief introduction to evolutionary theories, molecular evolution will be considered to show how similarities and differences between amino-acid sequences of particular proteins can give an indication of phylogenetic relationships between species. Changes in chromosomal arrangements will be treated in a similar way, and will lead on to a consideration of the various levels at which variation within a species can be studied and how it may be measured. The way such variation is propagated through various natural breeding systems will then be investigated (sexual versus asexual reproduction, inbreeding versus outbreeding). The enormous quantity of genetic variation within and between species provides a basis for a consideration of the evidence for natural selection, the way natural selection operates and the other factors which may affect the maintenance of genetic variations in a population. Geographical variation within species may be produced as an outcome of selection, and the conditions under which this may lead to speciation are discussed. Finally, there is a summary of the relevance to human populations and races of the principles of evolutionary change which have been developed in the course.

Although most students taking this course will have done at least one biological subject at A-level, this is not essential, but students who have not done an 'A' level in Biology are advised to consult their Colleges about doing some preliminary reading before coming up.

Chemistry. This is a general course containing aspects of organic, inorganic, and physical chemistry appropriate to provide an integrated background for the later study of chemistry as a whole. A previous knowledge of chemistry up to Advanced level in G.C.E. is assumed. Practical work is an essential part of the course and is continuously assessed. The course is geared towards the illustration of modern techniques and general principles.

This foundation course is designed to emphasize the scope of modern chemistry and its central position as an enabling subject for many other disciplines.

Crystalline Materials. This course introduces many important aspects of the study of solids. The lectures deal with the arrangement of atoms in crystals, with the symmetry and the defects of these crystal structures, and with their chemical stability and transformations. The way in which crystals grow together in polycrystalline aggregates ('microstructure') is also studied. This leads on to explanations of how the atomic arrangements and the microstructure together determine selected physical and mechanical properties of crystalline materials. Emphasis is placed on the experimental methods of characterizing crystals on scales from the millimetre to the nanometre, including X-ray diffraction, optical microscopy and high resolution electron microscopy; the scientific principles underlying these techniques are explained. The sequence of examples classes and experiments, which is expressly designed to help develop an understanding of the lectures, forms an essential part of the course. The facts and insights gained from the Crystalline Materials course can be applied widely, for example in the fundamental physics and chemistry of solids, transformations in rock-forming minerals, the strength of engineering materials, the behaviour of micro-circuit constituents, and the determination of the atomic architecture not only of simple crystals but also of glasses and macro-molecules including biological molecules.

In Part I A, Crystalline Materials is most commonly combined with both Chemistry and Physics, but significant numbers each year take it with Geology or Biology of Cells and either Chemistry or Physics. The background of anyone taking the course should include Physics and/or Chemistry or Physical Science to A-level.

Crystalline Materials provides a balanced introduction to the solid state, and is of direct value to those planning to specialize in Chemistry or Physics. It also forms a highly desirable preparation for those intending to read Crystalline State and Mineralogy & Petrology, or Material Science & Metallurgy in Part I B with a view to taking the Part II courses in Mineral Sciences or in Materials Science & Metallurgy.

The course is presented jointly by the Department of Materials Science & Metallurgy and the Department of Earth Sciences.

Geology. The course is an introduction to the whole field of earth science. It covers the nature and properties of the Earth, particularly of the mantle and the crust; observed and deduced processes of change; biological, physical, and chemical methods of dating; and major economic considerations. It illustrates the principles of geology as they apply to a broadscale picture of a segment of the Earth. Emphasis is placed on practical and field work including general identifications and interpretation of rocks, interpretation of geological maps of large areas, and the use of fossils and rocks in determining the successive changes in the crustal environment. Much of the course is concerned with application of principles of physics, chemistry, and biology to rocks and their distribution, so that a school background in some or all of these subjects is a good preparation. Previous knowledge of geology is not necessary. The course includes fieldwork carried out in part of the Easter Vacation.

Physics. This course presupposes familiarity with physics and mathematics equivalent to Advanced Level in GCE and aims to provide a general background suitable both for those going on to further study of physics and also for those whose main interests lie elsewhere. The lectures cover mechanics, relativity and fields; electric circuits and oscillations; waves; and thermal physics. It is assumed that those taking physics will also be taking either the A or B courses in NST mathematics. Practical work is an essential part of the course.

Physiology. The biology of living organism includes consideration of structure and function. Physiology is primarily the study of function, though it inevitably involves some study of structure, particularly of the fine structure of tissues and cells.

The course does not assume any previous knowledge of biology, and in fact, for many of the topics studied, those students who have read physics and chemistry and possibly mathematics at school find that these constitute a groundwork as useful as that given by biological subjects. Physiology therefore forms an eminently suitable third subject for those Tripos candidates who are primarily interested in the physical sciences but also wish to cover a biological subject.

The first-year course can be taken simply as a one-year course or as the first part of a two-year course. It does not attempt to cover all aspects of physiology but studies selected topics in considerable detail and these topics are not dealt with again in the second year. The course concentrates on vertebrate, mammalian, and human physiology. It starts with a detailed study of the mechanisms of nerve conduction and muscle contraction, both from the physico-chemical and biological aspects. The circulatory, respiratory, and excretory mechanisms and the processes of intestinal absorption, energy balance and thermoregulation, together with their control systems, are studied in relation to the need to maintain the stability of the internal environment. A considerable proportion of the course is devoted to practical work, particularly in experimental and histological studies.

Mathematics. This subject is principally designed for physical scientists who have studied mathematics to Advanced level in G.C.E. There are two courses which differ in their level.

The A course is the easier of the two and includes lectures on calculus, vector algebra, matrices, ordinary and partial differential equations, and computing techniques. The B course covers all the material of the A course but in more depth. It is more difficult than the A course, and it should only be attended by students who are well prepared in mathematics. Those who intend to continue with mathematics in Part I B of the Tripos will find it an advantage to attend the B course in Part I A but this is not a necessity.

The timetables of both courses are constructed so as to allow students to change from one to the other at certain times during the year without placing themselves at a disadvantage.

Biological Mathematics. This subject is designed to show how biological understanding can be enhanced by the sensible use of mathematical techniques. It is intended for students who have taken one subject mathematics at Advanced level in the G.C.E. (or its equivalent). The material is presented through particular biological examples drawn from biochemistry, animal and plant physiology, ecology, genetics. Mathematical topics include simple treatments of ordinary differential equations, the diffusion equation, vector algebra, matrix algebra, probability, statistics, and computing. The lectures are supplemented by classes.

Elementary Mathematics for Biologists. This subject is designed to cover those parts of elementary mathematics that are of immediate use to biologists. No knowledge of mathematics is assumed beyond that required for mathematics at Ordinary level in G.C.E. The course consists of elementary calculus, an introduction to differential equations, statistics and computing; the lectures are supplemented by classes.

Arrangements for the courses in Biological Mathematics and Elementary Mathematics for Biologists are at present under review.

Part I B

Candidates are required to offer either two subjects or three subjects for Part I B, not more than one subject being chosen from any one of the nine groups set out below. If only two subjects are being offered one of them must be Advanced Physics.

(i) Chemistry A.
(ii) Pathology; Physics; Advanced Physics.
(iii) Materials Science and Metallurgy; Ecology; Molecular Cell Biology.
(iv) Crystalline State; Physiology.
(v) Biochemistry and Molecular Biology; Mineralogy and Petrology.
(vi) Experimental Psychology; Fluid Mechanics; Plant Biology.
(vii) Mathematics; Pharmacology; Animal Biology.
(viii) Advanced Physics; Chemistry B; Stratigraphic Geology.
(ix) History and Philosophy of Science.

Advanced Physics may not be offered together with another subject from group (ii) or group (viii). Mathematics may not be offered together with only one other subject unless the candidate has

NATURAL SCIENCES

previously attained a qualifying standard in Mathematics in Part I A, or unless he has been placed in a class not lower than the second class in Part I A of the Engineering Tripos, or been classed in Part I A of the Mathematical Tripos, or is an Affiliated Student. A candidate may not offer Mathematics if he has previously obtained honours in Part I B of the Mathematical Tripos. No subject, other than Physiology, may be offered which has already been offered in the Medical Sciences Tripos.

Animal Biology. This course follows the Part I A courses in Biology of Cells, Biology of Organisms and Physiology. Many students will have read two of these in Part I A; some come across from the 'physical' side, having read only Biology of Cells in Part I A.

The overall aim of the course is to demonstrate the extraordinary diversity of ways in which the behaviour, physiology and development of animals are adjusted by evolutionary processes to result in adaptation to environment.

The Michaelmas Term begins with Behaviour and Ecology, which considers how different behaviour patterns will be favoured by natural selection under different ecological conditions. Life history strategies, foraging behaviour, habitat selection and mate choice are some of the topics covered. This is followed by Brains and Behaviour, which explores the ways in which brains are organized for the control of behaviour.

In the Lent Term lectures are concerned with Adaptation and Evolution, drawing first on vertebrate examples to show that integration of developmental and evolutionary studies can enhance the understanding of adaptation. In the second half of the term the lectures seek to explain the success of those most abundant land animals, the insects. Topics covered include endocrine systems, insect–plant relations and the evolution of insect societies.

In the Easter Term lectures on Environmental Physiology use the physiological similarity and differences between animals to illustrate adaptation to environment (especially with respect to water, oxygen and temperature), again within an evolutionary framework.

Practical work consists of experimental procedures, observation of specimens, behavioural experiments, dissections, films and talks as appropriate to the course. Particular emphasis is placed on the ways in which nervous systems function in the detection and discrimination of signals in the environment, during learning and memory and in the generation of various patterns of movement.

Biochemistry and Molecular Biology. This course can be read by any Part IB scientist, physical or biological, who wishes to pursue the study of biological processes at the molecular and cellular level. It builds on basic concepts discussed in the Part IA course on Biology of Cells, although that is not an essential prerequisite. The aims of the course are to describe how information is stored as DNA and expressed as specific proteins, how enzymes and other proteins exert their functions, how cells function as integrated and coordinated metabolic systems, and how the growth and differentiation of cells is controlled.

The Michaelmas Term is concerned with Molecular Biochemistry: genes and proteins in action. The three main themes are firstly the control of gene expression in prokaryotes and eukaryotes, secondly the structure of proteins, the molecular mechanisms of enzyme action and the manipulation of protein structure to modify function, and finally gene cloning and genetic engineering. The Lent Term builds on these basic molecular concepts to deal with Cell Biochemistry: properties and functions of membranes and organelles and the integration of metabolism. The first topic is bioenergetics, how cells obtain their energy supply on which all metabolism is based, which is followed by the biogenesis of organelles and the sorting problem: how are proteins targeted to the appropriate organelle or membrane? The mechanisms by which metabolism is controlled and integrated are then discussed with examples that include the application of modern NMR techniques. The hormonal control of metabolism and mechanisms of signal transduction across the cell membrane lead on naturally at the end of the term to an introduction to the control of eukaryotic cell growth, mitogenic signal transduction and how genes and metabolism can be activated. This topic is continued in the Easter Term with a discussion of transforming oncogenes, cell division and the genetic control of the cell cycle. The final topic of the course is the overall metabolic behaviour of microorganisms, including chemotaxis and substrate transport, and the exploitation of microbial properties in biotechnology.

Practical work involving experiments, the use of computers in the analysis of DNA and protein sequences, audiovisual presentations and discussion is designed to complement the lectures.

Chemistry A and Chemistry B. The new chemistry courses have been designed to cater both for students who wish to go on to specialize in chemistry in Part II, and for those whose main interest lies in one of the other physical or biological sciences. The course emphasizes the more modern aspects of the four main branches of the subject: organic, inorganic, physical, and theoretical. Chemistry A emphasizes aspects of physical, theoretical, and inorganic chemistry, and the options include 'Quantum Mechanics', 'Coordination Chemistry', 'Heterogeneous Catalysis' and 'Solid State Chemistry'. It is suitable for physicists, chemical engineers and metallurgists. Chemistry B develops aspects of organic, inorganic and theoretical chemistry, and the options include 'Organic Synthesis', 'Medicinal Chemistry', 'Coordination Chemistry' and 'Spectroscopy'. It is well suited to those with biological or biochemical interests. Chemistry A and Chemistry B, taken together, cover the complete range of chemistry offered in Part IB, and will be a suitable choice for many students proceeding to related subjects such as Biochemistry or Chemical Engineering as well as for those intending to take Chemistry in Part II.

The inherent flexibility within the course structure allows students either to maintain a general interest in all aspects of chemistry, by taking both subjects, or to concentrate on specific areas which are closely related to other scientific disciplines. In this way, it is possible to include chemistry in a course which crosses interdisciplinary boundaries, and that provides a foundation for new and developing fields of science and technology.

Students who propose to read chemistry in Part II are normally expected to take both Chemistry A and Chemistry B. However, it is possible to read Part II having taken either Chemistry A or Chemistry B alone, provided that additional reading is undertaken during the Long Vacation before Part II.

There are no practical examinations for either Chemistry A or Chemistry B but the laboratory work is continuously assessed.

Crystalline State. The purpose of this course is to extend the understanding of the basic theory of crystalline matter and of the techniques for its study acquired in Part IA Crystalline Materials, and to show how, with this more advanced knowledge, particular problems in the solid state can be tackled. Topics in the course include: the interaction of X-rays, electrons, and neutrons with crystals (both diffraction and image formation, including crystal structure determination); the anisotropy of physical properties; non-stoichiometry; the search for compounds with specific properties; solid-state transformations. Laboratory practicals and paper demonstrations are closely linked to the lectures.

This course, given in the Earth Sciences Department, is a valuable second subject for physicists and chemists. It is complementary to **Materials Science and Metallurgy** on the one hand, and to **Part I B Mineralogy and Petrology** on the other, and it is essential for the **Mineral Sciences option in Part II Geological Sciences.**

Ecology. The course, run jointly by the Departments of Botany, Genetics and Zoology, introduces a variety of approaches to the study of the relationship between plants, animals and the environment. After examining the determinants of global patterns of vegetation and productivity, it focuses on the structure and operation of some freshwater and terrestrial communities including details of the botanical consequences of climatic change and the greenhouse effect. Aspects of evolutionary ecology to be considered include optimal foraging theory, interactions between predator and prey, and the comparative ecology of mammals, with special reference to body size, life histories and mating systems. The section on population ecology deals with population genetics, emphasizing the way selection and other factors can affect the gene pool of populations and the genome of a species. It also introduces aspects of population dynamics, competition, and models of community structure. Principles introduced earlier in the course are developed further in lectures in the Easter Term on the relationship between insects and plants with special reference to herbivory and pollination, and on the management of wildlife, for whaling, sealing, game cropping, hunting and conservation.

Students taking the course are expected to attend two residential field courses during the Long Vacation. Most of the practical work will be done on the field courses, and termtime practical classes are reduced to about two per term, to include seminars, excursions and classes on data handling. Practical work will be examined on the basis of a project, normally based on work done during the field courses, as well as a conventional practical examination. Students unable to attend the field courses will be expected to submit for the examination an account of alternative project work completed during the year.

Experimental Psychology. Experimental Psychology uses the methods of natural science to understand the behaviour and mental processes of human beings and animals. The course is intended to provide an introduction to experimental findings and related theories on the following topics: how human beings perceive the world, process and remember information; language, thought, and intelligence and the development of these processes and abilities in childhood; motivation, learning, and memory, how these may be studied in animals, and what brain processes may underlie them; abnormal psychology and mental illness and how research in experimental psychology may help us to understand them. The course does not include any work in social psychology.

Most parts of the course are accompanied by practical work, which includes individual and group experiments on human or animal behaviour, demonstrations, and films. There is teaching on the applications of elementary psychological statistics and on basic neurobiology for non-biologists. It is useful, although not essential, to have some previous knowledge of biology such as would be gained by taking Biology of Organisms, Physiology, or both, in Part IA. Some knowledge of physical science or of mathematics is a valuable alternative preparation for the course.

Fluid Mechanics (and Transfer Processes). The course, which is taught in the Department of Chemical Engineering, provides a broad introduction to fluid mechanics and transfer processes. The emphasis is on the physical and practical aspects of the subject, and on getting numerical results. Laboratory work is provided throughout the year, and each student has the opportunity of doing 18 experiments.

The material is also relevant to any subject, e.g. Chemistry, Physics, Materials Science and Metallurgy where transfer processes (discussed below) are important. There are 60 lectures, 36 hours of laboratory work and 40 hours of example classes.

(1) *Fluid Mechanics.* The equations governing fluid dynamics are derived from the conservation of energy, momentum, mass and Newton's Law of Viscosity. Ideal, viscous and turbulent flow are discussed, with applications in pipe flow, centrifugal pumps, boundary layer theory. The importance of dimensional analysis is emphasized.

Non-viscous fluid flow is described by means of a potential function, and velocity fields and pressure distributions obtained. An example is the lift force on a wing.

The flow of fluids through packed beds of particles is described. Fluidization of the bed, and the dynamics of fluid bubbles passing through the bed are discussed.

(2) *Heat and Mass Transfer.* Heat conduction and convection, and diffusion of molecules are described. Models of heat and mass transfer in fluids are constructed, and the similarities between

heat and mass transfer are exploited, using dimensional analysis. Some applications are in heat exchangers, material transfer between gases and liquids, chimneys and central heating systems.

Humidity is discussed, with applications in drying.

(3) *Compressible Flow and Open Channel Flow.* This course covers the flow of an ideal gas through a duct, and the flow of a liquid along an open channel; the physics of the two are closely related. For gas flow, continuity, thermodynamics and the equation of state provide a description of the dynamics; there is a discussion of supersonic flow and shock waves. In open channel flow the fluid dynamics already covered provides a discussion of gravity waves, weirs and hydraulic jumps.

(4) *Surface Effects.* The physics and thermodynamics of interfaces are described, with applications in flotation, foams and wetting.

History and Philosophy of Science. The course is intended to introduce the student to some of the historical and philosophical problems relating to the rise of science in Western civilization and to the nature of scientific knowledge. Examples are taken from many different branches of science, and students will be able to concentrate to some extent on the history and philosophy of the sciences that interest them. Students are expected to read a substantial amount of material in the subject, including some original sources. Further details of the courses, and recommended reading for the previous Long Vacation, are available from the Department. The examination consists of two papers, one with questions of a primarily historical character, the other with questions on more philosophical topics.

Mathematics. This course is especially useful for students intending to study Physics and Theoretical Physics in Part II. It is also attended by students taking Chemistry. The following topics are included: introduction to group theory; more advanced matrix theory; Cartesian tensors; more advanced theory of differential equations (including solution in power series and expansions in characteristic functions); Fourier and Laplace transforms; calculus of variations; functions of a complex variable. An opportunity is provided for practical work in numerical analysis using a computer.

Materials Science and Metallurgy. Through a systematic study of the scientific principles involved this course aims to provide an

NATURAL SCIENCES

understanding of the reasons underlying the selection and use of materials, metallic and non-metallic, in a wide range of applications from electronic through structural to electrochemical. Topics covered include: the development and optimization of microstructures; extraction and production of materials; corrosion and other mechanisms of degradation; mechanical and physical properties and their control; processing and fabrication. Metals, ceramics, glasses, and polymers are all studied.

Study of the subject Crystalline Materials in Part I A is a desirable, although not essential, preparation. Whilst this course is self-contained and so can usefully be taken by those planning to proceed to Part II in another subject, it also forms an important prerequisite for Materials Science and Metallurgy in Part II.

Mineralogy and Petrology. **The nature and formation of igneous and metamorphic minerals and rocks form the core of this course,** together with methods of their determination such as optics, diffraction, isotope analysis and phase equilibrium studies. This traditional 'hard rock' geology course concludes by considering the build-up of a complete orogenic belt. Practical work and map analysis are emphasized, and there is a Field Course in the Easter Vacation.

The course develops one half of Geology but is complete in itself. Together with the complementary subject Stratigraphic Geology it leads on to Part II Geological Sciences.

Molecular Cell Biology. Part I B Molecular Cell Biology is a new course which is designed to build on the foundation provided in the first year by I A Biology of Cells and to extend and consolidate coverage of cell biology. The course is taught by members of the Departments of Botany, Genetics, and Zoology and it is designed to be taken in conjunction with any other subject in Part I B of the Natural Sciences Tripos except Ecology or Materials Science and Metallurgy, with which it shares slots in the lecture timetable. Arrangements have been made to minimize overlap between I B Molecular Cell Biology and I B Biochemistry and Molecular Biology as it is envisaged that many students will wish to take both courses.

The first term of Molecular Cell Biology considers how genetic information is organized and expressed, particularly within the nuclei of eukaryotic cells. The Lent Term emphasizes the cytoplasm. How are cytoplasmic organelles and the cytoskeleton organized and maintained? How are proteins targeted to particular sites in the cell? How do cells communicate with one another and how do the nucleus and cytoplasm influence each other's activities? The Easter Term focuses on Cell Differentiation. How do cells which contain similar genetic material diverge to make different specialized products and to perform different functions within a multicellular organism; and how do populations of cells become organized into complex body patterns?

Practical work involves experimental techniques which illustrate fundamental concepts and which are in current use in cell biology research.

Cell biology and molecular biology are advancing rapidly. This new course aims to illustrate the excitement of those advances.

Pathology. This is a course in general pathology, treated from the standpoint of abnormal biology. It includes the variations which may occur in disease in the structure and functions of living cells, tissues and organs and discusses the causes of such changes. The course includes cell pathology, immunology, microbiology and parasitology. Practical classes are an important feature of the course and are integrated as far as possible with the lectures. The course is equally suitable for all biological, medical and veterinary students.

Pharmacology. The emphasis of the course is on pharmacology considered as the action of chemical substances on biological systems and in particular the mechanisms by which drugs produce their actions considered at the molecular, sub-cellular, and cellular levels. A knowledge of the basic biochemistry and physiology of living systems is an advantage. The practical course is designed in parallel to the lecture course to illustrate the principles by which pharmacological actions can be assessed.

Physics and Advanced Physics. Both of these courses assume a knowledge of Part IA Physics.

The Advanced Physics course is mainly for those who intend going on to Physics and Theoretical Physics in Part II, but it is also a useful, though not essential, preparation for Materials Science and Metallurgy in Part II, or for the Electrical and Information Sciences Tripos. It includes six hours a week of practical work and six lectures a week. These cover electromagnetism, dynamics, wave mechanics, optics, experimental methods, quantum physics, thermodynamics, and solid state physics. These are lectures on symmetry properties of solids (for those who have not taken Crystalline Materials in their first year), on computational methods in physics, and on mathematical methods (for those who are not attending the Mathematics course for Part IB.

There are examples classes on computing and mathematical methods, and optional lectures on analytical dynamics and microcomputing in physics.

The Physics course is designed for those who intend to offer some subject other than Physics in Part II. It includes practical work (about four hours a week) and three lectures a week with courses on waves and imaging instruments, quantum physics, and physics of electronic devices.

Physiology. The course is designed as a continuation of the Physiology Part IA course but students who elect to read Physiology IB without having attended the Part IA course will not be placed at a significant disadvantage provided they have, or are prepared to acquire, a basic knowledge of biology approaching 'A' level in standard. The main topics studied are the physiology of reproduction in selected vertebrate species including man, and the physiology of the the two main vertebrate control systems, the central nervous system (together with the special sense organs feeding information into it) and the endocrine system.

Plant Biology. This subject continues the study, begun in the Part IA courses on Biology of Cells and Biology of Organisms, of higher and lower plants, their structures, physiology, biochemistry, genetics and ecology; there is no overlap with the subject *Ecology*. Centred on the Department of Botany, this course has a series of internal options, enabling the student to follow plant cell biology courses or whole organism plant biology courses through the year. The first term contains a course on plants, pathogens and partners with parallel courses on cellular microbiology and plant cell manipulation. The second term offers two parallel alternative courses, one on plant metabolism, the other on the dynamics and physiology of world vegetation. The third term's course also offers two alternatives, one dealing with plant variation and microevolution, the other with the regulation of development in plants. It will be noted that the options dealing with plant cell biology complement the cell biology of the *Animal Biology* and Molecular Cell Biology courses. Most students selecting this subject will have read Biology of Cells and/or Biology of Organisms in their first year.

Stratigraphic Geology. The study of sediments and sedimentary rocks, including palaeontology, palaeoceanography and sedimentary geochemistry, together with methods of study such as well-logging and seismic profiling, are accompanied in this course by sections on rock deformation and large-scale tectonic evolution. Practical geology, including map interpretation, is emphasized, and there is a Field Course in the Easter Vacation.

The course develops one side of Geology but is complete in itself. Together with the complementary subject Mineralogy and Petrology it leads on to Part II Geological Sciences.

Part II

Candidates are required to offer one of the following subjects or combinations of subjects:

Anatomy	Pathology
Biochemistry	Pharmacology
Botany	Physics and Theoretical
Chemistry	Physics
Genetics	Physiology
Geological Sciences	Physiology with Psychology
History and Philosophy of Science	Psychology
Materials Science and Metallurgy	Zoology

Entry in certain Part II subjects is limited by reason of the laboratory space available, and in most cases is conditional on taking certain courses in Part I B so that it cannot be guaranteed on entry to Cambridge that a student will always be accepted for the Part II subject of his choice.

Anatomy. The Anatomy Department offers an advanced course of lectures in two main modules. *The Cellular and Molecular Development* module includes a general consideration of the mechanisms underlying developmental processes (lineage analysis, mechanisms and consequences of spatial heterogeneity, cell interaction and movements, selective gene expression, the cell cycle and developmental time), as well as detailed analysis of current research on *Drosophila, Caenorhabditis, Dictyostelium* and vertebrates. The *Neurobiology* module offers lectures on the control of motor function, the neuroanatomy, -pharmacology and -endocrinology of sexual behaviour, aggression, reproductive function, thirst, hunger and mental disorder, and on the development and regeneration of the central and peripheral nervous systems.

NATURAL SCIENCES

Students undertake an ambitious research project in close cooperation with members of the academic staff and research workers. The research project is their sole experimental work and results in a dissertation. As part of these projects students have access to practical instruction in a variety of techniques including scanning and transmission electron microscopy and freeze-fracture replication, histochemistry, immunohistochemistry, tissue culture, computing, radioimmunoassay, neurosurgery and cell biology.

Biochemistry (including Molecular Biology). This is an advanced course in general Biochemistry, which includes topics in related physical, chemical and biological disciplines; it continues and extends the study of subjects introduced in Part I. The study of Biochemistry either in Part I B of the Natural Sciences Tripos (in which the course is designated Biochemistry and Molecular Biology), or in Part I A of the Medical Sciences Tripos, is the normal preparation for the Part II course.

The Part II course is divided into a 'core', taken by all students, during the Michaelmas Term; followed by a set of 'options' and a research project occupying the Lent Term.

The 'core' course lectures comprise two successive themes 'Biochemistry and Molecular Biology' and 'Biochemistry and Cell Biology', each of four weeks and about 36 lectures. Practical work in the Michaelmas Term is under successive headings 'Enzymology', 'Gene Cloning', 'Macromolecular Structure and Analysis' and 'Cell Biology', each of about 10 days.

'Options' lectures extend throughout the Lent Term; there are about 10 options of 15 lectures each – students have free choice and are expected to attend a minimum of three options. A major research project also occupies the Lent Term; each student has a unique project chosen from a list of about 55 – there is no other practical work in the term. The Easter Term has no formal teaching.

There are opportunities for students, who satisfactorily complete the Part II course in Biochemistry, to proceed to Higher Degrees by research; the Department is well equipped for research on a wide range of biochemical topics. The Part II course is also a good preparation for careers in Industry, Teaching and the Hospital Laboratory Service.

Botany. **The modern study of plants is dealt with comprehensively at an advanced level, timetabled to allow attendance at any combi-**

nation of courses. There are lectures and project work in: plant ultrastructure; plant pathology, mycology and microbial physiology; plant biochemistry; plant biophysics; developmental physiology; genetic manipulation; cytology and genetics; ecology; tropical botany; palaeoecology and flora history; genecology; taxonomy and systematics; statistics. The Department participates in the interdepartmental Part II Course in Developmental Biology (see p. 377). It is not necessary to take all the courses offered; students are encouraged to specialize by taking their own choice of about half of the total.

There is a two-week Long Vacation course primarily concerned with field work in ecology and taxonomy. Students intending to take the relevant options in Part II Botany are expected to attend the whole of this course.

There are extensive facilities in the Department for training in research in all the above aspects of the study of plants. Many openings exist for good botanists in biotechnology, agriculture, horticulture, forestry, industry and other fields at home and abroad; there is a particular shortage of persons with degrees in botany who have been trained in physics, chemistry, and mathematics up to advanced level in G.C.E.

Ecology. It is possible to devote the year to ecology, taking a mixture of courses from Botany and Zoology. There are two interdepartmental courses: population and community ecology, and tropical ecology. Students are registered under Part II Botany or Zoology, depending on where their primary interest lies.

Chemistry. It is a requirement of entry into the Part II course for students to have studied Chemistry in Part IB. The course is framed in a manner allowing maximum flexibility attuned to the individual choice of the student. It readily allows increased specialization for those who wish it, without restricting those who want a more general coverage. The initial lecture programme of Inorganic, Organic, Physical and Theoretical Chemistry courses lays the basis for an informed choice from fifteen more specialized 'packages' from which the student has an unfettered choice of five.

There are four papers in the examination. The first two deal with general material based on the IB course and the initial courses of Part II. The third and fourth papers examine material from each of the fifteen specialized 'packages' with wide freedom of choice. There are no practical examinations and the laboratory work of the year is continuously assessed; practical Inorganic Chemistry starts on the Monday before Full Term (2 October in 1989).

The success of the chemical industry in Britain means that companies compete to secure our graduates because of their excellence. Most graduates start work in industry as chemists but may later diversify into management, administration, marketing, and information technology. Less able or ambitious graduates may move directly into finance or management. The best graduates usually study for a Ph.D. before following their chosen career.

Genetics. The course in broad in scope, covering gene transmission and expression in both procaryotes and eucaryotes, genetic 'engineering', evolution and the genetics of populations, cytology and the genetics of cell differentiation and development. All Part II Genetics students attend the interdepartmental course in Development Biology (see p. 377). The time for practical work is divided between practical classes and individual projects. The project work is in the Lent Term and the reports prepared by students constitute part of the final assessment in the examination. An ideal preparation for those aspiring to Part II Genetics is Biochemistry, Molecular Cell Biology and another biological subject in Part I B, but these are by no means absolute requirements.

Openings for geneticists who have taken the Part II course occur in medical research, plant and animal breeding, biotechnology, and a variety of other areas of biological research, both basic or applied. The breadth of the course also makes it a good preparation for teaching in biology. Departmental facilities are available in a relatively wide range of topics for students wishing to do postgraduate research. Openings for those who go on to a higher degree have so far been readily obtained.

Geological Sciences. The courses cover all important aspects of the structure, composition and history of the earth: geophysics and structural geology; geochemistry, including isotope geochemistry; petrological processes and the use of experimental data in deducing thermal gradients and magma sources; topics in mineralogy, including mineral chemistry and physics; sedimentary petrology; historical geology; advanced palaeontology. A combination of courses emphasising mineralogy forms an option known as 'mineral sciences'.

There are openings for graduates with geological surveys, with oil and mining companies, and in connection with refractories, ceramics, cements, etc. For the best students there are research scholarships for advanced study and research leading to academic posts and senior positions in geological surveys and museums.

History and Philosophy of Science

The general aim of the course is to give insight into the historical and intellectual development of modern science (including medicine) within Western society, and into its philosophical structure and presuppositions. While a general knowledge of science is a valuable background for the course, students whose background is for example in the humanities will not be at a disadvantage: the insights they can bring from their previous training will compensate for any lack of knowledge of science. Students who have not already read the subject in Part I B are advised to attend the Part I B lectures in addition to those given specifically for Part II.

The Part II courses are normally arranged under eight groups, each of which corresponds to one paper in the examination. Candidates *either* take any four of Papers 1–8 together with Paper 9 (a three-hour essay on one of a number of general topics); *or* take any four of Papers 1–8 and submit a dissertation; *or* take Paper 9 and any three of Papers 1–8 and submit a dissertation in lieu of one of the remaining papers. The range of papers is such as to allow a measure of specialisation within the general field of history and philosophy of science. For example, papers may be chosen which focus primarily on history of science, on philosophy of science, on life sciences, or on physical sciences. A dissertation submitted in lieu of a paper must be on a topic that falls solidly within the subject area of that paper. A dissertation must be of not more than 15,000 words, and is expected to embody a substantial piece of study on a given topic; it must be submitted by the first day of Easter Full Term; possible topics should be discussed with any of the teaching officers, preferably before the preceding Long Vacation but otherwise as early as possible in the academic year. It is generally inadvisable for students who have not previously read the subject in Part I B to attempt a dissertation.

The scope of the courses is indicated by the titles of the papers, which are as follows:

1. Scientific ideas and practice from antiquity to the Renaissance.

2. The scientific revolution.

3. History of science since the seventeenth century: special topics

4. Philosophy of science: general principles.

NATURAL SCIENCES

5. Conceptual problems of the physical sciences.
6. Philosophy of the human and life sciences.
7. Medicine and Natural Philosophy from antiquity to the end of the seventeenth century.
8. Medicine, science, and society from the eighteenth century.

No candidate may offer Paper 7 or Paper 8 having previously offered the Special Subject History of Medicine in Part II (General) of the Medical Sciences Tripos.

Further details of the courses, and recommended reading for the previous Long Vacation, are available from the Department.

Materials Science and Metallurgy. The structure of this course provides for a broadly-based study of all aspects of Materials Science and Metallurgy in the 'Core' courses followed by greater specialization through optional courses. Individual courses within the Core cover the mechanical, chemical, and physical properties of materials and the selection and usage of materials in a wide range of technological applications. Optional courses involve further study of properties and applications in one of two important areas of the subject: materials processing or device materials. Members of staff in the Department will be happy to give advice on the option best matched to a student's particular interests and future plans. In addition to the lecture courses, there are demonstrations of specialized equipment, examples classes, microscopy and laboratory work, including a research project. During the Long Vacation between Part I B and Part II students are strongly encouraged to work in industrial or other research and development establishments. Advice and assistance in finding suitable positions is available through the Department. Successful completion of the Part II course provides a recognized professional qualification which is accredited for purposes of subsequent advancement to Chartered Engineer (C.Eng.) status.

There are many openings for materials scientists and metallurgists in the U.K. and abroad. The course provides a preparation for research or applied scientific work on problems over a wide field in many industries concerned with metallic and non-metallic materials. New opportunities are continually arising in industries based on advanced technologies, such as aerospace and electronics. The course also provides a good background for men and women looking for administrative or technical management posts in industry or business generally.

Study of Materials Science and Metallurgy together with one of Chemistry A (or B), Advanced Physics, Crystalline State, or Physics in Part IB is normally a necessary preparation.

Pathology. This course offers study in the four main constituent disciplines of Pathology. In order to facilitate study in depth each discipline is presented as an optional subject. Students take any two options.

(1) *Cellular and Genetic Pathology:* This is concerned with the function and structure of cells in disease. The principles are illustrated by a close study of cell behaviour and molecular biology in arterial disease, neoplasia, transplantation and genetic disorders.
(2) *Immunology:* This aims to give a comprehensive course in Immunology, dealing with such topics as the molecular biology of antibodies, the cellular basis of the immune response and its genetic control, the effector mechanisms, immunity and hypersensitivity, and immunopathology.
(3) *Microbial and Parasitic Disease:* This concerns the principles of infection and infectious disease. It deals with parasites both large and small (from helminths to viruses) and their relationships with vertebrate and other host species.
(4) *Virology:* This deals with molecular and general virology including structure and function of the virion, the processes of replication and its control, virus genetics, pathogenesis, epidemiology and oncogenesis.

Students take practical classes in each of their chosen options and undertake a research project in one of these. The course is a suitable prelude for those wishing to make research careers in the biological sciences as well as for those going on to do clinical and veterinary medicine. There are no particular requirements for entry though Part I courses in one or more biological disciplines are essential. Similar experience is required for entry by Affiliated Students.

Pharmacology. Lectures on selected topics in pharmacology, especially those of current research interest, are presented at an advanced level. The course emphasizes molecular mechanisms of drug action. Especially detailed attention is given to (*a*) effects of drugs upon cytomembranes and subcellular components, (*b*) pharmacology of the central nervous system and peripheral synapses, especially biochemical and biophysical aspects of transmitters, (c) drugs affecting transport processes, (d) physical processes involved in drug action, and (e) actions on cell growth and division.

There is no Long Vacation course. In the Michaelmas Term the practical laboratory work occupies $2\frac{1}{2}$–3 days a week and introduces the student to the application of advanced techniques and equipment to pharmacological problems. In the Lent Term each student is expected to undertake a practical research project supervised by a member of the staff. The results of these projects are presented by the student at a seminar in the Easter Term, and the work is written up as a short dissertation.

Normally students entering this course are expected to have attended the course in Pharmacology for Part I B of the Medical Sciences Tripos or the Natural Sciences Tripos.

The final examination consists of four written papers and a *viva voce* examination together with the submission of the project report. There are substantial vocational opportunities for natural scientists reading pharmacology as well as for medical students who do so before proceeding to clinical studies.

Physics and Theoretical Physics. The lectures continue the course for Advanced Physics given in the second year, and offer a wide choice of subject matter. The 'Core Course', during the Michaelmas Term and first two weeks of the Lent Term, completes coverage of the physics regarded by the Department as what every graduate in the subject should know. It includes lectures on solid-state physics, thermodynamics, electrodynamics and relativity, quantum physics, nuclear and particle physics, fluid dynamics, and systems. This is followed in the Lent Term by more than a dozen courses on specialized topics of which candidates are expected to attend three or four. These topics change from time to time but include at present: electrons in solids; materials; quantum transport in semi-conductors; particle physics; plasma physics; lasers and masers; advanced quantum physics; astrophysics; geophysics; medical physics; micro-electronics; and Science in Society.

Every candidate is required to carry out a project, and a course on computational methods in physics, in addition to a selection from: extended experiments; and lectures and class-work on mathematical physics. There are five examination papers, some parts of which may be substituted by the project work. Normally over 40 per cent of the class continue to higher education after graduating.

Physiology. The Physiology Part II Course has recently been completely reconstructed. There are two options: a *Neurobiology option* and a *Mammalian, Clinical and Reproductive Physiology option*. Those teaching in the course include not only members of staff of the Physiological Laboratory but also members of staff of other Departments in this University and in London University, as well as members of staff of the Medical Research Council and the Agricultural and Food Research Council.

The *Neurobiology option* has been designed to allow students to spend the whole of their third year studying different approaches to problems such as: How do nervous systems work? How do our brains control our behaviour? How are events in our brains related to our experiences? These approaches range from molecular biology and the investigation of molecular events in excitable membranes, at one end of the scale, to considerations of consciousness and the abnormal behaviour found in certain neurological diseases, at the other.

Lectures and seminars will be accompanied by practical classes designed to introduce advanced techniques used in the investigation of particular aspects of the subject. In addition, each student will be expected to do *either* a practical project *or* a library project under the supervision of a member of staff.

The course has been designed to be suitable for both natural scientists and medical students. While the majority of those taking it will probably have done the IA and IB courses in Physiology, those who have done only one of these courses will also be welcome; so will those who approach neurobiology from other directions and who have acquired, or are prepared to acquire, the necessary basis of physiology.

The *Mammalian, Clinical and Reproductive Physiology option* treats in greater depth, and with a wide range of practical techniques, many topics that were introduced in the IA course or in the Endocrinology or Reproductive Physiology lectures in the IB course. The option has been designed for medical, veterinary and science students. It is, primarily, a course in scientific physiology. At the same time, because it offers a rigorous scientific training in a large number of clinically important topics, it is highly suitable as a preparation for those who hope to specialize in medicine or surgery. The many aspects of whole animal physiology that it covers are also of particular interest to veterinary students.

The course consists of lectures, seminars and practicals, and students may undertake a practical project under the supervision of a member of staff.

Most of those taking the *Mammalian, Clinical and Reproductive Physiology option* will have done both the IA and IB Physiology

NATURAL SCIENCES

courses, but candidates who have acquired a suitable knowledge of physiology by other routes will be welcome.

Physiology and Psychology. The course is given in part in the Physiological Laboratory and in part in the Department of Experimental Psychology, and leads to an examination which includes two papers from the Part II Physiology examination and two papers in Psychology set specially for candidates taking this course. It is a combination suitable for those who wish to study sensory, neural and functional processes on the general border between Physiology and Psychology. Physiology and Experimental Psychology in Part IB, or the Medical Sciences Tripos Physiology and Neurobiology, are an essential preparation.

Psychology. Teaching is organized so that students may, if they so wish, concentrate upon specific areas studied in detail. The areas within which teaching is given may vary slightly from year to year but will include:

Sensory processes, psychophysics and perception.

Human performance (including signal detection, decision and choice, vigilance, selective attention, and reaction time).

Human learning and memory.

Language, thought and intelligence.

Comparative psychology of learning and cognition

Neuropsychology and physiological psychology.

Developmental psychology.

Abnormal psychology.

Students usually study about half the range of subjects listed above. The scheme of the examination is that four papers must be offered. Each paper is divided into five sections, four of which contain questions on a particular field of study drawn from those areas listed above. In paper 1, the fifth section contains questions on experimental design and analysis of data, and in the remaining papers, questions which call for a wider treatment and may also include questions on the history and philosophy of psychology. A dissertation on an approved topic may be submitted either in place of one paper or in addition to the four papers. If the latter, a candidate is assessed on the four highest marks from the five component parts of the examination.

There are no formal practical classes; instead each student conducts, under supervision, a single research project throughout the year and submits a report on the results obtained.

In the selection of applicants for this course, preference is given to those who have previously taken Experimental Psychology in Part I B of the Natural Sciences Tripos or Empirical Psychology in Part I B of the Philosophy Tripos, or to medical students who have completed the pre-clinical part of their medical studies after Part I B of the Medical Sciences Tripos. Other students, if they are in a position to devote two years to the course, are also considered. For the latter, transfer from previous study of an Arts subject may be practicable.

Students who have read Experimental Psychology in Part I B and Psychology in Part II, or those who have not read Experimental Psychology in Part I B but have devoted two years to the Part II course, are qualified to work in clinical or educational psychology; or may find their training relevant in other fields of activity, such as industrial psychology or market research. Some of these vocational opportunities may require attendance at a postgraduate course after Part II. For students who do well in Part II there are opportunities to take up research in pure or applied branches of the subject.

Zoology. The courses are arranged in 'modules' of which students select two (or more if they wish) in each of the Michaelmas and Lent Terms. The Michaelmas Term modules are: Vertebrate Evolutionary Studies; Aquatic Ecology; Population and Community Ecology; Eukaryote Cell and Molecular Biology; Behaviour; Sensory Systems and Animal Behaviour; Cellular and Molecular Neurobiology: neurotransmission and neuromodulation; Physiology and the Environment; and Cell Biology. The Lent Term modules are: Neural Mechanisms of Behaviour; Behavioural Ecology; Tropical Ecology; Mammalian Evolution and Faunal History; Animal Energetics: the cost of living; Control of Gene Expression; Cellular and Molecular Neurobiology: transduction, growth and regeneration; Developmental Biology; and Insect Biology. Students who wish to may take either the course Ecology and Ecophysiology of Plants (Michaelmas), offered by the Botany Department, *or* the course Population and Ecological Genetic Aspects of Evolution (Lent), offered by the Genetics Department, instead of one of the modules listed above. The Easter Term is kept free for reading and seminars, though there are a few non-examinable lectures on aspects of Human Biology.

In the Long Vacation between Part I B and Part II, students are expected either to attend a two-week Field Course, or to engage in some other approved biological work or to carry out a laboratory project. During the Field Course students carry out individual projects on the ecology and behaviour of animals living in a coastal habitat; instruction is given in statistics and experimental design, using microcomputers to deal with the data collected during the projects. In addition, there is also a short course on the field-collection and identification of insects.

Vertebrate Evolutionary Studies. The major features of evolution from fishes to birds are reviewed, using the evidence of both fossil and living forms. The functional significance of structural changes are explored, giving emphasis to controversial issues and problematical forms. Alternative approaches to classification and phylogeny are compared and practical work is based on exquisite material from the Museum research collections.

Aquatic Ecology: investigates the ecology of freshwater, saltmarshes and other intertidal systems, estuaries, and coastal and open-ocean waters from the level of the behaviour of individual species up to that of the structure of eco-systems. Accent is placed on whole-organism biology and on an integration of information from all relevant disciplines.

Population and Community Ecology. The course, which is taught jointly by staff from Botany and Zoology, explores the dynamics of plant and animal communities in theory and practice. Lectures cover patterns of stability and instability, density dependence and the regulation of population size, interactions between plants and herbivores, predators and prey and competing species. The course provides an introduction to theoretical approaches to population ecology, including the application of statistical techniques, the use of simple modelling techniques and the interpretation of demographic data. The final part of the course concerns the structure and distribution of communities and investigates patterns in plant and animal diversity, the differentiation of ecological niches and the control of relative abundance.

Eukaryote Cell and Molecular Biology: concentrates on the interdisciplinary nature of the subject and is illustrated by systems amenable to structural, physiological, biochemical, genetic and immunological approaches, e.g. (1) the mammalian cell *in vitro* and somatic cell genetics, including gene cloning; (2) aspects of the eukaryote genome including the replication of DNA and chromosomes, and DNA repair mechanisms; (3) cell transformation and malignancy, DNA and RNA tumour viruses and cellular oncogenes, the role of growth factors.

Behaviour: will give a broad view of the major ideas, methods and empirical observations of ethology (the biological study of behaviour), and establish links between studying the behaviour of whole organisms and the neurobiological analysis of the mechanisms underlying behaviour.

Sensory systems and animal behaviour. An animal's sensory capabilities are a fundamental determinant of its behavioural repertoire and are intimately related to its ecology and lifestyle. This module examines these relationships with respect to three important modalities, vision, hearing and olfaction and then examines the mapping and integration of sensory information. Fundamental sensory mechanisms are directly related to behaviour and lifestyle and adaptations of structure to function are demonstrated at a number of levels of biological organization, from protein sequences to maps in the brain. The examples chosen are straightforward and no previous specialization is required.

Cellular and Molecular Neurobiology: neurotransmission and neuromodulation. This module describes how nerve cells generate and transmit signals. The topics covered range from the molecular biology and biophysics of membrane ion channels and receptors involved in both axonal and synaptic transmission, as well as the modulation of synaptic interactions by local neurohormones and intracellular transduction by second messengers.

Physiology and the Environment: examines physiological systems within the context of their ability to promote survival in different environments. Emphasis is placed on the principles underlying the operations of physiological systems in a wide variety of animals and the ways in which they modify their physiology and behaviour in relation to the environment. This basic approach assumes little previous knowledge of animal physiology.

Cell Biology. This course concerns the cell and its interaction with its environment. The course will be divided into four major topics; (1) cell recognition, adhesion and signalling, (2) the extracellular matrix and the way it controls cell behaviour, (3) cell membrane synthesis and the control of targeting of molecules into the cell membranes, and (4) cellular motility and its control. Lectures will be given by experts in these fields. Most of the examples used will be from developing systems. There will be one practical, which will take approximately two weeks.

Neural Mechanisms of Behaviour: takes as its starting point the functioning of a single neurone and then attempts to explain how groups of neurones interact to produce simple patterns of behaviour. The functions of nervous systems with relatively small numbers of neurones are discussed before proceeding to more complex nervous systems and how these also function in the control and integration of behaviour.

Behavioural Ecology: evolution of behaviour in relation to ecology, optimality models, competition for food, mates and territories, mating systems, co-operation and conflict in animal societies; communication; reproductive strategies, and life history variables in mammals; social insects.

Tropical Ecology. The course is divided into two with a consideration of tropical forests, which is largely botanical in nature, and a survey of East African rangelands, in which the emphasis is on the large mammals. In both sections, the factors which make the tropical ecosystems distinct from those in temperate zones is emphasized. The structure of rain forests is described and compared with other types of forest. Ecological separation between the large mammals of the rangelands is considered in relation to feeding strategies.

Mammalian Evolution and Faunal History: starts with a consideration of structure, function, mode of life, relationships and basic systematics of mammals (and mammal-like reptiles). It then deals with modes of evolutionary change and changes in mammalian faunas during the Pleistocene.

Animal Energetics: *the cost of living*. Animals clearly show a broad range of behavioural activities and habitat choice, which inevitably calls for diverse physiological characteristics. This module explores such diversity in terms of the energetic costs to the animal: what are they, how are they met, and what restrictions do they place on the animal? Lecture topics include how activities are fuelled, how the respiratory and cardiovascular systems are adapted for oxygen uptake and delivery to the tissues, how muscles are adapted for economy and performance, and how they are used in animal locomotion. The energetic costs are compared for the more common forms of locomotion, and the implications for animal migration patterns are also discussed.

Control of Gene Expression. Zoology students may include this interdepartmental course as one of their modules. Details are provided in a separate entry in this handbook (see below).

Cellular and Molecular Neurobiology: transduction, growth and regeneration. The lectures describe how nerve cells interact within the nervous system. The functional implications of the cellular and molecular mechanism involved in transduction and integration within small networks of neurones are considered as well as the role of the supporting cells of the brain, the neuroglia, in neural signalling and brain metabolism. Other topics covered range from the molecular mechanisms of neural growth factors and synapse formation to neuronal targeting and the use of embryonic nerve grafts to alleviate pathological brain conditions.

Developmental Biology: Zoology students may include this interdepartmental course as one of their modules. Details are provided in a separate entry in this handbook (see below).

Insect Biology: presents a broad view of the biology of insects including the physiological control of growth and reproduction, the effect of behaviour-modifying chemicals on the ecological interactions of insects, the ways in which insects monitor the environment and the evolution of the behaviour of some insects.

Interdepartmental Courses

Control of Gene Expression. The first nine lectures consider approaches used to study control of gene expression in eukaryotes and are for students reading Part II Zoology. The following fifteen lectures are shared with students reading Part II Biochemistry. They are taught by members of both departments with additional lectures from members of the MRC Laboratory of Molecular Biology. The course examines various ways in which gene expression is regulated in eukaryotic cells. The power of recombinant DNA techniques (gene cloning and mutagenesis *in vitro*) for analysis of gene regulation is emphasized.

Developmental Biology. This course of 24 lectures is offered jointly by the Departments of Biochemistry, Botany, Genetics, and Zoology in the Lent Term as an optional course for students taking Part II subjects. It deals with development in both animals and plants at molecular and cellular level and brings together material previously taught for separate Part II subjects. The course includes practical work which will be arranged departmentally. Questions on the course may be set in the examination papers for individual Part II subjects.

Part II (General)

For Part II General candidates have to offer an essay paper and one of the following:

Either (*a*) Advanced Physics and one other subject from Part IB not previously offered;

or (*b*) One subject from Part IB not previously offered and one Special Subject;

or (*c*) Two Special Subjects.

The Special Subjects are as follows:

Chemistry Physics
Pathology

Candidates must choose their two subjects in such a way that not more than one is drawn from any one of the nine groups set out below:

(1) Chemistry A; Special Subject Chemistry.
(2) Pathology; Special Subject Pathology; Physics; Advanced Physics; Special Subject Physics.
(3) Materials Science and Metallurgy; Environmental Biology; Molecular Cell Biology.
(4) Crystalline State; Physiology.
(5) Biochemistry and Molecular Biology; Mineralogy and Petrology.
(6) Experimental Psychology; Fluid Mechanics; Plant Biology.
(7) Mathematics; Animal Biology; Pharmacology.
(8) Advanced Physics; Chemistry B; Stratigraphic Geology.
(9) History and Philosophy of Science.

In addition no candidate may offer
   (*a*) any subject which he has previously offered in Part IB of the Natural Sciences Tripos or in the Medical Sciences Tripos;
   (*b*) Special Subject Chemistry with Chemistry A or Chemistry B;
   (*c*) Mathematics if he has previously obtained honours in Part IB or Part II of the Mathematical Tripos;
   (*d*) Physics from Part IB if he has previously offered Advanced Physics;

(e) Physics or Fluid Mechanics from Part IB of the Natural Sciences Tripos if he has previously obtained honours in Part IB or Part II of the Engineering Tripos;

(f) Experimental Psychology from Part IB of the Natural Sciences Tripos if he has previously offered Paper 9 in Part IB of the Philosophy Tripos;

(g) Advanced Physics with any other subject from groups (2) and (8) specified above.

Details of the Special Subjects are as follows:

Chemistry. The course consists of about half the lectures and practical work attended by a candidate offering Chemistry in Part II. Candidates are free to make any selection from the courses available, except that some courses may be excluded because the lectures take place at the same times as those for the candidate's other subject. The examination requires a knowledge of some of the subject-matter covered by either of the Chemistry courses in Part IB. Candidates who have not taken Chemistry in Part IB may take the course, but they need special advice as to which lectures they are equipped to understand.

Pathology. The course consists of the lectures available in any one of the options in Part II Pathology, namely Cellular and Genetic Pathology, Immunology, Microbial and Parasitic Disease and Virology, Students take limited practical class work and undertake a literature research project. Special Subject Pathology can be read in conjunction with any other Part II General Special Subject course or with a subject offered in Part IB of the Natural Sciences Tripos. As the course contains limited practical work, it is less suitable than Part II Pathology for students wishing to follow a career in research.

Physics. The course consists of about half the lectures and practical work expected of a candidate offering Physics and Theoretical Physics in Part II. The lectures in the Michaelmas Term normally consist of an approved selection of the courses for physics and theoretical physics, and in the Lent Term, of one or more of the special topics. A prior knowledge of physics equivalent to the material covered in Advanced Physics in Part IB will be assumed.

The Preliminary Examinations for Part II of the Natural Sciences Tripos

The examinations are intended for the very few candidates spending two years preparing for Part II of the Natural Sciences Tripos.

The examination for Part II is in the subjects of that Part of the Tripos. The examination in Physics and Theoretical Physics consists of *either* (i) the written papers for Advanced Physics in Part IB of the Tripos, *or* (ii) the written papers for Advanced Physics and for Mathematics in Part IB of the Tripos. The examination in Chemistry consists *either* (i) of the written papers for the subjects Chemistry A and Chemistry B in Part IB of the Tripos, *or* (ii) of the first two of the four written papers for Chemistry in Part II of the Tripos. Candidates who previously offered Advanced Chemistry in Part IB offer the examination specified in (ii) and other candidates offer the examination specified in (i). The examination in Psychology consists of the papers and the practical examination in Experimental Psychology in Part IB of the Tripos. The examination in History and Philosophy of Science consists of Papers 1–8 set for that subject in Part II of the Tripos. Each candidate is required to offer four papers. In subjects other than Chemistry, History and Philosophy of Science, Physics and Theoretical Physics, and Psychology the examination consists of the written papers and, in subjects in which a practical or oral examination is set, the practical or oral examination set in Part II of the Tripos.

Examinations in the Natural Sciences for the Ordinary B.A. Degree

There are Ordinary Examinations in each of the subjects included in Part IB of the Natural Sciences Tripos. The examination and Schedule for each Ordinary Examination in any year is the same as that for the corresponding subject of Part IB of the Tripos.

A student may not count towards the Ordinary B.A. Degree an Ordinary Examination in Natural Science in

(*a*) any subject for which the Examiners for Part IB of either the Natural Sciences or the Medical Sciences Tripos have specified that his work deserved the allowance of an examination for the Ordinary B.A. Degree;

(b) Physics, if he has offered Advanced Physics in Part I B of the Natural Sciences Tripos;

(c) any subject, except Physiology, for which the Examiners for Part I A of the Medical Sciences Tripos have specified that his work deserved the allowance of an examination for the Ordinary B.A. Degree;

(d) any subject for which the Examiners for any examination (except the Natural Sciences or Medical Sciences Tripos) have specified that his work deserved the allowance of an examination for the Ordinary B.A. Degree;

nor if he has obtained honours in any Tripos other than the Natural Sciences Tripos may he count an Ordinary Examination in Natural Science in any subject which he has offered in that other Tripos Examination, except that a student who has obtained honours in Part I A of the Medical Sciences Tripos may count an Ordinary Examination in Physiology.

Certificate of Post-graduate Study in Natural Science

Certificates are awarded for advanced study and training in research in certain specific sciences. A candidate must have been admitted as a Graduate Student, on the recommendation of the Degree Committee concerned, by the Board of Graduate Studies, who will fix the date of commencement of his candidature. He must also *either* (a) have graduated, or have completed the examination and residence requirements for graduation, in the University, and have been classed in Part II of the Mathematical, Natural Sciences, or Engineering Tripos, or in the Chemical Engineering Tripos, *or* (b) if not a member of the University, satisfy the Appropriate Degree Committee of his fitness to study for the Certificate.

The course of instruction extends over three consecutive terms, but a candidate may be permitted in exceptional circumstances to spend up to two years in study for the Certificate.

Each candidate is required to submit a dissertation and to take an oral examination, which may include practical tests, on the subject of the dissertation and on the general field of knowledge within which it falls, and which may be supplemented by a written examination. In addition he may be required to take one or more written papers. By the end of the second term of his candidature a candidate must send to the Secretary of the Board of Graduate Studies the proposed title of his dissertation for approval by the Board. He must submit two copies of his dissertation to the Secretary of the Board of Graduate Studies before the division of the third term of his candidature, unless he has been granted an extension; a statement of the sources from which his information is derived must be included.

A candidate for a Certificate may be allowed to count the whole or some part of the period for which he has been a candidate towards a course of research for the degree of Ph.D., M.Sc., or M.Litt., but, if such an allowance is made, he will not be entitled to receive a Certificate so long as he remains on the register of Graduate Students, nor subsequently if he should submit a dissertation for the degree of Ph.D., M.Sc., or M.Litt. A candidate is not entitled to receive a Certificate until he has kept at least three terms.

A candidate who is not awarded a Certificate may not be a candidate again either in the same field or in any other field.

Subjects of examination

Certificates are awarded in Biochemistry, Biological Science, Chemistry, Genetics, Materials Science and Metallurgy, and Physics.

For a Certificate in Biochemistry, the study and training include courses of lectures proposed by the Head of Department, and a research investigation.

For a Certificate in Biological Science, the study and training include courses of lectures and one or more original research investigations; the department which the candidate will join will be determined by the research which he or she wishes to undertake. The original investigations may be practical, theoretical or combined. The examination consists of a dissertation of not more than 15,000 words in length, exclusive of tables, footnotes, bibliography and appendices. In it the candidates shall provide evidence to satisfy the Examiners that he or she can design and carry out investigations, assess and interpret the results obtained, and place the work in the wider perspective of the subject.

For Certificates in Chemistry, Materials Science and Metallurgy, and Physics the study and training includes (*a*) Courses of lectures, and (*b*) Practical work carried out in one or more of the following ways: (i) organized experiments or theoretical exercises of an advanced type, (ii) assistance with a piece of research, (iii) a small research investigation, (iv) training in some technique. The examination may include one or two written papers on subjects cognate to the lectures attended by the candidate; for Certificates in Chemistry and Materials Science and Metallurgy the written papers may include passages of scientific literature in a foreign language for translation into English, for which the use of a dictionary is allowed.

For a Certificate in Genetics, the study and training include a course of lectures, and training in research by means of one or more original investigations which may be practical, theoretical, or both combined.

M.Phil. courses (one-year) in Natural Science subjects

One-year courses leading to the M.Phil. Degree provide advanced study and training in research in certain specific sciences. A candidate must have been admitted as a Graduate Student, on the recommendation of the Degree Committee concerned, by the Board of Graduate Studies, who will fix the date of commencement of his candidature.

The course of instruction extends over three consecutive terms but a candidate may, in exceptional circumstances, be permitted to continue beyond that period.

The examination may consist of written papers or the submission of a dissertation or both written papers and a dissertation. Where the examination consists of the submission of a dissertation the candidate will be expected to take an oral examination on the subject of that dissertation and on the general field of knowledge within which it falls. By the division of the second term of his candidature a candidate must send to the Secretary of the Board of Graduate Studies

(*a*) the papers in which he is to be examined, and

(*b*) the subject of the dissertation, if any, which the Degree Committee have approved for him.

He must submit two copies of this dissertation to the Secretary of the Board of Graduate Studies by a date which shall be not later than the end of the third term of his candidature, unless he has been granted an extension.

A candidate for the M.Phil. will be allowed to count the whole of that period for which he has been a candidate for that degree towards a course of research for the degree of Ph.D. or M.Sc.

NATURAL SCIENCES

Subjects of examination

One-year courses for the M.Phil. Degree are provided in Biological Science, History and Philosophy of Science, Physics, Plant Breeding, Psychopathology, and Quaternary Research.
Research.

M.Phil. course in Biological Science

The course is designed to provide further study and training in research in biological sciences. The course may include lectures, instructions in specialized techniques and associated practical work. For part of the academical year the candidate will carry out a course of research in biological sciences under the supervision of a member of the staff of one of the biological departments; the department which the candidate will join will be determined by the research which he or she wishes to undertake. The examination consists of a thesis, of not more than 15,000 words in length, exclusive of tables, footnotes, bibliography, and appendices, on a subject approved either by the Degree Committee for the Faculty of Biology 'A' or by the Degree Committee for the Faculty of Biology 'B'. The examination includes an oral examination on the subject of the thesis and on the general field of knowledge within which it falls.

M.Phil. course in History and Philosophy of Science

The scheme of examination for the one-year course in History and Philosophy of Science consists of:

(*a*) a thesis, of not more then 15,000 words in length, including footnotes and appendices, but excluding bibliography, on a subject approved by the Degree Committee for the Faculty of Philosophy;

and

(*b*) four essays, each of about 3,000 words, and, except as provided below, each on a subject approved by the Degree Committee for the Faculty of Philosophy which is related to one or more of the following areas:

> Science from antiquity to the Renaissance
> The scientific revolution, 1500–1700
> History of the exact sciences since 1700
> History of the life, earth, and human sciences since 1700
> Philosophy of science: general principles
> Conceptual problems of the exact sciences

Philosophical problems of the human, life, and earth sciences
History of the philosophy of science

Not more than two essays may be chosen from any one area. With the permission of the Degree Committee one of the four essays may be offered in an area which is not listed above but is related to History and Philosophy of Science.

The examination will include an oral examination of the subjects of the thesis and of the four essays.

Further details regarding these areas for essays are as follows:

1. Science from antiquity to the Renaissance

The sciences in antiquity, the Middle Ages, and the Renaissance, including developments in mathematics, method, apparatus, institutions, and the dissemination of ideas and techniques

2. The scientific revolution, 1500–1700

The intellectual, social, and technical factors in the origin of modern science including changing views of science, method, and nature; the transformation of mathematics, mechanics, astronomy, optics, magnetism, pneumatics, anatomy, and physiology; the emergence of disciplines; seventeenth-century natural philosophies and the establishment of the mechanical world view; scientific instruments and technical change.

3. History of the exact sciences since 1700

Mathematical sciences and natural philosophy in the eighteenth century; physics from the nineteenth century, including electromagnetism, optics, field theory, thermodynamics, relativity, and quantum mechanics; the development of astronomy, chemistry, and mathematics; technology and instrumentation; other topics in the history of the exact sciences.

4. History of the life, earth, and human sciences since 1700

Human sciences since the seventeenth century, including theories of language; economics; sociology, anthropology, and archaeology; psychology and psychoanalysis. Life and earth sciences since the seventeenth century, including natural history, medicine, research techniques and instrumentation, taxonomy, animal behaviour, geology and cosmology, *Naturphilosophie*, evolutionary biology.

5. Philosophy of science: general principles

Recent history of philospohy of science; theories of scientific method, confirmation theory, and logical theory; problems of scientific objectivity;

realism and anti-realism; reduction, probability, laws, causation, and explanation; unity of science, fields, and disciplines; other general issues in the philosophy of science.

6. Conceptual problems of the exact sciences

Theories of space, time, and geometry; foundations of thermodynamics and statistical mechanics; cause, chance, and determinism; the interpretation of quantum mechanics; quantum field theory; philosophy of mathematics; other philosophical problems and aspects of the exact sciences.

7. Philosophical problems of the human, life, and earth sciences

Philosophical problems and aspects of psychology, psychoanalysis, history, the social sciences, sociology of science, biology, medicine, and the earth sciences.

8. History of the philosophy of science

The history of the philosophy and methodology of science from antiquity to the early twentieth century.

M.Phil. course in Physics

The course is designed to provide further study and training in research in Physics. It may include lectures and relevant practical work, which will not occupy a period greater than the equivalent of one full term. For the remainder of the academical year a candidate must pursue under supervision a course of research in Physics.

The examination consists of a thesis of not more than 15,000 words in length, exclusive of tables, footnotes, bibliography, and appendices, on a subject approved by the Degree Committee for the Faculty of Physics and Chemistry. The examination will include an oral examination on the thesis and on the general field of knowledge in which it falls. The thesis must provide evidence that the candidate can design and carry out investigations, assess and interpret the results obtained, and place the work in the wider perspective of the subject.

M.Phil. course in Plant Breeding

This is a one-year course, given by academic staff of the Departments of Genetics and by others. It is designed to provide a thorough grounding at advanced level in the principles of genetics and other disciplines relevant to plant breeding and is intended primarily as a training for research or for specialist employment in the field of plant breeding. The course comprises lectures, seminars, practical work, and individual research projects.

It is desirable that applications for the course should reach the Secretary, Board of Graduate Studies, by the beginning of April.

Requests for further information should be addressed to Professor J. R. S. Fincham, Department of Genetics, Downing Street, Cambridge.

M.Phil. course in Psychopathology

This one-year course provides much of the academic background necessary for clinical psychology and is linked closely with clinical psychology training within the East Anglian Regional Health Authority. Those who take the M.Phil. and who are selected to train as clinical psychologists will spend two further years undergoing in-service training, funded by the Health Authority. The areas of study are: Research methods, Psychopathology in Children, Psychopathology in adults, Cognitive deficits, Biological aspects, special topics, and History, philosophy and clinical practice. The course includes lectures, seminars, practical training and clinical attachments.

The examination consists of a thesis, three essays and two written papers. The thesis must be of not more than 15,000 words in length, including footnotes and appendices, but excluding bibliography. The essays must be each of about 3000 words in length, and falling respectively within the following fields: Cognitive deficits in children and adults; Biological aspects of abnormal psychology; and *either* Special topics in psychopathology *or* History and philosophy of the concept of mental illness, and professional issues in clinical psychology. The written papers comprise Psychopathology in adults and Psychopathology in children. There is an oral examination on the thesis and the essays, and on the general field of knowledge within which they fall.

Requests for further information should be addressed to Dr. B. Bradley, Department of Experimental Psychology, Downing Street, Cambridge CB2 3EB.

M.Phil. course in Quaternary Research

This one-year course is intended to provide training in fundamental aspects of Quaternary research and in selected fields of the subject, including biological, geological, geographical and physical aspects. The course consists of lectures, seminars and practical work, together with a research investigation. The examination consists of a thesis, not more than 15,000 words in length, and five essays or exercises on particular topics in Quaternary research. Requests for further information should be addressed to the Director, Sub-department of Quaternary Research, Botany School, Downing Street, Cambridge, CB2 3EA.

ORIENTAL STUDIES

In this subject there are courses of study followed by candidates for:

The *Oriental Studies Tripos*, which is divided into three Parts – Part I, Part II (General), and Part II.

The *Preliminary Examination* for Part I of the Oriental Studies Tripos (p. 397).

The *Ordinary Examination in Oriental Studies* for the Ordinary B.A. Degree (p. 399).

The *M.Phil. Degree* (one-year course) in Oriental Studies (p. 399).

The Oriental Studies Tripos

The Oriental Studies Tripos is an Honours Degree course dealing with the major civilizations which have flourished in Asia and adjoining areas during a period of over five thousand years. The teaching provided by the Faculty covers a number of Middle Eastern and Asian languages (Ancient Egyptian, Coptic, Akkadian, Sumerian, Hebrew, Aramaic; Arabic, Turkish, Persian; Sanskrit, Prakrit, Hindi; Chinese, Japanese) and also the literature, history, philosophy, religion, art, and archaeology of these widely differing civilizations.

Each student undertakes a course which is based on either one language or two related languages, and which also provides an introduction to the cultural background of the civilization concerned. The balance between the amount of language study and the study of the connected literature, history, philosophy, etc., naturally varies from course to course, but the main emphasis in all courses is laid on the attainment of a satisfactory knowledge of the language or languages studied, as the key to the original source material essential to the proper understanding of each civilization. Some of the courses pertain to civilizations that have passed away, others to civilizations with both classical and modern forms. Attention is also paid to the modern spoken forms of Arabic, Persian, Turkish, Hebrew, Hindi, Chinese, and Japanese.

The Tripos is divided into three Parts as follows:

Part I, normally taken at the end of two years, is mainly concerned with providing as thorough a knowledge as possible of the one or two languages being studied together with a general introduction to the literature, history, and general cultural background of the civilization. Knowledge of the languages is fostered by an intensive and detailed study of a number of set texts, which include significant examples of the literature concerned. At the end of the first year of the two years spent on Part I there is a Preliminary Examination.

Part II (General) is only available to students taking certain subjects, and is taken at the end of the fourth year of study. The purpose of Part II (General) is to permit certain subjects to be studied in succession: a student who has already gained a Part I in one subject may take a number of Part I-level papers in a second, related subject, together with a smaller number of Part II-level papers in his or her first subject.

Part II is taken at the end of the third or fourth year of study, depending on the particular course of study. In Part II knowledge of the language or languages is further advanced, normally by continued detailed study of set texts, while at the same time specialization is often permitted in one or more options. These options may range from philological and linguistic studies to the literature, history, art, and archaeology pertaining to the language and civilization concerned. In certain subjects a period of time – in some cases one term, in other cases an entire year – may be spent in study abroad at an approved institution in an appropriate country.

The courses which involve the study of a single civilization and the various forms of one language or language group include Part II Assyriology, and Parts I and II Chinese Studies, Egyptology, Hebrew Studies, Indian Studies, Islamic and Middle Eastern Studies, and Japanese Studies. There are in addition many courses which involve the concurrent study of two languages and their related civilizations: Arabic may be combined with Akkadian or Hebrew, Hebrew with Akkadian, Aramaic, or Egyptology, and Hindi with Persian; at Part II level Chinese may also be combined with linguistics. For the complete lists of possible concurrent combinations see pp. 388–9, 391–6. There are other combinations which can only be taken consecutively under the regulations for Part II (General); for these see pp. 390–1. Combinations of Middle Eastern or Asian languages with languages from the Modern and Medieval Languages Tripos may be permitted with the consent of the Faculty Boards concerned.

Since Middle Eastern and Asian languages are not generally taught in schools, all the courses leading to Part I start from the beginner's level. Oriental Studies does not demand a particular bent of mind or type of intellectual training. The courses are, however, intensive, and the learning of remote languages requires concentrated application and regular attendance at lectures. The most successful students are often those who have studied classical or modern languages or history at school. A complete course consisting of Parts I and II, or Part I followed by Part II (General), is the most desirable for those wishing to choose careers in fields directly related to Oriental Studies, but Part I alone is not infrequently taken in two years by those who have taken Part I in another Tripos in their first or second year.

The languages and civilizations covered in the Tripos are as follows:

The Ancient Near East

Egyptology. Egyptology is the study of the language, literature, history, religion, institutions, art, and archaeology of ancient Egypt. The civilization of ancient Egypt began during the fourth millennium B.C. and lasted until the Arab conquest in A.D. 640. The aim of the course is to become acquainted with, and to ask questions about, Egyptian civilization, through studying the various stages of the language (including Christian Coptic), through historical records, excavation reports, Egyptian art and architecture, and the collections in the Fitzwilliam Museum.

Assyriology. Historical records of the ancient civilizations of Mesopotamia which include documents written in the Sumerian and Akkadian (Babylonian and Assyrian) languages cover a period from about 3000 B.C. to the time of the fall of Babylon in the sixth century B.C. and beyond. A study of archaeology and of the ancient history of the Near East forms an essential part of Assyriology, and both archaeological and written evidence – inscriptions, annals, letters, contracts, myths, epics, hymns and prayers – throw light on the history, laws, religions, and customs of early Mesopotamian culture and society.

Hebrew. Cambridge has long been a leading centre of Hebrew scholarship. Hebrew has been taught since the middle ages; there has been a Professorship of Hebrew since 1540; and the University Library is the home of one of the most important collections of Hebrew manuscripts in the world. Hebrew literature has an uninterrupted history extending over a period of some 3,000 years until the present day. Classical Hebrew writings include the Old Testament, inscriptions and the literature of the sect of the Dead Sea Scrolls, and there are related texts in closely related languages (Ugaritic, Phoenician and Moabite). The rabbinical and medieval literature includes many of the classical texts of Judaism, as well as secular poetry and prose. Modern Hebrew is the main spoken and written language of Israel, with an important and rapidly growing literature. The course for the Tripos involves a study of Classical and Rabbinical Hebrew language and texts and related history for everyone, and allows a choice among other subjects.

Aramaic. The Aramaic language was originally current in Mesopotamia and the adjoining areas. Its literature, including texts written in Syriac, extends from the fifth century B.C. to the thirteenth century A.D., and inscriptions, dating from the eighth century B.C. and onwards, are also important for the study of archaeology, the Old and New Testaments, Rabbinics, early Church history, law, institutions, and philosophy.

Islamic Studies

Islamic civilization is approached through a study of its three major languages, Arabic, Persian, and Turkish. Of these, Arabic may be studied by itself, but a wide range of options is available for those who wish to combine it with another language. The Tripos lays stress on the continuity of the languages and all candidates are introduced to both their classical and their modern forms. The emphasis in the Part I course is placed on linguistic competence and background knowledge, while Part II allows for a measure of specialization. Optional sections within individual papers provide considerable flexibility. Stress is laid on the comparative approach, through the interconnections between Islam and Europe in history, literature and philosophy, but the main purpose of the course is to give a framework for an appreciation of Islamic civilization itself.

Arabic. Arabic is both the classical language of the Koran and the mother tongue of the modern Arab world. It has a vast literature, covering some fourteen centuries. It is an important source for the transmission of Greek philosophy, science and medicine and its study can be linked to medieval and modern history, medieval geography, medieval and modern languages (particularly Spanish), law, ecclesiastical history, and theology.

Persian. Since the beginning of the Islamic period in Iran and Central Asia, which dates from the seventh century A.D., Persian has been of next importance to Arabic as the language of literary, spiritual, and philosophic significance in the Islamic world. The 'classical' hegemony of Persian as the language of literature, poetry, historical annals, and legal documents also comprehends the study of Indian history since the fourteenth century; Persian was the court language of the Mogul emperors, Persian is today spoken in Iran, Afghanistan, and large areas of the U.S.S.R. and is still cultivated for scholarly and literary purposes in Pakistan.

[*Turkish*.[1] Turkic dialects are found wherever the Turks who came from Central Asia successfully infiltrated – from the south-east of Europe to the lands near the Yenisei river and the borders of China. The subjects studied include the dialect of an eleventh-century Islamic–Turkish civilization of Central Asia; the language, literature, and history of the Islamic Ottoman Empire (*c*. 1300–1918); and the written and spoken language of the subsequent modern Turkish Republic.]

India

Indian Studies: Vedic, Sanskrit, Pali, Prakrit, and Hindi. Vedic, Classical Sanskrit, Pali, and the various Prakrits extended over a period of 3,000 years of Indian history and contained three main literatures (Hindu, Buddhist, and Jain). A very large volume of literary output includes all types of composition – religious texts, epic poems, dramas, lyrics, novels, histories, and technical treatises on many subjects. Vedic and Sanskrit in particular are important for comparative Indo-European linguistic studies, as well as for study of the development of early Indian culture. Indian archaeology, of both the prehistoric and historic periods, includes the history of art and architecture, and may be read in conjunction with epigraphy and ancient history. Indian history and politics may be read with Hindi. The Hindi dialects of Northern India evolved from about A.D. 1000 with a rich literature including devotional verse. The literature of modern Hindi which developed from the nineteenth century illustrates the extent of changes in Indian life which have taken place since that time. Hindi is now spoken in one form or another by nearly 300 million people. Optional papers available in Part II of the Tripos include one in either Bengali or Urdu. It is usual for candidates studying Hindi for Part II to spend a year of study at an approved centre of instruction in India.

---

[1] Teaching in Turkish is currently not available.

East Asia

Chinese. China's written culture extends from the first period of writing (about 1500 B.C.) until the present day, but from a practical point of view the study of Chinese civilization may be divided into the periods before and after 1840. Several stages of development can be traced during the earlier period, which witnessed the organization of the Chinese empires, the evolution of society, and the growing application of technical skills. The modern period is characterized by more intensive contacts with western countries, and has been marked by external and internal conflicts in which other parts of the world have been increasingly concerned. China's rich and varied literature has influenced the growth of civilization in the traditional and the modern styles; and the study of art, history, literature, philosophy, and religion forms an integral part of the Tripos. Undergraduates are required to spend three months at an approved centre of instruction in East Asia before taking the Part II examination. Part I comprises a standard course, without options, in which undergraduates receive a basic training in the classical and modern (*Putonghua*) forms of the language and in aspects of China's cultural history; the examination includes an oral test in modern spoken Chinese. Part II includes some papers taken by all candidates which enable them to extend their knowledge of early and modern literature, and, in addition, allows a choice of specializing in literature, history, linguistics, archaeology or art. Among the requirements for the Part II examination are the presentation of a dissertation, and an oral test in modern spoken Chinese.

Japanese. Japanese civilization developed very rapidly under Korean and Chinese influence from about the middle of the first millennium A.D. and soon acquired a characteristic form of its own. The essential elements of the Japanese language are not related to Chinese and were retained despite the adoption of the Chinese script. A wide literature of merit dates from the seventh century onwards. The Cambridge course is distinguished by the emphasis placed on an all-round education which includes history, culture and study of the classical language to supplement work in modern Japanese. The language is difficult and the work arduous but students with a variety of academic interests have succeeded in mastering it. Japan is not only the third largest economic power in the world but has a culture as old and varied as our own and offers tremendous rewards for any student with intelligence and an open mind.

For Part I, as most students have had little or no former contact with Japan, the priority in the first year is to cover the basic elements of the modern spoken and written language as quickly and efficiently as possible. Extensive use is made of the language laboratory facilities. In the second year work in the modern spoken and written language continues. The student is also introduced to the classical language and has lectures on Japanese religion, literature and modern history, and can choose whether to concentrate on the classical or the modern option. For Part II students there is a compulsory period of study in Japan, normally covering the first term of the student's third year. By using the summer months as well, this period can be extended to six months, although it is at present up to the student to arrange this particular aspect. In Part II there is further work in advanced Japanese with video material, classical texts and modern prose of various kinds, depending on which option is chose. The student is also expected to work on one special subject offered by members of the faculty and to write a short dissertation on a subject of his/her choice.

Papers in the Tripos

The complete list of papers in the Tripos from which Papers in Part I, Part II (General), and Part II will be taken will be as follows (assuming candidates desire to present themselves therein):

Aramaic

    Am. 1. Aramaic specified and unspecified texts, 1.

    Am. 2. Aramaic specified texts and composition.

    Am. 3. Aramaic literature and its historical background.

    Am. 11. Aramaic specified and unspecified texts, 2.

    Am. 12. Aramaic specified texts.

    Am. 13. Aramaic unspecified texts and composition.

    Am. 14. Special subject.

Assyriology

    As. 1. Akkadian specified texts, 1 (may also serve as one of the papers set for Paper 5 in Archaeology of Part II of the Archaeological and Anthropological Tripos).

    As. 2. Akkadian unspecified texts, 1, and composition.

    As. 3. Introduction to the history and archaeology of the Ancient Near East.

ORIENTAL STUDIES

- As. 11. Akkadian specified texts, 2.
- As. 12. Akkadian unspecified texts, 2.
- As. 13. History of Mesopotamia (also serves as Paper 3G in Archaeology of Part II of the Archaeological and Anthropological Tripos).
- As. 14. Civilization of Mesopotamia.
- As. 15. Special subject in Assyriology (may also serve as one of the papers set for Paper 5 in Archaeology of Part II of the Archaeological and Anthropological Tripos).
- As. 16. Art and archaeology of Mesopotamia (also serves as Paper 4G in Archaeology of Part II of the Archaeological and Anthropological Tripos).
- As. 17. Practical examination in Mesopotamian archaeology.

Chinese Studies

- C. 1. Classical Chinese texts, 1.
- C. 2. Classical Chinese texts, 2.
- C. 3. Modern Chinese texts, 1.
- C. 4. Modern Chinese texts, 2.
- C. 5. Modern Chinese translation and composition.
- C. 6. Chinese history: specified subject, 1.
- C. 7. Chinese history: specified subject, 2.
- C. 11. Classical Chinese texts, 3.
- C. 12. Classical Chinese texts, 4.
- C. 13. Modern Chinese texts, 3.
- C. 14. Modern Chinese texts, 4.
- C. 15. Chinese literature (specified subject).
- C. 16. Chinese literature (specified readings).
- C. 17. Chinese history: specified subject, 3.
- C. 18. Chinese history (specified readings).
- C. 19. Chinese linguistics (specified subject).
- C. 20. Chinese texts on linguistics.

Egyptology

- E. 1. Middle Egyptian specified texts.
- E. 2. Middle Egyptian unspecified texts.
- E. 3. Coptic specified texts, 1 (Sa'idic dialect).
- E. 4. Coptic unspecified texts, 1 (Sa'idic dialect).
- E. 5. The development of early societies (Paper 1 of Part I of the Archaeological and Anthropological Tripos).
- E. 6. The archaeology of Europe and neighbouring areas (Paper 2 of Part 1 of the Archaeological and Anthropological Tripos).

- E. 7. Introduction to Egyptian civilization.
- E. 8. The archaeology of the Nile valley: predynastic and archaic periods.
- E. 11. Old, Middle, and Late Egyptian specified texts.
- E. 12. Old, Middle, and Late Egyptian unspecified texts.
- E. 13. Specified texts in hieratic book hands of the Middle and New Kingdoms.
- E. 14. Coptic specified texts, 2.
- E. 15. Coptic unspecified texts, 2.
- E. 16. Coptic composition, Coptic grammar, and literary history.
- E. 17. Ancient Egyptian civilization.
- E. 18. Special subject in Egyptology (may also serve as one of the papers set for Paper 5 in Archaeology of Part II of the Archaeological and Anthropological Tripos).
- E. 19. Art and archaeology of Ancient Egypt (also serves as Paper 4E in Archaeology of Part II of the Archaeological and Anthropological Tripos).
- E. 20. Early history of the Coptic church, monasticism, and art.
- E. 21. History of ancient Egypt (also serves as Paper 3E in Archaeology of Part II of the Archaeological and Anthropological Tripos).
- E. 22. Practical examination in Egyptian archaeology.

General Linguistics

- G. 1. General linguistics (Paper 111 of Part II of the Modern and Medieval Languages Tripos).
- G. 2. Phonetics (Paper 112 of Part II of the Modern and Medieval Languages Tripos).
- G. 3. The history of linguistic thought (Paper 113 of Part II of the Modern and Medieval Languages Tripos).
- G. 4. Historical linguistics (Paper 114 of Part II of the Modern and Medieval Languages Tripos).

Hebrew Studies

- H. 1. Hebrew specified texts, 1.
- H. 2. Hebrew unspecified texts and composition.
- H. 3. Israelite and Jewish history and literature.
- H. 4. Modern Hebrew, 1.
- H. 5. Modern Hebrew, 2.
- H. 11. Hebrew specified texts, 2.
- H. 12. Hebrew language.
- H. 13. General paper.
- H. 14. Post-biblical Jewish texts.

ORIENTAL STUDIES

- H. 15. Modern Hebrew, 3.
- H. 16. Modern Hebrew, 4.
- H. 17. Semitic specified texts.
- H. 18. Hebrew poetry.
- H. 19. Special subject.

Indian Studies
- In. 1. Classical Indian specified texts.
- In. 2. Classical Indian unspecified texts, 1.
- In. 3. Hindi specified texts, 1.
- In. 4. Hindi unspecified texts, 1.
- In. 5. Composition, and grammar or essay, in an Indian language.
- In. 6. Indian literature.
- In. 7. Indian religion, 1.
- In. 8. Indian cultural history.
- In. 11. Sanskrit specified texts, 1.
- In. 12. Sanskrit specified texts, 2.
- In. 13. Prakrit specified texts, 1.
- In. 14. Prakrit specified texts, 2.
- In. 15. Classical Indian unspecified texts, 2.
- In. 16. Hindi specified texts, 2.
- In. 17. Hindi specified texts, 3.
- In. 18. Hindi unspecified texts, 2.
- In. 19. Hindi essay, and history of the Hindi language.
- In. 20. Indo-Aryan philology.
- In. 21. Indian religion, 2.
- In. 22. Prehistory and protohistory of India (also serves as Paper 4F in Archaeology of Part II of the Archaeological and Anthropological Tripos).
- In. 23. Indian art and archaeology (500 B.C.–A.D. 400) (also serves as Paper 3F in Archaeology of Part II of the Archaeological and Anthropological Tripos).
- In. 24. Indian epigraphy.
- In. 25. Hindi literature.
- In. 26. Selected readings in a north Indian language.
- In. 27. Specified subject in nineteenth-century or twentieth-century Indian history.[1]
- In. 28. Specified subject in South Asian Studies (may also serve as one of the subjects for Paper 15 of Part II of the Economics Tripos, and as Paper 41 [26] of Part II of the Social and Political Sciences Tripos).

[1] This paper may be Paper 26 of Part II of the Historical Tripos.

CAMBRIDGE HANDBOOK

In. 29. Special subject in modern South Asian History, 1.[1]
In. 30. Special subject in modern South Asian History, 2.[1]

Islamic and Middle Eastern Studies

Is. 1. Middle Eastern languages, 1.
Is. 2. Middle Eastern languages, 2.
Is. 3. Arabic literature, 1.
Is. 4. Arabic literature, 2.
Is. 5. Persian literature, 1.
Is. 6. The formation of classical Islam.
Is. 7. The history of classical Islam.
Is. 8. The modern Islamic world.
Is. 11. Arabic language, 1.
Is. 12. Arabic language, 2.
Is. 13. Advanced Arabic language.
Is. 14. Arabic literature, 3.
Is. 15. Arabic literature, 4.
Is. 16. Persian language, 1.
Is. 17. Persian language, 2.
Is. 18. Persian literature, 2.
Is. 19. Persian literature, 3.
Is. 20. Islamic history, 1: specified subject.
Is. 21. Islamic history, 2: specified subject.
Is. 22. The history of the Arab world.
Is. 23. Arab and Middle Eastern themes: specified subject.

Japanese Studies

J. 1. Classical Japanese specified texts, 1.
J. 2. Classical Japanese texts, 1.
J. 3. Modern Japanese texts, 1.
J. 4. Modern Japanese texts, 2.
J. 5. Japanese composition and essay.
J. 6. Japanese cultural history.
J. 7. Japanese literature.
J. 8. Modern Japanese society.
J. 9. Modern Japanese politics.
J. 10. Modern Japanese economics.
J. 11. Classical Japanese specified texts, 2.
J. 12. Classical Japanese texts, 2.

[1] The subject of these papers may be a Special Subject for Papers 1 and 2 of Part II of the Historical Tripos.

J. 13. Modern Japanese unspecified texts.
J. 14. Japanese composition and essay.
J. 15. Modern Japanese texts, 3.
J. 16. Modern Japanese texts, 4.
J. 17. Modern Japanese texts, 5.
J. 18. Japanese literature: specified subject.
J. 19. Japanese history: specified subject.
J. 20. Modern Japanese society: specified subject.
J. 21. Modern Japanese politics and economics: specified subject.

In addition to the written papers, oral examinations will be held in the modern spoken forms of Arabic, Chinese, Hebrew, Hindi, Japanese, Persian, and Turkish.

Parts I, II (General), and II: General Conditions

The regulations for the Oriental Studies Tripos were revised in 1986 and the new Tripos consists of three Parts: Part I, Part II (General), and Part II.

Part I is normally taken in the second year, and there is a Preliminary Examination to Part I which is taken in the first year.

Part II (*General*) is always taken over two years.

Part II contains various options, some of which (including those involving a period of study abroad) are taken over two years, whilst others may be taken in a single year.

The Faculty Board have power to grant permission to candidates to present themselves for examination in Oriental languages and Oriental subjects and combinations of languages other than those specified in Part I or Part II (General) or Part II, provided that the Faculty Board are satisfied

(*a*) that any Oriental language which is thus offered possesses a literature adequate for the purposes of examination;
(*b*) that the general scope of an Oriental subject which is thus offered is similar to that of the Oriental subjects (Aramaic, Assyriology, Chinese Studies, Egyptology, Hebrew Studies, Indian Studies, Islamic and Middle Eastern Studies, and Japanese Studies) which are regularly included in the Tripos;
(*c*) that the requisite teaching is available.

An application for such permission must be made through the candidate's Tutor to the Secretary of the Faculty Board at the earliest possible date and in no circumstances later than 21 October next preceding the examination.

The Faculty Board have power to grant permission to candidates for Part I or Part II of the Tripos to present themselves for examination in an Oriental language and one of the languages available in the Modern and Medieval Languages Tripos, offering not more than three papers from that Tripos in place of the same number of papers from among those specified for Part I or in Part II. An application for such permission must be made through the candidate's Tutor to the Secretary of the Faculty Board at the earliest possible date and in no circumstances later than 21 October next preceding the examination.

No student may present himself as a candidate for more than one Part, or for any Part and also for another honours examination, in the same term. No student may present himself as a candidate for the same Part on more than one occasion.

Part I

A candidate for Part I must take the written papers specified for one of the following sections, together with any oral examinations specified, provided that no candidate may offer a paper that he has previously offered in another Honours Examination:

(1) Akkadian and Arabic
   As. 1–3; Is. 1, 3, 6.
(2) Chinese Studies
   C. 1–7, Chinese oral.
(3) Egyptology
   Either (i) if he is a candidate in the first, second, or third term after his first term of residence or after obtaining honours in an Honours Examination in the year previous;
   either (1) *philological option*:
      E. 1–4, 6, 7;
   or (2) *archaeological option*:
      E. 1, 2, 5–8;
   or (ii) if he is a candidate in the fourth, fifth, or sixth term after his first term of residence or after obtaining honours in an Honours Examination in the year next but one previous:
      E. 1–8.

(4) Hebrew Studies
    H. 1–5, Hebrew oral; Am. 1.
(5) Hebrew and Akkadian
    H. 1–3; As. 1–3.
(6) Hebrew and Arabic
    H. 1–3; Is. 1, 3, 6.
(7) Hebrew and Aramaic
    H. 1–3; Am. 1–3.
(8) Hebrew and Egyptology
    H. 1–3; E. 1, 2, 7.
(9) Hindi and Persian
    In. 3–5, Hindi oral; Is. 2, 5, Persian oral; *either* In. 8 *or* Is. 7.
(10) Indian Studies
    Either (i) In. 1, 2, 5; three papers chosen from In. 3, 4, 6–8; provided that a candidate who offers In. 3 shall also offer In. 4 and *vice versa*;

    or (ii) In. 3–5; three papers chosen from In. 1, 2, 6–8;

    provided that any candidate who offers In. 3 and In. 4 shall offer Hindi oral.
(11) Islamic and Middle Eastern Studies
    Is. 1, 2; four papers chosen from Is. 3–8; an oral examination in the language or languages that the candidate offers in the written papers.
(12) Japanese Studies
    Either (i) *classical option*: J. 1, 3, 5–7, and one paper chosen from J. 2, 4.

    or (ii) *modern option*: J. 3–6, two papers chosen from J. 7–10, Japanese oral.

Part II (General)

A candidate for Part II (General) must take the written papers specified for one of the following sections, together with any oral examination specified, provided that a candidate may not offer any paper that he has previously offered in Part I:

(1) Arabic with Hebrew
   (*a*) *Either* Is. 11 *or* Is. 12;
   (*b*) one paper chosen from Is. 13–15, 20–23;
   (*c*) H. 1–5;
   (*d*) Hebrew oral as set for Part I.

(2) Aramaic with Arabic
- (*a*) Am. 12, 13;
- (*b*) Is. 1, 2;
- (*c*) three papers chosen from Is. 3, 4, 6–8;
- (*d*) Arabic oral as set for Part I.

(3) Chinese with Indian Studies
- (*a*) One paper chosen from C. 11, 12;
- (*b*) one of the following pairs of papers; (i) C. 15, 16; (ii) C. 17, 18;
- (*c*) In. 1, 2, 5;
- (*d*) *either* In. 7 *or* In. 20.

(4) Chinese with Japanese
- (*a*) One of the following pairs of papers: (i) C. 15, 16; (ii) C. 17, 18;
- (*b*) J. 3–5;
- (*c*) two papers chosen from J. 6–10;
- (*d*) Japanese oral as set for Part I.

(5) Coptic with Arabic
- (*a*) E. 14–16, 20;
- (*b*) Is. 1, 3, 6.

(6) Hebrew with Akkadian
- (*a*) H. 11–13;
- (*b*) one paper chosen from H. 17, H. 19, As. 14, As. 15;
- (*c*) As. 1–3.

(7) Hebrew with Arabic
- (*a*) *Either* (i) H. 11 and one paper chosen from H. 12, 14, 17;

  or (ii) H. 15 and one paper chosen from H. 11, 14, 16;
- (*b*) Is. 1, 2;
- (*c*) three papers chosen from Is. 3–6;
- (*d*) Arabic oral as set for Part I.

(8) Indian Studies with Chinese
- (*a*) Four papers chosen from In. 11–14, 20, 21;
- (*b*) C. 1, 2, 6.

(9) Japanese with Chinese
- (*a*) J. 13;
- (*b*) one paper chosen from J. 18–21;
- (*c*) C. 3–7;
- (*d*) Chinese oral as set for Part I.

No candidate may offer:
(a) Arabic with Hebrew unless he has previously offered *either* Akkadian and Arabic *or* Islamic and Middle Eastern Studies in Part I;
(b) Aramaic with Arabic unless he has previously offered Hebrew and Aramaic in Part I;
(c) Chinese with Indian Studies unless he has previously offered Chinese Studies in Part I;
(d) Chinese with Japanese unless he has previously offered Chinese Studies in Part I;
(e) Coptic with Arabic unless he has previously offered Egyptology in Part I, including Papers E. 3 and 4;
(f) Hebrew with Akkadian unless he has previously offered *either* Hebrew Studies *or* Hebrew and Arabic *or* Hebrew and Aramaic in Part I;
(g) Hebrew with Arabic unless he has previously offered *either* Hebrew Studies *or* Hebrew and Akkadian *or* Hebrew and Aramaic in Part I;
(h) Indian Studies with Chinese unless he has previously offered Indian Studies in Part I;
(i) Japanese with Chinese unless he has previously offered Japanese Studies in Part I.

Part II

A candidate for Part II must offer the written papers specified for one of the following sections, together with any oral examinations specified, provided that no candidate may offer a paper that he has previously offered in another Honours Examination.

A candidate who takes the examination in the year next after last obtaining honours must offer one of the following sections:

(1) Akkadian and Arabic
    (a) As. 11–13;
    (b) Is. 11, 14, 15;
    (c) one of the following: As. 14; Is. 17; a dissertation.

(2) Hebrew Studies
    (a) H. 11, 12;
    (b) Hebrew oral;
    (c) four papers chose from H. 13–17, H. 19, Am. 1; provided that a candidate who offers H. 16 shall also offer H. 15.

(3) Hebrew and Akkadian
    (a) H. 11, 12;
    (b) As. 11–13;
    (c) one of the following: H. 13; H. 14; H. 15; H. 17; H. 19; As. 14; As. 15.

(4) Hebrew and Arabic
   - (a) H. 11, 12;
   - (b) Is. 11, 14, 15;
   - (c) one paper chosen from H. 13–15, 17, 19.
(5) Hebrew and Aramaic
   - (a) H. 11, 12;
   - (b) Am. 11–13;
   - (c) one paper chosen from Am. 14, H. 13–15, 17, 19.
(6) Hebrew and Egyptology
   - (a) H. 11, 12;
   - (b) E. 11, 12, 17;
   - (c) one of the following: Am. 11; H. 13; H. 14; H. 15; H. 17; H. 19.
(7) Indian Studies I

   Either (i) *classical Indian Studies*:
   - (a) In. 15;
   - (b) not less than three papers chosen from In. 11–14;
   - (c) additional papers chosen from In. 20–24, G. 1–4, so as to bring the total number of papers offered by the candidate to six, provided that a candidate who offers G. 2, G. 3, or G. 4 shall also offer G. 1;

   or (ii) *modern Indian Studies*:
   - (a) In. 16–19;
   - (b) Hindi oral;
   - (c) two papers chosen from In. 20–21, 25–30, G. 1–4; provided that
     - (1) a candidate who offers G. 2, G. 3, or G. 4 shall also offer G. 1;
     - (2) a candidate who offers In. 29 shall also offer In. 30 and *vice versa*;

   or (iii) *classical and modern Indian Studies* (*classical major option*):
   - (a) two papers cosen from In. 11–14;
   - (b) In. 15, 18;
   - (c) one paper chosen from In. 16–17;
   - (d) Hindi oral;
   - (e) one paper chosen from In. 20–26, G. 1; provided that a dissertation may be offered in place of one paper from In. 20–26;

ORIENTAL STUDIES

    or   (iv) *classical and modern Indian Studies (modern major option)*:
- (*a*) one paper chosen from In. 11–14;
- (*b*) In. 15–19;
- (*c*) Hindi oral.

(8) Islamic and Middle Eastern Studies I
- (*a*) Two papers chosen from Is. 11, 12, 16, 17;
- (*b*) **either** (i) four papers chosen from Is. 13–15, 18–23;
  - **or** (ii) three papers chosen from Is. 13–15, 18–23, and a dissertation;
- (*c*) an oral examination in the language or languages that the candidate offers in the written papers.

A candidate who takes the examination in the year next but one after last obtaining honours must offer one of the following sections:

(9) Aramaic and Hebrew Studies
- (*a*) Am. 11–13;
- (*b*) H. 11–13;
- (*c*) two of the following: Am. 14; H. 14; H. 15; H. 17; H. 19; a dissertation.

(10) Assyriology
- (*a*) As. 11, 12, 13, 14, 16, 17;
- (*b*) *either* As. 15 *or* a dissertation.

(11) Chinese Studies
- (*a*) C. 11–14;
- (*b*) one of the following pairs of papers: (i) C. 15, 16; (ii) C. 17, 18;
- (*c*) a dissertation;
- (*d*) Chinese oral.

(12) Chinese with linguistics
- (*a*) C. 13, 14, 19, 20;
- (*b*) G. 1 and one paper chosen from G. 2, 3, 4;
- (*c*) a dissertation;
- (*d*) Chinese oral.

(13) Egyptology
    Either (i) *philological option*:
          E. 11–15, 17, 21;
    or (ii) *archaeological option*:
          E. 11, 12, 17–19, 21, 22;
    or (iii) *Coptic and Syriac*:
          E. 14–16, 20; Am. 12–14.

(14) Egyptology and Hebrew Studies
- (*a*) E. 11, 12, 21;
- (*b*) H. 11–13;
- (*c*) two of the following: Am. 11; E. 17; H. 14; H. 15; H. 17; H. 19; a dissertation.

(15) Hebrew and Assyriology
- (*a*) H. 11–13;
- (*b*) As. 11–13;
- (*c*) two of the following: H. 14; H. 15; H. 17; H. 19; As. 14; As. 15; a dissertation.

(16) Hebrew and Islamic Studies
- (*a*) H. 11–13;
- (*b*) Is. 11, 14, 15;
- (*c*) two of the following: H. 14; H. 15; H. 17; H. 18; H. 19; Is. 20; a dissertation.

(17) Hebrew and Jewish Studies
- (*a*) H. 11–13;
- (*b*) Hebrew oral;
- (*c*) five of the following: Am. 11; H. 14; H. 15; H. 16; H. 17; H. 18; H. 19; a dissertation; provided that a candidate who offers H. 16 shall also offer H. 15.

(18) Hindi and Persian
- (*a*) In. 16, 17;
- (*b*) Is. 16, 17;
- (*c*) Hindi oral;
- (*d*) Persian oral;
- (*e*) four papers chosen from In. 18, 19, 25–27, 29, 30, Is. 18–21; provided that a candidate who offers In. 29 shall also offer In. 30 and *vice versa*.

(19) Indian Studies II

Either (i) *classical Indian Studies*:
- (*a*) In. 15;
- (*b*) not less than three papers chosen from In. 11–14;
- (*c*) additional papers chosen from In. 20–24, G. 1–4 so as to bring the total number of papers offered by the candidate to eight, provided that
    - (1) a dissertation may be offered in place of one paper from In. 20–24;
    - (2) a candidate who offers G. 2, G. 3, or G. 4 shall also offer G. 1;

ORIENTAL STUDIES

or
    (ii) *modern Indian Studies*:
        (*a*) In. 16–19;
        (*b*) Hindi oral;
        (*c*) two papers chosen from In. 20–21, 25–30, G. 1–4; provided that
            (1) a dissertation may be offered in place of one paper from In. 20, 21, 25–28;
            (2) a candidate who offers In. 29 shall also offer In. 30 and *vice versa*;
            (3) a candidate who offers G. 2, G. 3, or G. 4 shall also offer G. 1;

or
    (iii) *classical and modern Indian Studies* (*classical major option*):
        (*a*) two papers chosen from In. 11–14;
        (*b*) In. 15, 18;
        (*c*) one paper chosen from In. 16–17;
        (*d*) Hindi oral;
        (*e*) three papers chosen from In. 20–26, G. 1–4; provided that
            (1) a dissertation may be offered in place of one paper from In. 20–26;
            (2) a candidate who offers G. 2, G. 3, or G. 4 shall also offer G. 1;

or
    (iv) *classical and modern Indian Studies* (*modern major option*):
        (*a*) one paper chosen from In. 11–14;
        (*b*) In. 15–19;
        (*c*) Hindi oral;
        (*d*) one paper chosen from In. 20–28, G. 1, provided that a dissertation may be offered in place of one paper from In. 20–28;

provided that no candidate shall offer option (ii) or option (iv) of this section unless he has, during the academical year next before that in which he presents himself as a candidate, spent a period studying in India under conditions approved for this purpose by the Faculty Board.

(20) Islamic and Middle Eastern Studies II
    (*a*) Two papers chosen from Is. 11, 12, 16, 17;
    (*b*) **either** (i)   five papers chosen from Is. 13–15, 18–23;
           or (ii)   four papers chosen from Is. 13–15, 18–23, and a dissertation;

(c) an oral examination in the language or languages that the candidate offers in the written papers;

provided that no candidate shall offer this section unless he has, during the academical year next before that in which he presents himself as a candidate, spent a period studying in a Middle Eastern country under conditions approved for this purpose by the Faculty Board.

(21) Japanese Studies

Either (i) *classical option*:
- (a) J. 11–14;
- (b) one paper from J. 15–17;
- (c) one paper from J. 18–21;
- (d) Japanese oral;
- (e) a dissertation;

or (ii) *modern option*:
- (a) J. 13–17;
- (b) one paper from J. 18–21;
- (c) Japanese oral;
- (d) a dissertation.

Dissertations

A candidate who wishes, or is required, to submit a dissertation must submit his proposed title, together with a statement of the papers that he intends to offer in the examination, through his Tutor to the Secretary of the Faculty Board so as to reach him not later than the division of the Michaelmas Term next preceding the examination. Each candidate must obtain the approval of his title by the Board not later than the end of that term. A dissertation, which must be of not more than 12,000 words in length (inclusive of notes and appendices), should show evidence of reading, judgement, and a power of exposition, but not necessarily evidence of original research, and must give full references to the sources used. Two copies of each dissertation marked with the candidate's name and College must be submitted through the candidate's Tutor to the Secretary of the Faculty Board so as to reach him not later than the third day of the Full Easter Term in which the examination is to be held. The Examiners will have power, if they consider that a dissertation is not sufficiently legible, to require that it be resubmitted in typescript. Each copy of the dissertation must be accompanied by a summary of not more than 300 words in English, except that a candidate in Chinese Studies must furnish instead a summary in Chinese of not less than 600 characters.

The Preliminary Examination for Part I

In the Preliminary Examination each paper in the list given below is set if a candidate wishes to present himself for examination therein. The questions set are simpler than those set for the Tripos.

Arabic
- Ar. 1. Arabic composition and grammar.
- Ar. 2. Arabic texts and Arab history.
- Ar. 3. Arabic unspecified texts.

Aramaic
- Am. 1. Aramaic specified texts.
- Am. 2. Aramaic unspecified texts and composition.

Assyriology
- As. 1. Akkadian specified texts.
- As. 2. Akkadian unspecified texts, grammar, and syntax.

Chinese Studies
- C. 1. Classical Chinese texts.
- C. 2. Modern Chinese texts.
- C. 3. Modern Chinese translation and composition.
- C. 4. Chinese cultural history.

Hebrew Studies
- H. 1. Hebrew specified texts.
- H. 2. Hebrew unspecified texts, grammar, and syntax.
- H. 3. Modern Hebrew specified and unspecified texts.
- H. 4. Jewish history, 1800–1918.

Indian Studies
- In. 1. Classical Indian specified texts.
- In. 2. Classical Indian unspecified texts and composition.
- In. 3. Hindi specified texts.
- In. 4. Hindi unspecified texts and composition.
- In. 5. Introduction to Indian studies, 1: Art, archaeology, and history.
- In. 6. Introduction to Indian studies, 2: Language, literature, and religion.

Japanese Studies
- J. 1. Modern Japanese specified texts.
- J. 2. Modern Japanese unspecified texts.
- J. 3. Modern Japanese composition and grammar.
- J. 4. Japanese history and thought.

Persian
- P. 1.   Persian specified texts and grammar.
- P. 2.   Persian unspecified texts and composition.

Oral examinations are held in the modern spoken forms of Arabic, Chinese, Hebrew, Hindi, Persian, and Japanese.

A candidate must offer **either** the papers appropriate to one of the following sections: (*a*) Arabic; (*b*) Arabic and Persian; (*c*) Chinese Studies; (*d*) Hebrew Studies; (*e*) Hebrew and Arabic; (*f*) Hebrew and Aramaic; (*g*) Hebrew and Assyriology; (*h*) Hindi and Persian; (*i*) Indian Studies; (*j*) Japanese Studies; **or** special papers as may be approved by the Faculty Board of Oriental Studies if he proposes to offer himself for examination in the Tripos in Oriental languages and subjects which are not specified for the Tripos; provided that, if he offers the papers appropriate to sections (*b*), (*c*), (*e*), (*f*), (*g*), or (*h*), or offers special papers in two languages approved by the Faculty Board, he must pass in both languages. Applications to take special papers must be made to the Faculty Board not later than 21 October next preceding the examination.

In respect of each of the sections (*a*) to (*j*), a candidate must take the following papers and must take the oral examination in the modern spoken form of the language specified:

- (*a*)   Arabic: Ar. 1–3, Arabic oral.
- (*b*)   Arabic and Persian: Ar. 1, 2, Arabic oral; P. 1, 2, Persian oral.
- (*c*)   Chinese Studies: C. 1–4, Chinese oral.
- (*d*)   Hebrew Studies: H. 1–4, Hebrew oral.
- (*e*)   Hebrew and Arabic: H. 1–2; Ar. 1, 2, Arabic oral.
- (*f*)   Hebrew and Aramaic: H. 1–2; Am. 1–2.
- (*g*)   Hebrew and Akkadian: H. 1–2; As. 1–2.
- (*h*)   Hindi and Persian: In. 3, 4, Hindi oral; P. 1–2, Persian oral.
- (*i*)   Indian Studies: **either** (i) In. 1, 2 and two papers chosen from In. 3–6, **or** (ii) In. 3, 4 and two papers chosen from In. 1, 2, 5, 6, provided that any candidate who offers In. 3 or In. 4 must offer Hindi oral.
- (*j*)   Japanese Studies: J. 1–4, Japanese oral.

Specified texts for the Preliminary Examination for Part I for **1988** have been published in the *Reporter* and details may be obtained from the Faculty of Oriental Studies.

Examination in Oriental Studies for the Ordinary B.A. Degree

The papers for the Ordinary Examination in Oriental Studies, and the specified texts, are the same as those set for the Preliminary Examination for Part I. A candidate for the Ordinary Examination must offer all the papers that he would be required to offer if he were a candidate for that Preliminary Examination.

M.Phil. Degree in Oriental Studies (one-year course)

There will be a one-year course consisting of lectures, seminars, and individual supervision, leading to an examination in Oriental Studies for the M.Phil. Degree (one-year course). The scheme of examination will consist of:

(*a*) a thesis of not more than 15,000 words, inclusive of footnotes, appendices, and bibliography, on a topic approved by the Degree Committee for the Faculty of Oriental Studies, which must fall within one of the following subject areas:

   (i) Assyriology;
   (ii) Chinese Studies;
   (iii) Indian Studies;
   Either (*a*) Archaeology and epigraphy of the early historical period;
   or (*b*) Middle Indian Studies;
   or (*c*) Modern Indian Studies;
   or (*d*) Sanskrit;
   (iv) Islamic Studies;
   Either (*a*) Arabic;
   or (*b*) Islamic and Middle Eastern History;
   or (*c*) Persian;
   or (*d*) Turkish;
   (v) Hebrew Studies:
   Either (*a*) Classical Hebrew Studies;
   or (*b*) Rabbinical and Medieval Hebrew Studies;
   or (*c*) Modern Hebrew Studies,

and in respect of which the Degree Committee may in giving their approval specify a minimum length for the thesis;

and

(*b*) three written papers, which shall fall within the same subject area as the thesis offered by the candidate under section (*a*) above, and shall be chosen, subject to the approval of the Degree Committee for the Faculty of Oriental Studies, from the papers prescribed in the University *Ordinances* for each subject area. Details of these papers are obtainable from the Secretary, the Faculty of Oriental Studies.

PHILOSOPHY

In this subject there are courses of study followed by candidates for:

The *Philosophy Tripos*, which is divided into three Parts, IA, IB, and II.
The *Preliminary Examination for Part IB of the Philosophy Tripos*.
The *Preliminary Examination for Part II of the Philosophy Tripos*.
The *Ordinary Examination* in Philosophy for the Ordinary B.A. Degree.
The *M.Phil. Degree* in Philosophy.

The Philosophy Tripos

Philosophy is a study of problems which are ultimate and very general, being those concerned with the nature of reality, knowledge, truth, morality, and human purpose. In university courses it is studied in a manner which lays considerable emphasis on precise and careful argument. In the earlier stages of the Cambridge course, the central elements are logic, metaphysics, ethics, and philosophy of mind; while attention is also paid to political philosophy, philosophy of religion, philosophy of science, and aesthetics. As the course proceeds the number of optional elements increases, so that in Part II there are no compulsory papers.

The Tripos consists of three separate Parts, and it is possible for students to read the subject for one, two, or three years, and also either before or after reading another subject. It is not necessary for students to have done any work in philosophy before reading the subject at Cambridge and Part IA of the Tripos is taught on the assumption that they have not. Students with both Arts and Science A-levels are acceptable.

Part IA provides an introduction to the fundamental topics of metaphysics and the philosophy of mind, ethics, and logic, together with detailed work on prescribed texts.

Part IB contains further study of metaphysics, logic, and philosophy of mind. Candidates also take two further papers from a list comprising empirical psychology, ethics, prescribed texts, philosophy of science, political philosophy, and aesthetics.

Both Parts IA and IB also contain an essay paper.

In Part II, students who have taken IB must choose any four of eleven papers, together with an essay paper or a dissertation. Students who choose the essay paper may substitute two written essays for one of their four papers. The Examiners may call a candidate for interview in connexion with his dissertation or essays, and may require him to resubmit them in typescript if the original work is not sufficiently legible. The subjects covered are metaphysics, ethics, two papers in the history of modern philosophy from Descartes (for which works of different authors are prescribed), history of ancient philosophy, philosophy of science, mathematical logic, philosophical logic, political philosophy, and aesthetics. There is also provision for a special subject paper to be set from time to time.

Change to philosophy after one or two years in another subject:

(1) Students who change to philosophy at the end of their *first* year may attempt (i) Part IB in one year, (ii) Part IB in two years, or (iii) Part II in two years, with the following special arrangements:

Part IB in two years. The Part IA papers serve as a preliminary examination after one year.

Part II in two years. A preliminary examination is provided after one year.

(2) Students who change to philosophy at the end of their *second* year may attempt (i) Part IB in one year or (ii) Part II in one year, with the following special arrangements:

Part II in one year. Candidates who obtained honours in a Tripos examination in their previous subject the year before *must* take one fewer paper (other than the essay paper or dissertation).

Part II also caters for students able to study ancient philosophy in the original texts, especially those who have obtained honours in Part I of the Classical Tripos. Such a candidate may combine the essay paper or dissertation and any two other papers in Part II (except that in ancient philosophy) with Papers B1 and B2 of Part II of the Classical Tripos (if he takes Part II in one year) or with Papers B1, B2, and B3 (if he takes Part II in two years). But a candidate who has obtained honours in Part II of the Classical Tripos must not repeat papers from that Tripos.

Parts IA, IB, and II of the Tripos

Details of the topics prescribed for the various papers in Parts IA, IB, and II of the Tripos are given below. Although students are not expected to have studied any philosophy before embarking on the

Tripos, it is certainly useful for them to have read some books on the subject first, if only to enable them to get a better idea of what their work will be like. Any of the books in the following brief list, especially Russell's *Problems of Philosophy*, can be recommended as being a significant contribution to the subject, and representative of what is to be expected in studying philosophy:

Descartes, *Meditations*; Berkeley, *Principles of Human Knowledge*; B. Russell, *The Problems of Philosophy*; A. J. Ayer, *Language, Truth and Logic*; I. Hacking, *Why Does Language Matter to Philosophy?*; K. Campbell, *Body and Mind*; C. G. Hempel, *Philosophy of Natural Science*; Hume, *Enquiry Concerning the Principles of Morals*; J. S. Mill, *Utilitarianism*; B. Williams, *Morality*.

Part I A

Part I A may be taken only at the end of a student's first year as an undergraduate. All the following papers must be taken.

In Papers 1-4 candidates are asked to answer four questions out of at least ten set.

1. Metaphysics and philosophy of mind

Things and properties. Past, present, and future. Verification. Induction, evidence. Knowledge and scepticism. Deity, Identity, including personal identity. Free-will. Perception. Belief. Mind and matter.

2. Ethics

Introduction to the development of modern ethics. Fact and value. Theories of moral judgement. Problems of moral knowledge. Moral language. Amoralism. Consequentialism and deontology. Rights. Punishment.

3. Logic

Questions will be set on some of the following and related topics:

Logic and language: sentences, statements, and propositions; formal languages; object-language and metalanguage. Axiomatic method.

Propositional logic: truth-functions, tautologies, implication; problems of translation; formal proof, including methods of natural deduction; soundness and completeness.

**Introduction to predicate logic: translation into the language of quantifiers and variables; validity and counter-examples; elements of the logic of identity, descriptions, classes, and relations.

4. Set text or texts

Hume: *Dialogues Concerning Natural Religion*; Plato, *Meno*.

5. Essay

Part IB

A student may take Part IB in any but his first year. He must take Papers 1, 2, 3, and 10 and two other papers. No candidate who has previously offered Experimental Psychology in Part IB in the Natural Sciences Tripos may offer Paper 9.

1. Metaphysics (also serves as Paper O4 of Part II of the Classical Tripos)

Questions may be set on the topics for Part IA Metaphysics and on some of the following and related topics:

The nature of philosophy. Truth. Realism and idealism. Time. Primary and secondary qualities. Causality and change. Nature and grounds of religious belief. God.

2. Philosophy of mind

The general character of mind and the mental. Privacy, intentionality. Mental states, acts, dispositions. Behaviourism, functionalism. Memory, intellect, and will. The emotions. Pleasure. Sensation. Action. Motivation. Voluntariness. The unconscious. Self-deception. Mental illness.

3. Logic

Questions may be set on the topics for Part IA Logic and on some of the following and related topics:

Introduction to the philosophy of language. Logical form. Necessity and analyticity. Definition. Existence. Names and descriptions. Extensionality. Number.

Predicate logic, including the semantics of quantified sentences. Elements of modal logic. Elements of many-valued logic.

Selected topics or texts may be prescribed from time to time.

4. Ethics

The themes of Part IA, pursued in greater depth, with additional reference to:

Virtues and moral character. Rational choice, self-interest and altruism. Moral conviction and moral action. Responsibility. Morality and religion. Elements of the moral philosophies of Hume and Kant.

5. Set texts

Texts from the history of particular areas of philosophy are prescribed. More general questions may also be asked about some of the areas covered by the texts; such areas will be specified when the texts are prescribed.

In **1990** and **1991**: Plato: *Phaedo*; Aristotle: *Nicomachean Ethics*; Kant: *Religion within the Limits of Reason Alone*.

6. Philosophy of science

Questions will be set on some of the following and related topics:

Scientific method in natural and social sciences. Scientific explanation. Scientific theories. Scientific laws. Natural kinds. Causation in natural and social sciences. Probability.

7. Political philosophy

Questions will be set on some of the following and related topics:

Anarchism, authority, and power. Scope and legitimacy of government. Political obligation. Democracy. State of nature and social contract. Rights. Liberty, justice, equality, welfare. Law and morality. Elements of the political philosophies of Hobbes and Locke.

8. Aesthetics (also serves as Paper 11 of Part II)

A wide range of basic questions is set, on topics such as the following:

Nature of art. Understanding and evaluation. Individuation of works of art. Representation. Expression. Intentions. Imagination, originality. Art and morality. Art and nature.

9. Empirical psychology

The aims of empirical psychology. The relation of psychological studies to those of other biological sciences. Elements of the structure and function of the nervous system and sense organs.

Experimental and theoretical investigations within the general field of experimental psychology. These fall broadly into the categories of studies of instinct and maturation; sensory process and perception; learning and memory; language; reaction times and the control of human skilled behaviour; social development and studies of the behaviour of infants. In most of these areas reference is made to experiments on both animal and human behaviour.

10. Essay

Part II

Part II may be taken in one year after Part IB of the Philosophy Tripos or in two years or one after any other honours examination except Part IA of the Philosophy Tripos. In the first two cases a candidate must offer four out of Papers 1–11 and Paper 12.

A candidate who takes Part II one year after obtaining honours in another Tripos must offer three out of Papers 1–11, and Paper 12.

No candidate may offer Paper 11 if he has previously offered Paper 8 in Part IB and no candidate may offer Paper 5 if he has previously offered Paper B1 or B2 in Part II of the Classical Tripos.

If a candidate has either obtained honours in Part I of the Classical Tripos or has satisfied the Faculty Board of Classics that he has the necessary Greek and Latin to benefit by the course, he may offer two out of Papers 1–4 and 6–11 and Paper 12, together with papers taken from Group B of Part II of the Classical Tripos as follows:

(*a*) in the year after obtaining honours, Papers B1 and B2, or (*b*) in the year next but one, Papers B1, B2, and B3.

A candidate who has previously obtained honours in Part II of the Classical Tripos may not offer any paper that he offered in that examination.

Dissertation

A candidate for Part II has the option of offering in place of Paper 12 a dissertation on a topic of philosophical interest proposed by himself and approved by the Faculty Board. A dissertation must be of not more than 6,000 words and (except with the permission of the Faculty Board) not less than 3,000 words in length, including footnotes and appendices but excluding bibliography.

Essays

In place of any one of Papers 1–11 a candidate who has previously obtained honours in Part IB may submit two essays, each of not less than 3,000 words and not more than 4,000 words in length, including footnotes and appendices but excluding bibliography, on two topics proposed by himself and approved by the Faculty Board, which shall both fall within the scope of that paper, provided that

(i) a candidate may not submit both a dissertation and essays;
(ii) a candidate may not submit essays falling within the

scope of Paper 11 if he has previously offered Paper 8 in Part IB;

(iii) a candidate who chooses to submit essays may not write in Paper 12 an essay on a subject that overlaps significantly with either of his submitted essays.

Dissertations and Essays: General rules

A candidate who chooses to offer a dissertation or two essays must submit the proposed title of his dissertation or the proposed titles of his essays, together with a statement of the papers that he intends to offer in the examination, and in the case of essays a statement of the paper which they are intended to replace, through his Tutor to the Secretary of the Faculty Board not later than 30 November next preceding the examination. A candidate must obtain the approval of the Faculty Board for his title or titles not later than the last day of Full Michaelmas Term. A candidate must submit his dissertation or his essays through his Tutor to the Registrary so as to reach him not later than the last day of the Lent Term next preceding the examination. Each dissertation or pair of essays must bear a motto but not the candidate's name and must be accompanied by (*a*) a statement of the sources from which the candidate has obtained information, and (*b*) a sealed evelope bearing the motto outside and containing the name of the candidate and his College. The Examiners will have power to examine a candidate *viva voce* on his dissertation or his essays, and to require him to resubmit them in typescript if the original work submitted is not sufficiently legible.

The papers in Part II are:

1. Metaphysics

In **1990**: Questions may be set on the topics for Paper 1 of Part IA and Paper 1 of Part IB and on some of the following and related topics in metaphysics, theory of knowledge, the philosophy of mind, and the philosophy of religion:

Ontology. The rationality of belief. Miracles. God and human freedom. Mind and body. Consciousness. Understanding. Meaning. Images and imagination. Mental events, states and dispositions.

In **1991**: Questions may be set on the following topics: The Nature of Philosophy. Realism and Idealism. Substance. Universals. Facts. Relativism vs. Absolutism. Objectivity and Subjectivity. Space and Time. Causality and Change. Scepticism, Knowledge, and Rational Belief. Religious Belief. Mind and Body. Perception, Imagination, and Memory. Sensation and Consciousness. Mental Events, States and Representations.

2. Ethics

The paper will include, besides central questions in ethics, questions in the philosophy of mind (on such topics as decision, intention, the will, motivation, action, responsibility and self-knowledge).

3. History of modern philosophy I. The prescribed texts are:

In **1990** and **1991**: Questions will be set on the philosophy of the 17th and 18th centuries, including some of the following and related authors, texts and topics: Descartes (concentrating on the *Meditations*). Spinoza (concentrating on the *Ethics*). Leibniz. Locke (concentrating on *Essay concerning Human Understanding*). Berkeley (concentrating on *Three Dialogues between Hylas and Philonous* and *The Principles of Human Knowledge*). Hume (concentrating on Book 1 of the *Treatise of Human Nature*).
Knowledge and scepticism. Substance. Causality. Ideas and representation.

4. History of modern philosophy II. The prescribed texts are:

In **1990**: Kant: *The Critique of Pure Reason* to the end of the Transcendental Logic (A704, B732); Hegel, *The Essential Writings* (ed. F. Weiss, Harper Torchbooks); Nietzsche, *Genealogy of Morals, The Gay Science, The Birth of Tragedy, Thus Spoke Zarathustra*; Kierkgaard: *Either-Or*, Volume I, and *Concluding Unscientific Postscript*: Schopenhauer: *On the Basis of Morality*; *The Freedom of the Will*; *The World as Will and Representation*, Books 1 and 2.
In **1991**: The same texts as for 1990 but without Schopenhauer: *On the Basis of Morality*; *The Freedom of the Will*.

5. History of ancient philosophy

The prescribed texts for study in translation are:

In **1990**: Plato: *Hippias Major, Euthydemus*; Aristotle: *De Anima*; Cicero: *De Fato*, and related aspects of Hellenistic Philosophy.

In **1991**: Plato: *Hippias Major, Euthydemus*. Aristotle: *Physics* Book II. Cicero: *De Fato* and related aspects of Hellenistic Philosophy.

6. Philosophy of science

Questions may be set on the topics for **Part IB Philosophy of science** and on some of the following and related topics:
Objectivity in science. The role of values in natural and social sciences. The meaning and ontology of scientific theories. The reducibility of one science or theory to another. Scientific progress. The acceptance, confirmation, testing and refutation of hypotheses. Principles of decision-making. Space and time. Problems in the philosophy of physics; of biology; of psychology.

7. Mathematical logic

Questions will be set on some of the following and related topics:

First-order and second-order logic. Formal theories, consistency, completeness, axiomatisability, decidability, models and categoricity. Gödel's theorem. Recursive functions and computability. Proof theory. Intuitionism. Set theory. Infinity. Modal logic. Many-valued logic.

8. Philosophical logic

In **1990**: Questions may be set on the topics for Paper 3 of Part IB and on some of the following and related topics:

Semantics. Reference. Modality and quantification. Iterated modalities. Speech-acts. The semantic paradoxes. Identity. Subject and predicate. Conditionals. Anti-realism. Mathematical truth and the existence of mathematical objects. Proof. Pure and applied mathematics.

Selected topics and texts may be prescribed from time to time.

In **1991**: Questions may be set on the following and related topics: Semantics. Reference. Modality and quantification. Iterated modalities. Speech-acts. The semantic paradoxes. Identity. Subject and predicate. Conditionals. Anti-realism. Mathematical truth and the existence of mathematical objects. Proof. Pure and applied mathematics.

Selected topics and texts may be prescribed from time to time.

9. Special subject specified by the Faculty Board

In **1990** and **1991**: *Twentieth Century European Philosophy*

Questions may be set on the following topics and authors:

Phenomenology, Existentialism, Hermeneutics, Critical Theory, Deconstruction. Husserl, Herdegger, Sartre, Merleau-Ponty, Gadamer, Adorno, Habermas, Derrida.

10. Political philosophy

In **1990**: Questions may be set on the topics for Part IB Political Philosophy and on some of the following and related topics:

Representation, participation, social decision-making. Nature and justification of law and judicial punishment. Coercion. Paternalism. Civil disobedience. Fundamental concepts of marxist theory.

In **1991**: Questions may be set on the topics for Part IB Political Philosophy and on some of the following and related topics:

Representation, participation, social decision-making, Nature and justification of law and judicial punishment. Coercion. Paternalism. Civil disobedience. Topics in Marxist theory, including exploitation, ideology, alienation, revolution, communism and socialism, historical materialism.

Selected texts may be specified from time to time.
No texts are specified in **1990** or **1991**.

11. Aesthetics (Paper 8 of Part I B)

12. Essay.

The Preliminary Examination for Part I B

The examination consists of the same papers as compose Part I A. Candidates must offer the Essay paper and three or four of the other papers. A candidate who offers the Essay paper and four other papers will be classed on the basis of the Essay paper and the three best of his other papers.

The Preliminary Examination for Part II

Eleven papers are available. Papers 1–8 and 10 are the same as the correspondingly-numbered papers of Part I B. The others are:

9. Outlines of mathematical logic and philosophy of mathematics

Questions may be set on the topics specified for Paper 7 of Part II and on the topics in philosophy of mathematics specified for Paper 8 of Part II.

11. Outlines of modern philosophy

Questions will be set on philosophers from Descartes to Kant.

Candidates must offer Paper 10 and three or four of the other papers. A candidate who offers Paper 10 and four other papers will be classed on the results of Paper 10 and the three best of his other papers.

The Examination in Philosophy for the Ordinary B.A. Degree

The examination consists of the Essay paper and any three of the other papers set for Part I B of the Philosophy Tripos.

A student who has passed or received an allowance on Part I A or Part I B of the Philosophy Tripos may not be a candidate.

M.Phil. course in Philosophy

The scheme of examination for the one-year course in Philosophy consists of *either*:

(a) a thesis, of not more than 15,000 words in length, including footnotes and appendices, but excluding bibliography, on a subject approved by the Degree Committee of the Faculty of Philosophy; and:

(b) four essays, each of about 3,000 words and each in a subject approved by the Degree Committee which is related to one or more of the following areas of Philosophy (including in each case the History of Philosophy):

Metaphysics
Philosophy of Mind
Logic
Philosophy of Science
Ethics
Aesthetics
Political and Legal Philosophy
Not more than three essays shall be chosen from any one area.

or:

a thesis of not more than 30,000 words in length, including notes and appendices, but excluding bibliography. To adopt this scheme the candidate needs the special permission of the Degree Committee, granted after considering his experience, special qualifications and proposed topic.

The examination will include an oral examination on the thesis. Further details regarding the areas for essays are as follows:

1. Metaphysics

Metaphysics and Epistemology in the Western tradition, including topics such as deity, identity, time and scepticism.

2. Philosophy of Mind

Philosophical problems about mind, including topics such as perception, memory, will, emotions and action. Philosophical aspects of psychology.

3. Logic

Philosophical logic; philosophy of language; mathematical logic, including philosophical issues raised by its results and methods; foundations of mathematics; philosophy of mathematics.

4. Philosophy of Science

General principles, including theories of scientific method, probability, causation, realism, reducibility and other general issues. Conceptual problems of the exact sciences, e.g. theories of space and time and problems in the philosophy of physics and biology.

5. Ethics

Theories of ethics, including topics such as virtue, amoralism and the distinction between fact and value. Ethical aspects of medicine, business and other professions.

6. Aesthetics

Theories of art, including topics such as representation, expression, imagination and intention.

7. Political & Legal Philosophy

Theories of political authority, including topics such as democracy, the social contract, justice, equality and philosophical aspects of Marxism. Philosophical aspects of the law.

POLAR STUDIES

The M.Phil. (one-year course)

The course leading to the M.Phil. Degree in Polar Studies is intended to meet the needs of persons already working in the polar field who wish to broaden their knowledge on an interdisciplinary basis, and to enable others to gain knowledge of the polar regions in preparation for a career in which this will be relevant. Candidates need not have had any previous training in specifically polar areas of study. The possibility exists for further study towards a higher degree after completion of the M.Phil. course.

A candidate must write a thesis of up to 20,000 words on a subject proposed by him or her in consultation with his or her supervisor, and five essays on topics set by the Examiners. This work is to be done in the candidate's own time, with access to source materials, but must be submitted by specified dates. There will be an oral examination on the subject of the thesis and of the essays.

A candidate for the M.Phil. Degree must

(*a*) have been admitted to the status of Graduate Student and accepted as a candidate for the M.Phil. Degree by the Board of Graduate Studies on the recommendation of the Degree Committee of the Faculty of Earth Sciences and Geography; and

(*b*) have graduated at Cambridge or another university; *or*

(*c*) have produced other evidence to satisfy the Degree Committee and the Board of Graduate Studies of his or her fitness to study for the M.Phil. Degree.

An application for admission as a candidate for the M.Phil. must be sent to the Secretary of the Board of Graduate Studies and be accompanied by the names of not less than two referees and by a statement of the candidate's previous studies, attainments, and qualifications.

Subjects for essays are set by the Examiners from the following areas of study:

Environment

Environment; Peoples; History of exploration; Resources and problems of development; Administration; Research.

Social Sciences

Ethnography of indigenous and immigrant peoples of the Arctic and sub-Arctic; social change and human problems of development.

History

History of exploration of northern Eurasia, northern North America, Greenland, Arctic Ocean, Antarctica.

Resources and problems of development

Renewable and non-renewable resources. Engineering problems in snow, ice, and permafrost. Transport systems and techniques. Human adaptation and health.

Administration

Government administrative structure. Relations with native peoples. International law, treaties, political and strategic factors. Territorial claims.

Research

Importance of polar regions for scientific research. International organisation of polar science and scientists.

A candidate is required to select the subject of each essay or exercise from two subjects set and to submit his essay or exercise not more than two weeks of Full Term after the announcement of the subjects. The thesis must be submitted by an agreed date in the third term. In assessing a candidate's performance, the Examiners allocate half the marks to the thesis and half to the five essays or exercises.

SOCIAL AND POLITICAL SCIENCES

In this field the courses of study offered to candidates are:

The *Social and Political Sciences Tripos*, Part I.
The *Social and Political Sciences Tripos*, Part II.
The *Preliminary Examination* for the Social and Political Sciences Tripos, Part II.

The University of Cambridge has long had a distinguished record of teaching and research in politics, sociology and social psychology. The Social and Political Sciences Tripos enables undergraduates to study these subjects in a multi-disciplinary context over three years.

The Part I provides a systematic introduction to politics, sociology, and social psychology, and also includes an introduction to social anthropology. Within the framework of Part II it is possible to pursue many particular interests. Two compulsory papers ensure familiarity with the principal theories, findings and procedures of the social sciences, and emphasize the interdependence of theories, problems, and methods in the study of society. Class work in statistics is provided and some competence in statistical and other quantitative techniques of analysis is assumed in several of the papers.

The Tripos is distinguished from degree courses in the social sciences in many other universities by its concern with the logic and philosophy of the social sciences, the social institutions of past societies, the sociology of long-term historical change and various problems and topics requiring an approach from more than one discipline. Papers are also provided in standard subjects such as the family, the sociology of economic life, political philosophy, the psychology of development, and attitudes and personality. The papers set in Part II serve for the Preliminary examination as well. The Preliminary examination is composed of selected papers from Part II and a paper in data analysis.

Part II candidates may also submit a dissertation instead of one of the papers. In Part II, the student takes two papers devoted to theoretical and methodological issues in the social and political sciences and four other papers. These are chosen from a wide set of options which includes three papers in sociology, in political science, and social psychology, as well as a large variety of papers dealing with selected topics from a multi-disciplinary standpoint, plus single papers in international relations, linguistics, and development.

The papers in Part II can thus be combined in many ways to suit varied individual interests. It is possible to concentrate on the study of politics, including political philosophy, and political history; or on the study of developing societies; or on the application of quantitative methods to sociological problems in contemporary economics and political life; or on the social organization of personality, values, and culture. Accordingly, the Tripos should appeal to anyone interested in the disciplined study of different types of society or in the possibility of a scientific treatment of social phenomena.

Candidates for the Tripos Examination must be in their third or fourth year and must have been classed in either the Social and Political Sciences Tripos or another Tripos Examination either one or two years previously. Students transferring from a Tripos with a two-year Part I such as History can take the Social and Political Sciences Tripos Part II in one year, taking four papers. One-year candidates are classed separately from those who have followed the Social and Political Sciences Tripos for two years or more, who take six papers.

A degree in Social and Political Sciences offers a wide range of career opportunities. The Tripos can provide a suitable training for careers in the civil service, business, journalism and media, and social and public administration. It also qualifies people for the wide variety of challenging posts opening up for social scientists on the staffs of local authorities and development corporations both at home and abroad. Numerous international organizations and research institutes are also now seeking qualified social scientists.

Copies of the 'Guide to the SPS Part II" which provides fuller descriptions of the Papers and introductory reading lists may be obtained from the Secretary of the Department of Social and Political Sciences, Free School Lane.

PART I

There are four papers, all four of which must be offered. The papers are:

1. The analysis of the modern state

The historical development of western capitalist states: bourgeois revolution, state and civil society; liberal or laissez-faire states; crisis and transformation, 1870–1918; growth and characteristics of the interventionist state; world recession, political responses and the restructuring of contemporary states: U.S.A., Britain; France, Italy, West Germany; Sweden. The state in 'socialist' societies.

SOCIAL AND POLITICAL SCIENCES

2. Industrial societies (Paper 8 of Part I of the Archaeological and Anthropological Tripos)

3. Human society: organization, evolution, and development (Paper 5 of Part I of the Archaeological and Anthropological Tripos)

4. Society, interaction and the individual.

The scope of social psychology. Methods and levels of analysis. Selected topics from the following:

Nature–nurture issues in socialization. Cognitive and affective development. The self in social context. Social interaction processes. Attitudes and ideologies. The social psychology of work: occupational socialization, effects of work and its absence on individual and family life. Social psychology of domestic life: the family, parent–child relationships, marriage and divorce, sex roles. Cross-cultural variations in perception, thinking, and social behaviour.

PART II

There are twenty-six papers, divided into five groups, A, B, C, D, and E. Some papers are common to two groups. The papers are:

Group A: General papers

1. Methods of enquiry and analysis I

Basic principles of data analysis, including the importance of comparison, standardization, models, and appropriate levels of measurement. Techniques of analysing data, including single variable summaries of central tendency, dispersion and shape (including the normal distribution), comparing batches of data, frequency tables, percentages, two-way and three-way tables, elementary techniques of line-fitting. Sample design and elementary inference. Each year examples will be drawn from a delimited substantive area, and students will be expected to have a knowledge of the published statistics in that area.

2. Theoretical problems in social science I

Origins and development of social theory. Its connexion with the formation of social psychology. The political context of social thought. Selected coverage of major traditions of social theory from the late eighteenth to the early twentieth century. Contrasts between theoretical traditions in differing countries. Elementary analysis of philosophical problems in social science, including particularly: questions of the nature of knowledge claims in the social sciences; concepts of action and structure; modes of explanation in social science; individualism and holism.

3. Methods of enquiry and analysis II

Complex sample designs; stratification, clustering, and design effects. Analysis of variance. Multiple regression and causal modelling. Elementary factor analysis. Significance testing and its rôle in the social sciences. The theory of data, and various scaling techniques, such as Likert, Guttman, Thurstone, and Rasch. Issues in research design. Laboratory and field experiments, surveys and observational techniques, secondary analysis and cross-cultural comparisons. Qualitative methods in social science. The use of descriptive statistics. Ethical and political problems in social research. The use and effect of computers and computer packages in the social sciences for handling numerical and textual information.

4. Theoretical problems in social science II

Philosophical problems in social and natural science. Questions of laws and generalizations, induction and deduction, prediction, probability, and causality. Realism, relativism, and issues in the interpretation of meaning. Holism and individualism. Structuralism. Functional analysis and functional explanation. The point and nature of critical theory. Value-freedom in social science. Exemplifications of these issues in the work of selected theorists in social science and psychology.

Group B: Politics

5*. Political philosophy (Paper 5 of Part II of the Historical Tripos)

6*†. Comparative political systems (also serves as Paper 14 of Part II of the Economics Tripos)

The formation and structure of capitalist states; the economy and the polity; political institutions and culture; social classes and political representation; conservatism, liberalism, social democracy, communism; fascist movements, ideologies, and states; ruling classes, élites, forms of control and consent; working class politics, trade unions, and incorporation; the theory and practice of reformism; nationalism and regionalism; nation states and international capital.

Politics and society in Socialist states; theories of state socialism: Marxist–Leninist, totalitarian, convergence, mobilization; divergence and dissent: Yugoslavia, the Czech reform movement, the cultural revolution in China, Poland.

---

* See p. 440.
† Paper 6 will be set for the last time in 1990.

SOCIAL AND POLITICAL SCIENCES

7*. Revolution

Approaches to the understanding of revolution: history of ideas, political theory, political sociology, comparative history. The development of the concept of revolution: regime-transformation and historical process; the transition from sacred to secular conceptions of historial process. The English Revolution of the seventeenth century. The French Revolution. The concept of bourgeois revolution. The emergence of the rôle of professional revolutionary. The development of counter-revolutionary thought. Major theorists of revolutionary process: De Tocqueville, Marx, Lenin, Trotsky, Mao. The critical assessment of revolutionary political theory: the concept of proletarian revolution; the role of the party; permanent revolution; imperialism; the transition to socialism; cultural revolution. 'Theories' of revolution and social change in sociology: conceptual and methodological problems. The relationship between sociological explanation and revolutionary consciousness: Marxism and sociology. Fascist ideologies, movements, and states. The analysis of particular revolutions and attempted revolutions: England, France, Russia, China, Mexico, Germany, Italy, Yugoslavia, Vietnam, Cuba.

8*. State and society in developing countries

The nature of the 'Third World'. Problems of dependency. The history of the idea of 'development' for poorer countries since 1945. Theories of economic, social, and political change in poorer countries, including theories of development. Aspects of social and political change in selected countries, including strategies for and experiences of development.

9*. The history of political thought since *c.* 1750 (Paper 4 of Part II of the Historical Tripos)

16. The sociology and politics of welfare (option (*a*) of the subjects specified for Paper 15 of Part II of the Economics Tripos)

17. The history of political thought up to *c.* 1750 (Paper 3 of Part II of the Historical Tripos)

18. Europe and the rise of the superpowers: international relations since 1815 (whenever this subject is specified for Paper 7 of Part II of the Historical Tripos)

* See p. 440.

Group C: Social psychology

10*. The individual in society

The nature and scope of social psychology. Theories of relations between individuals and the societies they live in. Social interaction as a mediator between individuals and social structure. Relations between individuals and society as revealed by the study of substantive issues such as: intergroup relations; employment and unemployment; mental illness; marriage and divorce; socialization of the individual. The study of beliefs, attitudes, and social representations. The social psychological study of social issues.

11*. The psychology of development

The development of social relations.

Theories and concepts of development. Early experience and later behaviour. The origins of social behaviour; mother–child interaction. The growth of social relationships within the family and the wider social world. Sexual differentiation and sex rôles. The acquisition of social norms.

The development of cognitive abilities. Intelligence and I.Q. testing. Language acquisition. Social class differences in cognitive skills.

Social norms and abnormal behaviour. Some issues in psychopathology.

12*. Language and social interaction

The relationship between linguistic variation and various aspects of social stratification; social class, ethnicity, status, inter-group relations, and gender. Bilingualism and multilingualism. The motivations for, and consequences of, linguistic variation. Mass media. Language and sexism. The relationship between language, thought, and culture.

Interpersonal relationships. Interactional theories of personality. Persuasion. Politeness. Interactional style and affective state. Group processes. Language use in professional contexts. Inter-ethnic communication.

Conversational analysis. Discourse analysis. The ethnography of speaking. Conversational structure. Conversational inferences. Goals and strategies in social interaction. Mutual knowledge. Gricean pragmatics. Speech act theory.

Non-vocal communication; facial expression, gaze, gesture, and posture. The relationship between language and non-vocal communication. Universality and cultural relativity in non-vocal communication.

First language acquisition. The rôle of language in social development. Second language acquisition. Breakdown of interactional skills, and the consequences of their loss.

* See p. 440.

SOCIAL AND POLITICAL SCIENCES

13*. Empirical psychology (Paper 9 of Part IB of the Philosophy Tripos)

19. Social aspects of medicine

Conceptual models of health, illness, and disease used by doctors, administrators, and patients, including selected cross-cultural aspects. Medicine as social control. The definition of problems as the concern of doctors. The organization of health care in Britain and selected other countries. The rôle of professionals and non-professionals. Medical and para-medical education and training. Institutional structures and individual behaviour. Decision-making and organizational theories.

Economic factors. Doctor–patient relationships viewed from psychological, sociological, and historical perspectives. Social aspects of diagnosis and treatment, including discussion of self-medication, 'fringe' medicine, and the pharmaceutical industry.

20. Deviance

Definitions of deviance: crime, delinquency, sexual deviance, mental illness, drug use, aggression, and dishonesty. The creation of rules, laws, and morality: conflict or consensus? The relationship between legal and social change. Functions of deviance. Formal and informal systems of social control. Explanations of deviance: scientific theories and telling stories.

Psychoanalytic and social learning theories. The personalities of deviants. Social psychological experiments on deviance: factors promoting or inhibiting deviant behaviour, the effects of observing deviance, the evaluation of deviance, reactions of others to deviance, reactions of the individual to his own deviance.

Deviance and social structure: economic theories, culture conflict, social disorganization, anomie theory, subcultural theories. The interactionist approach; social reaction and the process of identification; the creation and maintenance of deviant identities; deviant careers. Accounts by deviants of their actions. Phenomenology and the study of deviance.

21. Women in society

Gender differences – their nature and explanation. The origins and acquisition of gender differences, and their relationship to biological, psychological, social, political, and economic factors will be considered. Specific but not exclusive attention will be given to the position of women. Particular emphasis will be given to problems of relating and integrating different approaches and different forms of explanation. The study of gender differences will be used to

* See p. 440.

illustrate and explore fundamental issues in the social sciences. The scope of the paper is as follows: biological factors associated with behavioural differences; the relevance of studies of animal social and sexual behaviour to human behaviour; gender differences in infancy, and parental behaviour and attitudes, and their possible explanation in terms of biological, motivational, and role considerations; the acquisition of concepts of social identity; the notions of sexual identification in psychoanalytic theory; the usefulness of concepts of 'identification' and 'rôle'.

Cross-cultural analysis of women's rôle within family and kinship systems, and its connexion with their rôles within the economic and political spheres, with reference to tribal, peasant, and industralized societies. Feminist movements and theories; the structure of women's rights and activities in present-day Britain and the legal, economic, and social determinants of this; the legal status of women in modern Britain, its historic development, with reference to property and divorce; the development of social security provisions in twentieth-century Britain and its effects on the family as a social and economic unit.

22. The family

This paper will provide a multidisciplinary analysis of family and domestic life in Britain. Among the major issues that will be discussed are: concepts of the family, kinship relations, and the interconnexion of the public and private spheres; the history of the family; demographic changes including birth, marriage, and death rates; migration and residence patterns; social policy and professional ideologies; divisions of labour within the home; socialization in the private sphere; marriage, cohabitation, and divorce; social and sexual relationships; sexuality, domestic violence; changes in relationships through the course of life; relationships within the wider kinship network.

Group D: Sociology

6*. Comparative political systems (also serves as Paper 14 of Part II of the Economic Tripos)

8*. State and society in developing countries

14*. The social structure of modern Britain (also serves as Paper 13 of Part II of the Economics Tripos)

Institutional patterns in the development of British society in the twentieth century. Distribution of population and basic demographic characteristics. Regional variations in social and economic organization. Relations between government and industry. Elite recruitment and class structure. The position of women in the class structure. The nature of urban development and change.

* See p. 440.

SOCIAL AND POLITICAL SCIENCES

Social control, crime, and deviance. Cultural organization and cultural institutions.

15*. Class, inequality and industrial conflict

Contending theories of industrial capitalism, its pre-conditions, development, and characteristic institutional order. The nature of class and status; theories of class division and conflict. The progressive differentiation of the division of labour. The industrial enterprise: the labour process, capital, ownership, and control; industrial democracy and participation, the regulation of industrial relations, strikes, and industrial conflict. The state, corporatism, and modern capitalism. The development and actions of trade unions. The development and nature of social classes in capitalism and state socialism; changes in class structure. The bases, rates, and avenues of social mobility. Social mobility and systems of education.

16*. The sociology and politics of welfare (option (*a*) of the subjects specified for Paper 15 of Part II of the Economics Tripos)

19. Social aspects of medicine

20. Deviance

21. Women in society

22. The family

Group E: The sociology and politics of particular areas

23. A subject specified by the Social and Political Sciences Committee
The subject of this paper in **1990** will be:

The politics and society of France and Italy since 1940

Political developments and ideologies: Vichy and the Republic of Salo; Resistance; post-war settlements. The Fourth French Republic and the Algerian crisis; Italian Christian Democracy in the 1950s. De Gaulle and the Fifth Republic; the Centre-Left in Italy. 1968: the May movement and the 'Hot Autumn'. French and Italian Communism. Pompidou and Giscard D'Estaing; Mitterand and French Socialism. Terrorism and historic compromise in Italy. French and Italian politics in the 1980s.

National and supra-national institutions and policies: State structures and buraucracies; education and welfare; economic planning and international trade; the Common Market; defence policies; autonomy and dependence.

* See p. 440.

Social and economic change: City and countryside; the Church and society; internal emigration and urbanisation; industrialisation and the tertiary sector; class structure and social inequality; women and society; family and collectivity; culture and the mass media; regionalism; environmental issues; immigration and racism.

24. The politics and society of the U.S.S.R. since 1917

Historical development of the U.S.S.R. The 1917 Revolution, the Civil War, the New Economic Policy, industralization and collectivization, the 1941–45 war, de-Stalinization, the Brezhnev era, modern economic reform.

The political system. The emergence of a one-party state, changes in the composition and rôle of the CPSU, the Stalin era, and the cult of the personality. Elites and groups in Soviet politics; consent, dissent, deviance; the politics of market and plan.

Social change. The evolution of the Soviet social structure, the Soviet cultural revolution, changes in the structure and function of the family, developments in education and the social services; religion, nationalities and ethnic groups, population, social stratification.

Ideology. The development of Soviet Marxism: Lenin's theories of revolution, party organization, and the state, Stalin's views on the construction of socialism, contemporary ideas about the transition to Communism. Critical theories of Soviet society: totalitarianism, state capitalism, workers' state, industrial society.

25. The sociology and politics of a specified area I. In 1990, Latin America (may also serve as option (*c*) of the subjects specified for Paper 15 of Part II of the Economics Tripos)

The emphasis of this paper is on the following topics: relations between Latin America and the world capitalist system; in particular, the effects of these on the social structure of Latin-American countries; patterns of agrarian change, rural social movements. Agrarian reform; the experience of populism and military government; urbanization and rural–urban migration; trade unions; the Mexican and Cuban revolutions. Students will be encouraged to concentrate on a limited number of countries.

26. The sociology and politics of a specified area II. In 1990, South Asia. (Paper In. 28 of Part II of the Oriental Studies Tripos)

Papers in Part II must be offered as follows:

(1) By a candidate taking Part II in the year after he obtained honours in another Honours examination:

SOCIAL AND POLITICAL SCIENCES

(*a*) one of Papers 1, 2, and 4; and (*b*) three additional papers, which must be

> *either* (i) three papers from any one of Groups B, C, and D, which must include at least two papers marked with an asterisk;
>
> *or* (ii) three papers marked with an asterisk from not more than two of Groups B, C, and D;
>
> *or* (iii) two papers marked with an asterisk either from Group B or from Group D, and one paper from Group E.

(2) By a candidate taking Part II in the year next but one after the year in which he obtained honours in another Honours Examination.

(*a*) Papers 3 and 4; and

(*b*) four additional papers which must be[1]

> *either* (i) three papers from any one of Groups B, C, and D, which must include at least two papers marked with an asterisk, and one paper which may be chosen without restriction from Groups B, C, D, and E;
>
> *or* (ii) two papers marked with an asterisk from each of two of Groups B, C, and D;
>
> *or* (iii) two papers marked with an asterisk either from Group B or from Group D, together with one paper from Group E, and one paper which may be chosen without restriction from Groups B, C, D, and E.

A dissertation may be offered under (1) above in place of any one of the papers, except a paper from Group A, on a topic which falls within the field of the paper concerned and which is approved by the Department. A dissertation may be offered under (2) above in place of any one of the papers, except a paper from Group A, on a topic which falls within the range of the Tripos as a whole (including a topic in the same field as that of a paper he is offering) and which is approved by the Department. A candidate offering such dissertations must submit a statement of the papers which he intends to offer, together with the title of his dissertation, through his Tutor, to the Secretary of the Department, not later than the division of the Michaelmas Term preceding the examination. He will obtain the approval of his proposed scheme of examination, and of the title of

---

[1] No candidate shall offer Paper 13 if he or she has previously offered either Paper 9 in Part I B of the Philosophy Tripos or the subject Experimental Psychology in Part I B of the Natural Sciences Tripos.

his dissertation, by the Department not later than the last day of the Michaelmas Term.

Dissertations

A dissertation must contain full references to any sources used in its composition, and must be of not less than 6,000 words and not more than 10,000 words in length, including footnotes and appendices but excluding any bibliography; one page of statistical tables will be regarded as equivalent to half a page of text of the same size. Each candidate must submit his dissertation through his Tutor to the Secretary of the Department not later than the end of the first week of the Full Easter Term in which the examination is to be held. Each dissertation must bear a motto but not the candidate's name and must be accompanied by (*a*) a sealed envelope bearing the same motto outside and containing the name of the candidate and his College, (*b*) a brief synopsis on a separate sheet of paper of the contents of the dissertation, and (*c*) a certificate signed by the candidate that it is his own original work. The Examiners may examine the candidate *viva voce* on the subject of his dissertation and on the general field of knowledge within which it falls, and require him to resubmit his dissertation in typescript if in their opinion the original work submitted is not sufficiently legible.

Preliminary Examination

There is a Preliminary Examination for Part II of the Tripos.

The examination will consist of Papers 1, 2, and 5–16 of Part II of the Tripos. A candidate who has previously obtained honours in Part I of the Archaeological and Anthropological Tripos, and has offered Paper 7, must offer Paper 1, and three papers chosen from among Papers 5–16. Any other candidate must offer Papers 1 and 2, and two papers chosen from among Papers 5–16, provided that a candidate who has offered either Paper 9 in Part IB of the Philosophy Tripos or the subject Experimental Psychology in Part IB of the Natural Sciences Tripos shall not offer Paper 13.

THEOLOGY AND RELIGIOUS STUDIES

In this subject there are courses of study followed by candidates for:

The *Theological and Religious Studies Tripos*, which consists of two Parts.

The *Preliminary Examination* for Part II of the Theological and Religious Studies Tripos (p. 457).

The *Ordinary Examinations* for the Ordinary B.A. Degree: the Ordinary Examination in Theology and Religious Studies I, and the Ordinary Examination in Theology and Religious Studies II.

The *Diploma in Theology* (p. 463).

The *M.Phil. Degree* (p. 470).

In all the relevant examinations the Examiners will in general use the following texts of the Bible:

Hebrew: *Biblia Hebraica Stuttgartensia*.

Greek: Nestle/Aland text (26th edition).

English: Revised Standard Version.

The Theological and Religious Studies Tripos

Note: The Faculty holds a one-day conference each year, in which senior and junior members try to give sixth-formers an idea of what reading Theology and Religious Studies involves; teachers are also welcome.

The courses in this Tripos are intended not only for prospective ordinands and teachers, but for all who are interested in asking basic questions about human existence and studying objectively answers that have been given. Emphasis is laid on the Jewish–Christian tradition but the Hindu and Buddhist religions are also studied. A wide variety of intellectual disciplines, philosophical, historical, literary, and linguistic, is involved, and school subjects which provide training in these are helpful as a preparation for the course.

The Theological and Religious Studies Tripos consists of two Parts. The Part I course is designed to be an introduction to theological and religious study with a high degree of flexibility, to provide both for those who have some background in the subject (e.g. at 'A' level) and for those who have none, and also for a wide variety of interests, biblical, historical, philosophical and comparative, as well as a mixture of any or all of these. The Part II course normally takes two years, and is designed to allow the exploration of areas not covered in Part I, or specialization in areas which have proved to be of particular interest. There is no single compulsory paper, but there are some restrictions on the choice of papers which a student may make, which are designed to avoid overlaps with similar papers in Part II or elsewhere.

Students who spend more than one year in the Faculty will be required to study either Greek or Hebrew or Sanskrit for at least one year and to offer it as an examination subject, so as to equip themselves for the detailed study of Scriptural texts of at least one world-religion. The regulations require that all candidates for Part II (except those who take it in one year) must either offer a language paper along with their other Part II papers or have been specifically exempted from this requirement, either by passing in a language paper in Part I or in the Preliminary Examination or by presenting evidence of satisfactory performance in one of the prescribed languages in an examination elsewhere. Thus, no students will be required to offer a language paper in their first year. But for all who intend to continue with Theology and Religious Studies (rather than, say, doing Part I before changing to another Tripos) this will be the logical point at which to undertake elementary language study, and most Directors of Studies will probably want to urge their students to do this. They will then have this skill available for use and development in their remaining years and will also be spared an additional burden in their second or third year.

Affiliated Students and those who transfer from another Faculty to read Theology and Religious Studies for two years will take Part II as indicated above, but they will have to include at least one biblical paper in their choices for Part II. They will also be well advised (unless they can gain exemption on the basis of work done elsewhere) to begin the study of a prescribed language at once and to offer a language paper in the Preliminary Examination.

Those who transfer from another Faculty to read Theology and Religious Studies for one year will be able either to take Part I or to take Part II in a shortened form. They will not be permitted to offer a dissertation or a paper which they have already offered in another Tripos or two overlapping papers. Candidates who transfer from the Faculties of Classics or Oriental Studies will not be able to offer an elementary language paper in a language in which they have previously sat for Honours.

The B.A. Degree can be obtained by taking honours in Parts I and II, or in any one Part, together with a Part of another Tripos.

Prospective candidates with no Greek, Hebrew or Sanskrit who intend to read Theology and Religious Studies for three years are advised to begin the study of one language before coming into residence. Introductory courses in Greek and Hebrew are provided in the Long Vacation Residence (July–August). Those who intend to begin the study of theology and religious studies in October may care to avail themselves of these, for, although classes are provided for beginners starting in October, the first year's work will be more profitable for those with some knowledge of at least one of the languages. In addition, they should read some books on the background to the study of religion, the methods of theology and the grounds for belief, and also on the background and the main lines of biblical history. Directors of Studies will give advice on particular books.

A Preliminary Examination is set at the end of the first year of the two years that may be spent preparing for Part II; it covers part of the syllabus, and affords a test of progress.

The M.Phil. Degree in Theology is an advanced course of study leading to an examination at the end of two years. A dissertation is also required. The M.Phil. in Theology is divided into six sections, corresponding to the main branches of Theology, and students may not offer more than one section. Application is made in the first instance to the Board of Graduate Studies.

For those who can spend only one year on an advanced course, a course leading to a Diploma in Theology is available. The syllabus is very similar to that for the M.Phil., but without the dissertation.

Theological and Religious Studies Tripos

Part I

A candidate for Part I should choose papers as follows:

(*a*) one paper must be a biblical paper (Papers 4–7);
(*b*) one paper must be a non-biblical paper (Papers 8–14);
(*c*) only one paper may be chosen from Group A, unless one is offered as an additional paper.

Among the biblical papers, Paper 4 is designed as a general introduction to the Bible for those who will probably specialize in other disciplines and its content will overlap to some extent with Papers 5 and 7. It is therefore not possible to offer Paper 4 together with either of these two papers. The papers available at this stage are divided into two groups, A (elementary language papers) and B (other introductory papers), as follows:

Group A

1. Hebrew I (Elementary Hebrew)

This paper contains (i) questions on Hebrew grammar, and (ii) passages for translation, linguistic comment, pointing, and retranslation from a portion or portions of the Old Testament.

In **1990**: Genesis xxxvii, xl–xlv.

2. New Testament Greek

This paper contains passages for translation from one or more portions from the Gospels, together with questions on the grammar of Hellenistic Greek. Copies of a Greek lexicon will be available in the examination for those who wish to make use of them.

In **1990**: Mark ix. i–xvi. 8.

3. Sanskrit

This paper contains (i) questions on Sanskrit grammar, and (ii) passages for translation, and for linguistic and exegetical comment from a portion or portions of the Hindu and Buddhist scriptures which the Board will prescribe.

In **1990**: *Kaṭhopaniṣad* chapters 1–3 (in J. N. Rawson, *The Katha Upanisad*, Oxford, 1934); *Mahābhārata* 2.66–68 (Poona edition, 1933–66). *Bhagavadgītā* ch. 12 with the commentaries of Śaṃkara and Rāmānuja (vrs. 1–6) (G. S. Sadhale ed., Bombay, 1935–38). *Buddhacarita* 3 (E. H. Johnston ed., Calcutta, 1935).

Group B

4. Biblical literature and theology

This paper introduces biblical literature and theology through a study of selected portions of the Old and New Testaments.

In **1990**: I Samuel; Psalms ii, xxix, xlviii, lxxiv, lxxviii, lxxx, lxxxi, xciii, xcvii, xcviii, cxix, cxxxii, cxxxv, cxxxvii, cxxxix; Mark.

5. Introduction to the Old Testament

This paper is a general introduction to critical Old Testament study, and requires a study of the outlines of the history and the history of the religion of Israel, from the settlement in Canaan to the end of the Persian period inclusive, with special reference to a selection of psalms and a portion or portions of the historical books in English as prescribed by the Board.

In **1990**: I Samuel; Psalms ii, xxix, xlviii, l, lxxiv, lxxviii, lxxx, lxxxi, xciii, xcvii, xcviii, cxix, cxxxii, cxxxv, cxxxvii, cxxxix.

6. Introduction to Judaism from 333 B.C. to A.D. 135

Candidates are required to show a general knowledge of the historical and political background and of such subjects as intertestamental literature; Philo; Josephus; Qumran; apocalyptic; Pharisaism and the early rabbis; biblical exegesis. The Board may from time to time prescribe particular texts for study.

In **1990**: II Esdras iii–xiv; the Wisdom of Solomon vi–xii; Ecclesiasticus xliv–li; I Maccabees i–ii; the Genesis Apocryphon; the Psalms of Solomon xvii, xviii; the Eighteen Benedictions. For the last three texts see G. Vermes, *The Dead Sea Scrolls in English* (3rd edn. Penguin books, 1987), pp. 252–9, H. F. D. Sparks (ed.), *The Apocryphal Old Testament* (Oxford, 1984), pp. 676–82; E. Schürer, G. Vermes, F. Millar and M. Black (ed.), *The History of the Jewish People in the Age of Jesus Christ*, vol. 2 (Edinburgh, 1979), pp. 455–63.

7. Christian origins: the emergence of the primitive Christian communities

This paper contains questions on the life, worship, and beliefs of the early Christian communities. Special attention will be given to such books of the New Testament as the Board may prescribe.

In **1990**: Matthew; 1 Corinthians.

8. Christian life and thought to 325

This paper includes questions on such subjects as: the development, organization, thought, art, and worship of the early church, its relations with the state, its mission, and its contacts with philosophy. Candidates will be expected to show knowledge of the literary and archaeological evidence for the period.

Candidates will be required to answer a question requiring comment on extracts from contemporary sources which will be drawn primarily but not exclusively from books prescribed by the Board.

In **1990**: J. Stevenson, *A New Eusebius* revised by W. H. C. Frend, London, 1987; H. Bettenson, *The Early Christian Fathers* (London, 1956, repr. 1958).

9. Christian culture in the western world

The subject set for this paper in **1990** is 'Popular Piety in England, 1400–1600'. The Board may from time to time prescribe texts for special study.

In **1990**: *The Book of Margery Kempe* (ed. B.A.Windeatt, Penguin Books) pp. 41–125, 141–4, 178–193, 212–227; *English Mystery Plays* (ed. P.Happe, Penguin Books) pp. 332–342; *English Gilds* (ed. L.Toulmin Smith, Early English texts Society) pp. 19–24, 37–41, 114–15; *Norfolk Archaeology* Vol I pp. 114–125, 257–271; *Bury Wills* (ed. S.Tymms, Camden Society 1850) pp. 15–45, 118, 130–133, 147–8; John Myrc, *Festival* (EETS) pp. 1–5, 21–6, 114–132, 168–175, 269–272, 275–7: E.Hoskins, *Horae ... or Sarum and York Primers* (London, 1901) pp. 107–118, 123–128, 147–148, 153–6, 159–173; W.Maskell, *Monumenta Ritualia* (Oxford 3 ed. 1982) Vol. III pp. 275–305, 408–19; T.Silverstein *Medieval English Lyrics* (London, 1971) pp. 99–126; Frere and Kennedy; *Visitation Articles and Injunctions* (Alcuin Club) Vol. II pp. 34–43, 103–130, Vol. III 97–110; Sir W.H.Parker, *History of Long Melford* (London, 1873) pp. 70–73; *Sermons or Homilies Appointed to be read in Churches* (of Salvation, Good Works, Worthy Receiving, Against Peril of Idolatry part III, Rogation Week); Thomas Cranmer, *Works* Vol. II (Parker Society, ed. J.Cox 1844) pp. 118–25, 163–187 ; J.Ketley (ed.) *The Book of Common Prayer* (Parker Society) pp. 17–22, 76–99, 155–158, 193–202, 265–283; J.Foxe, *Acts and Monuments* (ed. Townsend and Cattley 1837–41) Vol. III pp. 584–600, Vol. V p. 254, Vol. VI pp. 676–703, 492–7, 556–7, Vol. VIII, pp. 223–6; P. Northeast (ed.), *Boxford Churchwardens Accounts 1530–1561* (Suffolk Records Society Vol. 23, 1982) pp. 1–76; George Gifford, *A Briefe discourse .. termed the Countrey Divinitie* (1612, English Heritage Reprint 1973) pp. 1–100.

10. Background to modern theology

This paper will contain questions on the following aspects of changes in patterns of Christian belief during the nineteenth and early twentieth centuries:

(i) the authority and inspiration of scripture;
(ii) social, scientific, and moral critiques of religion;
(iii) the treatment of Christian beliefs, symbols, and values in novels and other literature of the period.

The Board may from time to time prescribe texts for special study.

Prescribed in **1990**:

Section (i): S. T. Coleridge, *Confessions of an Inquiring Spirit*, ed. H. St J. Hart, London, 1956; D. F. Strauss, 'Introduction', *The Life of Jesus*, trans. G. Eliot, ed. P. C. Hodgson, London, 1973, pp. 39–92;

THEOLOGY AND RELIGIOUS STUDIES

Benjamin Jowett, 'On the Interpretation of Scripture', in *Essays and Reviews*, London, 1860; W. Robertson Smith, 'Bible', *Encyclopaedia Britannica*, 9th edn., Vol. III, London, 1875; A. F. Loisy, *The Gospel and the Church*, London, 1903; K. Barth, Preface to the first six editions of *The Epistle to the Romans*, Oxford, 1968, pp. 1–26.

Section (ii): L. Feuerbach, *The Essence of Christianity*, trans. G. Eliot, New York, Harper Torch Books, 1957, Chapter I; K. Marx, Texts on 'Alienation' and 'Historical Materialism', in D. McLellan, *The Thought of Karl Marx*, 2nd edn, London, 1980, pp. 123–33, 138–49; C. Darwin, *On the Origin of Species*, London, 1859, Chapter XV; *The Descent of Man*, London, 1871, Chapter XXI; F. Nietzsche, *Twilight of the Idols and the Anti-Christ*, trans. R. J. Hollingdale, London, 1957; E. Durkheim, *The Elementary Forms of the Religious Life*, trans. J. W. Swain, London, 1915, Introduction, Book I, Chapter I, Conclusion; C. G. Jung, 'Sigmund Freud', in *Memories, Dreams and Reflections*, London, 1963.

Section (iii): F. D. E. Schleiermacher, *On Religion: Speeches to its Cultured Despisers* (1821), trans. J.Oman, intro. R.Otto, New York, 1958; Alfred Tennyson, *In Memoriam* (1850), ed. C. Ricks in *The Poems of Tennyson*, London, 1969; George Eliot, *Middlemarch* (1872); G. Flaubert, *Three Tales* (1877), trans. R. Baldick, Penguin, 1961, especially 'A Simple Heart'; F. Dostoyevsky, *The Brothers Karamazov* (1880), trans. and intro. D. Magarshack, Penguin, 1958; R. Wagner, *Parsifal* (1882).

11. Introduction to metaphysics

This paper is divided into two sections: (i) elementary metaphysics, especially the theory of knowledge, and (ii) the nature and grounds of religious belief. Candidates are required to answer questions from both sections of the paper. The Board may from time to time prescribe texts for special study.

Prescribed in **1990**:

Descartes, *Meditations*; Thomas Aquinas, *Summa Theologiae* 1a, 2.

12. Introduction to ethics

This paper is divided into two sections: (i) elementary moral philosophy, and (ii) morality and religion. Candidates will be required to answer questions from both sections of the paper. The Board may from time to time prescribe texts for special study.

Prescribed in **1990**:

Mill, *Utilitarianism*; Joseph Butler, *Preface, Sermons 1–3 and Dissertation on Virtue*.

13. Problems of truth and dialogue in religion

This paper contains questions on problems arising out of the encounter of Christianity and the world religions, such as the principles and approaches of inter-religious dialogue and truth-claims in religion. The Board may prescribe texts for special study. None are prescribed in 1990.

14. Introduction to the study of religion

This paper will be an introduction to anthropological and sociological understandings of religion.

Papers to be offered for Part I

A candidate for Part I must offer:

(a) one paper chosen from among Papers 4–7;

(b) one paper chosen from among Papers 8–14;

and

(c) two other papers chosen from Groups A and B, of which not more than one may be chosen from Group A;

provided that

(i) a candidate who offers Paper 4 may not offer Paper 5 or Paper 7;

(ii) a candidate may, if he so wishes, offer a total of five papers, provided that the additional paper is from Group A;

(iii) a candidate who has previously obtained honours in the Classical Tripos or the Oriental Studies Tripos may not offer a paper from Group A in a language in which he has previously offered a paper in an Honours Examination.

Part II

In Part II a student will normally offer *either* six papers *or* five papers and a dissertation. (If he has not already secured exemption from the language requirement, he will have to offer in addition one paper from Group A.) The papers must be selected from the following lists, and at least *two* of them (at least one if a dissertation is offered) must be from the more advanced papers (Group D). A student who has reached a satisfactory standard in one of the prescribed languages may offer an elementary paper (from Group A) in a different language as an additional paper, but not as one of his six main papers.

Group C

15. Hebrew II

This paper contains (i) questions on Hebrew grammar, and (ii) passages for translation, linguistic and exegetical comment, pointing, and retranslation from portions of the Old Testament.

In **1990** and **1991**: *Either* Genesis xxxvii, xl–xlv *or* Psalms viii, xix, xxii, xxiii, li, civ; Deuteronomy v–xv; Judges vi–xviii.

16. The religion and literature of the Old Testament

In this paper knowledge will be required of the contents of the canonical books of the Old Testament and their background, and of the main lines of Old Testament religion and literature. The Board will prescribe a selected portion or portions of the Old Testament for special study.

In **1990**: Genesis i–xi; Isaiah i–xii.
In **1991**: Genesis i–xi; Jeremiah i–xxv.

17. New Testament texts in Greek

This paper contains passages for translation, exegesis, and critical comment from such New Testament books as the Board may prescribe. Questions may be set on language, style, and text and also on background, content, theology, and problems of interpretation.

In **1990**: John; Ephesians.
In **1991**: John; Philippians.

18. Jesus

This paper will be concerned with the theology of the evangelists, and with the problems of discovering the historical Jesus and his teaching. In addition to the four Gospels, candidates will be expected to have studied Acts (as evidence for the theology of Luke) and to be familiar with such biblical and extra-biblical materials as may throw light on the historical problems. Questions may be set on literary-critical and interpretative problems, background, and problems of method.

19. Paul and the early church

This paper is concerned with the life and thought of the early church, as evidenced by Acts, the New Testament epistles, and the book of Revelation. Special attention will be paid to the theology of Paul. There will be questions on historical, literary, and critical problems, but the emphasis will be on the theology of the writers. The Board may also prescribe a particular text or texts for special study.

In **1990** and **1991**: Romans.

20. Study of theology

This paper contains questions on theological method as illustrated by writings of selected Christian theologians from the patristic period to the present day. The Board may prescribe texts for special study. The paper is divided into three sections: Section A (patristic, medieval and Reformation texts), Section B (modern texts), and Section C (general questions). Candidates will be required to answer questions from all three sections.

Texts prescribed in **1990** and **1991**: Athanasius, *Contra Gentes* (transl. by R. W. Thomson, Oxford, 1971); Augustine, *Confessions*, Books III, IV and VII (tr. R. S. Pine-Coffin in the Penguin Classics, London 1961 and later reprints); Aquinas, *Summa Theologiae* 1a, 1 (*Summa Theologiae*, Vol. 1, *Christian Theology*, transl. and ed. T. Gilby [London, 1964]); J. Calvin, *Reply to Sadolet* (*LCC*, Vol. XXII [London, 1954]); pp. 219–56); D. Waterland, *The Importance of the Doctrine of the Holy Trinity* (1734; *Works*, Vol. V, ed. W. van Mildert [Oxford, 1823], chs. I–II); F. D. E. Schleiermacher, *The Christian Faith* (Edinburgh, 1928), paras. 164–72; K. Barth, Church Dogmatics I/1 (2 ed., Edinburgh, 1975), paras. 8–9; K. Rahner, *Foundations of Christian Faith* (London, 1978), chs. IV–V.

21 A. Christian life and thought to 461, with reference to a special topic
21 B. Christian life and thought from 325 to 461, with reference to a special topic

These papers include questions on such subjects as: the development, organization, thought, art, and worship of the early church, its relations with the state, its mission, and its contacts with philosophy. Candidates will be expected to show knowledge of the literary and archaeological evidence for the period.

Candidates will be required to answer a question requiring comment on extracts from contemporary sources which will be drawn primarily but not exclusively from books prescribed by the Board.

The Board will prescribe a special topic for these papers, but only candidates for Paper 21 B will be required to answer questions on the special topic.

In **1990** and **1991**: J. Stevenson, *A New Eusebius* (revised by W. H. C. Frend, London, 1987), *Creeds, Councils and Controversies* (revised W. H. C. Frend, 1989).

The special topic for **1990** and **1991** is 'The life, times, and thought of St Augustine of Hippo'.

The following texts are prescribed in **1990** and **1991**: *The Confessions* (tr. R. S. Pine-Coffin in the Penguin Classics. London, 1961 and later reprints). *The Enchiridion* (tr. A. C. Outler in the Library of Christian Classics, vol. VII, London, 1955, pages 337–412). Epistle 185 'The Correction of the Donatists' (in vol. III 'On the Donatist Controversy' of the *Works of Augustine*, ed. Marcus Dods, Edinburgh, 1872, pages 479–520). *On Nature and Grace* (in vol. IV 'The Anti-Pelagian Writings. Vol. I', ed. Marcus Dods, Edinburgh, 1872, pp. 233–308).

22. Christian life and thought, 950–1300

This paper is concerned with Christian life, thought, art, and institutions in the central middle ages. There will be questions on such subjects as: the development of ecclesiastical institutions, especially the papacy; the religious orders, and the schools; society and its aspirations – celibacy and the pursuit of perfection; love and marriage; knightly and crusading ideas; Christian art and thought; popular religious movements; the twelfth-century renaissance and scholasticism; dissent and heresy.

The Board may also prescribe texts for special study.

In **1990** and **1991**: *The Epistolae vagantes of Pope Gregory VII*, ed. and trans. H. E. J. Cowdrey, OMT, 1972; Anselm, *Cur Deus Homo*; Eadmer, *Life of St Anselm*, ed. and trans. R. W. Southern, NMT, 1962, repr. OMT, 1980; *The Letters of Abelard and Heloise*, trans. B. Radice, Penguin Classics (1974); Peter Abelard, *Ethics*, ed. and trans. D. E. Luscombe, OMT, 1971; *The Life of Christina of Markyate*, ed. and trans. C. H. Talbot, Oxford, 1959; Walter Daniel, *The Life of Ailred of Rievaulx*, ed. and trans. F. M. Powicke, NMT, 1950, repr. OMT, 1978; *Magna Vita S. Hugonis: The Life of St Hugh of Lincoln*, ed. and trans. D. L. Douie and D. H. Farmer, 2 vols., NMT, 1961–2, repr. OMT, 1985; *Scripta Leonis, Rufini et Angeli, sociorum S. Francisci*, ed. and trans. R. B. Brooke, OMT, 1970; St Thomas Aquinas, *Summa Theologiae*, select passages: 1a. 1–11, 44–64; 1a 2ae. 1–5; 2a 2ae. 171–89; 3a. 66–83; Dante, *Commedia, Inferno*. (NMT = Nelson's Medieval Texts. OMT = Oxford Medieval Texts.)

23. Christian life and thought, 1500–1689

This paper includes questions on such subjects as: the political, economic, social, and intellectual background to the Reformation; humanism and the 'new divinity'; the advance of the 'new religion' with special reference to the principal persons and centres of 'protestant' activity; biblical authority, ministry, and sacraments; the 'radical' Reformation; the Catholic Reformation, the Council of Trent, and post-Tridentine Catholicism; lollardy and Luteranism in England; the Reformation in England and Scotland; puritanism and the Laudian revival; the Commonwealth and Protectorate; the Restoration settlement, 1662–65; nonconformity and the rise of dissent; the Catholic problem, the revolution of 1688–89, and the non-juring schism; religious toleration and its consequences.

Candidates will be required to answer a question requiring comment on extracts from contemporary sources which will be drawn primarily but not exclusively from books prescribed by the Board.

In **1990** and **1991**: J. Chandos (ed.), *In God's name: Examples of Preaching in England 1532–1662* (London, 1971); A. G. Dickens and D. Carr (eds.), *The Reformation in England to the Accession of Elizabeth I* (Documents of Modern History, London, 1967); H. J. Hillerbrand (ed.), *The Reformation in its own words* (London, 1964); J. C. Olin, *The Catholic Reformation: Savonarola to Loyola* (New York, 1971); Parker Society Edition, *Liturgies of Edward VI* (London, 1884); R. L. De Molen (ed.), *Erasmus* (Documents of Modern History, London, 1973); E. G. Rupp and B. Drewery (eds.), *Martin Luther* (Documents of Modern History, Arnold, 1970); G. R. Potter (ed.), *H. Zwingli* (Documents of Modern History, Arnold, 1978); H. J. Schroeder (ed.), *The Canons and Decrees of the Council of Trent* (New York, 1941); T. Corbishley (ed.), *The Spiritual Exercises of St Ignatius Loyola* (Anthony Clark, 1973); Teresa of Avila, *Autobiography* (Penguin pbk); Blaise Pascal, *Provincial Letters* (Penguin pbk); G. R. Potter and M. Greengrass (eds.), *John Calvin* (*Documents of Modern History*, London, 1983).

24. Christian life and thought since 1800

This paper includes questions on such subjects as: the history of the established and non-established churches in Great Britain; the relationship of church and state in Europe; ultramontanism, liberalism, and modernism in the Roman Catholic church; the churches and social questions; the missionary and ecumenical movements; the history of theological thought; the impact of biblical criticism on the church; the relationship between theology and the sciences; and the problems posed by secularization. Particular emphasis will be laid on the history of Christian life and thought in Great Britain.

Candidates will be required to answer a question requiring comment on extracts from contemporary sources which will be drawn primarily but not exclusively from books prescribed by the Board.

In **1990** and **1991**: H. Bettenson, *Documents of the Christian Church* (2nd edition), xi, nos. 7–12, xiii, xiv (London, 1967); A. O. J. Cockshut, *Religious Controversies of the Nineteenth Century* (London, 1966); S. Z. Ehler and J. B. Morrall, *Church and State through the Centuries*, vii and viii (London, 1954); R. P. Flindall, *The Church of England, 1815–1948* (London, 1972); J. Macquarrie, *Contemporary Religious Thinkers* (London, 1968); B. M. G. Reardon, *Religious Thought in the Nineteenth Century* (Cambridge, 1966); D. M. Thompson, *Nonconformity in the Nineteenth Century* (London, 1972).

25. Philosophical theology

This paper will be divided into two sections: (i) philosophical problems of theism, as illustrated and discussed in prescribed texts, and (ii) problems

THEOLOGY AND RELIGIOUS STUDIES 453

in philosophical theology including: the existence of God; analogical speech about God; the divine attributes; divine action and the relation of God to the world; and the problem of evil. Candidates will be required to answer questions from both sections of the paper.

In **1990** and **1991**: Plato, *Republic*, Book v, 475e4 to end of Book vii, in F. M. Cornford's translation, from p. 178: 'And whom do you mean by the genuine philosophers?'; D. Hume, *Dialogues Concerning Natural Religion*, ed. N. Kemp Smith (Oxford, 1935); I. Kant, *Critique of Pure Reason*, transl. by N. Kemp Smith (London, 1934), *Dialectic*, Book II, ch. iii, sections 4–7 and Appendix (pp. 500–70).

26. The comparative study of religions I

This paper contains questions on topics as they occur in one or more non-Christian religions. Reference to Christianity may be included. The Board may from time to time prescribe texts for special study.

In **1990** and **1991**: *Either* (*a*) The religious traditions of India: Hinduism and Buddhism. *Or* (*b*) Topics in medieval and modern Judaism.

Group D

27. Hebrew III

This paper will contain passages for translation, with grammar and exegesis, from portions of the Old Testament, including some parts of the prophetic and poetic books; unseen translation; composition, and pointing, not necessarily from the prescribed portions. Candidates will be required to offer either unseen translation or composition, but may not offer both. A candidate may not offer in Paper 27 any prescribed text that he has already offered in Paper 1 in Part I.

In **1990**: Deuteronomy v–xv; II Samuel xi. 1–xix. 9; Judges vi–xviii; Isaiah i–vii; Psalms viii, xix, xxii, xxiii, li, civ.

In **1991**: Deuteronomy v–xv; II Samuel xi.1–xix.9; Judges vi–xviii; Isaiah i–vii; Psalms xxiv, xlvi, lxxxii, xci, cvii, cxlv.

28. Old Testament and intertestamental studies

In **1990** and **1991**, candidates will be required to offer *two* of the following subjects:

(*a*) Old Testament theology;
(*b*) Intertestamental literature;
(*c*) Text, canon, and versions;
(*d*) Ancient Near Eastern texts in their relation to Old Testament studies;
(*e*) Biblical archaeology.

Candidates who offer Paper 29 may not offer subject (*b*) in this paper.

29. Jewish history, thought, and religion, 333 B.C.–A.D. 235, with reference to a special topic

The Board will prescribe a special topic for this paper and they may also prescribe texts for special study.

The special topic is:

In **1990**: Jewish Biblical Interpretation.

In **1990** the prescribed texts for the special topic are: *The Nash Papyrus* (F.C. Burkitt, 'The Hebrew Papyrus of the Ten Commandments', *Jewish Quarterly Review* xv (1903), 392–408; Philo, *On the Decalogue* (tr. F.H. Colson, *Philo*, vii (Loeb Classical Library, 1927), pp. 2–75); Exodus xx. 1–17 in the Targum of MS. Neofiti I (A. Díez Macho, *Neophyti I*, ii (1970), pp. 464–7; Mekhilta, Yithro, Bahodes iv end–vii (J.Z. Lauterbach, *Mekita de-Rabbi Ishmale*, ii (1933), pp. 227–66).

In **1991**: The Qumran Texts.

In **1991** the prescribed texts for the special topic are: The Manual of Discipline (1QS); the War Scroll (1QM) i.1–ii.14; The Temple Scroll (11QTemple) cols. ii, xvii–xxii, lvi–lx, Psalm 151; Apostrophe to Zion; David's Compositions; the Nahum Commentary (4Q 169).

See G. Vermes, *The Dead Sea Scrolls in English* (3rd Edn., London, 1987), pp. 61–80, 105–7, 129–30, 132–5, 150–54, 208–9, 212–4, 279–82.

30. New Testament exegesis

This paper contains passages for exegesis and critical comment from such portions of the New Testament in Greek as the Board shall prescribe. Questions may be set on background, content, theology, and also on problems of interpretation, translation, and text.

In **1990** and **1991**: Matthew xvi: 13–28; xviii: 1–20; 1 Corinthians x–xiv; 1 Timothy i–iii; Didache vi. 3–xv. 4.

31. Biblical authority and interpretation since 1800

This paper contains questions on the development of biblical criticism since 1800, the uses of scripture in theology, and the impact of new theories of interpretation on theology and the understanding of biblical authority.

32. Doctrine: special paper

The Board may from time to time prescribe texts for special study.

In **1990** and **1991**: The theology of the Church and sacraments in the twentieth century.

33. A special subject or subjects in Christian life and thought

For this paper the Board will prescribe one or two special subjects. With each of the subjects texts for special study will be specified.

THEOLOGY AND RELIGIOUS STUDIES

In **1990** and **1991**: *Either* (*a*) Thomas Cranmer as Archbishop and Liturgical Reformer; *Or* (*b*) The Churches and social problems in Britain from 1883 to 1914.

34. A subject or subjects in Christian life and thought specified by the Faculty Board

For this paper the Board will from time to time prescribe one or two subjects, and they may also prescribe texts for special study.

In **1990**: *Either* (*a*) Oxford and Cambridge: the University in the late Middle Ages. *Or* (*b*) The modern dialogue of science and theology.

In **1991**: *Either* (*a*) Religious Thought in Oxford and Cambridge 1350–1714; *or* (*b*) The modern dialogue of science and theology.

35. Philosophy, religion, and ethics

This paper is divided into two sections: (i) human nature, religion, and human destiny: concepts of transcendence; belief, practice, and commitment; religious language; the soul, freedom, and immortality, and (ii) Christian ethics: its form and content; its values and goals, both personal and social; and criticisms of Christian ethics. Candidates will be required to answer questions from both sections of the paper.

36. The comparative study of religions II

This paper will contain questions on topics as they occur in Christianity, and one or more other religions. The Board may prescribe texts for special study.

In **1990** and **1991**: *Either* (*a*) The self and salvation in Indian and Western thought. *Or* (*b*) Worship in Judaism and Christianity.

37. Religion, ritual, and ideology (Paper 2 in Social Anthropology of Part II of the Archaeological and Anthropological Tripos)

This paper will include questions on religion and magic, witchcraft, totemism, prophetic cults, mythology, and cosmology; morality in relation to ritual practices and beliefs; comparative religion; symbolism and thought.

Papers to be offered for Part II

(1) When a candidate has taken Part I of the Tripos, or of another Tripos, in his first year or if he is an affiliated student, he must offer for Part II:

(*a*) one paper from Group A.

Candidates may be exempted from this requirement if they have satisfied the Examiners in a paper from Group A in a previous examination or if they produce evidence that they have done work of a satisfactory standard in Greek *or* Hebrew *or* Sanskrit.

(b) *either* (1) two papers chosen from Group D;
  or (2) one paper chosen from Group D *and* a dissertation on a topic approved by the Faculty Board;

and (c) four papers chosen from Groups C and D;

provided that

(i) a candidate who has not obtained honours in Part I must offer under (c) at least one paper chosen from among Papers 16, 18, and 19;

(ii) a candidate who has offered Paper 1 in Part I may not offer Paper 15;

(iii) a candidate who has offered Paper 8 in Part I may not offer Paper 21 A;

(iv) a candidate may not offer both Paper 15 and Paper 27;

(v) a candidate may not offer both Paper 21 A and Paper 21 B;

(vi) a candidate may, if he so wishes and if he has been exempted from the requirement to offer a paper from Group A, offer a total of seven papers (or six papers and a dissertation), choosing one additional paper from Group A other than one from which he has been exempted;

(vii) a candidate may not offer a paper which he has already offered in another Tripos.

(2) When a candidate takes Part II of the Tripos in the year after he has obtained honours in another Honours Examination, he must offer:

either (a) four papers chosen from Groups C and D;

or (b) one paper chosen from Group A and three papers chosen from Groups C and D;

provided that

(i) a candidate may not offer both Paper 15 and Paper 27;

(ii) a candidate may not offer both Paper 21 A and Paper 21 B;

(iii) a candidate may not offer a paper which he has already offered in another Tripos;

(iv) a candidate who has previously obtained honours in the Classical Tripos or the Oriental Studies Tripos may not offer a paper from Group A in a language in which he has previously offered a paper in an Honours Examination.

If a candidate intends to submit a dissertation for Part II, he must give notice of his intention and of his proposed topic to the Secretary of the Faculty Board not earlier than the beginning of the Easter Term and not later than the first Monday of the Full Michaelmas Term next preceding the examination. The Secretary must inform him as soon as possible, and in any case before the end of Full Michaelmas

THEOLOGY AND RELIGIOUS STUDIES

Term, whether his topic has been approved by the Faculty Board. The dissertation shall be of not more than 10,000 words (inclusive of notes), and must be clearly marked with the author's name and College. The candidate must send his dissertation to the Secretary of the Faculty Board so as to reach him not later than the eighth day of the Full Term in which the examination is to be held, together with a written declaration that it is his own original work. The dissertation should show evidence of reading, judgement, and criticism, and of a power of exposition, but not necessarily of original research, and should give full references to sources used. It may be on any topic relating to the subject of any paper in any Part of the Tripos, but the Board may, when giving approval for a particular topic, impose the condition that a candidate who offers a dissertation on that topic may not offer a particular paper or a particular prescribed subject in a paper. It must be written in English unless the candidate has received permission from the Board to use some other specified language; a request for such permission must be made when the original notice of intention is given. The examiners have power, at their discretion, to require a candidate to resubmit his dissertation in typescript if in their opinion it is not reasonably legible, and to examine a candidate *viva voce* on his dissertation and on the general field of knowledge in which it falls.

Preliminary Examination for Part II of the Theological and Religious Studies Tripos

The papers are those in Groups A, B, and C of the Theological and Religious Studies Tripos.

A candidate must offer at least four papers, provided that he may not offer

(*a*) any paper from Group B which he has already offered in Part I of the Theological and Religious Studies Tripos;

(*b*) Paper 21 A if he offered Paper 8 in Part I of the Theological and Religious Studies Tripos;

(*c*) Paper 5 or Paper 7 if he also offers Paper 4;

(*d*) Paper 15 if he also offers Paper 1;

(*e*) Paper 21 A or Paper 21 B if he also offers Paper 8;

(*f*) both Paper 21 A and Paper 21 B.

In the case of any paper in which there is a choice of subjects a candidate must indicate in his entry which of the subjects he is offering.

The supplementary regulations for the papers in the Preliminary

Examination will be the same as the supplementary regulations for Papers 1–26 in the Tripos, except as stated below:

(i) Candidates for *Paper 15. Hebrew II* must offer only those texts which are prescribed for the Preliminary Examination.

(ii) Candidates for *Paper 16. The religion and literature of the Old Testament* must offer

  either (*a*) the full syllabus as prescribed for Tripos candidates but with a special study of a passage prescribed for for the Preliminary Examination in place of the passages prescribed for special study by candidates for the Tripos;

  or (*b*) a more restricted syllabus as follows: the religion and literature of the Old Testament with special reference to the prophets and in particular to the text prescribed under (*a*) above.

(iii) Candidates for *Paper 17. New Testament texts in Greek* must offer either or both of the set texts.

(iv) Candidates for *Paper 18. Jesus* and *Paper 19. Paul and the early church* will not be required to answer the questions requiring comment on or exegesis of the prescribed texts, one of which is compulsory for Tripos candidates.

(v) Candidates for *Paper 20. Study of theology* must offer a restricted syllabus consisting of the patristic, medieval, and Reformation texts, and general questions on theological method.

(vi) Candidates for the following papers must offer *either* the full syllabus as prescribed for Tripos candidates *or* a more restricted syllabus as follows:

Paper 22. Christian life and thought, 950–1300
Christian life and thought, 950–1200.

Paper 23. Christian life and thought, 1500–1689
Christian life and thought, 1500–1565.

Paper 24. Christian life and thought since 1800
Christian life and thought *either* (*a*) from 1800 to 1889 *or* (*b*) since 1889.

Paper 25. Philosophical theology
Philosophical problems of theism, as illustrated and discussed in prescribed texts.

(vii) Candidates for *Paper 26. The comparative study of religions I* must offer

  either (*a*) Introduction to the study of Hinduism and Buddhism;

or (*b*) Introduction to the life, thought, and worship of Modern Judaism.

In **1990** the following special subjects and prescribed texts have been selected.

1. Hebrew 1

Genesis xxxvii, xl–xlv.

2. New Testament Greek

Mark ix. i–xvi. 8.

3. Sanskrit

Kaṭhopaniṣad chapters 1–3 (in J. N. Rawson, *The Katha Upanisad*, Oxford, 1934); *Mahābhārata* 2.66–68 (Poona edition, 1933–66); *Bhagavadgītā* ch. 12 with the commentaries of Śaṃkara and Rāmānuja (vrs. 1–6) (G. S. Sadhale ed., Bombay, 1935–38). *Buddhacarita* 3 (E. H. Johnston ed., Calcutta, 1935).

4. Biblical literature and theology

I Samuel; Psalms ii, xxix, xlviii, l, lxxiv, lxxviii, lxxx, lxxxi, xciii, xcvii, xcviii, cxix, cxxxii, cxxxv, cxxxvii, cxxxix; Mark.

5. Introduction to the Old Testament

I Samuel; Psalms ii, xxix, xlviii, l, lxxiv, lxxviii, lxxx, lxxxi, xciii, xcvii, xcviii, cxix, cxxxii, cxxxv, cxxxvii, cxxxix.

6. Introduction to Judaism from 200 B.C. to A.D. 135

II Esdras iii–xiv; the Wisdom of Solomon vi–xii; Ecclesiasticus xliv–li; I Maccabees i–ii; the Genesis Apocryphon; the Psalms of Solomon xvii, xviii; the Eighteen Benedictions. For the last three texts see G. Vermes, *The Dead Sea Scrolls* (3rd edn., London 1987), pp. 252–9; H. F. D. Sparks (ed.), *The Apocryphal Old Testament* (Oxford, 1984), pp. 676–82; E. Schürer, G. Vermes, F. Millar and M. Black (eds.), *The History of the Jewish People in the Age of Jesus Christ*, vol. 2 (Edinburgh, 1979), pp. 455–63.

7. Christian origins: the emergence of the primitive Christian communities

Matthew; I Corinthians.

8. Christian life and thought to 325

J. Stevenson, *A New Eusebius* (revd. by W. H. C. Frend, London, 1957); H. Bettenson, *The Early Christian Fathers* (London, 1956, repr. 1958).

9. Christian Culture in the Western World
Popular piety in England, 1400–1600

Prescribed texts for special study: *The Book of Margery Kempe* (ed. B. A. Windeatt, Penguin Books) pp. 41–125, 141–4, 178–193, 212–227; *English*

Mystery Plays (ed. P. Happe, Penguin Books) pp. 332–342: *English Gilds* (ed. L. Toulmin Smith, Early English texts Society) pp. 19–24, 37–41, 114–15; *Norfolk Archaeology* Vol. I pp. 114–125, 257–271; *Bury Wills* (ed. S. Tymms, Camden Society 1850) pp. 15–45, 118, 130–133, 147–8; John Myrc, *Festial* (EETS) pp. 1–5, 21–26, 114–132, 168–175, 269–272, 275–7: E. Hoskins, *Horae ... or Sarum and York Primers* (London 1901) pp. 107–118, 123–128, 147–148, 153–6, 159–173; W. Maskell, *Monumenta Ritualia* (Oxford 3rd edn. 1882) Vol. III pp. 275–305, 408–19: T. Silverstein *Medieval English Lyrics* (London 1971) pp. 99–126; Frere and Kennedy, *Visitation Articles and Injunctions* (Alcuin Club) Vol. II pp. 34–43, 103–130, Vol. III pp. 97–110; Sir W. H. Parker, *History of Long Melford* (London 1873) pp. 70–73; *Sermons or Homilies Appointed to be read in Churches* (of Salvation, Good Works, Worthy Receiving, Against Peril of Idolatry part III, Rogation Week): Thomas Cranmer, *Works* Vol. II (Parker Society, ed. J. Cox 1844) pp. 118–25, 163–187 : J. Ketley (ed.) *The Book of Common Prayer* (Parker Society) pp. 17–22, 76–99, 155–158, 193–202, 265–283; J. Foxe, *Acts and Monuments* (ed. Townsend and Cattley 1837–41) Vol. III pp. 584–600, Vol. V p. 254, Vol. VI pp. 676–703, 492–7, 556–7, Vol. VIII pp. 223–6; P. Northeast (ed.) *Boxford Churchwardens Accounts 1530–1561* (Suffolk Records Society Vol. 23, 1982) pp. 1–76; George Gifford, *A Briefe discourse ... termed the Countrey Divinitie* (1612, English Heritage Reprint 1973) pp. 1–100.

10. Background to modern theology

Texts for special study: (i) S. T. Coleridge, *Confessions of an Inquiring Spirit*, ed. H. St. J. Hart, London, 1956; D. F. Strauss, 'Introduction', *The Life of Jesus*, trans. G. Eliot, ed. P. C. Hodgson, London, 1973, pp. 39–92; Benjamin Jowett, 'On the Interpretation of Scripture', in *Essays and Reviews*, London, 1860; W. Robertson Smith, 'Bible', *Encyclopaedia Britannica*, 9th edn., Vol. III, London, 1875; A. F. Loisy, *The Gospel and the Church*, London, 1903; K. Barth, Preface to the first six editions of *The Epistle to the Romans*, Oxford, 1968, pp. 1–26.

Texts for special study: (ii) L. Feuerbach, *The Essence of Christianity*, trans. G. Eliot, New York, Harper Torch books, 1957, Chapter I; K. Marx, Texts on 'Alienation' and 'Historical Materialism', in D. McLellan, *The Thought of Karl Marx*, London, 1971, pp. 123–33, 138–49; C. Darwin, *On the Origin of Species*, London, 1859, Chapter XV; *The Descent of Man*, London, 1871, Chapter XXI; F. Nietzsche, *Twilight of the Idols and the Anti-Christ*, trans. R. J. Hollingdale, London, 1957; E. Durkheim, *The Elementary Forms of the Religious Life*, trans. J. W. Swain, London, 1915, Introduction, Book I, Chapter I, Conclusion; C. G. Jung, 'Sigmund Freud', in *Memories, Dreams and Reflections*, London, 1963.

Texts for special study: (iii) F. D. E. Schleiermacher, *On Religion:*

THEOLOGY AND RELIGIOUS STUDIES

Speeches to its Cultured Despisers (1821), trans. J. Oman, intro. R. Otto, New York, Harper Torch books, 1958; Alfred Tennyson, *In Memoriam* (1850), ed. C. Ricks in *The Poems of Tennyson*, London, 1969; George Eliot, *Middlemarch* (1872); G. Flaubert, *Three Tales* (1877), trans. R. Baldick, Penguin, 1961, especially 'A Simple Heart'; F. Dostoyevsky, *The Brothers Karamazov* (1880), trans. and intro. D. Magarshack, Penguin, 1958; R. Wagner, *Parsifal* (1882).

Paper 11. Introduction to Metaphysics

Texts prescribed for special study in **1990** are:
Descartes. *Meditations*; Thomas Aquinas, *Summa Theologie* 1a, 2.

Paper 12. Introduction to Ethics

Texts prescribed for special study in **1990** are:
Mill. *Utilitarianism*; Joseph Butler, *Prefacce, Sermons 1–3 and Dissertation on Virtue*.

13. Problems of Truth and Dialogue

No texts for special study are prescribed for **1990**.

15. Hebrew II

Deuteronomy v–xv; Judges vi–xviii.

16. The religion and literature of the Old Testament

Jeremiah i–xxv.

17. New Testament texts in Greek

John; Philippians.

19. Paul and the early church

Romans.

20. Study of theology

Augustine, *Confessions*, Books III, IV and VII (tr. R.S. Pine-Coffin in the Penguin Classics, London 1961 and later reprints); Aquinas, *Summa Theologiae* 1a, o (*Summa Theologiae*, Vol. I, *Christian Theology*, transl. and ed. T. Gilby [London, 1964]); J. Calvin, *Reply to Sadolet* (*LCC*, Vol. XXII [London, 1954], pp. 219–56).

A candidate must show knowledge of these texts (in English), and must also answer at least one general question on theological method.

21 A. Christian life and thought to 461, with reference to a special topic

21 B. Christian life and thought from 325 to 461, with reference to a special topic

J. Stevenson, *A New Eusebius* (revd. by W.H.C. Frend, London 1987), *Creeds, Councils and Controversies* (revd. by W.H.C. Frend, London 1989).

The special topic for **1990** is 'The life, times and thought of St Augustine of Hippo'. Candidates for the Preliminary Examination need *not* answer questions on the special topic.

22. Christian life and thought, 950–1300

The Epistolae vagantes of Pope Gregory VII, ed. and trans. H. E. J. Cowdrey, OMT, 1972; Anselm, *Cur Deus Homo*; Eadmer, *Life of St Anselm*, ed. and trans. R. W. Southern, NMT, 1962, repr. OMT, 1980; *The Letters of Abelard and Heloise*, trans. B. Radice, Penguin Classics (1974); Peter Abelard, *Ethics*, ed. and trans. D. E. Luscombe, OMT, 1971; *The Life of Christina of Markyate*, ed. and trans. C. H. Talbot, Oxford, 1959; Walter Daniel, *The Life of Ailred of Rievaulx*, ed. and trans. F. M. Powicke, NMT, 1950, repr. OMT, 1978; *Magna Vita S. Hugonis: The Life of St Hugh of Lincoln*, ed. and trans. D. L. Douie and D. H. Farmer, 2 vols., NMT, 1961–2, repr. OMT, 1985; *Scripta Leonis, Rufini et Angeli, sociorum S. Francisci*, ed. and trans. R. B. Brooke, OMT, 1970; St Thomas Aquinas, *Summa Theologiae*, select passages: 1a, 1–11, 44–64; 1a 2ae.1–5; 2a 2ae.171–89; 3a. 66–83; Dante, *Commedia, Inferno*. Candidates may confine their attention to the period from 950 to 1200.

23. Christian life and thought, 1500–1689

J. Chandos (ed.), *In God's name: Examples of Preaching in England 1532–1662* (Hutchinson, 1971); A. G. Dickens and D. Carr (eds.), *The Reformation in England to the Accession of Elizabeth I* (Documents of Modern History, Arnold, 1967); H. Hillerbrand (ed.), *The Reformation in its own words* (SCM, Harper and Row, 1964); J. C. Olin, *The Catholic Reformation: Savonarola to Loyola* (Harper and Row, 1971); Parker Society Edition, *Liturgies of Edward VI* (C.U.P., 1844); R. L. De Molen (ed.), *Erasmus* (Documents of Modern History, Arnold, 1973); E. G. Rupp and B. Drewery (eds.), *Martin Luther* (Documents of Modern History, Arnold, 1970); G. R. Potter (ed.), *H. Zwingli* (Documents of Modern History, Arnold, 1978); H. J. Schroeder (ed.), *The Canons and Decrees of the Council of Trent* (New York, 1941); T. Corbishley (ed.), *The Spiritual Exercises of St St Ignatius Loyola* (Anthony Clark, 1973); Teresa of Avila, *Autobiography* (Penguin pbk); Blaise Pascal, *Provincial Letters* (Penguin pbk). Candidates may confine their attention to the period from 1500 to 1565.

24. Christian life and thought from 1800 to the present day

H. Bettenson, *Documents of the Christian Church* (2nd edn.), xi, nos. 7–12, xiii, xiv (London, 1967); A. O. J. Cockshut, *Religious Controversies of the Nineteenth Century* (London, 1966); S. Z. Ehler and J. B. Morrall, *Church and State through the Centuries*, vii and viii (London, 1954); R. P. Flindall, *The Church of England, 1815–1948* (London, 1972); J. Macquarrie, *Contemporary Religious Thinkers* (London, 1968); B. M. G. Reardon, *Religious Thought in the Nineteenth Century* (Cambridge, 1966); D. M. Thompson, *Nonconformity in the Nineteenth Century* (London, 1972). Candidates may confine their attention to *either* the period from 1800 to 1889, *or* the period from 1889 to the present day.

25. Philosophical theology

Plato, *Republic*, Book v, 475e4 to end of Book VII, in F. M. Cornford's translation, from p. 178: 'And whom do you mean by the genuine philosophers?'; D. Hume, *Dialogues Concerning Natural Religion*, ed. N. Kemp Smith (Oxford, 1935); I. Kant, *Critique of Pure Reason*, trans. N. Kemp Smith (London, 1934), *Dialectic*, Book II, ch. iii, sections 4–7 and Appendix (pp. 500–70).

26. The Comparative Study of Religions I

Either (a) Introduction to the Study of Hinduism and Buddhism;

Or (b) Introduction to the life, thought and worship of Modern Judaism.

Diploma in Theology *

To qualify for the award of a Diploma in Theology, a candidate must pursue the prescribed course of study and must pass the examination for the Diploma. He must also reside for three terms. A candidate for the Diploma must normally be a graduate and must have been admitted as a Graduate Student by the Board of Graduate Studies.

A candidate may not present himself for examination more than once and he may not be a candidate in the same term for any other University examination.

A candidate for admission to the course must apply to the Secretary of the Board of Graduate Studies normally not later than

---

* Lists of primary sources set for study and lists of recommended reading for Sections III–VI may be obtained from the Faculty Office.

31 July in the year before that in which he wishes his candidature to begin.

A candidate must pursue his studies in Cambridge under the direction of a Supervisor appointed by the Degree Committee of the Faculty of Divinity.

A candidate may be allowed by the Board of Graduate Studies to count all or part of the period during which he has been a candidate for the Diploma towards a course of research but, if he does so, he may not also be awarded the Diploma.

The scheme of examination consists of six sections, and an Essay paper common to all the sections (see p. 457). No candidate may present himself for examination in more than one section.

The sections are as follows:

Section I. *Old Testament and Hebrew*

1. Old Testament theology

This paper will include the theological ideas of the Old Testament Apocrypha. In preparing for this paper, the attention of students should be directed towards such subjects as the nature and methods of Old Testament theology, ideas of God, and Israelite monotheism; the formation of the Old Testament canon; the relationship between the Old and New Testaments; the relationship between the religion of Israel and the religions of other peoples of the ancient Near East; revelation, election, covenant, and universalism; holiness, righteousness, sin, and redemption; priestly and sacrificial institutions; the nature of prophecy; the kingdom of God, and the messianic hope; the Law; wisdom; the problem of suffering; life after death.

2. Old Testament general paper

This paper will be divided into two parts. The first will contain at least four essay questions on the texts prescribed for Paper 3. The second will contain at least ten questions on such subjects as the Hebrew language, and its relation to other Semitic languages; textual criticism, and the versions; archaeology and Old Testament study; Ugaritic and other ancient Near Eastern texts in their relation to Old Testament studies; inter-Testamental literature, including the Qumran scrolls. Candidates are required to attempt four questions, and to draw at least one from each part and at least two from the second.

3. A selected portion or portions of the Old Testament, including always some poetical texts.

This paper will contain questions on a selected portion or portions of the Old Testament in Hebrew concerning (*a*) translation; (*b*) grammar; (*c*) pointing; (*d*) textual criticism (questions involving a knowledge of the Septuagint translation of the prescribed texts may be included); (*e*) subject-matter. As an alternative to questions on some chapters of the selected portions of the Old Testament in Hebrew, candidates will be allowed to answer questions on either (i) a selected portion or portions of the Aramaic parts of the Old Testament, or (ii) a selected portion or portions of the Septuagint. The part of the paper concerned with (i) will contain questions on (*a*) translation; (*b*) grammar; (*c*) pointing; (*d*) textual criticism; (*e*) subject-matter. The part of the paper concerned with (ii) will contain questions on (*a*) translation; (*b*) grammar; (*c*) comparison of the Hebrew and Greek texts.

The selected portions of the Old Testament in **1990** will be: Exodus xvi–xxiv; Psalms cxx–cxxxii; Proverbs vii–ix; Song of Songs v–viii; and *either* Amos; *or* The Aramaic portions of Daniel; *or* The LXX of Isaiah xlv–lv.

4. Passages for translation from the Old Testament (Hebrew) generally, Hebrew composition, and pointing.

Candidates must offer all four papers and the Essay paper.

SECTION II. *New Testament*

1. General paper on the New Testament

This paper will contain questions on the background of the New Testament, on the authorship and date of the books of the New Testament, and on the circumstances in which they were written: on the general principles of the textual criticism of the New Testament; and on the outlines of the history of the formation of the canon. Some questions of a more advanced character will also be set on textual criticism and on the history of the canon, but candidates will not be expected to show detailed knowledge of more than one of those subjects.

2. **The Gospels in Greek, with special reference to a selected Gospel**

   For **1990**: John.

3. **The Acts, Epistles, and Apocalypse in Greek, with special reference to a selected portion**

   For **1990**: I–II Peter; James; Jude; Revelation.

4. **New Testament theology, with special reference to a selected subject**

   For **1990**: Church and Sacraments.

   Candidates must offer all four papers and the Essay paper.

Section III. *Church History*

1. History of the church, including doctrine, to A.D. 461
2. General church history, A.D. 461–1500
3. General church history, A.D. 1500–1800
4. General church history from 1800 to the present day.
5. **A subject in the early and patristic period**
   For **1990**: The rise and development of Monasticism up to A.D. 461.
6. **A subject in the medieval period**
   For **1990**: St Anselm of Canterbury.
7. **A subject in the Reformation and Counter-reformation period**
   For **1990**: John Calvin's Second Geneva Ministry, 1541–64.
8. **A subject in the modern period**
   For **1990**: The life and thought of William Temple, 1881–1944.

A candidate must offer the Essay paper and three papers as follows:

either (*a*) two papers chosen from Papers 1–4, and one paper chosen from Papers 5–8;

or (*b*) if the Degree Committee decide on the evidence supplied that he is already qualified in general knowledge of church history, one paper chosen from Papers 1–4 and two papers chosen from Papers 5–8. Application for such permission must be made not later than the end of the Michaelmas Term preceding the examination.

A candidate who in the judgement of the Degree Committee is not already qualified in general knowledge of the period covered in Paper 1 must offer Paper 1; a candidate whom they decide to be so qualified must not offer Paper 1. A candidate for this section must be informed by the Degree Committee as soon as his application is approved whether he must, or must not, offer Paper 1.

Section IV. *Dogmatics*

1. History of Christian doctrine to the close of the Council of Chalcedon

2. A subject from the patristic period in connexion with original documents

For **1990**: The Theology of Gregory of Nyssa.

3. A subject from the medieval period, i.e. A.D. 800–1500, in connexion with original documents

For **1990**: The Doctrine of the Trinity from Boethius to Aquinas.

4. History of Christian doctrine from Luther to the close of the Council of Trent

5. A subject from modern theology in connexion with original documents

For **1990**: The doctrine of the saving work of Christ in writings from 1870 to the present day (the ways in which theologians have represented the significance and continuing efficacy of the work of Christ in and for the individual, the community, and the world).

6. Selected portions of liturgies and service-books in their relation to the history of Christian doctrine

For **1990**: The action of the worshipping community as reflected in eucharistic and baptismal rites of the patristic, Reformation, and contemporary periods.

A candidate must offer the essay paper and three papers as follows:

either (*a*) Paper 1 and two other papers, provided that he offers at least one chosen from Papers 2, 3, and 5;

or (*b*) if the Degree Committee decide on the evidence supplied that he is already qualified in general knowledge of the subject covered in Paper 1, either or both Papers 4 and 6, and at least one paper chosen from Papers 2, 3, and 5.

A candidate for this section must be informed by the Degree Committee as soon as his application is approved whether he must, or must not, offer Paper 1.

SECTION V. *Philosophy of Religion and Christian Ethics*

1. The history of the philosophy of religion

2. Fundamental problems in the philosophy of religion

The subjects of Papers 1 and 2 are defined below. These subjects are to be studied historically and critically. Students are expected to have a general knowledge of the history of the subject, but alternatives to questions on the history before Descartes are set from the modern period.

The nature and grounds of religious belief: the functions of reason, feeling, and volition in producing faith; the theory of the relativity of knowledge as applied to man's knowledge of God; the different conceptions of divine revelation; the possibilities of revelation; reason and revelation.

The idea of God: the arguments for the existence of God; the value-judgement in religion; pluralism; pantheism; theism; divine personality and the absolute.

Theories of the universe: dualism; materialism; naturalism; idealism, law in relation to providence; prayer and miracle; the problem of evil.

Human nature: personality, freedom, immortality.

3. Christian ethics

   Types of moral theory, ancient and modern.
   Faith and morals.
   Christian ideals and motives.

4. *Either* (*a*) **Some major philosopher or school of philosophers or philosophical problem in its theological aspects**

   For **1990**: Time and eternity.

or (*b*) **A special subject in ethics**

   For **1990**: Sex and Gender.

A candidate must offer Papers 1–3, and the Essay paper. But the Degree Committee may permit a candidate who is already well qualified in general knowledge of the philosophy of religion to offer Paper 4(*a*) or Paper 4(*b*) in place of one of Papers 1–3. Application for such permission must be made not later than the end of the Michaelmas Term preceding the examination.

SECTION VI. *Christian Theology in the Modern World*

1. Church and society in England since 1800

   The relation between the Churches and civil society. History of the established and non-established Churches; the effects upon them of, and their reactions to, social change, including the conditions of life and labour, the development of political and economic democracy and the welfare state.

THEOLOGY AND RELIGIOUS STUDIES

2. Ecumenical movements since 1800

The history and theology of developments in inter-Church relations since 1800. This paper will also include some questions on the contribution of liturgical movements to closer relations between the Churches.

3. The Church's mission in the modern world

Developments since 1750 of Christian missionary thought and action in relation to non-Christian faiths and world-views. The paper will include two sections: (*a*) Missions and Society; (*b*) The Christian Faith and Other Faiths – A Study of Their Encounter. Candidates will be required to answer questions from both sections.

4. Religious thought since 1781

The impact of science, philosophy, and historical studies upon the understanding of the nature of religion and of theology.

5. Christian doctrine

The study in its setting in the twentieth century of *either* the thought of a selected theologian *or* the interpretation of a particular doctrine.

The subject of the examination in **1990** is: Eschatological hope in the twentieth century (Christian thought concerning the goal and outcome of human and cosmic history, in relation to other representations).

6. Christian ethics

The moral implications of Christian belief. The relation between Christian and other contemporary ethical attitudes with special reference to a select group of problems, such as crime and punishment, war and peace, sex and the family.

For **1990**: Sex and Gender.

Candidates must offer any three papers and the Essay paper.

AN ESSAY PAPER COMMON TO ALL THE SECTIONS

This paper contains subjects for an English essay, which are so chosen that each Section, for which there are candidates, is represented by at least three subjects. Candidates are directed to choose a subject cognate to their own section. No candidate may write on more than one subject.

The Examination in Theology for the M.Phil. Degree

To qualify for the award of the Degree of Master of Philosophy in Theology a candidate must pursue the prescribed course of study and must pass the examination for the Master of Philosophy. He must also reside for six terms. He must normally be a graduate and must have been admitted as a Graduate Student by the Board of Graduate Studies.

A candidate may not present himself for examination more than once and he may not be a candidate in the same term for any other University examination.

A candidate for admission to the course must apply to the Secretary of the Board of Graduate Studies normally not later than 31 July in the year before that in which he wishes his candidature to begin.

A candidate must pursue his studies in Cambridge under the direction of a Supervisor appointed by the Degree Committee of the Faculty of Divinity.

A candidate may be allowed by the Board of Graduate Studies to count all or part of the period during which he has been a candidate for the M.Phil. towards a course of research, but if he does so, he may not also be awarded the M.Phil. Degree.

The scheme of examination consists of six sections. No candidate may present himself for examination in more than one section. Every candidate is also required to submit a short thesis not exceeding 20,000 words, including footnotes, references, and appendices, but excluding bibliography. The six sections are as follows:

Section I. Old Testament and Hebrew

1. Old Testament theology

This paper includes the theological ideas of the Old Testament Apocrypha. In preparing for this paper, the attention of students is directed towards such subjects as the nature and methods of Old Testament theology, ideas of God, and Israelite monotheism; the formation of the Old Testament canon: the relationship between the Old and New Testaments; the relationship between the religion of Israel and the religions of other peoples of the ancient Near East; revelation, election, covenant, and universalism; holiness, righteousness, sin, and redemption; priestly and sacrificial institutions; the nature of prophecy; the kingdom of God, and the messianic hope; the Law; wisdom; the problem of suffering; life after death.

2. Old Testament general paper

This paper is divided into two parts. The first contains essay questions on the texts prescribed for Papers 3 and 5. The second contains questions on such subjects as the Hebrew language, and its relation to other Semitic languages; textual criticism, and the versions; archaeology and Old Testament study; Ugaritic and other ancient Near Eastern texts in their relation to Old Testament studies; inter-Testamental literature, including the Qumran scrolls.

3. A selected portion or portions of the Old Testament in Hebrew, including always some poetical texts.

This paper contains questions on a selected portion or portions of the Old Testament in Hebrew concerning (*a*) translation; (*b*) grammar; (*c*) pointing; (*d*) textual criticism (questions involving a knowledge of the Septuagint translation of the prescribed texts may be included); (*e*) subject-matter.

In **1990**: Exodus xvi–xxiv; Amos; Psalms cxx–cxxxii; Proverbs vii–ix; xxix–xxxi; Song of Songs.

In **1991**: Exodus xvi–xxiv; Amos; Psalms cxx–cxxxii; Proverbs vii–xii; Song of Songs.

4. Passages for translation from the Old Testament (Hebrew) generally, Hebrew composition, and pointing.

5. *Either* (*a*) Isaiah xl–lxvi in Hebrew,

   or   (*b*) Aramaic,

   or   (*c*) A selected portion or portions of the Septuagint, including both prose and poetical books of the canonical Old Testament.

5(*a*) contains questions on (i) translation; (ii) grammar; (iii) pointing; (iv) textual criticism (questions involving a knowledge of the Septuagint translation of Isaiah xl–lxvi may be included); (v) subject-matter.

5(*b*) contains questions on (i) translation; (ii) grammar; (iii) pointing; (iv) textual criticism (questions involving a knowledge of the Greek versions of the Aramaic portions of the Old Testament may be included); (v) subject-matter, and may contain a passage from an unspecified text for translation from Aramaic into English.

5(*c*) contains questions on (i) translation; (ii) grammar; (iii) comparison of the Hebrew and Greek texts; (iv) the history and criticism of the Septuagint Version.

The following Aramaic texts are prescribed for study in **1990** and **1991**: **The Aramaic portions of the Old Testament; Targum Neofiti on Genesis** xii–xiv, in A. Díez Macho, *Neophyti I*, i (1968); the Targum of Jonathan on I Samuel i–vi, in A. Sperber, *The Bible in Aramaic*, ii **(1959)**.

The selected portions of the Septuagint prescribed in **1990** and **1991** are: Exodus i–xii, Isaiah xlv–lv.

A candidate must offer all five papers in Section I.

Section II. New Testament

1. General paper on the New Testament

This paper contains questions on the background of the New Testament, on the authorship and date of the books of the New Testament, and on the circumstances in which they were written; on the general principles of the textual criticism of the New Testament; and on the outlines of the history of the formation of the canon. Some questions of a more advanced character are also set on textual criticism and on the history of the canon, but candidates are not expected to show detailed knowledge of more than *one* of those subjects.

2. The gospels in Greek, with special reference to a selected gospel

   The selected gospel in **1990**: John. In **1991**: Luke.

3. The Acts, Epistles, and Apocalypse in Greek, with special reference to a selected portion

   In **1990**: Revelation. In **1991**: 2 Corinthians.

4. New Testament theology, with special reference to a selected subject

   This paper will include passages for translation, explanation, or paraphrase.

   The selected subject in **1990**: Church and Sacraments. In **1991**: Death of Christ.

5. A selected portion or portions from (*a*) Philo, (*b*) Josephus

   This paper contains passages for translation from the prescribed portion or portions, with questions on relevant matters of language, history, or thought.

   The selected portion in **1990** and **1991** is: Philo, *de Opificio Mundi*.

6. A selected portion or portions of writings in Aramaic

This paper will be set on a portion or portions of one or more books in Aramaic. It will contain:
- (i) passages for translation from the prescribed portion or portions, with questions (mainly linguistic) on the passages set;
- (ii) general questions on the history of the language and of the Targums. Passages for retranslation may be set, but these will be optional.

The selected portion in **1990** and **1991**: Isaiah xlix–liii in *The Targum of Isaiah*, ed. J. F. Stenning (Oxford, 1949) and columns xx–xxi in *The Genesis Apocryphon of Qumran Cave 1*, ed. J. A. Fitzmyer (Rome, 2nd edn, 1971).

A candidate must offer Papers 1–4 and *either* 5 *or* 6 in Section II.

Section III. Church History

1. History of the church, including doctrine, to A.D. 461

2. General church history, A.D. 461–1500

3. General church history, A.D. 1500–1800

4. General church history, from 1800 to the present day
   A candidate must offer all four papers in Section III.

Section IV. Dogmatics

In **1990**:

1. History of Christian doctrine to the close of the Council of Chalcedon

2. A subject from the patristic period in connexion with original documents

    The subject in **1990**: The theology of Gregory of Nyssa.

3. A subject from the medieval period, i.e. A.D. 800–1500, in connexion with original documents

    The subject in **1990**: The doctrine of the Trinity from Boethius to Aquinas.

4. History of Christian doctrine from Luther to the close of the Council of Trent

5. A subject from modern theology in connexion with original documents

The subject in **1990**: The doctrine of the saving work of Christ in writings from 1870 to the present day (the ways in which theologians have represented the significance and continuing efficacy of the work of Christ in and for the individual, the community, and the world).

6. Selected portions of liturgies and service-books in their relation to the history of Christian doctrine

The prescribed subject in **1990** is: The action of the worshipping community as reflected in eucharistic and baptismal rites of the patristic, Reformation, and contemporary periods.

In Section IV a candidate must offer one paper from Papers 1, 4, and 6, one from Papers 2, 3, and 5, and two others chosen from Papers 1-6.

In **1991**:

1. The Doctrine of God.

2. The Doctrine of the person and work of Christ.

3. The Doctrine of the Holy Spirit.

4. A Special Subject in connexion wiith original documents.

5. A Special Subject in connexion with original documents.

6. Selected portions of liturgies and service books in their relation to the history of Christian doctrine.

In Section IV a candidate must offer four papers from Papers 1-6.

The prescribed subject in 1991 for Paper 4 is: Power, Kenosis and Sacrifice in Christian Theology; and in 1991 for Paper 5 is: Eschatological hope in the twentieth century (Christian thought concerning the goal and outcome of human and cosmic history in relation to other representations).

THEOLOGY AND RELIGIOUS STUDIES

Section V. Philosophy of Religion and Christian Ethics

1. The history of the philosophy of religion

2. Fundamental problems in the philosophy of religion

The subjects in these papers are to be studied historically and critically. Students will be expected to have a general knowledge of the history of the subject, but alternatives to questions on the history before Descartes will be set from the modern period.

   (a) *The nature and grounds of religious belief:* the functions of reason, feeling, and volition in producing faith; the theory of the relativity of knowledge as applied to man's knowledge of God; the different conceptions of divine revelation; the possibilities of revelation; reason and revelation.

   (b) *The idea of God:* the arguments for the existence of God; the value-judgement in religion; pluralism; pantheism; theism; divine personality and the absolute.

   (c) *Theories of the Universe:* dualism; materialism; naturalism; idealism; law in relation to providence; prayer and miracle; the problem of evil.

   (d) *Human nature:* personality; freedom; immortality.

3. Christian ethics

   (a) Types of moral theory, ancient and modern.

   (b) Faith and morals.

   (c) Christian ideals and motives.

4. *Either* (a) Some major philosopher or school of philosophers or philosophical problem in its theological aspects,

   In **1990** and **1991**: Time and eternity.

   or (b) A special subject in ethics.

   In **1990** and **1991**: Sex and Gender.

   A candidate must offer all four papers in Section V.

Section VI. Christian Theology in the Modern World

1. Church and society in England since 1800

The relation between the Churches and civil society. History of the established and non-established Churches; the effects upon them of, and their reactions to, social change, including the conditions of life and labour, the development of political and economic democracy and of the welfare state.

2. Ecumenical movements since 1800

The history and theology of developments in inter-Church relations since 1800. This paper will also include some questions on the contribution of liturgical movements to closer relations between the Churches.

3. The Church's mission in the modern world

Developments since 1750 of Christian missionary thought and action in relation to non-Christian faiths and world-views. The paper will include two sections: (*a*) Missions and Society; (*b*) The Christian Faith and Other Faiths – A Study of Their Encounter. Candidates will be required to answer questions from both sections.

4. Religious thought since 1781

The impact of science, philosophy, and historical studies upon the understanding of the nature of religion and of theology.

5. Christian doctrine

The study in its setting in the twentieth century of either the thought of a selected theologian or the interpretation of a particular doctrine. The Faculty Board will determine and announce which of the alternative subjects shall be the subject of the examination in a particular year.

The subject in **1990** and **1991** is: Eschatological hope in the twentieth century (Christian thought concerning the goal and outcome of human and cosmic history, in relation to other representations).

6. Christian ethics

The moral implications of Christian belief. The relation between Christian and other contemporary ethical attitudes with special reference to a select group of problems, such as crime and punishment, war and peace, sex and the family.

In **1990** and **1991**: Sex and Gender.

A candidate must offer four papers from Papers 1–6 in Section VI.

THEOLOGY AND RELIGIOUS STUDIES

Ordinary Examinations for the B.A. Degree

(i) The Ordinary Examination in Theology and Religious Studies I

The examination consists of any three papers chosen by the candidate from Group B of the papers specified for the Theological and Religious Studies Tripos.

A candidate who has obtained honours in, or has been allowed an Ordinary Examination on, Part I A of the Theological and Religious Studies Tripos should write to the Secretary of the Faculty Board to enquire which papers he may be allowed to offer.

(ii) The Ordinary Examination in Theology and Religious Studies II

The examination consists of Papers 16, 18, 19, 20, 21 A, 21 B, 22, 23, and 24 of the Theological and Religious Studies Tripos.

A candidate who has been classed in, or has been allowed an Ordinary Examination on, the Preliminary Examination for Part II of the Theological and Religious Studies Tripos must offer five papers. Every other candidate must offer three papers.

No candidate may offer Paper 21 A if he has previously offered Paper 8 in Part I of the Theological and Religious Studies Tripos. No candidate may offer both Paper 21 A and Paper 21 B.

A candidate who has obtained honours in, or has been allowed an Ordinary Examination on, Part I B or Part II of the Theological and Religious Studies Tripos, or the Preliminary Examination for Parts I B and II, under the old regulations, should write to the Secretary of the Faculty Board to enquire which papers he may be allowed to offer.

VETERINARY MEDICINE

The veterinary courses at Cambridge are divided into preclinical and clinical parts. The first three years[1] are concerned with the basic preclinical sciences and lead to the B.A. Degree. This part of the course is taught in the laboratories in Downing Street and lies mainly within the framework of the Medical Sciences Tripos (see p. 255 of the Handbook). The final examination for the degree of Bachelor of Veterinary Medicine (Vet.M.B.) is taken after clinical courses which extend over a further three years.

The Medical Sciences Tripos

Part I A

First-year veterinary students attend courses in Anatomy, Biochemistry, Medical Genetics, Medical Statistics, and Physiology, and take a written paper and a practical examination in Anatomy, Biochemistry and Physiology and a paper in Medical Genetics in Part I A of the Medical Sciences Tripos at the end of the year. There is in-course assessment of Medical Statistics in Part I B and Part II (General), Section 1. Students who have read Physiology in Part I A of the Natural Sciences Tripos take Pathology instead of Physiology.

Part I B

The courses available to second-year veterinary students offer an element of choice. Those students who, with the approval of their Directors of Studies, wish to study a single subject in depth during their third (Part II) year, will attend courses in Veterinary Anatomy, Pathology, Pharmacology, General Veterinary Physiology and Special Veterinary Physiology. They will be examined in all of these subjects in Part I B of the Medical Sciences Tripos at the end of their second year. At present the examinations consist of a practical examination and written paper in each of Pathology, Pharmacology, and Veterinary Anatomy, and General Veterinary Physiology, and the written paper in Special Veterinary Physiology. Alternatively, some students may prefer to spread the range of basic medical subjects over three years

---

[1] Two years for affiliated students, who must take the two-year course for Parts I A and I B of the Medical Sciences Tripos.

instead of two: these candidates postpone the courses in Pathology, and Pharmacology until their third year of residence but take a course of lectures in Animal Behaviour. For these students the subjects Pathology, Pharmacology, and Animal Behaviour are not examined in Part IB of the Tripos. Veterinary students taking the three-year option are not required to offer a second-year Elective Subject in Part IB.

Part II (General)

The choice of a Part II course in the third preclinical year will largely follow from the subjects taken in Part IB of the Medical Sciences Tripos. Those students who have postponed Pathology and Pharmacology from the second year will be required to offer both these subjects in Section I of Part II (General) of the Medical Sciences Tripos. They will also be required to attend a further course in Animal Behaviour and a course in an Elective Subject, and, with Pathology and Pharmacology, will be examined in these subjects at the end of the year. The list of Elective Subjects may change from one year to the next, but students will be informed of the choices available by the division of the Easter Term of their second year of residence. Section I of Part II (General) of the Medical Sciences Tripos will consist for veterinary students of one written paper and a practical examination in each of the subjects Pathology and Pharmacology, a short written paper in Animal Behaviour, and a written paper in an Elective Subject.

Students who have read Pathology and Pharmacology, in Part IB of the Medical Sciences Tripos are free to take any of the courses leading to Section II of Part II (General) of the Medical Sciences or to Part II of the Natural Sciences Tripos: the Clinical Veterinary Medicine Syndicate imposes no restrictions on candidates' freedom of choice. The courses for Part II of the Natural Sciences Tripos include Anatomy, Biochemistry, Genetics, Pathology, Pharmacology, Physiology, Psychology, and Zoology: full details of these courses may be found on p. 364 of the Handbook. Students who wish to read subjects from other Tripos examinations may in certain circumstances be allowed to do so, but they are strongly recommended to seek early advice from Tutors and Directors of Studies.

It should be noted that the choice between the two- and three-year courses for the Medical Sciences Tripos will normally be made at the end of the first year of residence, and that candidates who opt for the three-year course will be unable to read for any Part II other than Section I of Part II (General) of the Medical Sciences Tripos. On the other hand a student who chooses the two-year course and who subsequently regrets his decision should immediately consult his Tutor and Director of Studies. He may then be allowed to transfer to the three-year course, *provided he makes arrangements to do so before the middle of the Michaelmas Term.*

Transfers to Veterinary Medicine

In certain circumstances it is possible for students to transfer to Veterinary Medicine from other Triposes, but as places are in short supply it is essential for candidates considering the possibility of transfer to obtain early and detailed advice from their Colleges. Transfers to Veterinary Medicine read Part IA of the Medical Sciences Tripos in their second year and Part IB in their third year. If they have offered Physiology in Part IA of the Tripos in the first year they offer Pathology from Part IB of the Medical Sciences Tripos in Part IA instead of in Part IB.

Professional Training

The three years which follow the preclinical courses leading to degree of Bachelor of Arts (see Medical Sciences Tripos, p. 272, Natural Sciences Tripos, p. 347, as Affiliates, p. 13) are based on the Department of Clinical Veterinary Medicine at Madingley Road. During this time all students take the various parts of the Final Veterinary Examination which leads to the Vet.M.B. Degree.

Veterinary students, like medical students, must comply with certain standards laid down by the University in order to qualify for membership of the appropriate professional body. For veterinary students at Cambridge these standards are embodied in the First M.B. Examination, the Second Veterinary M.B. Examination and the Final Veterinary Examination, Parts I, II, and III.

The First M.B. Examination

Veterinary students normally gain exemption from the First M.B. Examination before they come up to Cambridge by obtaining appropriate passes in G.C.E. at 'O' and 'A' levels. Details of the examination and the exemption requirements may be found on p. 286 of the Handbook.

The Second Veterinary M.B. Examination

Candidates may obtain exemption from all subjects of the Second Veterinary M.B. Examinations by attaining the prescribed standards in the Medical or Natural Sciences Triposes. Details of the exemption requirements may be found on p. 281 of the handbook

The Final Veterinary Examination, Parts I, II, and III

No candidates are exempted from these examinations, nor may students take Parts II or III of the Final Veterinary Examination until they have successfully completed the previous Part or Parts. The examinations take place at the end of the Easter Term, and are held again at the beginning of the Michaelmas Term for candidates who may not have passed on previous occasions. The Vet.M.B. Degree is conferred on students who have passed Parts I, II, and III. It qualifies them for membership of the Royal College of Veterinary Surgeons and so to practise.

Part I

Part I of the Final Veterinary Examination is held at the end of the fourth academic year. A candidate for this examination must have satisfied the following requirements:

(a)* that he or she has passed all parts of the Second Veterinary M.B. Examination or has obtained exemption from the relevant parts by achieving the prescribed standards in Parts I A, I B, or Sections I or III of Part II (General) of the Medical Sciences Tripos or Natural Sciences Tripos, Transfers etc. can gain 2nd Vet. M.B. exemptions in Parts 1 A or 1 B of N.S.T.

(b) that he or she, since attaining the age of sixteen years, has spent a total of at least twelve weeks on a farm or farms working with the larger animals, and can produce the necessary certificates from the farmers concerned;

(c) that he or she has satisfied the requirements for the necessary certificates of attendance for the first three terms of clinical instruction.

* Requirement (a) must in practice be satisfied before the student starts the clinical courses.

The courses are divided into three sections as follows:

(i) *Animal Pathology and Microbiology*

This section includes morphological, histological, and clinical aspects of pathology, and the epidemiology, pathogenesis, laboratory diagnosis, and principles of control of viral, bacterial, and mycotic diseases.

(ii) *Animal parasitology*

This section includes helminth, arthropod and protozoal infections of domestic animals.

(iii) *Animal health and production*

This section includes the husbandry and management of healthy animals, including nutrition, livestock improvement, avian medicine, and housing.

The examination for each section consists of written papers, a practical examination and a *viva voce* examination. There are two three hour written papers for sections (i) and (iii) and one three hour written paper for section (ii).

Part II

Part II of the Final Veterinary Examination is held at the end of the fifth academic year. A candidate for this examination must have passed all sections of Part I of the Final Veterinary Examination and must have satisfied the requirements for the necessary certificates of attendance. The courses which lead to the examination cover public health (including meat and milk inspection), and the principles of diagnosis and therapeutics. The latter presents a common approach to medicine and surgery, with particular emphasis on the clinical examination of animals. The examination, now retitled *Veterinary Medicine* (preliminary clinical subjects), consists of two three-hour written papers, a practical examination, and a *viva voce* examination.

During this year students also complete the first three terms of a six-term course of instruction in the Principles and Practice of Animal Surgery. This part of the course is examined in Section (ii) of Part III of the Final Veterinary Examination at the end of the sixth academic year.

Part III

Part III of the Final Veterinary Examination is held at the end of the sixth academic year. A candidate for this examination (*a*) must have passed Parts I and II;

(*b*) must have satisfied the requirements for the necessary certificates of attendance;

(*c*) must produce written evidence of 26 weeks of practical veterinary experience as approved for this purpose by the Clinical Veterinary Medicine Syndicate.

The examination has two sections as follows:

(i) *Veterinary Medicine.* This section deals with the prevention and medical treatment of diseases in the domestic animals; it includes questions on jurisprudence.

(ii) *Animal Surgery.* This section deals with the principles and practice of animal surgery; it includes questions on anaesthesia, infertility, and obstetrics.

The examination for each section consists of two three-hour written papers, a clinical examination, and a *viva voce* examination.

5

RESEARCH AND COURSES OF ADVANCED OR FURTHER STUDY

The University offers the research degrees of Doctor of Philosophy (Ph.D.), Master of Science (M.Sc.) and Master of Letters (M.Litt.) to graduates, and in exceptional cases to non-graduates, who can show the ability to profit from a course of supervised research; and the degree of Master of Philosophy (M.Phil.) to similar candidates who can demonstrate their ability to profit from either a one-year course of further study and training in research or a two-year course of advanced study. In all cases the student works under the general direction of a Supervisor appointed by the Degree Committee for the Faculty concerned, and the resources of the University Library, the Departmental and College libraries and, in appropriate cases, the scientific laboratories, are open to him. For the Ph.D., M.Sc. and M.Litt. Degrees the student presents for examination a dissertation in English embodying the results of his research, and undergoes an oral, or in exceptional cases a written, examination on the dissertation and the general field of knowledge in which it falls. The M.Phil. Degree (one-year course) is examined by written papers, or by a thesis, or by written papers and a thesis, according to the subject; and the M.Phil. Degree (two-year course) is examined by written papers and a thesis.

General conditions of admission

Enquiries about admission as a Graduate Student and requests for application forms should be made to the Secretary of the Board of Graduate Studies, at 4 Mill Lane, Cambridge, CB2 1RZ from whom the *Graduate Studies Prospectus* may also be obtained. The application forms should be completed in accordance with the instructions, and returned to the Secretary of the Board of Graduate Studies, who will also handle the applicant's admission to a College, under the provisions of the Cambridge Intercollegiate Graduate Application Scheme.

In exceptional cases persons who are not graduates of a university may be admitted as Graduate Students, provided that they give such evidence of general educational qualifications as may be approved by the Board of Graduate Studies.

Applications for admission in any one academical year should, if possible, reach the Secretary of the Board of Graduate Studies, together with all the necessary documents, not later than the end of March in the preceding academical year, but those also applying for awards with early closing dates, including British Academy Studentships, may need to apply before this.

No application will be favourably considered unless (i) it appears at the time that the course proposed can conveniently be pursued within the University; and (ii) it appears that the applicant is well qualified for the particular course which he has proposed.

Candidates for the M.Phil. Degree are so registered on their admission, but the Board of Graduate Studies and the Degree Committee concerned almost invariably require a person who proposes to work for the Ph.D., M.Sc. or M.Litt. Degree to complete a probationary period before registration as a candidate for a degree, and may for this purpose require him to take a one-year M.Phil. or Certificate course in the first instance, or take a progress examination at the end of the first year. After the period of probation the Board may register a student retrospectively as a candidate for a research degree from the beginning of his course as a Graduate Student or from the beginning of any subsequent term.

Before anyone can be admitted as a Graduate Student and allowed to count residence or claim other privileges, he must have been admitted to one of the Colleges.

A Graduate Student is not admissible as a candidate for any University Prize, Scholarship, or Studentship which is open only to undergraduates.

Courses of research for the Ph.D., M.Sc., and M.Litt. Degrees

A person who has been admitted as a Graduate Student is required to pursue a course under the general responsibility of the Degree Committee which recommended his admission, and under such other conditions as may be laid down by that Degree Committee or by the Board of Graduate Studies.

He must pursue in the University under supervision a course of research, if he seeks the degree of Master of Science or of Master of Letters, for not less than six terms; if he seeks the degree of Doctor of Philosophy, for not less than nine terms, with the following exceptions:

(i) A Graduate Student who is a candidate for the Ph.D., M.Sc., or M.Litt. Degree may be exempted from three terms of research if, before he was admitted as a Graduate Student, he had been engaged either in full-time or part-time research or in other work done after graduation, which in either case is deemed by the Degree Committee and the Board to have provided satisfactory training for the course of research that he has undertaken.

(ii) The Board may allow a Graduate Student who is a candidate for the Ph.D., M.Sc., or M.Litt. Degree, to spend all but three terms of his course of research working under supervision outside the University under conditions approved by the Degree Committee and the Board.

(iii) The Board may allow a Graduate Student to intermit his course of research for one or more terms on account of illness or other sufficient cause.

(iv) The Board may allow a Graduate Student who is qualified to receive, but who has not received the Certificate of Postgraduate Study in Natural Science, or in Engineering, or in Chemical Engineering; the Diploma in Development Studies, or in Economics, or in Historical Studies, or in International Law, or in Legal Studies, or in Theology to count towards his course of research not more than three terms of the period during which he was a candidate for one of these Certificates or Diplomas.

(v) The Board may grant a Graduate Student, to whom an allowance of terms of residence has been made in respect of work done by him in the University before matriculation, a similar allowance towards the period during which he is required to pursue his course of research in the University.

All these exemptions and special privileges are exceptional and are not granted automatically. Further information about allowances is given in the *Memorandum to Graduate Students* issued by the Board of Graduate Studies. Specific application must be made to the Secretary of the Board whenever exemption or other allowance is applied for, and must be accompanied by a written opinion from the student's Supervisor on the proposal made.

At least three terms must have been kept by residence by any Graduate Student who is admitted to a degree, except any term which the Council of the Senate may allow on account of illness or other grave cause. Graduate Students who are graduates of the University may count for this purpose previous residence *in statu pupillari*, but they must in addition comply with the separate requirements about terms of research.

The Board of Graduate Studies have power to terminate a Graduate Student's course without notice if his work is not satisfactory, if he is no longer a member of a College, or if he has failed to pay the fees due from him.

Submission of dissertations for the Ph.D., M.Sc., and M.Litt. Degrees

A Graduate Student registered for a degree who has kept all but one of the terms required to be kept by him may submit a dissertation embodying the results of his research not earlier than the beginning of the term during which he expects to complete the period of research required under the regulations and not later than the end of the vacation following his twelfth term of candidature; by special permission of the Board of Graduate Studies a dissertation may be submitted later than this. An allowance of terms counts in calculating his standing.

Courses of advanced study for the M.Phil. Degree (two-year course), and of further study and training in research for the M.Phil. Degree (one-year course)

Candidates for the M.Phil. Degree are admitted as Graduate Students by the Board of Graduate Studies on the recommendation of the Degree Committee concerned.

One-year M.Phil. Degree courses are offered in a number of subjects, details of which may be obtained from the Secretary of the Board of Graduate Studies. Theology is the only subject for which candidates are currently being admitted to a two-year M.Phil. Degree course.

Candidates for both the one-year and the two-year courses follow a course under the general responsibility of the Degree Committee concerned and are examined in the case of candidates for the one-year course, by written papers, or a thesis, or written papers and a thesis, according to the subject, and, in the case of candidates for the two-year course, by written papers and a thesis.

A candidate who has been approved for the M.Phil. Degree (one-year course) may, with the approval of the Board of Graduate Studies, be allowed to count not more than three terms of his candidature for that degree towards the requirements of the Ph.D., M.Sc., or M.Litt. Degree. If this allowance is made, the candidate is not prevented from proceeding to the M.Phil. Degree.

A candidate who has been approved for the M.Phil. Degree (two-year course) may be registered for the Ph.D. Degree, but he will be required to complete five further terms of research, of which three terms must be spent in Cambridge. If the candidate has proceeded to the M.Phil. Degree, the Ph.D. Degree Examiners will take no account of any work which was included in the M.Phil. Degree thesis.

Fees and Expenses

Students in residence are charged both the University Composition Fee and College fees for each year of their course, and they must in addition pay for their own maintenance and for the living expenses of any dependants who may accompany them. Before an applicant's admission can finally be confirmed the Board of Graduate Studies must have proof that the applicant will have sufficient financial support to meet these expenses. The sum concerned will be specified as a condition of admission in formal offers of admission issued by the Board's office and will represent the estimated total of the following elements:

(1) University Composition Fees: for graduate students starting their course in October 1989 these will be as follows:

U.K. and EEC students:	£1,890 a year
Overseas students:	
Arts	£4,248 a year
Science	£5,571 a year
Clinical Medicine	£10,311 a year

All these sums could well have increased by October 1990.

(2) College Fees: students should allow a further £1,500 a year, **in addition to the sums mentioned above.** However, College fees vary from College to College; further information may be sought from the College concerned.

(3) Maintenance and living expenses

Apart from the costs of University and College fees, it is estimated that students admitted from October 1990 will need **at least** the following sums to cover their own maintenance and living expenses:

	£
A United Kingdom student staying for 12 months or more	3,325 a year
A United Kingdom student staying for 9 months	2,660
An EEC or Overseas student staying for 12 months or more	3,915 a year
An EEC or Overseas student staying for 9 months	3,130

These estimates do not include provision for travelling expenses.

In addition a student accompanied by a wife or husband will be required to show evidence that a further £1,950 a year will be available to meet the wife's or husband's living expenses, and those bringing children will be required to make provision of at least £310 a year for each child. The financial condition specified in an offer of admission takes account of the applicant's statement about accompanying dependants in his application for admission. No additional dependants may be brought to Cambridge before evidence of the extra financial support needed has been supplied and the consent of the College obtained. The figures mentioned above exclude the cost of child-minding, for which up to £60 a week extra should be allowed where needed.

Because of inflation, expenses including fees are likely to rise over a three-year period of research, and applicants and their sponsors should take this into account. Students from overseas should also allow for possible fluctuations in currency exchange rates.

Students pursuing research which requires the provision of abnormally expensive laboratory materials may sometimes be required to contribute towards the cost of their research, in addition to their paying the usual University and College fees. The Board of Graduate Studies will inform successful applicants for admission of any additional fees that they will be called on to pay for this purpose, and the Board will increase accordingly the amount of the financial support for which those students will be required to provide a guarantee.

UNIVERSITY SCHOLARSHIPS AND OTHER AWARDS
(i) UNIVERSITY SCHOLARSHIPS

Key: † Award published in the Awards number of the *Reporter*. Please consult this for further details, especially where indicated.
- B.G.S.: Board of Graduate Studies, 4 Mill Lane, Cambridge, CB2 1RZ.
- G.B.: General Board of the Faculties, The Old Schools, Cambridge, CB2 1TT.
- U.R.: University Registry, The Old Schools, Cambridge, CB2 1TN.
- * Awards also open to prospective members of the University. Other awards are open only to people who are already members of the University.

N.B. Due to the limited space available, certain details (e.g.) closing dates) have been omitted from the Table of Awards. Prospective candidates are strongly advised to make further enquiries before applying for funds or competing for a prize.

GENERAL AWARDS, RELATED TO MORE THAN ONE SUBJECT

Award	Subject/Purpose	Eligibility	When offered	Details (and forms when applicable) from:
†Allen Scholarships	Research in 'arts' subjects	Graduates of the University, under 29 on 1 October following application	Annually	B.G.S.
Bell, Abbott, and Barnes Fund/Exhibitions	Subject unrestricted. General financial assistance	Undergraduates needing assistance	Each Term	College Tutors
*Cambridge Commonwealth Trust Awards	Subject unrestricted	Graduates or undergraduates from the Commonwealth, Burma, Pakistan, or Sudan	Annually	B.G.S. (Graduates); College Tutors (Undergraduates)
*Cambridge Livingstone Trust Awards	Subject unrestricted. For Bachelor level degrees, or postgraduate courses	Graduates who are domiciled, resident, or normally resident in Botswana, Lesotho, Malawi, Namibia, South Africa, Swaziland, Zambia, or Zimbabwe		U.R.
*†H. M. Chadwick Studentship	For advanced study or research in the history, religion, and culture	Open to graduates or research students of universities in U.K.	Annually	G.B.

[1] Full details of the regulations governing awards are given in the *Statutes and Ordinances of the University of Cambridge*. Most University Scholarships, Studentships, and Prizes are advertised in the Awards number of the *Reporter* which appears annually in November. Notices also appear in the official and unofficial parts of the *Reporter* throughout the year.

Award	Subject/Purpose	Eligibility	When offered	Details (and forms when applicable) from:
H. M. Chadwick Studentship (*cont.*)	(all aspects) of any of the peoples of the British Isles or Scandinavian peoples before A.D. 1050, of the Teutonic/Celtic peoples before A.D. 600, of the peoples of the Near East before 1000 B.C., or of any modern primitive peoples, or the general history or comparative study of culture (*excluding* subjects wholly or mainly relating to Western Europe since A.D. 1050, the classical periods of Greece, Rome, or India, or other periods of advanced culture)	or Eire (preference to Cambridge candidates)		
†Bartle Frere Exhibitions	For study or research in any branch of knowledge requiring travel to any part of the Commonwealth except U.K., India, and Bangladesh	Preference given to Graduate Students intending to undertake research, but undergraduates may also apply	Annually	B.G.S.
*†Robert Gardiner Memorial Scholarships	Unrestricted	Undergraduates or graduates of Irish universities	Annually	U.R.
*†Le Bas Research Studentships	Research in Literature	Applicants must gain admission as Graduate Students	Annually	B.G.S.
†Lundgren Research awards	Research in scientific subjects, including Mathematics	Candidates for the Ph.D. Degree, who are not ordinarily resident in the U.K., and who have completed four terms of research as registered Graduate Students	Twice a year	B.G.S.
†W. A. Meek Scholarships	Research in 'science' subjects	Graduates of the University under 29 on 1 October following application	Annually	B.G.S.
†Mary Euphrasia Mosley Fund Grants	Travel to British Commonwealth countries for study or research	Members of the University below the standing of M.A.	Annually	U.R.
Prince Philip Scholarships	Any subject. To lead to a degree or other qualification of the University	Students domiciled, resident or ordinarily resident in Hong Kong	Annually	U.R.

Award	Subject/Purpose	Eligibility	When offered	Details (and forms when applicable) from:
†A. M. P. Read Scholarships	Research in 'arts' and 'science' subjects	Graduates of the University under 29 on 1 October following application	Annually	B.G.S.
†Research Maintenance Fund Grants	Research for the Ph.D. Degree	Those who have graduated (or about to graduate) with a B.A. Degree of the University. Applicants must gain admission as a Graduate Student and must apply within two academical years of graduating	Annually	B.G.S.
Schiff Studentship	Study or research in physics, engineering or related sciences	Open, but preferably British Nationals in financial need	Annually	U.R.
Sims Fund and Scholarship	Study or research in Physics, Chemistry, Mathematics, or Medicine	Graduates of the University born in Great Britain or N. Ireland, or whose parents were British subjects at the time of the candidate's birth. Registered Graduate Students, who are not graduates of the University, but are qualified in every other respect, may apply for a grant when the Scholarship is offered	When vacant	U.R.
†Smuts Memorial Fund Grants	Study or research in Commonwealth studies	Members of the University	Each Term	G.B.
C. T. Taylor Studentship	Advanced study or research in Earth Sciences and Geography, Engineering, Mathematics, Physics and Chemistry, Biology 'A', Computer Studies, Chemical Engineering, Land Economy or Biotechnology	Graduate Students or those about to become Graduate Students. Preference to candidates from Australia, Canada, New Zealand or the U.S.A.	Annually	U.R.
†Worts Travelling Scholars Fund Grants	Travel outside Great Britain investigating various subjects	Members of the University. Preference given to below standing of M.A.	Annually	B.G.S.

Award	Subject/Purpose	Eligibility	When offered	Details (and forms when applicable) from:
		AWARDS IN PARTICULAR SUBJECTS		
		Agriculture		
†A.J. Keith Studentships	Graduate studies in Agriculture	Members of the University	When vacant	Department of Applied Biology
		Anglo-Saxon		
†Dame Bertha Phillpotts Memorial Scholarships and	Advanced study or research in Old Norse or Icelandic	Members of the University	Annually	Faculty of Modern and Medieval Languages
		Archaeology and Anthropology		
*†Evans Fellowship	Research in Anthropology and Archaeology in relation to South East Asia	A graduate of any university	Annually	The Secretary of the Fund, Museum of Archaeology and Anthropology, Downing Street
†Fortes Fund Grants	Towards the expenses of publications in Social Anthropology	Members of the University. Preference given to those under 40 and those with children under 10	Annually	Department of Social Anthropology
†Mark Gregson Prize	For an essay on an archaeological subject	Undergraduates may compete in the year they are candidates for Part II of the Archaeological and Anthropological Tripos. See † for more details	Annually	U.R.
†Richards Fund	Fieldwork in Social Anthropology	Graduate Students registered for field research in the Department of Social Anthropology	Annually	Department of Social Anthropology
†Ridgeway-Venn Travel Studentship	Archaeology and Anthropology	Members of the University *in statu pupillari*. See † for more details	Annually	U.R.
Henry Ling Roth Scholarships	Research in Ethnology	Members of the University, who are working, or have worked, in the Faculty of Archaeology and Anthropology	When funds permit	Faculty of Archaeology and Anthropology
†Anthony Wilkin Studentship and Grants	Research in Ethnology and Archaeology	Members of the University who are not of standing to become M.A. Certain preferences apply. See †	When funds permit	U.R.

Award	Subject/Purpose	Eligibility	When offered	Details (and forms when applicable) from:
	Architecture and History of Art			
†Kettle's Yard Travel Fund	Travel abroad to study Art or Architecture	Members of the University who have graduated in Architecture or in History of Art. Preference given to those below standing of M.A.	Annually	Faculty of Architecture and History of Art
†Edward S. Prior Prize	For a portfolio of drawings which show the best understanding of building construction and use of materials	Students of Architecture who have completed the studio-work for Parts I B and II of the Architecture Tripos	Annually	Faculty of Architecture and History of Art
	Bibliography			
† Gordon Duff Prize	Essay on any of the following subjects: Bibliography, Palaeography, Typography, Book-binding, Book-illustration, or the Science of Books and Manuscripts and the Arts relating thereto. Subject must be approved	Members of the University, under 30	Annually	U.R.
	Classics			
†Craven, Prendergast Sandys, H.A. Thomas Studentships, and G.C. Winter Warr and Charles Oldham Scholarships	Various branches of Classical research in Cambridge and abroad	Graduates of the University. See † for more details	Annually	Faculty of Classics
†Henry Carrington and Bentham Dumont Koe Studentship	Travel in lands where Greek is spoken, preferably in connexion with the study of Greek literature	Graduates of the University, whose age on the first day of the term of the election is not more than 28	Annually	Faculty of Classics
†Walston Studentship	Travel to Greek lands for the furtherance of research in Classical Archaeology	Candidates who have obtained honours or have satisfied the Examiners in one or more of the following examinations (a) Diploma in Classical Archaeology	Annually	Faculty of Classics

Award	Subject/Purpose	Eligibility	When offered	Details (and forms when applicable) from:
†Walston Studentship (*cont.*)		(b) Part II of the Classical Tripos, including not less than 2 papers from Group D. (c) Part II of the Architecture Tripos (d) the History of Art Tripos and are not more than five years' standing from their matriculation.		
†Sir William Browne's Medals	For composition of a Greek ode or elegy, or epigram, or Latin ode or elegy, or epigram, on a prescribed theme	Resident undergraduates may compete not later than their third year	Annually	U.R.
†Montagu Butler Prize	For an original exercise in Latin Hexameter Verse on a prescribed theme	Resident undergraduates may compete not later than their third year	Annually	U.R.
†Porson Prize	For a translation of a set passage from an English poet into Greek verse	Resident undergraduates may compete not later than their third year	Annually	U.R.
†Hare Prize	A dissertation on an approved subject pertaining to the history, literature, philosophy, law, or archaeology of ancient Greece or Rome	Members of the University, under 30, who have either been admitted to a degree in the University or have been elected Fellows of a College or have been appointed University Officers	Triennially (next 1990)	U.R.
*†Jebb Scholarship	Approved course of Literary study either in Greek and Latin or in one of these languages, together with English, or some other European language and literature. Normally required to become an Affiliated Student, and a candidate for an appropriate Tripos Examination. In special cases a Scholar may be allowed to be a Graduate Student	British subjects who have completed a course in Classics (or Latin or Greek, together with English or some other European language or literature), who are graduates of a university in the Commonwealth (excluding Great Britain and N. Ireland) and who have received an approved degree	Annually	U.R.

Award	Subject/Purpose	Eligibility	When offered	Details (and forms when applicable) from:
†Members' Classical Essay Prizes	Two Prizes for essays on approved subjects, primarily concerned with the study of Ancient Greece or Rome. See † for more details	One Prize is open to members of the University *in statu pupillari* of not more than seven years' standing, other than Graduate Students or candidates for the Diploma in Classical Archaeology, who are eligible for the other Prize	Annually	U.R.
†Members' Classical Reading Prizes	For the reading out loud of Greek or Latin	Any member of the University *in statu pupillari*, other than a Graduate Student, who has not kept more than seven terms at the beginning of the academical year in which he competes	Annually	U.R.
†Members' Classical Translation Prizes	For translation of Greek or Latin verse	Any member of the University *in statu pupillari*, other than a Graduate Student, who has not kept more than seven terms at the beginning of the academical year in which he competes	Annually	U.R.
†F.S. Salisbury Fund	Grants for those engaged in excavations on Roman sites in Britain	Any member of the University *in statu pupillari*	Annually	Faculty of Classics
	Computing			
*ICL Research Studentship	Computing	Graduates of any university	When vacant	The Computer Laboratory, Corn Exchange Street
	Economics			
†Luca D'Agliano Scholarships	Research in the area of development economics	Any registered Graduate Student pursuing a course in the area of research specified	Annually	U.R.
†Price Waterhouse Prize	For an essay on some subject that is within the scope of any paper in Part II of the Economics Tripos, or on an approved subject	Any second year undergraduate. See † for more details	Annually	U.R.

Award	Subject/Purpose	Eligibility	When offered	Details (and forms when applicable) from:
†‡Adam Smith Prize	For an essay on some subject that is within the scope of the syllabus of any paper in Part II of the Economics Tripos	Any candidate for Part II of the Economics Tripos or any undergraduate who has obtained honours in Part I of the Economics Tripos and has kept by residence not less than six terms. See † for more details	Annually	U.R.
†Stevenson Prize	For an essay on some question in Economics, Economic History, or Statistics since 1800	Open to (a) any registered Graduate Student, provided that the minimum number of terms of research or study required for the degree or qualification registered for have not been completed; (b) B.A.s not of standing to become M.A.s	Annually	U.R.
†Wrenbury Scholarships	Study and research in Economics, Political Economy, or Economic History subsequent to 1800	Candidates for Part II of the Economics Tripos in the year of application	Annually	U.R.

Elocution

†Winchester Reading Prizes	Reading out loud passages in Classical English Prose and Poetry; in the Old and New Testament and English Liturgy. See † for more details	Students in their third and fourth years	Annually	U.R.

Engineering

†William George Collins Fund	Research in Engineering, but preference given to Electrical and Mechanical	Members of the University in the Department of Engineering	Any time	The Secretary of the Degree Committee for the Faculty of Engineering
†Ford of Britain Trust Fund	General financial support	Graduate Students in the Department of Engineering	Any time	The Secretary of the Degree Committee for the Faculty of Engineering
†Charles Hesterman Merz Fund	Grants for research	Members of the University in the Faculty of Engineering, who are citizens of the Commonwealth of Nations	Any time	The Secretary of the Degree Committee for the Faculty of Engineering

Award	Subject/Purpose	Eligibility	When offered	Details (and forms when applicable) from:
†Rex Moir Fund	General financial support	Postgraduate or Graduate Students in the Department of Engineering	Any time	The Secretary of the Degree Committee for the Faculty of Engineering
**†Taylor Woodrow Fund	Grants for Postgraduate Studies in Civil Engineering	Applicants must have obtained an honours degree in a U.K. university, or some other approved qualification, and must become members of the University	Any time	The Secretary of the Degree Committee for the Faculty of Engineering
†Hamilton Prize	(See Natural Sciences)			
†John Winbolt Prize	For a paper, already accepted for publication in an established professional or learned journal, on some subject related to the profession of a civil engineer. All subjects studied for Parts I B and II of the Engineering Tripos are deemed acceptable	B.A.s not of standing to become M.A.s, or registered Graduate Students holding the status of B.A. working under the supervision of the Degree Committee for the Faculty of Engineering	Annually	U.R.

English

Award	Subject/Purpose	Eligibility	When offered	Details (and forms when applicable) from:
†Chancellor's Medal for an English Poem	For an original English poem	Resident undergraduates may compete not later than their third year	Annually	U.R.
†Harness Prize	For an English essay upon some subject connected with Shakespearean Literature (See Classics)	Undergraduates, or graduates of not more than 3 years' standing from their first degree	Triennially (next 1989)	U.R.
†Jebb Scholarship	(See Modern and Medieval			
†Jebb Studentships	Languages)			
†Le Bas Prize	For an essay on an approved literary subject	Any member of the University, who is a graduate of this or another university, under 30	Annually	U.R.
†Members' English Prize	For an essay on a literary subject chosen by the candidate	Graduate Students working under the supervision of the Degree Committee for the Faculty of English, who were admitted not earlier than 1 August next but one preceding the academical year they compete	Annually	U.R.

Award	Subject/Purpose	Eligibility	When offered	Details (and forms when applicable) from:
†Charles Oldham Shakespeare Scholarship	For an examination and essay on the works of Shakespeare	Any member of the University *in statu pupillari* providing that on 1 January next preceding the examination (a) he has not attained the age of 25 years and (b) not more than ten complete terms have passed after his first term of residence, and (c) if he is a registered Graduate Student not more than one complete term has passed after the term of his admission as a Graduate Student	Annually	U.R.
		Geography		
Philip Lake Fund II Grants	Research or field-work in any approved branch of Geography	Graduate Students in the Department of Geography below the standing of M.A. Candidates for Part II of the Geographical Tripos may also apply at the beginning of the term they propose to present themselves	Annually	Department of Geography, Downing Place
†David Richards Travel Scholarships	Geography	British-born students who in the previous academical year have been classed in Part I A of the Geographical Tripos and are now reading for Part I B	Annually	U.R.
		History		
**†Stanley Baldwin Studentships and Grants	Study or research in British Political History in the years 1919 to 1939	Any person who is, or is about to become registered as, a Graduate Student in the University	Annually	Faculty of History, West Road

Award	Subject/Purpose	Eligibility	When offered	Details (and forms when applicable) from:
†Archbishop Cranmer Prize	For an essay on changes in doctrine, organization, and ritual within the Church of England between A.D. 1500 and A.D. 1700	Graduates of the University of not less than three years' standing from their first degree	Annually	U.R.
*†Archbishop Cranmer Studentships and Grants	For the furtherance of original research in English Ecclesiastical History between 1500 and 1700	Any person who is, or is about to become, registered as a Graduate Student in the University. Grants are also open to senior members of the University	When funds permit	Faculty of History, West Road
†Dr Lightfoot's Scholarship	For an examination in Ecclesiastical History. See † for more details	Members of the University who, having resided at least one year and being still in residence, or having taken their first degree, are under 25 when the examination begins	Annually	U.R.
†Ellen McArthur Prizes	Any work in Economic History	Any graduate of the University	Annually	Faculty of History, West Road
*Ellen McArthur Studentships	Original research in Economic History	Any person who is, or is about to become registered as, a Graduate Student in the University, with the intention of becoming a candidate for the Ph.D. Degree	Annually	Faculty of History, West Road
*Mellon Research Fellowships	Original research in American History	It is expected that candidates will either have completed a Ph.D. dissertation or be able to submit substantial written work if requested	Annually	Faculty of History, West Road
†Members' History Prize	For an essay on an historical subject chosen by the candidate	Graduate Students working under the supervision of the Degree Committee for the Faculty of History, who were admitted not earlier than 1 August preceding the academical year they compete	Annually	U.R.

Award	Subject/Purpose	Eligibility	When offered	Details (and forms when applicable) from:
†Sara Norton Prize	For an essay on an approved subject, on some aspect of the political history of the U.S.A.	Graduate Students and graduates of the University, under 25, who have kept not less than three terms	Annually	U.R.
†Prince Consort and Thirlwall Prizes	For a dissertation on an approved subject involving original historical research	Graduates of the University and those on the Register of Graduate Students provided they are under 30 on the last day for sending in dissertations and provided they have not previously won the prize	Annually (Prince Consort even years, Thirlwall odd years)	U.R.
Prince Consort Studentships and Thirlwall Studentships	Original Research in History	Anyone who is or is about to be registered as a Graduate Student	Annually. May be renewed for one year at a time up to 3 years	Faculty of History West Road
*†Holland Rose Studentship	Study of a subject approved by the Electors connected with the general history or constitutional, social or cultural development of the British Empire since 1815, of the Commonwealth or the present problems of the Commonwealth	Any citizen of a Commonwealth country, or of a country which was a member of the British Empire or Commonwealth in 1932, who has graduated in any University with high honours in History or in any other relevant subject. Candidates may apply if not more than three complete academical years have elapsed since they took their first degree, or if they have been registered Graduate Students for not more than nine terms The student, if not a member of the University, must become such by the end of the term after election and remain such during tenure	Annually	U.R.

Award	Subject/Purpose	Eligibility	When offered	Details (and forms when applicable) from:
*Harold Samuel Studentships	Research in economic, legal, or social matters relating to the use, tenure, or development of the land	Open, but tenure conditional upon the student being a registered Graduate Student of the University	Annually	Department of Land Economy, Silver Street
		Law		
*Humanitarian Trust Senior Studentship	Advanced study in International Law	Open to candidates of not more than 30 years, who hold or are about to obtain a degree or diploma of an approved university or college	Biennially (next 1989)	U.R.
†Arnold McNair Scholarships	Study or research in International Law	Members of the University, who have kept at least eight terms, who are candidates for, or have been classed in either Part I B or Part II of, the Law Tripos	Annually	U.R.
*F. W. Maitland Fund	Grants for research in the History of Law and of Legal Language and Institutions	Open to those appropriately qualified for research proposed	Any time	Faculty of Law, Old Syndics Building, Mill Lane
†Rebecca Flower Squire Fund	Grants for the study of law to those who declare their intention of practising the legal profession	Resident members of the University, under 25, who are British subjects and who are children of British subjects domiciled in England or Wales at the time of the candidate's birth	Any time	Faculty of Law, Old Syndics Building, Mill Lane
Rebecca Flower Squire Fund (*cont.*)				
*†Squire Scholarships	For those who declare their intention of practising the legal profession and are reading for an examination in Law	Undergraduates, or candidates for admission, under 25, who are British subjects and who are children of British subjects domiciled in England or Wales at the time of the candidate's birth	Annually	Faculty of Law, Old Syndics Building, Mill Lane

Award	Subject/Purpose	Eligibility	When offered	Details (and forms when applicable) from:
†Ver Heyden de Lancey Prizes	For an essay on any aspect of Medico-Legal Studies, approved by the Managers	Graduates of the University (in any subject), who are also professionally qualified in Medicine (including Dentistry, but not Veterinary Medicine) or in Law	Annually	U.R.
**†Whewell Scholarships	Awarded on examination of not less than three of the papers in International Law which have been prescribed for the LL.M. Examination, a fourth paper chosen by the candidate from among all the papers prescribed for that examination, and a paper on problems and disputed points in International Law	Open to persons who have not attained the age of 25 on the 1 January following the election in the Easter Term	Annually	U.R.
**†Wright Rogers Law Scholarships	Study or research relating to the Laws of England	Any person who has a degree of any university or polytechnic in the U.K., and has spent at least one year studying law	Annually	Faculty of Law, The Syndics Building, Old Press Site
†Yorke Prizes	For an essay on a legal subject (including the history, analysis, administration, and reform of law), approved by the Faculty Board of Law	Graduates of the University, or those who have been admitted or have been registered as a Graduate Student, who are under 32	Annually	Faculty of Law, The Syndics Building, Old Press Site
	Mathematics			
†Adams Prize	For an essay on a set subject in Pure Mathematics, Astronomy, or other branch of Natural Philosophy	Graduates of the University, and those who, on or before the closing date for entries, are Fellows of a College or University Officers. See † for more details	Biennially (next 1987–88)	U.R.

503

Award	Subject/Purpose	Eligibility	When offered	Details (and forms when applicable) from:
†J.T. Knight Prizes	For essays on any subject in Mathematics and its applications	Any member of the University who is not a graduate of the University. See † for more details	Annually	U.R.
†Smith's and Rayleigh Prizes	For essays on any subject in Mathematics and its applications	B.A.s of the University. See † for more details	Annually	U.R.
Medicine				
†Henry Roy Dean Prize	Awarded on the results of a special examination in Clinical Pathology	Any member of the University who is pursuing clinical studies in Cambridge and has been entered as a candidate for Part I of the Final M.B.	Annually	U.R.
Dept. of Pathology Studentship	Original research in Pathology	Open	From time to time	The Head of the Dept. of Pathology
†Denis Dooley Prize	For an essay on a subject in the field of Clinical Anatomy	Any member of the University pursuing a course of clinical study for the degrees of M.B. and B.Chir; and any who have passed the final M.B. Examination and are undertaking their pre-registration year.	Annually	The Department of Anatomy
*Elmore Medical Research Studentships	For research in Medicine	Certain restrictions apply	When funds permit	The Secretary of the Fund, The Clinical School, Addenbrooke's Hospital, Hills Road
†Glennie Prizes	For the best and next best annotated case history of a child with psychosomatic illness seen during the clinical course leading to the Final M.B. Examination	Any member of the University who is pursuing clinical studies in Cambridge and is a candidate for the Final M.B.	Annually	U.R.
*Grimshaw-Parkinson Studentships	Research in the diseases of the heart and circulation	Registered medical practitioners and holders of medical degrees approved by the Managers	When funds permit	The Secretary of the Fund, The Clinical School, Addenbrooke's Hospital, Hills Road

Award	Subject/Purpose	Eligibility	When offered	Details (and forms when applicable) from:
*†William Harvey Studentships and Grants	Clinical Medicine	Any student intending to pursue a course of clinical instruction in the University leading to the degrees of M.B. and B.Chir.	Annually	The Secretary of the Fund, The Clinical School, Addenbrooke's Hospital, Hills Road
†John and Margaret Henderson Memorial Prize	For an essay on a subject chosen by the candidate, in the field of either Gerontology or Geriatrics	Members of the University who are pursuing clinical studies in Cambridge for the degrees of M.B. and B.Chir., and have not yet presented themselves as candidates for Part III of the Final M.B.	Annually	U.R.
†Paediatric Prizes				
(a) Cow and Gate Prize	For best annotated case history or study in the field of Clinical Nutrition	Any member of the University pursuing clinical studies in Cambridge and who is a candidate for the Final M.B.	Annually	U.R.
(b) Fisons Prize	For best annotated case history or study concerning a child with allergic disease	Any member of the University pursuing clinical studies in Cambridge and who is a candidate for the Final M.B.	Annually	U.R.
*Pinsent-Darwin Studentship	Original research in Mental Pathology	Candidates must be qualified in medicine, psychology, or an allied subject	When funds permit	The Secretary of the Fund, The Clinical School, Addenbrooke's Hospital, Hills Road
*Gwynaeth Pretty Research Studentship	Research in Aetiology, Pathology, or treatment of diseases, with particular reference to those which disable in early life	A recent first degree is required	When funds permit	The Department of Pathology, Tennis Court Road
†Marmaduke Sheild Scholarship	Human Anatomy	Undergraduates of not more than three years' standing and B.A.s of not more than one year's standing, who have passed the First M.B. See † for more details	Annually	U.R.

Award	Subject/Purpose	Eligibility	When offered	Details (and forms when applicable) from:
Sims Scholarship	(See General Awards)			
†Eliot Slater Prize	Awarded on a special examination in Psychiatry	Any member of the University pursuing clinical studies in Cambridge and who was a candidate for Part I of the Final M.B. Examination at the last occasion it was held	Annually	U.R.
Oreste and Florence Sinamide Scholarship	Research directed to the mitigation of the diseases of the circulation related to other systems	Any member of the University who holds one or more of the degrees of M.B., B.Chir., M.Chir., and M.D.	Every 3 years	Regius Professor of Physics
†Department of Surgery Prize	For a dissertation on a subject of the candidate's choice related to Surgery	Any person who has pursued clinical studies in the University for the degrees of M.B. and B.Chir., provided that no entry shall be eligible if it is submitted more than two years after the candidate has passed the Final M.B.	Annually	U.R.
†Ver Heyden de Lancey Prizes	(See Law)			
*John Lucas Walker Studentship	Research, or for study and training for research in Pathology	Candidates must be of post-doctoral status	When funds permit	Department of Pathology, Tennis Court Road

Modern and Medieval Languages

Award	Subject/Purpose	Eligibility	When offered	Details (and forms when applicable) from:
*†Dorothea Coke Fund Grants	To aid publications contributing to the knowledge of the history and culture of Denmark, Iceland, Norway, and Sweden before A.D. 1500	British authors, who are not necessarily members of the University	When funds permit	The Faculty of Modern and Medieval Languages, Sidgwick Avenue
†Gibson Spanish Scholarship	Advanced study or research in Spanish Literature. See † for more details	Graduates of the University, provided that not more than 17 complete terms have elapsed after their first term of residence	Biennially (next 1988)	U.R.

Award	Subject/Purpose	Eligibility	When offered	Details (and forms when applicable) from:
†Jebb Studentships	Advanced study of some subject in the field of European Literature from the foundation of Constantinople onwards	Graduates of the University, under 26	Annually	U.R.
†Brita Mortensen Fund Grants	To visit Scandinavia to study culture, literature, and the arts	Undergraduates	Annually	The Faculty of Modern and Medieval Languages, Sidgwick Avenue
†Scandinavian Studies Studentship	Advanced study or research in Sweden, Denmark, Norway, or Iceland	Members of the University, who have passed some final examination for the B.A. Degree, provided that not more than 24 terms have elapsed since the end of their first term of residence	Annually	The Faculty of Modern and Medieval Languages, Sidgwick Avenue
†Tennant Studentship	Advanced study or research in Norway	Members of the University, who have passed some final examination for the B.A. Degree, provided that not more than 24 terms have elapsed since the end of their first term of residence	Annually	The Faculty of Modern and Medieval Languages, Sidgwick Avenue
*†Scandinavian Studies Fund Grants	For study connected with Scandinavian countries	Any member, or prospective member of the University	Annually	The Faculty of Modern and Medieval Languages, Sidgwick Avenue
†Tennant Fund Grants	For furtherance of study in Norway	Members of the University	Annually	The Faculty of Modern and Medieval Languages, Sidgwick Avenue
†Tiarks German Scholarship	Advanced study or research in German Language or Literature. See † for more details	Any graduate of the University, provided that not more than 17 complete terms have elapsed after the first term of residence	Annually	U.R.
†J. B. Trend Fund Grants	To visit Spanish- and Portuguese-speaking countries to study the language, literature, history, or music	Undergraduates or registered Graduate Students. See † for more details	Annually	U.R.

Award	Subject/Purpose	Eligibility	When offered	Details (and forms when applicable) from:
†Wallenberg Prize	For an essay on an approved subject connected with the language, literature, history, or civilization of one or more of the Scandinavian peoples	Members of the University who have kept seven terms, and if graduates, not more than nine complete terms have passed since they were admitted to their first degree at this, or any other university	Annually	U.R.
Music				
†Ord Travel Fund Grants	For travel in Europe and in the Mediterranean countries of Africa or Asia, or exceptionally elsewhere to increase interest and understanding of the art and practice of music	Members of the University, who have spent at least two terms studying for a Part of the Music Tripos. See † for more details	Annually	U.R.
†William Barclay Squire Essay Prize	For an essay on an approved subject relating to the history of music	Members of the University, *in statu pupillari*, other than Graduate Students, who have kept at least six terms	Annually	U.R.
John Stewart of Rannoch Scholarship in Sacred Music	For a dissertation on a set topic. A *viva voce* examination on the entry will also be held.	Students of not more than three years' standing	Annually	U.R.
NATURAL SCIENCES				
Astronomy				
**†Isaac Newton Studentship	Study and research in Astronomy (especially Gravitational Astronomy, but also other branches of Astronomy and Astronomical Physics). See † for more details	Graduates of any university, normally under 26 on 1 January in the year of the election	Annually	U.R.

Award	Subject/Purpose	Eligibility	When offered	Details (and forms when applicable) from:
		Biochemistry and Biophysics		
*†Broodbank Fellowships	Research in Biochemistry and Biophysics with special reference to the Principles and Practice of Food Preservation	Open, but preference given to postdoctoral applicants	When funds permit	U.R.
Benn W. Levy Studentship	Original research in Biochemistry	Graduates of the University	When vacant	The Secretary of the Fund, The School of Biological Sciences, 19 Trumpington Street
		Biology		
		Botany		
†Sir Albert Howard Travel Exhibition	For Botanical research	Students offering Botany in Part II of the Natural Sciences Tripos in the year of the award	Annually	U.R.
†Frank Smart Studentships	Research in Botany	Graduates of the University, not more than six years' standing from matriculation, or Graduate Students of not more than three years' standing from matriculation	When vacant	U.R.
		Colloid Science		
*Oliver Gatty Studentship	Whole-time study and training for research in Biophysical and Colloid Science	Graduates of all universities. Preference given to graduates of universities outside Great Britain	When vacant	U.R.
		Communications		
†Hamilton Prize	For a dissertation embodying research on the theory or practice of electrical physics associated with any aspect of communications using electromagnetic radiation, or with communication systems in general	Members of the University, who are, or have been, Graduate Students, provided that not more than nine terms of their course of research have been completed since admission as a Graduate Student. See † for more details	Annually	U.R.

Award	Subject/Purpose	Eligibility	When offered	Details (and forms when applicable) from:
		Entomology		
†Balfour-Browne Fund	For the advancement of study of entomology. Preference to studies in the field, especially in the U.K.	Any person working in the University, who need not be a member. Preference is given to persons *in statu pupillari*. Registered Graduate Students are not eligible for support with their courses of study or research	Any time	The Secretary of the Faculty Board of Biology 'A', The Department of Zoology
		Geology		
Cowper Reed Travelling Grants	Research in Palaeontology	Members of the University	Any time	Department of Earth Sciences, Downing Street
†Harkness Scholarship	Research in Geology, including Palaeontology	Members of the University, who have, within the previous 3½ years, passed a final examination for the B.A. Degree	Annually	U.R.
Philip Lake Fund I Grants	For travelling expenses incurred when on Geological studies	Students and University Officers in the Department of Earth Sciences	Any time	Department of Earth Sciences, Downing Street
†Marr Memorial Fund Grants	For study of Geology in the field	Members of the University. Preference given to those who have obtained honours in Part I B of the Natural Sciences Tripos	Annually	U.R.
†Sedgwick Prize	For an essay on a set subject in Geology or kindred sciences	Graduates of the University, who have resided 60 days during the 12 months preceding the date entries are sent in	Triennially (next 1988)	U.R.
		Metallurgy		
*Ulick Richardson Evans Fund Studentship and Grants	Research in the study and the prevention of corrosion and oxidation of metals and related fields	Any person who is, or is about to become, a registered Graduate Student	When funds permit	The Goldsmiths' Professor of Metallurgy, The Department of Metallurgy and Materials Science, Pembroke Street

Award	Subject/Purpose	Eligibility	When offered	Details (and forms when applicable) from:
		Organic Chemistry		
		Physics		
Clerk Maxwell Scholarship	Original research in Experimental Physics, especially Electricity, Magnetism, and Heat	Members of the University, who have been for one term or more in the Cavendish Laboratory	When vacant	The Department of Physics, Madingley Road
		Physiology (see also Medicine)		
†Michael Foster Studentship	Research in Physiology	B.A.s of the University, not of standing to become M.A.s	Annually	U.R.
†Gedge Prize	For an essay on original observations in Physiology or in any branch thereof. The subject must be approved	Members of the University, of five to seven years' standing, or, in the case of Graduate Students, of three to five years' standing from matriculation. See † for more details	Biennially (next 1988)	U.R.
		Zoology		
†Hanne and Torkel Weis-Fogh Fund Grants	(a) Research in Zoology and Zoophysiology at the Department of Zoology, Cambridge University, and the Departments of Zoology and Zoophysiology in the Universities of Copenhagen and Aarhus (b) To support exchange visits by those engaged in the above research in these departments	Those carrying out research in the specified fields in the Department of Zoology	When funds permit	Department of Zoology, Downing Street
J. Arthur Ramsay Funds Grants	For research in Experimental Zoology	Graduate Students in the Department of Zoology. Candidates for Part II of the Natural Sciences Tripos intending to offer Zoology, to pursue a course of experimental research in the vacation	When funds permit	Department of Zoology, Downing Street

Award	Subject/Purpose	Eligibility	When offered	Details (and forms when applicable) from:
		Oriental Studies		
†Professor A.J. Arberry Travelling Scholarship	For visiting Arabic or Persian speaking countries	Students whose mother-tongue is English, and are citizens of the Commonwealth. Must have acquitted themselves with distinction in Arabic or Persian or both languages in either Part of the Oriental Studies Tripos	From time to time	U.R.
†Bendall Sanskrit Exhibition	Awarded on an examination in Sanskrit	Any member of the University, not being a Graduate Student, of not more than four years' standing, or if still qualified to be a candidate for the Oriental Studies Tripos in the term of the award. More details may be obtained from the U.R.	Annually	U.R.
**E. G. Browne Memorial Research Studentship Fund Grants	Research in Persian Studies	Graduates of universities who have obtained honours in Persian or in Iranian	Annually	U.R.
**C.H.W. Johns Studentship	Whole-time and training for research in Assyriology	Graduates of any university	When vacant	U.R.
**Thomas Mulvey Egyptology Fund Grants	For field-work in Egyptology	Open	Annually	Herbert Thompson Reader in Egyptology, Sidgwick Avenue
†Rapson Scholarship	Study or research in Sanskrit, Pali, or Avestan	Any member of the University who has obtained honours in a Part of the Classical or Oriental Studies Tripos, but not of standing to become M.A. See † for more details	Annually	U.R.
†John Stewart of Rannoch Scholarship in Hebrew	Awarded on a special examination in Hebrew, including a test paper in Greek and Latin	Students of not more than three years' standing	Annually	U.R.

Award	Subject/Purpose	Eligibility	When offered	Details (and forms when applicable) from:
†Tyrwhitt's Hebrew Scholarships and Mason Hebrew Prize	Awarded on a special examination in Hebrew	B.A.s, LL.B.s, or LL.M.s under the New Regulations, if not more than seven years have elapsed since matriculation	Annually	U.R.
†Wright Studentship	Study of the Arabic language and literature and of subjects closely connected	Graduates of the University under 28	Annually	U.R.
†Ghulam Yazdani Essay Prize	For an essay on an approved topic in the field of Ancient Deccan History and Archaeology	Any member of the University *in statu pupillari*	Annually	U.R.
		Philosophy		
†Arnold Gerstenberg Studentship	Philosophical study	Members of the University, up to their sixth year, who have attained honours in Part IA, or Part IB or Section I of Part II (General) or Part II of the Natural Sciences Tripos, or Part Ib of the Medical Sciences Tripos	When vacant	U.R.
		Theology		
*†Bethune-Baker Fund Grants	Theological Studies	Open	Each Term	The Divinity School, St John's Street
†Gregg Bury Prize	For an essay on a set subject connected with the Philosophy of Religion	Members of the University in their second to sixth years	Annually	U.R.
†Burney Prize	For an essay on a set subject connected with the Philosophy of Religion	Members of the University in their third to sixth years	Annually	U.R.
†Burney Studentship and Fund	Study or research in the Philosophy of Religion	Members of the University in their third to sixth years N.B. Research Students ineligible for the Studentship may apply for grants	Annually	U.R.

Award	Subject/Purpose	Eligibility	When offered	Details (and forms when applicable) from:
†Carus Greek Testament Prizes	Awarded on a special examination to encourage the accurate study of the New Testament in Greek	Members of the University in their third to seventh years	Annually	U.R.
†Crosse Studentship	Advanced study or research for the furtherance of the knowledge of the Holy Scriptures in Hebrew and Greek, Ecclesiastical History, and Christian Theology	B.A.s of the University and Registered Graduate Students of not more then three years standing	Annually	U.R.
†Divinity (German Language Fund) Grants	For acquiring or developing knowledge of the German language	Members of the University pursuing or intending to pursue a course of study or research in Divinity in the University	Annually	The Divinity School, St John's Street
†Evans Prizes	Awarded on a special examination on selected Greek and Ecclesiastical writings earlier than A.D. 461	Members of the University in their third to seventh years	Annually	U.R.
*†Hort Memorial Fund Grants	For Biblical, Hellenistic, and Patristic research	Open	Each Term	The Divinity School, St John's Street
†Hulsean Prize	For an essay on an approved subject connected with the history of the Christian Religion	Members of the University, who are in their fourth year onwards, and who are under 27	Annually	U.R.
†Jeremie Prizes	Awarded on a special examination in either Septuagint or Hellenistic writings	Members of the University in their third to seventh years	Annually	U.R.
Kaye Prize	For a dissertation upon some approved subject relating to Ancient Ecclesiastical History, Biblical Studies which aid enquiry relating to the Scriptural authority for Christian doctrines, or advance the knowledge of Biblical History or Biblical Hebrew and Greek	Graduates of not more than 10 years' standing from their first degree	Every fourth year (next Nov. 1987 and then 1991)	U.R.

Award	Subject/Purpose	Eligibility	When offered	Details (and forms when applicable) from:
†Alasdair Charles Macpherson Fund Grants	Research expenses incurred by students in the Faculty of Divinity	Students of not more than ten years' standing from their first degree	Annually	The Divinity School, St John's Street
Peregrine Maitland Studentship	Comparative Religion	Graduates of the University, with preference to those preparing for missionary work	Triennially (next 1990)	U.R.
Norrisian Prize	For an essay on a set subject in Christian Doctrine.	Graduates of not more than 13 years' standing from their first degree	From time to time (next Nov. 1987 and then 1991)	U.R.
†Seatonian Prize	For a poem on a set sacred subject	Members of the Senate, and all persons who are possessors of the status of M.A. See † for more details	Annually	U.R.
†Steel Studentships	For further study in preparation for taking Holy Orders in the Church of England	Resident members of the University, who have completed the examination requirements for the B.A. Degree	Annually	U.R.
†Theological Studies Fund Grants	Pecuniary assistance to those engaged in the study of theology in the University or elsewhere	Students who have kept one term, but no grants are paid until four terms have passed after the first term of residence	Annually	U.R
†George Williams Prize	For an essay on an approved subject connected with liturgical study	Members of the University in their third to seventh years	Annually	U.R.
†Wordsworth Studentships	Divinity	Members of the University, intending to take Holy Orders in the Church of England. See † for more details	Annually	U.R.

Veterinary Medicine

Award	Subject/Purpose	Eligibility	When offered	Details (and forms when applicable) from:
†Jowett Fund Grants	Research into diseases of animals, especially those transmissible to man and tropical diseases of domestic animals	Members of the University	Annually	The Secretary, Department of Clinical Veterinary Medicine, Madingley Road

(ii) AWARDS OFFERED BY OTHER BODIES

Note: As the Awards change from year to year the attention of students is drawn to the '*Awards*' special number of the *Reporter* published annually at the beginning of November for up-to-date details.

With no restriction of subject, or for a wide field

Under the *Commonwealth Scholarship and Fellowship Plan* Scholarships are offered to Commonwealth students to enable them to study in countries other than their own in the Commonwealth. The Scholarships are normally for two years to be spent in advanced study or research, but some awards may be made to those who wish to follow undergraduate courses. Particulars of the Scholarships may be obtained from the Joint Secretary, Commonwealth Scholarship Commission in the United Kingdom, 36 Gordon Square, London, WC1H 0PF.

Harkness Fellowships are awarded annually to men and women between twenty-one and thirty years of age for study and travel in the U.S.A. Candidates should have completed both their schooling and university education within the United Kingdom. Information and application papers may be obtained from The Harkness Fellowships (U.K.), 38 Upper Brook Street, London, W1Y 1PE, and completed forms must be submitted by the beginning of October of each year.

One *Henry Fellowship* tenable at Harvard or Yale University (tenable for one year) is offered annually. Candidates must be unmarried British subjects, men or women, under twenty-six on 1 January of the year of the award, who are *either* graduates of a recognized university in their first year of postgraduate work *or* undergraduates of a British university who have completed at least six terms' residence in that university. Notice is given in the *Cambridge University Reporter*. Applications close in November.

Gladstone Memorial Trust Travelling Scholarships are offered annually to enable undergraduates in their first and second years to travel who would not otherwise be able to do so without some financial help. Candidature is limited to members of the Universities of Oxford or Cambridge who are in full-time residence. Applications from Cambridge applicants must be sent to Mr J. S. Morrison, Granhams, Granhams Road, Cambridge, CB2 5JX.

Jane Eliza Procter Visiting Fellowships at Princeton University, New Jersey (tenable for one year, with a possibility of re-election) are offered annually by Princeton University. Notices appear in the *Reporter*. Applications close in November.

The *Joseph Hodges Choate Memorial Fellow* at Harvard University (tenable for one year) is nominated by the Vice-Chancellor and is open to graduates of the University who are of British nationality. Applications are invited each year by notice in the *Cambridge University Reporter*, and close in November.

Frank Knox Memorial Fellowships (tenable for one year, but renewable for degree programmes of more than one year's duration), at Harvard University, are offered annually to graduate students from the U.K. who wish to pursue postgradute study in one of the Faculties of Harvard University. Details of the Fellowships and the method of application may be obtained from the Secretary, The Association of Commonwealth Universities, 36 Gordon Square, London, WC1H 0PF.

The Council of the *Royal Institution of Chartered Surveyors* offer awards for postgraduate study or research in the theory and practice of surveying, in any of its branches, subject to the candidates being accepted by the Board of Graduate Studies of the University. Applications should be submitted to the Honorary Secretary, R.I.C.S. Education Trust, 12 Great George Street, Westminster, London, SW1P 3AD. Full particulars may be obtained from the Head of the Department of Land Economy, Cambridge.

The Fishmongers' Company of the City of London award the Mark Quested Exhibition from time to time, to a student of the University of Cambridge, who is in need and deserving pecuniary assistance.

Philippe Wiener-Maurice Anspach Foundation offer grants for postgraduate study or research to graduate of Oxford or Cambridge Universities in law, economics or political sciences at the University of Brussels. Grants are tenable for one year and are not renewable. Details are available at the University Registry.

Classics

A Studentship, tenable at the British School of Archaeology in Athens, is offered to a student following a definite course of graduate study in some branch of archaeology, architecture, art, history, language, literature, religion or topography of Greece in ancient, mediaeval or modern times. The value of the Studentship may be supplemented in accordance with the needs of the student. Further information may be obtained from the Secretary, British School at Athens, 31-34 Gordon Square, London, WC1 0PY.

History

The *Royal Historical Society* offers annually the *Alexander Prize* for Historical Research. Particulars may be obtained from the Society at University College, Gower Street, London, WC1E 6BT.

Law

Harmsworth, Astbury, and Benefactors Law Scholarships (tenable for two years) may be awarded every October. Candidates must be members of the Middle Temple who intend to practise at the English Bar. The Harmsworth Scholarships are open to graduates or undergraduates of universities in England, Scotland, Wales, or Northern Ireland, whilst the Astbury Scholarships are limited to men who are members of Oxford or Cambridge Universities and who are or have been undergraduates in either of those Universities. Candidates must be nominated by the Vice-Chancellor of their university; the names of candidates should be sent to the Vice-Chancellor through Heads of Colleges before 30 June. Nomination forms for Scholarships can be obtained from the Under-Treasurer, Middle Temple, London, EC4Y 9AT.

Science

The *Smithson Research Fellowship* in Natural Sciences (tenable for four years, possibly renewable for a further period of one year) is administered by a Committee appointed by the Royal Society and the University of Cambridge. Copies of the regulations and forms of application for the Fellowship when this is being advertised (usually not more than once every five years) may be had from the Executive Secretary of the Royal Society, 6 Carlton House Terrace, London, SW1Y 5AG.

Fellowships of the Royal Commission of 1851. The Royal Commissioners for the Exhibition of 1851 award every year about four Research Fellowships, intended to give to a few young research workers, of proved capacity for original work, the opportunity of devoting their whole time for not less than two years to the prosecution of scientific research. These Fellowships are subject to some special provisions, and nominations can be made by a number of universities, including the University of Cambridge. A candidate must submit particulars of his or her academic record, and must present a published paper or thesis embodying the results of his or her work, together with a recommendation from the Professor or

Head of a Laboratory under whom he or she has worked. In considering the claims of a candidate, special importance will be attached to skill in original research.

The Secretary General sends annually to the Heads of all scientific Departments in the University circulars inviting recommendations for nomination. A candidate must be a citizen of the British Commonwealth or of the Republics of Ireland, Pakistan, or South Africa and should generally be under thirty years of age.

British Gas Research Scholarships are granted annually, through Heads of Departments or research schools, to graduates for research in the physical sciences or engineering at universities in the U.K. The Scholarships are tenable for three years. The closing date for applications is early December. Particulars and application forms may be obtained from the Manager, External Affairs Research and Development Division, British Gas plc, 148 Grosvenor Road, London, SW1V 3JL.

The Royal Society offers both senior and junior awards tenable in the U.K. and abroad, in most aspects of science, and in mathematics, medicine, engineering, technology and agriculture. Other awards offered are overseas research grants, scientific publications grants, history of science grants, marine science grants, grants for travel and study visits, and a European Science Exchange Programme. Application forms and full particulars may be obtained from the Executive Secretary of the Royal Society, 6 Carlton House Terrace, London, SW1Y 5AG.

A *Shell Scholarship in Geophysics* (tenable for two years, with possible renewal for a third year) is offered from time to time by the Royal Dutch/Shell Group of Oil Companies. The Student pursues a course of training in research in Geophysics in the University of Cambridge and must be or must become registered as a Graduate Student. Inquiries should be addressed to the Secretary of the Department of Earth Sciences, Madingley Rise, Madingley Road, Cambridge, CB3 0EZ.

The *George Henry Lewes Studentship* for research in Physiology (tenable for one, two, or three years: stipend at a rate determined by the Trustees) is awarded from time to time and is at present tenable in the Physiological Laboratory, Cambridge. Inquiries should be addressed to the Professor of Physiology, Physiological Laboratory, Cambridge.

The *Rolleston Memorial Prize* is offered each year for original research in Animal and Vegetable Morphology, Physiology and Pathology, and Anthropology, to certain members of the University of Oxford or to B.A.s, M.B.s, or Graduate Students of the University of Cambridge, of not more than six years' standing. Inquiries should be addressed to the Registrar, University Offices, Wellington Square, Oxford, OX1 2JD.

The Nuffield Foundation offers small grants of up to £2,500 to support research in the sciences and applied sciences (e.g. grants for short working visits, vacation research grants for undergraduates, grants for equipment and consumables, and grants for small working meetings of scientists). There are also one-year Science Research Fellowships (closing date 11 October) to provide young university scientists with a year's relief from teaching to help them in the early stages of their independent research careers; and awards for newly-appointed lecturers to help them in the early stages of their independent research careers (applications must be made within 12 months of appointment).

Similar grants are made in the social sciences.

Further details of these schemes are available from the Nuffield Foundation, Nuffield Lodge, Regents Park, London NW1 4RS.

Theology

Exhibitions are awarded from the *Cambridge Graduates Ordination Candidates' Fund* to graduates of the University who are preparing to take Holy Orders in the Church of England, and who undertake to study for such Part or section of a Part of the Theological Tripos, or for such other Theological Examination, as the awarders shall approve. Candidates should send their applications to the Regius Professor of Divinity at the Divinity School.

Candidates may obtain advice about other possible sources of financial assistance from the Secretary, Advisory Council for the Church's Ministry, Church House, Dean's Yard, London, SW1P 3NZ.

The Awards Information Service of the Association of Commonwealth Universities

The Service produces four publications which are listed below. They are revised every two years and are available for reference in many university and public libraries, and can be purchased from the A.C.U. office in London (John Foster House, 36 Gordon Square, London, WC1H 0PF).

1. *Awards for Commonwealth University Academic Staff*. Seventh edition (for 1986–88): price £9.90; 230 pages.

AWARDS

2. *Grants for Study Visits by University Administrators and Librarians*. Fourth edition (for 1987–9): price £3.50; 28 pages.

3. *Scholarships Guide for Commonwealth Postgraduate Students*. Seventh edition (for 1987–89): price £11.50; 345 pages.

4. *Financial Aid for First Degree Study at Commonwealth Universities*. Sixth edition (for 1986–88); price £2.90; 45 pages.

7

UNIVERSITY CAREERS SERVICE

Secretary: W. P. KIRKMAN, M.A.
Senior Assistant Secretaries: J. N. COOPE, M.A.; D. F. T. WINTER, M.A.
Assistant Secretaries: G. A. CURRY, M.A. (part-time); Mrs A. C. M. DINHAM, M.A. (part-time); A. J. FAWCITT, B.SC., M.A.; M. S. GAVIN, B.SC., M.A.; A. J. RABAN, M.A.: Mrs R. E. SMITH, M.A. (part-time): Mrs A. J. WALSHAM, B.A. (part-time).

Assistant to the Secretaries (Information Officer): MISS A. W. SYME, M.A.

The Cambridge Appointments Association was founded in 1899 and in 1902 was superseded by the University Appointments Board (for men, as women were not then full members of the University). In 1985 the Board in its turn was superseded by the Careers Service Syndicate.

The functions of the Service are:
(i) To provide a service of information and advice about careers in general, and individual employers in particular.
(ii) To help people to decide on their future plans.
(iii) To act as a link between employers seeking recruits and graduates and undergraduates seeking appointments.

The Service is open to past as well as present members of the University.

Men and women are welcome to consult the Service at any time during their period at Cambridge. Ideally they should first make contact well before their final year. Because the pressure of work with final year people is greatest in the first half of the academic year, it is helpful if first and second year people come from February onwards.

Those registering in their final year are put on mailing lists to receive details of specific appointments if they wish. Anyone who has had preliminary discussions before his or her final year should resume contact in the final year. The Careers Advisers do not automatically put on to their active lists those who have made preliminary contact in their first or second years.

The Service is in regular contact with well over 4,000 employers, covering an immense range of occupations, in the educational, professional, and non-commercial fields as well as in industry and commerce, and including small organizations as well as 'household names'.

UNIVERSITY CAREERS SERVICE

There is an Information Room containing a selection of literature about particular occupations and individual employers, and about postgraduate courses and training. It includes material produced by the staff, material provided by employers and material from other sources such as newspapers and is widely used by people at all stages in their University career. No appointment is necessary to use the Information Room, which may be consulted at any time during office hours.

Many people approaching the Service have little or no idea of what they want to do on graduating. The task of the Careers Advisers, therefore, is to help determine the possible range of choice, to suggest how more information can be obtained and to provide a frame of reference for judging the pros and cons of various fields of work. To this end, the Service arranges various courses and seminars, careers evenings, talks etc., as well as individual discussions.

In 1969 a joint committee was set up, consisting of the staff of the Service and a number of undergraduate and graduate representatives, to participate in the day to day work of the Service. It meets regularly.

The offices are at Stuart House, Mill Lane, Cambridge, CB2 1XE (tel. 338288). They are open from 9.15 a.m. to 5.15 p.m. Mondays to Fridays in Full Term. On Saturdays they are open from 10 a.m. to 12.30 p.m., during the Michaelmas and Lent terms. During vacations the offices are closed between 1 and 2 p.m., and in the Long Vacation from 5 p.m.

8

TRAINING FOR THE MINISTRY

Candidates for Holy Orders in the Church of England are advised to obtain from the Advisory Council for the Church's Ministry, Church House, Dean's Yard, London, SW1P 3NZ, a leaflet of general information entitled *Ordination in the Church of England*. Men and women who are in residence should consult the Dean or Chaplain of their College.

The normal course of training for the priesthood or the diaconate is for those who have read a degree, or a substantial part of their first degree, in Theology, to take a two years' course of theological, pastoral, and spiritual training at a recognized Theological College. Graduates in other subjects are expected to undertake three years of training, of which, in the case of suitable persons, two years may be spent in reading for Part II of the Theological and Religious Studies Tripos. Candidates must satisfy the requirements of the General Ministerial Examination insofar as they are not covered by university courses which have been taken. Members* of the Cambridge Federation of Theological Colleges take the Cambridge Federation Examination in Theology, which is a recognized equivalent of the General Ministerial Examination.

Candidates for the Ministry of the Methodist Church or the United Reformed Church may obtain information on the application procedure from the Principals of Wesley House and Westminster College respectively.

Ridley Hall

Ridley Hall is a Theological College, founded in 1877 mainly for the preparation of graduate candidates, men and women, for Ordination in the Church of England.

Applications for admission should be made to the Principal.

Further information may be obtained from the Principal: The Rev. Canon H. F. de Waal, M.A.

Wesley House

Wesley House is a Theological College for the training of accepted candidates for the ministry of the Methodist Church. Students of

* The members are Ridley Hall, Wesley House, Westcott House, and Westminster College.

TRAINING FOR THE MINISTRY

the College, who are usually graduates, become members of the University and read for a degree or take the Examination in Theology of the Cambridge Federation of Theological Colleges.

Applications for admission should be made to the Principal, Rev. Dr Ivor H. Jones, M.A.

Westcott House

Westcott House was founded as 'The Cambridge Clergy Training School' in 1881 by Dr B. F. Westcott, then Regius Professor of Divinity and subsequently Bishop of Durham. It received its present name after Dr Westcott's death. In 1972 it entered a Federation with the other theological colleges in Cambridge.

Most, but not all, members are graduates of a university and all must have been accepted for training by their diocesan bishop. Members of the University who are prospective ordinands may be accepted as Associates.

Applications from men or women desiring to become Members or Associates should be made to the Principal.

Westminster College and the Cheshunt Foundation

Westminster College, Cambridge, is a Theological College of the United Reformed Church, and it houses the Cheshunt Foundation which continues the work of Cheshunt College, founded by Selina, Countess of Huntingdon.

The College is open to receive candidates, men and women, for the ministry, not only of the United Reformed Church, but of any Church. It also welcomes, as residents, qualified persons who wish to pursue their own advanced or research studies in theology.

Detailed information about the conditions of admission may be obtained from the Principal of Westminster College, Rev. M. H. Cressey, M.A.

INDEX

Abbott Fund, 490
Academical dress, 39
Adams Prize, 503
Administrative officers, 2
Admission, undergraduates, 25: graduates, 484: overseas candidates, 26
Aeronautics: *see* Engineering
Affiliation, 13
Agriculture awards, 493
Alexander Prize (offered by the Royal Historical Society), 518
Allen Scholarship, 490
A. M. P. Read Scholarships, 492
Anatomy: *see* Medical Sciences *and* Natural Sciences
Anglo-Saxon, Norse, and Celtic, Courses of Study and Examinations in, 47: Scholarships and other awards, 493
Anthropology: *see* Archaeology and Anthropology
Arberry Travelling Scholarships, 502
Archaeology and Anthropology, Courses of Study and Examinations in, 53: Studentships and other awards, 493
Archaeology, M.Phil. Degree in, 53
Architecture, Courses of Study and Examinations in, 75: Scholarships and other awards, 494
Architecture, M.Phil. Degree in, 82
Astbury Scholarships, 518
Astronomy: *see* Mathematics
Awards Information Service, Association of Commonwealth Universities, 520

B.A. Degree, examinations leading to, 40: for courses of study, *see under the various subjects, e.g.* Architecture, etc.
Baldwin, Stanley, studentships and grants, 499
Balfour-Browne Fund, 510
Barnes Fund, 490
Bartle Frere Exhibitions, 491
Bell, Abbott, and Barnes funds/exhibitions, 490
Bendall Sanskrit Exhibition, 512
Benefactors Law Scholarships, 518
Bethune Baker Fund, 513
Biological Anthropology, M.Phil. Degree in, 68
Biology: *see* Natural Sciences
Biophysics: *see* Natural Sciences
Boards and Syndicates, 1
Botany: *see* Natural Sciences
British Gas Research Scholarships, 519
British Institute of Management, exemption from examinations of, 184
British School of Archaeology at Athens, Studentship, 517
Broodbank Fellowships, 509
Browne, E.G., Memorial Research Studentship (Persian), 512

Browne, Sir William, Medals (Classics), 495
Burney Fund, 513; Prize, 513; Studentship, 513
Bury, Gregg, Prize, 513
Butler, Montagu, Prize, 495

Cambridge Admissions Prospectus, 24, 25
Cambridge Commonwealth Trust Awards, 490
Cambridge Inter-collegiate Applications Scheme, 24
Cambridge Livingstone Trust Awards, 490
Cambridge University Reporter, 1, 2
Careers Service, 522
Carrington, Henry, and Bentham Dumont Koe Studentship, 494
Carus Greek Testament Prizes, 514
Celtic: *see* Anglo-Saxon, Norse, and Celtic
Certificate in Education, 140
Certificate in Diligent Study, 40
Certificate of Advanced Study in Chemical Engineering, 91
Certificates of Competent Knowledge in modern languages, 335
Certificates of degrees, 39
Certificates of Post-graduate Study in Chemical Engineering, 91; in Natural Sciences, 382; in Design, Manufacture, and Management, 186
Chadwick, H.M., Studentship, 490
Chancellor, 1, 2
Chancellor's Medals: for an English poem, 498
Chemical Engineering, Courses of Study and Examinations in, 85
Chemistry: *see* Natural Sciences
Cheshunt Foundation, 525
Choate, Joseph Hodges, Memorial Fellowship, 517
Classical Archaeology, Diploma in, 108
Classics, Courses of Study and Examinations in, 93: Scholarships, Studentships, etc., 494
Coke, Dorothea, Fund, 506
Colleges, general, 24
Collins, William George, Fund, 497
Colloid Sciences, awards in, 509
Commonwealth Scholarship and Fellowship Plan, 516
Commonwealth Trust Awards, 490
Comparative Pathology: *see* Natural Sciences
Computer Science Tripos, Courses of Study and Examinations in, 110
Computer Speech and Language Processing, M.Phil. Degree in, 185
Congregation, 1: general admission, 38; procedure for taking degrees at, 39
Council of Engineering Institutions (C.E.I.), exemption from examinations of, 184
Council of the Senate, 1
Cow and Gate Prize, 505
Cranmer, Archbishop, studentships and grants, 500
Craven Studentship, 494
Criminology, M.Phil. Degree in, 263
Crosse Studentship, 514
Czech (with Slovak) Language and Literature: *see* Modern and Medieval Languages

INDEX

D'Angliano, Luca, Scholarship, 496
Danish Language and Literature: *see* Modern and Medieval Languages
Dean, Henry Roy, Prize, 504
Degrade, permission to, 29
Degrees, 38: entry of candidates for, 38: presentation and admission to, 39: degrees by incorporation, 19: in virtue of office, under Statute B, III, 19; B.A., 40; B.D., B.Ed., LL.B., M.B., Mus.B., B.Chir., Vet.M.B., M.A., 42; LL.M., M.Litt., Mus.M., M.Phil., 43; M.Sc., M.Chir., D.D., LL.D., Litt.D., 44; M.D., Mus.D., Ph.D., 45; Sc.D., 46
Department of Surgery Prize, 506
Development Studies, 114
Diplomas, in Architecture, 81: in Classical Archaeology, 108: in Development Studies, 114: in Legal Studies, 261: in Computer Science, 112: in Economics, 137: in Education, 165: in Historical Studies, 224: in International Law, 261: in Mathematical Statistics, 270: in Theology, 463
Divinity, Bachelor of, 42: Doctor of, 44: *see also* Theology
Divinity (German Language Fund) grants, 514
Dooley, Denis, Prize, 504
Duff, Gordon, Prize, 494
Dutch Language and Literature: *see* Modern and Medieval Languages

Economics and Politics, Courses of Study and Examinations in, 115: Scholarships and Prizes, 496: Economics Qualifying Examination in Elementary Mathematics, 120
Education, Courses of Study and Examinations in, 140: Diploma in, 165
Education, Bachelor of, 42
Electrical and Information Sciences Tripos, 176
Elmore, F. E., Medical Research Studentships, 504
Elocution, prizes for, 497
Engineering, Courses of Study and Examinations in, 166: Scholarships, Studentships, etc., 497: exemptions from the examinations of Professional Institutions, 184
English, Courses of Study and Examinations in, 186: Scholarships, Studentships, etc., 498
Entomology grants, 510
Environmental Biology: *see* Natural Sciences
Ethics: *see* Philosophy
Ethnology: *see* Archaeology and Anthropology
Evans Fellowship, 493
Evans Prizes, 514
Evans, Ulick Richardson, Research Fund, 510
Examinations, dates, 35
Examination entry, 28: Allowances, 29
Examination requirements for matriculation, 10

Financial Board, 1
Fine Arts: *see* History of Art
Fisons Prize, 505
Fitzwilliam Museum, 22

Ford of Britain Trust Fund, 497
Fortes Fund grants, 493
Foster, Michael, Studentship, 511
French Language and Literature: *see* Modern and Medieval Languages

Gardiner, Robert, Memorial Scholarships, 491
Gas, British, Research Scholarships, 519
Gatty, Oliver, Studentship, 509
General Admission to Degrees, 38
General Board of the Faculties, 1
Genetics: *see* Natural Sciences
Geography, Courses of Study and Examinations in, 202: Scholarships, etc., 499
Geology: *see* Natural Sciences
German Language and Literature: *see* Modern and Medieval Languages
Gerstenberg, Arnold, Studentship, 513
Gibson Spanish Scholarship, 506
Gladstone Memorial Trust Travelling Scholarships, 516
Glennie Prizes, 504
Graduates Ordination Candidates' Fund, 520
Greek: *see* Classics *and* Modern and Medieval Languages
Gregson, Mark, Prize, 493
Grimshaw-Parkinson Studentships, 504

Hamilton Prize, 498, 509
Hare Prize, 495
Harkness Fellowships, 516
Harkness Scholarship, 510
Harmsworth Law Scholarships, 518
Harness Prize, 498
Harvey, William, Studentships, 505
Hebrew Scholarships and Prizes, 513
Henderson, John and Margaret, Memorial Prize, 505
Henry Fellowships, 516
History, Courses of Study and Examinations in, 208: Awards for study and research, 499
History and Philosophy of Science, 368, M.Phil. Degree in, 385
History of Art, Courses of Study and Examinations in, 228
History of Medicine, M.Phil. Degree in, 283
Holy Orders, Training of Candidates for, 524: Ridley Hall, 524: Westcott House, 525: Westminster College and Cheshunt Foundation, 525: Wesley House, 524: Exhibitions and grants for candidates for ordination, 524
Honours examinations: table of standing, 31
Hort Memorial Fund, 514
Howard, Sir Albert, Travel Exhibition, 509
Hulsean Prize, 514
Humanitarian Trust Senior Studentship, 502
Hungarian Language and Literature: *see* Modern and Medieval Languages
Hydraulics: *see* Engineering

INDEX

I.C.L. Research Studentship, 496
Incorporation, 18
Institution of Electrical Engineers, examption from examinations of, 184
Institution of Mechanical Engineers, exemption from examinations of, 184
International Relations, M.Phil. Degree in, 225
Irish Language and Literature, Early: *see* English *and* Anglo-Saxon, Norse, and Celtic
Italian Language and Literature: *see* Modern and Medieval Languages

Jebb Scholarship, 495 and Studentships, 507
Jeremie Prizes, 514
Johns, C.H.W., Studentship, 512
Jowett Fund, 515

Kaye Prize, 514
Keith, A.J., Studentships, 493
Kettle's Yard Travel Fund, 494
Knight, J.T., Prizes, 504
Knox, Frank, Memorial Fellowships, 517
Koe, Bentham Dumont, studentship, 494

Lake, Philip, Funds, 499, 510
Land Economy, Courses of Study and Examinations in, 236: Studentships, 502
Latin: *see* Classics *and* Modern and Medieval Languages
Latin-American Studies, M.Phil. Degree in, 247
Law, Doctor of, 44: Master of, 43
Law, Courses of Study and Examinations in, 252: Scholarships, Studentships, etc., 502: exemption from professional examinations, 257
Le Bas Prize, 498
Le Bas Research Studentship, 491
Letters, Doctor of, 44: Master of, 43: *see also Chapter 5*
Levy, Benn W., Studentship, 509
Lewes, George Henry, Studentship, 519
Lightfoot Scholarships, 500
Linguistics, M.Phil. Degree in, 335
Livingstone Trust Scholarships, 490
Logic: *see* Philosophy
Lungren Research awards, 491

McArthur, Ellen, Prizes and Studentships, 500
McNair, Arnold, Scholarships, 502
Macpherson, Alasdair Charles, Fund, 515
Madingley Hall, 23
Maitland, Frederic William, Memorial Fund, 502
Maitland, Peregrine, Studentship, 515
Management Studies Tripos, 181
Manfacturing Engineering Tripos, 179
Marr Memorial Fund, 510
Mathematics, Courses of Study and Examinations in, 265: Studentships, Prizes, etc., 503: *see also under* Natural Sciences

Matriculation, 10
Maxwell, Clerk, Scholarship, 511
Medical Sciences Tripos, 272
Medicine and Surgery, Courses of Study and Examinations in, 284: First M.B. Examination, 286, Second M.B. Examination, 289, Final M.B. Examination, 290: Studentships and Second Scholarships, etc., 504
Medicine, Doctor of, 45: Bachelor of Medicine, 42, of Surgery, 42: Master of Surgery, 44
Medieval Languages and Literature: *see* Modern and Medieval Languages
Meek, W. A., Scholarship, 491
Mellon Research Fellowships, 500
Members' Classical Essay Prizes, 496; Members' Classical Translation Prizes, 496; Classical Reading Prizes, 496; Members' English Prize, 498; Members' History Prize, 500
Merz, Charles Hesterman, Fund, 497
Metallurgy: *see* Natural Sciences
Meteorology: *see* Natural Sciences
Mineralogy and Petrology: *see* Natural Sciences
Modern and Medieval Languages, Courses of Study and Examinations in, 291: Scholarships, Studentships, etc., 506
Moir, Rex, Fund, 498
Mortensen, Brita, Fund, 507
Mosley, Mary Euphrasia, Fund grants, 491
Mulvey, Thomas, Prize, 512
Music, Courses of Study and Examinations in, 337: Scholarships and Prizes, 508
Music, Bachelor of, 42: Master of, 43: Doctor of, 45
Musical Composition, M.Phil. Degree in, 344
Musicology, M.Phil. Degree in, 345

Natural Sciences, Courses of Study and Examinations in, 347: Fellowships, Studentships, etc., 508
Newton, Isaac, Studentships, 508
Norrisian Prize, 515
Norton, Sara, Prize, 501
Norwegian Language and Literature: *see* Modern and Medieval Languages
Nuffield Foundation awards, 520

Oldham, Charles, Scholarships, 494
Oldham, Charles, Shakespeare Scholarship, 499
Ord Travel Fund, 508
Ordinances, 1
Ordinary B.A. Degree, 40: *for particulars of special Examinations, see under the several subjects*
Ordination Candidates Fund, 520
Organic Chemistry: *see* Natural Sciences
Oriental Studies, Courses and Examinations in, 390: Studentships, Scholarships, etc., 512
Oriental Studies, M.Phil. Degree in, 413
Overseas Candidates for Admission, 26

Paediatric Prizes, 505
Phillpotts, Dame Bertha, Memorial Fund and Scholarship, 493
Philosophy, Courses of Study and Examinations in, 415: Studentship, 513
Philosophy, Doctor of, 45, Master of, 43: *see also Chapter 5*
Physics, M.Phil. Degree in, 387
Physics and Theoretical Physics: *see* Natural Sciences
Physiology: *see* Medical Sciences *and* Natural Sciences
Physiology and Psychology: *see* Natural Sciences
Pinsent-Darwin Studentship, 505
Plant Breeding, M.Phil. Degree in, 387
Polar Studies, M.Phil. Degree in, 427
Polish Language and Literature: *see* Modern and Medieval Languages
Porson Prize, 495
Portuguese Language and Literature: *see* Modern and Medieval Languages
Praelectors, 38
Preliminary Examinations: *see under the various subjects*
Prendergast Studentship, 494
Pretty, Gwynaeth, Research Studentship, 505
Price Waterhouse Prize, 496
Prince Consort Prize and Studentships, 501
Prior, Edward S., Prize, 494
Proctor, Jane Eliza, Visiting Fellowships, 516
Proctors, 2
Professors, 3
Psychology: *see* Medical Sciences, Natural Sciences, *and* Philosophy

Quaternary Research, M.Phil. Degree in, 389

Ramsay, J. Arthur, Fund, 511
Rapson Scholarship, 512
Rayleigh Prizes, 504
Read, Amy Mary Preston, Scholarship, 492
Readers, 7
Reed, F. R. Cowper, Fund, 510
Regent House, 1
Registrary, 2
Research and courses of advanced or further study, 484
Research Maintenance Grants Fund, 492
R.I.B.A.: exemption from Examinations of, 75
Richards Fund, 493
Richards, David, Travel Scholarships, 499
Ridgeway-Venn Travel Studentship, 493
Ridley Hall, 524
Rogers, Wright, Law Scholarships, 503
Rolleston Memorial Prize, 519
Rose, Holland, Studentship, 501
Roth, Henry Ling, Scholarship, 493
Royal Commission for the Exhibition of 1851, Fellowships, 518
Royal Historical Society: Prize for Historical research, 518

INDEX

Royal Institution of Chartered Surveyors: postgraduate awards offered by the Council of, 517
Royal Society awards, 519
Russian Language and Literature: *see* Modern and Medieval Languages

Salisbury, F.S., Fund, 496
Samuel, Harold, Studentships, 502
Scandinavian Languages and Literature: *see* Modern and Medieval Languages
Scandinavian Studies Fund, 507
Science, Doctor of, 46: Master of, 44
Science, History and Philosophy of: *see* Natural Sciences
Seatonian Prize, 515
Secretary General of the Faculties, 2
Sedgwick Prize, 510
Senate, 1
Serbo-Croat Language and Literature: *see* Modern and Medieval Languages
Sheild, Marmaduke, Scholarship, 505
Shell Fund, Scholarship in Geophysics, 519
Sims Fund and Scholarship, 492, 506
Sinanide, O. and F., Scholarship, 506
Slater, Eliot, Prize, 506
Slavonic Languages and Literature: *see* Modern and Medieval Languages
Smart, Frank, Studentships, 509
Smith, Adam, Prize, 497
Smith's Prizes, 504
Smithson Research Fellowship, 518
Smuts Memorial Fund, 492
Social and Political Sciences, Courses of Study and Examinations in, 429
Social Anthropology, M.Phil. Degree in, 71
Sociology: *see* Archaeology and Anthropology *and* Economics and Politics
Spanish Language and Literature: *see* Modern and Medieval Languages
Squire Fund, Rebecca Flower, 502
Squire Law Scholarships, 502
Squire, William Barclay, Essay Prize, 508
Standing of candidates for examinations and degrees, 31
Statistics: *see* Natural Sciences
Status: of B.A., 19: of M.A., 19
Statutes, 1
Steel Studentships, 515
Stevenson Prizes, 497
Stewart of Rannoch, John, Scholarships for: Music, 508: Hebrew, 512
Surgery, Bachelor of, 42: Master of, 44
Surgery, Department of, Prize, 506
Swedish Language and Literature: *see* Modern and Medieval Languages

Teachers, Training of, *see* Education, 140
Tennant Fund, 507
Theological Studies Fund, 515
Theology and Religious Studies, Courses of Study and Examinations in, 441, Studentships, Prizes, etc., 513; *see also under* Holy Orders

Theology, M.Phil. Degree in, 470
Thirlwall Prize and Studentships, 501
Thomas, Henry Arthur, Studentships, Prizes, and Travel Exhibition, 494
Tiarks German Scholarships, 507: Fund, 507
Training for the Ministry, 524
Treasurer, 2
Trend, J.B., Fund, 507
Triposes, *see Chapter 4*: privileges accorded to Affiliated Students, 13
Tyrwhitt's Hebrew Scholarships, 513

University Careers Service, 522
University Classical Scholarships, 494
Universtiy Degrees, 38
University Examinations, dates of in 1989–90, 35
University Library, 20
University scholarships and other awards, 490

Ver Heyden de Lancey Prizes, 503
Veterinary Medicine, Bachelor of, 42
Veterinary Medicine, Courses of Study and Examinations in, 478
Vice-Chancellor, 1, 2

Walker, John Lucas, Studentships, 506
Wallenberg Prize, 508
Walston Studentship, 494
Warr, George Charles Winter, Scholarship, 494
Waterhouse, Price, Prize, 496
Weis-Fogh, Hanne and Torkel, Fund grants, 511
Welsh Language and Literature: *see* English *and* Anglo-Saxon, Norse, and Celtic
Wesley House, 524
Westcott House, 525
Westminster College, 525
Whewell Scholarships, 503
Wilkin, Anthony, Studentship, 493
Williams, George, Prize, 515
Winbolt, John, Prize, 498
Winchester Reading Prizes, 497
Woodrow, Taylor, Fund, 498
Wordsworth Studentships, 515
Worts Travelling Scholars Fund, 492
Wrenbury Scholarship, 497
Wright Studentship, 513
Wright Rogers Law Scholarships, 503

Yazdani, Ghulam, Essay Prize, 513
Yorke Prizes, 503

Zoology: *see* Natural Sciences